Alignment Despite Antagonism

STUDIES OF THE EAST ASIAN INSTITUTE,
COLUMBIA UNIVERSITY

The East Asian Institute is Columbia
University's center for research, publication,
and teaching on modern East Asia. The
Studies of the East Asian Institute were
inaugurated in 1962 to bring to a wider public
the results of significant new research on
Japan, China, and Korea.

.

Alignment Despite Antagonism

THE UNITED STATES-KOREA-JAPAN
SECURITY TRIANGLE

Victor D. Cha

Stanford University Press
Stanford, California

Stanford University Press
Stanford, California
© 1999 by the Board of Trustees of the
Leland Stanford Junior University
Printed in the United States of America
CIP data appear at the end of the book

For my parents, Moon Young and Soon Ock

Acknowledgments

This book could not have been possible without the help of many friends, colleagues, and institutions. I am grateful to the members of my dissertation committee at Columbia University, who supported this work in its first iteration, in particular, Professors Robert Jervis and James Morley. The initial idea for the book grew out of a graduate colloquium on Japanese Foreign Policy and an international relations theory course with these professors. They subsequently worked with me on this project throughout my time at Columbia and after. Their conscientiousness in reading countless drafts despite their busy schedules, their incisive comments, and their guidance and friendship have been invaluable. Simply put, one could not have asked for two finer scholars and gentlemen as teachers and mentors.

Other faculty at Columbia University and tutors at Hertford College, Oxford University, offered well-taken advice along the way. At Oxford Jeff Holzgrefe allowed me to explore my first interest in international security and Korea. At Columbia, Professors Jack Snyder and Andrew Nathan instilled in me an understanding of the importance of methodological rigor and rich case study research in any scholarly endeavor. Professor Gerald Curtis's crisp lectures and insightful writings sparked my interest in the United States-Japan alliance. Amy Lee at Columbia's East Asian Library deserves thanks for procuring numerous sources, as does Gari Ledyard for sharing his many historical insights. I have benefited immeasurably from the constructive criticism of my peers on the ninth floor ("The Friday Group"). I owe special thanks to Carol Y. S. Schulz of the Korean department for her infinite patience in teaching me a language that I often found impossible to learn, and to Peggy Freund for guiding me through the administrative maze of my graduate school years.

A variety of generous institutions have been behind this project. The

Weatherhead Foundation and SSRC/MacArthur Foundation supported the work in its formative stages at Columbia. The Fulbright Commission funded the project's initial year of field research in Korea and Japan. In Seoul Professors Hahn Bae-ho and Han Sung-joo of Korea University helped facilitate my field work. Professor Han, in particular, inspired me to embark on an academic career when I first met him over ten years ago; he remains a good friend, colleague, and mentor. Ambassadors Park Sang-yong and Lee Tong-won extended their courtesy in introducing me to numerous scholars and former policymakers knowledgeable on Japan-Korea relations. I benefited greatly from discussions with current and former journalists, including Shim Jae-hoon of the *Far Eastern Economic Review* and Professor Kim Jong-ki of Han'guk University of Foreign Studies. Professors Park Jae-kyu and Lee Su-hoon of the Kyungnam Institute for Far Eastern Studies and Moon Chung-in of Yonsei University also provided invaluable facilities. For follow-up research trips in 1996 and 1997 I thank Kim Wonsoo and Lee Chang-ho of the Ministry of Foreign Affairs and Yoo Jai-hyon at the Institute of Foreign Affairs and National Security.

My two research trips to Tokyo would have been fruitless without the guidance and support of Professor Nishihara Masashi of the National Defense Academy. Both he and Professor Okonogi Masao of Keiō University pointed me in the direction of the people I needed to meet. Among these individuals, Ambassador Sunobe Ryozo, Tsukamoto Katsuichi of the Research Institute of Peace and Security, Oikawa Shoichi of the *Yomiuri Shimbun*, and Takeichi Hideo of Sophia University were especially giving of their time and knowledge.

I had the good fortune of spending two enlightening pre- and postdoctoral years as a National Security Fellow at the John M. Olin Institute for Strategic Studies at Harvard University. The institute's director, Samuel Huntington, and associate director, Stephen Peter Rosen, gave unstintingly of their time and resources. They also allowed me to run a seminar on East Asian security and included me in a number of other Olin-related projects that broadened my perspective on international relations theory and its application to East Asia. Owing to the good graces of Coit Blacker, David Holloway, John Lewis, and Michael May, I spent a wonderful postdoctoral year in the unique environment of the Center for International Security and Arms Control at Stanford University, interacting with "real" scientists in the security field. I am no less indebted to the School of Foreign Service at Georgetown University and the Northeast Asia Council (Korea), Association for Asian Studies for summer support that allowed me to revise and reshape the work in its final stages.

As is the case for most young academics and their first major projects, this work has been presented in more forms and venues than I care to remember. I would be remiss in not thanking the individuals whose empirical and theoretical comments and criticisms have made this a better book. These include Thomas Berger, Michael Chambers, Thomas Christensen, Lynn Eden, Keith Hwang, Robert Immerman, John Mearsheimer, Jonathan Mercer, Katherine Moon, Edward Olsen, John Owen, Bruce Porter, Gideon Rose, Robert Ross, Randall Schweller, Sheila Smith, and Allan Song. In addition to my principal advisors at Columbia, special thanks go to Richard Betts, Ilpyong Kim, Gari Ledyard, Stephen Rosen, and Ezra Vogel for reading the dissertation and/or manuscript in its entirety and providing invaluable criticisms and recommendations for revision. Lindsay Jenkins, Hannah Lee, Juli MacDonald, and David Parker assisted with tables, maps, photos, and figures. Muriel Bell, John Feneron, and Jan Spauschus Johnson at Stanford University Press and Madge Huntington at the East Asian Institute deserve thanks for their careful shepherding of this manuscript to publication. Mitch Tuchman, the copy editor, did wonderful work on the manuscript, as did Doug Easton with the index. For no less invaluable guidance from colleagues and friends who were spared the burdens of the book project, I thank Robert Gallucci, David Kang, Young Whan Kihl, Eun Mee Kim, Joseph Lepgold, Robert Lieber, Dennis McNamara, Sam Mujal-Leon, Bonnie Oh, and James Reardon-Anderson. Sections of chapter one are derived from an earlier article and are published here with the permission of the journal in which it originally appeared, *Korean Studies*.

I thank my wife, Kim Hyun Jung, for her love and encouragement. She has endured many work-filled weekends, made multiple moves from New York to Seoul to Boston to Palo Alto and to Washington, all with superhuman optimism and good nature. Although he is too young to understand, I thank my son, Patrick Ellis, whose one incomprehensible baby word puts into perspective the hundreds of thousands of adult words in this book. I also thank my brother, Michael, who always keeps me laughing and seeing the bright side of things. Finally, I dedicate this book to my parents. The more I learn, the more people I encounter, and the more experiences I have, the more I understand and appreciate what they have done for me.

V.D.C.

Washington, D.C.

Contents

A Note to the Reader   xiv
Abbreviations   xv

Introduction: The Puzzle and Its Importance   1
1. The Enigma of History   9
2. The Argument: Quasi Alliances   36
3. Cooperation Under the Nixon Doctrine, 1969–1971   59
4. Detente and the Heightening Crisis, 1972–1974   100
5. Vietnam and the Carter Years, 1975–1979   141
6. The 1980s: Evolution and Friction During the Reagan Years   169
   Conclusion: Quasi Allies or Adversaries in the Post–
   Cold War Era?   199

Appendix Tables   235
Notes   243
Works Cited   335
Index   359

Map and Figures

Map

Japan and Korea   xvi

Figures

1. Realism Versus Reality in Japan-Korea Relations   18
2. Balance-of-Threat Theory Versus Quasi Alliances   49
3. Two-Tiered Model for Japan-Korea Relations   206

Tables

Text Tables

1. U.S. Military Personnel Reductions, 1969–1971   61
2. DMZ and Rear-Area Incidents, 1968–1971   64
3. Japan-ROK Regularized Bilateral Committees, 1966–1995   86
4. Quasi-Alliance Model for Japan-ROK Relations   201
5. Distribution of Overseas Koreans   218
6. Comparative Indicators: Japan and the Two Koreas, 1995   222
7. Recent Additional Japan-ROK Bilateral Policy Fora   224
8. Growth in Communication and Consultation   225

Appendix Tables

A.1. South Korean Trade with Japan, 1962–1995   235
A.2. North Korean Trade with Japan, 1962–1995   236
A.3. Japan-ROK Economic Treaties and Related Agreements, 1967–1991   237
A.4. Official and Unofficial Visits Between the Premier of Japan and President of South Korea, 1945–1996   238

A Note to the Reader

In this work I transliterate Korean words according to the McCune-Reischauer system. Personal names are cited in text, notes, and bibliography with surnames first. The exception to this are Korean names that appear as popularly Romanized in the Western-language literature, unless specifically cited within the context of a Korean-language source. For example, I refer to "Lee Tong-won" in the former context and "Yi Tongwŏn" in the latter. Japanese names and words are written as conventionally found in the Western literature.

Abbreviations

DSJP	Daily Summary of the Japanese Press, U.S. embassy
EIB	Export-Import Bank
embtel	embassy telegram
FBIS	Foreign Broadcast Information Service
FEER	*Far Eastern Economic Review*
IECOK	International Economic Consultation Group on Korea
JCF	Japan Country File
KCF	Korea Country File
KCIA	Central Intelligence Agency (ROK)
KPT	*Korea Press Translations*
LDP	Liberal Democratic Party (Japan)
memcon	memorandum of conversation
MITI	Ministry of International Trade and Industry (Japan)
MOFA	Ministry of Foreign Affairs (ROK)
NSC	National Security Council
NSCC	North-South Coordinating Committee
NSF	National Security File
OECD	Organization for Economic Cooperation and Development
PPPUS	*Public Papers of the President of the United States*
ROK	Republic of Korea (South Korea)
SCAP	Supreme Commander of the Allied Powers
SCC	U.S.-ROK Security Consultative Conference
SDF	Self-Defense Forces (Japan)
septel	State Department telegram

Japan and Korea

Alignment Despite Antagonism

Introduction: The Puzzle
and Its Importance

The Puzzle

At the 1988 Olympic Games in Seoul the overtones of the cold war were clear. The United States and Soviet Union had boycotted successive Olympic Games in Moscow and Los Angeles in 1980 and 1984. As a result, American and Soviet spectators and participants at the Seoul Games dutifully cheered the athletes and teams from their respective geopolitical spheres of influence. However, a peculiar sight astonished some observers of the host Koreans that year: in events pitting the Soviet Union against Japan, Koreans cheered their Communist adversaries, not their cold-war partners. While this may have defied logic for many, it is not surprising for those even vaguely familiar with Japan-Korea relations. Ask a Korean how she feels about Japan, and the response will almost certainly be overwhelmingly negative. Pose the question to a Japanese, and the response will most likely be one of ambivalence.

Such responses epitomize the puzzle that the Japan-Republic of Korea (ROK) relationship poses for East Asian security and international relations theory. Throughout the postwar era the security of Northeast Asia has figured prominently in U.S. geostrategic thinking. America's two key allies in this region are Japan and the ROK. The bilateral defense treaties concluded with these states in 1951 and 1953 have constituted the two legs of the U.S.-Japan-ROK security triangle and served as the foundation of the American-led defense network in East Asia. However, an important but precariously unpredictable third leg of this triangle has been the Japan-ROK bilateral relationship. Despite the existence of shared threats from the Soviet Union, China, and North Korea and generally convergent security interests, relations between Japan and Korea have been marred persistently by friction since normalization in June

1965, and normalization itself had been preceded by fourteen years of protracted and caustic negotiations before formal ties were established. The main channel of political dialogue, an annual joint ministerial conference, has been postponed or suspended on numerous occasions. Threats to sever economic ties have been initiated on several occasions by both Seoul and Tokyo. Despite their proximity and the tense cold-war environment in which the two states were recently situated, they remain averse to a bilateral defense treaty.

Explaining this seemingly irrational behavior is a difficult task for the Realist school of thought in international relations, according to which states with common allies and common enemies should be friendly. The reason Realism cannot account for the anomalous character of the Japan-ROK relationship, some argue, stems from its inability to comprehend the critical role that intangible factors, beyond a rudimentary calculation of power and national interests, play in state behavior in East Asia. In particular, it cannot account for the role played by historical animosity and psychological barriers in separating Japanese and Koreans. This enmity is rooted largely in the mutual distrust and negative images cultivated during Japan's occupation of Korea from 1910 to 1945.

This mutual animosity indeed accounts at least partially for the conflict between the two states; however, a number of lingering questions suggest that it does not provide a thorough explanation. Can such basic human emotions actually determine the policy of states? Is there something inherently distinctive about East Asian state behavior which eludes expression by Western social scientific theories? If Japan and Korea have contentious relations despite common enemies, is there anything peculiar perhaps about the way they define threats? How might historical enmity account for the role played by Seoul's and Tokyo's primary ally, the United States, in their bilateral relationship? How would such an argument account for variations in behavior, in particular, variations in *cooperative* foreign-policy outcomes? And if Japan and Korea do exhibit instances of cooperation, when and *why* do these occur?

This book develops a systematic model to explain the puzzling interaction between these two key states in the Asia-Pacific region. It considers the relevance of a strain of international relations theory, known as alliance theory, in exploring the structural foundations of the relationship. This body of literature posits that one of the determinants of state behavior is the fear of being "abandoned" or "entrapped" by the ally.[1] Employing these basic concepts, I develop the concept of quasi alliances to explain the triangular interaction among Japan, Korea, and the United States. A *quasi alliance* is one in which two states remain unallied but share a third party as a common ally. The principal characteristic of the model is its emphasis on policies of the United States as a key causal determinant of changes in Japan-ROK bilateral behavior.

By framing the relationship in this manner, the book acknowledges the critical role played by history in the Japan-ROK interaction but seeks to consider history's salience in the context of equally critical threat perceptions and notions of commitment that underlie the two states' triangular alliance dynamic with the United States. This endeavor yields two basic findings. First, the "normal" state of relations between Japan and the ROK is characterized by friction. This stems not only from historical animosity but also from a fundamental disparity in each state's perceptions of the surrounding security environment and expectations of support from the other. Despite the fact that Japan and the ROK are not allied, the friction they exhibit is typical of an asymmetrically dependent alliance. Second, variations from this baseline of contentious behavior are a function of the United States' defense commitment to the region. In particular, when there exists weak (or what is perceived to be wavering) American resolve, overarching security concerns compel Japan and the ROK to exhibit significantly less contention and greater cooperation over bilateral issues. However, when there exists an asymmetry in the two states' fears of being "abandoned" by the United States, Japan-ROK relations return to their "normal" state of contentious interaction. The argument does not purport to demonstrate that the only positive influence the United States has on these two East Asian allies is the threat of disengagement from the region. The United States has, in fact, been the strongest advocate of greater cooperation in Japan-ROK relations and has acted as a critical interlocutor during difficult times between the two sides. However, the quasi-alliance argument does specify the conditions under which American overtures have been most effective.

The Puzzle's Importance

Understanding Japan-ROK relations is important for several reasons. With the end of the cold war a decreased U.S. security presence in Asia is imminent in some form. As a result, stability will rest increasingly on the myriad bilateral relationships indigenous to the region. There is no relationship as important in this respect as that between Japan and

South Korea. In the post–cold-war era the strategic location, geographic proximity, and military preparedness of these market democracies make them a suitable anchor for continued regional stability and economic prosperity. Future power configurations, such as Sino-Japanese rivalry (or entente), will turn critically on the Japanese relationship with the Korean peninsula. Moreover, regional stability will be acutely determined by both the process and final product of Korean unification and, in particular, a united Korea's relations with its former cold-war partners, Japan and the United States. An understanding of what drives these relationships is therefore critical to future security of the region.

As a "theory-building" exercise the development of the quasi-alliance concept propounds a novel perspective on the study of alliances. In the predominant view alliances are the direct causal product of external threats. I argue, by contrast, that threat perceptions represent a far more complex dynamic, which requires unpacking for a better understanding of alliances. Specifically, I look at the way changes in external threat perceptions and alliance behavior not only emanate from enemy actions but are intimately tied to promises made by allies as well. Quasi alliances thus highlight more nuanced notions of threat and the interconnections between the alliance and adversary games in a manner not readily addressed by balance-of-power theories.

In addition, the model focuses, not on formal alliance contracts, but on the general dynamic of alignment. This is important because alignment patterns are a ubiquitous, yet insufficiently studied prerequisite for alliance formation. The quasi-alliance model also incorporates extensive exploration of the dual anxieties of abandonment and entrapment and their salience not only for states party to formal alliance treaties but also for behavior among less formally associated states. Finally, the model utilizes these concepts to explain the dynamics in a three-actor scenario (rather than the traditionally promulgated two-actor game). In this sense the quasi-alliance model attempts to refine a number of key tenets in alliance theory in the form of more specific and rigorously testable hypotheses for foreign-policy behavior.

With regard to area studies this book offers a much-needed objective and systematic explanation of Japan-ROK relations. The argument that two aligned but antagonistic powers will be driven together by shared concerns about a common major-power ally and will resume their hostile behavior only when the salience of these fears has diminished may not appear particularly startling or original, but it has not been stated before conceptually or applied systematically to the Japan-ROK case. In addition, the argument attempts a powerful and more causally precise understanding of the fundamental driving factors in the relationship than exists in previous literature. Indeed, despite the importance of this relationship there is a dearth of scholarship in English. In the existing studies cultural and economic perspectives, often strongly tinted by emotional and ethnocentric biases, have predominated. This is not to say that these factors are unimportant. An understanding of Japan-ROK relations that denied historical, emotional, and nationalist partialities would certainly be deficient. Nevertheless, an inclination to rest all arguments on the precedents of history has become apparent. For every failed effort at cooperation, scholars and practitioners have grown accustomed to throwing up their hands in frustration and blaming historical animosity. This has become a stale and over-utilized argument. By offering a theoretical perspective based on political-military variables, this book attempts a fresh look at an emotionally charged and deadlocked relationship in East Asia.

The quasi-alliance model of Japan-ROK relations also provides lessons regarding the explanatory power of the Realist view of international relations: the Japan-ROK anomaly highlights a broader concern that the East Asian region presents empirical cases beyond the explanatory domain of international relations theories. Interaction among states in the region is grounded in a history, culture, and value system that is distinctly Asian. By contrast, the Realist view generally assumes interest-based behavior drawn from Western experience. In analyzing the Japan-ROK case, this book accepts certain basic Realist tenets but also considers the roles played by history, perceptions, and commitments. This more precisely delineated version of Realism can explain seemingly anomalous behavior among East Asian states and, as a result, helps to close the gap between Western methods and Asian experiences.

About the Book

This book is divided into three parts. The first part (Chapter 1) is a statement of the research puzzle, followed by a survey of ways to look at Japan-ROK relations. Here I treat the historical issue of animosity and determine its explanatory vigor with regard to Japan-ROK interaction. The second part (Chapter 2) develops an alternative explanation, analyzing basic tenets of alliance theory and deducing general propositions for contentious and cooperative foreign policy behavior between quasi-allied states. In the third part of the study (Chapters 3–6) these propositions are tested against the Japan-ROK case. Chapters 3 and 4 are devoted to events occurring from 1969 to 1974, among the most volatile years of the relationship. I trace the changes in the external security environment brought about by the Nixon doctrine (1969–71) and detente (1972–74) and show how Japanese and South Korean perceptions of the commitment of the United States to its alliances under these changing conditions directly affected their bilateral behavior. Chapters 5 and 6 concern the manner in which the two states' perceptions of their common great-power patron's policies in the aftermath of the war in Vietnam (1975–79) and during the "new cold war" (1980–88) had an impact on attitudes toward one another. The Conclusion summarizes the quasi-alliance argument and deduces additional propositions for Japan-ROK relations and East Asian security in the post–cold-war era.

Empirical evidence for this book was collected from various institutions, including the South Korean foreign ministry archives (Institute for Foreign Affairs and National Security, Seoul); the Kyungnam Institute for Far Eastern Studies (Seoul); the Japanese National Diet Library (Tokyo); the Japan Cultural Office (Seoul); the United States Armed Forces Library at Yongsan (Seoul); various presidential libraries; the Harvard-Yenching Library; the Hoover Institution collection and Green libraries at Stanford University; the C. V. Starr East Asian Library at Columbia University; and government documents centers at Harvard and Columbia. In addition, I conducted approximately one hundred interviews with American, Japanese, and Korean government officials, journalists, and academics. These included former ambassadors, foreign ministers, vice-foreign ministers, director-generals of both the international relations and Asia bureaus of the ministry of foreign affairs, embassy deputy chief of missions, embassy political and economic counselors, embassy defense attachés, and newspaper correspondents assigned to diplomatic posts.

One encounters a number of methodological problems in undertaking a study of the Japan-ROK relationship. The literature generally lacks rigorous theoretical analyses. In addition, diplomatic histories of the relationship have a tendency to borrow chronologies from one another. As a result, the researcher encounters a repetition of events and no evidence of an attempt to discover new, potentially illuminating facts. This dearth of fresh materials presented a problem, as the process-tracing method used for this book required a great deal of historical detail. To overcome this dilemma, I relied on archival materials, daily newspapers, and government documents (some recently declassified;

others, internal documents not easily accessible to the public) to develop a more comprehensive chronology of Japan-ROK relations. Whenever possible, I also tried to confirm any conclusions drawn from a reading of these sources through interviews with decisionmakers active during the period.

The limitations of these research methods deserve mention. While I use primary and secondary sources in English and Korean, I do not use materials written in Japanese. I have tried to compensate for this in several ways. First, as is the case with the literature in Korean, a good portion of the studies written in Japanese appears in popular journals. While these works might be of interest, they are not necessarily scholarly or analytically rigorous. Second, the more substantive pieces on the relationship by Japanese authors or government officials have, with few exceptions, been translated and published in English or Korean academic journals. Third, because this study treats Japan within the context of its relations with the United States and Korea, a large portion of the government documents are available in English and Korean translations.[2] Fourth, I tried to compensate for the paucity of Japanese sources by interviewing Japanese journalists, specialists on Korea, and Japanese government officials who had served in Seoul.[3] By no means does this imply that Japanese-language sources are superfluous to a study of this nature. Rather, in the absence of access to these materials, the methods described offer an imperfect but adequate substitute.

Finally, there are inherent problems with information gathered through personal interviews. Among these are the interviewees' poor, biased, or instrumental recollections, self-aggrandizing accounts, and outright denial of involvement in events. The only way to overcome such difficulties was through careful preparation in advance of each interview. In most cases I established the decisionmaker's role in these events prior to questioning and limited discussions to specific events. In other cases I asked interviewees for more general impressions of certain periods in the relationship as these were useful in understanding the broader geostrategic environment in which they operated. Diplomatic correspondents were also a good source of information and helped fill in gaps in information or resolve conflicting accounts of events by interviewees. Such problems, however, were the exception rather than the rule. The individuals I interviewed were cooperative and did their best to recount events in Japan-ROK relations as accurately as possible. They welcomed a theoretical and objective approach to this enigmatic relationship in East Asia.

ONE

The Enigma of History

INTERACTION BETWEEN Japan and Korea offers a vexing anomaly for the Realist school of international relations. This dominant school of thought essentially views state behavior under the anarchic conditions of the international system to be the product of factors such as relative military and economic capabilities, threats to external security, geography, and ideology.[1] In the case of the relationship between Japan and Korea throughout the cold war, both states were staunch allies of the United States and sites of the greatest concentrations of American military forces in East Asia. For most of the postwar era Japan and Korea have faced hostile Communist adversaries in China, the Soviet Union, and North Korea. Under U.S. patronage they have espoused generally similar liberal-democratic aspirations, although the extent and success of democratization processes in the two countries differed (Japan's adoption of democratic governance being both earlier and more successful than Korea's). They have led East Asia with their exemplary postwar market economies based on state-guided industrialization and export-oriented strategies. Their high volume of bilateral trade and investment not only attests to the interdependence of their economies but also has fostered the creation of numerous domestic groups with strong interests in congenial relations. Geographic proximity and cultural familiarity also facilitate travel, communication, and policy coordination.

Given this general commonality of friends, enemies, political values, and economic systems, logic as well as a simple application of balance-of-threat theory suggests that cooperative relations should ensue. If states balance against threats, defined in terms of aggregate power, geographic proximity, offensive capabilities, and aggressive intentions, then Japan-ROK relations in the face of proximate Soviet, Chinese, and North

Korean threats, belligerent rhetoric, and offensive capabilities during the cold war should have been cooperative.[2] However, this has been far from the case. The Japan-ROK relationship has been marked by highly volatile behavior throughout its postwar history. This has ranged from intense friction to reluctant cooperation.

Historical Variations in Japan-Korea Relations

The late nineteenth century found an expansionist, modern, and Westernizing Japan in the midst of fulfilling its ambition to dominate a weaker and insular Korea. In the tradition of the West's imperialist gunboat diplomacy, Japan gained access to Korea through the Kanghwa Treaty of 1876, challenging China's traditional influence over the peninsula. Korea was torn between succumbing to the Western and modern ways of the Japanese and adhering to the more familiar Confucian traditions of its Chinese patron. This internal vacillation, coupled with the peninsula's geostrategic location, made Korea a coveted prize in the Sino-Japanese competition for regional hegemony, ultimately won by Japan through war in 1894–95. Russia was the next to obstruct the path to Korea yet fell to the Japanese navy in 1904–5. The last obstacle to Japanese control of the peninsula was removed while negotiating the Russian defeat at Portsmouth, when the United States conceded Japan's new sphere of influence in Korea in exchange for realizing its own colonial ambitions in the Philippines (Taft-Katsura agreement of 1904). These shifts in the East Asian balance of power culminated with Japan's claiming a protectorate over Korea by 1905, followed by formal occupation and annexation of the country by 1910. Thirty-five years of harsh colonial rule ensued, leaving an indelible imprint of resentment on the relationship. This has been instantiated on the Korean side in the synthesis of national identity and anti-Japanism and on the Japanese side in ambivalent but superior attitudes toward its former colonial subjects.

The two decades following Korea's liberation from Japanese colonial rule in 1945 were marked by intense enmity between the two states. Dialogue between Seoul and Tokyo did not advance beyond mutual recrimination over colonial reparations, territorial waters, fishing rights, and repatriation of conscripted Korean laborers from Japan. Mutual contempt was so severe that during the Korean war (1950–53), ROK president Rhee Syngman said he would rather concede defeat to the Communist North Koreans than enlist Japanese support in the war effort. Similarly, Japanese leaders such as Premier Yoshida Shigeru (1948–54) rejected Seoul's tirades over colonial injustices and refused to meet with Korean leaders despite American encouragement. In the end it took well over a decade of negotiations before a basic relations treaty was signed in June 1965. Even then both governments were ambivalent about the agreement, and mass demonstrations raged in both countries, particularly South Korea, against the settlement.

A temporary reprieve from this friction occurred in the early 1970s. In order to understand these changes, a brief overview of the economic and security aspects of Japan-ROK relations is required. The ROK was dependent on Japan for much of its postwar economic growth. In emphasizing the agricultural, chemical, and steel sectors as the backbone of development, ROK president Park Chung-hee's five-year development plans (1961–79) leaned heavily on Japanese capital and technology; in addition, Park drew much of his inspiration for these growth objectives from Japan's transformation during the Meiji period (1868–1912).

On the Japanese side, while profit motivations were certainly behind these economic ties, the intense cold-war environment also caused the Japanese to rationalize their support of the ROK as a wise investment in securing a more stable defense perimeter. Economic support for the ROK was also a means of currying favor with the United States by acquiescing in Washington's burden-sharing initiatives.

Several consequences flowed from this arrangement. Japan rapidly overtook the United States as South Korea's most critical source of trade and capital, giving rise to a chronic balance-of-trade deficit between the two countries, amounting during the early 1960s to hundreds of millions of dollars and by the 1990s tens of billions. Koreans blame Japan's protectionist policies, while the Japanese argue that the problem lies in the structure of trade relations. In particular, the Japanese argue, Korean reliance on Japanese investment, machinery, and other intermediate capital goods yields a division of labor in which ROK growth is structurally tied to imports from Japan. The onus to reduce the Korean trade deficit therefore rests, the Japanese maintain, with Korean efforts at reducing their dependence on Japan.

Another consequence of economic relations was the growth of extremely close links between the business and government elites of the two countries.[3] Many of these links were forged during the colonial years, and the friendships cultivated at elite levels contrast starkly with the animosity exhibited at the popular level. While these ties lubricated relations, they also laid both governments open to criticisms of corrupt backroom dealing (often for personal gain) and Japanese collusion in the perpetuation of ROK authoritarian politics, largely through the filling of Park's party coffers.

Japanese interest in bolstering ROK growth is not only economic but also implicitly related to security. Japan and the ROK have indirect, but not insignificant, defense ties. The complexity of their relationship is largely a function of the two states' sharing a common security ally in the United States but lacking an alliance with one another. This security triangle formed the basis of the West's anti-Communist defense network in Northeast Asia throughout the cold war. U.S. defense planning for contingencies in the region (primarily a resumption of hostilities on the peninsula) rested on effective integration of its air, naval, and ground presence in both countries. Regarding the dynamics of the Japan-ROK side of this triangle, the Republic generally views itself as providing Japan's forward line of defense against the North Korean threat. For Japan, Korea has historically been both a "dagger" pointed at the heart of Japan and the "bridge" to the Asian mainland. In spite of these immutable factors Japan acknowledges only implicitly the importance of the ROK's security. Constitutional limitations as well as desires not to concede the ROK bargaining leverage cause Tokyo to refrain from overt acceptance of this view. Instead, it occasionally has professed an equidistance policy toward the peninsula, in which maintenance of the balance of power between the two Koreas, rather than siding solely with the South, affords greater stability for Japan's proximate defense perimeter. Koreans criticize such policies, seeing them largely motivated by Tokyo's "economic animal" mentality and by latent Japanese preferences to keep the peninsula eternally divided.

It was during the late 1960s and early 1970s that many of the positive traits of Japan-ROK economic and security relations were established. From approximately 1968 to 1971 bilateral trade and Japanese investment in the South Korean economy increased dramatically. The former grew from $722.9 million to $1.22 billion, making Japan the ROK's most important import market and its second largest export market (see Appendix Table A.1). Japanese direct investment in Korea grew by over $30 million compared with a moderate growth of $4.7 million in the five years preceding this period. Plans were laid for Korean free-trade zones and technological training centers, all catering to and funded by Japan. The highlight of this upsurge in economic cooperation was a series of low-interest Japanese loans that aided Korea's ascension to double-digit growth rates. Japan undertook projects that other industrialized nations and international organizations considered unprofitable, justifying these as part of its "positive economic cooperation" policies to bolster ROK political stability. Official and semiofficial bilateral fora were created in which the nexus of business-government elites could grease the wheels of cooperation.

In the security arena the conservative prime minister Sato Eisaku adhered to a one-Korea policy, acknowledging the South as the only legitimate government on the peninsula, voicing support for the security triangle with the United States, and improving the bilateral security dialogue with Seoul through a series of high-level defense exchanges. Most important, the two governments affirmed a direct security link for the first time in the 1969 "Korea clause," and Japan publicly consented to the use of American bases in Okinawa for South Korean defense.

From mid-1971 to about 1974, however, relations soured. The Tanaka Kakuei government discarded the Korea clause and distanced itself from the agreement regarding the Okinawan bases. Indicative of a new equidistance policy for the peninsula, Foreign Minister Kimura Toshio declared the absence of a security threat from North Korea and intimated that Seoul was not the only recognized government in Korea. Spurred by Japan's normalization of relations with Communist China in 1972, elements within the Japanese Diet and ruling Liberal Democratic Party (LDP) lobbied for the normalization of relations with Pyongyang and in the process substantially expanded political dialogue. The Japanese public became equally infatuated with the North, increasing exchanges with Pyongyang in sports, culture, and education. The print media wrote glowingly about the North, enraging Seoul and resulting in the expulsion of Japanese journalists from the country.

In the economic arena Japan signed memorandum trade agreements with the North in 1972 reminiscent of the ones forged with China decades earlier. Bilateral trade increased from $58.4 million (1971) to $376 million (1974), constituting the period of greatest growth since 1965 (see Appendix Table A.2). By contrast, economic cooperation with the South dramatically decreased. Japan granted only 20 percent of ROK aid requests during the period and on one occasion rejected outright all proposals for additional "positive economic cooperation" projects, which had been so prevalent only a couple of years earlier.

In addition, during this period a number of controversies took diplomatic relations to an all-time low. The Japan-ROK political relationship is a delicate one, complicated by security and historical factors. For Seoul political relations cannot be divorced from security concerns. Because success in deterring the northern threat enhances Japanese security, Seoul expects whatever domestic authoritarian practices required to achieve this goal to be acceptable, at least tacitly, to Tokyo. One form of this Japanese acceptance is refraining from criticism of the regime in the South. Another is Tokyo's cooperation in preventing its substantial pro-North Korean resident population from undertaking acts that subvert the South. These desires are all part of the general ROK view that its more powerful and prominent neighbor should treat Seoul as an intimate partner, commensurate with the special security needs of two countries.

Japan, by contrast, has little tolerance for the ROK's authoritarian political practices. It has seen these, at best, as an overzealous obsession with the North Korean threat, which increases Pyongyang's fears of encirclement; at worst as a transparent and distasteful external security rationale for prolonging the regime's power indefinitely. While Japan could close one eye to such acts within Korean borders, it cannot tolerate acts that infringe on the civil liberties and safety of Japanese nationals. What emerges in the diplomatic arena is thus a continuum of Japanese views of Korean domestic politics, ranging from support of the regime for security and business reasons (usually from conservative elements of business and the LDP) to criticism for liberal-democratic and humanitarian reasons.

Another key determinant of the character of political relations is history. Koreans are perennially seeking apologies from Japan, whether formal statements of contrition for injustices associated with the colonial period or statements of regret for the way the period is portrayed in Japanese textbooks or for insensitive remarks by Japanese officials, not to mention for a host of other issues that arouse the ire of Koreans. Koreans also invoke history to gain leverage over Japan on unrelated matters, such as trade, equating Japanese concessions with evidence of its "genuine" repentance. Japanese reluctance to respond to complaints concerning historical policies and practices stems from constitutional constraints and domestic aversion to dealing with the past (unlike Germany). It also stems from an increasing popular and governmental frustration over "how much is enough" in terms of apologies and from a desire to avoid other parties' using Japan's past as a means of gaining bargaining leverage.

These conflicts over history and Korean domestic politics reached unprecedented levels in 1973 and 1974. The Park regime's draconian attempts to stamp out political opposition at home snowballed into a rancorous bilateral dispute when the Korean Central Intelligence Agency (KCIA) kidnapped the popular dissident leader Kim Dae-jung from Japan and then arrested Japanese nationals in Korea suspected of antigovernment activities. Relations further deteriorated when a North Korean resident of Japan attempted (unsuccessfully) to assassinate the ROK president in August 1974, validating ROK charges regarding Japan's lackadaisical attitude toward the North Korean threat within its borders. This succession of crises resulted in a near-rupture in bilateral relations. Ministerial conferences were canceled, ambassadors were temporarily recalled, and embassy compounds were attacked.

This friction was alleviated during another period of cooperation from 1975 to 1979. The Japanese government under Miki Takeo reaffirmed the Korea clause in 1975 along with its commitment regarding bases in Okinawa for ROK defense. This effectively disavowed Tanaka's and Kimura's earlier actions and returned Japan to a one-Korea policy. Japanese and Korean authorities resumed suspended joint ministerial conferences and sought diplomatic compromises to the Kim kidnapping and Park assassination cases. The two governments also sought a convergence of policies regarding North Korea. Tokyo heeded South Korean complaints about the potential danger posed by pro-Pyongyang groups in Japan and tightened its watch over suspicious activities. Optimistic Japanese assessments of economic opportunities in the North were replaced by pessimistic concerns that such ties might bolster the North's war potential; as a result trade volume declined to a five-year low in 1976. At the same time positive economic cooperation between Seoul and Tokyo was revived through various new commitments of aid and concomitant surges in bilateral trade. Park reestablished the collusive business-government ties of the Sato years with Premier Fukuda Takeo. On security affairs Park cut against the grain of history with unprecedented statements about the possibilities of defense coordination between Korea and Japan. A resumption of high-level military exchanges followed in 1978 and 1979, as did the creation of parliamentary consultative bodies committed to increasing security transparency on both sides. Finally, rather than criticizing the draconian and unstable authoritarian politics of the Republic after Park's assassination in 1979, the Japanese government and media expressed remorse and determination to help Korea through its crisis.

Further complicating the pastiche of Japan-ROK relations, the 1980s offered a strange mix of cooperation and friction. In 1983 President Chun Doo-hwan and Prime Minister Nakasone Yasuhiro held the first postwar summit. Complementing this new channel of dialogue, the two governments inaugurated a set of annual foreign-ministerial conferences. Economic interdependence reached new heights with the conclusion of a $4-billion-loan agreement during the period. In addition, in an unprecedented attempt to quell historical animosity, Emperor Hirohito offered a statement of regret for the colonial past in 1984. These events undoubtedly represented a positive evolution in relations. Collusive personal ties of the 1960s and 1970s were being replaced by formal and legitimate governmental channels. The Japanese leadership showed a greater willingness to look on Korea as a partner rather than a former colony and move relations out of the quagmire of the past. Nevertheless, undercutting these cooperative trends was a rash of old and new sources of friction. Chun's entourage, the product of a younger generation of confident and assertive Korean leaders, despised the supplicant attitudes of their predecessors and proclaimed themselves openly anti-Japanese. ROK suspicions mounted that contacts with Pyongyang by Nakasone and his predecessor, Suzuki Zentaro, were thinly disguised versions of Tanaka's equidistance policy. None of the 1978 and 1979 bilateral commitments to improve defense consultation were implemented, and high-level military visits were conspicuously absent. Instead, the hawkish Nakasone's calls for a more prominent Japanese defense role in the region drew protests from Seoul about the specter of renewed militarism.

As the ROK's bilateral trade deficit with Japan grew, accusations mounted in Seoul about Japanese semimercantilist trade practices. ROK officials also accused Tokyo of purposefully withholding technology and investment to undercut Korean growth and preempt challenges to Japan. The Japanese blamed Korea's own barren innovative efforts, rising labor costs, and macroeconomic mismanagement as the sources of the problem. In the diplomatic arena these years witnessed a flood of historical disputes, ranging from school textbook revisions whitewashing past colonial atrocities to Japanese veneration of its war dead, which crippled relations. These disputes inflamed public anger to such an extent that Korean taxi drivers and restaurateurs refused service to Japanese tourists, and Tokyo abandoned a visit to Seoul by Prince Akihito out of concern for his safety.

Realism Versus Reality

This chronology reveals a stark dichotomy between *Realism* and the *reality* of Japan-Korea relations. According to the former view, although the two states may have begun their relationship under contentious circumstances, common enemies, friends, and interests should have given rise thereafter to solid and steadily improving relations. Much to the contrary, however, the reality of the relationship hardly exhibits such consistency.[4] From the tumultuous start of relations in 1965, behavior vacillated, at times dramatically, between the poles of cooperation and friction. Improvements of relations in one period were followed by erosion in others, with any sense of a progressive evolution in ties, albeit again inconsistent, only emerging from during the 1980s. Notional conceptions of these two views are outlined in Figures 1A and B.

In general, past attempts at explaining this enigmatic relationship have been unsuccessful.[5] Beyond chronological treatments there are three "lenses" through which conflict and cooperation between the two states have been viewed: (1) structural and economic disparities, (2) domestic politics, and (3) historical animosity.[6]

The first of these establishes a dichotomy between Japan as a developed country, pluralist state, and regional/global power and South Korea as a newly industrializing economy, corporatist state, and peripheral power. These differences give rise to disparate perspective, or "perceptual gaps," over key issues. For example, problems in economic relations stem from the inability of either state to accept the legitimacy of the other's arguments on issues of trade liberalization, transfer of technology, and foreign investment. Perceptual gaps, in turn, stem from structural differences associated with the stage of economic development in each of the two countries.[7] Although this view accurately highlights the importance of power differentials between the two states as a causal factor in interaction, it exhibits a static bias incapable of accounting for the volatile swings of behavior witnessed in the relationship. In other words, structural incompatibilities in the nature of the two states may account for contentious behavior, but one would be hard-pressed to explain cooperative outcomes by the same causal variables.

One way of dealing with this volatility is by looking at domestic politics. Through this second lens of Japan-ROK relations friction or cooperation is largely a by-product of the ruling elites' domestic political needs. Although there is a general convergence of interests in Japan-ROK relations that fosters cooperation, this is often overshadowed by

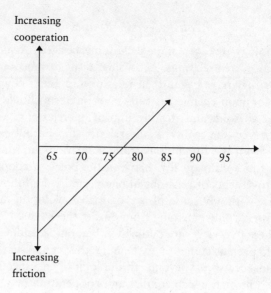

A. REALISM'S PREDICTIONS

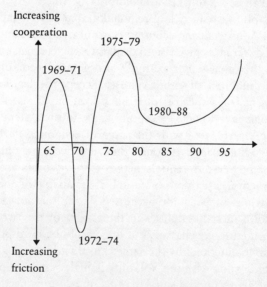

B. REALITY OF PREDICTIONS

Fig. 1. Realism versus Reality in Japan-Korea Relations

the disproportionate degree to which both sides, for domestic political purposes, allow minor differences to upset the entire relationship. For Korea this generally takes the form of the government's whipping up anti-Japan sentiment to consolidate public support and political capital.[8] For Japan policy convergence or divergence with Seoul is often a function of internal battles between liberal and conservative factions of the LDP about how best to serve Japanese economic and security interests (e.g., equidistance or one-Korea policy).[9]

The problem with this view is its "messiness." It is indeed possible to analyze Japan-Korea relations by tracing every policy decision to domestic causes unique to either Japan or the Republic; however, this provides little *a priori* understanding of interaction. Moreover, it generates a "laundry list" of possible causes without a clear sense of their relative importance. Indeed, the same foreign-policy decision may also be explained by common causal forces acting upon both states. In the end the domestic lens leaves us with situation-specific arguments that are not generalizable to the dynamics of the relationship as a whole.

The Historical-Animosity Lens

One very generalizable way of looking at Japan-Korea relations is through the lens of historical animosity. This has indeed been the prevailing characterization of those relations. In essence this view argues that deep-seated enmity and psychological barriers stemming from turbulent histories shared by the two peoples are the primary causes of friction.[10] Although disputes date back to the invasions by Hideyoshi Toyotomi in the late sixteenth century, the defining event in a modern context was Korea's colonial subjugation by Japan from 1910 to 1945. Occupation policies sought to assimilate the Koreans through the banning of their language, the enforced adoption of Japanese surnames, and the coerced worship of the Shintō state religion. The colonial police (many of whom were Korean) intruded extensively into every aspect of society and suppressed attempts at resistance, often brutally. Many colonial subjects were drafted into the Japanese military for the war effort. Even more were forced into labor-conscription programs, which abruptly transported nearly 20 percent of the rural population to low-skill mining and factory jobs in northern Korea, Manchuria, Sakhalin, and Japan under subhuman working conditions. All Koreans were the object of social discrimination and relegation to the lowest strata of society. In spite of these heavy-handed policies, the occupation also brought some benefits to Korea. Colonial policies aided the development of educational systems, an efficient government bureaucracy, and modernized agriculture and infrastructure.[11]

Distilled from this history is a peculiar "admiration-enmity" complex. On the side of admiration is the view in Korea of Japanese organization, efficiency, and economic prowess as models to be emulated. Similarly, the Japanese liken Korea's modern development to that of a younger sibling—one to be nurtured and through whom Japan vicariously relives its own earlier successes.

In spite of this mutual admiration, it is the enmity stemming from the colonial period that dominates. For Koreans this negative attitude is manifested in a direct association of Korean nationalism with anti-Japanism. The two principal national holidays in Korea, for example, March 1 (samilchŏl or Independence Day) and August 15 (kwangbokchŏl or Liberation Day), celebrate Korean patriotism through remembrance of the struggle for independence from Japanese colonial rule. Enmity is also manifested through a prevalent psychological complex known in South Korea as han, or "unredeemed resentment for past injustices."[12] In addition to the occupation, historical injustices recalled by Koreans include the 1923 Kantō earthquake, in which thousands of Koreans resident in Japan were scapegoated as responsible for the natural disaster and killed by angry Japanese. Many also hold Japan partially liable for the postwar division of the peninsula and are contemptuous of the economic benefits that accrued to the former colonizer as a result of the Korean war.[13] Han often surfaces in the form of overwrought lamentations at governmental meetings and in popular protests about the historical victimization of Korea. Typical of this complex was the opening Korean statement at the first postwar meeting between the two sides in 1951:

The years of Japanese occupation left us with problems which cannot be easily solved. . . . Our economic processes . . . were made to serve as subsidiaries to Japanese development. . . . Our own people were barred from technical and managerial training and experience. . . . We have never in our long history attacked you. We do not intend to do so. You have attacked us against our will and engulfed us.[14]

For the Japanese correspondingly negative attitudes surface in a superiority complex toward Koreans. Often described by Koreans and other Asians as "haughtiness," these sentiments are somewhat inherent in the collective mindset of Japan as a former colonizer of the region. And while not openly stated, such views occasionally are vocalized, as was the case in 1949 when Wajima Eiji, director of the Control Bureau of the Gaimushō (foreign ministry), stated with regard to the disposition of the Korean population in Japan:

The Japanese have always considered the Koreans to be an inferior race. [Wajima] said that a very elaborate study on the racial characteristics of Koreans had been prepared during the war and that it had concluded that the mental and social capacities of the Koreans were of a very primitive nature. He said that this feeling on the part of the Japanese that Koreans are inferior to a great extent motivates Japanese uncertainty and hostility in regard to the Koreans.[15]

Impressions of Koreans as "wild, savage, obstinate, and poor" and of Korea as a "country where there are many wars" were dominant among Japanese schoolchildren in 1956.[16] While a new level of respect for South Korean accomplishments is discernible today, the residue of these earlier impressions prevents complete Japanese acceptance of Koreans as equals. In addition, Japanese associations with things Korean today tend not to exceed the trivial: Korean cuisine, the Olympics, pop music. These "soft" Japanese impressions of Korea and its culture contrast with the "hard" Korean impressions of Japan that focus negatively on the colonial period and economic dominance.

For both peoples this contrast in impressions stems partly from mutual indifference and ignorance. *Tong-a/Asahi* newspaper polls in 1990, for example, found that 21 percent of Japanese respondents knew nothing about the occupation of Korea and 25 percent could not associate anything of significance with Korea. By the same token, Korean knowledge of Japan was also found to be wanting.[17] Augmenting this ambivalence is a general disinclination among the Japanese to contend with their nation's past and an annoyance at Korean attempts to hold the Japanese eternally responsible for their history. Some scholars have referred to this as Japan's "avoidance phenomenon" toward Korea.[18]

This clash of negative attitudes gives rise to the *Han-Il ŭng'ŏri* (Korea-Japan tangle), a fundamental lack of mutual understanding that plagues Japan-Korea interaction at both the common and governmental levels.[19] The two countries consistently fail to score as highly liked in each other's public opinion polls. Koreans see the Japanese as untrustworthy and unrepentant. The Japanese see the Koreans as overly emotional, blunt, and inferior. These animosities peak whenever bilateral issues arise that invoke memories of the colonial past.

For example, statements by Japanese leaders that even hint at justification for the occupation elicit strong protests from the South. In 1953 a senior Japanese official remarked that Japan's occupation policies provided many social and economic benefits to Korea. This statement precipitated a rupture in normalization talks which lasted more than four years.[20] Similar remarks by various Japanese cabinet officials in the 1970s and the 1980s elicited severe public reactions and government protests. Another source of friction is the constant bickering over the sincerity of Japan's apology for past aggressions against Korea. Koreans were dissatisfied with the text of the 1965 normalization treaty as it omitted any reference to Japanese contrition for the occupation, and they were far from placated by the ambiguous wording of the 1984 Hirohito apology.[21] Linked to this, recollection of the occupation is another persistent problem. The most prominent illustration of this was the Monbushō's (Education Ministry's) revision of Japanese history textbooks to reflect a less critical interpretation of Japanese aggression in Asia. Public outrage over this issue in 1982 resulted in formal protests from the South Korean government, suspension of concurrent bilateral loan negotiations, and spontaneous acts of discrimination against Japanese nationals in Korea.[22]

Colonial legacies are inextricably intertwined with a number of other ongoing issues in the relationship. One of these is the *chaeil kyop'o* (overseas Koreans in Japan). Numbering around 650,000, they constitute the largest minority group in Japan. Many were victims of Japanese labor conscription policies during the occupation and have been subject to social and legal forms of discrimination ever since. As a result, friction arises over Korean claims that Japan has a responsibility to redress the wrongs committed against this community.[23] Korean atomic bomb victims represent a related issue. As conscripted laborers who were innocent victims at Nagasaki and Hiroshima, these individuals (unofficially numbering around 10,000–20,000) claim the right to seek reparations and medical treatment from the Japanese government.[24] Additional matters associated with the occupation constantly arise. For example, the January 1992 revelations of the Japanese government's involvement in the conscription of Korean "comfort women" (*chŏngsintae*) during the Second World War revived dark colonial memories.

In each such dispute, dialogue degenerates into polemics, and resolution becomes infinitely more difficult because of the historical and emotional baggage attached. Moreover, reverberations from these disputes pervade all aspects of relations. For every failed diplomatic or trade negotiation, there arise Korean claims that Japanese intransigence reflects a lack of repentance for aggression and a desire to keep the Koreans in a subservient position. From the Japanese point of view there is disdain for Korean attempts to use the colonial legacy to extort concessions and a weariness over Korean emotional outbursts. In sum, a systematic rendering of this psycho-historical explanation for Japan-ROK friction could be expressed as follows: historical animosity produces systematic biases of a cognitive or affective nature on the part of government elites and the general public. These biases give rise to an atmosphere of distrust and contempt that makes compromise or concession in bilateral relations synonymous with treason (particularly for the Koreans). This, in turn, precludes the possibility of amiable or even rational negotiations.

The psycho-historical (or historical-animosity) approach is undoubtedly integral to an understanding of Japan-ROK relations. Indeed, many Koreans and Japanese still carry vivid memories of having lived through the painful period of Japanese colonization. Moreover, interviews with Korean and Japanese policymakers, as well as with American officials who have observed negotiations between the two sides, confirm that preexisting convictions of distrust and contempt constitute the starting point from which Japanese-Korean interaction begins.

As a systematic explanation of foreign policy, however, the argument exhibits some severe faults. One glaring shortcoming is its inability to account for change in the relationship. While mutual enmity may constitute the baseline of Japan-Korea interaction, the foreign-policy outcome of such interaction is not always contentious. Consequently, historical animosity may be useful for explaining instances of conflict between Japan and Korea; however, it does not prove useful in explaining instances of cooperation. The argument is essentially static; it uses a constant (i.e., mutual enmity) to explain a variable (i.e., cooperation/friction).

Advocates of the historical-animosity argument have tried to circumvent this criticism by embedding these negative images and psychological barriers in the belief systems of the particular incumbent elites of the respective nations. They then account for changes in foreign-policy outcomes (i.e., cooperation or friction) by citing changes in the leadership.[25] Among events in Japan-ROK relations offered by proponents of this argument, the 1965 normalization treaty is their best illustration.

1965 Normalization: Images or Realpolitik?

Signed on June 22, 1965, the Basic Relations Treaty formally reestablished diplomatic relations between the two governments after Japan's defeat in World War II and the surrender of its Korean colony in 1945. The treaty's basic provisions were: the abrogation of all colonial-era agreements; diplomatic recognition of the ROK; and an $845-million economic package of government and commercial loans ($200 million and $300 million, respectively), grants-in-aid ($300 million), and settled property claims ($45 million). There were also technical agreements on the return of cultural assets, alien-resident status, and the delineation of territorial waters.[26] The conclusion of this treaty, however, came only after a protracted, fourteen-year negotiation process marked by acrimony and numerous disruptions.

Treaty talks began in October 1951 but abruptly came to a halt over a clash of agendas.[27] Angered by Japan's uncooperativeness, ROK president Rhee in January 1952 unilaterally declared a sixty-mile zone of sovereign waters around the peninsula (the "Rhee line" or "Peace line"), which extended well beyond the three-mile international standard and enraged the Japanese as the political equivalent of an act of war.[28] Seoul subsequently imprisoned one thousand Japanese fishermen for violating the Rhee line (October 1952), and a one-year suspension in talks ensued.

Negotiations resumed in October 1953 only to founder over statements by the Japanese chief delegate, Kubota Kanichiro. Kubota responded to Korean demands for $2.7 billion in reparations by stating that Japan itself deserved compensation for its colonial development of Korean roads, railways, educational institutions, government facilities, and reforestation and irrigation projects. He added that the Allied powers' postwar seizure of Japanese assets in Korea was a violation of international law and that if Japan had not colonized Korea in 1910, "Korea would naturally have been occupied by some other country, and would have experienced a more miserable situation than under Japanese rule."[29] These remarks incensed the Koreans, resulting in another suspension of talks lasting nearly five years.

A tacit agreement involving Tokyo's retraction of Kubota's statements and Seoul's release of the detained Japanese fisherman (December 1957) enabled the resumption of the dialogue in April 1958. However, talks again stalled in March 1959 after the Kishi Nobusuke government's negotiation of a repatriation agreement with North Korea, returning over 80,000 Koreans to Pyongyang,[30] and did not make any progress until after Park Chung-hee took power in May 1961. High-level ROK visits to Japan resulted in a secret financial restitution agreement between KCIA director Kim Jong-pil and Foreign Minister Ohira Masayoshi in November 1962.[31] However, when the Kim-Ohira memo was made public, a vociferous public outcry over the ROK chief negotiator's "selling out" to the Japanese pressed him into an eight-month political exile (February–October 1963), which left negotiations at a standstill. Talks resumed in December 1964, and the following February Foreign Ministers Shiina Etsusaburo and Lee Tong-won held high-level meetings in Seoul, during which Shiina made a historic statement of regret for Japan's colonial aggression,[32] and the two sides initialed a preliminary treaty draft.[33]

At this point marathon subcommittee negotiations failed to reach agreements on three remaining technical issues: (1) the legal status of Koreans resident in Japan, (2) the exact amount of the financial-claims resolution package to be provided by Japan, and (3) the demarcation of exclusive and joint fishing zones.[34] Attempts by Foreign Minister Lee to seek a high-level solution in March 1965 proved unsuccessful.[35] Talks appeared to have reached a major impediment; however, shortly after a visit to the United States by Lee later that month (March 15–22) a breakthrough was reached by the fisheries subcommittee on March 24,[36] followed by resolution of the financial claims and residency issues four days later.[37] Clearing these last hurdles paved the way to a treaty signing, which finally took place in June 1965 despite mass antitreaty demonstrations in Seoul and Tokyo.[38]

How does one explain this extremely volatile path to normalization? Advocates of the historical-animosity approach attribute the inability to conclude a treaty, particularly during the period from 1951 to 1960, to the negative images and attitudes held by the leadership in Tokyo and Seoul.[39] Rhee, in particular, maintained strongly negative images of Japan. Intensely nationalistic, Rhee's entire political career before attaining the presidency was devoted to liberating Korea from Japanese occupation. In an often-cited example of his anti-Japanese sentiment, the ROK president once responded to Secretary of State John Foster Dulles's emphasis on forging an anti-Communist front in Asia by emphatically stating that Koreans were more worried about Japan than they were about the Soviet Union.[40] Similarly, Japanese Prime Minister Yoshida Shigeru (1948–54) held staunchly negative views of Korea, exemplified by statements once referring to Koreans living in Japan as "insects in the stomach of a lion with the potential to kill the lion itself if not checked"[41] His personal antipathy toward Rhee was so great that he once refused to attend a luncheon hosted in 1953 by the American ambassador to Japan, Robert Murphy, because he could not conceal his distaste for the South Korean president.[42] Mutual enmity held at the highest levels of government consequently precluded the possibility of businessslike or cordial treaty negotiations.

Similarly, advocates of this line of reasoning attribute the ability to achieve normalized relations in 1965 to the more pragmatic and positive attitudes that accompanied a change in leadership. Park Chung-hee, in particular, differed from his predecessors in his views of Japan. He had been raised during the occupation, spoke Japanese (his Japanese name was Takagi Masao), attended the Japanese military academy in Manchuria, and had been an officer in the Japanese army. Park's cabinet was staffed with younger, foreign-educated, cosmopolitan thinkers who were able to distinguish Korean nationalism from anti-Japanism.[43] For example, Premier Chung Il-kwon was a military academy classmate of Park's; business leaders like steel magnate Park Tae-joon were graduated from Waseda University in Japan; and four of the six ambassadors to Japan under Park were also graduates of Japanese universities. As interviews with some of Park's advisors confirmed, the former president, although strongly nationalistic, held an affinity and respect for Japan, manifest in his belief that South Korean economic growth could best be accomplished by following the Japanese model of development.[44] Park and his entourage saw relations in a junior/senior context (sŏnbae/hubae) wherein Japan would play a nurturing and supportive role in Korea's growth.[45] As a result, the dissipation of psychological barriers accompanying the change from Rhee to Park facilitated the signing of the normalization agreement in 1965.

While a plausible explanation, a more demanding test of this argument leads to some implausible propositions. To accept this psychohistorical interpretation of Japan-Korea normalization as true would also require one to argue that if a leader other than Park had been in power (i.e., ones with highly negative images of Japan), then normalization would *not* have occurred in June 1965. A review of the events preceding normalization finds such a proposition highly unlikely. The 1965 settlement was less a function of dramatic changes in the belief systems and attitudes of the leadership and more a product of: regional geostrategic conditions and the domestic political needs of the parties involved.

With regard to the latter factor, a confluence of domestic political imperatives pressed both Seoul and Tokyo to seek normalization.[46] By the mid-1960s the ROK faced a nearly desperate situation. The first five-year economic development plan (1962–66) had failed to extinguish the rampant inflation, high unemployment, and peasant unrest or to ameliorate the slow growth that plagued the economy. These conditions caused many to question the competence of the fledgling Park regime and look with envy on the then more prosperous North Korean system.[47] Banking the survival of his regime on an ambitious second five-year plan (beginning 1966), Park sorely needed massive infusions of capital and technology absent from Korea. Exacerbating this need was a steady decline in U.S. economic assistance from 1960, which reached a sixteen-year low in 1965.[48] On the security front the emergence of China as a nuclear power and the escalating conflict in Vietnam (heightened concerns about the threat from Pyongyang. Park's decision to deter this threat through an emphasis on economic growth rather than the *pukch'in t'ongil* (march north) strategy of his predecessors brought an important security rationale to Japanese infusions of capital. At the same time Korean business appetites were whetted by the prospect of tapping Japanese markets for export as well as by moving into new light industries made competitive by Japan's abandonment of them as it ascended the product/technology ladder.[49] This combination of economic and political imperatives compelled a more pragmatic attitude toward Japan. As Park stated in 1965, "It is wise that we should hold hands with even yesterday's enemy if it is beneficial to us today and tomorrow."[50] Upon appointing Lee Tong-won foreign minister, Park instructed him that normalization with Japan was his top priority and that the objective of this policy was national economic development, not obtaining historical repentance from Japan.[51] As one former foreign ministry official recalled, this became the "single-minded" purpose of Park, Lee, Premier Chung Il-kwon, KCIA Director Kim Jong-pil, and others of Park's inner circle of advisors.[52]

In Japan voices within the Gaimushō pressed emphatically for normalization. As a 1965 white paper stated, the reestablishment of ties with Korea was a "historical inevitability," and Park's urgent need for foreign capital and political legitimacy presented an opportune moment to extract an agreement at the lowest cost to Tokyo.[53] A core group of powerful conservative Japanese politicians also fervently promoted these views.[54] Their logic was that, regardless of how much financial compensation Japan provided with normalization, the Korean public would always demand more. As a result, striking a deal with Park (rather than, for example, the previous democratic Chang Myon government) was best for Japan as Park's iron-fisted rule was both less susceptible to popular demands for a huge Japanese reparations package and more easily persuaded to accept a smaller but immediate settlement.[55]

Additional pressure came from the powerful Japanese business lobby.[56] Although as many as sixty major trading and industrial firms had offices in Seoul by the mid-1960s, the ROK still represented a largely untapped market. Park's second five-year economic development plan offered Japanese firms a plethora of large-scale projects, all of which could be financed by the reparations and financial aid package arising out of a normalization settlement.[57]

Finally, security concerns provided further incentive for an improvement of relations with the ROK. As Fukuda recalled, cold-war dangers in Southeast Asia coupled with China's hostile rhetoric toward Tokyo made Japan's external environment increasingly threatening. Without Japanese support of the fledgling ROK economy, many believed that a collapse of government in Seoul might result in Communist-incited instability even closer to Japanese shores.[58]

In sum then, domestic political imperatives played an important role in pushing Japan and Korea to seek a "marriage of convenience" through normalization. Moreover, this occurred in spite of mutually held historical animosities.

The U.S. Role in Normalization

Another factor critical to the materialization of a treaty in 1965 was the subtle but significant efforts of the United States to consolidate the Japan-Korea axis in response to heightened cold-war tensions in the region.[59] This was particularly the case in the final eighteen months of talks when U.S. exhortations gave Seoul and Tokyo added incentives to reach a prompt settlement and overcome opposition at home. Prior to this period (i.e., from 1951 to 1963), the United States, with the exception of some regional experts, took a somewhat ambivalent position on Japan-Korea reconciliation.[60] While a U.S. lead may have helped move the talks along, many focused on the risks associated with such a policy: it would leave Seoul and Tokyo vulnerable to attacks from opposition groups for caving in to U.S. pressure and would undermine the perceived legitimacy of any final treaty.

By 1964, however, increasingly tense cold-war circumstances in Asia prompted a marked change in U.S. attitudes. First, the Chinese Communist threat loomed large. Beijing's split from the Soviet monolith, its signing of a mutual defense treaty with North Korea (1961), and its support of Southeast Asian revolutionary movements ominously signaled the consolidation of an "Asian communist front." Successful Chinese nuclear weapon tests in October 1964 and May 1965, coupled with harsh rhetoric on Taiwan and the radicalization of domestic politics, further heightened American perceptions of a Chinese threat.[61] Second, U.S. commitments to a deteriorating situation in Indochina became more encumbering. Congressional passage of the Gulf of Tonkin resolution in August 1964 authorized what had already grown secretly into a deepening entrenchment in the Vietnam conflict for the Lyndon Johnson administration. These commitments grew even deeper with the start of large-scale aerial bombardment campaigns on North Vietnam in February 1965 and the decision to deploy U.S. ground troops in April 1965.

Under these conditions a stable relationship between America's two principal allies in the region, Japan and Korea, became an immediate priority. From the perspective of U.S. grand strategy, Seoul-Tokyo reconciliation would reinforce what John Foster Dulles called the Pacific "anti-communist arc," stretching from the Philippines and Indochina up through Taiwan, Japan, and Korea. Japanese aid and trade deriving from a normalization settlement would bolster the fledgling South Korean economy and enhance political stability against the North as U.S. commitments in Indochina grew more burdensome.[62] A shoring up of the Japan-ROK link would also preempt any potential growth in Japan-North Korea ties.[63] Finally, a normalization treaty was a requisite step in the longer-term American vision of an eventual drawdown of ground forces after stabilization of the peninsula. While these views had been held, albeit less forcefully, in the past, by 1964 the majority of policymakers in the State Department and White House sought to encourage a treaty settlement within the year. Some reports even advocated Japan-ROK normalization as a prelude to a military alliance between the two powers. While such views were somewhat ambitious, they reflected the new enthusiasm in Washington for consolidating this Northeast Asian axis.[64]

In line with this policy the United States strongly pushed for an early conclusion to negotiations in three ways. First, Johnson officials made normalization the top priority in virtually all bilateral meetings with the ROK and Japan in 1964 and 1965. Second, Washington offered clear support for the treaty at pivotal moments to help boost the leadership in both countries over salient domestic opposition (this was particularly true on the Korean side). And third, the United States acted in various capacities to facilitate dialogue during critical impasses in talks. U.S. actions did not constitute direct intervention but were of a more subtle nature. As Ambassador Edwin O. Reischauer stated, Washington could not push its own policy objectives on its two allies yet had to meet competing demands from each of them:

A major difficulty is that, to get normalization over the very great hurdles of party conflict and public opposition in Korea, we will probably have to push more openly for it in Korea than we have in the past, but any seeming intervention on our part makes the problem more difficult in Japan.[65]

Undertaken within these constraints, American actions were therefore more visible in Seoul than in Tokyo; however, in both countries the U.S. role as a facilitator and interlocutor was critical to reaching an early conclusion to the talks.

For example, in January and February 1964 Secretary of State Dean Rusk made trips to Tokyo and Seoul and met with Japanese and Korean envoys in Washington specifically for the purpose of expressing "great interest" in an early normalization settlement.[66] In addition to these high-level exhortations, the United States took proactive steps in support of the treaty process. In particular, in response to massive anti-treaty demonstrations throughout Korea in the spring of 1964 Ambassador Samuel Berger made clear to ROK opposition leaders that attempts to derail the treaty process might jeopardize future U.S. support for the ROK as well as any economic benefits linked with normalization.[67]

The United States also sought to dampen an explosion of protest over ROK chief negotiator, Kim Jong-pil. Kim had become the focus of the spring 1964 antitreaty riots as well as the cause of a destabilizing polarization of factions within the ROK government. This was largely the result of his unpopular secret 1962 agreement with Ohira, corrupt practices as the ruling Democratic Republican Party (DRP) chair, and allegations of another secret deal that compromised the ROK treaty-negotiating position to Japan in exchange for personal profit.[68] Kim was ultimately removed from the political scene in June 1964 with an extended leave of absence. While this decision was taken by Park, the United States played an important supporting role. Confidential U.S. embassy telegrams in April 1964 flatly stated Ambassador Berger's concerns about Kim's debilitating effect on the prospects of a normalization settlement: "elimination [of] KCP [Kim Chong Pil] would deprive opposition of biggest club against government and would satisfy students. Resultant government strength would permit ROKG [to] resume ROK-Japan negotiations."[69] Kim's departure from Korea was hastily arranged through private American channels and extensively outlined in cables between the embassy and State Department.[70] As the following secret embassy cable reveals, U.S. officials also stated to Park later in the year their belief that Kim should not return until after normalization with Japan was completed.

After courtesy call by Senator Monroney December 21 I took President Pak [sic] aside and said that I had thought over very carefully what he had said to me on December 18 about return of Kim Chong P'il. I nevertheless continued to feel that it would cause a great deal of trouble for ROK-Japan negotiations and for political stability in Korea if KCP returned before the ROK-Japan negotiations were ended. I said I wanted him to know that what I had said to him on Saturday was not only my own personal opinion but that I had conveyed to him this message by specific instructions of the Department of State.[71]

Furthermore, in August 1964, Johnson sent a strongly worded personal letter to Park through the new American ambassador to Korea, Winthrop Brown, which focused solely on the normalization question despite a number of other pressing issues (e.g., currency devaluation, ROK troops in Vietnam, and status-of-forces agreement):

President Johnson asked me to give you his warm personal regards. He also asked me to speak to you for him about the negotiations for normal relations between Korea and Japan. . . . He hopes that you will move forward shortly to establish normal relations and reach a settlement with Japan. It is not healthy for Korea to continue long to be so exclusively dependent upon a single outside friend as it is at present. . . . It would also benefit the Free World position in the Far East. . . . The United States Government is prepared publicly to support such a settlement, and to make clear that it will not affect the basic United States policies of economic assistance to Korea. . . . It is because the President holds these views strongly that he authorized me to stress United States support of a Korea-Japan rapprochement in my public statement on arrival.[72]

American encouragement of Japan-ROK normalization continued through the first half of 1965. As noted earlier, the February 1965 meetings between Shiina and Lee in Seoul were decisive steps in the treaty process, as they produced Shiina's colonial apology, followed by the initialing of a draft treaty. However, a major obstacle to the staging of these meetings was the two sides' inability to agree on a venue. Although seemingly a minor logistical issue, this was one on which both sides remained fiercely intransigent. Seoul refused to follow the past practice of its officials traveling to Tokyo "begging" (*kugŏlhada*) for normalization.[73] The Japanese team considered dispatching its foreign minister to Seoul to "apologize" for the colonial past as equally humiliating.[74]

Low-profile efforts by the United States were key to resolving this dispute. In particular, Ambassador Reischauer sent a secret emissary, Deputy Chief of Mission John Emmerson, to Seoul at the end of September 1964 to persuade Lee to come to Japan. Lee discussed the issue over dinner with the emissary and Ambassador Brown but remained adamantly opposed. Having known Lee previously (and perhaps familiar with his stubbornness), Reischauer finally reasoned with Shiina to make the trip to Seoul despite strong opposition in Tokyo.[75] It was also as a result of exhortations by Reischauer and Assistant Secretary of State William Bundy that Tokyo conceded to including a colonial apology as part of Shiina's visit.

Had these issues not been resolved and the February 1965 meeting not materialized, the resulting stall in talks would have given antitreaty forces another opportunity to rally as they had done the previous spring. The absence of a dispute over these issues was therefore evidence of Reischauer's and Brown's subtle but indispensable efforts at facilitating progress in the talks. As Reischauer wrote, the normalization treaty was one of his "most important and long-lasting" accomplishments.[76]

At two critical moments in March and May 1965 the United States further encouraged the normalization process through high-profile statements and supportive actions. As noted, the last major hurdle after the February 1965 draft agreement was resolution of the three technical issues: residency rights, monetary claims, and the troublesome fisheries (territorial waters demarcation) question. Talks were deadlocked until ROK foreign minister Lee's mission to Tokyo (March 11–14), Washington (March 15–22), and then back to Tokyo, after which breakthroughs were reached on each issue (March 24 and 28).

It is clear that Lee's meetings in the United States contributed to these breakthroughs. High-level political compromises were the only way to break the impasse on technical issues; however, apprehensiveness about taking such a major step existed on both sides. For the Koreans the concern was that normalization with Japan might translate into a downgrading of U.S. commitments to Korea.[77] For the Japanese the concern was that, absent potent symbols of U.S. support, Park might not be able to withstand another barrage of antitreaty attacks similar to those of the spring of 1964. This would leave Tokyo in the unenviable position of having expended energies to get the treaty past a reluctant Japanese public, then having no results to show for it.[78]

As a result, it was extremely important for both governments that Lee's Washington visit result in unequivocal public statements of support for the treaty process. Rusk, Bundy, and other high-level officials provided such assurances in the joint communiqué issued at the time of the visit, explicitly stating that normalization would "in no way affect the basic U.S. policy of extending military and economic aid to the Republic."[79] President Johnson also took the time to consult personally with Lee on the status of the talks.[80] This was significant because administration officials had declined Seoul's earlier requests for such a meeting on the ground that the president rarely met with foreign ministers. A memo from Rusk to the president spelled out the rationale behind granting this exception:

Foreign Minister Lee's visit will come at a crucial stage in the Korea-Japan normalization negotiations. His meetings with Japanese Foreign Minister Shiina February 17–20 in Seoul led to the initialling of a Korea-Japan Basic Relations Treaty, a significant step forward in the negotiations. . . . He will return to Seoul through Tokyo to meet a third time with Shiina in an attempt to finalize a normalization agreement. . . . While in normal circumstances I would not recommend your receiving Foreign Minister Lee, I strongly recommend in this case that you do. . . . Your receiving him will significantly strengthen him personally and the Park Government as a whole in their efforts to advance this highly important project.[81]

To show the connection between the Washington meetings and Lee's return to Japan, the United States took the unusual step of having Reischauer present with Shiina to greet Lee at Haneda airport.[82] Newspapers all linked Lee's U.S. visit with the April breakthrough in normalization talks.[83]

Finally, in the critical month preceding the treaty's signing, U.S. officials were acutely aware that the antitreaty movement's last chance for obstructing the agreement rested on the argument that the American motive in forging a normalization pact was to shed commitments in the ROK, thereby subjugating Korea once again to Japanese dominance. Deflating this argument through a high-profile summit for Park (May 17–19) was therefore critical to public acceptance of signing a treaty in June and ratifying it thereafter.[84] At the summit Johnson's assurances were documented in a specific and lengthy section of the joint communiqué, which included assurances of continuing assistance programs, technical assistance and training, agricultural aid programs, and $150 million in development loan funds.[85] As Rusk bluntly explained to Park, the loan was tangible proof of American commitments and the final U.S. step in lubricating the wheels of normalization.

Secretary Rusk made the point that it seemed to him that the basic point to be made was that a Korea-Japan agreement would not mean that the U.S. would run away. We were trying to say so eloquently, and it seemed to him that $150 million was an eloquent figure.[86]

The History Variable: Necessary but Not Sufficient

The normalization treaty sheds light on the difficulties of using historical-animosity and leadership variables to explain conflict and cooperation in Japan-ROK relations. Proponents point to the treaty as a powerful validating case. They argue that the failure to normalize in the 1950s and early 1960s was due to the historical and emotional biases of the political leadership (i.e., Rhee and Yoshida) and that the ability to reach a settlement in 1965 was due to the more positive images held by new leaders (i.e., Park and Sato).

However, a review of the events finds such a proposition highly implausible. Contrary to the historical-animosity argument, it was not a change in attitudes or a lessening of enmity that produced this foreign-policy outcome in 1965; in fact, acute historical animosities and anti-treaty sentiments were present on both sides throughout the treaty's negotiation, signing, and ratification.[87] Instead, a confluence of U.S. cold-war security imperatives and domestic realpolitik in Tokyo and Seoul produced the settlement. Park Chung-hee dearly needed foreign capital for economic development and political legitimacy at a time when U.S. assistance was decreasing. Tokyo faced burden-sharing pressures from the United States. It knew normalization was inevitable and therefore assessed Seoul's desperate needs as an opportune moment to extract an agreement at least cost to Japan. And most important, America's deepening entrenchment in Vietnam made an immediate reconciliation between these two allies the top priority in shoring up the anti-Communist front in East Asia.[88] In short, a settlement would have been reached during this period in spite of historical animosity and regardless of whether the leadership held acutely negative or positive attitudes.

In essence, the preceding counterfactual exercise highlights the distinction between long-term policy outcomes and day-to-day interaction. Historical animosity is useful for showing that there are psychological barriers unique to Japan-Korea relations and that these barriers are manifested in a daily atmosphere of distrust and contempt. Personality, memory, and emotions do play a role. However, feelings of enmity cannot account for significant variations in longer-term Japan-Korea foreign-policy outcomes. The flaw in the historical-animosity argument becomes apparent when its advocates attempt to explain these types of outcomes and is clearly revealed in the case of the normalization treaty. These advocates cannot explain how this instance of cooperation arose from a baseline of mutual enmity. Therefore, as a systematic explanation of Japan-ROK relations, historical animosity alone is not sufficient. The next chapter proposes an alternative approach.

TWO

The Argument: Quasi Alliances

A N ANALYSIS OF the Japan-ROK relationship requires the development of a theory that can account for two weaker powers that share a common threat and common great-power protector but are afflicted by alliance hindrances (historical animosity). The quasi-alliance model aims to address the absence of an existing deductive theory for this. Quasi alliance is defined as the relationship between two states that remain unallied despite sharing a common ally. In order to understand the application of this concept to Japan-Korea relations, it is first necessary to assess briefly the literature on alliance theory.

Basic Elements

Alliances are a fundamental part of international relations. Under the self-help, anarchic conditions of the international system alliances serve as a means of attaining security through the deterring of aggressors, defending against attacks, or initiating offensive actions against others.[1] Three bodies of literature generally inform the study of this phenomenon.[2] The first of these, alliance formation, addresses issues such as the determinants of alliances and their termination in times of peace, crisis, and war.[3] Studies on alliance management generally focus on the dynamics within an alliance, looking at issues such as burden-sharing, free-riding between parties, and the degree to which alliance security is a public good.[4] The last, alliance effectiveness, looks at the degree to which alliances affect the frequency of war and the preservation of peace.[5] As Liska described, despite these efforts, a common criticism of the literature on alliances is its lack of progress toward a general theory:

"It is impossible to speak of international relations without referring to alliances; the two often merge in all but name. For the same reason, it has always been difficult to say much that is peculiar to alliances on the plane of general analysis."[6] One manifestation of this "delimitation dilemma" is a blurring of the analytical line distinguishing studies of alliances from those of balance of power.[7]

Attempts have been made at delineating areas of exploration for alliance theorists that advance beyond the domain of underdetermining balance-of-power theories. Christensen and Snyder, for example, looked at ways in which beliefs about the efficacy of offensive and defensive military doctrines affect the tightness ("chain ganging") and looseness ("buck passing") of alliance commitments. Schweller looked at the way the types of states (status quo or revisionist), their number (i.e., tripolar), and their relative capabilities cause dynamics like "distancing" among allies. And Christensen looked at the role that misperceptions of the distribution of capabilities play in determining the tightness, looseness, or avoidance of prewar alliance commitments.[8] What these studies highlight more fundamentally, as Glenn Snyder observed, are the numerous gray areas of interstate relations—gradations of alignment— that are left unexplained by theories that focus only on the balancing-bandwagoning dichotomy:

It should not be forgotten that the fundamental focus of analysis is, or ought to be, alignment rather than alliance. . . . There is a vast area of political interaction lying between the relatively static interests and conflicts in the system and the formation and management of formal alliances. In this area much turns on nuances . . . well short of alliance or even entente.[9]

In this regard Snyder developed the concepts of "abandonment" and "entrapment" to capture the expectations and anxieties of mutual support that underpin interaction between allied and aligned states.[10] Theories of alliance formation require further development of this concept of alignment because alignment patterns are a prerequisite to all forms of alliance creation and termination. Theories of alliance management need to develop variables that can be made operational and hypotheses that can be generalized in order to explain contentious and cooperative behavior within these alignment patterns. Furthermore, there exists a need to test the explanatory scope of alliance concepts outside the European and American cases traditionally used by way of example. Without such efforts the field of international relations cannot move closer to a more powerful and generalizable theory of alliances and alignment. The quasi-alliance model builds upon the theoretical contributions of Snyder. It explores the meaning and implications of the concepts of abandonment and entrapment and deduces more systematically testable hypotheses for allied and aligned foreign-policy behavior in both two- and three-actor games.

Alliance theory frames foreign-policy behavior between states within the context of a "game."[11] Behavior within the game varies between the two poles of cooperation and defection. I define *cooperation* as a strong commitment to alliance obligations. It includes material and verbal support for the ally in contingencies against the adversary. Defection is a weak commitment to the alliance, including little support for the ally in conflict with the adversary. The degree to which a state cooperates or defects in the game is dependent on its assessment of its abandonment and entrapment concerns.[12] These concerns reflect the combination of opportunity and obligation inherent in any alliance arrangement. Specifically, they reflect the degree to which a strong or weak commitment in particular contingencies is perceived to enhance a state's security interests. Abandonment is the fear that the ally may leave the alliance or may not fulfill obligations to it. In the extreme case abandonment means "dealignment" or realignment, but it generally occurs when the ally:

may fail to make good on his explicit commitments; or may fail to provide support in contingencies where support is expected. In both of the latter two variants, the alliance remains intact but the expectations of support which underlie it are weakened.[13]

Entrapment generally occurs when a commitment to an alliance turns detrimental to one's interests:

Entrapment means being dragged into a conflict over an ally's interests that one does not share, or shares only partially. The interests of allies are generally not identical; to the extent they are shared, they may be valued in different degree.[14]

Entrapment is also the overextension of one's commitments and resources to an ally.

Abandonment and Entrapment Further Examined

States engage in alliance behavior to attain security against, and only derivatively for, someone or something.[15] Consequently, a necessary condition for the existence and intensity of abandonment and entrapment fears is an external security threat, whether real or perceived. For example, in low-threat situations where security is abundant, contingencies that require support for or from an ally are less compelling than those in situations of high-threat or security-scarcity situations. As a result, such conditions generally engender less intense fears of abandonment and entrapment. Disparities in allied states' interests in defending against these threats affect the relative balance of abandonment/entrapment fears. For example, should allies identify a threat as compelling and define their security interests as wholly congruent, then both are fully committed to the alliance and will experience low fears of entrapment in any contingency. However, if only one of these partners defines its interests in this manner, then an imbalance in abandonment and entrapment fears will result.

The adversary game further illustrates these dynamics. For example, if one state practices hard-line containment against the enemy, this increases the state's abandonment fears in the alliance game because it increases the perceived need for allied support in deterring the adversary. But if the state's ally does not share the same threat perceptions, the ally's entrapment fears will increase as it will seek to avoid entanglement in the other state's policies. Conversely, if a state practices an accommodationist policy toward an adversary, this may heighten its entrapment fears in the alliance game as the state perceives tight alliance ties as unnecessarily provocative to the adversary; however, the same policy may also generate intense abandonment fears for the state's ally, particularly if the ally holds high-threat perceptions of the adversary. Strategies in the two games are therefore interlinked.

While security threats are necessary for abandonment and entrapment fears, formal alliance contracts are not.[16] Alliances are not the only form of interstate cooperation for security purposes. There are many less formal security arrangements that accomplish the same purpose and in some cases are more cohesive than formal alliance ties.[17] Prior to the outbreak of the First World War, for example, Italy did not honor commitments to Germany and Austria-Hungary in the Triple Alliance and instead showed stronger allegiance to the informal Triple Entente (France, Great Britain, and Russia). Alliances are merely part of a broader phenomenon known as alignment. *Alignment* is defined as "a set of mutual *expectations* between two or more states that they will have each other's support in disputes or wars with particular other states."[18]

The expectations states have regarding the likelihood and degree of

support from others are therefore at the core of alliance ties.[19] States do
not need formal alliance contracts to have such expectations and feelings of obligation; such contracts only reinforce and formalize alignment patterns that exist on the basis of perceived common interests.[20]
For example, after suffering an attack from China in November 1962,
India could rely on the United States for material and moral support.
Despite the absence of a mutual defense treaty, this alignment existed
because of a shared interest in preventing Chinese expansion in the region. Similarly, formal alliance ties did not undergird the United States-
Israel or Soviet Union-Egypt relationships prior to 1971; nevertheless,
expectations of support typical of alliance partners were quite substantive. Fears of abandonment and entrapment naturally derive from these
expectations and alignment patterns. The uncertain expectation of another state's support against an adversary generates abandonment fears.
The belief that another state will act intransigently against an adversary
or will expect full support from others in a given contingency can generate entrapment fears. In sum, abandonment and entrapment fears are
operative among unallied states given three basic conditions: (1) an external security threat, (2) a degree of commonly perceived interest in defending against this threat, and (3) resultant expectations of mutual
support.[21]

These anxieties constitute the "twin horns" of the security dilemma
in alliance politics.[22] For an individual state the abandonment/entrap-
ment complex is inversely constituted, as the high fears of one usually
mean lower fears for the other.[23] For example, *prima facie* if I fear losing my significant other to another, I generally have less fear of being
engulfed by this person. *Between* allies, abandonment and entrapment
anxieties are assessed in relative terms with regard to an adversarial
threat.

BALANCE OF ANXIETY

Three sets of factors in the alliance game influence the balance of
anxieties between states. The first set of factors relates to conditions
that affect a state's ability to "exit" from alliance arrangements deemed
unsatisfactory and "enter" into other means of assuring security.[24] The
lower a state's exit-entry potential, the higher the likelihood of abandonment or entrapment anxieties. For example, a state will experience
high abandonment fears if it is uncertain of an ally's support in the face
of salient threats and it lacks the capacity to exit the alliance for some

comparable form of protection. By contrast, a state can be immune from abandonment/entrapment anxieties regarding an ally if it has the capacity to easily enter into alternative arrangements that provide for security.

There are two basic structural determinants of a state's capacity for exit and entry: relative power capabilities and polarity. In general, strong states will experience less intense fears of abandonment, while weak states will experience more intense fears. This is because the power resources a state has at its disposal to provide for security influences its ability to exit alliances. Weak states, for example, that free-ride off the defense umbrella of an ally or value an alliance as a form of power accretion often cannot exit for a comparable form of protection (such as through internal balancing or alternative partners). As a result, weak states are susceptible to acute fears of abandonment, whereas a strong state with the ability to balance internally against outside threats will have greater choice and thus less intense abandonment fears with regard to the ally.

With regard to entrapment fears, the absence of exit capacity can raise intense entrapment fears for weak states on the one hand because the consequences of defecting from a valued partner (i.e., dealignment by that partner) can be more disastrous to one's security than being dragged into the partner's conflict with the adversary. For strong states on the other hand the consequences to one's security of abandoning an ally in need are less severe, hence entrapment fears are less intense. In short, power capabilities determine the degree of dependency on the alliance for security. If a state is highly dependent on the alliance or perceives the ally to be substantially less dependent, high fears of abandonment and entrapment result.

There are many exceptions to these rules, two of which deserve mention. First, the strategic interest one has in keeping the ally out of the adversary's camp can influence exit-entry choices and abandonment/entrapment concerns. If, for example, a strong state perceives dealignment or realignment by the weaker ally as highly beneficial to the adversary, then the former's abandonment fears are high. This differs from direct dependence in that abandonment fears are generated, not by the possible loss of the ally's intrinsic contribution to one's security, but by the desire to minimize the adversary's power.[25] Second, the degree to which the alliance partner offers benefits of significance also affects a state's exit-entry options. If, for example, a weaker state's contribution to the alliance is provision of bases, resources, and access to sea lanes that are crucial to the stronger ally's security needs, then the stronger state can have high fears of abandonment.

Linked to relative power capabilities, polarity also influences the options open to a state outside a given alliance. In general, the availability of alternative alliance partners in a multipolar system is higher than in a bipolar system. Exit and entry are therefore more feasible under conditions of multipolarity and, as a result, such conditions generate higher fears of abandonment. Higher entrapment fears also result under multipolarity than bipolarity because the number of conflict dyads are greater and hence the greater potential for being dragged into an ally's conflicts that do not directly involve one's interests. In bipolarity, by contrast, there is only one major conflict dyad around which allied interests generally converge.

The second set of determinants relates to conditions within the alliance itself. In particular, the explicitness of alliance contracts can influence abandonment/entrapment concerns. Vaguely worded agreements generate abandonment concerns because alliance obligations are not clear. Conversely, highly detailed contracts may raise a state's entrapment fears by committing it to support of the ally in contingencies.[26] For this reason, prudent statesmen usually seek agreements between these extremes, attempting to balance assurances against abandonment with risks of entrapment. In addition, the past behavior of allies affects abandonment/entrapment fears. If one perceives an ally's previous commitment to the alliance as weak, then higher fears of abandonment will ensue. Conversely, if one perceives an ally's past behavior toward the adversary as belligerent, then high entrapment anxieties will ensue.

The third set of determinants relates to the effect of domestic factors on attitudes toward an alliance. Downgrading of alliance commitments, necessitated by a state's domestic pressures for retrenchment, can raise allied abandonment fears. Conversely, a state may experience high abandonment fears with regard to an ally because of its need to gain political legitimacy against domestic opposition forces through the government's association with the outside power.[27] Values such as obligation, honor, and reputation can also influence abandonment/entrapment anxieties. For example, Dawson and Rosecrance show that history, affinity, and tradition are the only factors that can explain two puzzles in U.S.-British relations: Britain's 1949 decision to push for U.S. nuclear development and forgo autonomous production and the improvement in bilateral relations directly after American opposition to British actions during the Suez crisis.[28] A state that places a premium on maintaining a reputation as a trustworthy and fully committed partner would not only alleviate the abandonment fears of its allies but also render its own entrapment fears irrelevant.[29]

Finally, the factors listed above usually do not influence abandonment/entrapment concerns discretely but in combination.[30] For example, abandonment fears will be high for a weak state with high external threat perceptions, few alternative allies, no internal balancing capabilities, and an ally with a history of appeasement policies. Alternatively, entrapment fears will be high for a strong state with domestic pressures for retrenchment and a strategically valuable but belligerent ally, no salient security threats, little concern for maintaining reputation as a faithful partner, and an ally with a history of intransigence toward the enemy.

Strategies in the Game

What type of behavior emerges from anxieties of abandonment and entrapment? If a state believes that another will not support it in contingencies where it deserves support, it can cope with this in a number of ways. First, it may try to build up internal capabilities through increased military spending or weapons acquisitions.[31] For example, when DeGaulle said that the United States "would not give up New York to defend Paris," he was essentially expressing French abandonment fears regarding U.S. resolve in Europe. As a result, France pushed for an independent nuclear force as a means of alleviating these fears. Second, the state may seek out new allies, reinforce alternative ones, or appease the adversary. Among the many examples of this dynamic in nineteenth- and twentieth-century Europe, a classic case was France's formation of the Little Entente after World War I in response to what it perceived as lukewarm efforts by the allied victors to impose a harsh settlement on defeated Germany. These two policies aim to compensate for the shortfall in capabilities between the state acting alone and acting in conjunction with the abandoning ally.[32] As a third alternative, the state may try to elicit security cooperation from the ally by exercising leverage over other issue areas (e.g., economic). Fourth, the state may show a stronger commitment to the alliance in order to persuade the ally to reciprocate. Finally, it may try to bluff abandonment in order to obtain greater support for the alliance from the ally.[33]

States exercise any combination of these options when faced with the anxiety of abandonment. However, certain assumptions narrow the probable range of choice.[34] Because states are generally not risk takers, the likelihood of bluffing abandonment is low, as this might result in mutual abandonment. Appeasement also runs the risk of conveying weak resolve to an expansionist enemy, thereby raising more security problems than it solves. Budgetary and technological constraints often prohibit states from fully adjusting to abandonment fears solely through boosting internal capabilities. This also defeats the original purpose of the alliance as a form of power accretion. In addition, because of differing interests and threat perceptions it is generally difficult for a state to fully alleviate abandonment fears with respect to a specific ally and adversarial threat through ad hoc attachments to other powers. Another option is holding cooperation in another aspect of relations contingent on allied security cooperation; however, this assumes the state already possesses substantial leverage to issue credible threats in linking the two issue areas. Finally, the sunk costs states have in alliance relationships compel them to seek means of rectifying abandonment anxieties first from within the alliance rather than from outside of it. These considerations give rise to the following proposition regarding a state's reaction to abandonment anxieties:

Proposition 1: When a state fears abandonment, one of the options it will choose is to show a stronger commitment to the alliance in order to elicit a reciprocal response by the ally.[35]

A state can exhibit this commitment in positive and negative ways. It may make direct contributions to the alliance in terms of money, manpower, or military hardware.[36] It may enact policies reflecting unconditional support for the alliance and warning the adversary of its resolve.[37] On the negative side the state may express complaints about the ally's unsupportive behavior in order to elicit a reassuring response.[38]

A state can address the fear of entrapment in various ways. It may withdraw from the alliance thereby eliminating the fear altogether. Some argue that, with the exception of the postwar and cold-war eras, this has been the traditional American response to burdensome foreign entanglements. Washington's farewell address of 1796, for example, cautioned that the great rule of conduct for U.S. foreign policy was to avoid in Europe "a passionate attachment of one Nation for another," as this will lead to wars "without adequate inducement and justification."[39] An entrapment-ridden state may also conciliate the adversary in order to avoid entanglement in a conflict between the adversary and ally. This dynamic was evident, for example, in Europe in the 1980s as worsening relations between the United States and the Soviet Union prompted NATO allies to promote their own detente with the Soviets to avoid entrapment between the two superpowers.[40] Finally, the state may show a weaker commitment to the alliance in order to restrain the ally. In theory and practice states can exercise any of these options; however, certain assumptions again diminish the likelihood of all but one. The costs involved in developing an alliance generally prohibit states from abrogating ties every time entrapment fears become salient. Conciliation of the adversary involves high risks, particularly if the enemy is not oriented to the status quo and interprets such acts as signs of weak resolve. The desire to resolve anxieties first through intra-alliance rather than extra-alliance means also constrains the range of choice. These assumptions give rise to the following proposition:

Proposition 2: When a state fears entrapment, it will show a weaker commitment to the ally to prevent the ally from being intransigent toward the adversary.[41]

Ideally the state experiencing entrapment fears will attempt a "straddle strategy," in which it conveys to the ally a desire not to fight and conveys to the adversary a strong resolve to support the ally.[42] Short of this, it will communicate a weaker commitment in several ways. The state may directly restrain the ally;[43] it may not support the ally in acts of deterrence against the adversary;[44] or it may criticize the ally publicly for intransigence.[45]

The final element of the alliance game is the strategy. Under assumptions of classical economic rationality, states generally seek to maximize benefits and minimize costs in the alliance game. In other words, they will define their own responsibilities as narrowly as possible while defining those of their partner as broadly as possible.[46] This gives rise to the following proposition:

Proposition 3: The optimal strategy in the alliance game is to maximize one's security from the alliance while minimizing one's obligations to it.

Dynamics of the Game

Each state will have a unique set of abandonment/entrapment fears with respect to a given ally and adversarial threat. The relative strength of these fears, the level of external threat, and the employment of the optimizing strategy determine the dynamics of the alliance game. The following hypotheses can be deduced for explaining conflictual and co-operative behavior between allied or aligned states:

Hypothesis A: If relations between states X and Y reflect an *asymmetrical* structure of abandonment/entrapment concerns, then there will be *friction* between X and Y.

This is because the asymmetry or imbalance of abandonment and entrapment fears gives rise to opposing strategies. For example, if state X has a higher fear of abandonment than state Y, then X will show a stronger commitment to the alliance in order to get Y to reciprocate (Proposition 1). This lowers Y's abandonment fear, but it also increases Y's incentive to defect. Since Y practices the optimizing strategy of maximum security at minimum obligation (Proposition 3), Y's rational option is to show a weaker commitment—it can still preserve its security due to X's assured commitment; moreover, it can minimize its entrapment fears by minimizing obligations to the alliance. State X, expecting Y to reciprocate, remains unsatisfied. The result is friction.

Conversely, if state X has a higher entrapment fear than Y, then X will distance itself from the alliance (Proposition 2). This increases Y's fear of abandonment, and prompts Y to show a more cooperative strategy. This is the only rational play for Y such that it can minimize its abandonment fears.[47] Employment of a tit-for-tat strategy only results in mutual defection detrimental to its interests. Friction results as this disparity in strategies leaves Y unsatisfied.

Hypothesis B: If relations between states X and Y reflect a *symmetrical* structure of abandonment concerns, with respect to each other, or with respect to third party Z, then *cooperative* relations should ensue.

Symmetry means that the two states share comparable fears of abandonment. Two variants of this dynamic are possible. First, states X and Y share abandonment fears with respect to each other. This gives rise to a degree of distrust between X and Y as each is suspicious of the other's resolve. However, mutual abandonment fears also compel each state to show a stronger commitment to the alliance (Proposition 1). Moreover, each will expect—and receive—a similar commitment from the ally. As a result, relations run relatively smoothly.[48] A key assumption underlying this hypothesis is that states X and Y lack significant exit capacities. Neither is capable of fully alleviating abandonment anxieties through alternative security arrangements such as appeasement of the adversary, internal balancing, or the formation of new alliances.[49] In spite of the mutual suspicions that will arise from symmetrical abandonment fears, states X and Y therefore will be obliged to seek security through the improvement of bilateral relations.[50] Conversely, if states face symmetrically low fears of abandonment, then the likely outcome is friction. Low fears of abandonment can result from the lack of salient threats or from confidence in the ally's commitment to one's security. Friction results because these conditions of a perceived abundance of security give rise to high entrapment fears. Alternatively, allies, overly comfortable with the security benefits of the alliance, allow relations to be marred by domestic politics or bickering over responsibilities for the sharing of burdens in a more prominent manner than in security-scarce situations.

In the second variant states X and Y share abandonment fears with respect to a third party Z. This introduces the quasi-alliance aspect of the model. As noted, a quasi alliance is defined as the triangular relationship between two states that are not allied with one another but share a third party as a common ally. A key assumption is that the third state serves as the great-power protector of the two states, and therefore exit opportunities for the two are limited. In this case there are a number of options X and Y will consider. The first option exercised to alleviate abandonment fears will be to show a stronger commitment to Z (Proposition 1). However, an additional option X and Y will exercise, particularly if Z does not exhibit reciprocation, will be to show a stronger commitment to one another.

It may certainly be the case that such a situation could give rise to acute distrust between X and Y. States that fear abandonment by the common ally and are uncertain about their relationship with the quasi ally could find themselves in a prisoner's dilemma and seek the self-help alternative of across-the-board defection (e.g., internal balancing). However, the alliance game presumably would be an iterated one, and the lack of alternative security arrangements and the existence of sunk costs might press X and Y to explore cooperation with one another. Given the constraints on exit, at worst the situation could lead to hedging strategies of X and Y drawing closer but also arming themselves internally. Abandonment fears with respect to Z therefore can give rise to more cohesive relations between X and Y.

Moreover, this quasi-alliance dynamic regarding Z will occur regardless of X and Y's *bilateral* abandonment/entrapment makeup. For example, Hypothesis A proposed that asymmetrical structures of abandonment and entrapment between X and Y will lead to friction. However, the introduction of security concerns regarding state Z changes the dynamics between X and Y. Because X and Y lack alternative security arrangements that could replace Z, when fears of abandonment by Z become salient, this constitutes the primary security concern for both states and creates incentives for the two to draw closer (as well as internally build up). This is an imperfect, ad hoc choice for both X and Y that cannot necessarily replace Z's security contribution; however, it is the only one available to them given the lack of alternative arrangements. The forces for cooperation between X and Y arising out of mutual fears of abandonment by Z will therefore override any tendencies toward friction stemming from asymmetrical abandonment/entrapment structures at the bilateral level. However, if both states do not share abandonment concerns regarding Z, then the dynamics in Hypothesis A remain intact.

Quasi Alliances and Balance-of-Threat Theory

The quasi-alliance model offers two propositions for explaining conflictual and cooperative behavior. These hypothesize that an imbalance of abandonment/entrapment anxieties in the purely bilateral aspect of relations should give rise to friction (Hypothesis A) and that balance in the multilateral aspect of relations should give rise to cooperation (Hypothesis B). Friction at the bilateral level appears to constitute the baseline of the relationship. Variations from this baseline of behavior appear to be a function of mutually shared abandonment fears about the third party's defense commitments. Again, it should be noted that the effect of these abandonment fears on quasi-allied attitudes toward one another is in part, but not wholly derivative of, the level of perceived external threat. This is what makes the quasi-alliance argument analytically distinct from basic balance-of-power arguments about alliances.[51] It offers a related, but different treatment of the role that adversaries' actions play in determining alliance outcomes. The dominant work in this field, articulated by Stephen Walt, generally views alliance formation as the product of states balancing against threats.[52] The quasi-alliance dynamic, by contrast, does not see the causal connection between threats and alliance behavior as necessarily this direct. Alignments between two states are indeed motivated by the behavior of the adversary, but they are also motivated by the behavior of shared allies. In order to fully understand the nature of alliance relations, one needs to look beyond alliances as simply a ratifier of threats to the causal impact of assurances on behavior. External threats play a role in deter-

BALANCE-OF-THREAT THEORY

Threats ──────────────→ Alliance behavior

QUASI-ALLIANCE MODEL

Threats ──→ Abandonment/Entrapment complex ──→ Alliance behavior

Fig. 2. Balance-of-Threat Theory versus Quasi Alliances

mining alliance outcomes, but they are refracted through perceptions of commitment from the common ally and through resultant abandonment/entrapment complexes. In short, threats matter, but *promises* also matter.

The causal logic of the two views leads to different predictions. According to balance-of-threat theory, if two powers perceive high levels of threat from the adversary, then alliances will form. If states X and Y experience high threat levels and weak commitments by the common ally (i.e., high abandonment fears), then like balance-of-threat arguments, the quasi-alliance view predicts alliance formation between X and Y. However, if X and Y experience high threat levels but the shared ally's commitments are strong (i.e., low abandonment fears), then contrary to balance-of-threat predictions, this might not result in alliance formation between X and Y because security needs are fulfilled and additional commitments between X and Y only raise entrapment fears with marginal increases in security. Similarly, if X and Y experience low threat levels, balance of threat might predict no need for alliance formation. However, if threats are low but commitments by the shared ally are also weak (i.e., high abandonment fears), then the quasi-alliance argument sees cause for alignment between X and Y because the loss of the primary security guarantor is a compelling force for cooperation in spite of current security-abundant conditions. Conversely, if threats are low and abandonment fears are also low, then like balance-of-threat theory, the quasi-alliance argument predicts no cooperation between X and Y. The key difference is that the quasi-alliance argument sees outcomes emerging from the intersection of alliance and adversary games.[53] Perceptions of external threat are conditioned not only by objective conditions (i.e., behavior of the adversary) but also by the behavior of the shared ally. In addition, balance-of-threat theory implicitly assumes that the level of allied commitment positively correlates with the intensity of external threat (i.e., high threats mean strong allied commitments and hence low abandonment fears). However, the two may be wholly independent of one another. States may build up in low-threat situations or build down in high-threat ones for budgetary, domestic political, ideological, and isolationist reasons not related directly to the level of threat. Hence the causal impact of abandonment/entrapment fears on the shape of alliances can be analytically distinct from the level of threat.

Japanese and Korean Fears of Abandonment and Entrapment

The first step in testing the quasi-alliance hypotheses against the Japan-Korea case is to operationalize abandonment/entrapment variables for the two governments. Research of the postnormalization era in the relationship as well as interviews with policymakers active during this time yields two basic findings: within the *bilateral* context of the relations the ROK experienced a higher fear of abandonment than Japan, while Japan experienced a higher fear of entrapment across issue areas. Within the *quasi-allied* context of relations, however, both Japan and the ROK shared mutual abandonment fears regarding their common ally, the United States. A survey of issues in the security arena illustrates these points.

Japan and Korea are not party to a mutual defense treaty, but this does not preclude the existence of alignment patterns between the two states. As a result of their geographic proximity, prominence in the region, common security threats, and the triangular alliance arrangement with the United States, the two nations exhibit alignment patterns and de facto security ties that play an important part in their overall relationship.

For example, throughout the postwar and cold-war eras, the two states essentially comprised one integrated unit in U.S. defense planning in the region. The presence of American ground troops in South Korea was as much an extended frontline of defense for Tokyo as it was for Seoul. Similarly, the U.S. Seventh Fleet and marine units in Japan provided rear-guard support for the ROK. Joint United States-Korea military exercises regularly employed bases in Japan for logistic support; U.S. tactical air wing deployments rotated frequently between Japan and Korea; and air and naval surveillance of North Korea was operated out of bases in Japan. In addition, Seoul and Tokyo conducted periodic exchanges of defense officials, developed bilateral fora for discussion of security policies, and engaged in some sharing of military intelligence and technology.[54]

These informal defense links were first publicly enunicated in the joint communiqué issued at the conclusion of the November 1969 Nixon-Sato summit. Known as the "Korea clause," it stated that the security of the ROK was essential to Japan.[55] Concurrent with the enunciation of the Korea clause was the Okinawan-base agreement, which asserted that in the event of a second North Korean offensive, Japan would permit the United States unconditional access to bases in Okinawa for the defense of South Korea.[56] The two agreements constituted the closest approximation to a defense treaty between Japan and the ROK. Both agreements were subsequently restated in various forms in bilateral conference communiqués between Tokyo and Seoul.

Within this security relationship South Korea generally experiences high fears of abandonment on four accounts. First, anxieties run high when Japan fails to acknowledge the severity of the North Korean threat to South Korean security. Such anxieties become especially acute whenever the Japanese government permits trade with Pyongyang in goods deemed security-sensitive by the South.[57] Second, anxieties are exacerbated when Tokyo engages in contacts that convey de facto political recognition on the Northern regime.[58] Third, Seoul fears abandonment when Tokyo does not assent to the direct security link stated in the Korea clause or when Tokyo's attitude toward the Okinawan-base agreement appears ambivalent. Finally, Korean fears of abandonment also run high when Tokyo does not provide positive political support for the ROK regime or does not engage in intimate consultations with Seoul in a manner commensurate with the special security ties between the two governments.

Minimizing these abandonment fears serves three basic ROK needs. First and most obviously, it enhances containment of the North Korean security threat. Next to the United States, Japan is the key regional partner in deterring North Korea. As a result, South Koreans view Japanese contacts with Pyongyang as unilateral, self-centered acts, motivated by Japan's "economic-animal" mentality, which undermine Seoul's efforts at providing stability on the peninsula and in the region. At the baser level of historical animosity South Koreans interpret such contacts emotionally as reflective of latent Japanese desires to cement a permanent division of the peninsula and obstruct the resurgence of a united Korea.[59]

Second, by getting Japan to adhere to the Korea clause, Seoul ensures that the United States retains unimpeded access to bases in Okinawa for South Korean defense.[60] Without use of these facilities for logistical and air support, American defense of the ROK would be severely hampered.[61]

Third, Japanese acknowledgment of the Korea clause affords Seoul bargaining advantages over Tokyo with regard to certain forms of economic aid. The logic behind this leverage is known as the "bulwark-of-defense" argument. This essentially states that Japan should provide economic aid as a form of "security rent" to the Republic as the latter bears the burden of undergirding stability in the Japanese defense perimeter.[62] In addition to the bulwark-of-defense argument South Koreans reiterate issues of historical animosity in an effort to gain leverage over Japan. Seoul occasionally attempts to link concessions by Tokyo on economic and political issues with moral repentance for the colonial period. In this regard, Japanese acknowledgment of the ROK's defense contribution only strengthens Seoul's bargaining position in these endeavors.[63] The importance the ROK places on Japanese interpretations of the Korea clause therefore cannot be overstated. Any variations in wording, in Seoul's eyes, have implications for both Korean security and bargaining leverage over Tokyo, thereby heightening abandonment fears. One of the ways in which this is manifested is through internal foreign ministry reference manuals for the Japan section (Northeast Asia, Division 1) which carry sections wholly devoted to different readings of the Korea clause employed by Japan since 1969.[64]

While ROK abandonment fears regarding Japan are high, entrapment fears are low. It is difficult to imagine scenarios in which the ROK could become fully responsible for Japan's defense or could become entrapped by a Japanese conflict with another power which does not involve South Korean security interests. In the former case this is due to Japan's defense treaty with the United States and in the latter case due to the lack of a regional security threat directed primarily (and solely) at Japan.

Japanese fears of entrapment center on similar issues. An overcommitment to Japan-ROK defense ties, in the form of strong support for the 1969 Korea clause, could lead to formal acknowledgment of the ROK's indispensable security contribution to Japan's defense. In addition, although the region is relatively stable, an overcommitment to Japan-ROK defense ties could actually have second-order effects that are destabilizing. Strong backing of the South could *create* a more volatile situation on the peninsula by increasing North Korean fears of encirclement.[65] It could also embolden the South to become more provocative and intransigent toward the North. The result in either scenario could be a preemptive lashing out by the North, the consequences of which could be direct retaliation against Japan.

Minimizing these entrapment fears serves several Japanese needs. First, by promoting a stable status quo on the peninsula, Japan avoids having to contend with a host of politically difficult domestic issues. North Korean belligerency as a result of strong Japan-ROK ties would force Tokyo to contend with reevaluation of Article IX of the constitution, which legally delimits Japan's rearmament and presence as a military power. Japan would also have to deal with problematic issues such as internal monitoring of a substantial North Korean (*Chosen Soren*) resident population and absorbing the potential outflow of Korean refugees in the event of a second Korean war.[66] Entrapment into relations with the ROK which alienated Communist neighbors would close off potential export markets to Japanese economic interests. It also would run counter to the postwar vision of reestablishing relations with all nations Japan had warred with or victimized in the past.

Second, by refraining from acknowledging a direct Japan-ROK security link, Tokyo avoids becoming vulnerable to the bulwark-of-defense argument and ROK demands for "security rent."[67] An additional Japanese concern regarding such funds is to avoid Seoul's continual use of colonial contrition arguments as leverage to extract monetary forms of "moral repentance." Tokyo must also avoid succumbing to accusations that it withholds economic funds to stifle South Korea's rise as a rival in Japanese market sectors.[68] Finally, Japan must straddle entrapment anxieties vis-à-vis the ROK with burden-sharing pressures from the United States. These pressures often take the form of calls for Japanese assistance to South Korean economic development in order to promote prosperity and stability on the peninsula.[69] In sum, Tokyo's entrapment fears center on striking a balance between providing strong political and economic support for the ROK and abstaining from overt security ties that would leave it vulnerable to South Korean demands for security rent or moral repentance.

While Japanese entrapment fears regarding the ROK are high, fears of abandonment are low. A lack of Japanese support for the Republic could result in two scenarios. First, it could embolden a North Korean offensive. Second, it could prompt the ROK to abandon Japan's defense in some future security contingency. Neither of these is a salient concern as Japanese security is ensured by its defense treaty with the United

s. In addition, it does not perceive a North Korean attack as immi-

...n analysis of alignment dynamics would be incomplete without brief consideration of the adversary game. In Japan-ROK relations strategies in the adversary game reinforce the asymmetry of abandonment/entrapment fears in the alliance game. For example, the ROK strategy in the adversary game vis-à-vis North Korea is to stand firm. This reinforces abandonment fears regarding Japan as it increases the value placed by the ROK on strong Japanese allegiance in opposing the North. Japan's strategy in the adversary game has been, by contrast, less rigid. It seeks *seikei bunri* (separation of economics from politics) policies with Communist neighbors to tap potential economic markets and desires the latitude to adjust policies in accordance with changes in the international environment. This reasoning is well reflected in Tokyo's equidistance policy. This aims to preserve Japanese security by promoting relations with the two Koreas, thereby maintaining a balance of power on the peninsula.[70] Implicit in this is the view that Japan's security concerns on the peninsula are of a more multidimensional nature than those of the ROK. While the paramount concern for both is an unprovoked North Korean attack, Japan is also concerned about South Korean intransigence, which might provoke the North, and about a general war arising out of a U.S.-Soviet superpower confrontation in the region. These disparities in what is seen as threatening on the peninsula reinforce Japanese entrapment fears regarding strong ties with the ROK.

Therefore, in the bilateral context of Japan-ROK relations there is an asymmetrical structure of abandonment and entrapment concerns. According to Hypothesis A, this imbalance should result in friction between the two states. Before testing this proposition further, it is necessary to look at the quasi-allied (or multilateral) context of Japan-Korea relations.

The Quasi-Alliance Context: Japan-ROK Relations with the United States

It is difficult to analyze Japan-ROK relations without reference to the United States. American defense guarantees with each state make it the natural focal point of the three-way security triangle. The manner in which this triangular dynamic impacts Seoul-Tokyo relations has generally been described along two lines. The first is that American prominence as the underwriter of regional stability removes a major impetus for Seoul or Tokyo to take on greater burden-sharing responsibilities. The second is that dissatisfaction, particularly on the Korean side, with the lack of intimacy and peer respect in Japan-ROK bilateral relations stems from treatment of one another as secondary to, and an instrument of, each state's primary relationship with the United States.[71] The common theme underlying both views is that the primacy of the United States as an ally causes individual security perceptions as well as bilateral dynamics to be a function of each state's ties with the United States.[72]

The quasi-alliance perspective logically follows from these points. While Japan and the Republic have asymmetrical fears of abandonment and entrapment with respect to each other, they share the same or mutual fears of abandonment regarding the U.S. defense commitment to the region. It is in the supreme interests of Tokyo and Seoul to keep the United States actively engaged in the region. The absence of a U.S. security presence would dramatically change the strategic environment for both countries. In Korea's case the American ground troops, particularly those stationed in Panmunjom and in Seoul, represent the tripwire that guarantees a U.S. response to a second North Korean invasion. American air power and logistical support from Okinawa are also key to deploying large numbers of forces rapidly at decisive points in response to an invasion and limiting civilian casualties and industrial damage. Without this presence the ROK would have to devote a disproportionate percentage of its GNP to assuming the role as the primary deterrent force on the peninsula. This would entail not only a massive conventional arms buildup but also the development, most likely, of an independent nuclear capability. On the two occasions, in fact, when the United States contemplated a reduction in its security commitment to Korea, the South Korean government responded with covert programs to acquire the technology for nuclear weaponization.[73]

Military and strategic balances aside, the absence of U.S. forces would have profound economic and political implications as well. Regardless of whether the ROK exercised qualitative military advantages over the North or not, the psychological insecurities stemming from a U.S. withdrawal, after decades of support, would most likely create acute insecurities in Seoul, to the extent of possibly reducing tolerance for democratization at home. Full underwriting of its own defense would also have debilitating effects on Korea's cherished double-digit economic growth rates. Finally, South Koreans would be extremely concerned about how the lack of a U.S. presence would affect the North's mentality. ROK anxieties about the renewal of hostilities center less on whether it could win than on the collateral damage that would be incurred in the process. In other words, ROK abandonment fears center on the manner in which a withdrawal of U.S. commitments might embolden the North and force the ROK into a war-winning exercise it would dread. In this sense, the U.S. presence is valued as much as a *deterrent* to the North's contemplation of aggression as a defensive guarantee should such aggression take place.

Japan's concerns over U.S. disengagement are no less severe. The mutual defense treaty and nuclear umbrella form the basis of Japanese security. The American military presence in Korea also relieves Japan of concerns about proximate arenas of potential instability. The removal of any of these defense commitments would prevent Japan from buck-passing regional security issues to the United States. The withdrawal of the U.S. Seventh Fleet from Yokosuka and Sasebo and related units from Okinawa and other bases would make Japan responsible for defense of sea lanes stretching as far southwest of the home islands as the South China Sea and north through the Northern Pacific, the former having implications for Japan's lifeline to oil, gas, and commodity flows from Southeast Asia to the Persian Gulf. Without a U.S. presence control of the Yellow Sea, Sea of Japan, and exit routes for Soviet naval bases (during the cold war) would be strategic concerns suddenly thrust upon Japan. A contingency in Korea would require a total rethinking of Japan's role, which under U.S. auspices were limited to comfortable, noncommittal tasks like rear-area support and logistics. These and other concerns would force Japan, on the one hand, into massive conventional rearmament, acquisition of blue-water naval capabilities, and nuclearization or, on the other hand, into assigning greater value to the ROK for security. The latter option is unthinkable both strategically and politically. The former option would not only be internally problematic (e.g., requiring constitutional revision and revising nonnuclear principles) but also would elicit regional concerns about renewed Japanese militarism, anti-Japanese balancing coalitions, and unpredictable responses from rival powers, particularly China. In sum, as one astute specialist observed, "The United States' security guarantee allowed Japan to keep its defense expenditures low. Equally significant, it enabled the Japanese to postpone or moderate an extremely divisive internal debate over rearmament and the complications it would pose for Tokyo's relations with its Asian neighbors."[74]

The primacy of the U.S. alliance for Seoul and Tokyo raises an additional point regarding the causal connection between external threats, U.S. commitments, and fears of abandonment. As noted already, balance-of-threat theory sees changes in external threats generally giving rise to changes in abandonment/entrapment fears among allies. However, in the United States-Japan-Korea triangle security dependence is so acute for the latter two that in certain instances fears of U.S. abandonment can become salient regardless of objective changes in the levels of external threat. In other words, in an increasingly threatening environment decreased U.S. commitments would raise acute abandonment fears for Japan and Korea. However, abandonment fears would also arise if the level of threat remained constant but U.S. commitments weakened. Conversely, abandonment fears would not increase if the level of threat increased but U.S. commitments remained firm. These counterintuitive linkages between threats and fears of U.S. abandonment obtain largely because the alliance not only provides protection against adversaries but also affords both countries the luxury of sidestepping a host of problematic political and economic issues related to self-reliant defense. In this sense the value of the U.S. alliance exceeds its utility as simply a deterrent against immediate security threats.

BEFORE APPLYING the quasi-alliance model to Japan-Korea relations, two methodological notes are necessary. I have chosen to test the model against one case rather than many. A shortcoming of this method is its inability to offer the potentially large explanatory payoffs of a given theory or model over an array of cases.[75] To redress this deficiency, I look at numerous periods spanning some thirty years within my case. While such longitudinal testing does not fully compensate for the lack of additional cases, it does ensure tests that are empirically sound. Latitudinal testing over many cases runs the risk of historical inaccuracy, thereby undermining the integrity of the tests.

Second, the Japan-Korea case is particularly useful because the literature on alliance theory has focused almost exclusively on European cases. Therefore, testing against non-Western cases and outside great-power experiences has the potential for enhancing the explanatory scope of the theory. The Japan-Korea case also offers conditions that pose a "hard test" for the quasi-alliance model. The predominant view is that this relationship is deeply entrenched in, and wholly determined by, historical enmity. This enmity offers a potentially powerful intervening variable between the abandonment/entrapment structure of the quasi-alliance model and policy behavior. If the tests show that quasi-alliance dynamics determine outcomes in spite of this animosity, then the plausibility of the model is enhanced.[76]

My testing employs a combination of the congruence method and process tracing.[77] The former determines whether there is temporal covariation between the independent and dependent variables. As detailed above, the independent variable is abandonment/entrapment structures. The dependent variable is cooperation and friction in Japanese-Korean foreign-policy behavior. It is inherently difficult to measure the dependent variable during the cold war as *cooperation* and *friction* do not accord with the traditional definitions of allying with or against a state in a military confrontation. For the purposes of this study, I define the former as strong support for another state in contingencies against an adversary and the latter as the breakdown in the normal functioning of relations or the absence of interaction that would be beneficial to the parties involved. *Support* is broadly defined as both material and/or verbal commitments to another ally in accordance with the ally's expectations and the deliberate avoidance of friction over potentially contentious issues.

After establishing covariation, I use process tracing to determine whether a necessary causal connection exists between abandonment/entrapment concerns and foreign-policy outcomes. This requires a tracing of the intermediate cause-and-effect links in the chain between the independent and dependent variables.[78] I describe the external security environment and its relationship to Japan-Korea abandonment/entrapment complexes. I next try to show in real-time calculations that policymakers did, in fact, experience particular fears of abandonment and entrapment. I then retrace the behavior resulting from these perceptions and assess the conflictual or cooperative nature of the resulting interaction.

Process tracing requires a great deal of historical data. My evidence is drawn from daily newspapers, statements at press conferences and in diplomatic communiqués, and government documents (some internal and not generally available to the public) compiled from archives and government agencies in Washington, Seoul, and Tokyo. Whenever possible, extensive interviews were conducted with government officials directly involved in specific foreign-policy decisions as well as with journalists and scholars. Except for those interviewees who specifically requested anonymity, the identities of all respondents are provided.

THREE

Cooperation Under the Nixon Doctrine, 1969–1971

THE SIGNING OF a basic relations treaty between Japan and the Republic of Korea on June 22, 1965, hardly represented the start of a new era of amiable relations.[1] Mass demonstrations raged in both countries in opposition to the settlement. Moreover, residual animosity was evident in the absence of cooperation in the years immediately following normalization. Despite the establishment of diplomatic ties, the two governments sought neither to engage in formal summitry nor to create regularized channels of political dialogue. In spite of the hostile cold-war neighborhood in which the two states resided, they eschewed any discussion of common security interests. Economic relations were replete with accusations on Seoul's part of Japanese attempts at economic recolonization and complaints on Tokyo's part of Korean attempts at extorting economic assistance through perennial harping on colonial compensation. Disputes over territorial fishing rights led to South Korean harassment and capture of Japanese vessels in 1966, and in the ensuing years the two governments clashed over Japanese exports to North Korea, entry permits for North Korean visitors to Japan, and reentry visas for pro-Pyongyang (*Chosen Soren*) residents in Japan. These problems led to South Korean efforts at obstructing travel between the two countries, formal protests by both foreign ministries, and threats of recalling ambassadors.[2]

However, significantly different dynamics prevailed from 1969 to 1971.[3] Japan and the ROK entered into a brief but definitive phase of cooperative behavior. The two governments began discussions on common security issues. Binational committees to enhance political dialogue were established. Unprecedented amounts of Japanese aid and investment flowed into the South Korean economy.

Given the intense mutual animosities that continued to pervade attitudes in this early period of normalized relations, what accounts for the sudden trend toward cooperation? This chapter will argue that the quasi-alliance model offers a plausible explanation. To preview the argument, the United States implemented a number of policies in Asia that raised questions about the credibility of American defense commitments to the region. These policies gave rise to mutually shared fears of U.S. abandonment in Tokyo and Seoul and prompted the two governments to improve bilateral relations.[4] This cooperation was not the result of any new-found affinity or dissipation of historical enmity. Instead, it was an ad hoc, realpolitik response by two lesser powers, with no alternative means of security, to cope with anxieties regarding the resolve of their common great-power protector.

An elucidation of this argument requires three tasks. First, one must provide evidence of U.S. retrenchment policies toward the region. Second, one must verify that these policies actually instilled fears of U.S. abandonment in Tokyo and Seoul. And third, one must demonstrate that these abandonment anxieties translated into greater bilateral cooperation.

United States Retrenchment Policies:
The Nixon Doctrine

Upon entering office in 1969, the Nixon administration faced a foreign-policy agenda in substantial flux. Budgetary constraints and widespread opposition to the Vietnam war produced strong domestic pressures for U.S. retrenchment. On the international front Japan's and Germany's postwar economic growth presaged their increased role in world affairs commensurate with their capabilities. In addition, the advent of the Sino-Soviet split laid open the possibility of American diplomatic inroads into the once-united Communist monolith. Taken together, these international and domestic developments dictated the need for a reorientation of U.S. foreign policy.

The basic tenets of this new policy were spelled out during Nixon's five-nation tour of Southeast Asia in July 1969. At an informal news conference in Guam the president formulated what came to be known as the Nixon doctrine. This set out three precepts for the future U.S. role as a security guarantor. The United States would continue to honor all existing treaty commitments. It would continue to provide for the de-

TABLE I

U.S. Military Personnel Reductions, 1969–1971

	Authorized Strength		
	January 1969	December 1971	Reductions
Vietnam	549,500	159,000	390,500
Korea	63,000	43,000	20,000
Thailand	47,800	32,000	15,800
Japan	39,000	32,000	7,000
Philippines	28,000	18,000	9,100

SOURCES: Compiled from *United States Foreign Policy 1969–1970: A Report of the Secretary of State* (Washington, D.C.: G.P.O, 1971), 243; *United States Foreign Policy 1971: A Report of the Secretary of State* (Washington, D.C.: G.P.O, 1972), 50.

fense of any ally threatened by a nuclear power. However, in conventional military conflicts the United States would furnish some security and economic assistance in accordance with its treaties but would look to the ally to assume the *primary* burden of defense.[5]

Although the Nixon doctrine applied to all U.S. alliances, it was intended primarily for Asia. The pressing strategic need in this region was to avoid the entanglement of U.S. ground troops in future wars on the Asian mainland. This was also linked to a broader need to reorient U.S. strategic doctrine away from an unfeasible "two and one-half conventional wars" scenario to one more in line with U.S. capabilities.[6] As Nixon stated at the Guam news conference:

Asia is for Asians. And that is what we want, and that is the role we should play. . . . We must avoid the kind of policy that will make countries in Asia so dependent upon us that we are dragged into conflicts such as the one we have in Vietnam.[7]

The doctrine thus asserted the United States as an Asia-Pacific power but envisioned a new American role limited to assisting allies rather than dictating to them. It encouraged greater burden sharing by allies in the region, particularly calling on Japan to do so through increased economic aid to its neighbors.

AMERICAN FORCE REDUCTIONS IN THE ASIAN THEATER

In line with the Nixon doctrine American military personnel in Asia were decreased from 727,300 in January 1969 to 284,000 by December 1971. The cuts were most evident in Vietnam. In mid-1969 Nixon instituted a five-step troop withdrawal program that numbered 390,500 by the end of 1971. To localize hostilities and shift the primary burden of combat away from U.S. forces, the administration implemented a broad-based modernization of the South Vietnamese military as well as "pacification" programs in villages and hamlets designed to gain the favor of rural inhabitants and root out elements sympathetic to the North Vietnamese and Viet Cong.[8] These Vietnamization initiatives met with, at best, limited success; nevertheless, they provided definitive evidence of U.S. desires to extract itself from Asian conflicts.[9]

The second significant area where the United States sought retrenchment was on the Korean peninsula. In February 1969 Nixon authorized the continuation of a National Security Council (NSC) study, begun during the Johnson years, on phased troop reductions in Korea. Based on the recommendations of the NSC study and consultations with U.S. Ambassador to the ROK William Porter, Nixon in March 1970 issued National Security Decision Memorandum 48 calling for the withdrawal of one infantry division from Korea.[10] The South Koreans were notified of this decision in July 1970, and after lengthy and difficult discussions lasting until February 1971, the two governments issued a joint communiqué on February 6 stipulating the final terms of the withdrawal.[11] These included the deactivation of the American Seventh Infantry Division from reserve positions, removal of three Air Force squadrons, and pullback of the Second Infantry Division from front-line positions along the Demilitarized Zone (DMZ). This constituted a reduction of twenty thousand American troops; moreover, it fully transferred responsibility for defense along the DMZ to the ROK.[12] In addition to these reductions, the United States proposed a five-year $1.5-billion military assistance program to modernize the ROK military and eventually facilitate the total withdrawal of U.S. forces from Korea.

A key factor motivating both the Korean reductions and the new "Asia for Asians" policy was Nixon's need to respond to domestic political imperatives regarding Vietnam. The United States had considered troop pullouts in Korea as early as 1963–64 because the underwriting of a six hundred thousand strong Korean army and two U.S. divisions was seen as an expensive, overinsured position in deterring the North (whose army had not been rebuilt beyond three hundred fifty thousand since the Korean war). Internal White House memoranda suggest the United States was considering cuts in 1964 along the lines of seventy thousand for the ROK and twelve thousand for U.S. forces.[13] But because of the ROK's substantial troop commitment to the Vietnam war, Washington chose to shelve the issue. By 1970, however, antiwar sentiment in the United States had become severe, and positive evidence of American withdrawals from Asia was politically expedient. Vietnam was the most obvious theater, however, reductions there would appear like an unmitigated U.S. retreat. As a result, the United States sought to couch the Vietnamization program in a broader policy of American disengagement, which included force reductions elsewhere in Asia. Korea was the natural choice.[14]

NORTH KOREAN PROVOCATIONS

Passive responses by the Johnson and Nixon administrations to a number of hostile North Korean acts provided further evidence of American intentions to downgrade defense commitments to Asia. Provocations by the North Koreans were common at the time, largely in the form of inconsequential arms fire along the DMZ.[15] However, during the late 1960s these increased in boldness.[16] For example, on January 21, 1968, North Korean commandos attempted a raid on the South Korean presidential residence, the Blue House. U.S. and ROK forces barely managed to stop the operation in an armed clash one kilometer from the compound. Interrogation of the captured commandos found that the mission's purpose was to assassinate President Park Chung-hee and Ambassador Porter.[17] Despite the severity of this incident Washington responded with decided restraint. Porter stated that the United States would not retaliate and explicitly cautioned Park that any South Korean attempts at retribution would meet with strong U.S. opposition.[18]

Two days later North Korea seized a U.S. naval intelligence ship, the USS Pueblo, near the port of Wonsan. Even though the action was a clear violation of freedom of maritime conventions and the eighty-three American crewmen were subjected to torture and beatings during their captivity, the U.S. response was again passive.[19] Washington declined all requests from Park for retaliatory air strikes against Pyongyang.[20] The following month Deputy Secretary of Defense Cyrus Vance was sent to Seoul to clarify the U.S. position on the Pueblo seizure. As Vance recalled, his purpose was to

prevent any precipitate action in terms of a move to the North by Park and the Republic of Korea's army; . . . that President Park should be under no illusion as to the seriousness of any such action; and that if such a step were taken without full consultation with the United States that the whole relationships [sic] between our countries would have to be reevaluated.[21]

TABLE 2

DMZ and Rear-Area Incidents, 1968–1971

Year	Number (DMZ)	(Rear)	Casualties[a] (US)	(ROK)	(NK)
1968	542	219	68	395	13
1969	98	36	11	47	7
1970	71	35	0	55	6
1971[b]	11	4	0	0	1

SOURCE: Compiled from United States, House, Committee on Foreign Affairs, *American-Korean Relations* (92nd Cong., 1st sess., 1971), 11.
[a]Casualties include captured, killed, wounded, or missing in action.
[b]The 1971 figures are for January–June 1971.

The next major test of U.S. resolve occurred in early 1969. On April 15 North Korean MiG fighters shot down a U.S. EC-121 reconnaissance plane ninety miles off the North Korean coast. This was a calculated and unprovoked act of aggression against an unarmed U.S. aircraft operating in international airspace;[22] however, the United States again reacted mildly. In a news conference on April 18 Nixon said that armed countermeasures would not be forthcoming; instead EC-121 flights would continue under the protection of a specially mobilized naval convoy, Task Force 71, in the Sea of Japan.[23] Although this policy was commended by some as a measured and responsible reaction, many saw it as little more than empty posturing. Task Force 71 was scaled down from an initial deployment of twenty-nine vessels to a token nine only ten days after its inception; protests at Panmunjom were mild given the severity of the incident; and the crisis passed without any U.S. punitive actions or demands for compensation. As Henry Kissinger recollected:

Overall, I judge our conduct in the EC-121 crisis as weak, indecisive, and disorganized—though it was much praised then. I believe we paid for it in many intangible ways, in demoralized friends and emboldened adversaries.[24]

ROK Perceptions of American Abandonment

Washington's ambivalent response to the three North Korean provocations in 1968 and 1969 seriously undermined South Korean confidence in American defense commitments. As an aide to the prime minister recalled, the ROK leadership believed North Korean actions were probes to test the strength of the United States-ROK alliance.[25] Seoul consequently put a high priority on armed countermeasures to deter further provocations at the February 1968 Vance mission. Park officials demanded an explanation as to why their calls for "immediate retaliation" after the Blue House raid and *Pueblo* seizure were met only with Washington's promises for "immediate consultations."[26] From Seoul's perspective the meaning of U.S. inaction was clear: "If the most powerful country in the world would do nothing to retrieve its ships or the men in service of their own nation, what would it do on behalf of Koreans?"[27] Furthermore, when the United States eventually took some token measures to secure sea lanes in the aftermath of the *Pueblo* seizure, Defense Minister Kim Sung-eun cynically questioned why comparable actions were not appropriate after an assassination attempt on the chief executive of an American ally.[28] Koreans increasingly saw the United States as compartmentalizing its security interests and thereby selectively disengaging from future disputes on the peninsula.[29] As a member of the Korean negotiating team during the Vance visit recalled, "There was a true feeling of indignation and disappointment" at U.S. attitudes.[30] Han Sung-joo characterized the South Korean mindset at the time:

Doubts about US military credibility . . . increased with the North Korean seizure of US intelligence ship Pueblo in January 1968 and a US response that the South Korean government considered inadequate. The US failure to act forcefully in the Pueblo affair, as well as its refusal to permit the South Korean army to strike back in retaliation for the North Korean assassination attempt on President Park in January 1968, raised questions about the US determination to repel aggression in Korea if it ever became necessary.[31]

In retrospect, differing strategic concerns underlay Washington's and Seoul's attitudes toward the provocations. For the United States the desire not to open a second front on the Asian mainland and a need to appease growing domestic pressures for disengagement made retaliation against the North an undesirable option. The ROK viewed Pyongyang's provocations, however, from the narrow context of the North-South military confrontation on the peninsula. Punitive countermeasures were the only way to meet these challenges to the alliance.[32] The resulting disparity in the response deemed adequate by the two sides fueled concerns about U.S. credibility in Seoul.

1970 TROOP REDUCTIONS

The July 1970 decision on troop reductions confirmed Seoul's worst suspicions. Though this was only a partial withdrawal, it constituted the first major reduction of forces since the Korean war. Previous U.S. administrations had imparted the understanding that Washington would not alter force levels without prior consultations.[33] In addition, the general belief in Seoul was that the ROK was exempt from the Nixon doctrine largely because of its troop commitment in Vietnam. At its height this numbered fifty-five thousand and played an important part in portraying the conflict as a collective defense effort in the region.[34]

The South Korean reaction, as Assistant Secretary Marshall Green described it, was one of "shock" and "disbelief" at the abrupt and unilateral U.S. decision.[35] In meetings with Vice-President Spiro Agnew in September 1970 Park refused to accept the U.S. decision and raged that it would embolden the North and lead to "irrecoverable disaster."[36] A National Assembly resolution, unanimously passed within a week of the U.S. announcement, expressed the belief held by the ROK leadership and public that Korean loyalty, proven in Vietnam, had been betrayed by the United States.[37] The South Koreans were especially disturbed that the reductions entailed a pullback of the Second Infantry Division from front-line positions on the DMZ, as these troops effectively represented the tripwire deterrent that ensured an automatic U.S. response to a North Korean attack. To protest U.S. actions, Premier Chung Il-kwon wildly threatened not only to leave that portion of the border vacated by the United States undefended but also the resignation of his entire cabinet.[38]

ROK appeals to the Americans on the troop cut decision received little sympathy. At the third annual United States-ROK Security Consultative Conference (SCC) July 21–22, 1970, the United States rejected proposals for postponement of the reductions.[39] In addition, the SCC joint communiqué stated that, "The forces defending the Republic of Korea must remain alert and strong to deter North Korea from renewed aggression." This wording was markedly different from previous statements, such as the August 1969 Nixon-Park joint communiqué, which read, "[The] Republic of Korea forces and American forces stationed in Korea must remain strong and alert."[40] Protests over the deletion of the United States from this all-important clause ensued with Defense Minister Jung Nae-hyuk threatening at one point to pull Korean troops from Vietnam in retaliation.[41] As U.S. officials at these meetings described, ROK anxieties made the SCC proceedings "some of the most difficult [they] had ever attended."[42]

The United States was, of course, not oblivious to allied anxieties over the Nixon doctrine and consequently undertook a number of initiatives to shore up ties. In Korea this assumed the form of two large-scale joint military exercises, Operation Focus Retina (March 1969) and Operation Freedom Vault (March 1971), and in 1970 a five-year, $1.5-billion supplementary military assistance program.[43] In actuality, however, these policies only heightened South Korean insecurities. Joint operations such as Focus Retina certainly demonstrated the U.S. ability to deploy forces from across the Pacific rapidly, but they also underscored the operational superfluousness of maintaining the physical U.S. force presence on the peninsula deemed so crucial by Seoul.[44] Furthermore, the promise of military modernization did little to alleviate anxieties. Because the funds were to be provided in yearly installments subject to Congressional approval, monies would not only be vulnerable to partisan politics in the United States but also would be cut, in all likelihood, by a Congress generally resistant to additional security assistance beyond that already appropriated to the ROK on an annual basis.[45]

At the heart of ROK concerns was therefore a "proliferation of doubt" regarding U.S. dependability as a great-power patron.[46] Korea could no longer take for granted the notion of "automatic intervention," which had underpinned the United States-ROK alliance for decades. One reflection of this uncertainty was Seoul's demand, shortly after the troop reduction announcement, for a revision of the security treaty to include a NATO-type clause guaranteeing "automatic" U.S. intervention in the case of future hostilities.[47] Another was the secret South Korean decision, taken around the time of the U.S. announcement of troop reductions, to initiate development of clandestine nuclear weapons capabilities.[48] A U.S. embassy official best summed up the South Korean mindset at the time:

At the innermost ring of their concern is the fear that the announced American plan to reduce some troops from the ROK will lead to a total withdrawal, despite U.S. reassurances that a strong force will remain; that, although the Nixon Administration wishes to implement a long-term and massive program of modernization for their armed forces, the American Congress will trim this program so drastically as to render it meaningless; and that these early moves at troop reduction by the United States precure [sic] an eventual American desire to retreat from the terms of the defense security pact between the two countries on which the Koreans have based nearly everything.[49]

Japanese Fears of American Abandonment

Although U.S. policies during 1969–71 impacted Japanese security less directly than they did Seoul's, they nevertheless instilled concerns about U.S. resolve. Three general issues are relevant to a discussion of these anxieties: (1) perceptions of regional security threats, (2) assessments of the Nixon doctrine, and (3) reactions to U.S. force reductions.

As the Japanese defense attaché in Seoul at this time recounted, while North Korean provocations did not give rise to the same intensity of threat experienced in Seoul, they did foster an acute awareness of the volatility of events on the peninsula so close to Japanese shores.[50] For example, Sato Eisaku and Foreign Minister Aichi Kiichi strongly condemned the EC-121 downing and, despite harsh domestic criticism about Japanese entanglement in U.S.-North Korean conflicts, pledged continued support for reconnaissance operations based out of Japan.[51] When Washington mobilized Task Force 71 to protect further EC-121 flights, Japan provided use of naval ports at Yokosuka and Sasebo and waived the right of prior consultation for operations necessary for the escort or rescue of U.S. intelligence missions in the Pacific.[52]

Uncertainties regarding China added to Japanese threat perceptions.[53] By 1970 Japan faced a China that had emerged from the Cultural Revolution with extreme anticapitalist rhetoric, nuclear weapons, and an open conflict with the Soviet Union.[54] Chinese antagonism toward Tokyo's pro-Western policies became particularly strident after the "Taiwan clause," a product of the November 1969 Nixon-Sato summit, which implicitly permitted the use of Japanese bases for the American defense of Taiwan. Beijing harshly condemned this agreement as an affront to its one-China policy. Moreover, it saw the clause's formulation, just prior to renewal of the United States-Japan security treaty in 1970, as evidence of Tokyo's long-term commitment as an "unsinkable aircraft carrier" in America's "iron security triangle" of aggression against China.[55]

Concurrent with these events, in April 1970 China conducted its first state visit to Pyongyang since 1962. The visit marked a serious effort on China's part to consolidate the Asian Communist front and to counterbalance the Soviet threat.[56] Zhou Enlai and Kim Il-sung reaffirmed their alliance and criticized Japan for renewed militarism and for being a puppet of American imperialism in Asia.[57] While China never actually acted on its belligerent rhetoric, tensions in the relationship were palpable. As a Japanese participant in negotiations with Beijing during the period stated: "There can be no doubt that the [Taiwan clause] played a significant part in the Chinese decision to lump Japan with imperialist America as a major target for attack."[58] Under such conditions the absence of stable U.S. defense commitments engendered an environment ripe for the proliferation of abandonment fears.

JAPANESE PERCEPTIONS OF THE NIXON DOCTRINE

As former Japanese foreign ministry and defense agency officials stated, the government, although outwardly reticent about the Nixon doctrine, was undoubtedly concerned about the credibility of American resolve.[59] This apprehension stemmed in part from the ambiguity of the doctrine's message. In Asia Nixon spoke of the doctrine as a reaffirmation of American resolve—with only minor adjustments in the physical size) of its commitment. At home, however, Nixon sold his ideas to the American public as a policy of disengagement in Asia. Also disquieting to the Japanese was the doctrine's implicit Eurocentrism.[60] In his 1970 foreign-policy report Nixon referred to a U.S. withdrawal from Europe as unlikely as one from Alaska. Juxtaposed to this, he warned that the United States must learn from past costly wars in Asia. The insecurities sparked by these ambiguities were evident in the lack of success that Assistant Secretary Green and Vice-President Agnew had when trying to reassure allies of U.S. resolve. As Agnew testified in Congress after a three-week Asian tour in January 1970: "The Nixon Doctrine was [being] received by Asian leaders like a 'lead balloon.'" [He] believed that longtime allies of the United States felt a sense of abandonment because of the new policy."[61] Numerous statements by Japanese political leaders echoed Agnew's testimony. Moreover in early 1970 foreign ministry and defense agency officials began monthly policy planning meetings in which the main topic of discussion was U.S. disengagement from Asia. Influential Japanese leaders outside government such as former Prime Minister Kishi Nobusuke also commenced a series of dialogues with neighboring Asian government leaders on the importance of policy coordination in coping with the rapidly changing security environment.[62]

Japan was also troubled by the longer-term implications of the Nixon doctrine. Nixon believed that as the United States pared down its presence abroad, a new, global, five-power system—the United States, Soviet Union, China, Japan, and Western Europe—would emerge in which stability would derive, not from the iron-clad alliances of the cold war, but from the balance of power among the five powers themselves.[63] This vision effectively extended Japan's place in the world far beyond the conventional burden-sharing role in the economic realm, with which Japan was comfortable.[64] Even more troubling, the reference to Japan as one of the five equal poles implied that Nixon's ultimate objective might be a recasting of the United States-Japan alliance.[65] Numerous statements by Tokyo stressed that Japan possessed neither the capacity nor political will to take on such an independent role. Foreign Minister Aichi's 1969 *Foreign Affairs* article was representative:

A simple transfer of peacekeeping responsibilities in Asia from the United States to Japan is out of the question because of Japan's constitutional limitation and the great disparity in both actual and potential military power between our two countries. Japanese public opinion is simply not prepared for such an undertaking; nor, I believe, would the other free nations of Asia welcome it. . . . It is reasonable to assume that for some time to come there will be no substitute for the continuing presence of American deterrent power to counter effectively any designs for large-scale military adventures in the area.[66]

1970 TROOP REDUCTIONS: THE VIEW FROM TOKYO

Although the fall of Saigon in 1975 would eventually give rise to deep Japanese concerns about U.S. retrenchment (see Chapter 5), in this earlier, 1969–71 period Nixon's Vietnamization program drew mixed reactions from Tokyo. There was substantial ambivalence toward the Vietnam war because of the manner in which it entangled Japan. Throughout the conflict Japanese facilities were employed for logistic support of U.S. forces in Vietnam. This included hospitals, repair facilities, and fuel and ammunition depots in Okinawa for B-52 bombing runs originating in Guam.[67] While such operations fell under the terms of the United States-Japan defense treaty's Far East clause (Article IV),[68] they raised concerns that Japan's involvement at times bordered on combat operations, especially with regard to B-52 missions out of Okinawa.[69] These anxieties were reflected in public opinion polls that found 42 percent expressing general disapproval of U.S. policies in Vietnam and a rough split of 33 and 28 percent, respectively, supporting and opposing U.S. disengagement.[70] Anxieties were also manifest in Tokyo's vehement rejection of any mention of a security link between Vietnam and Japan in the 1969 Nixon-Sato joint communiqué.[71] Thus, while application of the Nixon doctrine in Vietnam raised concerns about U.S. credibility, these were somewhat mitigated by the decreased American and, in turn, Japanese entanglement in the conflict.

U.S. force reductions in Japan and Korea, however, were a different matter.[72] Regarding bases in Japan, the United States turned twenty-three facilities over to Japan in 1969 and implemented a substantial force rationalization program in December 1970. This included the withdrawal of over twelve thousand combat troops from bases on the home islands,[73] removal of a Tactical Fighter Group (F-4 Phantoms) from Misawa and Yokota air bases, reductions in EC-121 aircraft at Itazuke air base, and a general scaling down of operations at all U.S. installations on the islands, particularly Atsugi, Itazuke, and Yokosuka. This was one of the largest reduction and redeployment programs in the postwar era, putting total U.S. troop levels at approximately half their strength in 1960. In retrospect, this program constituted more of a realignment of forces than a reduction.[74] At the time, however, Tokyo's anxieties centered on the abrupt and nonconsultative manner in which the United States had proceeded. In August 1970 Ambassador Armin Meyer cabled Washington, urgently advising his superiors of Japanese concerns about American unilateralism.[75] In a December 1970 speech Defense Agency Director-General Nakasone Yasuhiro also cautioned against U.S. withdrawals from Japan "undertaken drastically and in an all out fashion without coordination with the Japanese side."[76] Such actions eroded the bases of trust and intimacy the Japanese deemed so important to the alliance.

Japanese reactions to the deactivation of the Seventh Infantry Division in Korea were not as severe as Seoul's; nevertheless Japan clearly linked the American troop cuts in Korea with its own security. Sato expressed his apprehension over the decision with uncharacteristic fervor in meetings with Secretary of State William P. Rogers just after the pullout announcement.[77] The urgency felt by the Japanese was also evident at the Japan-ROK ministerial conference in July 1970. Foreign Minister Aichi held extra meetings with his South Korean counterpart on the troop cuts. In addition, the joint communiqué they issued departed from past practice by explicitly stating that "U.S. military presence is a key factor in safeguarding the security of the Far East." Such overt references to the U.S. defense presence had never been issued in previous communiqués. In postconference press statements Aichi expressed sympathy with the ROK over the pullout and promised to reflect this attitude in future dealings with Washington.[78]

These concerns ultimately led to subtle but significant changes (at least in language) in Japan's security doctrine. The Japanese Defense Agency's first Defense White Paper in October 1970 called for a revision of traditional attitudes toward security relations with the United States. It argued that Japan should view the mutual security treaty as "complementing" rather than "substituting" for Japan's defense capabilities. In line with this the finance ministry's 1970 budget called for the largest increase in defense spending in the postwar era, 17.7 percent, focusing on the development of more autonomous self-defense capabilities.[79]

One additional point deserves mention with regard to Japan. The government publicly expressed abandonment fears regarding the United States despite numerous domestic political incentives against doing so. For example, a high priority issue for Sato at the time was the U.S. return to Japanese sovereignty of the Ryūkyū islands, administered by the United States since the occupation. The reversion of these islands symbolized for the nation the end of the painful memory of World War II.[80] One key issue in the negotiations was whether U.S. nuclear weapons would remain on the islands following the reversion.[81] The public vehemently opposed this, placing Sato in an awkward position regarding public comments on the Nixon doctrine. Expressions of anxiety over how Japan was to fill the security void left by U.S. retrenchment elicited public suspicions that this was an attempt to justify future concessions on the reintroduction of a American nuclear deterrent on Okinawa. Thus, in spite of igniting public skepticism over the Okinawa reversion agreement, the government voiced its concerns over Nixon's policies.

Another factor weighing against unambiguous expressions of U.S. abandonment was the impending renewal of the United States-Japan security treaty in 1970. Sato wanted to avoid a battle over treaty renewal resembling the debilitating crisis that had brought down the Kishi government ten years earlier. If Tokyo fervently expressed concerns about the Nixon doctrine, this would focus the public and political agenda on defense buildup issues as a means of coping with this fear. This, in turn, would fuel antirearmament forces in Japan and reignite popular support for Japanese neutralism, resulting in an environment hardly conducive to easy renewal of the treaty.[82] Sato's desire to pacify and preempt such forces (particularly in the midst of general elections in late 1969) was therefore best served by tempering, not amplifying, expressions of U.S. abandonment.[83]

In short, what should have deterred Sato from expressing fears about U.S. resolve was an abundance of political liabilities attendant on the logical *remedies* for these fears. Once the government voiced these anxieties, it would be obliged to offer some means of coping with them.

This, in turn, would spotlight the politically sensitive issues of rearmament and nuclearization. Moderating expressions of concern over U.S. policy was consequently the best way to circumvent such difficult issues. Actions and statements by the Sato government in spite of these domestic imperatives underlined the seriousness of concerns about U.S. resolve.

While allied fears of U.S. abandonment centered on the extent to which U.S. troop cuts compromised operational capabilities to promptly defend themselves, for both Japan and Korea these fears, at a deeper and more disturbing level, were rooted in a genuine loss of confidence in the United States. Japan and Korea questioned not only the capabilities but also the will and intent of the common ally to maintain its defense commitments. It was these shared fears that had a positive effect on the manner in which Japan and the ROK dealt with one another.

Japan-ROK Security Relations: Budding Cooperation

While Japan and the ROK are not parties to a bilateral defense treaty, they do exhibit de facto security ties as a result of their geographic proximity and common alliances with the United States. Concerns about U.S. retrenchment had a consolidating impact on these ties with regard to three issues: the reversion of Okinawa, the "Korea clause," and the volume of governmental interaction on military issues.

OKINAWA REVERSION

"As Okinawa goes, so goes Japan." The title of this cable transmission from the U.S. embassy in Japan to Washington well reflected the importance that the reversion of the Ryūkyū Islands held for U.S.-Japanese relations during the Nixon-Sato years.[84] A crucial element of the negotiations, lasting from June 1969 to the signing of the agreement on June 17, 1971, was the future status of U.S. bases on the main island of Okinawa. Japan's position boiled down to three points: the removal of all nuclear weapons prior to reversion, the placing of similar restrictions on U.S. use of the Okinawan bases as was applied to bases on the home islands, and the right of "prior consultation" regarding any changes in force deployment or use of the bases following reversion.[85]

The United States generally acceded to Japan's desires regarding the removal of nuclear weapons[86]; its primary concern was access to Okinawa after the reversion. The key forward post of U.S. operations in the

Asia-Pacific, Okinawa's air and naval bases were crucial to the defense of sea lanes, intelligence gathering, and logistical operations.[87] While there was no question about access to these bases in the defense of Japan, the salient concern was whether Japan would permit similar access for U.S. fulfillment of other defense commitments in Asia, particularly Korea. Without this, effective U.S. defense of the ROK would be severely hampered.[88] As a result, although Okinawa's reversion was a U.S.-Japanese bilateral concern, the issue refracted on United States-ROK and Japan-ROK security relations.

The South Korean government paid close attention to the reversion talks. American relinquishing of control of Okinawa was unnerving to Seoul as it might ultimately make U.S. defense of Korea contingent on Japanese approval. In addition, the reversion of this critical U.S. foothold in the region without a corresponding increase in capabilities elsewhere (logically in Korea) reinforced ROK anxieties. In April 1969 ROK Foreign Minister Choi Kyu-hah presented letters to the Japanese and American ambassadors in Seoul, requesting regular apprisals of the negotiations and calling on Japan to waive prior-consultation rights after reversion.[89] The ROK formally laid out this position at the Vietnam war allies conference the following month:

It is the opinion of the Korean Government that the question of the Ryūkyū islands should be dealt with in such a manner that the military value of the United States bases should in no way be impaired and that the speedy and effective utilization of the bases should at no time be disturbed. The question of Okinawa bases in this sense cannot remain to be a matter of interest solely between the United States and Japan. It is a matter directly linked with the security of the free Asian nations in this region, hence a vital matter of our common concern. In this regard, the Korean government feels it necessary to let its views on this question be known to the Governments of both the United States and Japan from time to time.[90]

The Sato government was generally receptive to these requests. Informally it consulted with the ROK on the reversion negotiations, and formally the two governments explicitly referred to the strategic value of Okinawa for ROK and Japanese defense. For example, the reversion issue and Nixon's retrenchment policies dominated the agenda at the February 1969 meetings of the Japan-ROK Cooperation Committee and the Japan-ROK Parliamentarians Conference.[91] In late March 1969 Premier Chung and former Japanese Premier Kishi discussed the issue in an unofficial capacity with Nixon and Rogers in Washington, and following this, Japan responded positively to Foreign Minister Choi's April

15 letter on Okinawa, stating that Seoul's concerns were duly noted.[92]

As Japanese-ROK anxieties over U.S. retrenchment heightened in the aftermath of the EC-121 incident and the announcement of the Nixon doctrine, Sato officials more openly acknowledged Seoul's and Washington's positions on Okinawa. In a May 1969 session of the Upper House of the Diet Foreign Minister Aichi stated for the first time that the strategic value of Okinawa, with respect to Korea, Taiwan, and Indochina, was an important criterion in Tokyo's negotiation of a reversion settlement.[93] The final communiqué of the third annual Japan-ROK joint ministerial conference in August 1969 also included a clause noting that the two delegations had exchanged views on Okinawa. This was a subtle but significant concession by Japan, as its previously stated position had been that Okinawa was strictly a U.S.-Japanese bilateral concern.[94] Moreover, in press statements following the conference Aichi asserted that Okinawa's strategic value would not be impaired after reversion to Japanese sovereignty. The ROK considered this a very positive sign, acknowledging its security interests, and refrained from its typical bluster and brinkmanship to pressure Tokyo further.[95] South Korean press reports widely heralded the conference as elevating bilateral cooperation to a new level.[96]

THE KOREA CLAUSE

The basic terms of Ryūkyū Islands reversion were laid out at the Nixon-Sato summit in Washington on November 19–21, 1969. The two governments agreed on return of the islands by 1972, removal of nuclear weapons prior to reversion, and administration of the bases under the *Hondonami* formula.[97] However, the issue of prior consultation could not be resolved without more specific delineation of Japan's security interests and obligations in the region. Discussions during the summit focused on this very issue and produced two agreements relevant to Japan-ROK relations.[98] The first was what came to be known as the "Korea clause" of the Nixon-Sato joint communiqué:

The President and the Prime Minister specifically noted the continuing tension over the Korean peninsula. The Prime Minister deeply appreciated the peace-keeping efforts of the United Nations in the area and stated that the security of the Republic of Korea was essential to Japan's own security.[99]

The second agreement concerned Japan's recognition of the vital role U.S. bases on Okinawa played in the region's security. This took the form of references in the communiqué stating that return of the islands

"should not hinder the effective discharge of the international obligations assumed by the United States for the defense of countries in the
Far East including Japan."[100]

The meaning of these statements with regard to Korean contingencies
became clear at Sato's National Press Club speech in Washington on November 21. Specifically addressing the prior-consultation issue, Sato said:

In particular, if an armed attack against the Republic of Korea were to occur,
the security of Japan would be seriously affected. Therefore, should an occasion
arise for United States forces in such an eventuality to use facilities and areas
within Japan as bases for military combat operations to meet the armed attack,
the policy of the government of Japan towards prior consultation would be to
decide its position positively and promptly on the basis of the foregoing recognition.[101]

This "positive and prompt" commitment of the Okinawan bases constituted an operationalization of the Korea clause. The reasoning was simple: based on the premise that the security of the ROK was essential to
Japan, Japan would grant the United States unconditional access to the
Okinawan bases in the event of renewed hostilities against the ROK.
While Sato's statements were made within the context of a speech, there
was a clear understanding that they constituted a de facto agreement. In
order to highlight this, Undersecretary of State U. Alexis Johnson held a
special briefing prior to the speech instructing the media to pay particular attention to Sato's remarks regarding ROK security as they were
of equal importance to the joint communiqué itself.[102] In addition, when
Nixon sent the Okinawa reversion treaty to Congress for ratification, he
included, as supporting documentation, the text of Sato's National Press
Club speech.[103]

The Korea clause and the Okinawan base agreement marked a watershed in cooperation in Japan-ROK relations. First, while references to
Japanese-Korean joint security had been made before, the Korea clause
constituted the first formal declaration of a direct security link between
the two states.[104] Second, as specialist Okonogi Masao argues, although
both statements were made within the context of a United States-Japan
summit, the intention was a consolidation of the third leg of the Wash-
ington-Tokyo-Seoul security triangle.[105] The ROK's positive reactions to
the Nixon-Sato summit further confirm this point. As an official in the
prime minister's office at the time recalled, Sato's National Press Club
speech wholly resolved Seoul's concerns over the Okinawa prior-
consultation issue.[106] In a press conference the day after the summit For-

eign Minister Choi voiced satisfaction with the joint communiqué, saying it reflected ROK interests well.[107] In addition, South Korean press reports all applauded the "awakening" of Japan and Korea to the need for closer cooperation in the face of the Nixon doctrine.[108]

Third, the Okinawan base agreement represented at a more substantive level a major readjustment in Japanese security policy. By effectively waiving its right of prior consultation, Tokyo provided the United States with a "blank check" for Japanese support of Korea's defense (from bases in Okinawa and on the main islands). This amounted to a de facto modification of Article V of the United States-Japan mutual defense treaty by explicitly including the Korean peninsula within Japan's immediate defense perimeter.[109] Furthermore, usage of the term *Republic of Korea* instead of *Korean peninsula* in the clause indicated that Japan's security interests were served by the defense of South Korea rather than by the maintenance of a balance between the northern and southern regimes.[110] The differences in the adjectives used to describe the importance of the ROK versus that of other countries also reflected the priority placed on the Japan-ROK security tie. While the ROK's defense was termed "essential" to Japan, Taiwan's defense was described only as being "important."[111] Sato reaffirmed this distinction in the National Press Club speech. Though he was definitive on Japan's reaction to an attack on the ROK, the extent of his remarks on defense of Taiwan and other regional neighbors was only that Japan "would deal with the situation" and that such scenarios "cannot be foreseen today."[112]

As former ambassador Meyer stated, this establishment of direct security ties between Japan and the ROK was invariably linked to Nixon's disengagement policies.[113] For example, during the Nixon-Sato summit the United States pressed for the communiqué to contain statements reflecting its expectation that Asia would be primarily responsible for its own defense. In response, the Japanese side called for the inclusion of statements expressing Tokyo's abandonment fears. These statements made up the section immediately preceding the Korea clause:

The Prime Minister . . . stressed that it was important for the peace and security of the Far East that the United States should be in a position to carry out fully its obligations referred to by the President. He further expressed his recognition that in light of the present situation, the presence of United States forces in the Far East constituted a mainstay for the stability of the area.[114]

Finally, Sato agreed to the Korea clause and Okinawan base commitment despite harsh domestic criticism. Upon Sato's departure for his summit with Nixon radicals in mass demonstrations claimed that the premier was going to enter into a "secret security deal" with the United States.[115] Moreover, after the summit the government faced protracted criticism in the Diet from December 1969 through March 1970. The opposition parties jointly denounced Sato for turning the country into a regional military base for the United States and for entrapping Japan into future conflicts in Korea and Taiwan.[116]

Despite this criticism Sato stood by the two agreements. Upon returning from the United States, he said that Japan could not treat hostilities against the ROK as simply those against any other foreign country and that consequently it would be natural for Japan to render cooperation to the ROK within constitutional bounds.[117] In subsequent Diet sessions in 1970 both Sato and Foreign Minister Aichi reaffirmed the Korea clause, adding that Japan would make good on these commitments even though it might incur direct North Korean retaliation. These statements constituted the most specific enunciation of the Korea clause and Okinawan base agreement and highlighted the new closeness of Japan-ROK security ties.[118]

1970 ANNOUNCEMENT OF AMERICAN TROOP REDUCTIONS IN KOREA

The July 1970 announcement of U.S. troop cuts in Korea increased Japan-ROK identification on common security issues. On the Korean side senior policymakers conceded that a "new thinking of Seoul's relationship with Tokyo and Washington was now necessary."[119] An immediate manifestation of this was a meeting between Ambassador Lee Hurak and Sato one week after the July 7 announcement of the pull out. Lee briefed Sato on the U.S. decision and requested Japan's increased cooperation, particularly economic cooperation, in light of the Nixon doctrine.[120] On the Japanese side ten days after the pullout announcement, Sato sent Vice-Minister for Defense Tsuchiya Yoshihiko to Seoul to assure his counterparts that Japan would not renege on its promises regarding Okinawa.[121] A *Tong-A Ilbo* editorial on July 11 aptly summed up the mindsets of Japanese and Korean policymakers at the time: "There is no question that the issue of a U.S. troop cut in Korea has made it urgent that Korea and Japan cooperate more closely with each other for their respective national security."

The culmination of these cooperative interchanges was the fourth annual Japan-ROK joint ministerial conference in Seoul on July 21–23. Fears of U.S. abandonment permeated the air at this meeting as it followed by only two weeks the pull out announcement and ran concurrently with the United States-ROK defense ministers conference in Honolulu, where the United States set forth the specifics of the Seventh Infantry Division cuts. Proceedings were marked by an atypical atmosphere of cordiality.[122] The ROK's opening statement emphasized the importance of "positive cooperation" with Tokyo, while Japan's highlighted its appreciation of the security ties between the two countries.[123] The conference joint communiqué specifically cited the North Korean security threat and stated with regard to the U.S. defense commitment and Japan-ROK security that

Both ministers reaffirmed that the security and prosperity of the two countries are closely interrelated and that their common goal is to attain peace and prosperity in Asia. . . . Noting that tension still exists in the Asia and Pacific region, the ministers of the two countries shared the view that the United States military presence in the region is a key factor in safeguarding the security of the Far East.[124]

These clauses represented a break from precedent. While not exact replications of the Nixon-Sato communiqué, they constituted the first Japan-ROK bilateral version of the Korea clause.[125] In addition, the two governments had never referred so affirmatively to the critical nature of the American regional presence, nor had they ever explicitly named Pyongyang as a threat. Together these statements reflected the extent to which Seoul's and Tokyo's threat perceptions had become more convergent and cooperative intentions made more salient by the overarching concerns about U.S. abandonment.

The 1970 joint ministerial conference also produced substantial economic agreements in support of the ROK's third five-year development plan. Tokyo provided $100 million in loans for the development of South Korean agriculture and medium-sized industries. In addition, it agreed to conduct a feasibility study for a second $100-million loan for South Korean heavy industrial development.[126] As Aichi stated at the close of the conference, these loans were intended as "positive assistance" to Seoul to help cope with the projected U.S. troop cutback.[127] Japanese press reports echoed the security motives behind the agreements, approving the ROK loans "as a wise investment in our defense."[128]

JAPAN-ROK SECURITY EXCHANGES

Security cooperation between Japan and Korea extended beyond atmospherics and policy statements at the annual ministerial conferences. During the 1969–71 period a number of bilateral military contacts took place for the first time. These consisted of Japan-ROK military activities within the context of U.S. defense mobilization in the region and direct exchanges of Japanese and South Korean military officials. Both symbolized the adherence to, and operationalization of, the Korea clause and Okinawan base agreement.

Coordination of Japan-ROK military activities took place during training exercises and actual crises in the region. Regarding the former, Japan played a key role in such exercises as Focus Retina and Freedom Vault.[129] Bases in Okinawa were indispensable for the coordination and staging of these exercises; they also facilitated the layover, refueling, and repair of U.S. transport planes involved in the maneuvers. Moreover, during the exercises inclement weather forced the postponment of the final, crucial airdrop stages of the exercise. Okinawa acted as an emergency layover point for U.S. paratroopers until these airdrops could be executed.[130]

Military coordination between Japan and the ROK also occurred during actual crises. For example, during the EC-121 incident Japanese Maritime Self-Defense Forces radar surveillance played a critical role in determining that the downed U.S. plane had been in international airspace when attacked by the North.[131] In addition, Tokyo permitted the Task Force 71 mobilization to use ports in Japan without prior consultation (access to which was very important to mission's success). During the *Pueblo* crisis, the positioning of a U.S. carrier off the North Korean coast to deter further provocations was facilitated through the use of Japanese ports, particularly Sasebo. Furthermore, an important aspect of the U.S. response to the *Pueblo* seizure was the extension of the 313th Air Division's permanent operational duty from Okinawa, at Kadena, to ROK bases at Kwangju and Suwon.[132] Each instance of Seoul-Tokyo coordination (in conjunction with Washington) represented an operationalization of the direct security link acknowledged by both governments and resulted in the effective use of the two states as a single strategic unit for defense operations in the region.

The Park government also undertook a number of initiatives to redefine its traditional security perspectives on Japan. These largely consisted of statements designed to reduce the stigma attached to an enlarged Japanese role in ROK defense. In his 1971 New Year's address Park said that he did not perceive Japan as a threat, nor did he oppose a larger Japanese defense presence in the region.[133] In addition, various ROK government agencies in 1970 recommended the promotion of closer security ties with its neighbor. A national security report in February 1970 and National Assembly Defense Committee report in June 1970, for example, called for joint efforts in military training, intelligence gathering, and other forms of defense integration to help fill the security vacuum left by the U.S. withdrawal. These recommendations even included considering a mutual defense treaty with Japan.[134] While such ideas were not acted upon, their mere discussion indicated the urgency attached to consolidating security ties.

Finally, cooperation in the defense sector was manifest in the direct exchange of military personnel. These bilateral contacts, although conducted with little publicity (for domestic political reasons), all involved relatively highly placed military officers. On June 10–15, 1969, Chief of the Ground Self-Defense Force General Yamada Masao visited the ROK at the invitation of General Kim Kye-won. Yamada inspected ROK army units and met with President Park. This was followed by an inspection of Japanese Self-Defense Forces (SDF) facilities by the chair of the ROK Joint Chiefs of Staff General Mun Hyong-tae on June 16. Mun met with his Japanese counterpart, Muta Hirokuni, as well as with Defense Agency Director General Arita Kiichi and Premier Sato.[135] As the Japanese defense attaché at the time later stated, these exchanges were largely ceremonial; however, they were intended to promote greater transparency between the two militaries and open an informal dialogue channel on security issues. As these visits occurred less than two months after the EC-121 incident, their purpose was also to improve military coordination in the event of further North Korean provocations.[136]

Similar exchanges took place in the aftermath of July 1970 announcement of the Seventh Infantry Division withdrawal. Around July 7 Tsuchiya Yoshihiko, SDF Political Affairs Division vice-chairman, met with Vice Defense Minister Yu Kun-chang in Seoul. The purposes of Tsuchiya's visit were to inspect ROK military facilities and to review contingencies regarding the Okinawan base agreement.[137] The following February 22 Yu made a one-week trip to Japan at the invitation of Director-General Nakasone, inspecting SDF facilities and visiting the National Defense College.[138] While the premise of these visits was again ceremonial, an official who accompanied Yu confirmed that the vice defense ministers did exchange views on the Nixon doctrine and on ways in which the two militaries were to cope with the vastly altered security environment resulting from U.S. force reductions in the region.[139]

In August 1970 the Park and Sato governments agreed on the assignment of a second Japanese defense attaché to Seoul.[140] The additional attaché made the Republic the only Asian country, other than the Soviet Union, with two defense attachés (ground and air). The assignment was made one year ahead of schedule and in spite of severe budgetary constraints imposed by the finance ministry. In fact, in meeting the budget cuts the Japanese Defense Agency scrapped plans for adding attachés in South Vietnam, Laos, and Cambodia but chose not to institute such cuts in Korea.[141] The link between the attaché decision and fears of U.S. abandonment was clear. As the Japanese defense attaché responsible for this assignment recalled, the measure was directly related to the JDA's increased priority on improved military coordination with the ROK in the wake of the Seventh Infantry Division pullout and the Korea clause.[142]

NONEVENTS: CIRCUMVENTED FRICTION

The characterization of Japan-ROK relations thus far has focused on instances of cooperation between the two governments. This does not mean, however, that relations were devoid of contention. There were, in fact, a number of disagreements over security issues during the 1969–71 period. These largely stemmed from Japan's contacts with North Korea. However, these disagreements on the whole did *not* cripple relations.[143] Instead, the two governments worked to avoid friction over such potentially divisive events. Three examples illustrate this point.

In June 1969 the ROK found that North Korean speedboats used to infiltrate the southern coastline had been purchased from Japan. In addition, in December 1970 the Japanese justice ministry detained an ROK army officer for attempting to defect to the North through Japan. Ten days later, however, the ministry reversed its decision and allowed the officer passage to Pyongyang on humanitarian grounds. Both of these incidents had a direct bearing on South Korean security.

Secret coastal landings by North Korean spies had been an especially effective means of aggression against the South. A rash of commando infiltrations on Cheju Island in July 1968 and in areas south of the DMZ, at Samch'ŏk and Ulchin in November 1968 and at Chu'munjin in early 1969, were testament to this.[144] ROK counterespionage forces could not check these activities precisely because they were incapable of tracking the high-speed boats used by the North. This issue so troubled Park that he commissioned the covert Agency for Defense Development, which answered directly to him and was mandated to close the weapons technology gap with the North through, among other projects, nuclear weapons. The discovery that Japan was supplying these boats therefore outraged the South Koreans and reinforced notions of the Japanese as untrustworthy "economic animals."[145]

Japan's acquiescence to ROK defectors had been vehemently criticized in the past on the ground that many of these individuals, after receiving training in the North, eventually reentered the ROK through Japan as spies. For this reason Seoul did not countenance similar actions in support of South Korean defectors in 1965 and 1966.[146] The fact that the December 1970 defection was by an individual from the military constituted an even greater affront to ROK security.

Given these considerations, one would expect Tokyo's actions to have elicited severe responses from Seoul, probably leading to a disruption in relations. This was not the case. In both incidents South Korean government reprisals were surprisingly restrained—token expressions of disapproval and a minor protest note filed with the Japanese embassy.[147]

Another potential Japan-ROK diplomatic crisis emerged in April 1970 when nine Japanese student radicals hijacked a civilian airliner (JAL Yodo) and demanded passage to North Korea. Through diversionary tactics Japanese aviation authorities fooled the hijackers into landing at South Korea's Kimpo airport, after which a tense standoff ensued, with the Yodo's ninety-nine passengers as hostages. The Park government unconditionally refused to grant the plane permission to fly through South Korean airspace to Pyongyang. The Japanese government pleaded with ROK authorities to allow the airliner free passage in exchange for the safe return of the hostages. With a resolution to the crisis appearing unlikely, Japanese negotiators, without consulting ROK authorities, secretly worked out an agreement with the hijackers exchanging the hostages for Vice Transport Minister Yamamura Shinjiro after which the plane would be allowed to go to North Korea. Japanese authorities then presented the final agreement to Defense Minister Chung post factum.[148]

These events certainly had the potential for disrupting Seoul-Tokyo relations. The hijacking was a major diplomatic incident, which brought officials from the highest levels of the foreign and transport ministries of both governments to Kimpo airport to negotiate personally. In addition, the ROK went to extraordinary lengths to accommodate Japanese requests during the crisis. It bypassed strict visa regulations and allowed a pro-North Korean Japanese Dietman to enter the ROK at the hijackers' request.[149] It also lowered the national flag at Kimpo airport in order to deceive the hijackers into believing they were landing in Pyongyang. Opposition parties in Seoul strongly criticized these measures as "degrading to the national character." Finally, the manner in which Japan presented their resolution of the crisis as a *fait accompli* was extremely embarrassing. As the hijacked plane was technically under South Korean jurisdiction, the final decisions should have been made by Seoul.

In spite of these factors Seoul chose not to condemn Japan's handling of the affair. Defense Minister Chung consented to the deal, quietly accepted apologies from the Sato government, and then allowed the airliner passage to Pyongyang.[150] As a member of the Japanese negotiating team recounted, the South Koreans were livid when they learned of the Japanese deal with the hijackers; nevertheless, in the interest of avoiding a diplomatic row, the ROK remained conspicuously silent in public.[151]

Japan reciprocated Seoul's cooperation in the aftermath of the incident. After the hijackers arrived in Pyongyang, the North Koreans returned the airliner (and Minister Yamamura) to Japan. Japanese opposition parties as well as the media saw this as a significant humanitarian gesture by Pyongyang and as an opportunity for Sato to improve relations with the North.[152] Tokyo had already increased contacts with Pyongyang through the reopening of repatriation talks, thus creating a political climate conducive to a warming of relations. Moreover, Japan wanted expanded dialogue with China for trade purposes, but Beijing's animosity toward the conservative Sato government made this difficult. Pyongyang's returning of the Yodo thus presented a political springboard for diplomatic inroads to Beijing via improved relations with the North.[153]

Rather than take advantage of this opportunity, Sato refused to alter his policy toward Pyongyang. In Lower House sessions, Sato and Foreign Minister Aichi expressed gratitude for the return of the airliner but definitively stated that Japan could not increase contacts with the North out of respect for the South and would always consult Seoul before undertaking any change in policy.[154]

It is, of course, difficult to isolate empirically the motives for Japanese and Korean self-control in the Yodo affair. On the South Korean side unusually conciliatory behavior could have been out of humanitarian concern, particularly after Japan's deal left the Koreans with little choice. On the Japanese side muted responses to North Korean acts of goodwill could have stemmed from ulterior concerns regarding Okinawa.[155] However, a couple of observations deserve mention. First, interaction over the Yodo represented an exercise of tacit, if not conscious, reciprocity.[156] And second, this behavior correlated with concerns about U.S. retrenchment from the region. As shall be seen in later chapters, behavior in the Yodo affair is striking because very similar incidents involving clashes over policy toward North Korea, at a time when joint fears of U.S. abandonment were less salient (especially 1973 and 1974), produced overwhelmingly contentious Japan-ROK behavior.

Political Cooperation

The link between anxieties about U.S. retrenchment and Japan-ROK cooperation was also evident in the political sphere. The 1969–71 period saw advances in the tenor and scope of bilateral channels of dialogue. The main arena in which policy was hammered out was the annual joint ministerial conference, and during the years concerned communiqués and proceedings of these meetings bore evidence of atypically high levels of cooperation.

Another significant forum for consultations was the *Han-Il hyŏpnyŏk wiwŏnhoe* (Japan-ROK Cooperation Committee). Sato and Park created this body in February 1969 to facilitate closer policy coordination between the two governments.[157] The committee was composed of elder statesmen and prominent business leaders who had the ear of government in Tokyo and Seoul. For instance, chairmanships were held by individuals like former Premier Kishi Nobusuke (Sato's half-brother) and former Premier Chang Key-young.[158] While historical animosity plagued relations between the two countries, members of this elite committee enjoyed enduring friendships through government service and business, which in some cases dated back to the period of occupation.[159] As a result of the camaraderie among its members, as well as the access enjoyed by these individuals to the highest levels of leadership in both countries, this body was highly influential in policymaking.

While the committee's formal agenda focused on economic issues, its true purpose was to discuss the most pressing issues in the relationship. Meetings seldom resulted in any tangible agreements; instead, they served as an invaluable channel for the exchange of views. Through this semiofficial dialogue the two governments sounded out one another's policy positions, ironed out differences, and laid the groundwork for the coordination of policy at the official ministerial conferences and other bilateral governmental meetings.[160]

TABLE 3

Japan-ROK Regularized Bilateral Committees, 1966–1995

Date	Title	Comments
1966	Economic Cooperation Committee	Delegation heads: Chang Key-young; Fujiyama Aiichiro
1966	Joint Fisheries Committee	
1967	Joint Ministerial Conference	Annual
1968	Cooperation Committee	Informally established
1968	Agriculture, forestry, and fisheries cooperation committee	First meeting in Tokyo
1969	Cooperation Committee	Formal inauguration (chairs: Sin Hyŏn-hwak, Sakurauchi Yoshio)
1971	Goodwill (friendship) association	Chairs: Cho Man-je, Hiranuma Takeo
1972	Parliamentarians Union (disbanded)	Chairs: Kim Yun-hwan, Takeshita Noboru
1972	Continental-shelf development talks	Working-level talks
1975	Sea disaster and rescue talks	Working-level talks
1977	Parliamentarians League	Replaced 1972 group
1977	Friendship Association	Chairs: Kim Su-han,Tanaka Tatsuo
1978	Women's Association	Chairs: Pak Chŏng-cha, Soma Yukiko
1978	Joint continental-shelf development committee	Formalization of 1972 working-level talks
1979	Parliamentary Defense Council	
1979	High-level defense exchanges	JDA chief Yamashita Ganri, Defense chief Jong-whan
1981	Legal Resident rights committee	For Korean residents in Japan
1981	Economic Committee	Chairs: Pak Yong-hak, Hakura Nobuya (reinaugurated under new name 1966, formerly Economic Cooperation Committee)
1981	Cultural Exchange Fund	Chairs: Lee Sang-woo, Maeda Toshikazu
1983	Cultural Exchange committee	Working-level committees
1984	High-level Policy meeting	Annual basis (different from joint ministerial conference)
1985	3rd Generation committee	Resident rights for 3rd generation Koreans in Japan
1986	Foreign Ministers Meeting	Annual basis (different from joint ministerial conference)
1988	Joint Olympics Security Committee	3 meetings (Apr.–Sept.)
1988	21st Century Committee	Annual basis (different from joint ministerial conference)
1991	Trade & Technology Cooperation Meeting	
1991	Assistant foreign ministerial meeting	Trilateral basis w/U.S. (started as a result of N. Korean nuclear dispute)
1992	Fishery working-level committee	Re-constituted body
1993	Korea-Japan Forum	
1994	Air defense working-level committee	4th meeting, orig. date not available
1994	Sakhalin Island committee	4th meeting, orig. date not available

SOURCES: Compiled from *Ilbon kaehwang* (Summary status: Japan), government publication no. 17000-20030-67-9607 (Seoul: Republic of Korea, Ministry of Foreign Affairs, Feb. 1996), 227–28, 230, 282–313; *Taehan min'guk woegyo yŏnp'yo: 1993 bu juyo munhŏn* (Major and minor diplomatic documents annual of the Republic of Korea) (Seoul: Republic of Korea, Ministry of Foreign Affairs, 1993), 486–88; and Cho Jung-pyo, director, Northeast Asia Division I, Republic of Korea, Ministry of Foreign Affairs, interview by author, 14 Feb. 1992, Seoul.

The proceedings of the Cooperation Committee therefore provide a good indicator of the policy priorities of both governments. During the 1969–71 period the agenda for these meetings reflected the need for increased cooperation in the face of U.S. regional retrenchment. For instance, the key topics at the meetings in February and November 1969 were the Nixon doctrine and the Okinawa reversion settlement. Similarly, at the 1970 meetings the main topics of discussion were the Korea clause and the promotion of greater security cooperation in response to the July 1970 U.S. pullout announcement.[161]

MUTUAL SUPPORT IN THE DOMESTIC POLITICAL ARENA

Japan-ROK cooperation was also exhibited in the form of mutual support in the domestic political arena. This was evidenced in such things as ceremonies conferring diplomatic honors on one another's politicians and the establishment of cultural and information centers in Tokyo and Seoul.[162] A more interesting example of this type of cooperation, however, related to South Korean domestic politics.

During the 1969–71 period a controversy arose over Park's plan to strike constitutional limits against his bid for a third consecutive presidential term. Nationwide student demonstrations erupted in the summer of 1969, forcing many universities to suspend classes, and the political opposition tried vigorously to block the third-term amendment in the National Assembly. These attempts failed, and Park eventually retained power; however, both the national referendum on constitutional revision in October 1969 and the April 1971 presidential election were met with widespread accusations of corruption and illegitimacy.[163]

In spite of the controversy surrounding these events, the Sato government was subtly but wholly supportive of Park's reelection bid. Ties between the two governments and big business ran deep, and a great deal of private financing of Park's party came from Japan.[164] Three days prior to the referendum on the third-term amendment, LDP Vice-President Kawashima Shojiro affirmed his party's support for the amendment and said that Park's continued rule was crucial to the ROK's political stability.[165] In addition, the day after the presidential election in April 1971, Chief Cabinet Secretary Hori Shigeru issued a statement hailing Park's victory as boding well for the preservation of strong Japanese-South Korean relations. (Hori's statement also did not question the legitimacy of the election.) As a further sign of support Sato attended Park's inauguration in July 1971 with promises of support for the ROK's upcoming third five-year development plan.[166]

These expressions of support were important for Park. His heavy-handed tactics in amending the constitution caused many South Korean voters to rally around the popular opposition candidate, Kim Dae-jung. In the end a key factor swaying voters toward Park was his promise of continued economic growth through the third five-year economic development plan. This plan was, in turn, contingent on massive inflows of Japanese capital and investment, which was implicitly guaranteed by Sato's support for Park's continued rule. To South Korean voters the availability of this aid, if the opposition party came to power, was less certain.[167]

Although the Park regime was not openly thankful for Japan's support, its appreciation was evident in Seoul's conspicuous silence following certain anti-Korean acts committed by Japanese radicals. For example, in October 1969 protests by anti-Park elements in Tokyo over the third-term amendment resulted in an attack on the Korean embassy. Communication facilities were firebombed, and the compound was ransacked.[168] In spite of this, foreign ministry officials did not issue a protest and quietly accepted an apology from Tokyo. Similarly, after Park's victory, demonstrations at the Japanese embassy in Seoul raged for an entire week against Sato's attending the inauguration and culminated with the burning of the embassy's flag. Tokyo did not lodge a protest over these acts and did not cancel Sato's visit to Seoul for the inauguration.[169]

Another instance of cooperation over potentially divisive issues was the Yun Yu-gil case. A Korean dissident who illegally immigrated to Japan in 1951, Yun was sought by the KCIA for alleged antigovernment activities. In January 1969 a Tokyo district court ruled against deporting Yun on the ground that he was a political refugee.[170] In May 1969, however, Yun disappeared after being summoned to the ROK embassy in Tokyo and turned up in Seoul a few days later in KCIA custody.[171]

The KCIA's abduction of Yun elicited denunciations in Japan. Demonstrations by civil rights and legal organizations condemned the ROK's blatant abuse of diplomatic privileges and violation of Japanese sovereignty. These groups put extreme pressure on Sato to protest the incident and demand a formal apology from Seoul.[172] Despite the intense public outcry over the incident, Tokyo's response was decidedly restrained. Not only did the justice and foreign ministries fail to file protests, but in the interest of maintaining good relations with Seoul, they refrained from any public criticism of the case. This reticence is striking when compared with Tokyo's reactions to similar incidents in other periods. In particular, the 1973 KCIA kidnapping of Kim Dae-jung from Japan was virtually identical in circumstance to the Yun case, yet Japanese behavior was noticeably different. In the Kim case Tokyo raised vociferous protests, temporarily recalled its ambassador from Seoul, and threatened to sever diplomatic relations (see Chapter 4). While this disparity is in part explained by the fact that Kim Dae-jung was a more prominent figure than Yun (some would argue that the kidnapping itself made Kim famous), it still does not explain how Japan's response in the Yun case could be so passive despite the KCIA's blatant show of disrespect for the authority of the Japanese judicial system.

It is admittedly difficult to link Japan-ROK cooperation over the Yun case directly with mutually shared fears of U.S. abandonment. This would require evidence that such anxieties occupied the minds of the decisionmakers precisely when they were dealing with these events. A more plausible characterization is to view these abandonment fears as providing the broad policy context in which decisionmakers dealt with events. This environment was one in which an overarching security imperative for greater cooperation infused both Seoul's and Tokyo's general outlooks and priorities. While U.S. abandonment fears may not have been the proximate cause of political cooperation in these cases, they provided the permissive condition for such cooperation to take place.

JAPANESE–NORTH KOREAN RELATIONS

Throughout the postnormalization era Japan's contacts with North Korea were perhaps the most disruptive factor in Seoul-Tokyo relations. While the 1969–71 period saw its share of disputes over such contacts, Japan-ROK interaction over this issue was marked on the whole by significantly less contention. The Park regime resisted the temptation to challenge every Japanese-North Korean encounter, and the Sato government showed greater cognizance of the ROK's containment policy by downplaying contacts with Pyongyang. This behavior was evident with regard to cultural/economic activities and pro-North Korean elements within the Japanese population.

Cultural/economic exchanges and, in particular, exchanges for humanitarian purposes, such as the reunification of families, served as the primary builder of goodwill in Japan-North Korea relations. However, during the 1969–71 period the Sato government became less receptive to these exchanges, largely to accommodate Seoul's security concerns.

For example, in the first half of 1969 the Japanese foreign ministry denied applications for exit and entry visas to a number of North Koreans as well as a seventy-three–person Chosen Soren cultural delegation on the ground that the trips were politically motivated.[173] The following June Tokyo also turned down a North Korean request to participate in the Japanese Communist party's annual convention on the ground that condoning such political exchanges was not in Japan's interests.[174]

Tokyo also addressed Seoul's complaints about economic contacts with the North. For example, in January 1969 the Japan-North Korea Trade Association concluded an agreement to export $40-million worth of plant equipment to Pyongyang. This was followed in February by a decision of the Ministry of International Trade and Industry (MITI) to subsidize Japanese participation in a science and technology trade fair slated for October in Pyongyang.[175] Both developments elicited complaints from Seoul about dual-use applications for some of the plant equipment and technology that could boost the North's military potential.

Tokyo usually would reject such complaints because: (1) these were private-sector decisions beyond government influence, (2) contacts with the North were strictly a Tokyo-Pyongyang bilateral concern, or (3) Japan's *seikei bunri* (separation of politics from economics) policy with the North posed no threat to Seoul. Rather than intone these arguments, MITI in March 1969 withdrew support for the trade fair in Pyongyang. This resulted in a substantial reduction in the scale of the exhibition and removed the appearance that the government was sanctioning trade relations with North Korea.[176] A *Han'guk Ilbo* analysis stated the reasons for MITI's reversal of its earlier decision: "Observers believe that Japan may have taken into consideration the possible deterioration of her relations with Seoul when she decided not to provide the subsidy."[177]

Even though Japan undertook efforts at ameliorating the ROK's anxieties over North Korea, this did not mean that relations were void of any disagreements. In defiance of Seoul's wishes, Tokyo did pursue contacts with Pyongyang on occasion throughout the 1969–71 period. But in certain key instances the ROK downplayed its dissatisfaction in the interest of keeping relations on an even keel. Two telling examples of this had to do with North Korean repatriation and the germ controversy.

In February 1971 the Japanese and North Korean Red Cross negotiated a followup agreement to a 1959 Calcutta protocol enabling the repatriation of some sixteen thousand North Koreans in the ensuing six months.[178] Simultaneously, from about March 1970, the foreign minis-try, as part of an initiative to reduce travel restrictions to Communist countries, dramatically liberalized visa approval guidelines for North Korean residents in Japan desirous of visiting their homeland (usually granted on a two-month basis).[179]

In Seoul's zero-sum mentality this agreement constituted a political victory for the North as they connoted Japan's de facto recognition of the Kim Il-sung regime. Furthermore, the issuing of reentry visas to Chosen Soren members was seen as encouraging North Korean espio-nage training and infiltration activities against the South. Given these circumstances, one would expect the ROK to have reacted resolutely. On the contrary, Park made a concerted effort to prevent these poten-tially inflammatory issues from damaging relations. Countermeasures did not go beyond an occasional statement of disapproval, and at worst, a diluted *note verbale* filed with the Japanese embassy.[180] In none of these cases did Seoul threaten retaliatory acts such as the suspension of bilateral conferences or recalling of ambassadors as had been the stan-dard practice.[181] The atypically magnanimous tenor of Park's statements was duly noted in a January 1971 *Chosŏn Ilbo* editorial:

The response of the [ROK] government to the latest news from Japan has been quite different. It has not sent protest notes or protest missions to Japan. It has even failed to announce protest statements. All this points to the fact that a quiet change has been taking place in the government's diplomacy toward Ja-pan.[182]

This behavior starkly contrasted with the ROK's vehement protests over the very same issues in other periods in the relationship. For example, when Kishi negotiated the first repatriation agreement in 1959, the ROK threatened outright to sink all repatriation ships out of Japanese ports.[183] Similarly, in December 1965 and February 1966 Seoul's severe reaction to Japan's reentry visa policy prompted American CIA assess-ments to cite this as a problem of significance between the two coun-tries.[184]

Circumvented friction in the political arena was also evident with re-gard to the germ controversy.[185] In early February 1970 a Japanese trad-ing company, Yanagida, underwent investigations for smuggling elec-tronic parts to North Korea. In the course of these probes the Japanese Maritime Safety Agency discovered that North Korea had at one time placed orders with Yanagida for various strains of bacteria including anthrax, cholera, and plague. The agency also found that Yanagida, along with ten other Japanese firms, was involved in the export of a number of Coordinating Committee for Export to Communist Countries (COCOM)-restricted goods to the North.[186]

The Yanagida revelations sparked a controversy, and the World Health Organization (WHO) immediately initiated an investigation. The ROK harbored serious concerns that Pyongyang was planning germ warfare, and this suspicion seemed all the more justified because South Korea had suffered an unexplained cholera epidemic the previous summer. Foreign Minister Choi's public statement on the controversy in February 1970 revealed the depth of ROK anxieties:

It was disclosed by the Japanese police authorities that the north Korean puppet regime had secretly placed an order, in the beginning of 1969, with a certain Japanese firm for shipment to north Korea for cholera and other epidemic germs. . . . We cannot but fear that those vicious germs might have already been in the hands of the north Korean communists. . . . In view of the above facts, it is not difficult to infer the origin of the cholera germs which caused the cholera epidemic in the west coast of the Republic of Korea in September 1969. . . . We condemn the north Korean communists for their acts of aggression and this inhumane design against the lives of innocent civilian population [sic].[187]

In spite of these concerns the Park government took a low-key posture throughout the incident. Although it filed two protests with Japanese authorities,[188] it took no punitive countermeasures such as suspending the February meeting of the Cooperation Committee or imposing economic sanctions. Moreover, the government sought to prevent public outrage over the incident from snowballing. The information ministry instructed the press to refrain from reports that might incite public indignation against Japan. As a Japanese official involved in resolving the dispute recalled, Park and Foreign Minister Choi also stated that their grievance was not with the Japanese government, but with Yanagida. As a further show of support, Park and Choi said they understood that Sato did not condone Yanagida's actions and expressed appreciation for Tokyo's prompt investigation of the incident.[189]

WHO investigations eventually confirmed that germ orders had been placed by North Korea with Japanese trading companies but that none of the orders had actually been filled. Again, while the South Korean media and general public were skeptical of these findings, the government was relatively conciliatory. It accepted the report as a satisfactory resolution of the dispute and only issued a note verbale requesting that Tokyo monitor trading companies' activities more scrupulously in the future.

In retrospect Seoul's muted response could be attributed to the fact that the germ orders were never filled. However, this explanation still does not account for Seoul's passive behavior regarding the export of other COCOM-restricted goods to Pyongyang by Yanagida and other Japanese firms (another of the findings of the WHO investigations). Nor does this explanation seem feasible given the ROK's long-standing sensitivity to any Japanese-North Korean contacts, let alone ones that directly undermine national security.[190] As a journalist who covered these events recalled, it was highly unusual that Seoul did not demand some form of economic compensation over the dispute.[191]

A permissive condition for the absence of friction in the germ controversy was U.S. disengagement from the region. As Shim Jae-hoon stated, there was a "basic underlying understanding" in Tokyo and Seoul at the time of the dispute, that the fluid security environment stemming from Nixon's retrenchment policies necessitated stable bilateral relations.[192] This was evident at the February 1970 Japan-ROK Cooperation Committee. Taking place concurrently with the germ scandal, the committee papered over difficulties arising from the incident and instead emphasized the need for cooperation. Shared fears of U.S. abandonment therefore prompted Japan and especially the ROK to downplay the potential damage the germ controversy could have done to bilateral relations.

Economic Relations

Japan-ROK cooperation in the economic arena took primarily three forms. First, both governments implemented policies promoting greater trade and investment. Second, while profit motives were behind much of this economic activity, an increasingly salient aspect was the security motive. Third, cooperation was also evident in the absence of friction over potentially contentious issues. In particular, this related to Japan's desire to increase trade relations with the PRC.

POLICY INITIATIVES

During the 1969–71 period Japan and the ROK undertook numerous efforts to promote bilateral trade and investment. On the South Korean side these included wide-ranging market liberalization initiatives, particularly regarding foreign ownership (December 1969); reductions in trade barriers for over 50 percent of Japanese imports (January 1970); and legislation allowing the opening of Japanese bank offices in Korea

(March 1971).[193] On the Japanese side measures included the establishment of technical-training institutes in various South Korean cities (February and May 1969),[194] the opening of a Japanese chamber of commerce in Seoul (December 1969), and the government-backed formation of financial consortia to increase commercial loans to the ROK.[195]

The culmination of these efforts was the Masan Free Export Zone. First proposed by the ROK Economic Planning Board in January 1969 and later established by economic ministers attending the Japan-ROK Economic Committee meeting in December, this watershed agreement provided for 100 percent Japanese foreign ownership in Korea and for the export of finished products out of Korea tax-free.[196] Masan was clearly designed to marry Japanese and South Korean economic interests. Its location at the southeastern tip of the peninsula was conducive to proximate Japanese trade and investment. The idea was originally part of a larger vision developed by Yatsugi Kazuo to form an EEC-type arrangement between Japan and the ROK, entailing the linking up of the Namhae and Chugoku regions of the two countries and the establishment of a vertical division of labor. South Korea would supply the cheap labor (wage rates were 15 percent of those in Japan) and land in return for Japanese capital and machine parts. South Korea benefited in terms of employment, technology and foreign capital, while Japan profited in terms of overseas plants and export markets.[197] As a result of these initiatives the 1969–71 period saw a vast increase in bilateral trade from $219.6 million in 1965 to $1.22 billion by 1971 (see Appendix Table A.1). While the ROK ranked thirteenth among Japanese export markets in 1965, it ranked second only to the United States during the 1969–71 period. ROK exports to Japan registered similar growth, increasing by only $55 million from 1965 to 1968, but by over twice that amount ($148 million) from 1969 to 1971.

P'OHANG IRON AND STEEL COMPLEX

Profit was, of course, a key motivation for the growth in economic cooperation. However, an equally important factor was related to security. This took the form of "positive" Japanese participation in the development of ROK infrastructure and heavy industries. The logic behind these activities followed from the Korea clause. As the security of the ROK was directly related to Japan's own, Japanese financing of Korean economic development contributed to the political stability of the Park regime, which, in turn, contributed to the security of both countries.

The shining example of "positive economic cooperation" was Japan's financing of the P'ohang Iron and Steel Works Project in 1969. The agreement to pursue this undertaking, signed on December 3, 1969, by Economic Planning Board Minister Kim Hak-ryul and Ambassador Kanayama Augustin, provided $123.7 million in Japanese grants and commercial credits for the design, construction, and operation of South Korea's first integrated steel mill.[198] Construction of the plant began April 1970, and the first blast furnace was erected by July 1973. The plant had an annual production capacity of 1.03 million tons and after additional stages of expansion (through 1983) reached an annual capacity of 9.1 million tons. At the time the project was the single most expensive undertaking in ROK history. It made South Korea an international supplier of steel virtually overnight and today is still considered one of the nation's most successful development projects.[199]

Several points support the argument that concerns about U.S. disengagement factored into the P'ohang deal. First, the project was initially rejected as economically unfeasible by a consortium of Western financiers from the United States, Great Britain, France, West Germany, and Italy and the International Bank for Reconstruction and Development. The fact that Tokyo went ahead with the project in spite of this evaluation suggests that motives other than profit were taken into account.

Second, the ROK's initial proposal for Japanese funding in August 1969 came less than two weeks after the Guam press conference and only a few days after Secretary Rogers's August 1 visit to Seoul to formally introduce the Nixon doctrine. Consequently, fears of U.S. abandonment were certainly salient at the time of the ROK request.

Third, within Japanese decision-making circles deliberations over providing assistance for P'ohang did not follow standard operating procedures. In aid decisions generally bureaucrats first conducted feasibility studies and fact-finding missions and drew up the terms of the loan for presentation at the ministry level. With P'ohang decisions on the feasibility and political will to support the project were made first at the ministry level and then sent through the bureaucracy for implementation.[200] The departments involved in the decision were the foreign ministry, MITI, and the finance ministry. The latter two groups generally opposed funding of P'ohang because they considered it economically unfeasible. The foreign ministry, whose views prevailed, favored the project, arguing that the Nixon doctrine and the impending U.S. withdrawal required a strong symbol of Japan-ROK cooperation. This was a purpose that P'ohang would serve very well.[201] As a Japanese negotiator for the deal stated, financing P'ohang was therefore as much a political and security-based decision as an economic one.[202]

Positive economic cooperation in Japan-ROK relations was not limited to the P'ohang project. During the period there were several additional agreements for ROK economic development. At the fourth annual joint ministerial conference July 21–23, 1970, the two sides concluded a $100-million Japanese loan for South Korean agricultural modernization and development of the small- and medium-business sector. Japan also committed $100 million in supplemental credits for the construction of the Ulsan shipyard and three additional projects upgrading the P'ohang complex. In addition funds were allocated for construction of the Seoul subway system, the Sogang River dam project, and the Seoul-Pusan highway.[203] Like P'ohang, the last project had also been rejected as unfeasible by the World Bank in 1966 but was taken up nonetheless by Japan.[204]

Security anxieties about U.S. commitments again played a role in these agreements. The ministerial conference took place just two weeks after the Korea pullout announcement and concurrently with the United States-ROK defense ministers talks on the logistics of the cuts. Foreign Minister Aichi's press statements also referred to these agreements as Japan's rendering of economic cooperation in lieu of direct security contributions to the ROK.[205]

This is not to deny that there were also counterpressures against such cooperation. Undoubtedly cases existed during the period in which Japanese companies and the government may have refrained from cooperating in projects with the ROK that might have been perceived as later undermining Japanese competitiveness and market share. This rationale from the Korean perspective was known as Japan's fear of the "boomerang effect."[206] These sorts of motives were certainly salient in later, followup projects at P'ohang as the Koreans became internationally competitive in the steel industry. However, two points deserve mention with regard to interaction in the 1969–71 period. First, it appears as if concerns about the boomerang effect were not salient, at least with regard to the initial P'ohang deal. As two specialists on the topic noted, the gap between the ROK and Japanese economies was so great and the former was still so underdeveloped that profit motives were not dampened by prospects of fueling ROK competitiveness. In addition, Japanese private-sector firms, the group most susceptible to fears of a boomerang effect, were the ones who sanctioned the feasibility of the project and pressed for the government's approval.[207] Second, even if boomerang dynamics were salient in the Japanese calculus, the approval of the project in spite of such concerns further testifies to the level of Japan-ROK cooperation and the security-based nature of economic decisions in the period. Press analyses confirmed the public perception, if not the actual government motive, for positive economic cooperation between the two countries:

[Having] demonstrated Japan's readiness to live up to the Japan-US joint communiqué of last November tying the security of South Korea with that of Japan ... Japan's reaffirmation of an identity of security interests with South Korea, given in the form of new aid commitments, has satisfied South Korean leaders who are concerned over the US plan to cut back its military presence in South Korea.[208]

CIRCUMVENTED ECONOMIC DISPUTES

The absence of friction over potentially disruptive issues found in the political and security arenas was also apparent in economic relations. This was particularly the case with regard to China's enunciation in April 1970 of four restrictive trade principles with Japan. Known as the Zhou principles, these stated that Beijing would not trade with companies that:

1. traded with the purpose of aiding Taiwan or the ROK
2. invested in Taiwan or the ROK
3. cooperated in U.S. aggression in Vietnam
4. participated in U.S.-related joint ventures in Japan[209]

The Zhou principles presented a potentially divisive issue in Japan-ROK economic relations. In effect they constituted an ultimatum to Japanese firms and the government to choose between the South Korean/Taiwanese market or the potentially more lucrative Chinese market.[210] However, despite Tokyo's temptations and Seoul's anxieties, Japan-ROK economic relations remained undisturbed over this issue. For example, when two prominent Japanese business leaders chose not to attend the May 1970 meeting of the Japan-ROK Economic Committee, the South Korean delegation did not boycott the conference.[211] Similarly, at the August 1970 Japan-ROK Cooperation Committee meeting the ROK did not make an issue of the Zhou principles. This was particularly unusual as the committee's membership of key business leaders and elder statesmen provided an opportune venue for the ROK to voice objections. South Korean reticence stood in stark contrast to the Taiwanese delegation's vehement protests over the same issue at the Japan-Taiwan Cooperation Committee meeting the previous month.[212] The extent of Seoul's protest was a note from the foreign ministry's Asia bureau chief, Kim Chong-tae, merely requesting that Tokyo ensure the Zhou principles not erode existing Japan-ROK economic ties.[213]

The Japanese government also sought to avoid a dispute over the issue. In November 1970 and January 1971 Sato, despite substantial pressure from liberal elements in the LDP and the powerful business lobby, assured the South Koreans that Japan's China policy would not be made unilaterally but would take into account the welfare of Japan-ROK relations.[214] In addition, in June 1970, despite a wave of small and medium firms bolting for the Chinese market, two key big business leaders, Nagano Shigeo, chair of Nihon Seitetsu, and Uemura Kogoro, president of Keidanren, stood with Sato against the Zhou principles.[215] Furthermore, at the August 1970 Cooperation Committee meeting the remaining Japanese delegates showed loyalty to Seoul by pushing for the establishment of a liaison committee. This group's ostensible purpose was to coordinate policy on continental-shelf exploration; however, the creation of the liaison committee in the midst of defections for the Chinese market symbolized a concerted effort by Japan and the ROK at increased cooperation in response to the Zhou principles.[216] Therefore, despite the strains and pressures put on Japan-ROK economic ties, interactions remained cooperative. Seoul tolerated the Japanese firms that defected to China, and key members of Sato's entourage maintained their allegiance to the ROK. The overriding cause for this behavior was the two governments' desire to consolidate relations in the face of U.S. retrenchment. As shall be seen in the next chapter, it was only *after* the United States opened relations with China that Sato and conservative business leaders like Nagano and Uemura succumbed to the Zhou principles.

THE YEARS 1969 TO 1971 offer confirming evidence of the causal role of abandonment structures in Japan-ROK cooperation (Hypothesis B). American retrenchment policies in Asia gave rise to shared abandonment fears between Japan and the ROK with regard to their primary ally. As a means of coping with this fear, both states sought an improvement in bilateral relations. It should be noted that the wider strategic environment was also a force for cooperation. Actions by North

Korea, rhetoric from China, and events in Vietnam gave rise to high threat perceptions on the part of both Seoul and Tokyo. However, as long as there existed confidence in the U.S. commitment, the incentives for dealing with these threats through alternative means were minimalized. It was only with the prospect of abandonment by the great-power ally that threat perceptions were exponentially exacerbated and incentives for cooperation were greatly increased between Tokyo and Seoul. This cooperation occurred not only on security issues but also spilled over into the political and economic spheres. As one observer wrote in 1971, the two governments exuded an optimism about their relationship that was unthinkable even a few years earlier.[217]

FOUR

Detente and the Heightening Crisis,
1972–1974

As RAPIDLY AS it emerged in the late 1960s, the newly instituted cooperation between Japan and the ROK soon faded. As relations developed during the 1970s, tensions surfaced over a reexamination of the defense links established in 1969. This was coupled with the emergence of deep differences over how to deal with North Korea. In addition, intense friction broke out over domestic political issues in both countries, driving relations to the brink of rupture. Interlaced with these numerous disputes, a resurgence of historical emotional tensions further strained already brittle ties.

How this abrupt downturn in the character of relations came about is the subject of this chapter. An underlying cause for the growth of friction in the years from 1972 to 1974 was, ironically, the lessening of cold-war tensions. In the language of the quasi-alliance model, regional and superpower detente brought change to the structure of abandonment and entrapment concerns at both the multilateral and bilateral levels of the relationship.[1] At the former level Japanese concerns about U.S. abandonment became less salient relative to the 1969–71 period, while ROK fears of U.S. abandonment remained unaltered by the tension-reducing effects of detente. This fundamental disparity affected Japanese and Korean attitudes toward one another.

In Seoul an increase in abandonment fears emerged with regard to Japan's relations with Communist neighbors. To alleviate these fears, the ROK pushed for tighter quasi-allied ties with Japan against the North. Meanwhile, Tokyo experienced heightened entrapment fears with regard to excessive ties with the ROK, as the Japanese felt threatened by different contingencies. Renewed conflict in Korea was not only a function of North Korean actions but also a potential outgrowth of superpower cold-war rivalries. With detente the latter concern was substantially ameliorated in Japanese eyes, and policy was shifted to avoid entrapment by obligations that impeded cultivating new relations with North Korea and China. To alleviate its own fears, Japan pursued policies aimed at obtaining equidistance between the two Koreas. Japan-ROK bilateral relations were thus characterized by an *asymmetrical structure* of abandonment and entrapment concerns during the detente years, a situation conducive to bilateral friction.

Unpacking the complex dynamics of this period requires answers to several questions. Over what issues did Japan and the ROK feel threatened? How did these threat perceptions change from those experienced in 1969–71? And how did these perceptions give rise to contentious events in the relationship? A prerequisite to answering these questions, however, is an understanding of the geostrategic environment as it emerged in 1972. Detente made the rigid line that divided cold-war allies from adversaries less distinguishable. The new dialogue of accommodation and coexistence was reflected, among other developments, in the U.S. detente with China and the Soviet Union and in North-South dialogue on the Korean peninsula.

The Proliferation of Detente

On July 15, 1971, President Richard Nixon surprised the world with a televised announcement of his intention to visit China.[2] The product of highly secretive contacts between National Security Advisor Henry Kissinger and Chinese Premier Zhou Enlai, the journey to Beijing was imbued with hopes of ending decades of Sino-American hostility and opening a dialogue based on mutual accommodation.[3] In Nixon's week of historic meetings with Chairman Mao Zedong and Premier Zhou February 21–28, 1972, the leaders exchanged views on the international system and discussed areas of common and conflicting interests. The resulting Shanghai communiqué affirmed the two states' adherence to principles of peaceful coexistence and antihegemonism in Asia. It also stated a mutual aspiration for normalized diplomatic relations.[4]

Nixon's visit marked a watershed event in the reduction of cold-war tensions in Asia.[5] Although the summit produced no tangible agreements, it facilitated a frank exchange of views on key issues after years without dialogue.[6] First, the two governments renounced the use of force in settling bilateral disputes and consented not to enter into agreements directed against each other. Second, Nixon and Zhou stressed the importance of pragmatism in bilateral affairs. They agreed that allies and enemies need not be defined by ideology but by the content of their foreign policy and consequently recognized their shared interests in avoiding a disruption of the status quo. Third, the two sides sought a workable accommodation on Taiwan; Nixon did not challenge Beijing's "one-China" principle, and Zhou tacitly accepted the U.S. need to maintain some form of defense commitment to Taipei. This "agreement to disagree" reduced the potential for conflict. Finally, each government clarified its purpose in Vietnam. While asserting its support for the South Vietnamese, the U.S. maintained that its actions there posed no threat to China. Similarly, China said it would continue to supply North Vietnam; however, it added that the purpose was not to undercut the United States, but to check Soviet influence in Hanoi. This disassociation of events in Vietnam from the United States–China relationship reduced the potential for the conflict's escalation into a direct United States-China confrontation.[7]

The Sino-American rapprochement initiated a "discernible escalation toward peace in Asia."[8] This trend extended to United States-Soviet relations as well. Three months after he announced his impending visit to China, Nixon disclosed his intention to visit Moscow. The May 1972 Nixon-Brezhnev summit was the first of four superpower summits during the 1972–74 period, an unprecedented number. At these meetings the two governments declared their adherence to principles of peaceful coexistence and nonaggression and reached economic agreements on U.S. grain credits, agricultural subsidies, and the restoration of most-favored-nation trading status for the Soviet Union. Moreover, the highlight of the May 1972 summit was the conclusion of the Strategic Arms Limitation accords (SALT), the Anti-Ballistic Missile (ABM) treaty, and the interim agreement on offensive arms limitations.[9]

Consequently, by 1972 the United States had entered into an accommodating dialogue with its two principal cold-war adversaries in East Asia. This change in the strategic environment was largely a function of balance-of-power dynaamics arising from the deterioration of relations on the Soviet-China axis. Brewing since the early 1950s, the Sino-Soviet conflict came to fruition with armed border clashes at Damansky (Zhenbao) Island in the Ussuri River and the Xinjiang/Kazakhstan border in 1969, causing Moscow and Beijing to view each other as proximate threats. As both powers wanted to preempt the other's collusive arrangement with the West, it became strategically incumbent on each to seek relations with Washington.[10] For the United States, occupying the central position in a United States-China-Soviet Union strategic triangle decreased the possibility of wars on two fronts in Asia and Europe.[11] In addition, relations with each power provided a counterbalance to the threat posed by the other. The most immediate benefit of this was in Vietnam, where the United States could heed domestic sentiment for disengagement with less concern about Chinese or Soviet designs on the resulting power vacuum. Detente therefore stemmed less from any benign desire for peace and more from basic balancing dynamics and strategic imperatives. The result, nevertheless, was a dramatic reduction in regional security tensions relative to the 1969–71 period.

The regional trend toward detente also extended to Korea. A month after Nixon's China announcement, North-South Red Cross delegations initiated meetings to discuss reunification programs for Korean families. In May–June 1972 ROK KCIA Director Lee Hu-rak met secretly with North Korean Vice-Premier Park Sung-chul to discuss means of reducing bilateral tensions. These meetings resulted in the release of a surprise joint communiqué on July 4, 1972, which set out several measures to facilitate detente between Seoul and Pyongyang.[12] The two governments renounced the use of force and agreed to seek unification through peaceful means only. They supported Red Cross efforts to reach agreements on family unification and visitation programs and asserted that the mutual trust built through these humanitarian ventures could then enable discussion on more substantive political and security issues. The two governments also established the North-South Coordinating Committee, whose mandate was to serve as the primary governmental channel for unification dialogue. Finally, to increase transparency and avert miscalculation, the two governments established a direct Seoul-Pyongyang telephone hotline. These measures represented the first attempt by the two regimes to seek improved relations since the division of the peninsula[13] and further instantiated the new turn in the regional strategic environment.

Japanese Security Perceptions in the Detente Era

Japan had little trouble adapting to the new security environment. Following the lead of their great-power patron, the United States, the Japanese saw tremendous opportunity in testing new relationships with Communist powers. The proliferation of detente consequently had an unprecedented soothing effect on Japanese threat perceptions and anxieties about U.S. defense commitments relative to the 1969–71 period. Evidence of these trends falls roughly into three categories: (1) laudatory Japanese statements on Sino-American rapprochement, (2) Japan's own improvement of relations with Beijing and Moscow, and (3) security reassurances from Washington.

The announcement of Nixon's journey to China initially shocked the Japanese. The government of Prime Minister Sato Eisaku was unaware of Kissinger's secret contacts with Beijing, receiving notice of events only minutes prior to Nixon's televised announcement.[14] Despite the severity of the China "*shokku*," however, the Japanese recognized Sino-American rapprochement as a positive development for regional stability.[15] Statements by Sato and Foreign Minister Fukuda Takeo immediately after Nixon's announcement made this clear. Although known for their hawkish, anti-Communist views, both supported Nixon's initiatives as consistent with Japan's own desire to break down cold-war barriers.[16] Foreign ministry white papers for the period contain phrases making note of the "remarkable trend" from "confrontation to dialogue" and the "dawning of a new age" in postwar Asia.[17] Prime Minister Tanaka's foreign minister, Kimura Toshio, succinctly summed up the rationale behind Japan's support of Nixon's rapprochement with he Chinese: despite the massive military capabilities that undergirded the cold-war balance of power in East Asia, the proliferation of detente revealed the benign intentions of all the regional powers and the potential for lasting peace.[18]

CHINESE RAPPROCHEMENT, SOVIET DIALOGUE

A key factor contributing to the amelioration of Japanese threat perceptions was Tokyo's advancement of relations with a number of regional adversaries, most notably China. Nixon's July 1971 announcement prompted Sato later that month to publicly express his own desire to meet with Zhou Enlai and to intimate his recognition of Beijing as the sole, legitimate representative of China.[19] This enthusiasm was reflected in 1972 foreign ministry white papers that stated forthrightly that normalization of relations with China was now Japan's most important foreign-policy objective.[20] The Tanaka government stepped up the pace of these overtures, calling for scrapping the all-important Taiwan clause, which had been fiercely opposed by Beijing as the primary impediment to amiable relations.[21]

The Chinese government responded positively to these overtures. It relaxed the five preconditions for dialogue with Japan established in 1953.[22] Moreover, in September 1972 Zhou stated that China no longer opposed the United States-Japan security treaty. In additional conciliatory steps Beijing ceased derogatory radio and newspaper propaganda against Japan, rampant during the 1969–71 period. It also assured Tokyo officials privately of its willingness to shelve historically sensitive disputes such as sovereignty over the Senkaku (Diaoyutai) Islands in the East China Sea and reparations of war.[23]

This process of rapprochement culminated with the September 1972 Tanaka-Zhou summit. The first visit by a Japanese premier to China in the postwar era, the event was hailed as a historic new chapter in relations. Summit proceedings took place in an atmosphere of extreme cordiality, and both Mao and Zhou made clear that China neither posed a threat to nor perceived a threat from Japan.[24] The joint communiqué issued at the conclusion of the summit affirmed the determination of both states to normalize relations and to uphold principles of peaceful coexistence and mutual respect for territorial integrity.[25] This new dialogue with China, after years of adversarial relations, contributed substantially toward easing Japanese threat perceptions.

Prior to 1972 Japan-Soviet Union relations were characterized by distrust and cold-war polemics. Dialogue had remained suspended since 1967 with disputed sovereignty of the Southern Kurile Islands (referred to by the Japanese as the Northern Territories) inhibiting relations. However, the period of détente saw considerable developments in this relationship as both governments sought to capitalize on the regional thaw. Beginning in the latter half of 1971, a series of Japanese-Soviet subcabinet-level meetings took place on economic cooperation, focusing largely on Japanese participation in the Tyumen petroleum resource development project in Western Siberia.[26]

January 1972 meetings between Sato and Soviet Foreign Minister Andrei Gromyko, the first official dialogue since 1967, produced agreements for substantive talks on a peace treaty (apropos to World War II) and the resumption of annual foreign-ministerial meetings.[27] In addition, Gromyko broke from Soviet precedent and intimated a willingness to discuss the Northern Territories issue.[28] Parliamentary exchanges took place the following spring and summer, and in March 1973 a letter from Tanaka to Leonid Brezhnev communicated directly the Japanese prime minister's desire for treaty negotiations and talks on Tyumen.[29] This led to summit meetings in October 1973, where additional agreements were reached on cultural and scientific exchanges and economic cooperation.[30]

Although an agreement on the Tyumen project did not eventuate, this did not detract from the congenial atmosphere that did develop between the two governments.[31] As analysts of the period concur, these increased contacts, after years of tense relations, went a long way toward reducing Japanese preoccupations with the Soviet threat relative to the 1969–71 period.[32]

PERCEPTIONS OF THE KOREAN THAW

Another arena in which Japanese security perceptions underwent change was Korea. During the preceding 1969–71 period reductions in U.S. troop strength and acts of North Korean belligerence caused Japan to have palpable security concerns about the potential renewal of hostilities on the peninsula. During the 1972–74 period, however, both of these became less critical factors in Japanese threat assessments.

As the 1972 foreign ministry white paper stated, the North-South communiqué substantially raised confidence that a workable detente for the Korean peninsula was within reach.[33] The United States also provided assurances throughout the period that it would not jeopardize Japanese security by leaving Korea unprotected. One example of this was a July 1973 policy statement by Secretary of State William P. Rogers before a Japanese audience, in which he asserted that the American security presence in Korea had aided, rather than impeded, the development of detente on the peninsula and that the United States therefore would continue to honor its commitments there.[34] Such assurances struck a chord of relief with the Japanese. A January 1974 Defense Agency report concluded there was "very little possibility" for additional U.S. force withdrawals from Korea. Similarly, a June 1974 Gaimushō (foreign ministry) report stated that Washington's numerous assurances had fostered confidence that neither U.S. troop levels in nor military aid programs to South Korea would undergo revision in the immediate future.[35] Finally, further assuaging Japanese threat perceptions was the improvement of relations with a number of other Communist states during the period. Particularly significant was the establishment of diplomatic relations with North Vietnam in September 1973. Throughout the Indochina conflict Japan harbored anxieties that American use of logistics facilities in Okinawa might result in direct retaliation against the home islands by either Hanoi, Beijing, or Moscow. Normalization with the North Vietnamese (in conjunction with the

January 1973 American ceasefire agreement and the February 1973 Laos peace agreement) eased these concerns.[36]

AMERICAN ASSURANCES TO JAPAN

The proposition that U.S. rapprochement with China and reassurances to Japan contributed to a decline in the fears of U.S. abandonment prevalent during the 1969–71 period may seem intuitively obvious; however, some alternative explanations of Japanese behavior during these years deserve brief consideration.

One view focuses on Japan's reaction to the China shock. Sato had no knowledge of Nixon's and Kissinger's secret overtures to Beijing.[37] This greatly upset the Japanese, and numerous government statements lamented that "Asakai's nightmare" had finally come true.[38] This interpretation therefore argues that the China shock engendered, not low, but high fears of U.S. abandonment in the detente years; that Nixon's actions undermined Japanese confidence in the United States as a trusted ally and raised concerns that Beijing would soon become America's primary partner in Asia.

While a plausible interpretation of Japanese behavior, the China shock did not foster rampant fears of U.S. abandonment. As the Japanese director-general of Asian affairs at that time recalled, anxiety centered more on the manner in which the China policy was revealed than on its content.[39] Nixon's announcement embarrassed Sato politically as the two leaders had agreed to consult closely with each other on China initiatives. Moreover, it made any subsequent Japanese moves toward Beijing look like blind obedience to U.S. policies rather than independent Japanese overtures. However, Tokyo officials did not view the July 1971 announcement by the United States as a form of security abandonment.[40] As Ambassador Edwin O. Reischauer testified, Japan, though upset with the "unnecessarily flamboyant" Kissingerian style of diplomacy, clearly supported the policy direction:

We are at long last moving on China policy in the direction [the Japanese] have always wanted us to. . . . They may feel some jealousy that we seem to be getting ahead of them in establishing better relations with China, but essentially the Japanese are pleased with the overall direction of the new policy.[41]

Foreign Minister Fukuda also acknowledged Tokyo's long-held desire to end the isolation of Communist China:

As regards Japan, this initiative by President Nixon, coincides in its basic lines, with her government's policy which stresses the necessity of relaxing tensions through rapprochement and friendly exchange with other countries regardless of differences in political systems and ideologies.[42]

The United States also went to extensive lengths to shore up Japanese confidence in the aftermath of Nixon's announcement. Administration officials apologized for the secrecy of the entire affair and fully debriefed Japan on the contents of the China meetings, assuring them that there were no "secret deals" undermining Japanese security.[43] As a former Gaimushō official recalled, these efforts helped restore Japanese confidence that U.S. overtures toward China did not imply a downgrading of relations with Japan.[44] In press statements after his January 1972 summit with Nixon, Sato stated that, "The Nixon shocks ended last year and any ill feelings that may have existed between Japan and America have been smoothed over."[45] Foreign Minister Ohira Masayoshi reaffirmed these views in May 1973 by declaring that the basis of Japanese foreign policy was still the special relationship with the United States and that mutual trust was still the guiding principle.[46]

A second interpretation grants that Japan experienced decreased threat perceptions during 1972–74 but claims this occurred *in spite of* heightened fears of U.S. abandonment. In other words, the mollification of Japanese threat assessments was not the product of U.S. assurances, but of Tokyo's balancing against the China shock and loss of trust in the United States by improving relations with Communist neighbors.

While some in Japanese decision-making circles may have held this view, the majority did not. The specific cause of Japan's diminished threat perceptions was indeed Sino-Japanese rapprochement and Japanese-Soviet dialogue, but the enabling condition was the Sino-American rapprochement. Without the latter, the former could not have occurred. As the former Gaimushō director-general of Asian affairs recalled, the situation Japan faced was not "win-lose"—in which Japan lost faith in the United States but gained better relations with China and the Soviet Union—but "win-win." Japan expanded diplomatic channels and probed new economic opportunities with Communist powers, yet still enjoyed the luxury of remaining within the penumbra of the U.S. security umbrella, especially after China dropped its explicit opposition to the United States-Japan defense treaty.[47] In this regard, the China shock was more of a boon than a blow to Japanese foreign policy.[48]

In sum, the detente years marked a major shift in Japanese security perceptions. Japan reached its own rapprochement with China, improved relations with the Soviets, and perceived a defusing of tensions in Korea. Reassurances from the United States also alleviated any lingering concerns about American resolve and credibility. This concatenation of developments did not wholly erase Japanese cold-war concerns; however, they did result in substantially lower fears of U.S. abandonment relative to the preceding 1969–71 period.

South Korean Reactions to Detente

In stark contrast to Japan, South Korea held ambivalent attitudes toward the proliferation of détente in Asia. From Seoul's perspective the various communiqués and declarations emerging in the name of this thaw in cold-war tensions were nothing more than political histrionics. The absence of any substantive confidence-building concessions by China and the Soviet Union revealed that Communist intentions were still aggressive. As a former foreign ministry official recalled, the equating of cryptic, lukewarm signals from these powers with a genuine burning commitment to peaceful coexistence required a tremendous leap of faith—one that was, at the most fundamental level, anathema to the ROK's grounding in a quarter-century of anticommunist ideology.[49]

As a result, while allies perceived a reduction in tensions, the ROK continued to see threats. Underscoring the difference between allied and South Korean perceptions, Park stated: "Only we, the Koreans who have had personal experience, can tell how terrible the Asian communist menace is."[50] And as the world marveled at Nixon's meetings with Zhou and visit to the Great Wall, Park urged Nixon to maintain a "correct sense of direction" and disparaged those who hailed detente as "illusionary romanticists."[51] The dynamic clearly emerging for the ROK was one in which others were getting swept up by the wave of detente, while the ROK was becoming increasingly isolated as the only remaining cold warrior in the region.

INEFFECTIVE NORTH-SOUTH DIALOGUE

South Korean wariness of detente was hardly surprising given its unchanged perceptions of the North Korean threat. The July 4, 1972, North-South communiqué was aimed at establishing a new era of reconciliation between the two regimes. However, the buoyant expectations that accompanied this document quickly dissipated as the two

main channels of dialogue, the Red Cross talks and the North-South
Coordinating Committee, deteriorated into exercises of mutual recrimination. By mid-1973 a total of three full-dress Coordinating Committee
sessions and six Red Cross sessions (in addition to countless preliminary
ones) had failed to achieve a single substantive agreement on even relatively simple issues such as mail exchange between separated families,
and continuation of these contacts was eventually suspended by both
governments.[52]

Exacerbating threat perceptions was a number of hostile North Korean acts during the 1972–74 period. Naval espionage operations along
the southern coast of the peninsula and attacks on unarmed ROK fishing vessels were commonplace.[53] In addition, in August 1974 North Korean elements in Japan organized an assassination attempt on South Korean president Park Chung-hee, and the following November United
Nations Command authorities discovered the first of what would later
turn out to be several North Korean infiltration tunnels in the DMZ.[54]
These developments offered little hope that detente might result in a
moderation of North Korean behavior. Moreover, they made clear that
attempts by Beijing, as a result of its rapprochement with the West, to
influence Pyongyang toward greater accommodation were not effective.
Thus, the July 1972 communiqué, as Premier Kim Jong-pil stated, was
nothing more than a "piece of paper" that did not change North Korea's basic aspiration to communize the South.[55] Foreign Minister Kim
Dong-jo echoed these sentiments, asserting that the peninsula was a
"marked exception" to detente.[56]

SOUTH KOREAN FEARS OF U.S. ABANDONMENT

The Park government grew increasingly worried that Washington's
embracing of detente would result in a downgrading of alliance obligations to Korea. A November 1972 United States Senate report was particularly revealing in this regard. Interviewing top South Korean foreign
ministry, defense ministry, ch'ŏngwadae (Blue House), and intelligence
officials, this U.S. fact-finding group reported that:

In particular, President Park was said to have felt increasingly, beginning with
the enunciation of the Nixon Doctrine, that Korea would not be able to rely on
the United States in the future as it had in the past. Many believe that this feeling intensified as . . . the new US policy toward China was revealed, and as
President Park concluded that US interest in Asia in particular, and in foreign
affairs generally, was decreasing.[57]

The ROK believed that superpower detente reflected a fundamental change in U.S. strategic doctrine. Peaceful coexistence between Washington and Moscow implied that U.S. policy would now be dictated by a maintenance of stability at the core of the international system (i.e., superpower relations) rather than by deterrence at the periphery.[58] In East Asia this meant that the United States would downgrade ties with traditional cold-war allies and elevate China as its primary partner in the region. Further fueling these worries was the belief that U.S. reconciliation with China was not motivated by the success of U.S. cold-war policies, but by their failure.[59] For Seoul then the United States-China rapprochement marked tacit U.S. acknowledgment of America's eroding influence in the region and a rise in Chinese influence.

Park also saw detente as giving North Korea strategic and diplomatic advantages over the South. While Seoul's relations with the United States were marked by disengagement and ambivalence, Pyongyang enjoyed a reaffirmation of alliance obligations from its Chinese patrons after a period of relatively strained relations. In addition to the Kim-Zhou summit in September 1971 Beijing provided Pyongyang with military grants-in-aid for the first time since the Korean war and rejoined the Military Armistice Commission at Panmunjom after a five-year absence. Equally troubling to the ROK was the political windfall North Korea enjoyed as a result of detente. By mid-1973 Pyongyang gained entry to several international organizations (e.g., the Interparliamentary Union in April 1973 and WHO the following May) and established relations with a number of noncommunist states.[60] Park's primary concern was that the North's new friends, coupled with Beijing's entry into the United Nations, would significantly increase the chances of a General Assembly resolution terminating the U.N. military and political presence in Korea. This, in turn, would undermine international support for a continued U.S. security contingent on the peninsula.[61]

An additional concern for the ROK was an unsympathetic United States Congress. Detente and the Nixon doctrine changed the tone of the policy debate in Washington from one of deterrence to drawback and cost saving. This directly affected the status of U.S. ground forces in Korea. In 1971 the Senate positively received Defense Secretary Melvin Laird's testimony that future conflicts in Asia should not involve U.S. ground forces. In addition, Congress favorably reviewed a 1971 Pentagon report recommending the reduction of standing U.S. army divisions from thirteen to eleven, including withdrawal of one division from Korea.[62] Unsympathetic congressional attitudes were also manifest in the

reluctance to appropriate funds for South Korea's military modernization program. During the period annual appropriations for the $1.5-
billion, five-year program consistently fell about 50 percent short of
ROK requests.[63] The following passage summed up the ROK perspective
at the time:

> Seoul's view is consistent and adamant. Despite the seeming worldwide mood
> of detente, it says Pyongyang has never changed its goal of unifying the divided
> country by force. A considerable credibility gap seems to exist between Seoul
> and the American public as to security conditions in this part of the world.[64]

In a series of off-the-record meetings with Blue House newspaper
correspondents at the time of Nixon's China announcement, Park
launched into diatribes about the loss of Korean trust in the United
States engendered by Kissinger's secret diplomacy and how Nixon was
sacrificing his faithful cold-war allies for atmosphere foreign-policy successes. When Park made a direct private appeal to Nixon later in the fall
of 1971 in the form of a letter urging the United States not to compromise ROK security interests in Nixon's upcoming February 1972 meeting with the Beijing leadership, he received an uninspiring response from
State Department and NSC staff only after three months which definitively declined a summit meeting with Nixon and contained token
statements about the continuing strength of the alliance.[65] In response to
these developments Park accelerated the pullout of ROK forces from
Vietnam to shore up defenses at home and in his 1974 summit with
President Gerald Ford further pressed for explicit commitments to repel
North Korean aggression.[66] At the September 1973 and 1974 United
States-ROK Security Consultative Conferences, the ROK provided the
United States with itemized lists of North Korean provocations and
urged its ally to meet this threat with increased annual appropriations
for South Korean military modernization.[67] A February 1974 U.S. study
group's interviews with Park's inner circle of advisors found emphatic
anxieties about a U.S. pullout from Asia.[68] Moreover, according to a
former foreign ministry official, the government remained skeptical of
Washington's countless reassurances. Such statements might have
shored up South Korean confidence in the past; however, the Nixon
doctrine, coupled with the disparity in ROK and allied perceptions
stemming from detente, instilled beliefs in Seoul that the United States
was making statements of support but would not actually deliver on
them.[69] According to an aide to Park, the intention behind U.S. actions

was crystal clear: "The message to the Korean people [was] that we won't rescue you if North Korea invades again."[70]

NUCLEAR AMBITIONS AND YUSIN REPRESSION

Fears of U.S. abandonment were also reflected in South Korean actions in the security and domestic political arena. By 1972 Park had decided to press forward with a clandestine nuclear weapons development program.[71] The program was operated out of the Agency for Defense Development and headed by senior Korean officials of the secret Weapons Exploitation Committee. This body had direct access to the Blue House and was created with the purpose of developing advanced and indigenous weaponry after the unsettling events of the 1968 Blue House raid and the U.S. Seventy Infantry Division pullout (1970–71). The program's purpose was to develop for Korea something akin to Japan's "recessed" nuclear capabilities, in other words, a Korea that did not exhibit a desire for harnessing nuclear weapons (i.e., by eschewing development of such weapons per se) but possessed the clear technological capability to do so.[72] ROK energies thus focused on acquiring the technology for nuclear fuel reprocessing, which would then enable the extraction of plutonium necessary for bomb production. The ROK sought negotiations in Belgium, Canada, and France and by 1974 reached an agreement with the French on the purchase of a reprocessing facility that was estimated to manufacture enough weapons-grade plutonium for two nuclear bombs. As part of the program Seoul also undertook campaigns to entice ethnic Korean scientists to return to Korea and to purchase various materials and equipment for nuclear-weapons production. The United States, after detecting its ally's covert program, was successful in eventually persuading Park to cancel the contract with France.[73] However, these defiant actions on the Park regime's part outside the bounds of the U.S.-ROK alliance were clearly motivated by ROK fears of abandonment. As Park explained in interviews with American journalists in June 1975, "If the U.S. nuclear umbrella were to be removed, we have to start developing our nuclear capacity to save ourselves."[74] High-level American officials involved in the delicate negotiations with Seoul to stop the program even admitted that, while Park's drive for nuclear weapons was ill-advised, emotional, and sloppy, particularly in terms of the view that the program could go undetected by the U.S., "given U.S. attitudes, one had to admit that

South Koreans had some reason for their concern over their future security."[75]

In October 1972 Park instituted the *Yusin* (revitalizing) reforms. Designed to expunge all political opposition and consolidate Park's hold on power, Yusin began with the imposition of martial law and dissolution of the National Assembly and expanded until Park's death in 1979 to the banning of all forms of antigovernment activity and the centering of all legislative, judicial, and executive powers in the presidency.[76] Opposition politicians and dissidents were imprisoned and tortured, and civil society in general was subject to the worst repression in the postwar history of Korean politics.[77]

A number of factors weighed in the president's decision to impose Yusin. Park saw precedents for such actions set by similar crackdowns in Thailand and the Philippines. In addition, the Japan-China summit a month earlier figured prominently in the timing of his decision. The ROK economy was simultaneously under strain from the oil crisis (gasoline prices increased 19.5 percent, rice by 7.3 percent, and the wholesale price index by 12 percent), and the trade deficit burgeoned as a result of 13 percent devaluation of the *won*.[78] Combined with these factors was a confluence of domestic political pressures. The closeness of the 1971 presidential and legislative elections, campus unrest, factionalism within the ruling party, and Park's personal ambition to hold the presidency indefinitely all led to the imposition and implementation of Yusin. In the end, however, as a former advisor to Park and others close to events of the time recounted, it was concerns about U.S. retrenchment that weighed most heavily on Park's mind.[79] His speeches throughout the period were replete with references to U.S. unreliability in the face of external threats as the rationale for tightening controls at home.[80] Providing U.S. Ambassador Philip Habib with twenty-four-hour advance notification of the Yusin declaration, Prime Minister Kim Jong-pil pointedly disparaged detente, stating that the primary rationale for the dramatic political crackdown was ROK concerns that "the interests of the third or smaller countries might be sacrificed for the relaxation of tension between big powers."[81] American fact-finding missions at the time reached similar conclusions after interviews with the regime's key advocates. The reports filed by these missions added that ROK abandonment fears were even more intense than those experienced during the 1969–71 period. Despite events such as the Blue House raid, *Pueblo* seizure, and withdrawal of the U.S. Seventh Infantry Division Park's reaction in the earlier period was not nearly as severe as his imposition of the Yusin system in 1972.[82]

From Seoul's perspective detente therefore raised the specter of Korea's victimization at the hands of colluding powerful nations. Fears of U.S. abandonment experienced in the 1969–71 period were exacerbated by the absence of tension reduction as a result of the 1972 North-South joint communiqué and continuing North Korean acts of aggression. This was the worst possible combination for Seoul: high threats and high fears of U.S. abandonment in the face of these threats.

Japan, by contrast, lost some confidence in U.S. trustworthiness as a result of Nixon's China shock but overall experienced both reduced threat perceptions and reduced fears of U.S. abandonment relative to the 1969–71 period. This occurred in spite of continued tensions on the peninsula because Japan responded to different contingencies regarding Korea. It was not just an unprovoked attack by Pyongyang but also conflict on the peninsula arising out of superpower confrontation that had worried Japan. The latter concern was ameliorated by detente. The result of these dynamics was one of the most contentious periods in the history of bilateral relations.

The Heightening Crisis, 1972–1974

Friction in Japan-ROK political-military relations occurred in two phases during the 1972–74 period. The first, from 1972 to mid-1973, saw clashes over the 1969 Korea clause, Japan-North Korea relations, and Sino-Japanese normalization. The second phase, from about mid-1973 to 1974, saw a succession of diplomatic crises. In each of these crises the asymmetry in the two states' abandonment and entrapment concerns lay at the core of a severe breakdown in relations.

THE KOREA CLAUSE REVISITED

As explained in Chapters 2 and 3, the 1969 Korea clause and Okinawan-base agreement constituted the two primary symbols of Japan-ROK defense ties during the cold war. As detente took hold of the region, however, friction immediately surfaced over differing interpretations of these agreements. For example, in the aftermath of Nixon's China announcement Prime Minister Sato stated that detente engendered a rethinking of Japanese security policy toward Korea, in particular that the use of Japanese bases for ROK defense should no longer be presumed as "automatic."[83] Sato's change in policy was also reflected in his January 1972 summit with Nixon, the communiqué from which conspicuously omitted the Korea clause terminology that had been used over the prior three years.[84] When questioned about this omission, Sato's response indicated a clear desire to undo the links between Japanese and ROK security:

1969 is 1969. This year is this year. To regard [the Korea clause] as a fixed condition is *not* appropriate. The [1969] statement was our feeling in regard to conditions at that time. It was not a treaty.[85]

Japan's desire to distance itself from the Korea clause was also evident at the fifth annual joint ministerial conference in August 1971. Taking place less than a month after Nixon's China announcement, the conference proceedings and joint communiqué contained little of the usual anticommunist rhetoric and no references to Japan-ROK defense ties. The latter omission starkly contrasted with the communiqués issued by the third and fourth conferences, which had highlighted the inseparability of the two nations' security.[86] In press statements after the fifth conference, Japanese chief delegate Kimura Toshio further emphasized that Japanese investment in ROK industries was strictly private-sector–based and not a symbol of government support for the ROK regime. These statements again contrasted with those of previous conferences, in which Japanese investment in ROK heavy industry and infrastructure was clearly meant to convey not only economic but also political and military allegiance with its neighbor.[87] Joint communiqués for both the Nixon-Tanaka (July–August 1973) and Ford-Tanaka (November 1974) summits also excluded any reference to the Japan-ROK defense link.[88]

Fears of entrapment clearly motivated this Japanese behavior. Detente effectively reduced the caliber of threats from China and the Soviet Union. In addition, U.S. reassurances moderated Japanese fears of abandonment. These developments did not, of course, make the United States-Japan security treaty irrelevant; however, they did make corollary agreements like the Korea clause unnecessary. From Japan's perspective adherence to this clause was actually detrimental to national security. It ran counter to the trend toward detente in the region; could only offend Pyongyang, Beijing, and Moscow; and therefore could foreclose a unique opportunity to expand relations with these powers. Finally, adherence to the clause entangled Japan in military contingencies that were not necessarily vital to Japanese security. A statement by Foreign Minister Kimura Toshio, published in 1975, summarized this new attitude:

Everyone agrees that Japan's security hinges on the security of Korea. But, when it comes to the question of how that security should be maintained, there are two opposing schools of thought. One is the very narrow preoccupation with Cold-war doctrines, while the other is the idea that if there is security and peace for the entire Korean peninsula, the Republic of Korea will be secure as well. From the perspective of the latter position, the statement in the United States-Japan joint communique of 1969 that the Republic of Korea is "essential to Japan's peace and security" is no longer valid.[89]

What resulted was thus a reinterpretation of the 1969 Korea clause by Japan: it was no longer the security of the *ROK*, but that of the *entire* Korean peninsula that was essential to Japan. Also implied in this new reading was a revision of the Okinawan-base agreement. This uncoupling of Japanese and South Korean security left ambiguous whether Tokyo would consent to American use of Okinawan bases for ROK defense.[90]

Japanese behavior raised intense abandonment fears in Seoul. For Koreans the prospect of superpower collusion (i.e., detente) and U.S. disengagement (i.e., Nixon doctrine) made Japan's continued adherence to the 1969 version of the Korea clause a critical component of a credible deterrent strategy. As a result, in opening statements at the fifth and sixth annual joint ministerial conferences the South Korean delegation expressed extreme disapproval of detente's dampening effect on Japanese enthusiasm for security cooperation with the ROK. On the contrary, ROK delegates argued, such rapidly changing security conditions should make closer Japan-ROK cooperation even more vital than before.[91] The ROK placed particular emphasis on Tokyo's acknowledgment of the Korea clause at the 1972 Nixon-Sato summit as this had been the original forum in which the clause was first enunciated three years earlier. Two days prior to that summit, Park had dispatched a special envoy, former premier Chung Il-kwon, to urge Sato to uphold the continued validity of the 1969 clause.[92] When these entreaties were not reflected in the United States-Japan communiqué, Park denounced Sato for revising the Korea clause without Seoul's prior consultation. A government-backed South Korean newspaper summed up Park's discontent:

Sato's negative view [regarding the 1969 Korea clause] voiced on the heels of his recent two-day talks with the U.S. president denotes an obvious, potentially precarious departure from the long-confirmed position of the two free world allies. . . . Whether Sato's statement took heed of the Republic of Korea's position is doubtful. If it did not, it contradicts the friendly and cooperative spirit embodied in the Korea-Japan amity treaty because it is bound eventually to spur the Pyongyang regime in its aggressive scheme toward this country. . . . Japan's growing tendency to appease and approach the Communist regime in north Korea in sheer disregard of the interests of this republic has drawn our alarming [sic] concern.[93]

Improvements in Sino-Japanese relations only exacerbated ROK anxieties about Japan. The government saw Tokyo's overtures toward China as a factor contributing to its revision of the Korea clause. (Beijing had vehemently criticized the clause as a symbol of United States-Japan-ROK aggression and impediment to Sino-Japanese dialogue.) In addition, the ROK was concerned that Tokyo-Beijing normalization would pave the path to Japanese-North Korean diplomatic and economic ties. This scenario would not only further isolate the ROK as the only regional power with hard-line cold-war policies but also boost North Korea at a time when U.S. resolve to defend the ROK was questionable.

As a result, in August 1972 ROK Premier Kim Jong-pil harshly criticized Japan's China policy as a hasty and irresponsible act that left Seoul in a "decidedly unfavorable" position.[94] Tokyo's response, given at the sixth annual joint ministerial conference (held two weeks prior to Tanaka's Beijing summit) was that the issue was strictly a bilateral concern between Tokyo and Beijing. Kimura's attempts to debrief the ROK leadership after the Tanaka-Zhou summit were largely unsuccessful. ROK officials chided Kimura about the ways in which Japanese actions were destabilizing to the balance of power in Asia and expressed skepticism at Kimura's assurances that Chinese normalization would not be a springboard for initiatives with North Korea.[95]

As further testament to the poor state of relations after Japan's China initiatives, the ROK did not take advantage of opportunities to consolidate ties with Tokyo.[96] One would expect that had relations been congenial during this period, the two governments would have patched up disagreements over China by reaffirming mutual support in subsequent bilateral meetings. This was the case, for example, with the Japan-ROK Cooperation Committee meetings that took place in the midst of the germ controversy and Yodo incident during the preceding period (see Chapter 3). However, in October 1972 Park abruptly canceled what was to have been a week-long state visit to Japan, the first by a South Korean president in the postwar era. The purpose had been to hold wide-ranging discussions on bilateral relations and to serve as a general reaffirmation of ties in the aftermath of Sino-Japanese normalization.[97]

Tokyo had planned to include in the week's events an unprecedented meeting between the ROK president and the Japanese emperor and thus was both embarrassed and angered by Park's cancellation. As the chief delegate of the Japan-ROK Parliamentary Committee Lee Tong-won recalled, "When Park canceled, the Japanese were very unhappy . . . it was very bad for relations."[98] *Ch'ŏngwadae* press secretaries cited the imposition of Yusin and martial law in Korea (October 17, 1972) as the reason for canceling the visit. However, as U.S. officials determined, the most salient factor leading to suspension of the summit was Park's indignation and insecurities over Sino-Japanese normalization.[99]

DIVERGENT POLICIES TOWARD PYONGYANG

During the 1972–74 period the issue over which Japan-ROK political-military relations experienced the greatest friction was North Korea. Park's fears of abandonment, precipitated by Tokyo's relations with Pyongyang were acute. South Korea essentially perceived a zero-sum situation in which improvements in Japan-North Korea relations could only come at the expense of Japan-ROK relations and a weakening of the anticommunist deterrent on the peninsula. In Japan's view, by contrast, a unique opportunity had emerged to forge more substantive ties with Pyongyang, which not only offered potential benefits in terms of export markets but also decreased potential security threats to Japan. As a result, Japanese entrapment fears caused it to avoid overcommitments to Seoul that might alienate Pyongyang.

Friction arising from this employment of opposite strategies was manifest in disputes over: (1) Japanese policy statements on North Korea, (2) visits to Pyongyang by various Japanese political groups, (3) North Korean reentry visa programs, and (4) activities of the Japanese mass media.

Although kept to a minimum in the past, both the frequency and positive tone of Japanese overtures to North Korea increased after Nixon's July 1971 China announcement. For example, at the fifth annual joint ministerial conference in August 1971 the Japanese delegation insisted on including in the joint communiqué a clause calling for the promotion of Japan-North Korean relations. It also called for the deletion of a customary clause naming the North as a security threat. These were unusual acts for the Sato government to take in a Japanese-South Korean forum and drew strong criticism. Foreign Minister Kim Yong-sik vehemently opposed any conciliatory clauses on North Korea and excoriated Japan's new-found positive posture toward the North.[100] Moreover, in strongly worded statements in the National Assembly the following month Premier Kim Jong-pil declared that the ROK was committed to "check[ing] any Japanese approach toward communist north Korea which would be conducive to increasing Pyongyang's war potential."[101]

Despite these protests the Japanese government continued its northern diplomacy. In November 1971 the staunchly anticommunist Fukuda said he did not regard the North with any hostility and would consider allowing Pyongyang officials to visit Japan. In his 1972 New Year's policy speech, Sato added that the 1965 Japan-ROK normalization treaty did *not* preclude improvements in contacts with Pyongyang.[102] Prime Minister Tanaka followed in Sato's footsteps by stating in Diet sessions in November 1972 that Japan needed a foreign policy approximating a more balanced treatment of the two Koreas.[103] And in 1973 Diet policy speeches Minister of International Trade and Industry Nakasone Yasuhiro declared that the time was right for promoting expanded economic, political, and cultural contacts with Pyongyang.[104] These statements by such conservative stalwarts as Sato, Nakasone, and Fukuda underscored the consensus within the Japanese polity that the new strategic environment eased the need for the hard-line, cold-war alignments with the ROK exhibited during the 1969–71 period.

THE MINOBE VISIT AND DIETMEN'S LEAGUE FOR THE PROMOTION OF JAPANESE-NORTH KOREAN FRIENDSHIP

Prior to detente the Japanese government generally discouraged visits by ruling or opposition party politicians to North Korea as these were seen as unnecessarily troublesome for Japan-ROK relations.[105] However, during the 1972–74 period these visits increased both in number and the level of contacts. For example, the government's approval of a visit to Pyongyang in October 1971 by Tokyo Governor Minobe Ryokichi resulted in the first formal meeting between Kim Il-sung and any national or local Japanese government official. At these meetings Minobe called for the opening of diplomatic relations and supported the North Korean view that Article 3 of the Japan-ROK normalization treaty—which recognized the South as the only legitimate government on the peninsula—should be nullified.[106] Japanese Foreign Minister Fukuda and Justice Minister Maeo Shigesaburo tacitly supported Minobe's visit by intimating they would consider granting entry visas to North Korean government officials and journalists should such opportunities arise in the future. This marked a significant departure from the practiced policy of banning any North Korean visits for expressly political purposes.[107]

Following Minobe's trip, in November 1971 246 Japanese legislators formed the Dietmen's League for the Promotion of Japanese-North Korean Friendship (Dietmen's League). This body called for the promotion of: (1) Japanese-North Korean trade, (2) "peoples' diplomacy" to increase bilateral ties, and (3) eventual negotiation of a normalization treaty. Particularly troubling to the ROK was the fact that the league's membership, unlike other procommunist Japanese legislative groups dominated by opposition parties, was suprapartisan and backed by the ruling LDP.[108] As one of its first acts, the league dispatched a goodwill delegation in January 1972 to meet with Kim Il-sung and signed a memorandum trade agreement with him, which entailed methods of deferred payment for Japanese exports to North Korea and favorable financing terms for those firms doing business in the North. The delegation also extended an invitation to North Korea Foreign Minister Kang Ryang-wook to visit Tokyo.[109]

The visits by Minobe and the Dietmen's League initiated a wave of Japan-North Korea contacts. In January, June, and July 1972 Japan Socialist party and Kōmeitō party delegations returned with messages from the North Korean leadership of its readiness to respond to any offers from Tokyo for expanded cooperation.[110] Further complementing this trend was Japan's hosting of a series of cultural and educational exchanges with Pyongyang and the emergence of a number of pro-North Korean political groups at the local government level modeled on the Dietmen's League.[111] These exchanges contributed to the growth in "peoples' diplomacy" envisioned by the Dietmen's League as the foundation for formal diplomatic relations in the future.

Amidst this tide of enthusiasm, the LDP finally voiced its own support for North Korean contacts, announcing in January 1972 its intention to send a mission to Pyongyang. The decision was unprecedented as past LDP policy had decried any political contacts with the North.[112] The LDP mission was eventually postponed in July 1973; however, this did not detract from its significance. That the LDP carried preparations for the visit to its final stages, including meetings of senior LDP and Korean Worker's Party officials and an agenda for establishing regularized political channels, was testament to the seriousness of the Japanese push toward North Korea.[113]

Although the 1972 memorandum trade agreement, Dietmen's

League, and other political contacts between Japan and North Korea were ostensibly "private" in nature, for the ROK they were uncomfortably similar to the arrangements of the 1950s and 1960s that opened the door to eventual Sino-Japanese normalization. As a result, the ROK launched a barrage of protests against Japan. Foreign Minister Kim Yong-sik's condemnation of Sato's October 1971 conciliatory statements on North Korea was typical of the tone of these criticisms:

Japan's moves for personal and material exchanges with North Korea, which is bent on preparing a war against the Republic, will help strengthen the combat readiness of North Korea and, at the same time, weaken the security of both Korea and Japan.[114]

Foreign Minister Kim Young-sik, Vice Foreign Minister Yun Suk-huen, and Ambassador Lee Ho filed protests with the Gaimushō over the relaxation of policies regulating entry visas for North Korean politicians and over the proposed LDP mission to Pyongyang.[115] In response to Governor Minobe's North Korea visit Kim warned that continued contacts of this sort would severely damage Japan-ROK relations. To further express its discontent, the ROK denied entry to a number of Japanese officials associated with the Dietmen's League on the ground that such advocates of an equidistance policy toward the two Koreas could not be considered as welcome visitors.[116]

REENTRY VISAS

North Korean reentry visas constituted another source of friction in Japan-ROK relations. During the 1972–74 period Japan, despite ROK complaints, showed greater flexibility in visa policies, moving beyond the traditional criteria of granting visas only on humanitarian grounds. For example, in late 1971 Justice Minister Maeo called for an increase in humanitarian reentry visas as well as an expansion of the categories for which visa applications would be accepted.[117] The ministry promptly approved reentry visas for more North Korean residents in September 1971 than the total granted for all of 1969 and 1970.[118] In March and August 1972 the justice ministry approved reentry visas for an additional number of prominent Chosen Soren leaders with full knowledge that the visits were for political rather than filial purposes.[119]

The ROK saw Japan's new reentry visa policy as a threat to national security. Relaxed restrictions on travel for individuals to and from North Korea—most of whom could then freely enter the South—provided an unrestricted avenue for infiltration activities. The ROK strongly denounced Japan's lack of understanding on this issue and in August 1971 lodged formal protests with the Japanese justice ministry.[120] As an ROK foreign ministry press statement read, this amounted to Japan's de facto political support for the North Korean regime.

We cannot but regard the action as signifying a virtual change in the Japanese government's policy toward communist North Korea, since Japan has so far permitted travel to N. Korea only for visiting families and graves.[121]

Park denounced Japanese actions as a violation of the 1965 normalization treaty, and Yun lodged additional protests with Ambassador Ushiroku Torao, threatening that Seoul would consider some form of retaliation against Tokyo's practices.[122]

South Korean and Japanese behavior over this issue starkly contrasts with that exhibited during 1969–71. During that period salient external security threats and mutual concerns about U.S. disengagement caused Japan and the ROK to seek a degree of mutual accommodation on reentry visas (Tokyo held these to a minimum, while the ROK did not raise protests over the few that were approved). However, in the period of detente that followed, the thaw in cold-war tensions caused Tokyo to employ the visa policy as a means of engaging Pyongyang. Moreover, desires to avoid entrapment by rigid anti-North Korean policies caused Tanaka to ignore Seoul's complaints. Meanwhile South Korean abandonment fears gave rise to the belief that Japan's new reentry visa policy, in conjunction with reinterpretation of the Korea clause, indicated the pursuit of an equidistance policy regarding the two Koreas. This represented an "incrementalist" tactic by Japan utilizing all forms of contact (short of direct governmental meetings) to lay the foundation for eventual normalization.[123]

THE YOMIURI INCIDENT

Exacerbating Japan-ROK friction during the 1972–74 period were heated disputes over the Japanese media. Laudatory articles on North Korea, spurred by the proliferation of cultural and political exchanges, cultivated great curiosity about and infatuation with the North among the Japanese public. To further these channels and build goodwill, Tokyo and Pyongyang promoted the exchange of journalists, which eventually led to discussions on the permanent stationing of news bureaus in each country.[124]

South Korean opposition to these developments centered on two issues. First, the Park government was extremely upset at the North's enterprising use of the Japanese media to convey its "peace offensive." Second, the ROK was angered by the Japanese newspapers' sympathetic reports on North Korea and, by contrast, their increasingly negative coverage of Park's Yusin system. A scathing March 1972 editorial in a South Korean newspaper illustrated the depth of this anger:

The decision on [exchanges of] journalists . . . appears as if Tokyo's thrust to Pyongyang knows no limit and they care little about Korean reactions. . . . Japan should pause to think hard whether its present stance toward Pyongyang is not near or already on the line that will damage and destroy the goodwill, political and economic cooperation . . . achieved in its relations with the ROK under the 1965 treaty.[125]

To protest these developments, the South Korean information ministry abruptly closed the Seoul offices of the *Yomiuri Shimbun* news organization, banned circulation of its publications, and ordered the expulsion of all its correspondents.[126] Vice Foreign Minister Yun Suk-huen filed protests with Ambassador Ushiroku denouncing the Japanese news media's favorable coverage of North Korea as "intolerably slander[ous] and debas[ing] our people and sovereignty."[127] Yun further declared that a similar fate would befall any other newspapers that criticized the Park regime.[128]

The Nadir of Japan-ROK Relations

Between 1973 and 1974 Japan-ROK relations regressed to their lowest point in the postnormalization era. The source of this friction was a series of political incidents that involved the direct clash of sovereignty and security issues for the two governments. Because much of the literature on Japan-Korea relations makes only topical reference to these events, and even fewer provide detailed accounts in English, the analysis that follows provides a basic chronology of each dispute.

THE KIM DAE-JUNG KIDNAPPING

On August 8, 1973, South Korean opposition politician Kim Dae-jung was abducted from a Tokyo hotel room. An outspoken critic of the Yusin regime, Kim garnered strong support from antigovernment groups in the ROK. The popularity of this young, charismatic leader was manifest in the surprisingly large, 46 percent share of the popular vote (60 percent in Seoul) he had received in the 1971 presidential elections. At the time of the incident it was widely suspected that the KCIA orchestrated the kidnapping to terminate Kim's political activities and permanently remove him as a threat to the Park regime.[129] Kim's location remained unknown for five days, during which his captors transported him back to Seoul and placed him under house arrest. Public access to the opposition figure was restricted for two months, and in a coerced statement read October 26, 1973, Kim apologized for his antigovernment activities and promised not to engage in politics in the future. It is widely believed that the KCIA's initial plan was to murder Kim en route from Osaka to Seoul; however, public outrage over the incident and strong pressure from the United States led to the aborting of that plan. American intelligence officials in Japan closely followed the kidnapping and apparently communicated their concerns about Kim's welfare to the Park government. Ambassador Philip Habib learned of the KCIA's involvement within twenty-four hours of the kidnapping and in no uncertain terms made clear that Kim's death would have a profoundly negative impact on relations with Washington. A very blunt and forceful man, Habib saw his role in Korea as a proconsul as much as ambassador. When these events transpired without his prior knowledge, Habib excoriated the Koreans in a manner far beyond the usual diplomatic demarche.[130] Informed observers believe that this prompt U.S. action was the key to the KCIA's aborted plan to kill Kim, although these subtle but significant interventions in the end were only manifested in an American official statement upon Kim's reappearance in Seoul expressing pleasure that he was still alive.[131]

The kidnapping drew heated reactions in Japan from both the government and general public. Premier Tanaka immediately pinned Japan's reputation as an upholder of social order and constitutional principles of free speech on resolution of the case.[132] Park officials showed little enthusiasm for helping with the Japanese investigation, denying numerous pleas by Vice Foreign Minister Hogen Shinsaku, Ambassador Ushiroku, and Justice Minister Tanaka Isaji for opportunities to question the two eyewitnesses, Yang Il-dong and Kim Kyong-in, as well as Kim Dae-jung himself.[133] When preliminary results of the South Korean investigation, released two weeks after the crime itself, clearly demonstrated that the Park government was not acting in good faith,[134] Justice Minister Tanaka openly accused the KCIA of orchestrating the kidnapping, and Foreign Minister Ohira warned that Japan "would take a firm stand against South Korea if Seoul was found to have been involved."[135]

These accusations set off a wave of recriminations. Lee, Yun, and special envoy Park Kun issued numerous statements denying government involvement in the abduction and lodged protests against Ohira's and Tanaka's accusations.[136] In retaliation against Japanese press reports implicating KCIA agents in the kidnapping, on August 24, 1973, ROK Information Minister Yun Ju-young ordered the closing of *Yomiuri Shimbun* offices (for the second time in eleven months) and the expulsion of all its correspondents.[137] Tanaka responded by recalling Ambassador Ushiroku from Seoul for consultations and postponing the seventh annual joint ministerial conference, which significantly raised the stakes in the dispute as Japan now linked resolution of the affair with $200 million in Japanese economic funds that were to have been provided at the conference.[138]

Matters grew worse when the Gaimushō revealed that fingerprints of the ROK embassy's first secretary, Kim Tong-won, were found at the kidnapping scene and demanded his release for questioning by Japanese authorities.[139] Flatly denying this request, Foreign Minister Kim Yong-sik lodged counterprotests over Japan's false accusations and immediately recalled thirteen government officials from Japan, including Kim Tong-won, maintaining that none would be made available for questioning.[140] The following quotation aptly characterizes the atmosphere of this diplomatic crisis:

Japanese officials tonight had increasing irritation with the South Korean position on the [Kim Tong-won] issue. . . . Today's newspapers carried not just columns but pages of reports on the affair. . . . It dominated television news and was the subject of much conversation among Japanese citizens. . . . Indeed, the kidnapping affair has begun to look something like the Watergate scandal in the United States. The Japanese appear to be deeply disturbed because a capital crime has been committed and because it appears more and more evident that it was a political crime by a foreign government thereby violating Japan's national sovereignty.[141]

By October 1973 a series of fruitless meetings made clear that a substantial gap separated Seoul's and Tokyo's positions on the case. The Japanese demanded: (1) Seoul's acknowledgment of KCIA complicity in the kidnapping, (2) punishment of the conspirators, (3) an apology for violation of Japanese sovereignty, and (4) the release of Kim Dae-jung to Japan for questioning. Moreover, Premier Tanaka asserted that he would suspend the annual joint ministerial conference and withhold Japanese economic funds pending a satisfactory resolution of the case.[142] The ROK for its part maintained that: (1) there was no government involvement in the kidnapping, (2) Japan should apologize for its spurious and irresponsible accusations, (3) Kim Dae-jung would not be permitted exit to Japan, and (4) Japanese actions amounted to a blatant interference in ROK internal affairs. A *New York Times* article summed up the crippled state of relations at this time:

Recent conversations with Korean officials here [in Seoul] and Japanese officials in Tokyo clearly indicate that positions on both sides have hardened to a point where political and economic relations are threatened. Moreover, the Kim Dae Jung affair has revived resentments springing from the legacy of the 40 years of Japanese colonial rule over Korea—in the Koreans their hatred and distrust of the Japanese, in the Japanese their contempt and scorn for the Koreans.[143]

In the end Park's need for Japanese economic funds led to an ad hoc compromise in November 1973.[144] The ROK lifted Kim Dae-jung's house arrest conditional on a public apology for his antigovernment activities; Premier Kim Jong-pil delivered a statement of regret (but not apology) over the affair; and Kim Tong-won was relieved of his post in Japan, pending further investigation of his alleged role in the kidnapping. This constituted a de facto acknowledgment of the first secretary's guilt; however, it implied that he acted alone, therefore absolving the government of any charges of violating Japanese sovereignty. Finally, while the ROK persisted in refusing Kim Dae-jung's exit to Japan, it agreed not to charge him for antigovernment activities conducted while in Japan.[145]

The degree to which Japan-ROK relations remained poor was manifested in the absence of cooperation even after resolution of the kidnapping affair. Although the postponed joint ministerial conference eventually did take place in December 1973, cooperation was limited. Meetings were held for one day rather than the usual two to three; moreover, the new ROK foreign minister, Kim Dong-jo, criticized Tokyo's inability to sympathize with the intensity of security threats felt by South Korea. In response Japan canceled a loan for the ROK steel industry and provided only $80 million in loans for various other projects. This figure was 75 percent less than the previous year and fell substantially short of the $200–400 million that the ROK desired. Moreover, in a stinging expression of disapproval, the Japanese delegation refused to include in the final communiqué the customary clause on economic cooperation and instead announced that the bulk of future interaction would be on the part of the private sector rather than government based.[146] It was clear that the scars left by Kim Dae-jung affair on bilateral relations would not soon heal.

Friction between Japan and the ROK only intensified in 1974. Two dynamics were involved. First, Seoul grew increasingly impatient with Tokyo's uncooperativeness in curbing subversive, anti-Park elements operating in Japan, while Japan became more critical of the ROK's continual exaggeration of security threats as justification for its authoritarian regime. These reactions became especially vehement when Yusin's strong-arm tactics touched Japanese nationals. Second, the hostile atmosphere engendered by these disputes provided fertile ground for the resurrection of historical animosities.

The Kim Dae-jung affair and the burgeoning of Japan-North Korea contacts fed resentments among South Koreans, which found expression in historical emotional issues. Throughout the period, for example, the ROK claimed that Japan's equidistance policy toward the two Koreas was intended to perpetuate the division of the peninsula and keep Koreans subservient to Japan. The Kim Dae-jung kidnapping revived public protests against Japanese economic imperialism as Koreans felt their government capitulated on a settlement because of Japanese threats to sever economic ties. South Korean *han* (unredeemed resentment) exploded in January-February 1974, when Premier Tanaka inadvertently remarked in the Diet that the Japanese occupation of Korea had, in fact, provided benefits, particularly in education and agriculture.[147] Still harboring resentment over the Kim Dae-jung affair, the Korean National Assembly excoriated Tanaka for his remarks, and public demonstrations raged at the Japanese embassy for several days. Foreign Minister Kim Dong-jo lodged formal protests with Ambassador Ushiroku and Vice Foreign Minister Hogen, demanding an apology for Tanaka's thoughtlessness.[148]

Augmenting the revival of historical antagonism was the ongoing dispute over Japanese journalists. As the news media continued to attack the repressiveness of Yusin, Park grew more angered with Japan's lack of appreciation for South Korean security concerns. Highlighting the differences between Korea's "semiwar" conditions and Japan's "peaceful environment," he warned Japanese journalists in January 1974 to respect ROK security imperatives and cease their negative reporting.[149] Finally, in February the information ministry banned circulation of the *Asahi Shimbun*, charging the paper with disseminating false propaganda and acting as a "spokesman" for North Korea.

A series of events in the spring and summer of 1974 led to further de-

terioration of relations. In April the KCIA arrested two Japanese students, Tachikawa Masaki and Hayakawa Yoshiharu, visiting Seoul, on
charges of conspiring with indigenous radical groups to overthrow the
Park regime. A South Korean military tribunal sentenced them to
twenty years' imprisonment. In June the Park government arrested Kim
Dae-jung on trumped up violations of electoral campaign laws, stemming from the 1971 presidential elections.

These events again took Seoul-Tokyo relations to the brink. The arrest of Tachikawa and Hayakawa constituted a direct infringement of
the civil rights of Japanese nationals.[150] Foreign Minister Ohira and
Ambassador Ushiroku were infuriated that the ROK took such actions
without prior consultation and condemned the roughshod handling of
the case, protesting that the trial produced no conclusive evidence of the
students' guilt.[151] The arrest of Kim Dae-jung was taken in direct defiance of Japanese entreaties to allow Kim safe passage out of Korea and
was a violation of the November 1973 diplomatic settlement.[152]

South Korean authorities vehemently rejected Japanese requests for
extradition of the two students, maintaining that they would serve their
full sentences.[153] After conviction of the students, mass demonstrations
broke out at the South Korean embassy in Tokyo, and the Gaimushō
yet again recalled Ambassador Ushiroku in protest.[154] Park retaliated by
recalling his ambassador to Japan on the ground that Tanaka's weak
posture toward pro-North Korean groups in Japan was making the
country a "relay station for communist activities."[155] By August 1974
the future of Japan-ROK bilateral relations remained, at best, uncertain.[156]

THE MUN SE-KWANG AFFAIR

As Park Chung-hee delivered an address at Korean Liberation Day
ceremonies (*kwangbokchŏl*) on August 15, 1974, a twenty-two-year-old
South Korean resident of Osaka sprinted down the aisle of the National
Theater firing gunshots wildly at the stage. The president's life was
spared, but in the exchange of gunfire that ensued his wife, Yook
Young-soo, was fatally wounded. The assassin, Mun Se-kwang, had apparently received instructions and financial compensation for the assassination attempt through pro-North Korean groups in Japan.[157]

For South Koreans this a yet another tragic result of Japan's lackadaisical attitude toward the North Korean threat. The assassination
had not only been planned in Japan, but Mun had gained entrance to

South Korea with a fake Japanese passport and had used firearms stolen from an Osaka police station.[158] For several weeks after the incident demonstrations raged at the Japanese embassy and consulates nationwide. Premier Kim Jong-pil, in a nationally televised address, demanded Japan bear "legal and moral responsibility" for the incident.[159] Foreign Minister Kim Dong-jo and Ambassador Kim Yongson called for the outlawing of pro-North Korean organizations in Japan.[160] The National Assembly issued a resolution advocating the severing of diplomatic relations if Japan refused to assume responsibility for the incident.[161]

The Tanaka government resisted South Korean demands for an apology. It saw the assassination attempt as an expression of anger against the repressive Yusin system rather than a North Korean-backed attempt to overthrow Park. The Gaimushō offered condolences for the tragic death of the ROK first lady but maintained that Japan bore no legal or moral responsibility; moreover, it refused to take extralegal measures against anti-South Korean activities in Japan simply to appease Seoul.[162]

With emotions already raw, Foreign Minister Kimura made a number of controversial remarks, in the context of reaffirming Japan's detente policies, which exacerbated tensions with Seoul. In the Diet just two weeks after the assassination, Kimura expressly stated that Japan did *not* perceive a security threat from North Korea. He also said that the recent thaw in regional tensions made the 1969 version of the Korea clause invalid and that it was now the security of the *entire* Korean peninsula, not just the ROK, which was important to Japan. The following week, on September 5, Kimura added that in this new era of detente he did not consider the ROK the *only* lawful government on the peninsula, thereby implying de facto recognition of the North.[163]

As a Western newspaper described them, Koreans considered these remarks "one of the sharpest putdowns ever uttered by a ranking Japanese official," as they undermined Park's single most important justification for his authoritarian regime.[164] More important, the overtly proNorth Korean flavor of Kimura's remarks, so close in time to an assassination attempt on the ROK head of state, clearly signaled Japan's abandonment of cold-war alignments and its move toward a policy of equidistance for the peninsula. From Japan's perspective the Kimura remarks and his obdurate behavior in the Mun case, stemmed from a change in Tokyo's geostrategic threat perceptions as well as from entrapment fears regarding the ROK. As Kimura stated, detente generated the need for new foreign policies based on "social justice" and multilateral diplomacy. This meant firmly venturing into new relationships without being fettered by old ones. The application of this policy to the ROK was twofold. Japan would challenge rather than submit to draconian South Korean acts that infringed human rights. In addition, it would not consent to repressive actions, such as persecution of pro-North Korean groups in Japan, which might preclude improving relations with Pyongyang.[165]

This disparity in ROK and Japanese perspectives gave rise to the worst friction in the history of normalized relations. On August 30, 1974, the ROK foreign ministry lodged protests against Kimura's remarks, criticizing them as "reckless" and a violation of the spirit of the 1965 normalization treaty.[166] The same day Park held a private meeting with Ushiroku, in which he is said to have delivered an ultimatum demanding: (1) Japan show better faith in the Mun case and (2) a government crackdown on anti-South Korean activities in Japan. Park warned that absence of cooperation on these points would force the ROK to take steps toward severing diplomatic relations and nationalize all Japanese assets in Korea.[167] Close associates of Ushiroku recalled that while the ambassador had grown accustomed to Seoul's bluster and brinkmanship in the past, he believed Park was genuinely serious about carrying out these particular threats.[168] In the weeks following the Mun affair and the Kimura remarks (August 20–September 13), nearly five hundred anti-Japanese demonstrations, involving more than three million Koreans, raged throughout large cities in Korea. The most violent of these resulted in the ransacking of the Japanese embassy on September 6. Demonstrators set fire to offices and tore down the Japanese flag. Several Korean students attempted suicide, and twenty-five students cut off their fingers in an act of protest outside the embassy.[169] Foreign Minister Kimura criticized the destruction of the embassy as "deplorable" and recalled Ambassador Ushiroku from Seoul. In a move exemplifying the deteriorating state of relations, both governments canceled the 1974 joint ministerial conference.[170] Under increasing threats that Seoul would recall Ambassador Kim Yong-son as the first step toward severing relations, Gaimushō officials took the extraordinary step of developing contingency plans for the protection and withdrawal of Japanese nationals from Korea.[171]

By September 1974 protracted negotiations boiled down to a deadlock on the contents of a letter to be delivered by special envoy Shiina Etsusaburo to Park. South Korea demanded that the letter contain: (1) Japanese acknowledgment of responsibility for the assassination, (2) an apology for allowing the plot to be fomented in Japan, and (3) a commitment to curb Chosen Soren activities. Japan maintained that it: (1) did not bear legal responsibility for the assassination, (2) would not deliver the formal apology Park demanded, and (3) would not specifically persecute the Chosen Soren. Bilateral relations had deteriorated so greatly that U.S. State Department officials expressed genuine concern that a breakdown in relations was imminent. President Ford sent communications to this effect to Park and dispatched the American ambassador to Korea, Richard Sneider, to Tokyo to meet with Japanese officials.[172]

An uneasy settlement was eventually reached on September 19, in which the Japanese acquiesced to expressing "regret" over the assassination. In addition, special envoy Shiina provided a *note verbale* that Tokyo would monitor future activities of anti-ROK groups in Japan (including, but not exclusively implying, the Chosen Soren) more closely. Individual efforts by American embassy officials played a key role in brokering this settlement. Although the two most important U.S. allies in Asia were on the brink of severing relations, little in the way of direction was forthcoming from Washington as the Japan-Korea crisis took place less than a month after Nixon's resignation. Deputy Chief of Mission Richard Ericson and incoming ambassador Richard Sneider, who replaced Philip Habib, therefore improvised, secretly mediating negotiations between Foreign Minister Kim Dong-jo and Ushiroku. The author's interviews with various foreign ministry officials found that the U.S. role generally consisted of applying pressure on the Park government to accede to an early settlement while imploring the Japanese, under any circumstances, not to lose patience and sever dialogue with Seoul. The Japanese ambassador to the United States at this time, Yasukawa Takeshi, specifically recalled conversations to this effect with Sneider. Ericson was a critical facilitator of the final package settlement that enabled both sides to claim some sense of victory and to step back from the brink of diplomatic rupture. CIA station chief Donald Gregg also played a role in support of Ericson, exhorting his counterparts in the KCIA to be amenable to a prompt settlement. Two close colleagues of Ushiroku recalled how the Japanese ambassador to Korea likened the indispensable role of the United States in the settlement to "much needed rain during a long drought."[173]

The Shiina mission to Seoul formally concluded the Mun Se-kwang affair; however, it neither quelled animosities nor represented a meeting of minds on the dispute. After the settlement Premier Kim Jong-pil continued to denounce Japan's attitude toward the incident. Moreover, Japan announced that its own investigation revealed no tangible links to any illegal Chosen Soren activities in Japan.[174]

In sum, the causes for the diplomatic crises from 1973–74 can be traced to asymmetrical abandonment/entrapment concerns and differing strategies in the alliance and adversary games. At the core of these disputes was a basic gap in threat assessments regarding North Korea, which was exacerbated by disparate abandonment anxieties regarding the common ally, the United States. In the case of Kim Dae-jung the disagreement centered on the danger posed by Kim's unrestricted antigovernment activities in Japan. In the arrest of the two Japanese students it centered on whether radical activities by these individuals constituted a bona fide threat to the Park regime. At issue in the *Yomiuri* shutdowns were South Korean concerns about sympathetic reporting on North Korea. Similarly, friction over the Kimura remarks stemmed from ROK complaints about Japan's overt disregard of North Korea's aggressive designs on the peninsula. Finally, at the root of the Mun Se-kwang affair was the question whether Japan's negligence was responsible for hatching the plot by North Korean groups in Japan. In each of these cases South Korea's hard-line cold-war attitudes in the adversary game against North Korea, reinforced by fears of an absent United States, gave rise to intense abandonment fears in the alliance game with Japan. This caused the ROK to protest Japan's ambivalent attitude toward security threats to the ROK and denounce Japan as a "relay station" for North Korean aggression.

Japan's attitudes in the adversary game caused it to hold intense entrapment fears in the alliance game. Detente, decreased fears of U.S. abandonment, and new diplomatic opportunities helped to alleviate Japan's external-threat perceptions. At the same time this heightened Tokyo's sensitivity to restrictive ties with the ROK that might alienate budding relations with Pyongyang. While the facts at dispute in each case were the immediate cause of friction, the underlying forces propelling the deterioration of relations were these contrasting attitudes and employment of opposing strategies in the alliance and adversary games.

Economic Relations: The Politics of Profit

During the 1972–74 period contentious Japan-ROK behavior was also evident in the economic aspect of the relations. This surfaced over three general issues: (1) the Zhou principles, (2) Japan's expanding economic interaction with North Korea, and (3) decreasing Japanese economic commitments to the ROK.

THE ZHOU PRINCIPLES

The Zhou principles stated that Japanese companies maintaining economic ties with South Korea and Taiwan were not welcome in China. Japan initially resisted the temptations of the vast Chinese market in deference to maintaining allegiance to Seoul and Taipei. However, during the 1972–74 period a number of leading Japanese companies abided by the Zhou principles and abandoned ties with Seoul and Taipei. This "wave of defections" began in the immediate aftermath of Nixon's July 1971 announcement on China, when Toyota and C. Itoh stopped sending representatives to the Japan-ROK Economic Cooperation Committee. Both companies explicitly pointed to the prospects of regional detente as prompting their decisions.[175] The following September a number of Japanese steel companies announced their acceptance of the Zhou principles, and accordingly several key Japanese business leaders began plans to lead an economic delegation to Beijing in October. These developments marked a significant step in the gravitation of Japanese businesses toward China. First, Japanese steel companies had been staunch supporters of economic ties with the ROK, their investment in the P'ohang complex having been the primary reason for the success of the South's burgeoning steel industry. Second, members of the October business delegation included key Japanese *zaikai* (big-business) leaders like Nagano Shigeo, Hasegawa Norishige, and Iwasa Yoshizane. These men wielded powerful influence over the Japanese business community by virtue of their companies' holdings as well as their executive positions in organizations such as Keidanren (federation of leading Japanese industrial- and service-sector organizations) and the Japanese Chamber of Commerce.[176] Many of these magnates had been pro-South Korea and had aligned themselves with the conservative Sato and Fukuda factions in resisting pressures for advances into the Chinese market prior to Nixon's July 1971 announcement.[177]

The decision of the zaikai leaders to accede to the Zhou principles set off a second wave of defections. In October 1971 and January 1972 two prominent Japanese banks, Fuji and Daiichi-Kangyō, agreed to restrict business dealings with the ROK and Taiwan. Another noteworthy defection, occurring in October 1971, was that of Keidanren president Uemura Kogoro, who was was not only a zaikai leader but had also been an outspoken opponent of the Zhou principles and a member of the Japan-ROK Cooperation Committee.[178] Finally, in November 1971 and June 1972 two major Japanese trading companies, Mitsui and Mitsubishi, announced their adherence to the principles and dispatched trade missions to China.[179] As an analyst of these events summarized the situation: "President Nixon's announcement that he would visit China was of critical importance and the single most important cause of change in the Japanese business community."[180]

Park grew anxious over this gravitation of Japanese commerce to China. Friction was most evident at the bilateral Japan-ROK Cooperation Committee and Economic Cooperation Committee meetings, the two principal fora through which economic agreements were facilitated. At their July 1971 and March 1972 meetings the ROK protested the absence of Japanese firms, such as Nippon Steel, Nippon Electric, Hitachi, C. Itoh, and Toyota, which had regularly sent representatives) in the past. In addition, the South Koreans were extremely upset with the Japanese delegation's unusual request not to issue customary joint communiqués.[181] After concluding $200-million worth of economic agreements at the fifth annual joint ministerial conference in 1971, acting Foreign Minister Kimura now made clear that these funds should not be interpreted as aggressively targeted against China or as posing an obstacle to Sino-Japanese economic relations. Such statements, Koreans complained, had never been made at previous conferences and typified Japan's loyalty-deficient "economic animal" mentality.[182]

Seoul-Tokyo friction over the Zhou principles starkly contrasts with the cooperative behavior exhibited during 1969–71. In the earlier period Japan discouraged firms from acceding to the Zhou principles, and the ROK did not raise protests over the few that did (see Chapter 3). The sheer increase in the number of firms that defected to China offers the most immediate explanation for the shift from cooperation to friction in the 1972–74 period. However, the underlying cause for this change can be traced to the external security environment and asymmetrical abandonment and entrapment structures. During 1969–71 shared fears of U.S. abandonment in the face of intense cold-war threat perceptions caused both Japan and the ROK to suppress the Zhou principles as a source of friction. However, during 1972–74 detente effectively lowered cold-war barriers to trade with China and prompted a change in the Japanese business community's attitude toward the Zhou principles.[183] In this new environment Japan sought to avoid entrapment in economic relations with the ROK and Taiwan at the expense of the potentially lucrative Chinese market. This naturally elicited protests from the South Koreans and Taiwanese as they perceived the Japanese abandoning support of key domestic industries necessary for development and stability.

JAPAN–NORTH KOREA TRADE

Friction between Seoul and Tokyo also mounted over the dramatic rise in economic interaction between Tokyo and Pyongyang. This expansion in trade began immediately after Nixon's July 1971 China announcement and the Japanese business community's acceptance of the Zhou principles. In August 1971, for example, the Kuraray Company, a major Japanese synthetic-fiber manufacturer, commenced arrangements for the export of textile plants to the North. This was followed in October 1971 by a $1.2-million contract for the export of a beverage-canning plant by the Nichiryū Shōji Company and in November 1971 by a third lucrative contract for the export of air-conditioning equipment to North Korea by the Daikin Kōgyō Company.[184] In January 1972 the Dietmen's League for Japan-North Korean Friendship negotiated a memorandum trade agreement with Pyongyang that provided for trade expositions and was ultimately aimed at the establishment of trade missions.[185] From January to March 1972 regularized shipping routes were established.[186] In addition, multimillion-dollar contracts were concluded for the export of Japanese trucks as well as the development of the North Korean steel and cement industries.[187]

The effects of these agreements were immediate. In the year following the memorandum trade agreement, Japanese trade with North Korea reached $137.6 million, more than double the volume in 1971, the year before the agreement. Overall from 1971 to 1974 bilateral trade increased more than sixfold, from $58.4 million to $376 million, constituting the period of highest trade growth since 1965. By contrast, total trade for the preceding 1969–71 period had increased by less than $3 million (see Appendix Table A.2).

South Korean anxieties over these developments centered on four issues. First, concerns proliferated that Japan's trade with North Korea and China could potentially displace that with the South. Second, although memorandum trade was conducted through private business channels, Park was concerned that it had the unofficial backing of the Japanese government. He felt that such private activities were part of the incrementalist policy aimed ultimately at full economic and diplomatic relations with Pyongyang in much the same fashion that memorandum trade had laid the foundation for Sino-Japanese relations. Third, the composition of Japanese-North Korean trade was threatening to national security. Although Japan imported raw materials and marine products from the North, it exported plant equipment for such industries as steel, cement, and chemicals, all of which had the potential to enhance North Korean military capabilities. Finally, of particular concern to the South Koreans was the Ministry of International Trade and Industry's (MITI's) contemplation of Export-Import Bank (EIB) financing of North Korean contracts. Pyongyang's dearth of hard currency placed outer limits on its volume of trade as Japanese companies could negotiate contracts only on a deferred-payment basis. MITI's approval of long-term, low-interest EIB loans for these companies would substantially increase the scale, volume, and scope of business contracts.

For these reasons the Park government registered the "strongest protest possible" over the 1972 memorandum trade agreement.[188] It recalled its ambassador to Japan for consultations and charged that the agreement was tantamount to Japanese de facto recognition of North Korea.[189] Regarding the EIB issue, in nearly every bilateral forum between 1972 and 1973 the Park government linked ROK security with a decision on EIB financing. Indeed, one of the first communications to the new premier, Tanaka, in August 1972 concerned Seoul's deep opposition to any favorable government inclinations toward financing North Korean trade.[190] During the sixth annual joint ministerial conference the following month Foreign Minister Kim Yong-sik held a set of unscheduled meetings with Foreign Minister Ohira specifically to reiterate these concerns.[191]

In spite of these entreaties MITI finally approved EIB financing for the export of a $1.2-million towel-manufacturing plant to North Korea in December 1973. In addition, it declared that it would now welcome applications for all future EIB financing of North Korean contracts. This decision outraged the Park government. Park had spent much political capital in discouraging such a decision and was doubly embarrassed that MITI's decision came only two days after rescheduling the postponed seventh joint ministerial conference (at which the two governments had committed to mending relations damaged by the Kim Dae-jung controversy). For South Korea these actions amounted to a blatant abandonment of anticommunist ties with the ROK.

MITI's explanation of the EIB decision clearly highlighted a different perspective:

Behind the Government's approval of the use of the official funds in exports to North Korea are the China-US detente, the normalization of relations between Japan and China, and the progress of dialogues [sic] between the two Koreas.[192]

A tight Japanese alignment with the ROK would alienate potentially lucrative markets in Communist nations; it would also forgo the ameliorating effect that interdependent economic ties with these Communist powers could have on Japan's external security environment. This was an entrapment scenario that the Tanaka government sought to avoid.

JAPAN-ROK AID AND INVESTMENT

The final source of friction in Japan-ROK relations concerned Japanese aid and investment. By 1972 Japan had become the largest foreign investor in the ROK, surpassing the United States. The criticality of Japanese capital to the South Korean infrastructure was manifest in agreements such as a $80-million loan for construction of a subway system and a joint offshore oil exploration pact.[193] Japanese credits were also crucial to continued development of the steel and shipbuilding industries, both of which were crucial to the legitimacy of Park's authoritarian rule.

In spite of these factors Japanese aid and investment in the ROK dramatically declined during the 1972–74 period, with Tokyo fulfilling only $210 million out of approximately $1.4 billion in Korean credit requests, a far smaller percentage than in previous years.[194] This lack of cooperation stemmed from two factors. First, as was the case with trade, detente raised Japanese concerns about being entrapped by ties with the ROK that might impede cultivation of new interdependent ties with Communist adversaries. For this reason Japan stated at the fifth and sixth annual joint ministerial conferences in 1971 and 1972 that credits provided to the ROK had no political or military implications and did not rule out similar packages with China or North Korea.[195] This behavior stood in marked contrast to the preceding 1969–71 period, when the Japanese government did not deny that economic credits for ROK industry connoted an investment in stability of the Park regime.

The second cause for the decline in Japan-ROK economic cooperation was the numerous diplomatic disputes that plagued relations during the period. For example, in protest over the Kim Dae-jung kidnapping, Tanaka postponed the seventh annual joint ministerial conference for four months and then limited the conference to only one day. Japanese credits totaled only 20 percent of ROK requests, representing a drop of more than 50 percent from the previous year. Japan also suspended a 1972 agreement to provide $135 million in loans for the second stage of the P'ohang steel project.[196] Taking even more stringent actions after the arrest of the two Japanese students and the Mun Se-kwang case, Tanaka canceled the 1974 joint ministerial conference altogether. Moreover, he wholly rejected ROK requests for $300 million in credits.[197]

Fears of entrapment and resentments arising from diplomatic disputes led Tanaka in March 1974 to institute a major revision in economic policy toward the ROK. The government announced that future government credits to the ROK would be provided through a nine-nation World Bank consortium known as the International Economic Consultation Group on Korea (IECOK). Under this program Japan would provide a fixed percentage (approximately 33 percent) of the total funds annually allocated to the ROK by the World Bank body.[198] As the amounts recommended by IECOK were already lower than average yearly Japanese credits to the ROK, this formula drastically reduced the volume of Tokyo's contributions.[199] Latent Japanese concerns about growing South Korean competitiveness may have been a factor in Japan's decision, but given the events of the period, the IECOK arrangement's true value was in its depoliticization of Japan-ROK economic cooperation by no longer subjecting the funds to bilateral negotiation, thereby distancing Japanese credits from any interpretation of political support for, or security links with, the regime.

THE 1972–74 PERIOD was an unprecedentedly poor one in Japan-ROK relations. While the specifics of each dispute fueled the acrimony of this period, the common causal variable for this friction was a basic asymmetry in Japanese and Korean abandonment/entrapment fears. Despite detente the Park government faced waning defense commitments from its security guarantor, which only exacerbated already virulent threats from North Korea. This combination of security concerns prompted Seoul to suffer intense abandonment fears regarding Japan's relations with regional adversaries. It was precisely these concerns that caused Park to implement Yusin measures at home and persecute anti-government forces abroad. Assuming Japan would harbor similar security concerns, Park sought Tokyo's understanding that actions taken against Kim Dae-jung, Japanese newspapers, and the two Japanese students were necessary evils to ensure stability against subversive threats.

When such sympathetic comprehension did not materialize, the ROK criticized Japan's reneging on the Korea clause and Okinawan-base commitment and its equidistance policy as hypocritical attitudes that still permitted Japan to enjoy the security benefits that accrued from the ROK's defense efforts.

For its part Japan capitalized on the new-found detente with regional adversaries, felt reassured by U.S. defense commitments, and perceived similar opportunities for a workable detente on the Korean peninsula. As a result, Tokyo experienced heightened entrapment anxieties regarding the avoidance of stifling and anachronistic security alignments with the ROK that could only alienate North Korea, China, and the Soviet Union. It scorned Park's draconian domestic practices, overzealous preoccupation with the Korea clause, and demands for crackdowns on the Chosen Soren in Japan. When Park's policies infringed on Japanese sovereignty and the safety of Japanese nationals, Tokyo could not fathom a rational justification for this other than a blatant violation of civil rights and affront to Japanese goodwill. Thus, while the particulars of each dispute were important, it was the gap in security perceptions that was the true catalyst for friction.

The implication of such an argument is that in periods when Japan and the ROK held *similar* threat perceptions behavior over such incidents would have been *different* from that exhibited in 1972–74. Counterfactuals are, of course, difficult to confirm, but the Yun Yu-gil kidnapping incident of May 1969 offers one example supporting such a proposition. That incident occurred at a time of high threat perceptions and fears of U.S. abandonment for both Japan and the ROK. The KCIA abduction of Yun from Japan was almost identical to the Kim case, yet Japanese and South Korean reactions in the former were marked by a conspicuous absence of contention.[200] The argument here does not purport to maintain that the degree of symmetry in abandonment/entrapment concerns will be the only determinant of cooperative or contentious outcomes in cases such as Kim Dae-jung and Yun Yu-gil. Rather, the degree of symmetry or asymmetry in these concerns can act as a mitigating or exacerbating influence on the dispute. In the Yun case overarching security imperatives caused both governments to minimize the significance of the issue as a source of friction in relations. In the Kim case the disparity in threat perceptions infused each side's intransigent attitudes, causing each to see the other's position as unreasonable. The result was a spiraling of emotions and ill will that took relations to the brink of rupture.

FIVE

Vietnam and the Carter Years,
1975–1979

THE SECURITY ENVIRONMENT in East Asia underwent dramatic changes in the latter half of the 1970s. The frailty of detente became apparent as Soviet intransigence in the peripheries of Africa, the Middle East, and the Eurasian continent raised questions about the feasibility of peaceful coexistence between the two superpowers and about the true nature of Soviet intentions. The Sino-American rapprochement too was cut short in its infancy. Although Richard Nixon's and Henry Kissinger's initiatives in the early 1970s would eventually bear fruit in the form of normalized relations by the end of the decade, the process was a slow and painful one, and the by-product, a reservoir of heightened mistrust and frustration on the parts of both Washington and Beijing. The issue of Taiwan, in particular, posed the main obstacle, deflating the hopes and expectations that accompanied the Shanghai communiqué in 1972.

The most wrenching event for the United States in these years was, of course, the war in Vietnam. The unceremonious fall of Saigon in the spring of 1975 both crushed the myth of American invincibility in the minds of Asian allies and raised intense American questioning of the costs, both moral and substantive, of America's commitments abroad. For Japan and Korea the post-Vietnam security environment was one of considerable uncertainty. The demise of detente engendered a return of unmitigated cold-war tensions to the region. Coupled with this was a demoralized and domestically torn United States, which was at best unenthusiastic with its continued overextension in the region. To the concern of many Asian leaders this American ambivalence translated into a new policy under Jimmy Carter for complete U.S. disengagement from the Korean peninsula.

This chapter shows how these troubling trends fostered an improvement in Japan-ROK bilateral relations. Heightened threat perceptions and fears of abandonment regarding the common great-power ally caused the governments in Seoul and Tokyo, despite lingering historical animosity and contentious bilateral issues, to renew efforts at cooperation. This was evident in the political, economic, and security aspects of relations and marked a significant improvement from the detente years, which were filled with friction. The story begins with a look at the regional security environment that helped foster this change.

The Demise of Detente

Detente reached its limits in the latter half of the 1970s. Superpower relations deteriorated as a result of Soviet policies in Africa, the Middle East, and later Afghanistan.[1] The Soviet and Cuban military presence in Angola, in particular, marked the retrogression of superpower relations from 1975. These interventions drew strong criticism from U.S. policymakers and revealed the Soviets' continued pursuit of expansionist policies aimed at undermining the West.[2] In addition, despite the signing of the SALT I arms limitations accords, the Soviet buildup of conventional and strategic forces and Moscow's lack of cooperation in the SALT II negotiations made clear that it did not equate detente with peaceful coexistence and the abandonment of political and ideological struggles.[3] As congressional hearings at the time concluded, detente became for the Soviets an opportunity to exploit the temporary thaw in security tensions and achieve a decisive shift in balance of power through all means short of direct superpower confrontation:

Constructive interdependence which was to be the cornerstone of United States-Soviet detente has not materialized. Rather while the Soviets benefited from relaxed credits, technology transfers, and lulling of Western opinion into a false sense of security, they stood unprepared to engage in any reciprocal restraint. . . . Thus in spite of the achievements of the Nixon-Kissinger diplomacy in engineering a shift from overt bipolar containment to a sort of triangular balance of power, it would seem that the United States is locked more than ever in a global bipolar military struggle with the Soviet Union.[4]

Similarly, the optimistic light cast on United States-China relations after the historic Nixon-Zhou meetings grew progressively dimmer during the 1975–79 period. Beijing rejected numerous U.S. proposals for confidence-building measures, such as an arms control dialogue, economic relations encountered a number of obstacles, and government-facilitated cultural contacts sputtered.[5] Bilateral meetings during the period failed to produce much beyond a reiteration of principles stated in 1972. President Gerald Ford's December 1975 visit to Beijing yielded no substantive cooperative agreements and did not even produce a joint communiqué. In addition, Chinese officials accused President Jimmy Carter of reneging on commitments made in the Shanghai communiqué.[6] Despite commitments by both governments to achieve normalization, a settlement did not come about until January 1979. As congressional hearings in 1977 found, the initial momentum attending Nixon's 1972 rapprochement had slowed to a crawl:

Our present relationship remains very limited, and in many respects it is still quite fragile. Unless it is consolidated in the period ahead, it could well retrogress. There has been no significant forward movement in the relationship for almost four years.[7]

A number of factors contributed to the deterioration in Sino-American relations. As United States-Soviet relations degenerated, Richard Nixon and Henry Kissinger became concerned that rapid improvements in Sino-American relations might raise encirclement fears in Moscow and upset the delicate triangular balance that they were trying to maintain (with the United States holding the pivotal position).[8] Domestic political turmoil in both countries also reduced enthusiasm for pushing relations forward. Crippled by the Watergate scandal, Nixon could not advance China policy because of his vulnerabilities to attacks by a critical mass of strongly anticommunist senators. After the U.S. withdrawal from Vietnam, the Ford administration was equally constrained by the conservative backlash from supporters of Ronald Reagan. In China the death of Mao Zedong, attacks on Zhou Enlai by the radical left (and later Zhou's death), the purge of the Gang of Four, the purge and reinstatement of Deng Xiaopeng, the April riots, and the rise of Hua Kuofeng all focused Beijing's attention inward rather than on deepening the rapprochement with America.[9]

The key issue deterring the improvement of relations, however, was Taiwan. It became clear that any augmentation of dialogue with China was not possible as long as the United States maintained full security and political commitments to Taiwan. As an analyst testified concerning Ford's 1975 trip to Beijing, the Chinese, "took the position implicitly that if you cannot move on Taiwan, we will not move on anything else."[10] Particularly after the communist victory in Indochina, U.S. hesitance about the effect on allied confidence and regional stability of severing thirty-year-old ties with a model cold-war ally dampened enthusiasm for pursuing relations with Beijing to the extent implied in the Shanghai communiqué.[11] China consequently grew impatient with U.S. backtracking and criticized the Ford and Carter administrations resoundingly for reneging on the spirit of the 1972 meetings. As U.S. congressional hearings in 1977 concluded:

Although Peking has been patient over U.S. policy on the Taiwan issue for six years, this patience may soon wear thin. . . . The current Chinese leaders place top priority on obtaining U.S. acceptance of the three conditions dealing with Taiwan. They note that Peking's current conditions represent a moderation of past People's Republic of China conditions for normalization of relations with the U.S. and that Peking is justified in feeling that it is now Washington's turn to compromise in order for normalization to proceed. . . . The alternative to U.S. compromise could be a potentially explosive situation developing in a few years, in which Peking would become increasingly inclined to use force to obtain jurisdiction over Taiwan.[12]

The 1975–79 period therefore witnessed a general downturn in U.S. relations with its two cold-war adversaries in Asia. As Assistant Secretary of State Winston Lord affirmed in 1976, "détente" was no longer part of U.S.-Soviet foreign-policy vocabulary.[13] On the China front the expectations and hopes that surrounded the 1972 Nixon-Zhou meetings remained unfulfilled. As a U.S. congressman in 1975 commented, the communiqué was not a binding treaty commitment but a piece of paper signed in 1972 by two leaders, one of whom had died and the other of whom was no longer in office.[14] The result of these dynamics was a return of regional cold-war tensions.

U.S. DISENGAGEMENT — THE CARTER PLAN

Concurrent with detente's demise was growing evidence of American disengagement from Asia. The United States terminated its involvement in the Vietnam conflict and helplessly watched the fall of Saigon in the spring of 1975. Following this event, President Carter announced a plan for the complete withdrawal of U.S. ground forces from South Korea. He first broached the plan as a presidential candidate in 1975 and continued raising it throughout his 1976 campaign.[15] Appearing early on in the new president's agenda with his National Security Council team, Presidential Review Memorandum/NSC13 (PRM-13, January 26, 1977), directed relevant agency and departmental heads to outline preliminary plans for troop withdrawals from Korea. This was followed on May 5, 1977, by Presidential Directive/NSC12 (PD/NSC-12), which laid out the timetable for withdrawals. Carter's plan called for the immediate pullout of one combat brigade (six thousand troops) of the Second Infantry Division by 1978, followed by the withdrawal of a second brigade and all noncombat support personnel (nine thousand troops) by the end of June 1980. Complete withdrawal of remaining personnel, U.S. headquarters, and nuclear weapons was expected by 1982.[16] In press conferences announcing the plan, Carter maintained the pullout decision was not subject to negotiation and would proceed without delay.[17]

The President's convictions on Korea stemmed from a number of factors. First, Carter sought to shed the economic burdens of overly dependent U.S. allies and believed ROK defense capabilities (in conjunction with U.S. air, naval, and marine deployments there) provided sufficient justification for the pullout of redundant and costly ground troops. Second, he believed the American presence on the peninsula, while a stabilizing force in the short term, was detrimental to any long-term prospects for reconciliation and peace between the two Koreas. Third, in line with his moralistic vision of foreign policy Carter questioned standard justifications for stationing U.S. forces overseas; moreover, he linked the pullout decision with U.S. objections to the Park regime's human rights violations. Carter noted the last point explicitly in a June 1976 Foreign Policy Association speech:

I believe it will be possible to withdraw our ground forces from South Korea on a phased basis over a time span to be determined after consultations with both South Korea and Japan. At the same time, it should be made clear to the South Korean government that its internal oppression is repugnant to our people and undermines the support of our commitment there.[18]

Finally, and perhaps most important, Carter's pullout decision reflected the general American neoisolationist determination to avoid future entanglements on the Asian mainland after the demoralizing outcome in Vietnam.[19] After the fall of Saigon in April 1975 opinion polls in the United States found only 14 percent of the American public favoring U.S. intervention in another Korean conflict and 65 percent opposing it. These were sentiments that any presidential candidate could not ignore.

The plan met with strong criticism. High-level administration officials like Defense Secretary Harold Brown, Secretary of State Cyrus Vance, National Security Advisor Zbigniew Brzezinski, and Assistant

Secretary for East Asia Richard Holbrooke all had to support a policy in public while they sought to change the president's iron-willed convictions in private. The chief of staff for U.S. forces in Korea, Major General John Singlaub, publicly opposed Carter's decision and was promptly relieved of his duty in 1977.[21] The Joint Chiefs of Staff also questioned the plan, recommending a partial withdrawal of seven thousand troops over a five-year period. In addition, Carter's bypassing of the interagency policy review process upset officials as he consulted with the NSC, Pentagon, State Department, and CIA more on the means of implementing the policy rather than on the merits of it.[22]

In the end a combination of congressional pressure, revised intelligence assessments of North Korea, and criticism from Asian allies led Carter to suspend the pullout plan in 1979.[23] However, this did not diminish the disengagement atmospherics that pervaded U.S. policy toward Asia during the period. From the plan's inception in 1975, through the debates that caused Carter to hesitate and eventually rescind the policy, the administration steadfastly maintained that the only aspect of the pullout at issue was the phasing, that is, when, not whether, the United States would withdraw from Korea.[24] Moreover, the actual postponement of the Carter plan did not ensure a renewed U.S. commitment to Korea but simply left matters ambiguous. Carter's policy reversal was based on revised intelligence estimates showing an increase in North Korean military strength.[25] The reversal, however, merely left U.S. commitments at their current levels.[26] The decision to retain the U.S. combat presence in Korea therefore amounted to a weakened U.S. deterrence posture despite the new information showing an increased threat. In sum, during the 1975–79 period policies of U.S. disengagement and the demise of regional detente engendered a security environment in East Asia wholly different from that of the preceding 1972–74 period. These changes instilled acute fears of U.S. abandonment in Japan and South Korea.

The Allied Reaction to Vietnam

The American withdrawal from Vietnam in 1975 raised serious doubts in Seoul and Tokyo about U.S. intentions in the region. The Ford administration attempted to assert continued strength through numerous statements and actions, most notably the retaking of the *Mayaguez* and the enunciation of the Pacific Doctrine in 1975.[27] The latter, formally stated in December 1975, assured allies of the United States' intention to remain in Asia despite the Vietnam debacle (but offered no new tangible defense commitments). In line with this Ford officials also reassured allies of the U.S. deterrent posture against North Korea.[28] Ford himself personally reassured Park of U.S. commitments during a brief meeting in November 1974. Defense Secretary James Schlesinger also privately tried to rationalize with Park during an August 1975 meeting in Seoul that there would be no basic changes in U.S. policy over the next five years regardless of whether the incumbent administration or (ironically) the Democrats won in the next election.[29] However, from the Japanese and Korean perspectives these words paled in comparison with the disheartening events in Southeast Asia.

For Japan the late 1970s were a time of heightened external threat perceptions. Although the 1972–74 period had seen an improvement in Tokyo's relations with China and the Soviet Union, both relationships stagnated by 1975. In the former case the initial euphoria over rapprochement and normalization gave way to the reality that there were limits to Japanese-Chinese cooperation, particularly over Taiwan.[30] Soviet-Japanese relations also deteriorated. Peace treaty talks between the Miki Takeo and Leonid Brezhnev governments in 1975 stalled over the northern territories and fishing rights issues.[31] Moreover, the Soviet military buildup and naval exercises during the period demonstrated such an ominous Russian threat in the Pacific that Japan Defense Agency (JDA) Director-General Kanemaru Shin once quipped that the Sea of Japan should be renamed the Sea of Russia.[32] In line with this, Japanese Defense Agency white papers in 1976 and 1977 acknowledged the demise of regional detente and expressed deep concern about the Soviets replacing the U.S. as the preponderant military power in the region.[33]

In light of these developments the fall of Saigon graphically illustrated to the Japanese government and public a general U.S. retreat from Asia. As Thomas Havens described it, Vietnam was Japan's "fire across the sea" (taigan no kasai)—a conflict which caught the attention of many yet one from which the Japanese desired to remain aloof.[34] The danger with the U.S. retreat was that this fire might now lap onto Japanese shores. Japan's reaction to these events was typical of a state fraught with anxieties of allied abandonment. Doubts proliferated about American credibility; at the same time the conviction grew that Japan must draw closer to its great-power protector. In April 1975 three key policy-making branches of the LDP passed a joint resolution calling for reconfirmation of American security commitments to Japan given the events in Vietnam. Foreign Minister Miyazawa Kiichi unambiguously reiterated the contents of the LDP resolution in meetings with Ford and Kissinger later that month.[35] In uncharacteristic fashion opposition parties and the press remained almost completely silent about the U.S. use of Japanese bases in the *Mayaguez* incident. While Japan had its own problems and incentives as a result of the outcome in Southeast Asia, it also shared security concerns with Korea.[36] In particular, in meetings with Ford and Defense Secretary James Schlesinger in August 1975 Miki pointedly asked what bearing the Vietnam pullout would have on U.S. forces in Korea.[37] As analysts of the period observed, anxieties were at a much more intense level than those experienced during the 1969–71 period of the Nixon doctrine.[38]

The Koreans had similar reactions. While the actual withdrawal of U.S. forces from Vietnam was disturbing to Seoul, of equal concern was congressional opposition to appropriating security assistance to South Vietnam in conjunction with the pullout. The latter action raised anxieties that the same fate would befall U.S. financing of the ROK's military modernization program. In addition, legislation in the form of the War Powers Act in 1973 and the Angolan Resolution in 1975 fueled concerns that Congress was imposing legal restraints on further U.S. military involvement abroad.[39] Ambassador Richard Sneider in June 1975 drafted a twelve-page secret telegram to Washington urging both a rethinking of policy and reaffirmation of commitments to Korea in light of the turn of events in Vietnam; it elicited little in the way of a supportive reaction from Ford officials. American uncertainty about what was next in Asia was evident in an inconclusive secret study conducted by the Ford administration at the time of Sneider's cable.[40] Heightening ROK threat perceptions was a consolidation of the North Korea-China axis. Concurrent with the fall of Saigon in April 1975 Kim Il-sung held extremely positive talks with the Beijing leadership, obtaining a joint communiqué in which the two countries asserted their military alliance in the face of the West's demoralizing defeat.[41]

ROK officials expressed their fears of abandonment in various bilateral fora with the United States in 1975 and 1976. At the eighth and ninth security consultative conferences, Defense Minister Suh Chong-chol provided detailed lists of North Korean armed provocations, urging that U.S. retrenchment in Southeast Asia not translate into a downgrading of commitments to Korea.[42] In retrospect the Ford administration did issue strong statements of continued support for alliance ties. Defense Secretary Schlesinger publicly acknowledged the presence of U.S. nuclear weapons in Korea in June 1975 and declared that they could be used to defend South Korea if necessary. The annual U.S.-ROK Team spirit exercises were also started under Ford in June 1976.[43] These actions, however, failed to allay anxieties over the magnitude of events in Indochina. Moreover, South Koreans found little comfort in the fact that Ford's National Security Council staff criticized as overstating administration policy certain assurances to Park by Schlesinger foreseeing no changes in the U.S. presence in Korea for the next five years. Korea reacted very much like an ally stricken with insecurities of abandonment. The ROK defense budget doubled from 1975 to 1976 and saw sharp increases through 1979, totaling in that year four-fold the budget in 1975. Park levied a new defense tax on the country and passed laws tightening even further the controls of Yusin and effectively putting the nation on a wartime footing. The secret nuclear weapons program initiated in 1972 looked even more appealing to Park as the route to securing national defense as doubts proliferated about the U.S. commitment, and it was only after a very strong set of American inducements and threats that Park begrudgingly gave in to suspending the program.[44] Further exemplifying their abandonment fears, Koreans wanted substantive reassurances such as a revision of the bilateral defense treaty along the lines of a NATO-type automatic-response commitment by the United States in future contingencies.[45] Portions of the text of a five-point resolution, unanimously passed by the National Assembly, also revealed the extent of Korean concerns:

We hope that the United States . . . will demonstrate by deeds its firm determination not to commit the same failure on the Korean peninsula as it did on the Indochinese peninsula. Without such a demonstration, the United States will lose all credibility in its foreign commitments and this will lead to a debacle in the order of world peace.[46]

In short, the ROK perceived in Southeast Asia nothing short of an American "defeat" that shook confidence in the United States as a great-power protector.[47] The predominant view of America's post-Vietnam policy was one of ambivalence, indecision, and retrenchment.[48]

ROK Disengagement Fears and the Carter Plan

Carter's pullout plan exponentially heightened South Korean anxieties.[49] At the heart of these concerns was the belief that the United States sought to shed its all-important tripwire presence on the peninsula, thereby relieving itself of any immediate entanglements in future contin-

gencies. Equally troubling to the ROK was Carter's unilateral implementation of this policy without first seeking Moscow's and Beijing's
assurances to restrain Pyongyang from adventuristic acts.[50] In lengthy
meetings with Undersecretary of State Philip Habib and Joint Chiefs of
Staff Chairman George Brown in May 1977 President Park was "in-
credulous" at the decision and expressed deep anger at Carter's lack of
prior consultation on the issue. He believed the new United States president was essentially abandoning Korea's well-being to gain domestic
political credibility.[51] Park was upset by the priority the new administration placed on implementing the Korea policy as a symbol of Carter's
making good on campaign pledges, that is, barely one week after inauguration. Also angering Park was Carter's decision to notify Japan of
the plan during Mondale's February 1977 Tokyo visit, a month before
notifying Korea. This was despite Park's invitation to the vice-president
to include Seoul in his February itinerary. In summit meetings with Carter, Park urged the U.S. president in blunt terms to better understand
the sensitivities of the Korean situation.[52] Park's anger with Carter
gradually worsened from March 1977. Park was astonished that just
prior to meeting with Carter, the U.S. president in news conferences
held firm to the pullout plan, overruling Joint Chiefs of Staff recommendations for a partial withdrawal and then proceeded in his meetings
with Park to excoriate the ROK president for human rights violations.
Park's distaste for Carter's attitudes were even made clear in a state
dinner toast at their June 1979 summit: "I also believe that President
Carter's visit to Korea, one of the most conspicuous conflict areas of the
world today, will give him a valuable opportunity to deepen his understanding of the heart of the problem in this area." It was at this summit
that Park, unbeknownst to American planner of the summit agenda,
launched into a forty-five-minute soliloquy scolding the American president for his ill-advised plan to pull out of Korea. Carter, who had already been made aware of the intelligence reassessments of North Korean military strength and had become reluctantly resigned to the fact
that the plan might have to be dropped, requested beforehand through
his aides that the summit meeting with Park not include specific discussion of the troop withdrawal issue.[53] Carter grew furious with Park's actions and passed a note to Secretaries Vance and Brown, saying, "If he
goes on like this much longer, I'm going to pull every troop out of the
country." The U.S. president then responded with his own oration criticizing the Park regime's human rights violations.[54] At the tenth security
consultative conference in July 1977 Defense Secretary Harold Brown,

in the ultimate understatement, admitted the Carter plan was raising doubts among ROK defense officials at the highest levels.[55] These trepidations were so great that Park at one time reportedly considered moving the South Korean capital to a location south of Seoul to better survive an attack from the North.[56]

Furthermore, as was the case after Vietnam, U.S. attempts to reassure the ROK did little to quell abandonment fears. Numerous statements to the effect that the United States would maintain its treaty commitments as well as retain the nuclear umbrella over the ROK impressed the Koreans as nothing more than "ritualistic guarantees" that did not boost U.S. credibility.[57] As a government-backed newspaper stated after such guarantees by United States Ambassador William Gleysteen in September 1978:

We are hardly convinced that the US commitment will not diminish while its military presence in Korea continues to dwindle. To the contrary, we are inclined to regard the troop phaseout as a definite sign of weakening US resolve to fight in case the north Korean Communists invade this Republic again.[58]

Moreover, promises to maintain air and naval deployments in Korea as well as provide military assistance packages offered little consolation.[59] From Seoul's perspective American air and naval power failed to deter North Korea in 1950; the United States also appeared unwilling to employ this power to punish a recent string of provocations (i.e., the 1968 *Pueblo* seizure and Blue House raid, the 1969 EC-121 shootdown, and the 1976 poplar tree incident, in which two U.S. soldiers were killed in an altercation with North Koreans over the trimming of a tree in the Joint Security Area of the DMZ).[60] In addition, revelations in 1976 regarding South Korean attempts to illicitly influence U.S. congressmen (known as Koreagate) raised the added threat of economic abandonment by the United States. In particular, Seoul's lack of cooperation in the Koreagate investigations caused Congress to become increasingly unwilling to approve additional funds for ROK military modernization and autonomous defense capabilities. One manifestation of this was a unanimous resolution in November 1977 declining the transfer of $800 million in armaments to Korea and threatening to cut off all additional assistance.[61] Further exacerbating ROK concerns were reports of letters exchanged between Kim Il-sung and Carter through third parties in Romania and Yugoslavia in the spring of 1978 exploring the possibility of expanded contacts.[62] These anxieties permeated every level of South Korean government and society, far surpassing those experienced over

Nixon's retrenchment policies in 1970–71.[63] *Joongang Ilbo* newspaper polls at the time found that 65 percent of the Korean public cited the withdrawal of American troops as their greatest concern.[64] Opposition parties also decried Carter's policies, not only because of the security implications but also because it would enable Park to justify further prolonging his repressive Yusin rule. As a Joint U.S. Military Assistance Group-Korea policy officer present at the United States-ROK security consultative council meetings during the period recounted in no uncertain terms, "[ROK] belief in us as a military power worth its name was at its lowest."[65]

KOREAN RETRENCHMENT AND THE JAPANESE REACTION

Chief of the Self-Defense Force (SDF) Sakata Michita described Japanese fears of U.S. abandonment after Vietnam as undoubtedly substantial, but it was with the Carter plan that these anxieties became critical and led to changes in security thinking.[66] Tokyo's concerns regarding U.S. troop withdrawal from Korea centered on four issues. First, the pullout plan, coming so soon after U.S. disengagement from Vietnam, reinforced perceptions of a widespread retreat from Asia. Second, high threat perceptions regarding the Soviet military buildup during the period made Japan feel even more vulnerable to U.S. retrenchment.[67] Third, Carter's lack of advance consultations on such a major policy decision rattled faith in the United States as a trusted ally. Fueling this anxiety was an underlying feeling in Tokyo (as well as in Seoul) that the Carter administration was neglecting the region and focusing priorities on Europe. This was manifest in policy statements by top administration officials omitting any mention of the Asian theater. The Japanese were very troubled, for example, by the fact that even though the Korea pullout plan was one of Carter's first and most controversial policies in Asia, he turned down the offer of a CIA briefing on Korea upon taking office and rarely attended NSC sessions on Korea during his presidency.[68] The Japanese were equally troubled by admissions by National Security Advisor Brzezinski in a March 21, 1978, *New York Times* interview that the administration had largely ignored Asian problems in its first year in office.[69] Such behavior not only disheartened Tokyo in its aspirations for intimate relations with Washington but also heightened skepticism at U.S. attempts to reassure allies of its credibility.

Finally, the Carter plan engendered a number of unattractive scenarios for Japanese security policy. American withdrawal from Korea meant that Japan could no longer buckpass defense concerns to the United States and would be forced to bear a greater share of the defense burden in the region. Moreover, it raised the specter of renewed hostilities on the peninsula, which, in turn, forced Japan to contend with difficult issues concerning conventional rearmament and nuclearization. Renewed Korean hostilities would also raise the dreaded problem of stemming massive inflows of Korean refugees.[70]

From this confluence of anxieties arose acute expressions of U.S. abandonment. Vice-President Walter Mondale informed the Japanese of the pullout decision during his February 1977 trip to Tokyo. As a *Yomiuri* newspaper correspondent who covered the trip recalled, the government's formal reaction (*tatemae*) was subdued support for the plan, saying the issue was a United States-ROK bilateral concern. However, its actual views (*honae*) were far less positive.[71] As early as 1976 both Prime Minister Miki and Foreign Minister Kosaka Zentaro publicly expressed apprehension at Carter's campaign pledges on Korea.[72] According to a U.S. intelligence officer, Prime Minister Fukuda Takeo's "face dropped" when news of the withdrawal decision first reached him.[73] In a January 1977 *Newsweek* interview, Fukuda cautioned that a U.S. pullout from Korea would be "particularly unwise," and during Mondale's visit the next month he reiterated that the Carter plan could have potentially devastating repercussions on the regional balance of power.[74]

As a former Japanese defense attaché recalled, the finality of Carter's withdrawal plans especially disturbed Tokyo. Unlike past U.S. troop reductions, Carter's called for a complete and relatively immediate pullout within four or five years.[75] In response, JDA white papers for 1976, 1977, and 1978 highlighted Korea as "one of the highest threat areas in the world in terms of military tension" and urged a continued American presence.[76] In addition, a number of Japanese defense officials in uncharacteristic fashion openly opposed the plan. In 1977 former SDF Chief Minister Sakata forewarned that a U.S. pullout would have a severe psychological impact on its Asian allies. Vice Defense Minister Maruyama Takashi and former Vice Defense Minister Kubo Takuya flatly called for the plan's postponement, stating that the withdrawals, if implemented, would necessitate a wholesale review of Japanese security policy.[77]

The outspoken nature of Japan's response to the Carter plan starkly contrasted with its normally reticent response to defense issues. The plan sparked a national debate on the normally taboo topic of security among the public and press, with the common reaction being that Carter was "cutting Japan's lifeline."[78] Nowhere were these fears better illustrated than in *Yomiuri* and *Asahi* newspaper polls in early 1978 that found only 19–20 percent of the general public expressing confidence in U.S. defense commitments to Japan.[79] After meetings with Premier Ohira Masayoshi, Foreign Minister Sonoda Sunao, and Defense Minister Yamashita Ganri, a January 1979 study group led by Senator Sam Nunn confirmed the unprecedented severity and unanimity of Japanese opposition to the Carter plan.[80] Additional trips by other U.S. leaders reinforced this view. Representative Stephen Solarz's remarks were particularly illustrative in this regard:

As someone who supported . . . [the Carter plan] on the basis of what was then the intelligence assessment with respect to the indigenous balance of power on the Korean peninsula . . . I was struck by the fact that even in what was perceived to be a relatively acceptable indigenous balance of power on the Korean peninsula, the Japanese nonetheless seemed to be quite disturbed over the president's plan to withdraw troops.[81]

The Renewal of Cooperation, 1975–1979

The reemergence of mutually shared fears of U.S. abandonment pressed Seoul and Tokyo to improve relations significantly from the friction-filled 1972–74 period. A discussion of Japan-ROK interaction in these years is best divided into two subperiods. The first, from 1975 to 1976, saw bilateral cooperation emerge largely in response to the events in Indochina. The second period of cooperation, from 1977 to 1979, came in response to the Carter plan. The enhancement of relations in the earlier period was manifest in: (1) the "new" Korea clause, (2) political reconciliation between Tokyo and Seoul, (3) a revival of economic ties, and (4) convergent attitudes toward North Korea.

THE "NEW" KOREA CLAUSE

As an analyst of the period stated: "After the [Vietnam] war came to its dramatic end, it was openly feared in South Korea, Japan, [and] other countries of Asia . . . that what happened in South Vietnam would next befall South Korea."[82] It was these anxieties that gave rise to a consolidation of relations between Seoul and Tokyo in the "new" Korea clause. In meetings with Ford and Kissinger in April 1975 and with ROK Premier Kim Jong-pil the following May, Prime Minister Miki stated that Japan would no longer view Tanaka's 1974 reinterpretation of the clause as relevant.[83] Influential elder statesmen, such as LDP Vice-

President Shiina Etsusaburo, also reiterated these views, thereby affirming to their South Korean counterparts Japan's ruling party's support for Miki's views.[84] This turnabout in policy culminated with meetings between Foreign Ministers Miyazawa and Kim Dong-jo in July 1975 and with the Ford-Miki summit the following August, where Japan officially stated the revised version of the clause:

The security of the Republic of Korea is essential to the maintenance of peace on the Korean peninsula, which in turn is necessary for peace and security in East Asia, including Japan.[85]

The phrasing effectively marked a return to the original 1969 version, stating a direct defense link between the two quasi allies. Although the wording was not identical with Sato Eisaku's version,[86] the operational meaning of the statement remained the same. By reestablishing a direct security link with the ROK, Miki reaffirmed Japan's commitment to allow American access to bases in Okinawa for ROK defense.[87] Miyazawa made clear Japan's support for this arrangement in statements after the summit, as did SDF Chief Sakata in security talks with Schlesinger during the same month.[88]

Strongly opposed to Tanaka's 1974 revision of the Korea clause, the ROK government welcomed Tokyo's new cooperative attitude and sought to reciprocate the reaffirmation of security ties. In meetings with Ford officials in August 1975, Park put forth the idea that Japan should be included in any security dialogue on Korea. In interviews with the *New York Times* (August 1975) and the *Mainichi Shimbun* (November 1975) the South Korean president elaborated that, despite the absence of a bilateral defense treaty between Japan and the ROK, the two states nevertheless had a "special" security relationship stemming from their common alliance with the United States; as a result, he supported consolidation of triangular defense ties. Moreover, in private conversations with Tokyo officials Park reportedly was amenable even to expanding direct Japan-ROK dialogue on defense issues.[89] Interviews with top-level South Korean government officials by an American study group in 1977–78 echoed these sentiments. These officials expressed avid interest in discussion of defense issues not just through the United States, but on a bilateral basis as well.[90]

These examples of cooperation are even more striking given two additional considerations. On the Japanese side Miki and Miyazawa haled from the liberal wing of the LDP. Miki, in particular, had never previously supported the 1969 Korea clause and had been an advocate of dissociating Japan from hard-line anticommunist policies. In the late 1960s Miki was, in fact, one of the first faction leaders to support normalization with China and severance of relations with Taiwan. His taking a pro-South Korean line on the new Korea clause, more typical of the conservative wing of the LDP, therefore marked a definitive shift from past policies.[91] On the Korean side collective memories of past colonial aggression made any endorsement of a greater Japanese security role in Korea anathema to the national conscience. Given the nation's historical disdain for its neighbor, Park's urging of security ties with Japan was therefore unprecedented. The extent to which such taboo notions had become part of the everyday agenda was reflected in a progovernment newspaper editorial's prognosis of relations prior to the eighth annual joint ministerial conference, scheduled for September 1975:

Notably in view of the fact that Japan is under the protection of the U.S. nuclear umbrella and that she wants American troops to remain in Korea, Korea and Japan may well reach an agreement to establish a cooperative security posture through earnest dialogue. Korea-Japan security cooperation is indispensable to cope with communist expansion in Asia.[92]

It should be noted that a motive behind Park's statements was to gain additional economic aid as a form of Japanese security cooperation. Nevertheless, the couching of such requests in the language of openness toward bilateral defense links with Tokyo was unprecedented.

POLITICAL RECONCILIATION

Seoul and Tokyo also sought to shore up diplomatic ties severely crippled after disputes during the 1972–74 period. In policy speeches in the Diet in January 1975, Premier Miki singled out the ROK as one country with which Japan needed to improve relations. After the April 1975 North Vietnamese victory, Miyazawa formally set out this policy of reconciliation with Seoul:

In the past year or so there have been several unhappy developments in Japanese-Republic of Korea relations, but the importance of close Japanese-Republic of Korea relations in our foreign policy has not diminished at all. Our government sincerely hopes that there will be peace and stability on the Korean peninsula. Our government also intends to make greater efforts to improve friendly relations with the Republic of Korea.[93]

Miyazawa reiterated in a major policy address to the foreign press the following July that ROK security was of "great concern" to Japan and that Japan would "strengthen and deepen" relations with its neighbor.[94] Reciprocating this change in attitude, South Korean Foreign Minister Kim Dong-jo emerged from meetings with top Japanese officials the same month stating that the avoidance of harping on the unhappy past was now a priority.[95]

Accordingly, the two governments made mighty efforts at resolving disputes outstanding from the earlier period. May 1975 meetings between Miki and Kim Jong-pil produced an agreement to reinstate the annual joint ministerial conferences, suspended since 1973,[96] and subsequent meetings of the conference were marked by an atmosphere of congeniality. The eighth conference in 1975 was especially significant not only because it was the first in more than twenty-one months but also for a number of equally important reasons. It constituted the first meeting between the two sides since the turn of events in Vietnam. It marked the tenth anniversary of normalized relations. And it took place at the conclusion of Japan's initial program of economic assistance, begun in 1965 and ending with the ROK's third five-year development plan (1972–76). Using the adage "the soil firms up after a long rain," the head of the Japanese delegation, Fukuda Takeo, stated in his opening remarks that the past two years of friction between Tokyo and Seoul, while intense, would only make future relations stronger. Foreign Ministers Kim Dong-jo and Miyazawa also declared that increased triangular defense cooperation was of paramount importance given the region's uncertain security environment, and in this vein Japan promised renewed economic support for the ROK's fourth economic development plan (1977–81) and later provided a substantial loan for expansion of the Korean steel industry.[97] Joint communiqués for the ninth and tenth conferences, in September 1977 and September 1978, also contained clauses expressing "deep satisfaction" with the recent improvement in relations and stressed the criticality of continued "close, intimate cooperation" between the two countries for regional stability.[98] Such remarks represented a significant change from the combative atmosphere that had pervaded bilateral meetings from 1972 to 1974.

The governments undertook efforts to revive other channels of political dialogue as well. In June 1975 Seoul established the Federation of Japan-South Korea Diet Members. This binational group replaced the Friendship Society of Japan-ROK Legislators, which had largely become ineffective after the Kim Dae-jung and Mun Se-kwang affairs. The new federation's mandate was to promote improved ties between the two legislatures and to coordinate policy positions on North Korea. Meet-

ings between opposition parliamentarians during the period also
stressed the "closely interwoven" nature of Japan-ROK security and
political ties, thereby showing suprapartisan support for bilateral cooperation in both countries.[99] In addition, other semiofficial binational
groups, such as the Japan-Korea Cooperation Committee (composed of
elder statesmen and business leaders), criticized the previous Tanaka
government's policy of equidistance between the two Koreas as
"irresponsible" and reaffirmed their support of the South.[100]

In addition to proactive cooperation, the two governments sought to
downplay friction over potentially inflammatory issues. This was particularly evident in four instances. The first concerned Tokto/Takeshima
Island. Located between Korea and Japan, the island has been claimed
historically by each government as its rightful territory. Composed of
two half-submerged rock outcroppings, Tokto has no natural resources
or strategic value other than as a docking point for fisherman. Despite
this, nationalist sentiment was so strong that the two governments could
not reach an amicable settlement in the 1965 normalization treaty and
left the issue unresolved.[101] During the 1975–79 period territorial disputes over Tokto resurfaced, stirring up intense irredentist and emotional animosities between the two nations, yet Seoul and Tokyo dealt
with the problem with a conspicuous absence of protest or inflammatory language.[102]

The second issue concerned fishing rights. In August 1975 Japan concluded a fisheries agreement with China. This had potential for friction
between Seoul and Tokyo. First, the delineation of territorial waters was
a delicate issue among the regional powers as all had thriving fishery industries. In the case of Japan and the ROK this had been the last and
most contested issue under negotiation prior to conclusion of the 1965
normalization treaty.[103] Skirting the historical sensitivities surrounding
this issue, Tokyo did not show the courtesy of consulting Seoul prior to
its agreement with Beijing. Second, the Japan-China agreement extended to portions of the Yellow and East China seas. This potentially
imposed on Korean fishing waters off the southern and western coasts
of the peninsula. And third, the ROK had protested several incidents involving Chinese harassment and detainment of ROK fishing expeditions
during the period. A Tokyo-Beijing agreement consequently undermined
Seoul's efforts at gaining Japanese support in opposing Chinese actions.
Again, in the interests of maintaining cooperative relations, ROK
authorities raised only minor protests over the issue.[104]

The third issue concerned past diplomatic disputes. In February 1975 the ROK granted clemency to the two Japanese students, Tachikawa Masaki and Hayakawa Yoshiharu, sentenced to twenty years' imprisonment in 1974 for anti-Yusin activities. The case had raised a myriad of contentious issues regarding activities of pro-North Korean groups in Japan and draconian violations of foreign nationals' civil rights. Park's explicit rationale for the release of the students was the positive effect he hoped it would have on bilateral relations. Miyazawa thanked Park for removing a persistent "trouble spot" in relations and rescinded Japanese protests over the case, asserting that the trial had indeed been a fair one. These statements marked a complete reversal of the Japanese and Korean positions during the trial the previous year, providing further evidence of concentrated efforts at mending relations.[105]

Finally, the two governments sought to resolve outstanding issues related to the Kim Dae-jung kidnapping. In July 1975 Miyazawa met with Park officials in Seoul, and in a *note verbale* agreed to drop charges against the ROK embassy's first secretary, Kim Tong-won, for his involvement in the affair. In return, the ROK reaffirmed its pledge not to bring charges against Kim Dae-jung for any antigovernment activities conducted in Japan.[106] Upon returning to Tokyo, Miyazawa declared that the closing of the Kim Dae-jung case officially brought Japan-ROK relations back to "normalcy."[107]

In retrospect, this constituted a significant effort at cooperation by Seoul and Tokyo. Park and Miki faced strong internal criticism, charging each with capitulating on the settlement. On the Japanese side Tokyo had conclusive evidence implicating Kim Tong-won and during the dispute in 1973 had vehemently protested Seoul's denial of the first secretary's guilt.[108] By dropping the issue, Miyazawa essentially absolved the ROK government from any legal responsibility for the kidnapping. On the South Korean side the agreement not to hold Kim Dae-jung responsible for antigovernment activities in Japan amounted to a tacit acceptance of Japanese intervention in a ROK domestic matter. This was a point on which the South Koreans had remained fiercely intransigent in 1973. Moreover, the Park government accepted without protest Tokyo's requests for Kim Tong-won's dismissal despite the government's maintaining his innocence throughout the affair. This cooperative behavior reflected both governments' desire to consolidate relations in the face of U.S. disengagement from the region. As Fukuda stated in reference to the settlement at the eighth annual joint ministerial conference: "The world is yet to see peace and stability. In this situation closer Japanese-Republic of Korea cooperation is all the more important."[109]

ECONOMIC REJUVENATION

At the end of the detente era, linkage between Japan-ROK political disputes and economic relations caused economic ties at the government level to reach an all-time low. This situation was completely reversed in the 1975–79 period. At the eighth and ninth annual joint ministerial conferences the two governments agreed to reinstate Japanese participation in aid, loan, and investment programs for the ROK. In line with this, Tokyo provided government credits for the fourth South Korean five-year economic development plan (1977–81) and various loans for ROK heavy industry and infrastructural projects. These agreements effectively nullified the 1973 suspension of such funds as a result of protests over the Kim Dae-jung affair.

An upturn in economic relations, reminiscent of the 1969–71 period, ensued. In August 1975 agreements were reached on a 12.5-billion-yen government loan for the development of South Korean port facilities and an 11-billion-yen low-interest, long-term Export-Import Bank (EIB) loan for agricultural industries.[110] The following month Japan provided another $300 million in EIB loans to finance the third expansion of the P'ohang Steel Complex, the flagship of Japan-ROK economic cooperation in the 1969–71 period.[111] In addition, in February 1977 the two governments concluded three major loan agreements totaling over 30 billion yen for the South Korean infrastructural, energy, and agricultural sectors.[112] Tokyo also supported South Korean loan applications to international organizations such as the International Bank for Reconstruction and Development and the Asian Development Bank.[113]

Similar improvements occurred in the private sector. During the 1972–74 period acute bilateral friction emerged over Japanese firms that had: (1) abandoned the ROK market for China in accordance with the Zhou principles and (2) expanded trade with North Korea. Both problems largely dissipated during the 1975–79 period. In June 1975 Uemura Kogoro led a *zaikai* (big-business) mission to Seoul and agreed to major aid and investment programs for South Korean chemical and other heavy industries. In addition, the Japan-ROK Economic Cooperation Committee meetings during the period were well attended with few Japanese business leaders absent or represented by proxies, as had been the case in the years of detente. Moreover, the ROK delegation abstained from protests over the companies that continued to boycott the meetings or maintain trade with the North.[114]

INTERACTION OVER NORTH KOREA

Cooperation between Seoul and Tokyo was especially evident with regard to North Korea. During the preceding period the ROK registered vocal protests over the growth in Japanese-North Korean trade; however, during the 1975–79 period these complaints disappeared. This was largely the result of a stagnation in Tokyo-Pyongyang trade. While the detente years saw bilateral trade multiply more than sixfold, total trade for the 1975–79 period increased by only 73 percent (see Appendix Table A.2). This decline correlated with Japanese security anxieties over the U.S. retreat from Vietnam and the announcement of the Carter plan. Total bilateral trade dropped from a high of $376 million in 1974 to $199 million in 1977 with Japanese imports falling from $98 million to $61 million and exports from $277 million to $138 million. Pyongyang's delaying repayment of debts to Japan during the period was certainly one cause for the decline in trade; however, the decline was also motivated by business leaders' desires not to alienate Seoul further. Two manifestations of this were the powerful zaikai group's canceling of a trade mission to Pyongyang and the Miki government's decision to suspend sales of heavy-industrial plant and equipment to the North in 1975.[115]

The expansion of Japan's political contacts with Pyongyang had also been a prominent source of friction between Tokyo and Seoul in the detente years. However, during the 1975–79 period the Miki and Fukuda governments substantially decreased contacts with the North. For example, JDA Chief Yamanaka Sadanori publicly stated that Japan was in no position to assess North Korean military intentions on the peninsula. This effectively nullified the highly controversial statements made in August 1974 by Tanaka's foreign minister, Kimura Toshio, averring that Japan did not perceive a security threat from North Korea. In November 1976 former JDA Vice-Minister Kubo Takuya reaffirmed Yamanaka's views by stating that the potential for a North Korean "miscalculation," that is, an invasion of the South, was still very real. Japan's ambassador to the ROK, Nishiyama Akira, showed the Gaimushō's (foreign ministry's) support for this position in July 1975 with statements to the effect that Japan should not be fooled by North Korean propaganda and that it was "singularly important" for Japan to deter the northern threat. In response to Kimura's other controversial statements implying Japanese de facto recognition of the legitimacy of the North Korean regime, the Miki government declared unreservedly that it had no intention of normalizing relations with Pyongyang.[116]

These changes in Japan's orientation toward the North were clearly a function of increased fears of U.S. abandonment. The demise of detente, fall of Saigon, and prospect of a new United States president who intended to withdraw the American military presence from Korea caused the Miki government to become increasingly anxious about renewed North Korean aggression. The following passage by a Japanese analyst illustrates these perceptions:

If the United States, by abandoning Indochina, gave the world the impression that it would also leave Korea, the allies' confidence would fast decline. . . . It would be a matter of grave concern if an American pullout from the Republic of Korea should lead to a "misunderstanding" on the part of North Korea that the United States had virtually given up its commitment to the Republic of Korea, resulting in reinforcement of the North's willingness for aggression against the South.[117]

A *Yomiuri* correspondent who accompanied a Japanese political delegation to Pyongyang in 1975 confirmed these views. Many of the LDP officials on this trip voiced concern that North Korea was more menacing given the North Vietnamese victory and the Carter plan and expressed skepticism at assurances to the contrary by Pyongyang officials.[118]

As a result of these abandonment fears Japan took two additional actions against the North in 1975. In May the government discontinued the use of EIB funds for financing trade with North Korea. Following this, it instituted restrictions against activities of the Chosen Soren in Japan.[119] Accordingly, the LDP executive board in late 1974 undertook a study on anti-ROK political activity in Japan. Among measures taken by the government as a result of the study were restrictions on activities associated with the organization's twentieth-anniversary celebration and the denial of entry visas to foreign delegations' seeking participation in the event.

The Park government had demanded the disbanding of this organization for its involvement in subversive activities throughout the 1972–74 period. In July 1975 foreign ministerial meetings between Kim Dong-jo and Miyazawa, Japan provided a note verbale promising to give the problem greater attention.[120] While subsequent restrictions by Tokyo did not go to the extreme of banning the organization, the actions did acknowledge for the first time that the Chosen Soren was a political organization tied to Pyongyang rather than a independent Korean residents' body in Japan.

These were subtle but important acts of allegiance to the ROK. The decision on EIB funds expunged the notion prevalent in the 1972–74 period that such funds represented the government's de facto endorsement of trade with North Korea.[121] In announcing its decision to suspend the export of heavy-industrial plant equipment to the North in 1975, the government cited trepidations about the role such exports could play in enhancing Pyongyang's war potential. Deputy Foreign Minister Togo Fumihiko, in addresses to Japanese business groups, also discouraged private-sector trade with North Korea as upsetting to the balance of power on the peninsula. Moreover, both of these policies were undertaken at a time when Japan was *increasing* trade with other Communist states, particularly North Vietnam.[122]

Cooperation in the Face of the Carter Plan

The Carter plan prompted both the Japanese and ROK governments to continue efforts, begun in 1975 and 1976, to consolidate bilateral relations. Cooperation in these years took three general forms: (1) joint opposition to the troop pullout plan, (2) the absence of friction between Tokyo and Seoul over potentially contentious issues, and (3) greater bilateral dialogue on security issues.

As soon as Carter's campaign pledges on Korea became established U.S. policy, Japan and the ROK closed ranks in opposition to the plan. As the Japanese ambassador to Seoul recalled from his conversations with Park, both he and the ROK president shared a "deep displeasure" over Carter's unilateral decision.[123] At the ninth and tenth annual joint ministerial conferences, in 1977 and 1978, both delegations placed defense, rather than economic, issues at the top of the agenda and stressed that their joint security hinged on the U.S. troop presence in Korea.[124] Conference joint communiqués stated that the Japanese delegation had a strong "interest" (*kwansim*) in and paid "close attention" (*yuŭihada*) to South Korean explanations of the plan. Such statements not only broke from the practice of not mentioning third parties in bilateral talks but also made clear that the Carter plan was not simply a United States-ROK issue but one that bore directly on Japanese interests as well. The only time that the United States had been mentioned in such a manner before was in the communiqués during the 1969–71 period following the Nixon doctrine and withdrawal of the Seventh Infantry Division from Korea (see Chapter 3). In addition, in "demanding" that the Carter plan not be harmful to the two nations' security, the communiqués used the word *myŏnghada* (demand) rather than the more indirect expression *kyŏnhaerŭl malhada* (expressed opinion). The choice of stronger language reflected the intensity of the two governments' abandonment fears.[125]

Furthermore, a number of prominent Japanese officials spoke out on behalf of the ROK against Carter's policies. The Japanese ambassador to the United States, Togo Fumihiko, issued numerous public statements to the effect that U.S. ground troops in Korea singularly represented America's defense commitment to its Asian allies.[126] These remarks were repeated by the LDP security affairs council, led by former SDF Chief Sakata.[127] In a November 1976 *Newsweek* interview, Foreign Minister Kosaka opposed the plan and cautioned that it could lead to a dangerous power vacuum that would be threatening not only to Korea but also to Japan.[128] In addition, in February 1977 just prior to Vice-President Mondale's trip to Tokyo, the newly formed Japan-ROK Parliamentary Federation sent a letter to Carter saying any American withdrawals risked destabilizing the Korean peninsula. During his visit Mondale was presented with a petition opposing the withdrawal signed by members of the Diet and the Fukuda cabinet.[129] This was a striking act by the Japanese given that the vice-president's visit was meant to be the forum in which the plan would be formally announced in Asia.

Cooperation between Seoul and Tokyo over the Carter plan was also evident in the *absence* of friction. In particular, two major issues arose that potentially threatened bilateral relations. The first was the Koreagate scandal, which involved South Korean attempts to illicitly influence members of the United States Congress. While this was a U.S.-ROK bilateral concern, in the course of the investigations Korean officials implicated Japan in the scandal. In congressional testimony former KCIA chief Kim Hyung-wook explicitly stated that similar South Korean bribery practices were used with members of the LDP in Japan.[130] A former ROK public information officer, Lee Jae-hyon, made similar statements to the American and Japanese press. U.S. officials subsequently discovered that Korean influence-buying networks in Japan existed on a far larger scale than those in the United States and extended portions of the Koreagate investigations to Japan.[131] These revelations were both embarrassing and debilitating to the Japanese government's already tarnished image in both domestic and international circles as a result of the Lockheed scandal.[132]

The second issue was the *nikkan yuchaku* (Japan-Korea adhesion) controversy. Partly a result of the Koreagate revelations, this movement among the Japanese media, opposition parties, and liberal wing of the

LDP charged the government with profiting from illicit ties with Korean businesses, government, and the KCIA. When Fukuda, who had been known for his conservative, pro-South Korean policies, took office in December 1976, he faced immediate accusations of having such improper ties with the ROK. The Diet held special investigations into nikkan yuchaku in December 1977, and sentiment was so strong that it resulted in the blocking of various pieces of pro-South Korean legislation in the Diet.[133]

The Koreagate revelations and the nikkan yuchaku controversy therefore put tremendous pressure on Premier Fukuda to temper his ties with the ROK. While it was in Japanese interests to oppose the Carter plan, these two controversies should have made Fukuda much less willing to exhibit vocal and visible allegiance to South Korea in lobbying against the pullout plan. Such blatant support for Seoul would only confirm accusations of Japan-ROK adhesion and fuel the domestic opposition.

In spite of these pressures Fukuda maintained cooperation with the ROK. He did not raise protests over the Koreagate revelations; moreover, he played an instrumental role in opposing the Carter plan. During Mondale's February 1977 visit to Japan, Fukuda called for a compensatory military-aid package for the ROK in the event of troop withdrawals. At the March 1977 Carter-Fukuda summit the Japanese premier urged Carter to opt for a phased "reduction" of troops over the long-term rather than a complete withdrawal over four to five years. In May 1978 Fukuda again pressed Washington not to commence with force reductions on the peninsula and reiterated the need for compensatory aid and arms and equipment transfers to the ROK.[134]

These efforts were effective in influencing U.S. policy. Fukuda's insistence on compensatory aid for the ROK was critical in motivating U.S. officials to add such a package to the final terms of the pullout plan.[135] In addition, Japan's uncharacteristically outspoken reaction was one of the key factors behind Carter's eventual suspension of the plan. Japan's strategic importance to the United States generally accorded its views great weight. Washington also saw Tokyo's assessment and concerns as rational and those of the ROK as self-serving and emotional.

Fukuda's efforts did not go unappreciated by the South Koreans. Seoul's own lobbying abilities were emasculated as a result of the Koreagate investigations. In addition, friction over the Park regime's human rights violations increasingly impaired relations with the Carter administration. The government therefore viewed Tokyo's support as crucial.[136] This was confirmed by the Japanese ambassador to the United States at that time, Yasukawa Takeshi, who recalled that ROK officials in Washington expressed their concerns about the pullout plan on numerous occasions and appreciated Japanese efforts at prevailing upon the Americans not to carry it out.[137]

Although the accuracy of historical counterfactuals is difficult to ascertain, one can with reasonable certainty surmise that had Seoul's implication of Japan in the Koreagate hearings and the nikkan yuchaku controversy taken place in a period when U.S. disengagement was not salient, the likely outcome would have been Japan-ROK friction. Instead, the overarching fear of U.S. abandonment in Tokyo and Seoul during the 1975–79 period caused the two governments to put aside these inflammatory issues and opt for cooperation.

Another by-product of these overarching security anxieties was positive changes in Japan's overall image of the ROK. Since the Kim Dae-jung kidnapping in 1973 the Japanese media had been extremely critical of the Park regime's authoritarian practices and human rights abuses. These critical reports reinforced the general public's negative images of Korea.[138] As the Carter plan raised public debate within Japan on security issues, however, the tone of reporting on Korea changed substantially. The media was replete with laudatory reports on South Korean economic growth as well as stories on the ROK defense industry and military capabilities.[139] This new attitude was also evident in the aftermath of Park's assassination.[140] In statements made after the incident Foreign Minister Sonoda stressed the importance of continuing stable relations with the successor government. In addition, Sonoda urged the public not to harp on the negative aspects of South Korean politics and instead to respond with "flexibility and understanding" to the fluid situation in Seoul.[141]

These trends toward cooperation culminated in 1978 and 1979 with two events unprecedented in Japan-ROK relations. In 1978 two visits to Seoul by former JDA heads led to the establishment of the Joint Parliamentary Security Consultative Council. Composed of Diet and National Assembly members, this body served as the first formal intergovernmental forum on security issues. This group's mandate was to coordinate views and increase the transparency of the two nations' defense policies. This was followed in 1979 by a series of exchange visits by senior-level defense officials. In April General Kim Jong-whan, in his official capacity as ROK chairman of the joint chiefs of staff, accepted an invitation from the Japanese Defense Agency to tour Japanese military facilities. In

May Chief of the Ground Self-Defense Forces, General Nagano Shigeto, reciprocated General Kim's visit with inspections of ROK forward military bases and tours of defense industry complexes.[142]

Finally, in July 1979, JDA Director-General Yamashita Ganri paid an official visit to Seoul at the invitation of the Park government. This was the first visit by a cabinet-level Japanese defense official to Seoul in the postwar era. Yamashita received a national service decoration; moreover, in a gesture of support for ROK security the director-general toured the infiltration tunnels excavated at the DMZ by the North Koreans. During these meetings the two governments committed to expand military exchanges, participate regularly in U.S.-led joint defense exercises, develop cooperative arrangements on the production of military hardware, establish joint early warning systems, and exchange visits of warships. There were also reported sharing some military intelligence and technology.[143]

As former defense attachés concurred, these activities marked the first serious step in the promotion of direct Japan-Korea interaction on security issues.[144] The visits by Nagano and Yamashita marked the only time since the occupation that Japanese military personnel entered Korea in their official capacity. Moreover, that the South Koreans, despite historical animosities, allowed these individuals to visit Korea represented a significant sign of cooperation. As an analyst of the period agreed, the single most decisive factor in this upswing in security contacts was anxiety over the Carter plan.[145] The historical significance of these events was apparent:

These were clear signs that the two countries were moving toward closer cooperation on security matters. Japanese-South Korean relations had come a long way since the days of the Korean War, when President Syngman Rhee had threatened to conclude a truce with the North Korean communists to repel any Japanese troops that might set foot on Korean soil—even if they were sent to provide support for South Korea.[146]

The latter half of the 1970s therefore provides plausible evidence of the explanatory power of the quasi-alliance dynamic in Japan-ROK-United States relations. As was the case during the 1969–71 period, convergent perceptions of U.S. disengagement provided the overarching security imperative that compelled Tokyo and Seoul to seek greater bilateral cooperation. This behavior stood in marked contrast to the intervening 1972–74 detente years, when divergent threat perceptions and asymmetrical abandonment/entrapment structures resulted in contentious interaction. The 1969–71 and 1975–79 periods also reveal the counterintuitive nature of interaction in the Japan-ROK-United States alliance triangle. Although U.S. policy has always been to promote better relations between its two key East Asian allies, this has historically obtained only when the United States, for reasons related to domestic politics and the costs of overextension, shows ambivalence in its commitments to the region. In this sense Japan-ROK cooperation is something of an unintended consequence of U.S. disinterest.

As Japan-ROK relations entered the 1980s, however, this new-found cooperation proved short-lived. The counterintuitive link between bilateral cooperation and U.S. disengagement on the one hand and between bilateral friction and U.S. engagement on the other would again become salient as a new American president, Ronald Reagan, took office with a wholly different security vision for East Asia.

SIX

The 1980s: Evolution and Friction During the Reagan Years

I N   T H E   1 9 8 0 S Ronald Reagan assumed the presidency with a mandate to reestablish American global strength and stature. In Asia this "peace through strength" message translated into a reaffirmation of defense commitments to U.S. allies. Reagan's invitation to ROK President Chun Doo-hwan as one of his first official state guests in 1981 and his explicit assurances that U.S. combat forces would remain indefinitely in Korea were strong pronouncements of this policy. The message also rang clearly in Japan, where the administration's initiatives for a deepening strategic relationship with Japan, coupled with the development of a personal rapport between Reagan and Premier Nakasone Yasuhiro, engendered a new, intimate partnership that the Japanese had long desired. These actions reestablished U.S. credibility in the region and effectively supplanted fears of U.S. abandonment prevalent in Seoul and Tokyo during the Jimmy Carter years.

Concurrent with these developments Japan-ROK bilateral relations experienced a number of watershed events. In 1983 the two countries held summit talks for the first time in the history of normalized relations; in 1984 Emperor Hirohito offered a historic public apology for Japan's past aggression against Korea; and economic interdependence during the period was highlighted by the conclusion of an unprecedented $4-billion-loan agreement. These developments led many to herald the start of a new era of cooperation in bilateral relations.

The confluence of these two trends appears to pose an anomaly for the argument advanced by the quasi-alliance model, according to which decreased fears of U.S. abandonment in the 1980s should have given rise to *contentious*, not cooperative behavior between Japan and the ROK. This chapter addresses the 1980s in Japan-ROK relations in the context of this apparent inconsistency between the empirical evidence and the quasi-alliance argument. It first establishes that the Reagan years were indeed a period of decreased concerns about U.S. resolve for Japan and the ROK. It then argues that a closer look at Japan-ROK bilateral behavior during the period raises questions as to whether relations were truly as congenial as they have been popularly depicted. This analysis does not deny that certain watershed events instantiated a positive evolution of Japan-ROK relations but argues that a focus solely on these developments obscures significant evidence of contentious behavior over very substantive issues. This friction and the inability to overcome it can be explained in part by the model's predictions.

Peace Through Strength

The election of Ronald Reagan in 1980 ushered in a sea change in U.S. foreign policy. The Soviet Union's military buildup, coupled with its refusal to withdraw from Afghanistan, made clear the hollowness of the previous administration's aspirations for a renewal of detente. For Reagan the pursuit of cooperative resolutions to superpower disputes was still the objective; however, the means of achieving this required a new approach.[1] As Reagan stated in a foreign-policy address to Congress, the source of the problem was the drift and complacency into which America's global leadership had fallen:

The failure to maintain our military capabilities and our economic strength in the 1970's was as important as any other single factor in encouraging Soviet expansionism. By reviving both of them in the 1980's we deny our adversaries opportunities and deter aggression. . . . [The American people] want an effective foreign policy, which shapes events in accordance with our ideals and does not just react, passively and timidly, to the actions of others.[2]

Out of these convictions grew a clear strategic and ideological vision for U.S. foreign policy. The Soviet Union was no longer a misunderstood adversary that could be coaxed into mutual accommodation with the United States, but an inherently "evil empire," best deterred by the overwhelming and unchallengeable disposition of U.S. power.[3] America would reclaim strength and confidence through achieving, not parity, but across-the-board military superiority over its rivals. It would reassert leadership through the reaffirmation and extension of security commitments to both traditional allies and anticommunist insurgencies.[4]

Reagan's vision was distinguishable from the previous administration's in several ways. First, his administration explicitly dropped Carter's "weaker is stronger" rhetoric and under the new mantle of peace through strength, embarked on a massive rearmament program. During Reagan's first term defense spending increased in real terms by 32 percent, from $199 billion to $264 billion. This constituted an unprecedented peacetime increase from 5.2 percent to 6.6 percent of total GNP. The Reagan brain trust pressed for weapons programs such as the MX and Trident II missiles and the Strategic Defense Initiative (SDI) and held off on arms control dialogue like Intermediate-Range Nuclear Forces and Strategic Arms Reduction Talks. These policies reflected the belief that a strategic counterforce doctrine and offensive conventional-force capabilities would provide the United States with the escalation dominance at all levels of warfare necessary to deter the Soviets.[5]

Second, Reagan rejected the notion that Third World conflicts were outside the arena of direct superpower competition and instead expanded the U.S. defense mission into the periphery. This meant not only containing Soviet-backed revolutionary movements but also actively rolling back communism through support of rebel insurgencies and direct U.S. intervention. American actions in Grenada, Nicaragua, Libya, and Afghanistan were testament to this new policy.[6]

Finally, in a marked departure from policy during the Carter years Reagan placed less emphasis on a nation's human rights record as a condition of U.S. support. As advocated by officials such as United Nations Ambassador Jeane Kirkpatrick and Secretary of State Alexander Haig, virtuous means and objective ends were two conduits of foreign policy that did not always converge in the real world. To lose track of the latter for the sake of the former was not in the interests of the United States. As a result Reagan was less averse than Carter to the support of loyal, staunchly anticommunist states with politically repressive domestic systems and proclaimed this at the outset of his presidency:

To those neighbors and allies who share our freedom, we will strengthen our historical ties and assure them of our support and firm commitment. We will match loyalty with loyalty. We will strive for mutually beneficial relations. We will not use our friendship to impose on their sovereignty, for our own sovereignty is not for sale.[7]

The objective of these policies was clear: to demonstrate to both allies and adversaries a definitive end to the era of American drift, decline, and disengagement.

Reaffirmation of the United States-ROK Alliance

The Reagan administration sought to regenerate relations with the ROK from their deteriorated state at the end of the 1970s. Unlike Carter, Reagan viewed the U.S. presence in Korea as neither an economic drain on the United States nor an impediment to tension reduction on the peninsula; instead, he saw the ROK as a loyal ally that had held the front-line in East Asia against the Soviet threat. Moreover, it was South Korea's embracing of anticommunist and capitalist ideals, rather than its human rights record, that took priority as the rationale for U.S. support.[8] For this reason administration officials invited Chun as one of the first heads of state for summit talks with Reagan in February 1981. The cordial atmosphere that pervaded their meeting contrasted starkly with the tense dialogue between Carter and Park Chung-hee in June 1979. In toasts and press statements Reagan highlighted the two nations' ideological affinities and called for a return to the deep bonds of alliance that had typified relations in the 1950s and 1960s.[9] The resulting joint communiqué used unusually explicit language to reaffirm U.S. alliance commitments and lay to rest any residual trepidations regarding the Carter plan.

President Reagan reaffirmed that the United States, as a Pacific power, will seek to ensure the peace and security of the region. ... President Reagan assured President Chun that the United States has no plans to withdraw US ground combat forces from the Korean peninsula.[10]

In additional symbols of support the United States resumed the previously suspended security consultative conferences (SCC) between defense departments and reinstituted Team Spirit joint military exercises.[11] Furthermore, to downplay Carter's emphasis on human rights in U.S. policy, Secretary Haig postponed release of a human rights report on the Chun regime until after the summit.[12]

The United States consistently reaffirmed these commitments in 1983 and 1985. In November 1983 Reagan personally inspected forces at the DMZ and standing in full view of the North, declared that American support for the ROK provided "vital protection against a system hostile to everything we believe in as Americans." Similarly, in a speech at the National Assembly the president further pledged: "Let me make one thing very plain. You are not alone, people of Korea. America is your friend and we are with you."[13] The clarity of these presidential statements contrasted unequivocally with the ambivalent pronouncements of the Carter years, further highlighting the new turn in U.S. policy.

The period also saw a steady stream of high-level State and Defense Department officials to the region to consolidate Reagan's commitments. Secretary of Defense Caspar Weinberger's pair of visits to Seoul in the span of just eight months, March and October 1982, were the most frequent by any defense secretary since the 1960s.[14]

In a major policy address in San Francisco in March 1983 newly appointed Secretary of State George Shultz clearly maintained that the American strategic vision for Asia focused priority on strong ties with traditional cold-war allies. Significantly his remarks constituted the first detailed policy statement on the region in six years and quelled Seoul's and Tokyo's nagging dread that Reagan might proceed along the path of past Republican administrations (not only that of Richard Nixon and his advisor Henry Kissinger but of Reagan himself during the tenure of Alexander Haig, Shultz's own predecessor), which emphasized pragmatic great-power diplomacy with China as the primary means of counterbalancing the Soviet threat rather than prioritizing relations with the ROK, Japan, and Taiwan.[15] As the June 1988 SCC communiqué stated, the U.S.-ROK alliance was firmly grounded under Reagan's stewardship; moreover, regarding the primary symbol of the alliance—the presence of U.S. ground troops—the United States would remain engaged "as long as the threat from North Korea continues and [the U.S. troop] presence is desired by the South Korean government and people."[16]

American policy initiatives and allied perceptions of such policies are, of course, two separate matters. In the latter vein Reagan was successful in greatly reducing South Korean fears of U.S. abandonment, prevalent during the preceding 1975–79 period. Although the ROK welcomed Carter's eventual shelving of the pullout plan with relief, the general drift and indecision that pervaded U.S. policies during those years caused many Koreans to yearn for a clearer, more assertive U.S. leadership role. Reagan's anticommunist fervor and his campaign promises to revitalize the American military effectively reduced lingering fears that tentative steps toward reengagement at the end of the Carter years might backslide under a new administration. As one senior ROK official remarked upon Reagan's election victory: "It took us three years to educate the Carter people in the realities of the security situation in the Korean peninsula. I think we are that much further ahead with Reagan already."[17]

The Reagan-Chun summit in 1981 was particularly important in this regard. Strongly supportive language in the joint communiqué left no doubt in South Korean minds that the United States fully appreciated and stood behind ROK defense efforts on the peninsula. The Korean premier also deeply appreciated the timing of the summit for domestic political reasons. Chun's wresting of power through a military coup after Park's October 1979 assassination, his subsequent imposition of martial law, and violent suppression of demonstrations in the southern city of Kwangju, had met with widespread charges of illegitimacy. Reagan's summit invitation was as powerful a symbol of United States-backed legitimacy for the regime, despite its authoritarian practices, as Chun could have hoped for.[18] As the ROK president stated upon his return from Washington: "My trip to the US has been both satisfactory and successful ... I can call the result of the visit a restoration of trust."[19] One knowledgeable observer more aptly described Seoul's reactions:

Koreans ... both official and private ... recognize that the current Administration could not have been more emphatic in its firm reiteration of the security pledge, its swift dismissal of Carter's troop withdrawal concept, and its heavy emphasis on greater U.S. military capacity.[20]

In addition to these statements of commitment, substantive U.S. policy measures enacted by Reagan further assuaged South Korean anxieties. There were basically two reasons for this. First, many of the policies were definitive reversals of actions previously taken by Carter. For example, while Carter denied ROK requests for F16 Falcon Fighters, Reagan approved the sale as one of his first acts. Similarly, the ROK welcomed the reopening of the SCC dialogue in 1981, as Carter's canceling of these bilateral defense consultations had effectively closed off the primary channel for deliberation on U.S. military assistance. Second, U.S. actions showed a clear desire to augment deterrent capabilities on the peninsula. U.S. security assistance to the ROK during the period increased while that toward other countries either leveled off or decreased. In addition, the sale of advanced F16s in 1981, deployment of Lance missile systems in 1986, and other efforts to support the ROK's five-year Force Improvement Plan (1982–87) shifted the qualitative North-South military balance in Seoul's favor.[21] These measures made clear to Koreans that the United States sought not just the restoration but the strengthening of the alliance from the *status quo ex ante* under Carter.[22]

Finally, U.S.-ROK bilateral exchanges during the period that did not produce new commitments of military hardware or new forms of security assistance were no less effective in restoring faith in the United States as a reliable ally. Reagan's November 1983 visit to Seoul was especially significant in this regard. Prior to these meetings two events had stimulated ROK threat perceptions. In September 1983 the Soviet Union shot down a civilian Korean airliner that had strayed into Soviet airspace, killing all passengers. A month after this tragedy a North Korean assassination attempt on Chun during a state visit to Rangoon, Burma, resulted in the deaths of half the ROK cabinet.[23] As Shultz recalled, Chun officials expressed concern that these events would result in an embarrassing cancellation of the U.S. presidential visit planned for November; however, Reagan's conviction to follow through with the trip was an important sign of U.S. resolve.

President Reagan was scheduled to visit Korea the very next month, from November 12 through 14, 1983, after a four-day visit to Japan. [After the Rangoon incident] the South Koreans immediately asked whether the president intended to go through with his planned visit. He assured them that he was more determined than ever to stand at their side: his support registered.[24]

In light of the Rangoon bombing Reagan's visit to the DMZ and his statements condemning the North were particularly appreciated by Koreans. As press coverage of the summit noted: "Although Reagan's visit was high on rhetoric and low on substance, his emphatic reiteration of the strong US security commitment to Seoul left both the government and general public here reassured."[25]

This assessment does not deny that United States-ROK relations encountered their share of problems during the 1980s. In particular, increasing trade friction, alleged U.S. complicity in Chun's brutal May 1980 suppression of civil unrest in Kwangju,[26] and the stamp of approval provided to Chun by the 1981 summit all spawned an outgrowth of anti-American sentiment that found expression in several attacks on American embassy and consular offices during the period. However, such events constituted a reaction on the part of students and dissident political elements to the renewed American presence in Korea. As a political counselor at the ROK embassy in Washington at this time noted, security was no longer a problematic issue during the Reagan-Chun years as two anticommunist leaders now shared a common mindset absent during the Carter administration.[27]

Consolidation and Expansion of the
United States–Japan Alliance

Reagan's peace-through-strength policies had similar effects on Japan. Japanese security perceptions at the end of the Carter years were molded by two issues. First, by the beginning of the 1980s Soviet military deployments in Asia had placed more than 160 SS-20 intermediate-range ballistic missiles in immediate range of Japanese cities.[28] Equally ominous was the deployment of Soviet ground forces and the significant upgrading of airpower capabilities on the northern territories in 1978–79.[29] Second, Vietnam and the Carter plan shook confidence in the United States as a reliable ally in Tokyo as it had in Seoul. While Japan held less concern than South Korea about an absolute American retreat from the region, it remained troubled by the general lack of advance consultation by Washington on Asia policy throughout the 1975–79 period.

Against this backdrop of uncertainty Reagan entered office with three objectives regarding the United States-Japan alliance: (1) to reaffirm defense commitments and restore U.S. credibility, (2) to delineate more clearly and expand each party's defense roles and responsibilities, and (3) to prevent heightened bilateral trade friction from negatively impacting security relations. Reagan's policy team signaled early and clearly these intentions. In the administration's first meetings with Foreign Minister Ito Masayoshi in March 1981 and Reagan's summit with Premier Suzuki Zenko the following May the United States declared that the cultivation of solidarity with Tokyo constituted the "anchor" of America's reassertion of leadership in Asia. Secretary of State Haig added that this meant not just notifying Japan of U.S. policies after the fact (as had been the case in the past) but conferring with its ally in advance of enunciating such policies.[30] Defense Secretary Weinberger further avowed U.S. commitments in March 1982 meetings with Japanese leaders, stating that the primary pillars of American policy in Asia were the continued U.S. presence as a dominant Pacific power and a strong defense partnership with Japan.[31]

These statements registered positively in Japan. Foreign Minister Ito proclaimed the restoration of Japanese faith in the United States after his meetings with top Reagan officials,[32] and in the Reagan-Suzuki joint communiqué Tokyo departed pointedly from past practice and for the first time used the word *alliance* to denote full Japanese allegiance with the West in deterring Moscow.[33]

Regarding Korea, Tokyo officials appreciated Reagan's swift and decisive scrapping of the Carter plan and, in particular, his efforts to keep
the Japanese informed at every step along the way. At his summit with
Reagan, Premier Suzuki also thanked the United States for its continued
engagement in Korea and stated: "Through the 2 days of talks with you,
Mr. President, we have been able to establish between us an unshakable
basis of friendship and mutual trust. And this is the greatest treasure
that I take home from my visit to the United States to Japan."[34] And
upon assuming his post as ambassador to Korea, Maeda Toshikazu declared that such practices had finally expunged the era of confusion over
the Carter plan.[35]

THE "RON-YASU" FRIENDSHIP

After Nakasone Yasuhiro succeeded Suzuki as premier in November
1982, the consolidation of relations gained even greater momentum. A
long-time advocate of Japan's defense buildup and proactive role in
world affairs, Nakasone found in Reagan a fellow conservative leader
with appealing anticommunist views. Similarly, Reagan found in his
counterpart a new outspoken leader willing to shoulder greater responsibilities within the alliance and move to a more equal partnership with
Washington. The result was a much more explicit emphasis on the security aspects of relations. The Japanese Defense Agency's (JDA's) five-
year defense plan (1983–87) increased the defense budget by 7 percent
and eventually raised total defense spending as a percentage of GNP to
the 1 percent ceiling. In 1983 Nakasone amended Japanese law to allow
the transfer of Japanese military technology to the United States and
later joined in support of SDI. Nakasone also expanded intelligence
sharing and increased Japanese host-nation support for U.S. forces. In
support of U.S. military contingency planning in the region Japan expanded capabilities to defend sea lanes of communication around the
home islands. The Self-Defense Force (SDF) branches also took part for
the first time in a series of joint military exercises with the United States
to improve interoperability of forces.[36]

High-level political symbols of the alliance were also put forth by the
two leaders. At January and November 1983 summits Nakasone responded to U.S. affirmations of alliance by asserting his own ideological
affinities with Reagan and making the controversial reference to Japan
as an "unsinkable aircraft carrier" in the Pacific, drawing protests from
Moscow.[37] The new partnership was also manifested in Reagan's invita-

tion for Nakasone to play a more prominent role at the Organization for Economic Cooperation and Development (OECD) and G-7 summits.[38] In total the two leaders met an extraordinary twelve times during their tenures, and the "Ron-Yasu" personal friendship reinforced the popular image of the new closeness in United States-Japan ties.[39]

One might argue that the significant increases in Japanese defense spending during the 1980s and desires to improve autonomous defense capabilities reflected continuing concerns about U.S. disengagement.[40] However, this reasoning is inaccurate if one considers the context in which these rearmament policies were implemented. While Reagan reaffirmed alliance ties with Japan, he also called for the assignment of certain defense roles and missions to Japan. Two key components of this new mission were the more equitable sharing of the cost of supporting U.S. forces in Japan (host nation support) and the acquisition of capabilities to defend air and sea lanes of communication up to one thousand miles east and south of the home islands.[41] The primary purpose of the latter was to enlist Japanese air and antisubmarine support to deter a potential Soviet advance in Northeast Asia while the U.S. Seventh Fleet met contingencies in the Persian Gulf.[42]

Seen in this light, Japanese rearmament policies constituted a response to these new burden-sharing responsibilities. As one Japanese newspaper described it, this was burden sharing in a "positive" rather than "negative" sense.[43] Under past U.S. administrations Asian allies normally equated an increase in U.S. pressures to share costs with U.S. desires to pare down expensive commitments to the region. Under Reagan, however, Japanese rearmament supplemented, rather than substituted for, U.S. regional engagement and therefore did not reflect increased fears of U.S. abandonment.

TRADE CONCERNS

The final factor affecting Japanese abandonment fears was the Reagan administration's policy on trade. During the 1980s economic friction between the United States and Japan reached new heights. The annual trade deficit with Japan during Reagan's first term ballooned from $16 billion in 1981 to $49.7 billion in 1985. In addition, in 1985 and 1986 Congress passed resolutions demanding retaliation against unfair Japanese trade practices in such sectors as automobiles, telecommunications, medical equipment, pharmaceuticals, tobacco, and forestry products. In spite of the imposition of voluntary export restraints on Japanese auto exports, begun in 1981, the initiation of the MOSS (market-oriented, sector-specific) talks in 1985, and a sweeping market liberalization program by Nakasone also in 1985, calls for more punitive measures reached a fevered pitch on Capitol Hill, and "Japan-bashing" pervaded policy debates.[44]

While the Reagan administration acknowledged trade issues as a major problem in United States-Japan relations, it took great care to prevent these from dominating the bilateral agenda. For Reagan the clear priority was consolidation of the security relationship. The president himself made this clear in a quintessentially Reaganesque sound bite during his November 1983 summit with Nakasone:

We know we have trade problems with Japan but is it worth jeopardizing the strategic relationship with our most reliable Asian ally in order to sell a few more oranges and steaks?[45]

The administration's objective was therefore to maintain parallel tracks of diplomacy in which the executive handled the more vital security dialogue while Congress dealt with economic issues. Even when issues arose that forced a convergence of these two tracks, Reagan officials sought to accentuate the primacy of the strategic partnership. A case in point was the Toshiba affair in September 1987. This involved the Japanese sale of sophisticated milling-machine technology to the Soviet Union, which would enable the production of quieter submarine propellers. While Congress chided Tokyo for providing such sensitive military technology to Moscow, Reagan officials tried to play down the issue, emphasizing instead Japan's relatively prompt response in tightening export controls and its increased financing for the Coordinating Committee for Export to Communist Countries (COCOM).[46] As one analyst argued, this separation of security and trade issues boosted Japanese confidence that American defense commitments would not fall prey to domestic politics.

Because Reagan has stressed America's global strategy to contain the Soviet Union, Japanese fears of American abandonment have been minimal. Moreover, Americans who talk of withdrawing from Japan have lost their persuasiveness since the Reagan administration has emphasized the importance of Japan to America's own forward deployment strategy.[47]

As George Shultz described it, the 1980s therefore saw "the best government-to-government relations with Japan in many a year."[48] U.S. commitments to defend Japan against the Soviet threat were firm; Tokyo enjoyed treatment as a fully consulted partner; and economic friction, however severe, remained separate from the alliance. Tokyo had obtained the close, intimate partnership with the United States it had long desired.

Evolution and Friction in Japan-ROK Relations

According to this book's argument, decreased fears of U.S. abandonment during the Reagan years should have impacted Japan-ROK bilateral relations negatively. This is because strong commitments by the common great-power ally would have removed the overarching security imperative for Seoul and Tokyo to improve bilateral relations. Under such conditions of security abundance the two states should have been more likely to allow contentious issues and historical animosities to mar interaction.

However, events during the 1980s appear to disprove this proposition. Concurrent with the renewed vitality of the United States-ROK and United States-Japan alliances, Japan-ROK relations experienced an unparalleled and positive evolution. On the diplomatic front this took the form of a general institutionalization and expansion of consultation channels. In 1984 and 1986 the two governments inaugurated regular, high-level policy consultations and foreign-ministerial meetings to augment the annual joint ministerial conferences, the primary fora for political dialogue. More significantly, in January 1983 and September 1984 they conducted the first executive-level summits in the history of normalized relations. At these meetings Chun and Nakasone proclaimed a new, forward-looking vision that sought to overcome historical legacies. The summit joint communiqués and press statements heralded the start of a "new chapter" and "one-thousand years of friendship" between the two countries.[49] As evidence of these new ties, in January 1983 the two governments concluded the largest loan contract for ROK economic development since the 1965 normalization treaty. Composed of $4 billion in Japanese official development assistance ($1.85 billion), commercial bank loans ($350 million), and Export-Import Bank loans ($1.8 billion), this landmark agreement took interdependence between the two economies to new levels of cooperation.[50] During the period the two governments also made an unprecedented attempt at closing the historical emotional chasm. In September 1984 Emperor Hirohito for the first time offered statements of regret over the Japanese occupation of Korea. Chun accepted the emperor's apology on behalf of the Korean people and proclaimed an end to the colonial legacy in bilateral relations.[51]

The progress in Japan-ROK relations was also manifest in changes in the nature of diplomacy between the two governments. Chun and Nakasone generally sought to increase the transparency of policies through more frequent consultations and through such newly established mechanisms as a diplomatic hotline. As a result of the growing political and economic prominence of both states discussion of issues no longer took place only in a bilateral context but on a wider regional scale. New leaders were less imbued with the colonial era. Unlike the days of Park Chung-hee, Sato Eisaku, and Fukuda Takeo, they did not speak a common language (i.e., Japanese) and did not relate to one another based on personal relationships and informal diplomacy conducted at *kisaeng* houses. The result was a greater emphasis on more objective and businesslike diplomacy through institutional channels. Finally, on the security front Japan took unusually restrictive measures in allegiance with the ROK over aggressive acts by communist powers during the period. In particular, Tokyo joined Seoul and Washington in condemning the Soviet downing of a civilian Korean airliner in September 1983. It also imposed sanctions against North Korea for its assassination of half the Chun cabinet in Burma in October 1983 and terrorist bombing of a Korean airliner in November 1987.[52] These events have led a number of scholars to characterize this period as an overwhelmingly cooperative one in Japan-ROK relations.[53]

The 1980s therefore pose an anomaly for this book's explanation of Japan-ROK relations. On the one hand, decreased fears of U.S. abandonment should give rise to contentious Japan-ROK interaction. On the other, the conventional conception of this period is one of new-found cooperation. The remainder of this chapter attempts to reconcile this apparent incongruity. While it does not deny that there were instances of cooperation contributing to an overall progression of relations during the 1980s, it does argue that a closer analysis of the evidence raises questions as to whether relations were as congenial as have been popularly depicted. In fact, a number of incidents severely disrupted relations, and on balance, these outweighed those of a cooperative nature.

THE IMPACT OF DOMESTIC POLITICS:
RESURRECTION OF THE KIM DAE-JUNG CASE

South Korean domestic politics were often the source of friction in Japan-ROK relations. The Japanese generally looked down on the

authoritarian acts of the Yusin regime and became particularly incensed
when repressive ROK political practices affected Japan in some manner.
During the 1972–74 period this was a particularly salient concern when
Kim Dae-jung was spirited out of Japan and later two Japanese students
visiting Seoul were seized and convicted of antigovernment acts. Both
incidents were perceived as violating the sovereignty of Japan and its
civil rights principles. For Seoul events such as Mun Se-kwang's attempted assassination of Park Chung-hee in 1974 infuriated the Koreans as representative of Japan's ambivalence toward pro-North Korean
activities by the Chosen Soren and its affiliates. These sorts of issues
again plagued relations in the 1980s, the most prominent example occurring in September 1980. As part of a wide-ranging crackdown
against dissident elements, an ROK military court sentenced Kim Dae-
jung to death on charges of sedition.[54] This act immediately rekindled
animosities from 1972–74 and elicited mass anti-ROK demonstrations
in Japan.[55] The Japanese were already perturbed by Chun's expulsion of
several Japanese news organizations as part of his "purification" campaign against all elements critical of the government.[56] Moreover, the
military court's charges against Kim included his role as founder of the
Hanmintong, an antigovernment organization operating out of Japan.[57]
In Japan's view this constituted a direct violation of the diplomatic settlement reached after the 1973 kidnapping.[58] The result was a revival of
the Kim Dae-jung controversy, which again took Japan-ROK relations
to the brink of rupture.

In an NHK television interview days after the sentencing, Premier
Suzuki stated that the execution order against Kim Dae-jung would not
bode well for bilateral relations:

We have clearly stated (to the ROK side) that in case a situation, which Japan is
concerned about, arises as to (the person of) Kim Dae-jung, various restrictions
will be enforced on (Japan's) economic cooperation and technical aid (to the
ROK).[59]

Foreign Minister Ito and Vice-Minister Takashima Masuo warned that
Seoul's reneging on the 1973 settlement would cause a "serious split" in
diplomatic relations.[60] Initially Tokyo's desire not to have the dispute
spill over into lucrative economic relations tempered its protestations.
However, after an ROK appellate court upheld the death sentence
against Kim on November 3, 1980, Japanese protests grew more insis-
tent. The foreign ministry demanded commutation of the sentence, recalled its ambassador to Korea, Sunobe Ryozo, for consultations, and

declared that the outcome of "the Kim Dae-jung problem has now become a symbol of Japan-ROK relations."[61] In a confidential meeting between Suzuki and ROK Ambassador Choi Kyung-nok on November 21 the Japanese premier personally warned that Kim's execution would be looked upon with utmost gravity by Japan and would force the government to alter its diplomatic and economic policies toward Korea. Ambassador Sunobe also cautioned Chun officials that public outcry to the execution would be so severe that the government would have no choice but to reevaluate its entire relationship with Seoul.[62]

The Chun regime responded to these protests intransigently. It criticized Japan's intervention in a domestic matter as a "remnant of Japanese colonial behavior." ROK officials leaked the contents of the Suzuki-Choi meeting to the press, accusing Japan of threats to expand relations with North Korea if Seoul did not capitulate on the case. Tapping into the public's well of historical resentment, the government-controlled media carried banner headlines of "Suzuki's diplomatic blackmail" and mobilized nationwide anti-Japan protests.[63] In response to these actions, Ito on November 28 flatly threatened to suspend all Japanese economic aid if Chun executed Kim.[64] In the end U.S. mediation facilitated an uneasy secret compromise to the dispute in January 1981. Washington made commuting of Kim's death sentence a precondition for Chun's February 1981 summit with Reagan. The sentence was eventually reduced to twenty years' imprisonment, and Kim was permitted passage in December 1982 to the United States, where he remained, ostensibly for health reasons, until February 1985.[65]

In hindsight Japanese and Korean capacities to avoid a rupture of relations over the renewed Kim Dae-jung dispute could be seen as an instance of cooperation; however, neither side emerged with such an assessment. On the contrary, resentments over the case set a precedent for confrontational relations between the Chun and Suzuki governments. As Ambassador Sunobe recalled, the resurrection of this dispute brought acrimony back to Japan-ROK relations after a relatively calm period from 1975 to 1979.[66] While this outbreak of friction cannot be directly tied to wider security factors in the region, reduced anxieties about U.S. disengagement in Seoul and Tokyo certainly played a role. Removal of the immediate imperatives for bilateral cooperation effectively made the perceived consequences of crippled diplomatic relations over the Kim dispute much less severe than would have otherwise been the case. In this sense, U.S. commitments removed constraints on the two governments to allow domestic politics to determine bilateral relations.

THE LOAN DISAGREEMENT: SLOW BIRTH OF
GREATER ECONOMIC COOPERATION

The ill will created by the Kim Dae-jung affair hardly subsided before polemics surrounding the $4-billion-loan agreement rattled relations. There is no denying that this agreement marked a watershed in Japan-ROK economic interdependence. However, these loans materialized at the expense of political goodwill and two years of extremely contentious negotiations, which were often suspended. Furthermore, it was the residual bitterness engendered by these negotiations rather than euphoria over the final agreement which left a lasting impression on bilateral relations.

For example, the Chun regime's initial loan proposal in August 1981 emphasized that the ROK "demanded" these funds, not merely "requested" them.[67] Among the justifications for this demand, Foreign Minister Lho Shin-yong stated that Japan owed "security rent" to Seoul after having enjoyed a free ride for years because of the ROK's service as the "bulwark of defense" in the region. Chun also argued that the 1965 normalization settlement short-changed the Korean people, and these new loans therefore constituted a "second round" of material repentance for Japan's colonial atrocities. Proclaiming itself "anti-Japanese," the Chun regime further threatened that if funds were not forthcoming, it would embarrass the Suzuki government by exposing the involvement of many of its officials in illicit *nikkan yuchaku* (Japan-Korea adhesion) ties prevalent during the Park years.[68]

Chun's position on the loan deal stemmed largely from his understanding of U.S. reengagement policies. At Reagan's 1981 summits with Chun and Suzuki the United States not only reaffirmed allied security commitments but also outlined a United States-Japan-ROK united-front strategy against the Soviet Union which required Japan to assume larger defense responsibilities. From the Korean perspective one of the tasks incumbent on Japan under this strategy was to provide economic support for the ROK military deterrent on the peninsula.[69] Insertion of the term *alliance* for the first time in a joint communiqué issued by the United States and Japan, coupled with Suzuki's enunciation of a "comprehensive security strategy" for Japan, signaled to Seoul Tokyo's full acceptance of its new burden-sharing role.[70] As a result the Chun regime conceived this as an opportune time to invoke the security-rent argument and gain a large sum of money from Japan as well as the upper hand in bilateral relations.

The Japanese were outraged at the ROK's demands. Seoul's initial $6-billion proposal amounted to more than half of the total Japanese official development assistance budget for Asia and fourteen times its annual average outlay for Korea.[71] The extravagant amount as well as Seoul's haughty attitude prompted the newly appointed Foreign Minister Sonoda Sunao to express indignation: "The side which wishes to borrow money says, 'I can't knock off even a dime.' This is not possible by Japan's common sense."[72] Tokyo officials chided the ROK for attempting to extort funds from Japan and pointed to the incompetence of South Korean macroeconomic policy planners as the reason South Korea needed Japanese aid.[73] Moreover, the Japanese government emphatically rejected classification of the loans as security rent. In August 1981 Asia Bureau Director-General Kiuchi Aritane publicly denied the validity of the ROK's bulwark-of-defense rationale. Suzuki, Sonoda, and Chief Cabinet Secretary Miyazawa Kiichi added that a precondition for discussing the loan was its segregation from security issues.[74]

Intransigent behavior on both sides was exhibited at the August 1981 foreign-ministerial meeting and the annual joint ministerial conference the following month. Media coverage of the former described the atmosphere as "extremely tense," with the ROK foreign minister threatening to walk out after the first day,[75] while at the joint ministerial conference Sonoda opened his remarks with a definitive statement reiterating Japan's rejection of economic-aid requests on security grounds. The ROK retorted that Tokyo should acknowledge the ROK's service as a "citadel" of Japanese defense as the "guiding principle" for bilateral relations.[76] Heated exchanges took place, and the conference ended, as one paper described it, in "virtual rupture."[77] The two delegations did not issue the customary joint communiqué and effectively suspended loan talks, with both sides proclaiming the need for a cooling off period.[78] Negotiations resumed in late 1981; however, these reached yet another impasse as historical emotional issues consumed relations the following summer.

OUTBREAK OF HISTORICAL ANIMOSITY:
THE TEXTBOOK DISPUTE

The Chun-Suzuki years saw heightened tensions over the growth of anti-Japan sentiments and the resurgence of historical antagonisms. These stemmed from a confluence of factors. First, generational changes were relevant. Declaring themselves the *han'gŭl* (Korean language) generation, Chun and his entourage did not identify with the old ROK elite's personal ties with Japan growing out of the colonial era but saw themselves as nationalistic leaders seeking to elevate Korea out of its traditionally submissive relationship with Japan. They prided themselves on not speaking Japanese (the ultimate sign of the previous generation's subservience) and sought to establish a new tone of confidence and assertiveness over Tokyo.[79] Second, domestic political imperatives also fostered anti-Japanism. The draconian means by which Chun assumed the reins of power in 1979–80 and the authoritarian practices of his regime did not sit well with the Korean people. The promises of security against the North Korean threat and of double-digit economic growth were the traditional means by which to "buy" political legitimacy; however, anti-Japanism also became a convenient hook upon which the regime could hang the hat of political legitimacy. Yet a third related causal factor for the growth of historical antagonisms was the abundance of security engendered by renewed U.S. defense commitments to the region. While the causal link between security and historical animosity is indirect, the absence of U.S. abandonment fears certainly provided Chun with a much wider political space in which to contemplate the use of anti-Japanism for domestic political consumption.

What most symbolized the outbreak of historical animosity in these years was the controversy over revisions in Japanese history textbooks. In June 1982 rumors surfaced that the Monbushō (Education Ministry) intended to issue new guidelines for the national certification of history textbooks. These guidelines would allow the authors of secondary-school texts more freedom to depict Japanese aggression in Korea and China less critically than had been the case in previous texts. In theory this meant publishers could market works that whitewashed the 1905 annexation of Korea as an "advance," the March 1, 1919, demonstrations as an isolated "riot" (rather than a nationwide independence movement), and Shintō worship in colonial Korea as "encouraged" rather than coerced. The proposed guidelines would also allow texts to delete references to other occupation policies, such as the banning of the Korean language and the institution of labor conscription.[80]

The textbook revisions provoked outrage in Korea. Seoul filed numerous protests with the Japanese foreign and education ministries demanding retraction of the guidelines.[81] It also suspended the $4-billion-loan talks at a critical point, just after major deadlocks had been broken over the security-rent question and the total sum of the loan package.[82] Tokyo's rebuttal to ROK protests only worsened friction. In August

1982 Japanese officials asserted the ROK had no right to intervene in a domestic matter, and citing Korea's own practices of historical revisionism, criticized the hypocrisy of Seoul's demands.[83] Premier Suzuki worsened the situation by stating that "evaluation of our country's actions in the past needs to await the judgment of future historians."[84] As Lee Chong-sik stated, these developments prompted an eruption of anti-Japanese sentiment in Korea.

The mass media launched a massive campaign during which the press serialized long articles on past Japanese atrocities and carried reports of rallies and statements denouncing Japan. Taxis, restaurants, and other establishments normally catering to Japanese tourists posted signs refusing them service. Campaigns against Japanese goods were launched in some localities.[85]

Chun canceled a scheduled Japan-ROK binational sporting event, postponed the autumn 1982 Japan-ROK parliamentarians conference, and threatened to recall his ambassador to Japan.[86] In one of the most visceral public condemnations ever by an ROK leader, Chun's August 15, 1982, Independence Day speech was replete with diatribes against Japanese colonial injustices. Media coverage described the state of affairs at the time: "Relations between Japan and South Korea have sunk to one of the lowest points since the two nations established diplomatic ties in 1965."[87]

In the end both issues reached uneasy resolutions. The Monbushō temporarily ended the textbook dispute by dropping its plans for revision. Following this, loan talks resumed, and a compromise over final terms materialized in January 1983. In assessing these events, however, a distinction must be made between process and outcome. While a snapshot of the two resolved disputes might project an image of Japan-ROK cooperation, a closer look at the process reveals an entirely different picture. In spite of the agreement on loans the lasting impression for most was the predominantly negative atmosphere in which these talks were mired for two years. In spite of the Monbushō reversal on textbooks, the two governments admitted that the tremendous friction over the issue severely estranged relations.[88] Moreover, the mutual contempt felt by Chun and Suzuki was also manifest in the rejection of distinct opportunities to consolidate relations in the aftermath of such disputes. For example, following the February 1981 Reagan-Chun meetings, the idea of a Chun-Suzuki summit was floated. This was to be the first such meeting between the two countries and would symbolize the United States-Japan-ROK united-front strategy strongly desired by Washington. However, the ROK government emphatically rejected the idea. Still harboring resentments over the Kim Dae-jung affair the previous month, it showed no desire to mend relations, arguing that a summit so shortly after the Kim controversy would give the impression that the ROK had capitulated to Japanese demands on the dispute and was now seeking forgiveness.[89]

Suzuki raised the possibility of a Japan-ROK summit after his meetings with Reagan in May 1981. The ROK responded positively this time, extending an invitation for the Japanese premier to visit Seoul in late September.[90] Again, the summit would have been an important step in consolidating relations, especially following a series of bilateral exchanges, which would begin with foreign-ministerial talks in March and August 1981 and the annual joint ministerial conference in September. However, after the stormy loan negotiations resulted in extremely contentious conclusions to all these meetings, both governments promptly dropped the summit initiative.[91] Seen in this light, while the outcome of the loan deal and textbook issue was cooperative, the processes behind these events provided little evidence of a new chapter of cooperation. In fact, they were testament to the mutual animosity and historical emotionalism that still underlay relations.

THE CHUN-NAKASONE ERA: WINDS OF CHANGE?

A new wave of optimism appeared to overtake Japan-ROK relations in 1983 and 1984. Nakasone Yasuhiro, who succeeded Suzuki as premier, set improved relations with the ROK as a top priority. Unlike past leaders, the new premier of Japan personally telephoned his Korean counterpart and proposed Seoul rather than Washington as his first overseas visit. The sight of Japanese flags flying in Seoul, not seen since the colonial era, laid the backdrop for the Nakasone-Chun summit of January 1983, the first state visit by a Japanese premier in the postnormalization era. The charismatic Nakasone delighted his hosts with his use of Korean phrases in speeches, his singing of Korean songs, and his expressions of regret over the colonial past. The two leaders finalized the $4-billion-loan agreement and declared a new era of bilateral cooperation. This theme continued during Chun's visit to Japan in September 1984. The two leaders pledged close consultations with one another and established a diplomatic hotline for this purpose. Emperor Hirohito's statement of regret regarding the colonial era highlighted the summit's proceedings. Concluding his trip, Chun declared a "historic turning point" in relations and the start of a "new partnership" based on amity and friendship.[92]

There is no doubt that the Chun-Nakasone summits were important events in Japan-ROK relations. However, the common conclusion that these events indicated true cooperation is a contestable one. Again the distinction between process and outcome is useful. A closer analysis of the former reveals serious bilateral friction on several fronts, cordial atmospherics notwithstanding. Of the four key issues plaguing relations at the time—treatment of Korean residents in Japan, trade, technology transfer, and most importantly North Korea—not a single substantive agreement emerged from the Chun-Nakasone summits or from bilateral negotiations in their immediate aftermath.

The ROK had long pressed for improved treatment of Korean residents in Japan. The practice Seoul especially protested was Japan's fingerprinting of Koreans, as part of the alien registration process, calling it degrading and suggestive of criminal suspicion. The issue became particularly salient during the mid-1980s as the quinquennial registration of aliens approached in July 1985 and a movement to boycott the fingerprinting process grew among the *kyop'o* (overseas Korean minority) community. The Chun-Nakasone summits failed to make any headway on this problem. Despite ROK demands for abolition of the fingerprint requirements at the January 1983 and September 1984 summits Japan only agreed to a vague reference to an exchange of opinions on the issue in the 1983 communiqué.[93]

The two governments also failed to resolve disputes on trade and technology. By 1983 the ROK's annual trade deficit with Japan reached $2.9 billion, and its cumulative deficit (since 1965) climbed above $26.8 billion.[94] Seoul claimed the imbalance was due to unfair Japanese trade practices and demanded market-opening measures such as reductions of tariff and nontariff barriers on Korean goods and expansion of Japan's Generalized System of Preferences list. While Japan offered some token tariff reductions at the July 1984 foreign-ministerial talks and the September 1984 summit, it rejected the majority of Seoul's requests.[95] On technology transfer the ROK sought liberalization in the flow of technology from Japanese companies in areas such as steel, textiles, paper manufacturing, computers, videotape recorders, and other consumer electronics. This was a key issue at both the twelfth annual joint ministerial conference in August 1983 and the 1984 Chun-Nakasone summit. While the latter resulted in government commitments to negotiate a science and technology treaty, the ROK did not obtain the more critical commitment from Nakasone to pressure the Japanese private sector to liberalize technology transfer to Korea.[96]

FRICTION OVER NORTH KOREA

Perhaps most important the Chun-Nakasone summits failed to overcome the two governments' inability to reach policy consensus on North Korea. The 1980s not only made clear how Japan and the ROK perceived reduced fears of U.S. abandonment (in spite of continued threats from the Soviet Union) but also how the two countries perceived different degrees of threat from North Korea. The Nakasone government saw stability on the Korean peninsula as best served by promoting peaceful coexistence between the rival regimes. This meant traditional ties with Seoul while at the same time providing inducements for Pyongyang to interact with the Western powers. Although Tokyo stood ready to condemn blatant acts of aggression by the North (e.g., the 1983 Rangoon bombing and 1987 attack on a Korean airliner), it maintained that a policy of isolation and lack of dialogue only exacerbated the North's fears of encirclement and increased the likelihood that it might lash out in a belligerent manner.[97] As a result Tokyo undertook an expansion of contacts with Pyongyang during the 1980s. As in the past many of these were in the educational and cultural spheres;[98] however, an increasing number were political. These took the form of visits exchanged between government officials, ostensibly traveling privately, and between individuals from the private sector with ties to the government. In June 1984 former chair of the Dietmen's League for Japan-North Korean Friendship, Kuno Chuji, paid a goodwill visit to Pyongyang, where he discussed issues such as a fisheries agreement, reciprocal trade and journalist delegations, and civil aviation routes. In September 1984 a visit to North Korea by Ishibashi Masashi, Japanese Socialist party chair, included an unprecedented six meetings with Kim Il-sung.[99] A month later the Japanese foreign ministry enraged Seoul by announcing the lifting of sanctions against the North for the October 1983 Burma terrorist bombing.[100] And in June 1985 Kim U-jong, president of the North Korea-Japan Friendship Association, met with a number of prominent Japanese politicians, including former premier Miki and speakers of both Diet houses, and discussed such issues as the establishment of trade liaison offices and expanded political exchanges.[101]

These contacts drew strong criticism from Seoul, although the ROK also sought an improvement of relations with North Korea during the

period, overtures that met with moderate success in the form of a resumption of North-South dialogue in October 1984 and a limited number of family reunions and cultural exchanges in September 1985.[102]
However, the North's continued military buildup, belligerent rhetoric,
and perpetration of the 1983 Rangoon bombing and November 1987
terrorist airliner attack, betrayed its continued aggressive intentions.[103]
Consequently, at both the January 1983 Chun-Nakasone summit and
August 1984 joint ministerial conference the ROK emphatically rejected
Tokyo's proposals for expanded contacts with the North and as a symbol of this opposition closed its ports to Japanese shipping companies
doing business with Pyongyang.[104] Divergence of policy over North Korea became particularly acute at the September 1984 Chun-Nakasone
summit in Tokyo. Japan resisted ROK pressure for a joint statement
specifically designating the North as a security threat. Nakasone and
Foreign Minister Abe Shintaro instead maintained that their support of
North-South dialogue did not preclude Japan from cultivating its own
channel of contacts with Pyongyang. This issue became such a contentious point in communiqué negotiations that the ROK side held up the
final draft (albeit unsuccessfully) until hours before Chun's return to
Seoul. Japanese negotiators also vehemently denied ROK postsummit
press statements that Japan had privately agreed to reduce nongovern-
mental contacts with North Korea.[105] The ROK was further incensed at
Ishibashi's September 1984 mission to Pyongyang, as it took place only
weeks after the Chun-Nakasone summit. Coupled with Japan's subsequent decision to lift sanctions against Pyongyang, the Ishibashi visit
flew in the face of the supposed new chapter of cooperation between
Seoul and Tokyo. Moreover, although the Japanese envoy went to Pyongyang on behalf of the Japanese Socialist party, his briefings with
Nakasone and Abe indicated the government's de facto support.[106]

ROK protests over Japanese-North Korean exchanges reached an
apex with the January 1986 mission of Tani Yoichi, chair of the Dietmen's League for Japan-North Korean Friendship, to Pyongyang. Tani
held extensive talks with Foreign Minister Ho Dam and Kim Il-sung on
a variety of topics, including North-South dialogue, North Korean participation in the 1988 Seoul Olympics, and economic cooperation.[107]
The ROK rejected Tokyo's claim that Tani traveled in an unofficial capacity, noting that he was a member of both the ruling LDP and Nakasone faction and had been briefed by the premier and Abe. ROK embassy officials further denounced the mission as revealing Japan's desire
to establish de facto political ties with the North and demanded Tani's

invitation for a reciprocal visit by Ho Dam be retracted.[108] Despite the atmospherics of the Chun-Nakasone summits, little was therefore truly accomplished in removing the North as a perennial source of friction in bilateral relations.

An important causal factor behind this friction was the disparity in Japanese and Korean security perceptions. Although Reagan's reengagement policies reduced fears of U.S. abandonment in Tokyo and Seoul, these policies had the unintended effect of exacerbating fundamental gaps in perspectives on dealing with the North. For Tokyo relaxed concerns about U.S. disengagement and resulting perceptions of security abundance fostered a more open policy toward Pyongyang, somewhat akin to the equidistance policies of the early 1970s. The notion here was that Japanese security was best served by an engaged, rather than isolated, North Korea. This contributed to a stable balance on the peninsula, which was then reinforced by the renewed U.S. security guarantee to the region. By contrast, Seoul, although equally relieved at Reagan's reversal of Carter's disengagement policies, did not perceive such policies as providing the requisite security cushion for venturing any form of engagement with the North. The only viable policy remained hard-line containment, and Japanese acts at quasi-official dialogue with Pyongyang amounted to self-serving measures that undercut Seoul's deterrent posture. The rigidity of these perceptions made friction unavoidable. Japan saw ROK complaints as overzealous preoccupations with crushing its northern rival, often for domestic political consumption, and ultimately harmful to peace on the peninsula. For its part Seoul saw Japanese acts as free-riding on ROK and U.S. defense efforts on the peninsula and in the region generally.

This absence of consensus in the political-military arena was also manifest in the two governments' inability to avoid friction over other potentially contentious issues as well as their inability to extend the cooperation established in the preceding 1975–79 period. On several occasions during the period, for instance, the two governments became embroiled in disputes over Tokto/Takeshima Island. In spite of implicit understandings since 1965 to shelve this issue, in 1981 the ROK protested a relatively insignificant incident involving Japanese patrol boats docking on the island. In 1983 Japan filed counterprotests over Korean fishermen illegally occupying the island. As one analyst correctly stated, "Neither the Japanese nor the South Korean government refers to Tokto or Takeshima when their relations are cordial."[109]

Finally, security cooperation present during the 1975–79 period was noticeably absent in later years. While there were isolated incidents of allegiance particularly with regard to North Korean terrorist acts, these paled in comparison with the general downturn in security dialogue. For example, although the two governments began a series of high-level defense exchanges in 1978–79, these were not pursued further in the 1980s. JDA Director-General Yamashita Ganri's July 1979 trip to Korea produced several commitments to upgrade bilateral defense exchanges, yet Seoul and Tokyo failed to implement any of these measures during the 1980s.[110] Moreover, in spite of U.S. entreaties for a united front against the Soviets, the ROK exhibited, not support, but opposition to Japan on security issues. Japan's increased military spending during the period, expansion of its sea lane defense perimeter to one thousand miles, and Nakasone's hawkish rhetoric revived traditional Korean concerns about Japanese aggression.[111] South Koreans perceived the conservative groups behind these policies as reflecting a resurgent nationalism in Japan, and in spite of Nakasone's efforts to appease complaints over these disputes, Koreans believed he tacitly supported these groups.[112]

RESURGENCE OF HISTORICAL ANIMOSITY

Even on issues where Chun and Nakasone made progress, the results were suspect. For example, the most celebrated accomplishment of the summits was Emperor Hirohito's September 6, 1984, statement on the colonial period. Delivered at a state banquet in honor of Chun, the emperor said:

> Your country and Japan are neighbors, separated only by a narrow strip of water, and practiced exchanges in various fields since ancient times. Japan learned many things through exchanges with your country. . . . Our two countries were thus bound by deep neighborly relations over the ages. In spite of such relations, however, it is indeed regrettable that there was an unfortunate past between us for a period in this century and I believe that it should not be repeated again.[113]

Although Chun welcomed these remarks as the Korean people's long-sought colonial apology, in actuality, Hirohito's statement did little to quell animosities. Many rejected the emperor's remarks as little more than a duplication of Foreign Minister Shiina Etsusaburo's lukewarm apology at the time of normalization in 1965.[114] Others wanted a direct admission of guilt and rejected the emperor's ambiguous reference to "an unfortunate past." Still others focused on Hirohito's choice of the passive "it is regrettable" rather than the more active form "I regret," and questioned whether the statement qualified as an apology at all. The Japanese answered that the text of the apology was indeed similar to past statements, but the significance lay in the fact that the emperor was making it. Tokyo also reasoned that a more direct political statement by the emperor was forbidden by the constitution.[115] Nevertheless, a *Han'guk Ilbo*-Gallup poll at the time found less than 50 percent of the Korean general public satisfied with Hirohito's remarks.[116] Positive histrionics aside, Chun officials also claimed that the remarks, while unprecedented, lacked the clear expression of repentance that Koreans had hoped for.[117] In sum, Hirohito's apology only confirmed Korean suspicions about Japanese reluctance to show true repentance for the colonial period. It therefore rekindled more historical emotional fires than it extinguished.

The Shōwa (or Hirohito) apology's ineffectiveness was apparent in the resurgence of historical emotional disputes in the mid-1980s. Relations deteriorated over disparaging remarks about the colonial era by a Japanese education minister, renewal of the textbook dispute, and controversy over visits by Japanese government officials to the Yasukuni shrine to the nation's fallen soldiers. These disputes further demonstrated that the much-lauded new chapter in Japan-ROK relations retained much of the old script.

In the summer of 1985, as part of ceremonies commemorating the end of the Pacific War the Nakasone government announced an official visit by the premier to the Yasukuni shrine. This became an immediate cause of controversy. Although the Yasukuni shrine served only as a national cemetery, its original incarnation as a monument to state Shintō-ism inexorably tied it with the practices of imperial Japan. Both the Korean and Chinese governments filed protests over the visit. While previous Japanese premiers had paid tribute at Yasukuni,[118] Seoul decried Nakasone's visit as the first by a premier in his official capacity. Tokyo insisted that the visit would not entail engaging in Shintō rituals; however, the ROK protested the visit as a revival of militarism and state-sanctioned glorification of imperial Japan's actions during the Second World War.[119]

Persistent Korean and Chinese protests eventually led Nakasone to put off a second official visit to Yasukuni in 1986;[120] yet this did little to soothe relations as another controversy erupted over Japanese Education Minister Fujio Masayuki in July 1986. The conservative and outspoken minister criticized the government's capitulating to foreign pressure on the Yasukuni shrine visits and 1982 textbook row and proclaimed the need for more positive assertions of Japanese identity.[121] Lamenting the lack of reverence for Japan's historical accomplishments, Fujio intimated the need for massive reform of the education system: "It is necessary to consider whether the good traditions of Japan . . . have not come to be distorted in the course of the post-war Occupation policies."[122] In an interview with the Japanese monthly *Bungei Shunjū*, he further argued that:

The unification of Korea and Japan [in 1910] was based upon an agreement between Japan's representative Hirobumi Ito and the Korea representative Kojong. Formally, and in actual fact, it was agreed upon by both countries. Of course, there is doubt whether Kojong really represented his country, and there may have been Japanese pressure on him to agree. But the least one can say is that Ito's counterpart in negotiations did represent the Yi court. And so there was some responsibility on the Korean side too.[123]

These comments predictably drew irate responses from South Korea. Foreign Minister Choi Kwang-soo denounced Fujio's remarks as "absurd and reckless."[124] Polemics over the issue reached such a fevered pitch that the ROK postponed (and then threatened cancellation of) the inaugural session of the widely anticipated new foreign ministers' meeting in September 1986 and a scheduled visit by Nakasone to Seoul to attend the Asian Games.[125]

Fueling polemics over the Fujio affair was a chain of events resurrecting the textbook controversy. In January 1984 the Japanese education ministry approved a primary-school text without first requesting the revision of controversial passages whitewashing occupation policies in Korea.[126] Following this, in March 1986 the Tokyo High Court ruled that the ministry's exclusive control over textbook contents did not constitute a violation of academic free speech.[127] The issue came to a head in the summer of 1986, when the education ministry approved another textbook for classroom use, this time authored by the conservative Kokumin Kaigi, or National Council to Protect Japan (NCPJ).[128] While the ministry requested some revisions, the book's basic characterization of historical events were markedly more right-wing than those of previously certified texts. In June 1986 both the ROK and China filed protests, denouncing the NCPJ textbook as reactionary and bellicose. ROK officials expressed concern that the glorification of Japan's past reflected an ominous growth of nationalism among the younger LDP elite.[129] While this dispute was not as severe as that in 1982, in conjunction with the Yasukuni shrine controversy and the Fujio affair, it revealed the full-fledged resurgence of historical emotional issues.

The two governments also passed up golden opportunities to improve relations which presented themselves in spite of these historical disputes. One of these was Japan's cancellation of a visit to Korea by Prince Akihito. Originally scheduled to take place in October 1986, the visit was to mark the next step in the new era of cooperation following the Chun-Nakasone summits and Hirohito apology. In addition, it was to provide an opportunity for some choice reflective statements by the prince on the colonial era to relieve heightened animosities stemming from the Yasukuni shrine controversy, the Fujio affair, and the textbook dispute.[130] Chun had personally pressed for the Akihito visit, seeing a potentially historic event that would further mark his regime's foreign-policy successes.[131] As a result, Japan's canceling of the visit in August 1986 and choice of Southeast Asia as an alternative venue angered Seoul. Moreover, Tokyo's stated reason—that the battle over democratic reforms and constitutional revision in South Korea presented an "inopportune moment" for the visit (i.e., fear for Akihito's personal safety)—was a political embarrassment for Koreans. Chun chided Vice Foreign Minister Sunobe, noting that he went ahead with his visit to Japan in 1984 despite strong domestic opposition. He also expressed offense at Japan's lack of confidence in his government's ability to host Akihito's visit without incident.[132]

Another foregone opportunity for improved relations came in conjunction with the widespread *Kankoku būmu* (Korea boom) in Japan, the surge of Korean music, language, and food in popularity beginning in the mid-1980s. Japanese filmmakers became intrigued with the social plight of the kyop'o community, formerly a taboo topic, and books about Korea as well as about the Korean perspective on Japan grew in demand. In spite of this development the ROK showed little reciprocal interest in cultural exchanges. It continued to ban Japanese films and music from Korea and expressed concerns about a new Japanese television satellite making "cultural inroads" into Korea. Seoul also rejected Foreign Minister Abe's 1983 proposal for a bilateral cultural committee, and conservative Korean pundits criticized the Kankoku būmu as the beginning of Japan's second cultural absorption of Korea.[133]

The Quasi-Alliance Argument in
the 1980s—A Difficult Test

To what extent is the quasi-alliance model helpful in understanding Japan-ROK relations during the 1980s? Although scholars have generally depicted the events of this period as wholly congenial, this chapter has shown that a closer analysis of events reveals significantly more contention than is commonly recognized. This assessment does not deny a positive progression in Japan-ROK relations during the 1980s. Such developments indeed greatly changed the texture of the relationship from the 1960s and 1970s. However, the popular depiction of cooperation belies the stubborn and at times intense friction that existed between the two states. Despite the fanfare and histrionics that accompanied such events as the Chun-Nakasone summits, the Shōwa apology, and the $4-billion-loan agreement, substantive issues remained unresolved, historical animosities persisted, relations nearly ruptured over diplomatic disputes, and security ties remained tenuous. Leadership variables cannot account for this friction as Nakasone and Chun both aimed to improve relations. Threat-based variables also cannot explain this friction as the Soviet buildup and the "new cold war" in Asia provided sound incentives for the two powers to consolidate relations.

This friction can be explained by the quasi-alliance model. Japan-ROK interaction over North Korea vividly illustrates this point. In the 1969–71 and 1975–79 periods anxieties about U.S. retrenchment caused Seoul and Tokyo to agree on containment policies vis-à-vis Pyongyang. In the 1980s, however, decreased fears of U.S. abandonment gave rise to a divergence of policy on North Korea. Under these new conditions of abundant security Japan saw an opportunity to forge contacts with Pyongyang and consequently reinstituted peaceful coexistence policies from the detente era. The ROK, despite a reaffirmation of U.S. security commitments, continued to pursue hard-line containment of the North and demanded the same from Japan.

The quasi-alliance model also helps explain the problems associated with the $4-billion-loan negotiations and the foregone attempts at cooperation. Seoul's resorting to the security-rent argument as entitling it to greater Japanese economic support took place in the context of a more secure position in its reinvigorated alliance with the United States. Japan, bolstered by U.S. support in the form of recognition as a world leader, awakened to the possibility of exerting greater influence in the region and thus could only alienate Seoul as it came to be regarded less a critical ally than as simply a part of the region. These factors acted to slow economic cooperation over the loan deal. Similarly, while opportunities to consolidate bilateral relations, such as the Chun-Suzuki summit and Akihito visit, presented themselves to both governments, neither side saw them as critical given Reagan's renewed alliance commitments. As fears of U.S. abandonment decreased, enthusiasm in Seoul and Tokyo for consolidating the third leg of the United States-Japan-ROK triangle dampened.

It is admittedly difficult to draw direct causal inferences between the model's predictions and contention over specific incidents such as the Kim Dae-jung controversy or the general resurgence of historical animosity during the period. This would require evidence showing that fears of U.S. abandonment were specifically in decisionmakers' minds as they interacted over these issues. Nevertheless, one can infer that Japan-ROK perceptions of security abundance during the 1980s effectively removed the overarching imperatives for bilateral cooperation that had existed in 1969–71 and 1975–79. In this sense decreased fears of U.S. abandonment provided, not the specific, but the *permissive* conditions for such friction to arise.

Finally, the model is admittedly incapable of explaining instances of Japan-ROK cooperation during the 1980s. Changes in leadership, the fading of colonial legacies with time, and a general maturing of interaction were important trends that engendered a positive evolution of relations. Nevertheless, one is led to question why this evolution was not more pronounced. In conjunction with the trends listed above, one would expect that watershed events such as the Chun-Nakasone summits and Hirohito apology would have provided the springboard for much higher levels of cooperation. Moreover, strong U.S. encouragement of a united-front strategy should have led to greater consolidation of security ties. The absence of such heightened cooperation may have stemmed from domestic political constraints or historical mistrust; however, a plausible contributing factor may have been the reduced fears of U.S. abandonment and the lack of compelling reasons to move to higher levels of cooperation.

Conclusion: Quasi Allies or Adversaries in the Post–Cold War Era?

Summation of the Argument

Throughout the postwar era Northeast Asian security has rested on the triangular defense network of the United States, Japan, and the Republic of Korea. While U.S. security treaties with Japan and the ROK have formed two stable legs of this triangle, the third leg has been at best tenuous. Explaining this enigmatic relationship is difficult for the Realist school of thought in international relations theory. Despite the existence of common enemies and generally common interests, Japan-ROK relations have been extremely volatile since 1965. While the prevailing explanation correctly highlights the undercurrent of ill will between the two states as a reason, this cannot systematically account for the alternating periods of contention and cooperation.

This book offers a theoretical model for Japan-Korea relations that looks at interaction within the context of a quasi-alliance game, consisting of two states that remain unallied but share a third party as a common ally. The model operates at the intersection between Realism's emphasis on adversarial threats and the quasi-alliance emphasis on actions of the third, or common, ally in determining state behavior. In particular it argues that Japan's and the ROK's fears of being abandoned or entrapped in their quasi-alliance relationship is a key causal variable for policy outcomes. *Abandonment* is defined as the anxiety that an ally may leave the alliance or may not provide support in contingencies where support is expected. *Entrapment* is defined as the concern that commitments to an alliance may end up being detrimental to security interests.

Two hypotheses were deduced for explaining conflict and cooperation. Hypothesis A maintains that, if relations between states reflect an asymmetrical structure of abandonment/entrapment concerns, then friction will result. This is because the imbalance of abandonment/entrapment concerns gives rise to the employment of opposing strategies in the game. Hypothesis B maintains that, if relations between states reflect a symmetrical structure of abandonment fears with regard to one another or with regard to a third party, cooperation will result. In this case the latter variant of the hypothesis—a symmetrical structure of abandonment fears with regard to a third party—is the more relevant of the two. Shared abandonment fears with regard to a third party cause each to show a stronger commitment to that party; however, an additional option, particularly if the third party does not reciprocate, is to show a stronger commitment to one another.[1]

These hypotheses were then empirically tested against Japan-ROK relations. Table 4 summarizes the results. While the tests reveal abandonment/entrapment dynamics *within* four distinct periods in Japan-ROK relations—1969–71, 1972–74, 1975–79, and the 1980s—comparison of behavior *across* the periods yields some supplementary conclusions. First, cooperation between Japanese and Koreans in the 1969–71 and 1975–79 periods did not reflect a new-found mutual affinity, but an imperfect, ad hoc attempt at alleviating perceived abandonment fears regarding their primary security guarantor, the United States. Neither Japan nor Korea had the capacity to internally balance, appease the adversary, or create alternative alliances in response to U.S. abandonment. At the same time both states sought to accommodate U.S. pressures to share the burdens of providing security against the North Korean threat. The only option available to Seoul and Tokyo was a strengthening of the quasi-alliance triangle and in particular, their bilateral relations.

Second, in contrast to these four periods, the early normalization years, 1964–65, appear to offer a contradictory causal dynamic. The United States played a key role in facilitating normalization between Seoul and Tokyo in 1965. This appears to challenge the causal arguments advanced for the other four periods: while the 1969–71 and 1975–79 periods show U.S. *disengagement* producing greater cooperation in Japan-ROK relations, the mid-1960s seemingly offer a period in which U.S. *engagement* also produced cooperation.

One cannot deny that in this early period of relations, when mutual distrust was high, a combination of U.S. exhortations and reassurances was required for Seoul and Tokyo to move bilateral relations forward. However, whether these U.S. actions truly constituted engagement is open to question. While the United States asserted a continued and un-

TABLE 4

Quasi-Alliance Model for Japan-ROK Relations

Period	AB/ENT structure	Historical animosity	Outcome
1969–71	Symmetrical AB (H:B)	Yes	Cooperation
1972–74	Asymmetrical AB/ENT (H:A)	Yes	Friction
1975–79	Symmetrical AB (H:B)	Yes	Cooperation
1980–88	Asymmetrical AB/ENT (H:A)	Yes	Friction (mixed)

ABBREVIATIONS: AB = abandonment; ENT = entrapment; H:A = Hypothesis A; H:B = Hypothesis B.

changing presence, it clearly saw normalization as a means of reducing commitments in Korea as the war in Vietnam grew more encompassing. Reductions in economic aid to the ROK were already being implemented while U.S. assistance programs to Vietnam and Latin America were increasing. A normalization settlement would enable the United States to shift some of its Korea burden to Japan and in the long term be a positive factor in stabilizing the region and enabling a reduction of American troops on the peninsula. These objectives were clearly expressed by the President Johnson's advisors during the period.[2] Moreover, although the $150 million provided by the United States to the ROK in May 1965 was trumpeted as evidence of additional assurances of U.S. engagement, these funds were in actuality an early allocation of monies already earmarked for Korea.[3] In the end, therefore, the conditions that gave rise to cooperation in Japan-ROK relations in 1969–71 and 1975–79 were also present in the mid-1960s: a U.S. desire to reduce commitments, albeit not as obviously as in other periods, in the face of a threatening cold-war security environment.

Third, the causal dynamic highlighted in the four periods sheds light on the relationship between security and economics in Japan-ROK relations. The latter, in the form of trade, aid, and investment, is the most active and visible component of relations. However, contrary to popular opinion, it is not the primary driver of outcomes in the relationship. If one looks at the aggregate of governmental economic treaties and agreements between Seoul and Tokyo since 1965 (see Appendix Table A.3), there appears to be no discernible trend across periods. However, when figures are adjusted for amendments and ancillary agreements, a pattern does emerge. In periods when mutual fears of U.S. abandonment compelled Japan and the ROK to improve bilateral cooperation, the number of government-backed economic agreements also increased. Even if one factors in the varied durations of the periods, it is clear that between the Nixon doctrine and the detente years the number of agreements dropped from ten to six and then dramatically increased to fifteen during the years of the Carter plan and Vietnam debacle. In addition, while the total amount of assistance in the 1980s outstrips that of the other periods, if one considers that developmental loans from 1983 to 1988 were part of the original $4-billion-loan agreement of 1983, then in actuality a total of only four new agreements were reached in the entire decade. This odd combination of cooperation (largest assistance totals) and friction (absence of other agreements) in the 1980s correlates with the mixed nature of relations in the political and military realms as well. These trends, in conjunction with other government-supported economic initiatives, such as the P'ohang Iron and Steel Works project, 1969, and the Japanese suspension of plant exports and Export-Import Bank loans to North Korea, 1975–79, show that overarching security imperatives, occasioned by fears of U.S. abandonment, drove economic behavior in Japan-ROK relations.[4]

Fourth, behavior exhibited over the four periods reinforces how it is fears of abandonment and entrapment, not other factors like domestic politics, leadership, or external threats, which are the primary causal variable in binational relations. For example, skeptics might charge that balance-of-power logic could explain variations in Japan-ROK behavior across the periods and that the abandonment/entrapment framework is unnecessary baggage. When threats were high, Japan and the Republic drew closer, and when threats declined, the two grew apart.

However, the evidence suggests otherwise. External threats affected Japanese and Korean behavior to the extent that they were filtered through Seoul's and Tokyo's perceptions of U.S. commitments and their respective abandonment/entrapment complexes. *Threats* certainly matter in alliance behavior, but *promises* also matter. Threat-based balancing logic, for instance, would have predicted vast improvements in Japan-ROK cooperation in the 1980s as the new cold war against the Soviet "evil empire" in Asia provided imperatives for cooperation. Yet, these predictions did not obtain; although cooperation existed, there was also substantial friction in the relationship. This was because Japanese and ROK threat perceptions were somewhat muted by sound promises and decreased abandonment fears stemming from Reagan's alliance policies in the region. Similarly, in the post–cold-war era the quasi-alliance argument, more so than balance-of-threat theory, would see U.S. disengagement postures substantially affecting Japan and ROK security perceptions despite the end of the Soviet threat.[5] Abandonment/entrapment complexes thus have a conditioning effect on threat perceptions. They link the alliance and adversary games. Developments in the alliance game can exacerbate threats, as they did in 1969–71 and 1975–79, when there was a confluence of increased threats and U.S. disengagement, or they can dampen threat perceptions, as they did in the 1980s. Seen this way, the quasi-alliance model can help explain dynamics that a focus solely on threats as the independent variable cannot.

Similarly, a focus solely on leadership or domestic political factors to explain Japan-ROK relations produces a number of inexplicable anomalies. For example, during the 1969–71 period Park Chung-hee's Japanophile inclinations, his good relationship with Sato Eisaku, and Sato's pro-South Korean conservative political backing cannot explain why Sato agreed to the Korea clause in 1969 and then reneged on the pro-South Korean interpretation of the clause in 1972. During the 1975–79 period Miki Takeo's hailing from the liberal wing of the LDP and his previous opposition to Japanese policies that alienated relationships with China and North Korea cannot explain why he strongly backed a reaffirmation of the anticommunist Korea clause in 1975. After the *nikkan yuchaku* (Japan-Korea adhesion) and Koreagate revelations Fukuda Takeo faced strong domestic political pressure to distance himself from the Koreans. Nevertheless, he played a key role as an interlocutor for Seoul in opposition to the Carter plan in 1977. In the same period mass public resentments over the Kim Dae-jung and Mun Se-kwang affairs provided domestic political incentives for the two governments to take intransigent positions on the disputes. Yet Seoul and Tokyo both made unpopular concessions in resolving them. During the 1980s improvements in bilateral relations could be traced to Nakasone Yasuhiro's and Chun Doo-hwan's personal initiatives; however, their efforts cannot explain the numerous instances of friction also seen in relations at that time. In short, leadership or domestic political variables provide at best a partial picture of relations. Each of these anomalies, however, can be explained by the quasi-alliance model's predictions. Contentious or cooperative outcomes that contradict leadership preferences and domestic political imperatives, in fact, do correlate with variations in Japanese and Korean fears of U.S. abandonment.

Finally, the cases of Japan-Korea cooperation and friction show how the quasi-alliance argument takes a different view of alliance behavior than balance-of-threat/power arguments. One of these differences is the emphasis on commitments of allies (in addition to threats by adversaries) as a causal variable. However, another difference is the relationship between alliances and *structure*. Balance-of-threat theory generally sees alliances as a *product* of the security architecture in the region; the quasi-alliance model sees alliances not only as a product but also a *producer* of this structure.[6] For example, the United States-ROK and United States-Japan alliances are the product of security threats in the region, *à la* balance-of-threat theory, but the nature of the threats and promises in these two bilateral relationships produces variations in the structure. In particular it produces new alignments in the Japan-ROK relationship, which, in turn, influence each power's relationship with the United States. Thus, alliances do more than ratify threats, they also produce behavior that can have secondary and tertiary effects on structure.

Implications for American Policy: Disengagement or "Gradual Finality"?

The quasi-alliance dynamics laid out in this book are *not* an argument for U.S. disengagement from Asia. I do acknowledge that the existence of a dominant U.S. presence may effectively relieve Tokyo and Seoul of a host of responsibilities they would otherwise incur in securing their own defense. One of these is the need to expunge emotionalism from their bilateral relationship. In this sense, the U.S. presence may foster a "freedom of irresponsibility," in which the incentives for the two states, especially Korea, to approach relations in a more rational and constructive manner are low and the temptation to utilize bilateral animosities for domestic political purposes is high.[7]

This does not mean that the only possible constructive role for the United States in Japan-ROK relations is as a passive disengager. Throughout the postwar and cold-war eras the United States, more than any other power, sought to promote closer ties between Japan and Korea, not only out of self-interest but also for the interests of its allies. In times of dispute between the two Washington actively encouraged dialogue and occasionally intervened to pull the two governments back from diplomatic rupture. Instead, I argue that the degree to which Seoul and Tokyo *respond positively* to American entreaties for Japan-ROK bilateral and trilateral cooperation with the United States is a function of whether the United States is perceived to be in a disengagement mode. This was the case in 1969–71 and 1975–79, when U.S. reductions made it difficult for Japan and the ROK to respond negatively to calls for improvements in bilateral relations. By contrast, in the 1980s Ronald Reagan's full-engagement policies effectively reduced the imperatives for the two to respond positively to U.S. entreaties for closer bilateral ties. Therefore, the success of the United States as an active bargainer in the Japan-ROK relationship is inexorably linked to allied fears of U.S. abandonment in the region.

An additional point follows: although the United States has pressed for improvements in Japan-ROK relations, and this has been effective during periods of U.S. disengagement, the United States has never deliberately used the latter to achieve the former. In this sense changes in Japan-ROK bilateral behavior are an unintended consequence of changes in U.S. security policy. Alterations in the level of U.S. defense commitments are often made for reasons wholly separate from Japan-ROK relations (e.g., isolationist sentiment, budgetary constraints, hegemonic overextension). Yet Seoul and Tokyo respond to U.S. retrenchment by seeking a consolidation of alliance ties with the United States, and one of the means of doing this is by addressing American burden-sharing demands for improvements in relations with one another. As a result, U.S. disengagement policies unintentionally improve Japan-ROK relations by virtue of the quasi-alliance nature of the United States-Japan-ROK security triangle.

The most prudent policy for the United States might therefore be one that does not signal full and immediate disengagement, possibly driving Japan and Korea apart, but one that explicitly bespeaks withdrawal over a deliberately long time horizon. This provides the incentive for consolidation of the Japan-Korea axis but allows this consolidation to take place within the context of a residual, gradually decreasing American presence. Full American disengagement, especially if done in an abrupt manner that left alliance obligations only in words, would not necessarily lead to greater Japan-ROK cooperation. In sheer power calculations neither Japan nor the ROK will see alliance with the other as substituting for levels of security attained under the U.S. defense umbrella. Power factors aside, the two will not find in each other the same qualities of trust and virtues as an honest broker they find in the United States. As a result, the reaction to total U.S. abandonment may be for each state to internally balance, including full rearmament and nuclearization.[8] This outcome would reduce American influence in the region considerably; moreover, it might create more security problems than it solves, particularly with regard to reactions from China and Russia. Instead, a disengagement policy based on the notion of "gradual finality"

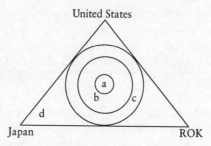

Fig. 3. Two-Tiered Model for Japan-Korea Relations: (a) historical enmity;
(b) government/business elite perceptions; (c) purely bilateral Japan-ROK relations ("inner core"); (d) multilateral aspect of Japan-ROK relations ("outer
layer")

would strike a balance between raising enough abandonment fears to
discourage the freedom of irresponsibility among allies but not overly
rampant fears that might drive them to choose unilateral internal balancing over reinforcement of the quasi-alliance triangle. The latter outcome could take the form of either consolidation of the bilateral axis
(Japan-ROK) or overall improvements in trilateral coordination.

In sum, this study offers a two-tiered model for United States-Japan-
Korea relations (Fig. 3). The relationship consists of an inner core and
outer layer. The inner core is the purely bilateral aspect of Japan-ROK
relations. At this level interaction is characterized by asymmetrical
abandonment/entrapment concerns (Hypothesis A) and friction (1972–
74 and 1980s). The outer layer is the multilateral aspect of relations.
This second tier highlights Japan's and the ROK's common alliance
with the United States. At this level relations are characterized by symmetrical abandonment fears (Hypothesis B) and cooperation (1969–71
and 1975–79). Friction constitutes the baseline of Japan-Korea interaction. This stems from the asymmetry of abandonment/entrapment concerns as well as historical enmity at the inner core. However, variations
in this behavior will occur. The primary determinant of these variations
is the fear of U.S. abandonment. When this fear is high, as a result of
weak U.S. defense commitments and/or salient external threats, Japan
and Korea are more willing to put aside friction arising from conflicting
abandonment/entrapment concerns and show greater cooperation.
When this fear is low, the outer layer of the relationship is stripped
away to reveal the inner core. At this level Japan-Korea contention
dominates bilateral interaction. This argument does not deny the impor-

tance of historical animosity in Japan-ROK relations. Such animosity constitutes the permanent baseline of friction at the inner core. However, the argument does distinguish between historical enmity at the mass and elite levels. At the mass level psychological barriers and mutual distrust plague any and all interaction between the Japanese and Korean people. However, the degree to which this friction surfaces in full-blown disruptions at the level of the governing elite is a function of abandonment/entrapment dynamics. When fears of U.S. disengagement are not salient, then the likelihood of historical emotional disputes disrupting interaction is substantially greater.

DYNAMICS IN THE POST–COLD-WAR ERA:
QUASI ALLIES FOREVER?

The end of the cold war dramatically changed the international security environment that had evolved since 1945. In Asia many of the traditional chasms of rivalry have been bridged in some manner. The ROK's *nordpolitik* efforts produced normalization with the Soviet Union in 1990 and China in 1992. On the peninsula the two Koreas held the first substantive dialogue since 1972, resulting in the Basic Agreement on Reconciliation in 1991, and have probed, albeit haltingly, initial steps toward a peace process in the Four Party Talks begun in 1997. Moreover, the cold-war military and economic competition between the two Koreas is effectively over, with the South emerging victorious, while the North suffers from negative economic growth, near-famine conditions, and the loss of proprietary support from Beijing and Moscow. Japan too saw modest improvements in relations with the Soviet Union in the form of summits with Mikhail Gorbachev and subsequently with the new Russian entity as well as with North Korea, where Tokyo opened normalization talks with Pyongyang.

Accordingly, several questions arise regarding the relevance of this book's argument to future Japan-ROK relations: Is the quasi-alliance argument, based on cold-war data, at all applicable to post–cold-war relations? Does it offer any predictions as to whether this new security environment portends greater cooperation or friction between the two states? And does the argument say anything about *Unified* Korea-Japan relations?

Although the 1990s offer a vastly different set of circumstances, perhaps rendering the quasi-alliance model less useful in its specific applications, the model does offer some preliminary assessments of relevance.

The argument advanced thus far has set out a two-tiered structure for Japan-ROK relations. The purely bilateral context, where issues and expectations between Seoul and Tokyo are salient, and the multilateral context, where issues regarding the common ally, the United States, are salient. With the end of the cold war, factors at both levels suggest that relations, on balance, will be more cooperative than contentious.

At the multilateral level two key factors are American disengagement and residual security threats in Northeast Asia. The end of the cold war brought with it U.S. commitments to decrease its military presence in the region. Beginning with the George Bush administration, this policy was reflected in the closing of Clark and Subic Bay bases in the Philippines and the Defense Department's East Asian Strategic Initiative (EASI), which in Korea called for the transfer from U.S. authority of the joint command structure to the South and phased removal of troops from the peninsula.[9] Mitigating circumstances from 1992 caused the Bush and Bill Clinton administrations to postpone further reductions in Korea and restate the importance of defense commitments to the region.[10] Nevertheless, regardless of U.S. declaratory policy, the perception throughout Asia is that some form of withdrawal from the region is inevitable in the post–cold-war era. As one expert stated:

Recent Pentagon announcements that the Clinton administration plans no further reductions for an indefinite period may squelch current fears of retrenchment. . . . But Asians know that administrations come and go and that such decisions are regularly revisited. In fact, there is nothing magic about the current level of our forces either in Korea or Japan. They were established under quite different circumstances. There is no reason to rule out future adjustments.[11]

This is problematic for Japan and the ROK as the strategic environment remains unsettled in a post–cold-war Asia, most immediately in North Korea. In spite of various inter-Korean tension-reducing measures and the South's military superiority over its adversary, the North still harbors noncooperative intentions vis-à-vis the South, supports international terrorism, and maintains an arsenal of ballistic missiles and biochemical weapons capable of targeting not only South Korean but also Japanese cities.[12] In addition, the potential for the regime's violent implosion as a result of food shortages, economic degradation, or leadership struggles makes it the most salient source of instability in the region. The 1992–94 dispute over Pyongyang's drive to acquire nuclear weapons only amplifies this threat.

In the long term concerns about China also abound. While there is considerable debate on Beijing's post–cold-war intentions, its military buildup, economic growth, and sheer size make it the one power in the region that others cannot balance alone. These factors, coupled with Chinese ambitions in the South China Sea, irredentist claims, nuclear modernization, expanding force-projection capabilities, and a demonstrated proclivity to use force to achieve its goals, make its consideration as one of the most likely threats in post–cold-war Asia unavoidable.[13] According to the quasi-alliance model, U.S. policies of disengagement under such conditions give rise to mutually shared abandonment fears in Tokyo and Seoul. These fears of abandonment should give rise to greater bilateral cooperation.

With some exceptions, evidence of such cooperation was visible in the first half of the 1990s. Reminiscent of the dynamics of 1969–71 and 1975–79 the two governments in 1990 resumed high-level defense exchanges for the first time since the Yamashita Ganri visit eleven years earlier.[14] And in an unprecedented move to improve security coordination in 1991, Seoul and Tokyo established high-level trilateral policy-planning talks with the United States. As was made clear to President Bush and Secretary of State James Baker during visits to the region in 1989 and 1991, a key motive for these actions was Korea's and Japan's expressed concerns about whether U.S. post–cold-war "peace dividends" would be sought in Asia.[15]

This new-found cooperation between Japan and the ROK also carried into the Clinton administration. After Clinton's election in November 1992, Roh Tae-woo and Premier Miyazawa Kiichi held consultations in Kyoto which dispensed with protocol and preset agendas. These informal and extraordinarily frank conversations were intended by both sides as a sign of more intimate relations and produced a joint statement, directed at the incoming U.S. administration, which communicated the two leaders' abandonment fears. As a typical press report of the Kyoto summit stated:

In an unusual statement tinged with anxiety, Prime Minister Kiichi Miyazawa of Japan and President Roh Tae Woo of South Korea agreed that a continued active United States role is indispensable to stability in the region, and voiced the expectation that the coming new United States Administration will not change this policy.[16]

In addition, cooperation on defense matters continued to expand in regularity and scope. ROK Defense Ministry white papers and the Advisory Defense Council Report for Japan (1994) both singled out improvement of bilateral relations as a priority for the post–cold-war era. Revealing the degree of absolute convergence with ROK security perceptions absent in Japanese Defense Agency white papers during the 1980s, the 1995 version, as well as the foreign ministry blue book, explicitly cited North Korea as Japan's most worrisome concern.[17] Visits exchanged by Japanese defense chief Eto Seishiro and Korean defense chief Lee Byong-tae and his successor Lee Yang-ho as well as working-level talks in April, July, and October 1995 resulted in agreements to consider joint training for peacekeeping operations and mutual use of transport aircraft. Exchange training programs of naval fleets were inaugurated in 1993, and in an understated but significant step toward maritime defense coordination a flotilla of three ROK naval vessels in December 1994 made the first port calls between the two countries.[18] In addition, in 1997 unprecedented steps were taken toward moving beyond periodic, ceremonial defense exchanges to instituting a formal channel for security dialogue, the Military Information Consultative System, initially at the director-general level but with plans to upgrade its meetings to the ministerial level.[19] Operational coordination between the two militaries on noncombatant evacuation, search and rescue, and maritime interdiction in response to security contingencies, which had been unthinkable in the past as topics of discussion, are now freely contemplated as future benchmarks for evolving Japan-ROK bilateral security cooperation.[20]

INTERACTION ON THE NORTH KOREAN AND NUCLEAR QUESTIONS

Japan-ROK cooperation was especially evident with regard to North Korea. Although initially appearing as a major source of friction in Seoul-Tokyo post–cold-war relations, the two governments promptly coordinated policies along two tracks.[21] First, Japan consented to conducting its normalization dialogue with Pyongyang at a pace acceptable to Seoul and in a manner not detrimental to the North-South dialogue.[22]

The second track on which coordination was evident was with regard to the North's nuclear program. Although U.S. intelligence was aware of the North's clandestine drive to develop atomic weapons since the early 1970s, it was not until 1989 that it began expressing concerns that the regime might be capable of producing a bomb. What followed from 1992 were two years of tense on-again, off-again negotiations among North Korea, the United Nations, and the United States in which the

North resisted International Atomic Energy Agency (IAEA) inspections, reneged on Non-Proliferation Treaty obligations, and defied U.S. and UN threats to impose economic sanctions. Events came to a head in April 1994, when Pyongyang removed eight thousand spent fuel rods from its five-megawatt reactor in Yongbyon and refused to segregate rods that held evidence of the nation's plutonium-reprocessing history. The United States began consultations with Seoul and Tokyo to pursue sanctions, and plans were laid for the movement of minesweepers and amphibious vessels from Hawaii to the region. In what was most likely the final effort at negotiation, President Clinton approved a "private" mission to Pyongyang by Jimmy Carter, who brought back proposals for a freeze on the North's nuclear activities in exchange for a new round of United States-North Korea talks and a summit between the two Koreas. A period of uncertainty followed after the death of Kim Il-sung in July 1994; however, United States-North Korea talks resumed between Assistant Secretary of State Robert Gallucci and Vice Foreign Minister Kang Sok-ju, ultimately leading to the October 1994 Agreed Framework. This set out the exchange of civilian light-water nuclear re-actors and interim energy sources for a freeze on the North's nuclear program, compliance with IAEA monitoring, and future dismantling of the North's gas-graphite nuclear facilities.[23]

Japan and the ROK presented a united front throughout this crisis. As North Korea's intransigence on IAEA special inspections mounted in the dispute's early stages, Japan, in accordance with Seoul's desires, sus-pended normalization talks with Pyongyang and set resolution of the nuclear issue as a precondition to further dialogue (December 1992). Throughout the protracted negotiations between the United States and North Korea in 1993–94 Seoul and Tokyo jointly urged Washington to emphasize carrots rather than sticks in dealing with the North's brink-manship. They also opposed earlier talk (among some in Congress and the U.S. intelligence community) of a preemptive strike and urged Washington and the IAEA to exhaust all possible avenues of diplomacy before moving toward sanctions.[24] Finally, the two governments pledged full cooperation in implementing the Agreed Framework. As cochairs with the United States of the Korean Energy Development Organization (KEDO), charged with replacing the North's nuclear reactors (and as the primary underwriters of the estimated $5.1-billion project), the two states effectively sit at the forefront of the first post–cold-war multilat-eral security effort in Northeast Asia. As U.S. officials noted, KEDO consultations and the meetings of assistant foreign ministers have taken

Japan and the ROK to levels of in-depth dialogue and policy consensus not known in the past.

The intention here is not to argue that all is rosy in Japan-ROK post–cold-war relations. Indeed, interaction could just as well turn contentious over a number of issues. For instance, the significant arms buildup in the region makes the potential for insecurity spirals between the two states quite real. Japan continues to pursue a strategy of "recessed deterrence" through development of dual-use advanced rocket and nuclear technologies.[25] Similarly, some have argued that the ROK's post–cold-war buildup eschews conventional ground-war capabilities necessary for a North Korean contingency and instead emphasizes force-projection capabilities, such as blue-water navy and satellite technology, in preparation for future regional conflicts, potentially with Japan.[26] Fueling these tensions, many argue, will be the resurrection of historical and territorial disputes. During the Gulf War, for example, the ROK voiced concerns about the renewal of Japanese militarism when Tokyo contemplated, and eventually sent, minesweepers to the Persian Gulf and subsequently passed bills allowing Self-Defense Force participation in UN peacekeeping operations. Disputes continue over interpretations of the colonial period and sovereignty of Tokto/Takeshima.[27] In addition, although cooperation over policies toward the North have thus far gone smoothly, potential problems still abound. Unilateral Japanese steps to improve relations with Pyongyang, for instance, through humanitarian food relief or the reopening of normalization talks, without parallel improvements on the North-South front, are bound to upset Seoul. Japanese economic assistance to North Korea resulting from a normalization settlement and in particular the transparency regarding the use of these funds offer an additional potential source of friction. The use of sanctions against the North in the event of the failure of the Agreed Framework offers yet another.[28]

Skeptics of Japan-ROK relations have history in support of these arguments; however, given the conditions of the early post–cold-war period, the balance still appears to weigh in favor of cooperation for the near future. North Korea's wedge-driving strategy to cultivate ties with the United States and Japan to the exclusion of the South has been unsuccessful. While issues of history may arise, these isolated disputes pale in comparison with the broader and deeper cooperative trends in relations. The number of executive, foreign-ministerial, and legislative exchanges have expanded exponentially over recent years (see Appendix Table A.4 and Table 7), as has the capacity of these meetings to resolve many issues that have perennially plagued relations.[29] A degree of rearmament by Japan and the ROK is certainly a natural response by security-conscious states to the uncertainties arising after the cold war, and the overlay of history could exacerbate insecurity spirals between the two. However, the "Enemy Japan" advocates in Seoul are a vocal minority, motivated as much by preserving organizational interests against calls for post–cold-war budget cutting as by true perceptions of military threats.[30] More important, these buildups are occurring against the backdrop of the unprecedented frequency and regularity of high-level bilateral defense consultations, maritime coordination, military-academy exchanges, and positive statements of security cooperation.

U.S.-ROK-Japan Trilateral Coordination Under Conditions of "Gradual" Finality

Ultimately, which way the balance between greater cooperation or friction falls may hinge on perceptions of U.S. policy in the region. Abrupt and total U.S. abandonment engenders conditions conducive to greater friction. Explicit but gradual disengagement fosters greater cooperation. A sudden U.S. withdrawal would make Japan and the ROK acutely aware of the absence of any immediate alternative security arrangements. There are no regional partners that could replicate the U.S. commitment. The option of bandwagoning with China is at best a risky one. Conditions would be akin to a severe prisoner's dilemma in which Japan and the ROK might seek shortsighted, self-help strategies of internal balancing through full-scale rearmament.

Alternatively, explicit but gradual U.S. disengagement—the notion of "gradual finality"—might foster greater bilateral cooperation. Components of such a strategy might include: (1) controlled and modest force reductions achieved according to a definite timetable, (2) a focus on personnel cuts in the immediate future and combat units at the end, (3) the couching of a drawdown policy in terms of an initiative rather than as a response to domestic politics, (4) prior and full consultations with Seoul and Tokyo throughout the process, and (5) the encouragement of institution building of both a bilateral and trilateral nature in conjunction with gradual reductions. The details fall to the military planners, but the conceptual objective is to create an environment in which the incentives for Japanese-ROK incremental security cooperation are reinforced by the cross-pressures of modest concern about filling security vacuums in the long term after the American departure and confidence in the short and medium term in the safety net provided by a residual American presence during the process of building bilateral cooperation. In this manner the United States balances raising abandonment fears just enough to discourage allied complacency but not so much as to drive Japan and the ROK to mutual distrust and to self-help behavior.

Under U.S. policies of gradual finality the primary form of cooperation likely to emerge in the quasi-alliance triangle is trilateral coordination initially, followed later by consolidation of the bilateral Seoul-Tokyo axis. With regard to trilateral dialogue the U.S.-ROK-Japan triangle has already seen the development of channels in both the security and diplomatic arenas in the post–cold-war era.[31] Policy-planning talks on longer-term regional issues have taken place among the U.S. State Department and South Korean and Japanese foreign ministries. In conjunction with the 1997 start of four-party talks for a peace treaty on the peninsula among the United States, China, South Korea, and North Korea a second trilateral channel at the level of deputy assistant secretary of state in Washington and foreign ministry Asia bureau director in Seoul and Tokyo was created to enhance policy coordination. Informal defense dialogue on regional security issues among the U.S. Department of Defense, ROK Ministry of Defense, and Japan Defense Agency started in the early 1990s and was formalized at meetings in Seoul and Washington in March and May 1997. The growth of Second Track Security Dialogue (Track II) through research institutes in the three countries has added fora in which more substantive issues can be discussed informally.[32] Track II discussions have shown that arenas of operational cooperation for the future agenda of official U.S.-Korea-Japan trilateral dialogue include minesweeping, noncombatant evacuation operations, intelligence sharing, maritime search and rescue operations, and maritime interdiction operations.[33] For Seoul and Tokyo the primary motivation for the form and substance of the trilaterals is contingency planning for a North Korean collapse, and, in fact, some observers argue that the only way to get the Japanese and Koreans to consider operational coordination is with guarantees of U.S. commitment, not abandonment. However, again the distinction must be made between temporary safety nets of American support that facilitate Japanese-Korean confidence in initial steps toward cooperation on the one hand and long-term unadulterated American security guarantees that encourage allied complacency on the other. On the surface these two forms of American support may look similar; however, U.S. entreaties for trilateral coordination carry more weight with Seoul and Tokyo when the perceived endgame behind such acts of support is neither rapid withdrawal or unconditional engagement, but gradual and final retrenchment.

Are there indications that an American policy of gradual but final retrenchment will push Japan and Korea toward the mutual-help option rather than the self-help, internal-balancing option? This is difficult to determine; however, initial evidence justifies some optimism. In direct response to reports about the one-sided, anti-Japanese intentions behind the South's post–cold-war defense strategy, the ROK defense minister emphatically stated that the ROK does *not* perceive Japan as its new post–cold-war enemy and that, in fact, ROK defense priorities regarding Japan seek to expand cooperation in the military arena given the uncertainties attendant upon an inevitably reduced U.S. presence.[34] In addition, gradual shifts in governmental and popular thinking about the Japan-ROK relationship are now evident. One telling example of the latter is recent South Korean opinion polls that found that more than 50 percent of respondents said they did not oppose the dispatch of Japanese military forces to the peninsula in the event of a North Korean attack.[35] Similarly, the transformation of views among the future generation of South Korea's policymakers was especially evident in a 1996 paper from the ROK foreign-ministry–related think tank, the Institute of Foreign Affairs and National Security (IFANS). A Japanese newspaper article, entitled "Time to Consider the Unimaginable," quoted from the IFANS paper:

A rather shocking article, written by Prof. Yun Duk Min of South Korea's Institute of Foreign Affairs and National Security [stated] "US forces deployed in East Asia are certain to pull out eventually. . . . While the US forces are here, South Korea should think about forming direct security ties with Japan—the sooner, the better. It is time for us to ponder bilateral security relations between Japan and South Korea." . . . When it comes to security issues, both countries can only think of a three-way relationship with the United States at the center. We tend to think this situation is appropriate and will last forever. Some Foreign Ministry and Defense Agency officials do speak privately of the need for direct Tokyo-Seoul security ties, but it is not something they would discuss publicly. . . . In that sense, Yun's article is epochal. It is also logical.[36]

Korean Unification and Japan

Some closing comments regarding Korean unification and East Asian security are in order.[37] The conventional wisdom generally argues four basic points with regard to relations between a united Korea and the

major powers. First, a united Korea, by choice (i.e., resurgent nationalism) or by necessity (i.e., post–cold-war burden shedding by the United
States), will be more independent of American influence. In addition, by
virtue of its military and economic capabilities, it will be a key regional
player. Second, a change in the status quo on the peninsula coupled
with a lessened U.S. regional presence will give rise to the release of historical rivalries between Japan and China over Korea. Third, in this new
Sino-Japanese-Korean triangle, there will be a consolidation of relations
between China and Korea based on economic ties and historical affinities (stemming from a common Confucian heritage and history of tribu-
tary relations). And fourth, the release of deep-seated historical resentments with the end of the cold war will make relations between a united
Korea and Japan more contentious. Moreover, the resurgent nationalism accompanying unification will be vented negatively toward Japan,
further exacerbating the erosion of relations.[38]

In juxtaposition with this dominant view, the quasi-alliance argument suggests an alternative set of propositions. These argue that relations between China and Korea will deteriorate and those on the Japan-
Korea axis will see steady improvement. The primary causal mechanism
again is Japan-Korea security perceptions in the face of a diminished
U.S. presence.

With regard to the Sino-Korean axis South Koreans certainly welcomed normalization with Beijing in 1992. This marked a triumphant
crossing of the cold-war divide and the opening of tremendous economic opportunity. Perhaps more significantly, however, Seoul welcomed normalization because in the South's zero-sum mentality, it
amounted to the ultimate diplomatic coup over the North.[39] Along with
Soviet normalization in 1990, Seoul succeeded in effectively isolating
Pyongyang from its two primary cold-war patrons. In this sense the existence of the North Korean state has acted as a sort of buffer for unbri-
dled ROK enthusiasm for relations with Beijing.

In a unification scenario, however, this buffer disappears, and a
united Korea faces the prospect of an eight-hundred-mile, contiguous
border with a militarily and economically burgeoning Communist China, whose intentions are not transparent. Moreover, it faces this without the same U.S. security guarantees enjoyed during the cold war. In
addition, renewed Korean nationalism as a result of unification may
translate into animosities and suspicions regarding China. As one observer noted, often-cited Korean resentments toward Japan seem equally
relevant in the Chinese case:

When Koreans get around to nursing grudges, they might consider which neighbor [Japan or China] saddled them with Kim Il-sung, which gave the go-ahead for the Korean War, and which prevented non-Communist unification in late 1950 by massive, undeclared intervention.[40]

Traces of this sort of problem were already apparent in the negotiations leading up to the 1992 normalization treaty. As an ROK foreign ministry official recalled, China's outright rejection of expressing remorse or repentance for the Korean war in the treaty left a sobering subtext to the fanfare of the moment.[41] The political mood of a unified Korea would also be distrustful of a Chinese government as it stands today. In particular, once North Koreans realize the extent of their relative deprivation under the Kim Il-sung ideology, any residual affinity for socialism that might be harbored in a united Korea would fall by the wayside. The possibility therefore arises that the new Korean state might view China with concern and might heavily fortify its northern border.

Similar threat perceptions are not unthinkable on the Chinese side as well. Of all the powers in the region, Beijing has the most direct stake in the status quo on the peninsula. As two Chinese analysts noted, loss of the North would leave China "deprived of an indispensable security buffer proximate to both the nation's capital and to one of its most important industrial regions."[42] A united Korea presents Beijing with the unwanted prospect of another noncompliant neighbor (like Vietnam) with a competing ideological and social system. China would not pass lightly over the security implications of such a situation. It has already expressed concerns about the buildup of South Korean and Japanese naval forces, and such concerns are likely to be heightened in the case of a united Korea.[43] Moreover, if relations between Beijing and the United States are tense, then the Chinese perception that the West might utilize Korean unification as a means of containing China is far from remote. For these reasons, a lengthy 1992 report on future peninsular strategies by the Communist Party Central Committee stated that despite Seoul-Beijing normalization, North Korea was still "China's Northeast Asian strategic bulwark." It stated that the North's absorption by the South would have a "devastating psychological impact" on China, and therefore Beijing's priorities center on preventing Korea from becoming "the route for the overthrow of socialism by peaceful means from the West."[44]

Finally, nationalist fervor from a united Korea might also raise Beijing's concern about the two-million–strong ethnic Korean community

TABLE 5

Distribution of Overseas Koreans

Country (Region)	Overseas population	Percentage
Africa	2,693	0.1
Australia	39,572	0.8
Canada	70,181	1.4
China	1,927,278	39.0
Europe	60,216	1.2
FSU	458,923	9.3
Japan	712,519	14.0
Latin America	92,864	1.9
Middle East	11,612	0.2
New Zealand	3,049	0.6
United States	1,533,577	31.0

SOURCE: Compiled from *Status of Overseas Koreans* (Seoul: Republic of Korea, Ministry of Foreign Affairs, 1995); reprinted in *Korea Focus* 4.1 (Jan.–Feb. 1996), p. 26.

in Manchuria's Jilin province, the largest contingent of overseas Koreans in the world (Table 5). Unification raises a plethora of unpleasant scenarios for Beijing regarding mass migration or ethnic identification of this group with the new Korean state. As early evidence of this China has already expressed disapproval at former President Roh's advocacy in 1989 of an international community of Koreans. Sensitivities were also manifest in Beijing's harsh criticism in 1995 that seemingly innocuous Korean tour groups to Manchuria might incite secessionist movements among the ethnic minority.[45] In addition, during normalization talks in 1992 Beijing rejected ROK proposals for establishment of consular offices in Jilin and remains reluctant to permit ROK heads of state to tour this area during summit visits.[46] As one specialist noted, for these and other reasons the Chinese perception of a united Korea is therefore far from one of unadulterated optimism.

From a longer-term perspective, China is apprehensive about potential threats to its interests from a reunified Korea. In the economic sphere, Beijing is wary of competition from a united Korean economic powerhouse. Politically, the Chinese are uncertain about the role that a united Korea might play in the region and worried that Japan could eventually dominate the peninsula and undermine China's growing influence in Korea. Militarily, the prospect of a reunified Korea with at least a potential if not an actual nuclear capability is also cause for Chinese concern. In addition, some Chinese foresee the possibility that a reunified Korea would seek to reclaim Chinese territory bordering Korea that both North and South view as the birthplace of the Korean nation.[47]

History has shown that states with contiguous borders, whether intentionally or not, often lapse into competition driven by security fears.[48] In this regard the most proximate threat to a united Korea may emanate from China, not Japan.[49] A united Korea would not have the autonomous capabilities to balance against China; in addition, in the post–cold-war era it would not have the luxury of certain U.S. security guarantees. Furthermore, while a united Korea would certainly harbor its share of animosities toward Japan, this relationship (presumably between Tokyo and a united government under Seoul) would still be grounded in the decades of Japanese-South Korean normalized relations that preceded unification. It would also be grounded in a familiarity bred through common security ties with the United States for the entire postwar and cold-war eras.[50] By contrast, the cumulative experiences undergirding a united Seoul-Beijing relationship would not extend further back than 1992. Compelled to balance against the more proximate and unfamiliar threat, Korea could look to Japan with greater fondness.

THE ECONOMICS OF UNIFICATION

Optimists point out that the rapid growth in ROK-China economic relations throughout the 1980s and 1990s will multiply with unification, thereby mitigating a deterioration in relations. However, unification also brings certain disheartening economic realities for Koreans to contend with. Although bilateral trade has grown at a dramatic pace since normalization, the ROK's trade deficit with China surpassed $1 billion in the mid-1990s and promises to be a source of friction. Comparative advantages in labor costs also enable China to challenge Korea for cherished export market shares in Japan and the United States. From the late 1980s to early 1990s Korea's advantage over China in exports to the United States declined from $11.6 billion to $3.3 billion. Similarly, while ROK exports to Japan outpaced China's by $1.9 billion in the late 1980s, by the 1990s China surpassed the ROK by $400 million, particularly in sectors like shoes and toys.

These trends could seriously undermine Korean long-term economic competitiveness. As one scholar noted, the challenge posed by China is that its sunrise industries increasingly clash with sunset industries of the more advanced economies in the region.[51] The mechanism for this dynamic is Chinese economic growth and the changing composition of trade with the region. In the early 1990s, for example, bilateral trade from China to Korea largely consisted of exports of primary products and raw materials for imports of consumer electronics and manufactured goods. However, the combination of Chinese growth and scarcity of arable land will eventually make China a net importer of food and raw materials. In order to pay for these imports, the Chinese economy will increasingly shift toward export of manufactured goods.[52] Two implications for the Korean economy follow from this. Korea will be faced with a flood of price-competitive Chinese manufactured goods that challenge its own firms (most likely in declining industries). This dynamic will be exacerbated by China's new commercial base after Hong Kong's 1997 reversion, liberalization pressures on the ROK market as a result of Organization for Economic Cooperation and Development (OECD) membership, declining ROK trade surpluses, and rising labor costs. In addition, tremendous pressure will mount on the Korean economy to avoid getting squeezed out of low- and medium-technology markets taken over by China and losing pace with high-technology sectors held by Japan. It should be noted that these are long-term considerations for Korea; and, in fact, in the short term the overlap between firms is currently greater between Japan and Korea than China and Korea. Nevertheless, the point remains that current views of China as an economic partner can in the future turn into views of China as an economic threat.[53]

In contrast to the uncertain outlook for a united Korea's relations with China, prospects for cooperation with Japan appear bright. A key factor in this regard is the future cost of unification. Estimates by the ROK finance ministry put the cost of unification at $980 billion. Even spread over ten years, this would absorb a good portion of the South Korean annual budget.[54] South Koreans are also fully aware that any attempt to underwrite unification would be infinitely more difficult than the German case. ROK per capita GNP totals only 25 percent that of West Germany (prior to reunification); moreover, the gap between the East and West German economies was much smaller than that between the two Koreas.[55]

In spite of the range of figures on unification costs, the clear message is that the ROK does not possess the capacity to finance unification alone. It will need substantial inflows of foreign aid and investment.[56] The most likely source of this is Japan. Neither the United States, Europe, the United Nations, nor international financial institutions are capable of undertaking such a task in any substantial form.[57] By contrast, Japan has a history of economic success in South Korea and the most familiarity among the developed economies with the North.[58]

More important, the incentive provided to Japan by the cheap, literate, and proximate North Korean labor force after unification and the market for commercial exports and investment would be great.[59] In short, just as Japan fulfilled ROK foreign-capital needs during the economic growth of the 1960s and 1970s, it may do so again during unification. Strong Korean resentment of a primary Japanese role in the historic moment would be great, but there may be little choice in the matter. Furthermore, these economic imperatives would have feedback effects on security dynamics in the Japan-Korea-China triangle. When unification comes, China would prefer to see itself first, the United States second, and Japan third in exercising influence over the peninsula. The larger Japanese role in Korea engendered by the cost of unification would therefore only heighten Chinese concerns about the new Korean entity on its border. Even if a united Korea sought better relations with China, the resulting insecurity spirals in Beijing about Japan's prominent place in the economic aspects of unification might make this more difficult to achieve.

MYTHS OF UNIFICATION

Would Japan cooperate with a united Korea? There have been two basic arguments (advanced largely by Koreans) that Japan would oppose unification. The first states that a united Korea would possess the military capabilities and the motive (i.e., revenge) to threaten Japan. The second argues that a united Korea would challenge Japan economically.[60]

Both of these are overstated. The economic argument is at best only partially true. As was the case with the South Korean economy, Japanese aid to a united Korea would pose challenges to Japan in certain sectors. However, in total a united Korea does not threaten to overtake Japan. By any indicator the ROK economy is only one-fourteenth to one-tenth the size of Japan's and the 1997–98 Asian financial crisis, in which the ROK has been a principal victim, has only expanded this differential. The addition of North Korean industry and natural resources only marginally closes this gap.

Second, while historical arguments for a united Korean security threat to Japan abound, historical precedents are absent.[61] While Korea has often been referred to as a "dagger pointed at the heart of Japan," aggression has historically come from China *through* Korea, not from Korea itself. A united Korea would be more preoccupied with threats on

TABLE 6

Comparative Indicators: Japan and the Two Koreas (1995)

	Japan	ROK	DPRK
Population (millions)	125.5	45.2	24.3
GDP (U.S.$ billions)	$4,700	$422	$21
GDP/per capita	$21,600	$12,100	$1,000
Defense budget, 1996 (U.S.$ billions)	$45.1	$15.6	$2.4
Defense expenditures (U.S.$ billions)	$50.2	$14.4	$5.2
Active-duty armed forces(millions)	0.24	0.66	1.05
Armed forces reserve (millions)	0.05	4.5	4.7

SOURCE: Compiled from *The Military Balance 1996–97* (London: International Institute for Strategic Studies [1996]: 184–89).

its northern border than with any designs on Japan. In addition, arguments that Japan would be threatened by a joint North-South Korean military are unfounded. The two Korean militaries currently total around 1.7 million men, a number indeed intimidating to Japan (see Table 6). However, in a unification scenario a rationalization of the two militaries is likely. The more appropriate military force would number around 650,000, which is comparable to current ROK levels.[62]

Finally, the same cross-pressures that figure in Japanese geostrategic thinking in the post–cold-war era are also relevant in a unification scenario. Japan faces uncertain relationships with Russia and China, obligations to play a larger leadership role in the region commensurate with its economic capabilities, and the need to move beyond its one-dimensional security dependence on the United States. At the same time, pursuit of more proactive defense policies must not contradict constitutional principles, must not disregard domestic aversion to rearmament, and must not raise regional concerns about renewed Japanese militarism. A thriving relationship with Korea seems to fit well with these needs. It provides for Japanese security and regional stability and at the same time strikes a balance between a policy not too strong to raise regional suspicions and incite anti-Japan balancing coalitions but not too weak to embolden China to seek to enhance its influence.

Whether unification results in a Japan-Korea-China triangular dynamic that isolates Japan (the dominant view) or China (the quasi-alliance argument) is admittedly a close call. Ultimately, a key determinant of the balance is again the manner in which the U.S. presence recedes from the region. Incremental and gradual disengagement provides enough of a residual American presence to make Japan and Korea feel comfortable with expanding and deepening the quasi-alliance triangle as a means of maintaining security. Abrupt and total withdrawal, however, "shocks" the region, raises insecurities and suspicions, and promotes self-help strategies to the detriment of Japan-United Korea relations.[63]

Democratic Maturation and East Asia's Democratic Peace

A final factor to consider in future Japan-Korea relations is domestic politics. The quasi-alliance argument has established that at the purely bilateral level of relations, residual animosity, and negative images give rise to persistent low-level friction. Pessimistic arguments that this friction will worsen in the post–cold-war period must be measured against certain mitigating factors. Most important among these is the trend toward democratization, particularly in South Korea. Since 1987 the ROK has seen a peaceful transition from military authoritarianism to two successive popularly elected civilian governments under Kim Young-sam and in 1998 Kim Dae-jung.[64] These developments put South Korea firmly on the path of democratization for the first time in the Republic's history.[65] Barring a major calamity and backslide to authoritarianism, there is little reason to believe that a united Korea would abandon this path. In Japan, although one-party dominance characterized postwar politics, by most traditional indicators a democratic tradition is well established.[66] The LDP's fall from grace in 1993 and rise, albeit short-lived, of the coalition Hosokawa Morihiro government reinforced this tradition.

Should these trends continue, interaction between Tokyo and Seoul may increasingly mature into that between two established democracies. As the "democratic peace" literature suggests, liberal-democratic culture, values, and political institutions, commonly respected and adopted by states, positively affect relations between them.[67] The establishment of democratic institutions at home, particularly in Korea, and acceptance of practices such as the peaceful resolution of disputes through compromise may be externalized in the form of greater cooperation between Seoul and Tokyo.[68]

Evidence of this is already surfacing. The post–cold-war era has seen a voluminous increase in bilateral channels of dialogue. As Appendix

TABLE 7

Recent Additional Japan-ROK Bilateral Policy Fora

Forum	Year established	Frequency
Joint Ministerial Conference (*Chŏnggikakryo hoeŭi*)	1967	annual
High-level Foreign Policy Council (*Han-il kowi woegyochŏngch'aek hyŏpŭihoe*)	1984	annual
Foreign Ministerial Meetings (*Chŏnggi woemuchanggwan hoedam*)	1986	annual
21st Century Committee (21st *segi wiwŏnhoe*)	1988	occasional
Asia Bureau Directors Meetings (*Han-il chŏnggi ajukukchang hoedam*)	1991	occasional
Korea-Japan Forum	1993	occasional
Director-General Security Dialogue	1997–98	annual

SOURCES: Compiled from *Ilbon kaehwang* (Summary status: Japan), government publication no. 17000-20030-67-9607 (Seoul: Republic of Korea, Ministry of Foreign Affairs, Feb. 1996), 227–28, 282–313; *Chosŏn Ilbo*, 15 Apr. 1997.

Table A.4 shows, while there were only thirteen executive-level meetings, official and unofficial, over the four decades following the end of the Pacific War in 1945, a total of seventeen took place in a span of less than seven years since the end of the cold war and the liberalization of domestic politics (particularly in Korea). Similarly, cabinet- and sub-cabinet-level exchanges exhibited substantial increases in both scope and number from the days when the annual ministerial conference was the sole official meeting of significance between the two sides.

Another indicator of the growing emphasis on mutual consultation is the number of high-level meetings held outside regular bilateral channels of communication (Table 8). These can range from goodwill visits by special envoys to meetings in third countries (usually the result of attending international organizational meetings) and brief stopovers en route from business in other countries. In the twenty years from 1968 to 1988 contacts of this sort numbered approximately 86, but in the six years from 1989 to 1995, there were 105. A similar increase in activity is evident at the foreign-ministerial level, where the total number of meetings from 1969 to 1988 was surpassed in the six years thereafter.

Both the proliferation and regularization of these dialogue channels are a direct result of democratization in Korea. Back-channel politics of the authoritarian era are rapidly being replaced by modes of interaction typical of two liberal democracies. These foster expansive opportunities to deliberate, debate, and reach consensus on decisions of policy. They

TABLE 8
Growth in Communication and Consultation

Type of consultation	1968–88	1989–95
High-level meetings outside regular bilateral policy channels (special envoys, goodwill visits, advisory meetings, flight layovers, third-country venues)	86	108
Foreign-ministerial consultations (outside summits, annual joint ministerial conferences, and regular foreign-ministerial meetings)	31	35

SOURCE: Compiled from *Ilbon kaehwang* (Summary status: Japan), government publication no. 17000-20030-67-9607 (Seoul: Republic of Korea, Ministry of Foreign Affairs, Feb. 1996), 282–313.

promote institutional familiarity and cultural, educational, and sports exchanges, which reinforce the cooperative maturing of relations. These continue to expand into areas like the environment, disaster relief, and civilian nuclear energy.[69] Perhaps most important these multiple channels provide an institutional foundation to relations that is increasingly difficult to uproot and that can withstand bouts of friction over troublesome historical and trade issues.

In addition to institutional factors the cultivation of democratic norms and perceptions casts an optimistic light on future relations. In particular, the ROK's democratic consolidation and economic prosperity transform Japanese images of its neighbor. While yesterday's media coverage condemned the ROK's martial-law brutality, political repression, and human rights abuses, particularly beginning with the Kim Dae-jung kidnapping in 1973, today's reports praise Korean political liberalization, economic development, the Seoul Olympics, and the Taejon World Expo.[70] This gradually influences the Japanese government and general public to hold more positive images of Korea and Koreans. One manifestation of this was the *Kankoku būmu* (Korea boom), in which Korean language, food, and music experienced an upsurge in popularity in Japan in the late-1980s.[71] Plans to start Korean-language broadcasting in Japan by the end of the century have also been implemented.[72] A study of the Korean minority in Japan noted additional ways in which perceptions are changing: "A new image is emerging for Koreans in Japan. This new image is vibrant, dynamic, and self-confident, backed not only by growing economic power but by changing cultural attitudes."[73]

On the Korean side, as the country embraces democracy and progresses toward economic prosperity, its enhanced international prestige—reflected in events such as the 1988 Seoul Olympics, United Nations membership in 1991, OECD membership in 1996, and the 2002 World Cup to be cohosted with Japan—fosters a growing self-confidence among Koreans that reduces national insecurities and xenophobia and nurtures a less petty, less emotional attitude in dealings with Japan. As generations of Koreans, in the South or a unified entity, live in a democratic society, they will cultivate norms of compromise, nonviolence, and respect for opposing viewpoints, which will become externalized in their attitudes toward Japan. In addition, future Korean leaders, not having experienced the occupation of the first half of the century, are less apt to carry the historical and emotional baggage borne by their predecessors and are more apt to engage in rational and less emotional dialogue.[74]

These points raise a potentially negative effect of democratization on Japan-Korea relations. The ties between Korean nationalism and anti-Japanism are inextricable, and these might be even more pronounced with unification. One characteristic of democracies is the rally-'round-the-flag effect, or the mobilization of popular support against outside elements, particularly prior to an election or in relation to consensus building for a particular policy.[75] In the Korean case one could envision the use of anti-Japanese sentiment, especially over historical issues that arouse animosity, for such purposes.

While a precedent for an anti-Japanese, rally-'round-the-flag effect does exist in Korean politics and will continue in some form in the future, particularly among the older generations,[76] this should not debilitate bilateral relations to the same extent as in the past. Norms of compromise, coupled with generational changes and growing Korean self-confidence, can prevent emotional animosity from clouding realpolitik concerns.

One example of this is the Korean ban on import of Japanese popular culture.[77] Whereas older generations support this policy as a hedge against Japanese "cultural imperialism," younger generations are less supportive. A 1994 opinion poll found that over 50 percent of the population as a whole favored doing away with the antiquated policy, and an additional 23.7 percent saw the importation of Japanese pop culture as beneficial to Korea. Moreover, of those that continued to support the ban, the majority cited economic competition rather than historical reasons.[78] Commentary by one observer of the relationship illustrates this more magnanimous and self-critical transformation taking place in the view of younger, educated Koreans:

Many Koreans argue that the ban [on import of Japanese culture] should be lifted only if Japan shows "satisfactory" evidence of contrition for its colonial-era behaviour. . . . But it is hard to see how allowing in Japanese consumer brands such as Sony and Panasonic can contribute to progress on these issues, while lifting the ban on Japanese movies won't. The so-far unresolved colonial-era wrangles—and Japanese foot-dragging on them—are indeed a serious mat-ter, but Koreans ought to realize that countering one unreasonable policy with another is no solution. . . . Making difficult choices is what growing up is all about. If Koreans have demonstrated anything . . . it is that they have the ma-turity and confidence to chart their own destiny. The ball is now in South Ko-rea's court . . . get rid of a senseless and defunct policy and at the same time convince the Japanese and the world that [Korea] is serious about forging a truly "future-oriented" diplomacy.[79]

In addition, many of the outstanding issues that provide rallying points for anti-Japan mobilization in Korean domestic politics are being dealt with. For example, both the content and number of colonial apologies by Emperor Akihito (1990) and Premiers Hosokawa (1993), Murayama Tatsuo (1994), and Hashimoto Ryutaro (1996) attest to the Japanese government's earnest efforts to placate Korean complaints about Ja-pan's lack of colonial repentance.[80] Agreements on expanded alien-resident rights for the Korean minority community in Japan in 1991 as well as attempts to minimize friction over the comfort-women issue of-fer other examples of efforts to shed rational light on historical dis-putes.[81] In the ultimate step at dealing with the past, the two govern-ments agreed in 1996 and 1997 to the establishment of binational his-tory committees.[82] ROK and Japanese foreign ministry officials admitted that these new outlooks and actions starkly contrast with the past po-lemics over historically tainted issues.[83]

Attitudinal changes among the general public naturally lag behind those at the elite level; nevertheless, transformations are apparent. A newspaper editorial was exemplary in this regard after the 1996 Kim Young-sam–Hashimoto summit:

Wiping off old scores is inevitable and necessary. . . . From a logical or practical point of view, emphasis ought naturally to be switched from the past to the fu-ture. . . . In spite of the prevailing consciousness and commitment [of Japan and Korea] in favor of future-oriented and positive partnership, some aberrant ele-ments occasionally speak out and act to disrupt growing amity and partnership through erroneous or malicious references to some old wounds. They should learn from the lessons of history and the requirements of current history for all parties concerned to work together with a sense of empathy and common good. Chauvinism is no patriotism for both countries.[84]

Finally, one area of continued friction between Japan and Korea will be the economic arena. South Korea's trade deficit with Japan has increased exponentially over the last decade, accounting for some 90 percent of the ROK's total trade deficit. However, as contentious as this issue may become, it is not likely to rupture relations. Though alarmingly large, the trade imbalance also attests to the volume of interaction between the two economies, consequently causing cooler heads to prevail in trade negotiations. In addition, the maturation of Korean democracy should engender a demeanor in trade talks less obsessed with dredging up colonial issues and emotional demands for trade concessions. At his November 1993 summit with Premier Hosokawa, for example, President Kim Young-sam acknowledged that a decline in Korean competitiveness was partially responsible for the mounting trade deficit with Japan and assured his counterpart that Korean attitudes toward trade negotiations would henceforth be based on "economic logic" not historical emotionalism.[85]

Another source of friction in current and future economic relations is advanced technology. Koreans claim that the Japanese have been reluctant to transfer high technology as the ROK has become increasingly competitive in international markets. Japan has deflected these complaints, arguing that technology transfer is a private-sector matter and therefore beyond government influence. However, recent changes in attitudes also bode well for resolving this problem. The ROK's efforts to develop an autonomous technological base through increased government and private-sector investment in research and development[86] and the establishment of various Japan-ROK cooperative science and technology projects reflect both governments' desire to approach this issue on a more rational and equal footing in the future.[87]

In sum, the quasi-alliance model predicts greater cooperation in future interaction between Japan and Korea. This optimism, most likely problematic for many students of the relationship, stems from a gradual transformation in the underlying abandonment/entrapment structure of relations. At the multilateral level, or outer layer, the period following the cold war presages a decreased U.S. presence in the region despite lingering security threats from North Korea and China. This raises mutual abandonment fears in Tokyo and Seoul and provides the external conditions conducive to greater cooperation. At the bilateral level, or inner core, emotions are giving way to realpolitik concerns. Complementing this trend, a less prominent U.S. role as a mediator of disputes between its two allies provides the enabling condition for more rational and responsible behavior between Seoul and Tokyo. Finally, nonstructural factors such as Japan's attempts to come to terms with its past and the ROK's democratic maturation further reduce potential areas of friction at the inner core of relations.

Final Thoughts

Theoretical models of international relations aim to explain systematically, rather than describe historically, the policies of nation states. This book seeks to identify the causal variables that drive Japan-ROK bilateral behavior. Rather than recount instances of cooperation and contention between the two states, I have tried to highlight the underlying abandonment/entrapment structure of relations and the importance of the two states' ties with their common ally, the United States, as the key determinants of *why* variations in behavior occur. To an astute observer of the region this book's basic argument may appear intuitively evident. However, it has not been stated before in the literature. Indeed, while many have talked about United States-Japan-Korea relations, the dynamics of this triangle have not been theoretically conceptualized or causally analyzed.

In this regard the quasi-alliance argument offers a systematic and rigorous explanation of Japan-ROK relations. It avoids the static nature of the prevailing approach based on historical animosities by accounting for both contentious and cooperative foreign-policy outcomes. Moreover, it aims for parsimony by explaining more about Japan-Korea behavior without a multitude of causal variables. The model also offers policy-relevant applications to the future state of the relationship.

This book also taps into a broader debate between those who study international relations and those who study East Asia. The origins of this debate began in the 1960s and 1970s. Authors such as James Morley (1965) and Lee Chae-jin (1976)[88] advanced the realist argument (without naming it as such) that basic strategic and economic interests would cause South Korea and China to strengthen future relations with Japan. This was followed by a second wave of authors—most notably Lee Chong-sik (1985) and Allen Whiting (1989)[89]—who argued that such national-interest–based arguments underestimated the negative impact that memories of Japan's past aggression would continue to have on Korean and Chinese behavior. This book responds to this second wave of authors by arguing that a more nuanced version of Realism, incorporating an appreciation of the causal importance of perceptions of threat and commitment, can explain seemingly anomalous behavior in Asia. It therefore argues that Western social scientific tools are useful in understanding East Asian international relations.

Admittedly the next step in assessing the usefulness of the quasi-alliance concept is to test its applicability to other international relationships. The argument appears most relevant to regions of the world in which small powers are geographically proximate, share external security threats, and need the support of a common great-power protector. Aside from the Japan-Korea case, other relationships in Northeast Asia exhibit these traits. Relations between Japan and Taiwan prior to the Sino-Japanese normalization represent a potential example. Other regions of the world where the quasi-alliance dynamic may be applicable are the Middle East and Eastern Europe, where a host of proximate states with high security concerns whose interaction is influenced by the level of commitment provided by a great power exists.

Some final remarks regarding Japan-Korea relations are in order. The model best explains Japan-ROK relations during the 1960s and 1970s and somewhat explains relations during the 1980s when external threats were high and security dependence on the United States was acute. Changes in the nature of the bilateral relationship and the external environment in the 1990s and into the new millennium may modify the causal effects of the model. For example, the cooperation imperatives vis-à-vis Japan produced by U.S. abandonment fears might be muted in Seoul because of the changed nature of the military balance on the peninsula since the 1960s, now greatly favoring the ROK, and the withering of traditional threats to the ROK in China and Russia. These imperatives may also be obstructed by the changing nature of domestic politics. In particular, democratization in the South weakens the traditional capabilities of ROK leaders to act with alacrity in responding to security needs. As alluded to earlier, democratization also can give rise to populist, nationalist views against Japan. As a result, future U.S. preferences for a diminished presence in Asia may not have the same causal impact on ROK policies toward Japan as they did in 1969 with the Nixon doctrine or in 1975 with U.S. disengagement from Vietnam.

In short, times have changed, and the theory, in its specific applications, might be more applicable to the cold-war era; however, this does not mean that the model is totally irrelevant in the post–cold-war era. Indeed, there are many aspects of the United States-Japan-ROK security triangle that remain the same. For example, in spite of the South's military superiority over the North, threats are still salient with regard to rash, isolated acts of belligerence by Pyongyang, which target ROK and Japanese cities, such as attacks with ballistic missiles or other weapons of mass destruction. Regardless of Japan's and the ROK's current economic status and potential inclinations toward military self-sufficiency in the future, the withdrawal of U.S. ground forces would still elicit some form of abandonment fear because of the forces' historic symbolism, first, as the physical bond that tied U.S. security interests with those of its allies and, second and more broadly, as the protective enclosure that enabled the two to avert difficult domestic political and grand strategy issues. Thus, the core behavioral tendencies in the model are not necessarily irrelevant to current and future scenarios for the region.

Moreover, I should note that I aim for a theoretically plausible, not historically definitive, explanation of the relationship. A legitimate criticism of such arguments is their underdetermining nature. They are generally more adept at determining the enabling conditions for events rather than the proximate causes. Accordingly, the quasi-alliance argument cannot explain every idiosyncratic historical wrinkle in Japan-ROK behavior. Nevertheless, as a systematic, generalizable argument that takes a first cut at analyzing foreign-policy outcomes in the relationship, it might prove useful.

Finally, this book does not deny the importance of the history that has passed between Japan and Korea and the emotionalism that continues to plague interaction. Instead, it has shown that this enmity is not the sole determinant of bilateral behavior. While history may tinge interaction between Japan and Korea, it is the larger geostrategic concerns that ultimately determine outcomes. This being said, there are two reasons why scholars have tended to focus so heavily on historical animosity. First, at least on the Korean side, this enmity has become inextricably intertwined with national identity: Korean patriotism is anti-Japanism. Second, the focus on historical enmity as an explanation is analytically convenient. For any given issue—whether it be a historical dispute, failed trade negotiation, or diplomatic protest—the pat explanation of Japan-Korean mutual distrust and contempt could be given. This indeed was the first reaction of many of the interviewees for this study. However, when pushed beyond this initial reaction for explanations as to why friction occurred in a particular instance or why friction was more intense in one period than another, these individuals admitted that broader realpolitik concerns were at work.

There are undoubtedly many in the school of historical animosity who would disagree with my emphasis on realpolitik over emotionalism. However, there are numerous historical precedents that lend credence to this message. In real-time calculations few would have figured during the Napoleonic wars that Britain and France would ever enter into cooperative arrangements or in the eighteenth century that Britain and the American colonies would become allies. In the aftermath of the Second World War few would have expected France and Germany to engage in cooperation despite their intense mutual enmities. And during the 1950s many did not envision the causal effect that realpolitik concerns would have on the ideological ties within the communist monolith. While different circumstances and events inform each of these historical examples, the basic point is same. As deep as historical animosity and emotionalism may run, they are not in the long term all-determining in state behavior.

Appendix

Appendix Tables

TABLE A.1

South Korean Trade with Japan, 1962–1995

Year	(US$ million)		
	Imports	Exports	Total
1962	109.2	23.5	132.7
1963	159.3	24.8	184.1
1964	110.1	38.2	148.3
1965	175	44.6	219.6
1966	293.8	64.9	358.7
1967	443	84.7	527.7
1968	623.2	99.7	722.9
1969	753.8	113.3	867.1
1970	809.3	234.3	1,043.6
1971	953.6	261.9	1,215.5
1972	1,031.2	409.6	1,440.8
1973	1,726.8	1,169.4	2,896.2
1974	2,620.5	1,379.6	4,000.1
1975	2,433.6	1,292.9	3,726.5
1976	3,099	1,801.6	4,900.6
1977	3,926.6	2,148.3	6,074.9
1978	5,981.5	2,627	8,608.5
1979	6,656.7	3,353	10,009.7
1980	5,857.8	3,039.4	8,897.2
1981	6,373.6	3,502.8	9,876.4
1982	5,305.3	3,388.1	8,693.4
1983	6,328.4	3,403.6	9,732
1984	7,640.1	4,602.2	12,242.3
1985	7,560.4	4,543.4	12,103.8
1986	10,869.3	5,425.7	16,295
1987	13,656.6	8,436.8	22,093.4
1988	15,928.9	12,004.2	27,933.1
1989	17,448.6	13,456.8	30,905.4
1990	18,573.9	12,637.9	31,211.8
1991	21,120.2	12,355.8	33,476

Year	(US$ million)		
	Imports	Exports	Total
1992	19,457.7	11,599.5	31,057.2
1993	20,015.5	11,564.4	31,579.9
1994	25,390	13,522.9	38,912.9
1995	32,606.4	17,048.9	49,655.3

SOURCES: Compiled from *Major Statistics of the Korean Economy* (Seoul: Economic Planning Board), vol. for 1982; and *Major Statistics of the Korean Economy* (monthly) (Seoul: National Statistical Office, Sept. 1996).

TABLE A.2

North Korean Trade with Japan, 1962-1995

Year	(US$ million)		
	Imports	Exports	Total
1962	n/a	n/a	
1963	n/a	n/a	
1964	12.4	18.2	30.6
1965	18.1	13.2	31.3
1966	5.3	20.6	25.9
1967	6.3	29.6	35.9
1968	20.7	34	54.7
1969	24.1	32.1	56.2
1970	25.6	31.3	56.9
1971	31.6	26.8	58.4
1972	103.8	33.8	137.6
1973	110.7	65.8	176.5
1974	277	99	376
1975	199	58.8	257.8
1976	106	65.1	171.1
1977	138.7	61	199.7
1978	203	98	301
1979	309.6	137.1	446.7
1980	414	165	579
1981	319	127	446
1982	344	137	481
1983	360	115.8	475.8
1984	279.5	131.1	410.6
1985	274.4	160.9	435.3
1986	203.9	154	357.9
1987	237.7	217.7	455.4
1988	263	293	556
1989	216	267	483
1990	194	271	465
1991	246	250	496
1992	246	231	477

	(US$ million)		
Year	Imports	Exports	Total
1993	243	222	465
1994	188	297	485
1995	n/a	n/a	n/a

SOURCES: Compiled from *Direction of Trade* (Washington, D.C.: International Monetary Fund, 1967, 1975); *Direction of Trade Statistics* (Washington, D.C.: International Monetary Fund, 1981, 1988, 1995); and Lee Chong-sik, *Japan and Korea*, 78.

TABLE A.3
Japan-ROK Economic Treaties and Related Agreements, 1967-1991

1967–71

Content: Civil Aviation (1967)
Technical assistance (1967)
Trademarks (1968)
Tax exemption (1969)
Double taxation (1970)
Agriculture/fishery (1971, ¥7.2 billion loan)
Small/medium firms (1971, ¥10.8 billion loan)
Kumoh technical training center (1971, ¥130 million grant)[a]
Kumoh technical training school (¥390 million loan)
Rail/subway construction (1971, ¥27.2 billion loan)

Aggregate total: 12
Adjusted total: 10

1972–74

Content: Telecommunications (1973, ¥6.2 billion loan)
Export-industry promotion (1973, ¥15.4 billion loan)
Kumoh technical training center (1974, ¥563 million grant)
Agricultural technological cooperation (1974)
Rural development (dam) (1974, ¥19.4 billion loan)
Laboratory equipment (1974, ¥500 million grant)

Aggregate total: 9
Adjusted total: 6

1975–79

Content: Pukpyong port (1975, ¥12.4 billion loan)
Seoul National University laboratory equipment (1975)
Taejon training institute (1976)
Seoul National University laboratory equipment (1976, ¥1 billion grant)
Telecommunications development (1976, ¥6.6 billion loan)
Agricultural development (1977, ¥12.6 billion loan)
Electricity transmission lines (1977, ¥6 billion loan)
Wheat and barley research (1977, ¥100 million grant)
Medical equipment (1977, ¥600 million grant)
Language laboratory equipment (1977, ¥17 million grant)
Continental shelf (1978)

Continental shelf II (1978)
Medical equipment (1978, ¥440 million grant)
Agricultural and medical equipment (1978, ¥14 billion loan)
Language laboratory equipment (1979, ¥15 million grant)

Aggregate total: 16
Adjusted total: 15

1980–88[b]

Content: Sewage treatment (1980, ¥19 billion loan)
Hospital and educational facilities (1981, ¥19 billion loan)
Development loan (1983, ¥45 billion loan)
Development loan (1984, ¥49.5 billion loan)
Double taxation (1985)
Development loan (1985, ¥54.4 billion loan)
Scientific and technological cooperation (1985)
Development loan (1987, ¥44.6 billion loan)
Development loan (1988, ¥27.2 billion loan)

Aggregate total: 12
Adjusted total: 9

1989–91

Content: Development loan (1989, ¥7.6 billion loan)
Maritime science/research (1990)
Nuclear energy (1990)
Development loan (1990, ¥99.5 billion loan)

Aggregate total: 6
Adjusted total: 4

SOURCE: Compiled from MOFA, *Taehan min'guk choyakjip: yangja choyak* (Bilateral treaties and agreements of the Republic of Korea), government publication no. 17000-25100-17-9459, vols. 2–14 (Seoul: Republic of Korea, Ministry of Foreign Affairs, International Treaties Division, 1962–91).

NOTE: Figures do not include 1965 normalization treaty or related agreements/amendments. Enumerated agreements are those listed under the adjusted total. Adjusted totals were calculated by subtracting from aggregate totals those agreements that were amendments or revisions of earlier agreements.

[a]Agreement signed in 1972 but negotiated during the 1967–71 period.
[b]Development loan agreements for 1983–87 are annual installments of the original 1983 $4-billion-loan agreement.

TABLE A.4

Official and Unofficial Visits Between the Premier of Japan and President of South Korea, 1945–1996

Year	No. of visits	Nature of visits	Visitors, dates, and purpose (if known)
1945	0	—	—
1946	0	—	—
1947	0	—	—
1948	1	unofficial	Rhee Syngman (Oct. 19 to Japan)
1949	0	—	—
1950	1	unofficial	Rhee (Feb. 16 to Japan)

Year	No. of visits	Nature of visits	Visitors, dates, and purpose (if known)
1951	0	—	—
1952	0	—	—
1953	1	unofficial	Rhee and Yoshida Shigeru meet (Jan. 16 in Tokyo)
1954	0	—	—
1955	0	—	—
1956	0	—	—
1957	0	—	—
1958	0	—	—
1959	0	—	—
1960	0	—	—
1961	1	unofficial	Park Chung-hee and Ikeda Hayato meet (Nov. 11 in Seoul)
1962	0	—	—
1963	0	—	—
1964	0	—	—
1965	0	—	—
1966	0	—	—
1967	1	unofficial	Sato Eisaku attends Park's inauguration (June 30 in Seoul)
1968	0	—	—
1969	0	—	—
1970	0	—	—
1971	1	unofficial	Sato attends Park's inauguration (July 1 in Seoul)
1972	0	official	Park-Sato summit (Nov. 11 in Tokyo) canceled
1973	0	—	—
1974	1	unofficial	Tanaka Kakuei attends Mrs. Park's funeral (Aug. 19 in Seoul)
1975	0	—	—
1976	0	—	—
1977	0	—	—
1978	0	—	—
1979	0	—	—
1980	0	—	—
1981	0	—	—
1982	0	—	—
1983	1	official	Nakasone Yasuhiro–Chun Doo-hwan summit (Jan. 11–12 in Seoul)
1984	1	official	Chun-Nakasone summit (Sept. 6–8 in Tokyo)
1985	0	—	—
1986	1	unofficial	Nakasone attends Asian Games (Sept. 20 in Seoul)
1987	0	—	—
1988	3	unofficial	Takeshita Noboru attends Roh Tae-woo's inauguration (Feb. 24–25 in Seoul) Former Prime Minister Nakasone (Feb. 10–12 to Seoul) Takeshita attends Olympics (Sept. 16–17 in Seoul)
1989	0	—	—
1990	3	unofficial	Former Prime Minister Nakasone (Mar. 23–25 to Seoul) Former Prime Minister Takeshita (Apr. 15–17 to Seoul)
		official	Roh summit (May 24–26 in Tokyo)

Year	No. of visits	Nature of visits	Visitors, dates, and purpose (if known)
1991	1	official	Kaifu Toshiki–Roh summit (Jan. 9–10 in Seoul)
1992	2	official	Miyazawa Kiichi–Roh summit (Jan. 16–18 in Seoul) Roh-Miyazawa summit (Nov. 8 in Kyoto)
1993	2	unofficial	Former Prime Minister Nakasone to APEC meetings (May 25–26 in Seoul)
		official	Hosokawa Morihiro–Kim Young-sam summit (Nov. 6–7 in Kyongju)
1994	3	unofficial	Kim (Mar. 24–26 to Japan) Muruyama (July 23–24 to Korea) Kim and Muruyama Tatsuo meet (Nov. 14 in Jakarta)
1995	5	unofficial	Former Prime Minister Hosokawa (Jan. 9–10 to Korea) Former Prime Minister Hata Tsutomu (May 15–18 to Korea) Former President Roh (May 19–30 to Japan) Former Prime Minister Hosokawa (Oct. 8–10 to Korea) Kim and Hosokawa meet (Nov. 18 in Osaka)
1996[a]	1	official	Hashimoto Ryutaro–Kim summit (June 23–24 in Cheju)

SOURCE: Compiled from *Ilbon kaehwang* (Summary status: Japan), government publication no. 17000-20030-67-9607 (Seoul: Republic of Korea, Ministry of Foreign Affairs, Feb. 1996), 223–26, 297, 300.
    [a]Through June 1996.

Reference Matter

Notes

Introduction: The Puzzle and Its Importance

1. In particular I draw heavily from the works of Glenn Snyder: "Alliances, Balance, and Stability," "Alliance Theory: A Neorealist First Cut" (hereafter "Alliance Theory"), "The Security Dilemma in Alliance Politics," and *Alliance Politics*.

2. The stigma attached to the mandatory imposition on Koreans of the Japanese language during the occupation, coupled with the lingering mistrust between Seoul and Tokyo in the early post-colonial period, resulted in both governments' acceptance of English for the official texts of all bilateral agreements until recently.

3. For example, as I was unable to access the works of former defense attaché Tsukamoto Katsuichi or Keiō University professor Okonogi Masao, I sought them out for interviews during research trips to Tokyo. I also interviewed such former Japanese ambassadors to the ROK and United States as Sunobe Ryōzō and Yasukawa Takeshi.

Chapter 1. The Enigma of History

1. For classic and more recent expositions of Realism, see Mearsheimer, "The False Promise"; Morgenthau, *Politics Among Nations*; and Waltz, *Theory of International Politics*.

2. This is, for illustrative purposes, a simple application of balance-of-threat logic as developed by Stephen Walt in *Origins of Alliances*. The quasi-alliance argument is not a refutation of Walt's theory, but a modification of some of its basic tenets.

3. This book focuses on Japan-ROK relations at the government level. Private channels of dialogue between Japan and the ROK also play an important role in policymaking. These channels are semiofficial and have involved influential political insiders and business leaders. From the 1950s to the 1970s key participants included Kishi Nobusuke, former premier and half-brother of Sato Eisaku; Chang Key-young, former premier; Uemura Kogoro, chairman, Keidan-

ren; Nagano Shigeo, chairman, New Japan Steel; Lee Tong-won and Shiina Etsusaburo, both former foreign ministers; and other individuals, such as Ono Banboku, Kono Ichiro, Iseki Yujiro, Paek Nam-ok, Funada Naka, Nakagawa Ichiro, Tokuyasu Chijucho, Sukimiji Cho, Hasagawa Jin, Paik Tu-jin, Kaya Okinori, Iishi Mitsujiro, Kim Song-kun, Yatsugi Kazuo, and Nakamura Kikuo. On many bilateral issues they conducted the preliminary groundwork that enabled agreements to be reached at official fora, such as the annual joint ministerial conferences. I focus on government-level interaction rather than private channels because the latter were always initiated at the direction of the former, and in no case did such private channels determine policy in contradiction to government preferences.

4. Balance-of-threat theory might explain the absence of good relations between the two states as the result of free-riding or buck-passing dynamics (Walt, 30–31); however, this still does not explain why relations between the two are antagonistic and subject to such wide variations.

5. Many works on the relationship have tended more toward diplomatic histories than analytical inquiries. These books have provided richly detailed descriptions of key events but generally have not sought out the deeper causal dynamics behind relations, those that not only describe conflict but explain why and how it occurs. The seminal work is still Yi Chŏngsik, *Han'guk kwa Ilbon* (hereafter cited by the English edition, Lee Chong-sik, *Japan and Korea*). Also see Bridges; Hahn Bae-ho and Yamamoto Tadashi, *Korea-Japan Relations: A New Dialogue*; and Hahn, ed., *Korea-Japan Relations: Challenges and Opportunities*; Kim Kwan-bong; Lee Chae-jin and Sato, *U.S. Policy*; and Shin. Some of the better articles include Kil Sŭnghŭm, "*Han-Il kukkyo chŏngsanghwa 20-nyŏn ŭi pansŏng*" (Reflections on 20 years of normalization between Korea and Japan); and Okonogi, "A Japanese Perspective." Other works that provide detailed historical chronologies of the relationship include Kim Hong-nak, "Japan's Policy Toward the Korean Peninsula"; Koh, *Foreign Policy Systems*; and Youn.

6. These categories are in no way distinct, as authors will often combine arguments from each approach; however, they are representative of the previous attempts to analyze contemporary Japan-Korea relations.

7. Representative of this argument are Ahn Byung-joon, "Political and Economic Development"; Bridges, ch. 3; Cho, "A Korean View"; Hahn, "Japan's International Role"; Hirono, "A Japanese View"; Sato Seizaburo, "Indispensable but Uneasy Partnership"; and Tanaka Akira.

8. For example, some attribute the generally poor relations between Japan and the ROK in the immediate postwar years to President Rhee Syngman's use of anti-Japan sentiment to rally support and consolidate power in a politically unstable environment (see Cheong).

9. In a related vein one widely used argument during the postwar era was that the continuity of LDP rule was itself a source of friction with the ROK, especially with regard to historical disputes. This was largely because the conservative LDP was less willing to criticize Japan's past aggression than the more

liberal opposition elements, fostering continuing anger and resentment in Korea. As a result, those holding this view argued that there was little chance of improvement in relations as long as the opposition in Japan remained out of power (see Kobayashi Keiji et al.). Other works that highlight the importance of domestic politics include Ahn Byong-man, "The Internal Political Change in Japan"; Han Sung-joo, "Convergent and Divergent Interests"; Kim Hong-nak, "Japanese-Korean Relations in the 1980s"; Kim Kwan-bong, *The Korea-Japan Treaty Crisis*; and Watanabe Akio "Political Change in Japan and Korea-Japan Relations."

10. Virtually every work on Japan-Korea relations includes these as key obstacles to genuinely amiable relations.

11. The coercive policies were more prevalent during the initial and late stages of the occupation, 1905–19 and after 1934. As historians have shown, Japan's colonial policies in the interim were more moderate and at times benevolent. Nevertheless, it is the harsher periods that remain most vivid in Korean collective memories. For studies on this period, see Eckert et al., chs. 15–17; Conroy; Grajdanzev; Lee Changsoo and de Vos, ch. 2; and Lee, *Japan and Korea*, ch. 1.

12. For a readable clinical introduction to this concept, see Luke Han, "Han: Unquenched Woes of the Oppressed," *Korea Times*, 5 Dec. 1990. Also see Kim Sŏnyŏp; and Lee Jung-hoon.

13. See Hahn, "Japan's International Role," 9–11; and Lee and de Vos, ch. 1.

14. Cited in Cheong, 104.

15. Conversation with U.S. official, Richard Finn, on 3 Feb. 1949, as cited in Cheong, 72.

16. Hahn, "Japan's International Role," 10–11.

17. See 1984, 1988, and 1990 public opinion polls by *Tong-a* and *Asahi*, cited in Bridges, 22–26; also see Kim Tongsŏn; and Tsujimura, 75–78.

18. See Hong, 198–208; Imazu, "A New Era," 359; Tanaka Akira, 30; Tanaka Yasumasa; and Wakatsuki, 48.

19. See Kil, "*Han-Il kukkyo chŏngsanghwa 20-nyŏn ŭi pansŏng*," 146; and Kobayashi Keiji et al., 260–75.

20. Similarly, at the 1951 talks chief delegate Iguchi Sadao silently listened to a litany of emotional ROK demands (personally written by Rhee) that Japan bear responsibility for "burying the hatchet" of the past. He then responded by indifferently asking what hatchets the Koreans were referring to (Cheong, 104).

21. For the Shōwa apology, see Republic of Korea, Ministry of Foreign Affairs (hereafter ROK-MOFA), *Ilbon kaehwang* (Summary status: Japan), 363. For South Korean dissatisfaction with the wording, see Kil Sŭnghŭm et al., "*Han-il kwan'gye ŭi chiha sumaek chindan*" (Examining the hidden pulse of Korea-Japan relations). Emperor Akihito's apology in 1990 attempted to address these semantic criticisms by providing a more direct expression of Japanese regret.

22. For a concise overview of this issue see Kim, "Japanese-South Korean

Relations in the 1980s"; Kim Hosup, "Policy-Making of Japanese Official Development Assistance," ch. 6; and Lee, *Japan and Korea*, especially ch. 6.

23. For the dispute between the two governments over this issue, see Hoffman; and Lee and de Vos. For an interesting ethnographic study on the North
Korean population in Japan, see Ryang.

24. See Victor D. Cha, "Forgotten by History."

25. For representative works that either implicitly or explicitly use this approach, see Bridges, 9–11; Fuccello; Hahn, "Policy Toward Japan"; Lee, *Japan
and Korea*; and Nam Koon Woo, 9–10. Fuccello's dissertation is one of the
earliest attempts to develop a theoretical model for this argument.

26. For the treaty text see ROK-MOFA, *Taehan min'guk woegyo yŏnp'yo:
1965* (Diplomatic documents annual), 321–23. For a comprehensive analysis of
the contents of the treaty, corresponding documents, and the history of negotiations see Kim Kwan-bong, ch. 2; ROK-MOFA, *Ilbon kaehwang*, 314–41; and
Yi Tongwŏn and Fukuda, 244–58.

27. The ROK demanded a comprehensive settlement that included, in true
Confucian tradition, a formal expression of Japanese repentance for their im-
moral past actions, financial reparations as a tangible admission of this guilt, a
Japanese promise of nonaggression, return of cultural assets and gold reserves,
and financial restitution for conscripted laborers. The Japanese agenda focused
on two legal issues requiring immediate settlement: the repatriation of Koreans
living in Japan and the demarcation of territorial waters. Japan rejected ROK
demands for a full settlement on the legal grounds that the country was technically still under Supreme Command of the Allied Powers (SCAP) occupation in
October 1951 and therefore did not exercise sovereignty to negotiate a settlement. (For an interesting discussion of the clash between Korea's Confucian
ideals and Japan's legalistic, Western attitude toward the treaty talks, see Kim
Kwan-bong, 41–48; and Lee, *Japan and Korea*, 40–42.) Although the ROK negotiators were fluent in Japanese as a result of the occupation, these talks were
held in English; in addition, the prevailing legal text of the treaty, although
written in both Japanese and Korean, was the English version. U.S. officials described the South Korean attitude at these first meetings as so laden with emo-
tion and anger that negotiation was virtually impossible (see Lee and Sato, *U.S.
Policy*, 28; and Yi and Fukuda, 249).

28. The immediate need for the demarcation of waters between Seoul and
Tokyo stemmed from the end of the SCAP occupation. The San Francisco
treaty terminated a postwar arrangement that barred Japanese vessels from operating in waters beyond the halfway point, the MacArthur line, between Korea
and Japan. In negotiations over a new line of exclusive and joint waters Koreans wanted to keep the MacArthur line intact, as this would ensure exclusive
rights over fishing and mineral resources in waters that normally would be
designated as open seas. Japan refused to recognize such a line and sought a
three–twelve-mile demarcation. On the origin of the MacArthur line and the
early stages of this dispute, see Cheong, ch. 2, especially 22–25, 32–34, and
109–10.

29. For the text of the Kubota statement see ROK-MOFA, *Korea-Japan Relations: Korean Views, Related Documents*, 145–52; also see Yi Tongwŏn, *Taet'ongryŏngŭl kŭrimyŏ* (Yearning for the president), 184. SCAP authorities estimated in August 1945 that Japanese properties and assets seized in Korea totaled $2.9 billion in the North and $2.3 billion in the South; Japan's counter-offer for reparations was $70 million.

30. Japan's labor conscription policies during the Second World War brought two million Koreans to Japan. Many of them returned home after the occupation, leaving approximately six hundred thousand who chose to reside in Japan. Tokyo first treated this entire population as nationals but in 1950 adjusted the policy to provide permanent residence status only to those settling in Japan before 1945. It sought a repatriation agreement with Seoul, but talks stalled over Korean demands that repatriates be allowed to bring all assets out of Japan and receive sizable compensation. For a synopsis of this issue, see Cheong, ch. 5; and James Morley, *Japan and Korea*, 60–61.

31. This stipulated a total of $300 million in grants and $300 million in loans to the ROK, classifying these funds as "economic aid" rather than "colonial restitutions." For the contents of the memo, see *Han-Il kwan'gye charyojip* (Collected materials on Korea-Japan relations) 1: 143; and *Korean Republic Sunday Magazine*, 1 Jan. 1963, 8.

32. In remarks delivered upon his arrival at the airport, Shiina stated: "We must express our regret, however, over the unhappy relations which have existed between our two nations during a certain period in the long history of the two countries, and over which Japan is engaged in serious self-reflection." (See ROK-MOFA, *Ilbon kaehwang*, 363; and *Japan Times*, 17 and 18 Feb. 1965.) This constituted the first public apology for the colonial period by Japan and fulfilled an important precondition laid down by Seoul for normalization (Yi, *Taet'ongryŏngŭl kŭrimyŏ*, 207, 232).

33. This draft laid out the basic relations text of the treaty and outlined points of agreement and disagreement on the remaining technical issues (see *Japan Times*, 21 Feb. 1965). Two key issues resolved in conjunction with the basic relations agreement were (1) the invalidation of all previous treaties associated with Japanese annexation and (2) Japanese recognition of the ROK as the sole legitimate government of Korea, as specified in Resolution 195 (III) of the United Nations General Assembly. For the Lee-Shiina joint communiqué see ROK-MOFA, *Taehan min'guk woegyo yŏnp'yo: 1965*, 78–79. For an account of the eleventh-hour negotiations among Lee, Shiina, Ushiroku Torao, and Yŏn Ha-gu over these issues, see Emmerson, *Arms, Yen and Power*, 263–64; Yi, *Taet'ongryŏngŭl kŭrimyŏ*, 222–31; and Yi and Fukuda, 253. South Koreans assumed the latter agreement to mean that Tokyo recognized theirs as the only government on the entire peninsula; however, the resolution technically recognized the ROK only in that area over which UN authority was accepted (i.e., South Korea). This ambiguous wording left open the possibility of Japanese recognition of North Korea in the future, which became an issue of contention between Seoul and Tokyo during the detente period.

34. The key issue in each of these subcommittees was, respectively, (1) permanent residency rights for Koreans living in Japan; (2) the balance among grant aid, government loans, and commercial loans; and (3) abolition of the Rhee line. Regarding the latter, the key sticking points centered on Korean claims to the rich fishing areas around Cheju Island, regulations on the number of vessels and haul size of catches allowed in joint fishing zones, and monitoring and enforcement procedures (see *Korean Republic*, 3, 4 Mar. 1965; and *Korea Times*, 4 Mar. 1965).

35. An archival note: Lee's memoirs are unclear on this point. He verifies that the deadlock over the fisheries issue was particularly severe but implies that there was a very vague meeting of minds with Shiina over a settlement (*Taet'ongryŏngŭl kŭrimyŏ*, 243). Contemporary newspapers reported that no breakthroughs were achieved on this trip. The author's interviews with Lee did not elicit a definitive answer to this. However, given intense U.S. pressures for an early settlement (discussed below), one would surmise that had Lee achieved any semblance of an agreement with Shiina during this Tokyo trip, he would have played this up in advance of his meetings with Johnson and Rusk (see *Japan Times*, 11, 12 Mar. 1965; *Korean Republic*, 11 Mar. 1965; and Yi, *Taet'ongryŏngŭl kŭrimyŏ*, 238–44).

36. See *Japan Times*, 25 Mar. 1965; *Korean Republic*, 25–26 Mar. 1965; and *Stars and Stripes*, 26 Mar. 1965.

37. *Japan Times*, 4 Apr. 1965; and *Korean Republic*, 4 Apr. 1965. For the Shiina-Lee joint communiqué see ROK-MOFA, *Taehan min'guk woegyo yŏnp'yo: 1965*, 122–23. The fisheries agreement included a twelve-mile exclusive fishing zone around the ROK and exclusive rights to the resource-rich corridor between Cheju Island and the peninsula. Jointly regulated fishing zones were also established in the high seas formerly under the Rhee line. Regarding the issue of overseas Koreans, residency status was granted to those settling in Japan before World War II and to descendants of families subject to labor conscription programs during the occupation. The formula for financial claims was as stated in the final terms of the treaty. The last outstanding issue was the disputed sovereignty of Tokto/Takeshima, a small islet between the two countries (for a synopsis of each side's postwar claims to this territory, see Cheong, 38–45). The two governments exchanged notes affirming that the issue would be settled through diplomatic mediation at a future date. See Emmerson, *Arms, Yen and Power*, 264–65; *Japan Times*, 23, 26 June 1965; Morley, *Japan and Korea*, 58–62; and United States, Central Intelligence Agency (hereafter CIA), "Special Report."

38. In total these antitreaty movements in Korea involved over 3.5 million individuals from March 1964 to September 1965 (see *Japan Times*, 14, 16 Apr., 7 May 1965; and Kim Kwan-bong, 111–12, 116).

39. For example, see Bridges, 10; and Lee, *Japan and Korea*, 23–42.

40. Cited in Lee and Sato, *U.S. Policy*, 26. For a study of Rhee as a Korean nationalist see Oliver.

41. Lee Jung-hoon, 176.

42. See Fuccello, 102; and Lee and Sato, *U.S. Policy*, 28. The two leaders eventually did meet in Tokyo at the behest of UN Commander General Mark Clark.

43. For a profile of the personalities that made up the Rhee and Park governments see Fuccello, 92–121.

44. Former personal secretary of Park Chung-hee, interview by author, 29 June 1992, Seoul.

45. Park often used the honorific term for "senior" (*sŏnbaenimdŭl*) to address his Japanese counterparts (see Yi, *Taet'ongryŏngŭl kŭrimyŏ*, 184–85).

46. For representative examples of this argument see Cheong; Kil Soonghoom, "South Korean Policy," 35–50; Kim Kwan-bong, ch. 3; Kim Tongjo; Welfield, *Empire in Eclipse*, 200–214; Woo, ch. 4; and Yi and Fukuda.

47. For an example of ROK insecurities regarding their northern counterpart's economic success at the time see *Washington Post* (Rafael Steinberg, "ROK Looks to the North"), reprinted in *Japan Times*, 7 Mar. 1965.

48. South Korea private savings rates were only 1.6 percent of GNP, and government savings were in perpetual deficit (Woo, 81). In addition, the 1961 Foreign Assistance Act established that future U.S. aid to Korea would be in the form of loans rather than grants. Total economic and military assistance for 1960 and 1965 declined from $529 million to $309 million, respectively (figures quoted in Lee and Sato, *U.S. Policy*, 24–25, 35).

49. These business magnates formed the pronormalization Korean Businessmen's Association in 1961. They included individuals such as Lee Byong-chol, Lee Chong-rim, Chong Chae-ho, Lee Han-ung, and Pak Hung-shik, all of whom had already reaped substantial profits from the redistribution of Japanese colonial holdings after liberation and from pocketing U.S. economic aid during the Korean war. They saw normalization as another opportunity to make substantial profits through both legal and illicit business ventures (see Kim Kwan-bong, 87–88).

50. *Japan Times*, 24 June 1965.

51. Lee Tong-won, interview by author, 27 May 1992, Seoul (hereafter Lee Tong-won interview, 27 May 1992). For specific recollections of Lee's meetings with Park regarding the urgent and pragmatic need for normalization with Japan, see Yi, *Taet'ongryŏngŭl kŭrimyŏ*, 184, 186–87.

52. Ambassador Park Sang-yong, political counselor, Korean embassy, Washington, 1961–64, and prime minister's office, 1964–66, interview by author, 30 Mar., 19 May 1992, Seoul. Also see Yi and Fukuda, 250.

53. The quotation is from the Gaimushō's first white paper on the Japan-ROK normalization talks, as reported in *Korea Times*, 20 Mar. 1965. For similar assessments by other Japanese officials, see Lee, *Japan and Korea*, 48.

54. Many of these were former colonial officials who still retained considerable influence within the conservative wing of the LDP. They included individuals such as Yagi Nobuo, former premiers Kishi Nobusuke and Yoshida Shigeru, LDP Vice-President Ono Banboku, former Defense Agency chief Funada Naka, Iseki Yujiro, Justice Minister Ishii Mitsujiro, and Noguchi Uichi. Most

were part of a pro-South Korean LDP study group formed in April 1961, known as *Nikkan Mondai Kondankai* (Roundtable on the South Korean problem), also known as the *ch'in han p'a* (friends of Korea).

55. Former Premier Kishi's reasoning after Park's 1961 coup reflected this view: "South Korea is under a military regime where a small number of leaders under Park Chung Hee can decide things. . . . So, if [we] persuaded Chairman Park at a certain level, [that will be all]. They have no National Assembly. Even if the newspapers opposed it, Chairman Park can seal them off" (cited in Lee, *Japan and Korea*, 47).

56. This included individuals such as Uemura Kogoro, Adachi Tadashi, Doko Toshio, Ando Toyoroku, and Anzai Masao, who held key positions in major Japanese organizations, such as the Japan Chamber of Commerce, the Federation of Economic Organizations, and the Japan Federation of Employer Associations. This lobby allied with conservative *ch'in han p'a* (pro-south Korean) politicians (Kishi Nobusuke, Ishii Mitsujiro, Ono Banboku, former Minister of Finance Shibusawa Keizo, and Funada Naka) in pushing pro-ROK policies (see Kim Kwan-bong, 88–89).

57. For example, companies such as Nisshō Trading, Mitsubishi Trading, Marubeni Trading, Hitachi, and Nippon Kōei had all staked out projects to undertake once normalization occurred.

58. Yi and Fukuda, 250.

59. This is a tremendously understudied aspect of Japan-ROK normalization. The most complete work on the treaty, by Kim Kwan-bong, acknowledges that "one of the most important factors working toward the normalization of relations between the ROK and Japan was the pressure applied by the United States" (78); however, he does not delve into the nature of this pressure. For recent works that attempt to fill this gap, see Victor Cha, "Bridging the Gap"; Cha, "1965 nyŏn Hanil sugyo hyŏpchŏng" (1965 Korea-Japan normalization); and Kim Jiyul, ch. 7.

60. For example, efforts by such individuals as Edwin Reischauer to convince administration officials of the need to push for normalization in 1960 and 1961 met with little response (see letter, Edwin Reischauer to McGeorge Bundy, 21 Aug. 1964 [secret, declassified 2 July 1993], "Korea, Vol. I," Korea Country File [hereafter KCF], National Security File [hereafter NSF], Box 254, Lyndon Baines Johnson [hereafter LBJ] Library, Austin, Texas).

61. Exacerbating the situation, France's recognition of China (January 1964), Japan's growing economic relations with Beijing, and SEATO's failure as a collective security organization represented a weakening of the Western anticommunist front in the region.

62. At the time the ROK received $185 million in economic aid and $147 million in military assistance. These made up a disproportionate 9 and 14 percent, respectively, of total U.S. aid outlays.

63. For U.S. concerns regarding this particular point see State Department telegram (hereafter septel) 97 (Washington), Rusk-embassy, Seoul, 2 Aug. 1964 (confid., declassified 2 July 1993), "Korea, Vol. II," KCF, NSF, Box 254, LBJ

Library. For background on contacts by Japanese opposition groups and trade associations with North Korea in these early years see Morley, *Japan and Korea*, 63–65.

64. See "Department of State Policy on the Future of Japan," 26 June 1964 (secret, declassified 29 May 1991), "Japan, Vol. II-Cables," Japan Country File (hereafter JCF), NSF, Box 250, LBJ Library, 86. For internal White House memoranda to this effect see Briefing Paper, The White House, 7 May 1965 (confid., declassified 7 Aug. 1992), "Park Visit Briefing Book," KCF, NSF, Box 256, LBJ Library, 1.

65. Reischauer-Bundy, 21 Aug. 1964 (declassified 2 July 1993), "Korea, Vol. I," KCF, NSF, Box 254, LBJ Library. Also see Reischauer, 206.

66. The treaty issue sat at the top of Rusk's agenda in meetings with Premier Ikeda and President Park; in the former case ahead of other important pending issues such as port calls for U.S. nuclear submarines, relations with China, and trade liberalization. See memorandum of conversation (hereafter memcon), Rusk-Ohira, 26 Jan. 1964 (confid., declassified 30 May 1991), "Japan, Vol. I-Memos," JCF, NSF, Box 250, LBJ Library, 1; memcon, Rusk-Ohira, 28 Jan. 1964 (secret, declassified 22 June 1993), "Japan, Vol. I-Memos," JCF, NSF, Box 250, LBJ Library, Part 1, 1–2; embtel 989 (Seoul), Berger-Rusk, 30 Jan. 1964 (secret, declassified 30 June 1992), "Korea, Vol. I," KCF, NSF, Box 254, LBJ Library, 2; and memcon, Rusk-Takeuchi, 29 Feb. 1964 (confid., declassified 29 May 1991), "Japan, Vol. I-Memos," JCF, NSF, Box 250, LBJ Library, 1. Rusk's visit to Asia received front-page headlines as indicative of new U.S. support for the embattled treaty process (e.g., see *Korean Republic*, 26, 30 Jan., 2 Feb. 1964).

67. See embtel 1761 (Tokyo), Reischauer-State, 17 Nov. 1964 (secret, sanitized 23 Dec. 1975), "Asia and Pacific," NSF 1963–69, Johnson Administration microfilm, reel 10, frame 226–30; and memo, Komer-the president, 9 Apr. 1964, "Asia and Pacific," NSF 1963–69, Johnson Administration microfilm, reel 10, frame 122.

68. According to a U.S. assessment of the demonstrations in late March 1964: "The riots were against Kim Chong Pil as well as against continuation of the talks with Japan . . . many of the people believe that KCP (Kim Chong Pil) is too close to the Japanese" (telegram, CINCPAC-JCS, 5 Apr. 1964 [secret, declassified 22 Jan. 1992], "Korea, Vol. I," KCF, NSF, Box 254, LBJ Library). Accusations against Kim charged that he had bargained down the financial restitutions package in 1962 in exchange for $20 million in Japanese funds for financing the DRP; had illicitly imported Japanese autos, cement, and sugar duty-free, which were then sold in Korea for huge personal profits; and had received bribes from Japanese companies for exclusive monopoly rights in Korea after normalization. U.S. intelligence reports showed that Japan indeed financed as much as 66 percent of the DRP's 1961–65 budgets. On these points see Cha, "Bridging the Gap," 135–36; CIA, "Special Report"; 6; Kim Se-jin, 115–16; and Woo, 107.

69. Embtel 1330 (Seoul), Berger-Rusk, 20 Apr. 1964 (confid., declassified

30 June 1992), "Korea, Vol. I," KCF, NSF, Box 254, LBJ Library. For other communications to this effect see embtel 1374 (Seoul), Berger-Rusk, 27 Apr. 1964 (secret, declassified 10 Aug. 1992), "Korea, Vol. I," KCF, NSF, Box 254, LBJ Library, 1; and embtel 1277 (Seoul), Berger-Rusk, 9 Apr. 1964 (confid., declassified 30 June 1992), "Korea, Vol. I," KCF, NSF, Box 254, LBJ Library, 3 (sec. 1).

70. Outlined in a June 11, 1964, State-embassy cable, Kim's departure for the United States was ostensibly to participate in a summer seminar at Harvard run by Henry Kissinger and was arranged through a private foundation in Dallas by R. Douglas Payne of the Southwestern Research Society. The letter to Kissinger (reprinted in the cable) attests to the urgency of the arrangement: "I apologize that for you to accept a nomination at this late date presents you with real difficulties. I would be less than frank, as well, if I did not admit Kim Chong P'il suffers certain deficiencies as participant in your seminar. . . . Notwithstanding obvious difficulties, I sincerely hope you can decide to accept Kim Chong P'il . . . and extend an invitation at once to him." See septel 1133 and 1134 (Washington), Rusk-Berger, 11 June 1964 (secret, declassified 10 Aug. 1992), "Korea, Vol. I," KCF, NSF, Box 254, LBJ Library; and embtel 1660 (Seoul), Berger-Rusk, 15 June 1964 (confid., declassified 10 Aug. 1992), "Korea, Vol. I," KCF, NSF, Box 254, LBJ Library.

71. Embtel 557 (Seoul), Brown-Rusk, 21 Dec. 1964 (secret, sanitized 27 May 1992), "Korea, Vol. I," KCF, NSF, Box 254, LBJ Library, 1–2. For additional details see Cha, "Bridging the Gap," 135–36.

72. Contents of the letter as reported in septel 99 (Washington), Rusk-embassy, Seoul, 2 Aug. 1964 (confid., declassified 23 June 1993), "Korea, Vol. II," KCF, NSF, Box 254, LBJ Library. Also see memcon, the president-Brown, The White House, 31 July 1964 (confid., declassified 23 June 1993), "Korea, Vol. II," KCF, NSF, Box 254, LBJ Library. Internal communications between National Security Advisor McGeorge Bundy and Robert Komer reflected the intensity of U.S. efforts at the time: "I think I've got rolling another effort at ROK/Jap settlement, utilizing arrival of new ambassador and LBJ's willingness to weigh in personally . . . when Brown explained our ROK/Jap scenario he [LBJ] warmly endorsed, said he regarded settlement as 'top priority' (thank God), and told Win 'I'll pray for you.' At any rate, we now have State brought around to the point where it agrees US should take a direct hand in pushing settlement through. We've got LBJ saying so orally to Pak through Brown, and we've got Brown ginned up and willing to fire up Reischauer" (memo, Komer-Bundy, 3 Aug. 1964 [secret, declassified 23 June 1993], "Korea, Vol. II," KCF, NSF, Box 254, LBJ Library). For details of additional efforts by Assistant Secretary for East Asian Affairs William Bundy in October 1964, see Cha, "Bridging the Gap," 137–38.

73. Upon becoming foreign minister in July 1964, Lee personally communicated these objections to Park (see Yi, Taet'ongryŏngŭl kŭrimyŏ, 186–88). The information below is also based on interviews with former Foreign Minister Lee Tong-won, 19, 27 May 1992 and 19 Dec. 1994, Seoul; and Yi and Fukuda, 252.

74. Yi, *Taet'ongryŏngŭl kŭrimyŏ*, 192–93, 203.

75. Bundy also put pressure on the new premier, Sato, in November 1964 to send Shiina to Korea. Shiina's decision met with strong protest from both ultra-conservative and liberal elements in Japan. The former criticized the trip as degrading to the national character; the latter charged that Shiina was seeking an alliance with the ROK. The Japan Socialist Party (JSP) later introduced a no-confidence motion in the Diet against the foreign minister over the trip.

76. Reischauer, 206–7, 281. For a similar recollection of the U.S. mediating role see interview with William Bundy in Lee and Sato, *U.S. Policy*, 30.

77. Lee Tong-won, interview by author, 19 May 1992, Seoul (hereafter Lee Tong-won interview, 19 May 1992).

78. As Reischauer stated, Tokyo's hesitance in this regard stemmed from the fact that with each forward step, it had to overcome public skepticism over repeated disappointments in the past, strong nationalist sentiment not to concede on certain issues in the talks (e.g., the fisheries), and charges by opposition politicians of forging anticommunist alliances that would entangle Japan in America's war efforts (see embtel 1761 [Tokyo], Reischauer-Rusk, 17 Nov. 1964 [secret, sanitized 23 Dec. 1975], "Asia and the Pacific," NSF 1963–69, Johnson Administration microfilm, reel 10, frame 226–30).

79. See ROK-MOFA, *Taehan min'guk woegyo yŏnp'yo: 1965*, 108–9; also see memcon, Lee-Rusk, 15 Mar. 1965 (confid., declassified 10 Aug. 1992), "Korea, Vol. II," KCF, NSF, Box 254, LBJ Library, 3.

80. See memcon, the president-Lee Tong-won, 17 Mar. 1965 (confid., declassified 23 June 1993), "Korea, Vol. II," KCF, NSF, Box 254, LBJ Library.

81. Memo, Rusk-the president, 1 Mar. 1965 (confid., declassified 15 Apr. 1991), "Korea, Park Visit 5/65," KCF, NSF, Box 256, LBJ Library.

82. Yi, *Taet'ongryŏngŭl kŭrimyŏ*, 247.

83. See U.S. embassy reports of press coverage in embtel 879 (Seoul), Doherty-Rusk, 18 Mar. 1965, "Korea, Vol. II," KCF, NSF, Box 254, LBJ Library. For elaboration of these points see Cha, "Bridging the Gap," 140–41.

84. As White House briefing papers stated: "Park has come to Washington for one paramount reason: he seeks the strongest possible indication from us, both through our courtesies to him and through tangible evidence of continuing U.S. assistance, that *we have no intention of abandoning Korea to Japanese control* in the wake of a Japan-Korea settlement. Whatever reassurance we can give him will ease the severe problems he faces in gaining the support of his people for the ratification and acceptance of such a settlement" (original emphasis) (memo, James C. Thomson, Jr.-the president, 17 May 1965 [secret, declassified 23 Apr. 1991], "Park Visit Briefing Book," KCF, NSF, Box 256, LBJ Library).

85. For the Johnson-Park communiqué see *American Foreign Policy: Current Documents, 1965*, 779–81, especially clauses 7–9 (subsecs. A–D); also see *Japan Times*, 18–20 May 1965; and memcon, the president-Park Chung Hee, 17 May 1965 (secret, declassified 24 Aug. 1989), "Korea, Vol. II," KCF, NSF, Box 254, LBJ Library.

86. Memcon, Rusk-Park Chung Hee, 18 May 1965 (confid., declassified 2 July 1993), "Korea, Vol. II," KCF, NSF, Box 254, LBJ Library, 3. In the aftermath of the treaty signing the United States also steered clear of raising other politically sensitive bilateral issues with Seoul and Tokyo which might fuel efforts to block ratification. For examples of these see Cha, "Bridging the Gap," 142; and Kim Jiyul, ch. 7. It should be noted that while U.S. actions were couched in the language of commitments and assurances, policymakers clearly saw the normalization treaty as a way of paring down U.S. commitments to Korea as events in Vietnam unfolded. These subtleties in U.S. policy are taken up in the concluding chapter.

87. As Lee recalls, antitreaty sentiment was so acute that inner circles of leadership in both Seoul and Tokyo opposed any conciliatory moves at each step in the negotiations and even cautioned Shiina and Lee before their February and March 1965 visits of possible assassination attempts by antitreaty fanatics (see Yi, Taet'ongryŏngŭl kŭrimyŏ, 203–4, 245–46).

88. South Korean and Japanese officials involved in the normalization process acknowledged that U.S. pressures for an early settlement became noticeably stronger during this period. For example, while normalization was the primary agenda item in 1964 and 1965 high-level meetings with the United States, it was at best a side issue, not even covered by newspapers, during Park's 1961 summit with Kennedy (see Kim Kwan-bong, 79–80; Korean Republic, 18, 25 Nov. 1961; Yi, Taet'ongryŏngŭl kŭrimyŏ, 190–91; and Yi and Fukuda, 250). Lee Tong-won interview, 19 May 1992; Ambassador Park Sang-yong, interview by author, 30 Mar. 1992, Seoul; and Sunobe Ryōzō, interview by author, 10 July 1992, Tokyo (hereafter Sunobe interview).

Chapter 2. The Argument: Quasi Alliances

1. For a definition of alliance see Snyder, Alliance Politics, 4; Wolfers, "Alliances," 268; and Walt, 1.

2. For concise reviews of the literature on alliances see Holsti et al., ch. 1; Kegley and Raymond, "Preservation of Peace," 270–89; Snyder, "Alliances, Balance, and Stability," 121–22; Snyder, Alliance Politics, ch. 1; and Walt, 6–11.

3. George Liska's book Nations in Alliance still stands as the seminal work. Glenn Snyder's new book, Alliance Politics (just released as this book went to press) is certain to be the next classic. Other studies in the Realist vein include Holsti et al.; Morgenthau, "Alliances in Theory and Practice"; and Walt. For formal modeling approaches that include economic, coalition, and game theoretic applications, see Cross; Niou et al.; Olson and Zeckhauser; Riker; Wagner; and Zinnes. For examples of institutionalist approaches see Duffield; Keohane, International Institutions; and McCalla.

4. The dichotomy of alliance formation and management belongs to Snyder (see Alliance Politics, chs. 2, 6; and "Alliance Theory," 104). Representative examples of the latter include Bennett et al.; Fox and Fox; Goldstein; Olson and Zeckhauser; Osgood, Alliances; and Sabrosky.

5. This aspect of alliances is less a focus of this book than alliance formation and management. For the pioneering work on the causal relationships among alliances, deterrence, and war, see Singer and Small; also see Huth and Russett; Levy; and Vasquez.

6. Liska, 3.

7. For the core works on balance of power see Claude; Gulick; Morgenthau, *Politics*; Waltz, *Theory*, ch. 6; and Wolfers, *Discord*.

8. See Christensen, "Perceptions"; Christensen and Snyder, "Chain Gangs"; and Schweller, "Tripolarity."

9. Snyder, "Alliance Theory," 116; also see Snyder's criticism of Walt's book in "Alliances, Balance and Stability," 121–42, especially 125–32; and *Alliance Politics*, 6–16. For another study that specifies distinctions among balancing, bandwagoning, and neutrality and the causal importance of learning in minor-power alliance choices see Reiter. On variations in bandwagoning behavior that look in particular at gain-based incentives (rather than purely defensive ones) see Schweller, "Bandwagoning."

10. This aspect is developed largely in Snyder's "Alliance Theory," *Alliance Politics*, 180–99, and "The Security Dilemma in Alliance Politics."

11. I do not employ a mathematical usage of game theory but use the term to illustrate the strategic interaction between two allies acting as players (see Snyder, "Alliance Theory," 106, n. 15).

12. The concepts of abandonment and entrapment were introduced by Mandelbaum, 151–52. However, Mandelbaum uses the terms only cursorily in a discussion of tensions within NATO.

13. Snyder, "The Security Dilemma in Alliance Politics," 467.

14. Ibid.

15. Liska, 12.

16. As Liska stated, the "ambivalence" arising from the two conflicting requirements of "consensus to ensure joint efficacy" and "independent identity to retain the ability to act separately" exist in all forms of association (71–72).

17. See Kahn, 611.

18. Snyder, "Alliance Theory," 105. For a further discussion of what connotes alignment see Duncan and Siverson; Modelski; and Snyder, *Alliance Politics*, 6–16.

19. Snyder, "Alliance Theory," 105, 116. Also see Weinstein, 43.

20. The three general determinants of alignment patterns are (1) strength inequalities, (2) the degree of conflicting and common interests, and (3) past interaction (see Snyder, "Alliances, Balance, and Stability," 123–25).

21. Note that because Japan and Korea are unallied states does not preclude the existence of common security interests and alignment patterns between them. Expectations of support arise from these dynamics, as do consequent anxieties of abandonment and entrapment.

22. Snyder, "Alliance Theory," 113. The concept of the security dilemma was devised by Herz; for a fuller treatment see Jervis, "Cooperation Under the Security Dilemma."

23. Exceptions to this are noted below with regard to power inequalities between allies (see Snyder, "Alliance Theory," 113, and "The Security Dilemma in Alliance Politics," 466, 474).

24. I thank Randy Schweller for suggesting the use of this terminology.

25. This dynamic has been highlighted in the counterintuitive notion that small powers can exert disproportionate influence over their great-power allies (see Keohane, "The Big Influence"; Park Chang-jin; and Rothstein). For an analysis of why larger allies bear a disproportionate share of alliance costs see Olson and Zeckhauser.

26. Liska, 75–76.

27. For examples of other arguments on the effect of domestic politics on alignment patterns, see Michael Barnett and Levy, "Domestic Sources"; and David, 233–56.

28. Dawson and Rosecrance; and Kegley and Raymond, "Alliance Norms."

29. For an excellent work on the issue of reputation see Mercer, especially ch. 2. Mercer argues that allies acquire reputations for lacking resolve but generally not for having resolve. This largely stems from an attribution dynamic in which the observer explains undesirable behavior of the ally (e.g., weak commitments) in dispositional terms (i.e., a character-based choice) and desirable allied behavior (e.g., strong commitments) in situational terms (i.e., circumstance-based choice). If Mercer is right that reputations for resolve among allies rarely obtain, then fears of abandonment would not be ameliorated through supportive actions by reputation-conscious allies.

30. Moreover, this list is not exhaustive; for another discussion of the determinants of abandonment and entrapment fears see Snyder, "The Security Dilemma in Alliance Politics," 471–77.

31. For similar reactions by China and Great Britain to abandonment fears regarding the Soviet and U.S. nuclear umbrellas see Goldstein.

32. For some of the trade-offs states face between internal balancing and external alignments see the analysis by Morrow of Austria's and France's choices in response to German unification in the 1860s.

33. In 1970, for example, the ROK reacted to news of U.S. troop reductions in Korea by threatening a concurrent withdrawal of its combat forces supporting the United States in Indochina. As discussed in Chapter 3, this was an empty threat.

34. These assumptions logically follow from a state's incentives for entering into an alliance. They are (1) accretion of power, (2) deterrence of the adversary, (3) preventing accretion of the adversary's power, and (4) restraint and control of allies (see Liska, 26–27, 30; Morgenthau, "Theory and Practice," 185; Osgood, *Alliances*, 21–22; and Sabrosky, 2–3).

35. Probability estimates for these options are, of course, difficult to make as the option chosen by the abandonment-ridden state will differ depending on individual capabilities, allies, and strategies. However, for the purposes of the model, as long as *one* of these options is to show a stronger commitment to the alliance, the dynamics we are concerned with are set in motion. For a related

exposition of responses to abandonment fears see Snyder, *Alliance Politics*, 183–85.

36. For example, in order to discourage U.S. force reductions in their countries, the Japanese and South Korean governments have increased their share of the maintenance costs for U.S. troops and installations.

37. Lack of Russian support in the 1911 Moroccan crisis engendered French fears of Russian abandonment in a future confrontation with Germany; as a result, France expressed unadulterated support for Russia in standing down the Austrian threat in the Balkans (see Christensen and Snyder, 151–53). Similarly, Castro's radicalization of the revolutionary struggle in Cuba in 1959–60 was in part due to a desire to show allegiance to, and become a beneficiary of, the Soviet regime (see Gonzalez).

38. For example, Kennedy's 1960 statement "Ich Bin ein Berliner" was a classic case of the United States addressing European complaints about the credibility of U.S. resolve (see Mandelbaum, 154).

39. See DeConde, 62–63. Similar anxieties about unwanted entanglements in remote conflicts motivated the United States to opt out of membership in the League of Nations in the interwar years.

40. In a related vein Liska observed: "Parties to adversary alliances may exchange reassuring interpretations and these reduce the danger of both provocation and miscalculation" (53).

41. See Snyder, *Alliance Politics*, 185–86, for an analysis of how states deal with entrapment fears.

42. Snyder, "The Security Dilemma in Alliance Politics," 483. This is generally the case for major-power alliances. Minor powers generally seek the strongest possible commitment from the major power with minimal reciprocal obligation.

43. For example, in the immediate aftermath of the Korean war the United States maintained forces on the peninsula not only to deter the North Koreans and Chinese but also to restrain Rhee Syngman from adventuristic acts that might embroil the United States in a second confrontation.

44. This was the case in the aftermath of World War I, for example, when the United States and Great Britain distanced themselves from France's desires for harsh postwar arrangements to stifle the future rise of German power.

45. During the Suez crisis the Eisenhower administration strongly condemned British and French actions against Egypt and supported a UN resolution demanding troop withdrawals. These policies stemmed from desires to minimize the potential for escalation of the conflict into a direct United States-Soviet confrontation in the region.

46. Most alliance theorists make this assumption of classical economic rationality (see, for example, Bueno de Mesquita and Singer, 251; Kahn, 611; Liska, 26–27; and Reiter, 503).

47. Again, the assumptions here are that state Y has limited exit capacities (i.e., lacks internal balancing capabilities and alternative security partners) and faces a salient security threat that is too risky to appease.

48. This dynamic is referred to as the "integrative spiral," whereby states with mutual abandonment fears grow progressively closer (see Snyder, "The Security Dilemma in Alliance Politics," 477, 494). Jervis has shown that "insecurity spirals" can result where adversary perceptions of alliance cohesion set off a reciprocal fear that leads to further cohesion in the adversary bloc (see Jervis, *Perception*, ch. 3).

49. Otherwise the existence of exit capabilities can result in substantially different behavior in the face of mutual abandonment fears. The classic example here is the atmosphere of distrust and the use of internal balancing and appeasement that characterized relations among France, Germany, Great Britain, and the Soviet Union during the interwar period.

50. I do not consider the hypothesis of symmetrical entrapment fears as the logical result would be mutual disalignment by the parties. Or, as Michael Altfield observed, alliances that offer no security benefits to both partners almost never form ("The Decision to Ally: A Theory and Test," *Western Political Quarterly* 30 [Mar. 1984], 107–14, as cited in Kegley and Raymond, "Preservation of Postwar Peace," 272).

51. This section benefited from conversations with Bob Jervis, Jon Mercer, and Steve Rosen.

52. Walt, especially chs. 1–2, 5, and 8. Walt argues that balancing is a more common security phenomenon than bandwagoning and that states form alliances in response to imbalances of threat rather than imbalances of power. The level of threat is a function of four interrelated factors: aggregate power, proximity, offensive capabilities, and perceived intentions. Walt's findings help repair balance-of-power theory to explain why allies did not balance against dominant U.S. power in the postwar era and why the alignment choices of smaller powers have little to do with the global distribution of power. Other findings are that ideology, foreign aid, and political penetration are not powerful causes of alignment.

53. For additional discussion of the interplay between these two games see Snyder, *Alliance Politics*, 192–99.

54. These points are all discussed in greater detail in the ensuing chapters.

55. See "Joint Communique Between President Richard Nixon and Prime Minister Eisaku Sato," 21 Nov. 1969, United States Embassy transcript, sec. 4.

56. This commitment was originally made in Sato's National Press Club address in Washington after release of the Nixon-Sato joint communiqué. For the text see "Transcript of Proceedings: The Japanese Embassy, Press Conference of the Honorable Eisaku Sato," 13. Also see Sato Eisaku, 333–40, especially 335. These agreements are further discussed in Chapter 3.

57. For example, in June 1969 South Korean authorities found that speedboats used by North Korea to infiltrate peninsular coastlines were purchased from Japan (*Tong-A Ilbo,* 3 July 1969). In addition, in Feb. 1970 Japanese trading companies were found to have exported COCOM-restricted goods on a private basis to North Korea. For this incident see *Far Eastern Economic Re-*

view (hereafter *FEER*), 4 Feb.–5 Mar. 1970; Foreign Broadcast Information Service (hereafter FBIS), 2–20 Feb. 1970; and *Japan Times*, 2–20 Feb. 1970.

58. Although Tokyo does not yet have formal diplomatic relations with Pyongyang, it has often hinted at informally recognizing the regime. A representative example was when Tanaka reinterpreted the 1965 Japan-Korea normalization treaty to read that South Korea was not necessarily the only legitimate government on the peninsula. Numerous LDP officials have also made "private" visits to Pyongyang. For example, in 1986 Tani Yoichi met with North Korean Foreign Minister Ho Dam ostensibly in an unofficial capacity, although Tani was both a member of Prime Minister Nakasone's faction and a Gaimushō (foreign ministry) official.

59. Imazu Hiroshi, "Uniting a Divided Korea," 140–42. A further discussion of Japanese attitudes toward unification is in the Conclusion.

60. For the implicit link between the wording of the Korea clause and the validity of the Okinawan base agreement, see Blaker, 54.

61. Conflict simulation studies in the 1960s and 1970s forecast that a second North Korean offensive, similar to 1950's, could gain air control over northern portions of the ROK and penetrate the first line of defense north of Seoul within two days. From bases in Okinawa U.S. airpower and marine support could fully augment U.S. forces in the ROK within two days to stop this advance. However, the inability to launch operations from Okinawa would lengthen the response time to five days, thereby substantially increasing the likelihood that Seoul would fall (Weinstein and Kamiya, *The Security of Korea*, 40).

62. The best-known example of South Korean attempts to exercise this leverage was the Chun regime's request in 1981 for $6 billion in loans from the Japanese government. South Korea initially considered such funds a form of "security rent" based on the bulwark-of-defense argument (see Lee, *Japan and Korea*, 115–20).

63. While some Korean calls for Japanese repentance are sincere, there is no doubt that this issue is used also to gain leverage in other issue areas. For example, the ROK utilized the alleged revision of Japanese history textbooks by the Monbushō (education ministry) to stall and extract further concessions in concurrent bilateral loan negotiations in 1982 (see Kim, "Policymaking," ch. 6; and Lee, *Japan and Korea*, ch. 6). Similarly, in 1990 the South Koreans used colonial-contrition arguments to obtain concessions over naturalization rights of Korean residents in Japan (see Lee Jung-hoon).

64. ROK-MOFA, *Ilbon kaehwang*, 380–82.

65. For this reason Prime Minister Sato in January 1972 and Foreign Minister Ohira in August 1973 stated publicly that the Korea clause should not be interpreted as a bilateral defense treaty between Japan and the ROK (see *Korea Herald*, 9–11 Jan. 1972 and 4 Aug. 1973).

66. Monitoring of the Chosen Soren was a constant source of friction between Tokyo and Seoul during the 1960s and 1970s, as North Korean infiltra-

tion of the South was largely conducted through Japan. The refugee issue, though less openly discussed by the Japanese, is nevertheless a very salient concern. Korean refugees to Japan numbered between 200,000 and 500,000 during the Korean war.

67. For example, during the 1981–83 loan negotiations Japan adamantly stated that it would not negotiate an agreement if the funds were classified as security related (see Lee, *Japan and Korea*, 118).

68. This is termed the "boomerang effect." For example, South Korean authorities accused Tokyo of denying funding of the Kwangyang steel complex because Japan's earlier support of the P'ohang steel complex in 1969 made the ROK a rival supplier of steel. More recently the ROK has used this argument in connection with Japanese reluctance to provide technology. Japan does not want to give in to South Korean complaints and become locked into investment projects in the ROK when cheaper sources of labor exist elsewhere (e.g., Southeast Asia). In addition, Tokyo sees technology transfer issues as private-sector matters that are beyond the realm of direct government influence (see Cho, "A Korean View"; Kubota; and Lee Hy-sang).

69. One manner of contending with these forces is the "comprehensive security strategy." First conceptualized by Ohira in 1973 and later formalized by Suzuki in 1981, the strategy maintains that Japan will promote regional peace and stability through nonmilitary means.

70. *White Papers of Japan: 1973–74*, 55.

71. For representative examples see Hellmann, "US-Korean Relations"; and several works by Edward Olsen, including *U.S. Policy*, "Japan-South Korea Security Ties," and "Japan and Korea." Also see Ahn Byung-joon, "The United States"; and Hurst, "The United States and Korea-Japan Relations."

72. For two of the earlier conceptualizations of this triangle see Morley, *Japan and Korea*; and Kamiya, "The US Presence." Other general works in this vein include Clough; Young C. Kim; Lee and Sato, *U.S. Policy*; Sigur and Kim; and Weinstein and Kamiya, *The Security of Korea*. For radical perspectives that see U.S. desires to integrate the region through cultivating Japanese security dependency on the United States and ROK economic dependency on Japan, see Bix; and Chang.

73. See Chapter 3; also see Oberdorfer, *Two Koreas*, ch. 3.

74. Armacost, 28.

75. See Eckstein; George; and Lijphart.

76. On the importance of choosing hard or "critical" cases against which to test theories, see Eckstein, 111–12; and Posen, *Sources*, 38.

77. See Farnham, 16–18; and George, 57–58.

78. Because of the complex causal connections between threat perceptions and allied commitments in the quasi-alliance triangle, it is sometimes difficult to distinguish the relative causal importance of external threats and abandonment/entrapment complexes as the root cause of alliance behavior.

Chapter 3. Cooperation Under the Nixon Doctrine

1. For the treaty's provisions see Chapter 1.

2. For an overview of these events see "Chronology of Relations," 685–715, especially, 686–91.

3. A note on periodization: the 1969–71 period has not been carefully analyzed in previous studies of Japan-ROK relations. Authors have subsumed these years under an early-postnormalization period stretching from 1965 to 1972 and within this have focused only on the normalization treaty and the era of detente (e.g., Lee, *Japan and Korea*). Others have entirely omitted the 1969–71 period and started their analyses from detente (e.g., Weinstein and Kamiya, *The Security of Korea*).

4. This accords with Hypothesis B of the quasi-alliance model in Chapter 2.

5. See *Public Papers of the Presidents of the United States* [hereafter *PPPUS*], *Richard Nixon: 1969*, 544–56; and *New York Times*, 27 July 1969. For the document formally laying out the doctrine see Nixon, *United States Foreign Policy*, 55–56. For Nixon's initial exploration of the idea (after lengthy discussions with then-Ambassador to Indonesia Marshall Green), see Nixon, "Asia After Viet Nam."

6. The former doctrine called for the United States to mount an initial ninety-day defense of Western Europe against a Soviet attack while simultaneously sustaining a credible deterrent against a Chinese attack in Korea or Southeast Asia as well as meeting a third contingency, possibly in the Middle East (see Kissinger, 220–22).

7. Nixon, *Setting the Course*, 304.

8. For an overview of these programs, see Nixon, *United States Foreign Policy*, 68–71.

9. A full discussion of U.S. policy in Vietnam is beyond the scope of this book. Instead, I give greater attention to U.S. policies in Korea as these were more immediately relevant to Japan-ROK interaction.

10. U.S., Congress, House, Committee on International Relations, *Investigation of Korean-American Relations*, 1977, 62–63; and *Tong-A Ilbo*, 6 July 1970. Porter was favorable to the idea of troop withdrawals, provided they occurred at a moderate pace.

11. The key issue in these discussions was Seoul's demand that Washington modernize the ROK military before commencing with reductions. The United States refused to link these issues, as it would have effectively delayed withdrawal for at least five years (see *Korea Herald*, 24 July 1970; and *Tong-A Ilbo*, 24 July 1970). For the communiqué outlining the reductions see ROK-MOFA, *Taehan min'guk woegyo yŏnp'yo: 1971*, 648.

12. The Seventh Infantry Division was inactivated in March 1971. Before its pullback the Second Infantry Division manned an eighteen-mile stretch of the DMZ. The only front-line area in which U.S. forces remained after 1971 was Panmunjom (see U.S., Congress, Senate, Committee on Armed Services, *Korea: The US Troop Withdrawal Program*).

13. In August 1964 the White House briefed Ambassador-designate Win-throp Brown prior to his posting to Seoul to seek a feasible time at which to carry out force reductions. For discussions of this issue see memo, Bundy-Johnson, 20 Dec. 1963 (secret, declassified 14 July 1993); and memo, Komer-the president, 22 Jan. 1964 (secret, declassified 14 July 1993), both in "Korea, Vol. I," KCF, NSF, Box 254, LBJ Library; memo, Bundy-the president, 29 July 1964 (confid., declassified 23 June 1993), and memo, Komer-the president, 31 July 1964 (secret, declassified 23 June 1993), both in "Korea, Vol. II," KCF, NSF, Box 254, LBJ Library. Also see account by Porter's deputy, George New-man, in U.S., Congress, House, Committee on International Relations, *Investigation of Korean-American Relations*, 1977, 61.

14. Testimony of John Dunn, Agnew's foreign policy advisor, in U.S., Con-gress, House, Committee on International Relations, *Investigation of Korean-American Relations*, 1977, 33, 60–63. Also see Hellmann, "Japanese Security," 332–34; and Levin and Sneider, 45–50.

15. Graves, 7; and Gregor, 69–71.

16. As shown in the table, the sharp drop off in incidents between 1968 and 1969 was due to (1) construction of a barrier wall along the DMZ and (2) changes in North Korean tactics from provocations on land to offshore infiltra-tion. Despite this quantitative reduction the gravity of North Korean provoca-tions intensified.

17. All but one of the thirty-one North Korean commandos were killed. U.S.-ROK civilian and military casualties numbered more than one hundred, including thirty-six dead (see Lyndon Baines Johnson, 535; and Koh, "The Pueblo Incident," 272). In secret meetings between North and South Korean envoys four years later Kim Il-sung apparently disavowed responsibility for the raid and conveyed his regrets for the incident to Park. Kim attributed the com-mando raid to radical groups in the military, certain elements of which he claimed he fired after the event. A purge in the North Korean military did take place in the Blue House raid's aftermath, but this did not make Kim's disa-vowal seem more genuine because the purge could have been for Kim's stated reasons or simply because the mission failed. See transcripts of 1972 North-South secret meetings released in *Joongang Wŏlgan* (March 1989) as cited in Oberdorfer, *Two Koreas*, 23–24. One of the battalion commanders of the Capi-tal Security Command (responsible for security of central Seoul) which led the fight against the commando raid was Chun Doo-hwan.

18. In meetings with Porter, Park apparently called for armed U.S.-ROK re-taliation against Pyongyang and claimed South Korean forces could be readied in two days. For American statements see U.S., Department of State [hereafter State], *Department of State Bulletin*, 12 Dec. 1969. On the Porter-Park meet-ings see Lee and Sato, *U.S. Policy*, 44; and U.S., Congress, House, Committee on International Relations, *Investigation of Korean-American Relations*, 1977, 54–55.

19. In order to obtain release of the crew, the United States consented to an apology for provoking the incident but later issued a statement repudiating this

coerced admission of guilt (see U.S., State, *Department of State Bulletin*, 6 Jan. 1969). During the crisis Johnson did order the dispatch of the *USS Enterprise* to South Korea, pledged $100 million in special aid, and activated reservists; however, observers characterized this as only "muscle-flexing" and viewed U.S. behavior as marked by "singular restraint" (see Koh, "The Pueblo Incident," 273–74). For official statements of the U.S. nonretaliatory position during the crisis, see U.S., State, *Department of State Bulletin*, 12 Feb.–4 Mar. 1968.

20. U.S., Congress, House, Committee on International Relations, *Investigation of Korean-American Relations*, 1977, 30–31. Johnson's stated reason for this was to ensure the safe return of the detained American crewmen (Lyndon Baines Johnson, 536); also see Rusk, 392, 396.

21. *Oral Histories*, "Interview of Cyrus R. Vance, December 26, 1969, Part II," tape 2 (26 Dec. 1969), 13–16. For the joint communiqué see U.S., State, *Department of State Bulletin*, 11 Mar. 1968.

22. The EC-121, with thirty-one crewmen, operated out of Atsugi airbase in Japan and was on a routine surveillance mission monitoring Sino-Soviet communications and North Korean troop movements (see *Stars and Stripes*, 18–20 Apr. 1969; and *Washington Post*, 16 Apr. 1969, 1 ["N. Korea Claims It Downed US Plane"]).

23. *Japan Times*, 19 Apr. 1969; *Stars and Stripes*, 20 Apr. 1969; and *Washington Post*, 20–21 Apr. 1969. Initially Nixon did consider a variety of armed responses, including air strikes, mining of North Korean harbors, and reciprocal seizure of vessels, but later succumbed to Rogers's and Laird's counseling against this (Nixon, *RN*, 384; and U.S., Congress, House, Committee on International Relations, *Investigation of Korean-American Relations*, 1977, 58).

24. Kissinger, 320–21.

25. Ambassador Park Sang-yong, prime minister's office, 1968–70, interview by author, 7 Feb. 1992, Seoul.

26. *New York Times*, 10–18 Feb. 1969, quoted in Koh, "The Pueblo Incident," 278–79, n. 46.

27. Interviews with ROK officials quoted in Jean Egan, "Wider Thoughts of Park Chung Hee," *FEER*, 8 Jan. 1972.

28. Shim Jae-hoon, Seoul bureau chief, *FEER*, interview by author, 29 Feb. 1992, Seoul (hereafter Shim interview, 29 Feb. 1992); and U.S., Congress, House, Committee on International Relations, *Investigation of Korean-American Relations*, 1977, 57–58.

29. For foreign ministry statements see *Han'guk Ilbo*, 20 Apr. 1969; Koh, "The Pueblo Incident," 276–77; *Korea Herald*, 16 Apr. 1969; and *Tong-A Ilbo*, 17 Apr. 1969. South Korean insecurities were so high that even a placard displayed at U.S. military facilities after the EC-121 shootdown wryly stating, "North Korea: 2, US Navy: 0," elicited angry complaints at the apparently lighthearted attitude toward ROK security (see Jean Egan, "Wider Thoughts of Park Chung Hee," *FEER*, 8 Jan. 1972).

30. Ambassador Park Kun, director-general, MOFA, International Relations Bureau, 1966–69, interview by author, 15 Jan. 1992, Seoul (hereafter Park Kun

interview). As Ambassador Park recalled, the atmosphere during these meetings was extremely tense. In the end the South Koreans were able to secure commitments for additional military assistance and the creation of regular bilateral defense consultations (also see *Oral Histories*, "Interview of Cyrus R. Vance, December 26, 1969," 13–15). For similar observations see Rusk, 394; testimony of Richard Ericson, embassy political counselor, in U.S., Congress, House, Committee on International Relations, *Investigation of Korean-American Relations*, 1977, 54–55; and testimony of Gari Ledyard, professor of Korean Language and History, Columbia University, 15 Mar. 1978, in *Investigation of Korean-American Relations*, 1978, 8.

31. Han Sung-joo, "Past, Present, and Future," 211.

32. It should be noted that Park did reap gains from playing up the severity of these incidents. For example, ROK complaints after the *Pueblo* affair won it $100 million in supplementary U.S. military aid. In addition, Park could consolidate domestic support for his regime by underscoring the northern threat. While the ROK was undoubtedly concerned about the Blue House raid, *Pueblo* seizure, and EC-121 shootdown, some of Seoul's bluster could be seen as theatrics for these political purposes.

33. Johnson and Park reached such an understanding at their May 1965 summit. See memcon, Johnson-Park, 17 May 1965 (secret, declassified 29 Aug. 1989), "Korea-Vol. II," KCF, NSF, Box 254, LBJ Library; also see testimony of William Porter in U.S., Congress, Senate, Committee on Foreign Relations, *United States Security Agreements*, 2: part 6, 1525–26.

34. See Han Sung-joo, "South Korea's Participation in the Vietnam Conflict," 893–912. For statements reflecting this belief see remarks by Foreign Minister Choi Kyu-hah and Premier Chung Il-kwon during Rogers's August 1969 Seoul trip in ROK-MOFA, *Taehan min'guk woegyo yŏnp'yo: 1969*, 325–29, 334–36.

35. U.S., Congress, House, Committee on International Relations, *Investigation of Korean-American Relations*, 1977, 123; also see *FEER*, 23 July 1970.

36. "Report by Prime Minister Chung to the National Assembly in Regard to the Recent Visit by Vice President Spiro Agnew, Seoul, September 7, 1970," in ROK-MOFA, *Taehan min'guk woegyo yŏnp'yo: 1970*, 344–47; for similar accounts of ROK reactions see Emmerson, *Arms, Yen and Power*, 273–74. Defense Secretary Laird later issued a statement clarifying that U.S. decisions on troop presence in Korea did not require prior approval of Seoul.

37. *Japan Times*, 17 July 1970; and *Korea Herald*, 17 July 1970. Interviews with Korean diplomatic and military officials confirmed this point. The ROK generally assumed that the two U.S. divisions would remain on the peninsula as long as ROK troops were engaged in Vietnam (General Kim Jae-myong [ret.], interview by author, 19 Dec. 1990, New York [hereafter Kim Jae-myong interview]; and Ambassador Park Sang-yong, interview by author, 7 Feb. 1992, Seoul [hereafter Park Sang-yong interview, 7 Feb. 1992]).

38. Interview with Porter in U.S., Congress, House, Committee on Interna-

tional Relations, *Investigation of Korean-American Relations*, 1977, 64; and *Japan Times*, 14, 21 July 1970.

39. *Japan Times*, 25 July 1970; and *Korea Herald*, 24 July 1970. South Koreans later attempted to claim the United States had agreed to modernize the ROK armed forces before proceeding with reductions, but the Defense Department issued statements denying this (see *FEER*, 30 July 1970; *Japan Times*, 24 July 1970; and *Tong-A Ilbo*, 24 July 1970). The SCC is the highest bilateral consultative body on United States-ROK security issues (begun on an annual basis after the 1968 Vance mission).

40. For the SCC text see "Joint Statement of the 3rd Annual Meeting of the US and ROK Defense Ministers, July 21, 1970," ROK-MOFA, *Korea-US Relations*, 23–25, especially clause 4. For analysis of the text see *Korea Herald*, 24 July 1970; and *Taehan Ilbo*, 24 July 1970 in *Korea Press Translations* (hereafter *KPT*), 6. For the Nixon-Park communiqué see ROK-MOFA, *Taehan min'guk woegyo yŏnp'yo: 1969*, 382–84.

41. This could be seen as an attempt to alleviate abandonment fears by bluffing reciprocal abandonment in order to elicit cooperation from the ally (Chapter 2). The United States, however, was fully aware that ROK troops in Vietnam were an extremely profitable enterprise for Seoul, based on various U.S. compensation incentives totaling some $546 million from 1965 to 1969 (see U.S., Congress, Senate, Committee on Foreign Relations, *United States Security Agreements*, 2: part 6, 1532–59).

42. See accounts by Donald Ranard (Korean Desk director) and Deputy Defense Secretary David Packard in U.S., Congress, House, Committee on International Relations, *Investigation of Korean-American Relations*, 1977, 65–66.

43. Operations Focus Retina and Freedom Vault tested U.S. rapid reaction capabilities through the airlift of battalions and support equipment from bases in the United States to combat zones south of Seoul. The former exercise involved more than ten thousand troops, constituting the largest airlift operation since "Big Lift" in West Germany in 1963 (see *FEER*, 27 Mar. 1969; and U.S., Congress, Senate, Committee on Foreign Relations, *United States Security Agreements*, 2: part 6, 1697–98). The supplementary assistance program provided funds for ROK military modernization and self-sufficiency, including the supply of F-4 and F-5 jet fighters, naval patrol aircraft, and S-2 reconnaissance craft (for details of the program see U.S., Congress, House, Committee on International Relations, *Investigation of Korean-American Relations*, 1977, 69–70, 76–88).

44. Kim Jae-myong interview; and comments by General John Michaelis (testimony of William Porter) in U.S., Congress, Senate, Committee on Foreign Relations, *United States Security Agreements*, 2: part 6, 1698. Also see *Han'guk Ilbo*, 7, 14 Mar. 1969; and *Tong-A Ilbo*, 6, 22 Mar. 1969.

45. Agnew explained this to Park during the former's visit to Seoul on August 22–23, 1970, and a marathon, six-hour discussion ensued in which Park harangued the vice-president for being unable to guarantee the funds in

advance (see *FEER*, 5 Sept. 1970; and U.S., Congress, House, Committee on International Relations, *Investigation of Korean-American Relations*, 1977, 66–67, 70). In the end ROK concerns were justified. Congress did not provide the total amount originally promised in the modernization program until 1977 (two years behind schedule) largely because salient political trends—most notably the 1972 North-South joint communiqué and the Park regime's human rights violations—resulted in decreased annual appropriations. Congressional clout over the distribution of such funds set in motion a process of illegal South Korean lobbying practices in the United States, later known as the "Koreagate" scandal (see Chapter 5).

46. Park Sang-yong interview, 7 Feb. 1992.

47. *Tong-A Ilbo*, 9 July 1970.

48. Park's nuclear decision came on the heels of a series of provocations by armed, high-speed North Korean boats against ROK vessels in June 1970 and in the context of a new secret government agency devoted to weapons development. This issue is discussed in greater detail in Chapter 4; see also Oberdorfer, *Two Koreas*, 68.

49. U.S., Congress, House, Committee on International Relations, *Investigation of Korean-American Relations*, 1978, 66.

50. General Tsukamoto Katsuichi (ret.), Japanese defense attaché, Seoul, 1967–71, interview by author, 8 July 1992, Tokyo (hereafter Tsukamoto interview).

51. *Japan Times*, 14–16 Apr. 1969.

52. The port calls were crucial to the operation's success (see *Japan Times*, 24 Apr. 1969). For Sato's declaration waiving prior consultation, see U.S., Congress, Senate, Committee on Foreign Relations, *United States Security Agreements*, 2: part 5, 1156–59.

53. An in-depth analysis of Japan-China relations is beyond the scope of this study. For two comprehensive works see Lee Chae-jin, *Japan Faces China*; and Whiting, *China Eyes Japan*.

54. Beijing detonated its first atomic bomb in 1964 and demonstrated delivery capabilities by 1970. For dissenting views that assess Japan's reaction to China's attainment of nuclear capabilities as mild, see Meyer, 81; and Totten, 13–14.

55. Many of these points were made at the March–April 1970 Japan-PRC memorandum trade talks. For concurring views see Ito, 1035; *Japan Times*, 18 Apr. 1970; Matsumoto Shun'ichi's recollections of his meetings with Liu Hsi-wen in "Our Neighbor China," 151–52; and Whiting, "Japan and Sino-American Relations," 225.

56. The latter motive became especially salient after border clashes over the Ussuri in 1969 made a firming up of regional support against the Soviet threat imperative. Prior to this North Korea-China relations had deteriorated during the Cultural Revolution, culminating in 1969 with skirmishes that led to tight control of border areas. I thank Ezra Vogel for highlighting the dual motives of this summit.

57. Ito, 1035; also see Emmerson, *Arms, Yen and Power*, 270–73.

58. Matsumoto, 151. For concurring views on Japanese perceptions of North Korea and China see Hellmann, *Japan and East Asia*, 172–76; and *Japan Times*, 15 Mar. 1970 (Tadao Ishikawa, "Japan and Her Neighbors" [special supplement]).

59. Sunobe interview; and Tsukamoto interview.

60. Kobayashi Katsumi; and Osgood, *The Weary*, 45.

61. See Agnew's testimony in U.S., Congress, House, Committee on International Relations, *Investigation of Korean-American Relations*, 1977, 60, n. 37; also see *FEER*, 5 Sept. 1970.

62. The importance of foreign ministry-defense agency meetings was seen in their attendance by top government officials, including Foreign Minister Aichi, Defense Director-General Nakasone, and Chief Cabinet Secretary Hori Shigeru (see *Japan Times*, 4 Feb. 1970). For Kishi's efforts see *Tong-A Ilbo*, 12 Feb. 1970. For statements by Ambassador to the United States Ushiba Nobuhiko and Foreign Minister Aichi about the doctrine see *Japan Times*, 21–24 July, 4 Dec. 1970.

63. See Clough, 91–92, 97–98; Kissinger, 748–49; and testimony of Undersecretary of State George Ball, 16 May 1972, in U.S., Congress, House, Committee on Foreign Affairs, *The New China Policy*, 169. For a contrasting view see U.S., Congress, House, Committee on Foreign Affairs, *National Security Policy*, 1–62.

64. For statements on Japan's willingness to share the financial burden through economic support of regional development see Aichi, 30–31, 34–35; and Ito, 1031–36.

65. As Foreign Minister Ohira Masayoshi stated: "What we must remember is that even though we may speak of a quintipolar world, the relationship among the five poles is one of inequality" (Ohira, 414–15). For similar statements see Kanazawa, 71–72.

66. Aichi, 31. For additional examples see Hirasawa, 341–42; Ito, 1031–36; Saiki, 602–24; and testimony of George Ball, 16 May 1972 in U.S., Congress, House, Committee on Foreign Affairs, *The New China Policy*, 169.

67. Blaker, 31. The Japanese public's ambivalence toward the American war effort in Vietnam had been evident as early as 1965. The seminal work on this topic is Thomas R. H. Havens, *Fire Across the Sea*. Also see *Oral Histories*, transcript, Edwin O. Reischauer interview, 8 Apr. 1969, 6–7, 9–11; and Reischauer, ch. 39, especially 284–91.

68. This basically stated Japan's obligation to provide its facilities and bases in support of U.S. defense efforts in the Far East. The boundaries of the "Far East" defense perimeter were never delineated. For an analysis of this clause see Emmerson, *Arms, Yen and Power*, 82–84; and Lee and Sato, *U.S. Policy*, 18–19.

69. Japanese concerns over this were particularly high in 1965, when the United States began its initial bombing missions over North Vietnam. See Emmerson, *Arms, Yen and Power*, 84–85, 178–80; and Havens, ch. 1; also Oi-

kawa Shoichi, editor, *Yomiuri Shimbun* (political correspondent, 1970–72), interview by author, 9 July 1992, Tokyo (hereafter Oikawa interview).

70. *Kyodo* opinion poll, Oct. 1969, cited in U.S., Congress, Senate, Committee on Foreign Relations, *United States Security Agreements*, 1422.

71. As former Ambassador Meyer stated, the Japanese accepted such links with Korea, and to a lesser extent, Taiwan; however, opposition to further Japanese involvement in Vietnam was so strong that Tokyo would only agree to a vague mention in the communiqué of aspirations for peace in Indochina (see Meyer, 35–36).

72. The following details were compiled from Blaker, 25–27; Emmerson, *Arms, Yen and Power*, 90–97; *FEER*, 26 Dec. 1970; *Japan Times*, 22 Dec. 1970; U.S., Congress, House, Committee on International Relations, *Investigation of Korean-American Relations, Appendices*, 1978, 104; *United States Foreign Policy: 1969–1970*, 36–42; and *United States Foreign Policy: 1971*, 50–61. For a concise overview of United States-Japan security relations during this period see Sneider; and U.S., Congress, Senate, Committee on Foreign Relations, *United States Security Agreements*, 1147–1525.

73. Ground troop levels were reduced by 7,000 in 1971 and an additional 5,000 through mid-1972, putting total troop levels at 24,500, lower than average levels of some 40,000 since 1964.

74. For example, F-4 Phantoms and EC-121 craft were redeployed at Kunsan and Kwangju bases in Korea, thereby leaving them in proximate locations. In addition, a large contingent of U.S. forces was added to bases in Okinawa after reversion of the Ryūkyū Islands to Japan in 1972.

75. Meyer, 95–96.

76. "Defense of Japan," text of a speech by Nakasone Yasuhiro at the Foreign Correspondents' Club of Japan, 1 Dec. 1970, 18, 32.

77. These meetings took place directly after Rogers's attending the Vietnam War Allies Conference in Saigon, where he informed ROK Foreign Minister Choi of the pullout decision (see *Japan Times*, 17 July 1970; and *Korea Herald*, 17 July 1970).

78. For the text of the joint communiqué see *Han-Il kwan'gye charyojip*, 1: 653–58. For proceedings of the conference see *Japan Times*, 21–24 July 1970; and *Seoul Haptong* press releases, 20–23 July 1970, in FBIS, 21–23 July 1970. For the press conference see *Seoul Kyŏngje Sinmun*, 29 July 1970, in *KPT*, 29 July 1970, 6.

79. Makato, 347, 356–61; Meyer, p. 87; and *New York Times*, 25 Jan. 1970 (Philip Shabecof, "Japanese Budget for 1970 Includes the Sharpest Increase in Defense Since World War II"). Actual increases over the 1969–71 period were from 453.4 billion yen to 630.2 billion yen (Japan, Ministry of Finance, *The Budget in Brief*, 1970, 36–38 and *The Budget in Brief*, 1971, 34–35).

80. See Emmerson, *The Japanese Thread*, 376–77; and Havens, 4.

81. Tokyo's position was that reversion should be under the same terms as those used for the home islands. Known as the *Hondonami* formula, this meant

that nuclear weapons had to be removed prior to reversion. Despite this, Japanese opposition parties, the press, and public were wary that the conservative Sato might concede on the nuclear issue in order to facilitate the early return of the islands.

82. On the 1960 treaty crisis see Packard; and Sneider. On Japanese neutralism see Stockwin.

83. For an example of the Sato government's desire to prevent a domestic crisis over the treaty renewal and Okinawan reversion issues see Finance Minister Fukuda's "Japan in the 1970's," 137–48.

84. Meyer, 27. A concise history of the Okinawan reversion issue is in Sneider, 1–66.

85. The "prior consultation" clause was established in an exchange of notes between Premier Kishi and Secretary of State Christian Herter concurrent with the revision of the 1960 mutual defense treaty. It stated that any changes in deployment, equipment, or use of facilities in Japan for U.S. combat purposes were subject to prior notification of the Japanese government. The clause was always double-edged for Japan. On the one hand, it was Japan's sovereign right to be informed of U.S. activities; on the other, prior consultation made Japan implicitly accountable for U.S. military activities outside Japan proper (see Armacost, 81).

86. Recent documents released on the Japanese side purportedly reveal evidence to the contrary. According to these sources, Sato consented to a secret agreement with Okinawan reversion which allowed the reintroduction of nuclear weapons in future contingencies in the region. I thank Sheila Smith for bringing this evidence to my attention.

87. Situated some six hundred miles south of Korea, five hundred miles east of China, and four hundred miles northeast of Taiwan, Okinawa's strategic location was critical to U.S. defense planning in the region. For the United States Navy Okinawa facilitated defense of the East China and Yellow Seas. Bases at Kadena and Futenma provided a forward presence for the United States Air Force and Army, and rear area support functions (e.g., reconnaissance, refueling tankers, and movement of transport planes). In particular, Kadena was a repair facility and dispatch point for B-52 bombers in the Vietnam war. The United States Marine Corps presence in Okinawa came about later in the course of its expanded role in the Vietnam war. Major U.S. bases on the home islands were Misawa and Yokota air bases on Honshu, serving as headquarters for United States Air Force and later United States Forces in Japan [USFJ]; Yokosuka, Atsugi, and Sasebo naval bases on Honshu and Kyushu, serving as headquarters of the United States Navy (Yokosuka) and port facilities for the Seventh Fleet; Iwakuni and Fuji on Honshu, serving as the Marine Corps Air Station; and Itazuke and Camp Zama, United States Air Force and Army, on Honshu.

88. The indispensability of Okinawa for the U.S. defense of the ROK was reflected in its support role in U.S.-ROK military exercises and in operational roles during the EC-121 and *Pueblo* crises. This strategic importance was also

historically evident during the Korean war (1950–53), when Okinawa (and Japan in general) was used for operations such as naval landings on the Korean coast, minesweeping and dredging of Korean harbors, and communication and repair. The UN Command during the Korean conflict was also stationed in Japan (Lee and Sato, *U.S. Policy*, 16).

89. *Japan Times*, 16 Apr. 1969. Prime Minister Chung also met with Assistant Secretary Green for this purpose in April and with Deputy Defense Secretary David Packard in June (*Tong-A Ilbo*, 12 Apr., 4 June 1969). Concern over these issues was so acute that Park offered a small South Korean island (Chejudo) for U.S. use as a substitute for Okinawa (see Park's interview in *U.S. News and World Report*, 25 Aug. 1969; and U.S., Congress, House, Committee on Foreign Affairs, *American-Korean Relations*, 14). While the island's terrain and weather conditions made it impractical as a military base, the offer in itself was a clear manifestation of ROK abandonment fears regarding the Okinawa reversion.

90. See "Statement by H. E. Kyu Hah Choi, Minister of Foreign Affairs of the Republic of Korea, at the Third Ministerial Meeting of the Seven Troop-Contributing Nations in Vietnam, Seoul, May 22, 1969," ROK-MOFA, *Taehan min'guk woegyo yŏnp'yo: 1969*, 179.

91. The former were periodic conferences involving prominent business leaders and retired high-level politicians who held influence in policy-making circles. The latter were biannual meetings of legislators for the purpose of policy consultations. For details of these meetings see FBIS, 26 Feb. 1969, C3; and *Japan Times*, 26–27 Feb. 1969.

92. *Han'guk Ilbo*, 3 May 1969. Foreign Minister Aichi and Asian Affairs Director Sunobe Ryōzō reaffirmed this view at the June 1969 ASPAC Conference (Sunobe interview; also see FBIS, 11 June 1969, A9; and *Japan Times*, 10–12 June 1969). The occasion for the Chung-Kishi consultations in the United States was Eisenhower's funeral (see *Japan Times*, 30 Mar. 1969).

93. *Seoul Kyŏngje Sinmun*, 9 May 1969, in *KPT*, 9 May 1969.

94. *Han-Il kwan'gye charyojip*, 2: 639–2, especially 640, clause 7. Also see *Japan Times*, 27, 29–30 Aug. 1969; and *Tokyo Jiji* (newswire), 29 Aug. 1969, in FBIS, 29 Aug. 1969, C1–3.

95. For Aichi's press statements see *Japan Times*, 29 Aug. 1969; and *Tokyo Kyodo*, 29 Aug. 1969, in FBIS, 29 Aug. 1969, C2–3.

96. For example see *Tokyo Jiji* (newswire), 28 Aug. 1969, in FBIS, 29 Aug. 1969, C1.

97. See secs. 6–11 of the joint communiqué, U.S., State, *Department of State Bulletin*, 15 Dec. 1969.

98. For an account of these negotiations see the memoirs of U. Alexis Johnson, 540–48.

99. "Joint Communique Between President Richard Nixon and Prime Minister Eisaku Sato," United States Embassy transcript, 21 Nov. 1969, sec. 4 (I thank James Morley for this document). Also see *Han-Il kwan'gye charyojip*, 2: 643–46, or U.S., State, *Department of State Bulletin*, 15 Dec. 1969.

100. Secs. 6 and 7 of the communiqué, U.S., State, *Department of State Bulletin*, 15 Dec. 1969, or *Han-Il kwan'gye charyojip*, 2: 644.

101. "Transcript of Proceedings: The Japanese Embassy, Press Conference of the Honorable Eisaku Sato," 13. Also see Sato Eisaku, 335.

102. *Han'guk Ilbo*, 22 Jan. 1970, in *KPT*, 23 Jan. 1970, 20; and U. Alexis Johnson, 546. For the text of Johnson's briefing see U.S., Congress, Senate, Committee on Foreign Relations, *United States Security Agreements*, 1439–46.

103. The latter act in particular showed that Sato's statements were considered part of the conditions under which the United States endorsed the agreement (Robert Immerman, former political counselor, United States Embassy, Japan, interview by author, 19 Aug. 1991, New York [hereafter Immerman interview]). For the treaty see *United States Treaties*, 447–574.

104. De facto acknowledgment of the Korea clause had been made as early as the San Francisco Conference, when Yoshida agreed to provide Japanese facilities in support of UN military action in the Far East. However, never before the Nixon-Sato summit had the link between Japan and the ROK been stated so explicitly (see U. Alexis Johnson, 546; his testimony in U.S., Congress, Senate, Committee on Foreign Relations, *United States Security Agreements*, 1182–83; and Langdon, xiv).

105. Okonogi, "A Japanese Perspective," 7; and Okonogi, interview by author, 31 Jan. 1992, Tokyo (hereafter Okonogi interview). Both the Korea clause and Okinawan base agreement were reaffirmed in subsequent Seoul-Tokyo fora (discussed below).

106. Park Sang-yong interview, 7 Feb. 1992.

107. See *Japan Times*, 23 Nov. 1969; and Okonogi, "A Japanese Perspective," 27.

108. *Seoul Kyŏngje Sinmun*, 4 Dec. 1969, in *KPT*, 7 Dec. 1969, 18. A November 23 *Han'guk Ilbo* editorial noted the government's conspicuous silence in the aftermath of the Nixon-Sato summit as a sign of satisfaction over the results of the summit. For other examples see *Chung'ang Ilbo*, 22 Nov. 1969, in *KPT*, 23–28 Nov. 1969; *Korea Herald*, 22 Nov. 1969; *Sina Ilbo*, 24 Nov. 1969; and *Tong-A Ilbo*, 25 Nov. 1969.

109. Undersecretary Johnson's press briefings and congressional testimony highlighted this as a "considerable change" in Japan's previous positions (see U.S., Congress, Senate, Committee on Foreign Relations, *United States Security Agreements*, 1162–63, 1442, 1444). The significance of these agreements was also manifest in the two governments' negotiating positions on the reversion treaty and the Nixon-Sato communiqué. U.S. officials originally wanted the Korea clause and the Okinawan base commitment written into the reversion treaty, as they believed this was necessary to obtain ratification from Congress. Sato opposed this and instead offered to include the Korea clause in the joint communiqué. The United States then pushed for inclusion of the base commitment clause as well. Sato, for domestic political reasons, could not accept this and proposed the innovative idea of the press club speech (Immerman interview).

110. This designation would change under the Tanaka government (Chapter 4).

111. As former Ambassador Meyer recalled, it took little convincing to get Japan to accept the word *essential* to describe the Japan-ROK security link, but Japan was adamantly against similar wording for Taiwan (Meyer, 35–36). For the discussion of Taiwan see sec. 4 of communiqué in U.S., State, *Department of State Bulletin*, 15 Dec. 1969.

112. Sato Eisaku, 335.

113. Meyer, 25–45.

114. *Han-Il kwan'gye charyojip*, 2: 643–44, sec. 3; or U.S., State, *Department of State Bulletin*, 15 Dec. 1969.

115. *Japan Times*, 19–20 Nov. 1969.

116. The political damage done by these criticisms was partially offset by Sato's facilitating the return of Okinawa and the removal of nuclear weapons prior to reversion. Sato dissolved the Lower House on December 2, and the LDP won the Diet elections by the largest majority since 1960 in a test of the popularity of the Nixon-Sato communiqué and Sato's continued rule.

117. Sato's statements came at an airport press conference upon returning to Tokyo (see *Tokyo Jiji* [newswire], 26 Nov. 1969, in FBIS, 28 Nov. 1969, C2).

118. *Japan Times*, 15, 24–25 Feb. 1970; *Tokyo Kyodo*, 18 Feb. 1970, in FBIS, 18 Feb. 1970, C3–5, and 24 Feb. 1970, in FBIS, 24 Feb. 1970, C1–2.

119. *FEER*, 23 July 1970.

120. *Japan Times*, 15 July 1970; and *Tokyo Kyodo*, 14 July 1970, in FBIS, 14 July 1970, C1. In addition, Lee and Sato met in March 1970 to discuss in detail the Nixon-Sato joint communiqué (see *Seoul Haptong*, 6 Mar. 1970, in FBIS, 9 Mar. 1970, C3).

121. Tsukamoto interview. Also see *FEER*, 30 July 1970; *Japan Times*, 17 July 1970; *Korea Herald*, 17 July 1970.

122. *Japan Times*, 25 July 1970 ("Japan-ROK Cooperation," editorial).

123. Opening speeches were delivered by Deputy Premier Kim Hak-ryul and Foreign Minister Aichi. For the former's statements see ROK-MOFA, *Taehan min'guk woegyo yŏnp'yo: 1970*, 243; for the latter's statements see *Japan Times*, 21, 24 July 1970.

124. See ROK-MOFA, *Taehan min'guk woegyo yŏnp'yo: 1970*, 254, clauses 7–8. Also see *Japan Times*, 24 July 1970; and *Seoul Haptong*, 23 July 1970, in FBIS, 23 July 1970, E3–6.

125. The Japanese Foreign Ministry blue paper for 1970 also reaffirmed this direct security link (see *White Papers of Japan: 1969–70*). A Japanese foreign ministry official present at the joint ministerial conference could not recall the specific negotiations behind this clause; however, he believed that mutual security concerns stemming from the recent U.S. troop pullout announcement caused both delegations to show greater bilateral cooperation through statements of this nature (Sunobe interview).

126. *Han-Il kwan'gye charyojip*, 2: 653–58, clause 9. The first project with Japanese assistance, P'ohang, is discussed in the section on economic relations.

127. *Japan Times*, 24 July 1970, and *Seoul Haptong*, 22 July 1970, in FBIS, 22 July 1970, E1.

128. *Japan Times*, 25 July 1970. The cooperation evident at the 1970 joint ministerial conference elicited harsh criticism from the Japan Communist party, Socialists, and Kōmei, all denouncing the communiqué and economic agreements as leading to a de facto military alliance between Japan and Korea (*Tokyo Kyodo*, 23 July 1970, in FBIS, 23 July 1970, C1).

129. As noted earlier, these tested the ability to deploy forces in the ROK rapidly through massive airlifts of United States-based ground forces.

130. For details of these exercises see FBIS, 3 Mar. 1969; and *Japan Times*, 5–11 Mar. 1971.

131. *Japan Times*, 16–17, 20 Apr. 1969.

132. On these points see *Japan Times*, 24 July 1969; *Tokyo Kyodo*, 23 Apr. 1969, in FBIS, 23 Apr. 1969, C1, and 30 July 1970, C1; Langdon, 114; and U.S., Congress, House, Committee on International Relations, *Investigation of Korean-American Relations*, 1977, 57–58.

133. *Tong-A Ilbo*, 12 Jan. 1971.

134. See *Korea Herald*, 27 Feb., 25 June 1970.

135. *Japan Times*, 11, 18 June 1969, and *Tong-A Ilbo*, 14 June 1969.

136. Tsukamoto interview. Tsukamoto was responsible for arranging the Yamada and Mun visits. Also see *Japan Press Service*, 5 June 1969, in FBIS, 5 June 1969, C2.

137. *FEER*, 30 July 1970; and *Tong-A Ilbo*, 8 July 1970. Tsukamoto recalled that both governments were extremely mindful of the political sensitivities of these exchanges, and therefore kept them low-profile. In particular Tokyo appreciated Seoul's difficulties in allowing Japanese military officials to visit Korea and therefore made a point of not offering, and only reciprocating, invitations extended by the ROK (Tsukamoto interview).

138. *Japan Times*, 23 Feb. 1971.

139. Tsukamoto interview. Tsukamoto stressed that these discussions were not a formal part of the agenda. Japan and the ROK conducted a third set of military visits in the summer of 1971. General Kinugasa Hayao, chief of the Ground SDF, toured ROK front-line ground units in June; this was followed by a visit by General Suh Chong-chol, ROK Army Chief of Staff, to Tokyo (see *Tokyo Kyodo*, 1 June 1971, in FBIS, 4 June 1971, E4). In addition, in July a forty-two-man JDA observer group visited the ROK National War College and military facilities. This four-day mission was for the purpose of educating the Japanese on ROK defense strategy (see *Japan Times*, 4 July 1971). More important, this mission began an annual exchange program between military academies that continues to flourish today (Colonel Fukuyama Takashi, Japanese defense attaché, Seoul, 1992, interview by author, 29 May 1992, Seoul [hereafter Fukuyama interview]; and anonymous JDA official, interview by author, 7 July 1992, Tokyo).

140. The attaché was officially assigned on January 2, 1971 (see *Japan Times*, 2 Jan. 1971). For the initial JDA announcement see *Tokyo Kyodo*, 1

Aug. 1970, in FBIS, 4 Aug. 1970, C4–5; and *Tokyo Kyodo*, 30 Dec. 1970, in
FBIS, 31 Dec. 1970, C2.

141. The JDA had initially requested three attachés solely for Korea, one for
each branch of the military. These attachés generally acted as liaisons between
the JDA and the ROK defense ministry. At the time three ROK attachés were
assigned to Tokyo.

142. Tsukamoto interview. Tsukamoto stated that after the United States
announced drawdown plans for Korea, the JDA gave the ROK the highest policy priority, less only than that of the United States and Soviet Union.

143. A distinction must be drawn between a minor "disagreement" and
large-scale "friction." The latter is defined as either the absence between two
states of relations that would be beneficial to both or a major disruption (e.g.,
breakdown) in existing relations.

144. See ROK statements at the fourth ministerial meeting of the Asian and
Pacific Council (ASPAC), June 10, 1969, in ROK-MOFA, *Taehan min'guk
woegyo yŏnp'yo: 1969*, 263–64. For a comprehensive listing of North Korean
infiltrations see "Report of the United Nations Commission for the Unification
and Rehabilitation of Korea, U.N., August 13, 1970," in ROK-MOFA, *Taehan
min'guk woegyo yŏnp'yo: 1970*, 271–74.

145. Kim Ki-sok, editor, *Korea Herald*, foreign ministry correspondent,
1969–74, interview by author, 29 Apr. 1992, Seoul (hereafter Kim Ki-Sok interview).

146. The ROK foreign ministry filed numerous protests and threatened to
recall its ambassador in this earlier period. See "Chronology of Relations,"
685–89; and CIA, "Special Report."

147. See *Tong-A Ilbo*, 3 July 1969, for the incident involving North Korean
speedboats, and see *Japan Times*, 27 Dec. 1970 for the repatriation case.

148. For additional details of the hijacking see *Japan Times*, 1–6 Apr. 1970;
also see FBIS, 1–7 Apr. 1970.

149. Before the exchange of hostages for Yamamura the hijackers wanted
Socialist Dietman Abe Sukuya to come to Kimpo to verify that Yamamura was,
in fact, the vice-minister for transport.

150. See *Seoul Haptong*, 1 Apr. 1970, in FBIS, 1 Apr. 1970.

151. Sunobe interview. Sunobe remarked that Seoul's attitudes were "extremely generous." Another specialist also confirmed that the ROK's behavior
was "extremely cooperative" (Okonogi interview).

152. For example see *Japan Times*, 4–6 Apr. 1970.

153. For South Korean concerns on this see *Chosŏn Ilbo*, 6 Apr. 1970;
Chung'ang Ilbo, 6 Apr. 1970, in *KPT*, 7 Apr. 1970, 6; and *Japan Times*, 8 Apr.
1970.

154. *Japan Times*, 8 Apr. 1970; *Tokyo Kyodo*, 6 Apr. 1970, in FBIS, 7 Apr.
1970, C6; and *Tong-A Ilbo*, 8 Apr. 1970.

155. In particular Sato understood that it would have been extremely difficult for the United States Congress to ratify the Okinawa reversion agreement if
Japan was concurrently seeking a rapprochement with Pyongyang.

156. For example, Ambassador Sunobe did state with regard to the government's decision on North Korea policy: "We expressed appreciation to North Korea through the Red Cross for the return of the plane and hostage. But we could not improve relations with the North. We did not do this because it would have made the South Korean government very unhappy" (Sunobe interview).

157. *FEER*, 20 Mar. 1969. As noted in Table 3, the committee met in 1968 before its formal establishment in 1969.

158. Other key participants not listed in the table included Paek Nam-ok and Funada Naka (political subcommittee chairs); Hong Song-ha and Noda Uichi (economic subcommittee chairs); Yi Son-kun and Uemura Kentaro (cultural subcommittee chairs); and Kim Chu-in and Hasegawa Jin (chief spokesmen). Other influential committee members included Lee Tong-won (former foreign minister), Paik Tu-jin (former premier), Kaya Okinori (former finance minister), Uemura Kogoro (president, Keidanren), Nagano Shigeo (chair, Nippon Steel), Ishii Mitsujiro (former Diet speaker), Kim Sang-yong, Kim Song-kun, Tanaka Tatsuo, Yatsugi Kazuo, Shinin Kinai, and Nakamura Kikuo.

159. Lee Tong-won interview, 19 May 1992.

160. Cho Jung-pyo, director, Northeast Asia Division I, Ministry of Foreign Affairs, interview by author, 14 Feb. 1992, Seoul (hereafter Cho interview).

161. Other pressing issues discussed at these meetings are detailed below.

162. During the period the two governments conferred diplomatic service awards on Sato, Shiina Etsusaburo, Funada Naka, Kishi Nobusuke, Ishii Mitsujiro, Chung Il-kwon, and Lee Tong-won. In addition to the Japanese information center in Seoul, other significant examples of goodwill included the establishment of a Shimonoseki-Pusan ferry line (June 1970) and an interest-free loan of 333,000 tons of Japanese rice to South Korea in March 1969.

163. For an overview of these events see Y. C. Han.

164. These activities were later revealed during the *nikkan yuchaku* (Japan-Korea adhesion) controversy in the late 1970s (see Tamaki, 349–55, especially 354). Nikkan yuchaku is discussed in Chapter 5.

165. *Japan Times*, 15 Oct. 1969.

166. For Hori's statements see *Japan Times*, 28 Apr. 1971. For Park's inauguration see *Japan Times*, 2 July 1971. Sato's delegation included such high-level figures as special envoy Shiina Etsusaburo, Deputy Chief Cabinet Secretary Kimura Toshio, Deputy Vice-Minister for Foreign Affairs Hogen Shinsaku, and Ministry of Foreign Affairs Director of Northeast Asian Affairs Nakahira Noburo. (Sato also attended Park's inauguration in July 1967.)

167. This is not to imply that Japanese support was the primary reason for Park's victory in April 1971. Park used a variety of tactics to sway voters, a favorite being an emphasis on how a change of government would embolden North Korean aggression. Park played up the northern threat just prior to the national referendum on constitutional revision in October 1969 and threatened the resignation of his entire government if the referendum outcome was negative. Therefore, diverse factors were involved in Park's victory. The relevant

point here is that, despite the questionable legitimacy of Park's tactics, Japan chose to associate itself with his bid for a third term. While this support may not have been the key factor behind Park's victory, it certainly was not an insignificant one.

168. *Tokyo Jiji* (newswire), 20 Oct. 1969, in FBIS, 21 Oct. 1969, C2.

169. *Japan Times*, 26 June 1971.

170. *Japan Times*, 26 Jan. 1969. This was one of the first rulings by a Japanese court on political refugees in Japan. The court based its decision on the case of Cho Yong-su. While in Japan Cho led a dissident movement against the South Korean government and was executed when he returned to Korea in 1961.

171. Yun at first said he went voluntarily but upon returning to Japan, claimed that he was kidnapped by KCIA operatives (see *Japan Times*, 9 May, June 1969).

172. *Tokyo Press Service*, 12 May 1969, in FBIS, 12 May 1969, 91–92. The Japanese organizations involved in the protest movements included the Association for the Protection of Human Rights of Korean Residents in Japan, the Association of International Lawyers, the Democratic Lawyers Association, the Free Bar Association, Sohyō, and the Young Lawyers Association.

173. These decisions were in accordance with requests made by ROK envoys and were strongly protested by Pyongyang (see *FEER*, 9 Jan. 1969 [Derek Davies, "Seoul Searching"]; and *Japan Times*, 30 Jan., 31 Aug. 1969, and 1 Aug. 1970).

174. *Han'guk Ilbo*, 20 June 1970, in *KPT*, 21 June 1970, 4. For other examples see *Chosŏn Ilbo*, 28 Mar. 1970, in *KPT*, 28 Mar. 1970, 5; and FBIS, 27 Mar. 1970, E1.

175. *Korea Herald*, 5 Feb. 1969; and *Tong-A Ilbo*, 6 Feb. 1969. The plant deal included equipment for such items as synthetic fibers, petrochemicals, and oil refining.

176. For example, while 360 items were displayed at a similar exhibition in 1965, only 120 were displayed at the October 1969 event (see *Han'guk Ilbo*, 25 Mar. 1969; and *Tong-A Ilbo*, 18 Apr. 1969).

177. *Han'guk Ilbo*, 25 Mar. 1969. In an editorial on the growth of Japan-Korea cooperation in 1969 the *Han'guk Ilbo* later cited this decision as an important instance of the new cooperation between the two governments (1 May 1969, in *KPT*, 6 May 1969).

178. The Calcutta agreement led to the repatriation of eighty-eight thousand Korean residents. This expired in November 1967 and left some sixteen thousand applications outstanding (see *FEER*, 20 Mar. 1969; *Japan Times*, 20 Feb. 1969; and Moon). While the second agreement set a deadline of six months, it also stated that groups of 250 or more would still be eligible for repatriation after the initial period expired. The program began in May 1971 with monthly departures via Niigata.

179. *Japan Times*, 9 Mar. 1970 and 23 Jan. 1971. For example, while only a handful of applications were dealt with prior to 1970, the justice ministry was

screening more than two thousand applications under the new initiative. The liberalized visa policy was lobbied for by the Chosen Soren through the Socialist party. Sato obliged these groups in part because he wanted to ensure a sedate domestic political climate prior to the upcoming World Expo.

180. See *Japan Times*, 10 Mar. 1970 and 7 Feb. 1971.

181. See Park's press conference on the repatriation agreement, reentry visas, and Japanese plans to export plant equipment to North Korea reported in *FEER*, 9 Jan. 1969 (Derek Davies, "Seoul Searching").

182. *Chosŏn Ilbo*, 29 Jan. 1971, in *KPT*, 29 Jan. 1971, 24.

183. For an informative account of Korean reactions see Kim Tongjo, ch. 8; and Moon.

184. See CIA, "Special Report," 55–63.

185. The following data was compiled from FBIS, 2–20 Feb. 1970; *FEER*, 4 Feb.–5 Mar. 1970; *Japan Times*, 2–20 Feb. 1970; *KPT*, 2–20 Feb. 1970; and Shim interview, 29 Feb., 19 Mar. 1992.

186. The initial investigation centered on the Yanagida Trading Company's alleged sale of nine-million-yen worth of transistors and electronic parts to the North. A key figure in the case was Sano Hirohiro. Sano was a Korean resident in Japan who worked for the firm's Osaka branch. He received two requests from the North Koreans for germs in January and March 1969. COCOM-restricted goods sold to the North included machine parts, electrical appliances, maps, and telephone directories.

187. "Statement Made by Minister of Foreign Affairs Kyu Hah Choi on the Reported North Korean Attempt to Smuggle Epidemic Germs from Japan, Seoul, February 3, 1970," ROK-MOFA, *Taehan min'guk woegyo yŏnp'yo: 1970*, 55.

188. ROK protests were filed with Ambassador Kanayama on February 3 and with Vice-Minister Ushiba on the 4th.

189. *FEER*, 5 Mar. 1970; and Sunobe interview.

190. There is an additional domestic reason that should have made the government react strongly to the germ issue. At the time the major opposition party, the NDP, was boycotting the National Assembly to protest the government's handling of the constitutional revision bill. The ruling party, the DRP, wanted to break the boycott and bring the NDP back into the legislative body. By playing up the germ issue as a national emergency, the DRP could have forced the NDP to abandon its boycott and close ranks behind the government or risk criticism as allowing politics to cloud national security concerns.

191. Shim interview, 29 Feb. 1992.

192. Ibid.

193. See FBIS, 3 Feb. 1970, E2; and *Japan Times*, 26 Dec. 1969 and 27 Jan. 1970.

194. These were established in Taegu in February 1969 and in Inchon in May 1969 and (see *Japan Times*, 2 Feb. and 24 May 1969).

195. See *Japan Times*, 27 Aug. 1969; and *Seoul Kyŏngje Sinmun*, 24 Dec. 1969, in *KPT*, 25 Dec. 1969, 8.

196. See Paul Chan, 153–54; and *Japan Times*, 13 Dec. 1969.

197. For these and related points see Paul Chan, 153–66. Also see Warr. For an alternative view see Chang.

198. Economic Planning Board authorities first requested Japanese financing of P'ohang on August 5, 1969. At the third joint ministerial conference (August 26–28, 1969) the two governments reached an agreement in principle on Japanese funding of the project pending a feasibility study. The following month (September 17–26) a survey team consisting of representatives from the foreign ministry, MITI, finance ministry, and Japanese steel industries approved the project, and the agreement was formalized in December. Of the total, $73.7 million derived from an early allocation of funds promised in the 1965 normalization settlement, and the remaining $50 million in Export-Import Bank credits (the final amount was also $24 million more than originally requested by Seoul). Two key individuals throughout the negotiations were Park Tae-joon and Sunobe Ryōzō.

199. A concise study of P'ohang is in Kim, "Policy-Making," 111–51. For a detailed account of the decision making behind P'ohang, also see *P'ohang Chech'ŏl Simnyŏnsa* (A ten-year history of the POSCO Project).

200. Kim, "Policy-Making," 150–51.

201. Aichi even reportedly declined requests from economic advisors for any negative or conditional language in Japan's statements on P'ohang at the August 1969 joint ministerial meeting (*Japan Times*, 29 Aug. 1969; and *Tokyo Kyodo*, 28 Aug. 1969, in FBIS, 28 Aug. 1969, 2–3. For the communiqué see *Han-Il kwan'gye charyojip*, 2: 639–43).

202. Sunobe interview; confirmed by Okonogi interview. Also see *Japan Times*, 29 Aug. 1969; and Kim, "Policy-Making," 137.

203. On these points see Paul Chan, 166; *Japan Times*, 5 Feb., 24 July 1970; *Tong-A Ilbo*, 22 July 1970. For the conference communiqué see *Han-Il kwan'gye charyojip*, 2: 653–58.

204. Kim, "Policy-Making," 89.

205. *Han'guk Ilbo*, 24 July 1970, in *KPT*, 24 July 1970, 6–7.

206. Such "nonactions" are by nature difficult to document.

207. Kim, "Policy-Making," 124; and Woo, 124.

208. *Japan Times*, 24 July 1970 ("Seoul Meet Results Show Japan Living Up to Vows").

209. See Langdon, 177; and Ogata, 185.

210. Total Japan-ROK trade in 1971 was $1.2 billion, while that between Tokyo and Beijing was around $578 million (see Japan-MOFA, *Statistical Survey of Japan's Economy*, 45; and Lee, *Japan and Korea*, 58–62).

211. *Chosŏn Ilbo*, 16 May 1970, in *KPT*, 16 May 1970, 7; and *Japan Times*, 16 May 1970. Doi Masaharu, chair of Sumitomo Chemicals, and Makita Yoichiro, president of Mitsubishi Heavy Industries, were the two magnates who opted out of the conference.

212. *FEER*, 20 Aug. 1970; and *Japan Times*, 5 Aug. 1970.

213. *Seoul Press Service,* 5 Mar. 1971, in FBIS, 12 Mar. 1971, E1; and *Tong-A Ilbo,* 5 Mar. 1971.

214. *Japan Times,* 21 Jan. 1971; and *Tokyo Kyodo,* 20 Jan. 1971, in FBIS, 20 Jan. 1971.

215. *Seoul Kyŏngje Sinmun,* 4 June 1970, in *KPT,* 5 June 1970, 9–10.

216. *FEER,* 20 Aug. 1970. The liaison committee included Taiwan.

217. Emmerson, *Arms, Yen and Power,* 266.

Chapter 4. Detente and the Heightening Crisis

1. As explained earlier, these terms delineate the triangular relationship among Japan, the ROK, and the United States. *Bilateral* refers to Japan-ROK relations, the base of the triangle; *multilateral* refers to each state's ties with the common great-power protector, the United States, the two legs of the triangle.

2. For the text of the announcement see *Weekly Compilation of Presidential Documents,* 19 July 1971, 1058; and Nixon, *RN,* 544–45.

3. Kissinger's two-day, secret trip to Beijing (July 9–11), while ostensibly on a weekend retreat with Pakistan president Yahya Kahn, laid the groundwork for Nixon's visit. For additional details see Freeman, 7; Kissinger, 723, 781–82; and Nixon, *RN,* 555–56.

4. For the communiqué text see U.S., Congress, House, Committee on International Relations, *Normalization of Relations with the PRC,* 361–63. For a description of the meetings see Freeman, 9–10; and Kissinger, 1072–87.

5. A note on periodization: while I utilize 1972 as the starting point of detente, the reduction in regional security tensions strictly should begin from Nixon's July 1971 China announcement. The reader should assume the detente period to include events from mid-1971 to 1974. I use 1972 only for clarity in distinguishing this period from the preceding 1969–71 period. Some may argue periodization for detente should begin even earlier with United States-China rapprochement probes dating back to 1969; however, the contacts at this time were highly secretive, and success was far from certain. As a result, a thawing effect on regional security tensions was not really salient until after Nixon's announcement. For a chronology of these early contacts see Freeman, 1–9; Kissinger, 687–782; Meyer, 131–33; Nixon, *RN,* 544–52; and Whiting, "New Perspectives," 261–76.

6. Prior to the China summit the only dialogue channel (established in 1954) was at the consular level in Geneva. This was upgraded to ambassador level and moved to Warsaw in 1955 but produced only one agreement on repatriation in September 1955.

7. Before the rapprochement with China U.S. policymakers held serious concerns that actions in Vietnam (e.g., May 1970 incursions into Cambodia and bombing of North Vietnamese supply routes near the Chinese border) might provoke China. The likelihood of such a scenario substantially lessened after the China summit (see testimony of Marshall Green in U.S., Congress, House, Committee on Foreign Affairs, *The New China Policy,* 40–43). For

similar arguments see Kissinger, 1051, 1086–87; Nam Joo-hong, 110; Nixon, *RN*, 547–48; and Whiting, "New Perspectives," 263–65.

8. Testimony of Marshall Green in U.S., Congress, House, Committee on Foreign Affairs, *The New China Policy*, 27.

9. A detailed exposition of United States-Soviet detente is beyond the scope of this work. While superpower detente had global implications, the effects of the Sino-American rapprochement were more immediately relevant to security dynamics in Japan-ROK relations. See Garthoff, 289–472; Kissinger, 788–841, 1124–64, and 1202–57; U.S., Congress, House, Committee on Foreign Affairs, *Detente: Hearings*; and U.S., Congress, Senate, Committee on Foreign Relations, *Detente*.

10. In particular China saw the border clashes, Moscow's actions in Czechoslovakia in November 1968, and the enunciation of the Brezhnev doctrine as threats to national security. The Chinese expressed concerns about Soviet expansionism on numerous occasions during Nixon's visit, and these concerns were reflected in the "antihegemony" clause of the Shanghai communiqué (see Kissinger, 1072–74; and Nam Joo-hong, 112).

11. U.S., Congress, House, Committee on International Relations, *United States-Soviet Union-China: The Great Power Triangle, Part II*, 155–56.

12. For the text see "7-4 Nam-Puk kongdong sŏngmyŏngsŏ" (7-4 North-South joint communiqué), ROK-MOFA, *Taehan min'guk woegyo yŏnp'yo: 1972*, 203–6. Contrary to diplomatic historical accounts this event was not sprung by Seoul and Pyongyang on the regional governments and the Korean public in complete surprise. According to Oberdorfer and former KCIA officials, the U.S. embassy in Seoul had received and reviewed advance copies of the document. News leaks were so rampant in Seoul that the deputy U.S. ambassador's son learned of the impending communiqué from locals at a tea house. See Oberdorfer, 23–25; and interview, former KCIA official involved in the secret 1972 exchanges, 11 Aug. 1997, Seoul.

13. For details on North-South dialogue see *White Paper on South-North Dialogue*. For analyses of the July 4 communiqué see Saito, 88–98; and U.S., Congress, Senate, Committee on Foreign Relations, *Korea and the Philippines*, 11–13.

14. For details of this see Meyer, 111–13.

15. Japanese reactions to the "China shock" are dealt with in greater detail in the section on U.S. reassurances. In short, while the China shock dealt a blow to Japanese trust in the United States, it did *not* raise Japanese fears of U.S. military abandonment.

16. In Diet sessions three days after Nixon's announcement, Sato stated: "The proposed visit of President Nixon to Peking will contribute to the easing of world tensions, especially in Asia, and is to be welcomed" (*Japan Times*, 28 July 1971; and *Korea Herald*, 18 July 1971). Sato also made these points at his January 1972 summit with Nixon (see *White Papers of Japan: 1972–73*, 68–69; also see Fukuda, "The Future of Japan-US Relations," 242).

17. For examples see *White Papers of Japan: 1973–74*, 53–57; and *White Papers of Japan: 1974–75*, 74–77.

18. Kimura, 108–17. Japanese defense planning during the period also exhibited evidence of relaxed threat assessments. In December 1971 the JDA decreased by 10 percent its draft budget for the fourth five-year defense plan (1972–76) and even considered postponing the plan until 1973 because of changes in the security environment. The JDA did eventually implement the plan as scheduled; however, Director-General Esaki Masumi explicitly stated this action stemmed, not from any perceived increase in security tensions, but from the need to show Japanese efforts at burden sharing before the upcoming January 1972 Nixon-Sato summit (see *Japan Times*, 2–7 Dec. 1971).

19. See Sato's statements in the July 1971 Diet plenary sessions in *Japan Times*, 23 July 1971, and his October 1971 policy speeches in *Japan Times*, 20 Oct. 1971. For additional statements see *FEER*, 2 Oct. 1971; and Hsiao, 164–65. This was a major policy change for the conservative, pro-Taiwan Sato. China was a topic of intense policy debate for many years between the conservative wing of the LDP (led by Kishi, Ishii, and Fukuda favoring Taipei) and liberal wing (led by Miki and Ohira). Sato had sided strongly with the former group and changed his position only *after* Nixon's July 1971 announcement. See Hayashi, 259; and Ogata, 195, 199.

20. See *White Papers of Japan: 1972–73*, 63; also see *FEER*, 8 July 1972; and *White Papers of Japan: 1971–72*, 36–37. By contrast, the 1969–70 white papers made no mention of Chinese normalization (see *White Papers of Japan: 1969–70*, 54–55). In additional steps to gain Beijing's goodwill, the foreign ministry offered to apologize for past aggressions against the Chinese, and MITI considered reinstating long-suspended Export-Import Bank financing of trade with China. For foreign ministry statements see Hsiao, 164–65; for MITI statements see *FEER*, 16 Nov. 1971, and Ogata, 200.

21. For Tanaka's statements see *FEER*, 26 Aug. 1972; *Korea Herald*, 6–8 July 1972; and Ohira, 416–17.

22. These preconditions were (1) recognition of the PRC as the legitimate government of China, (2) recognition of Taiwan as a part of mainland China, (3) abolition of the Japan-Taiwan treaty, (4) support for U.S. withdrawal from Taiwan, and (5) support for China's entry into the UN and Taiwan's expulsion.

23. On these points see A. Doak Barnett, 27; Burleson, 21; Hsiao, 167–69; Kimura, 112; and Whiting, "Japan and Sino-American Relations," 229.

24. Kissinger, 1061–62; Lee and Sato, *U.S. Policy*, 61–62; and Whiting, "Japan and Sino-American Relations," 226.

25. For the communiqué text and summit analyses see Hsiao, 171–73; *Korea Herald*, 26, 30 Sept. 1972; and *White Papers of Japan: 1973–74*, 61–62. Also see *FEER*, Oct. 21, 1972 (Nakamura Koji, "Introducing Positive Defense"); and Matsumoto, 150.

26. For details see Curtis, "Tyumen Oil," 154; and Meyer, 144–45.

27. See *FEER*, 5 Feb. 1972.

28. The long-held position was that these territories—Habomai, Shikotan, Kunashiri, and Etorofu—were Soviet and therefore not subject to discussion (see Harako, 81–82). The decision to dispatch Gromyko to Japan instead of a concurrent Warsaw Pact conference also reflected Soviet intentions to upgrade relations with Japan. An additional motivating factor for Moscow's overtures was the desire to balance Sino-Japanese rapprochement. Sino-Soviet currying of Japanese favor was manifested in a bidding competition in 1973 over Tokyo's search for secure energy resources. The Chinese offered offshore oil facilities, while the Soviets offered the Siberian project. This put Tokyo in the position of being courted by two former adversaries and further contributed to its decreased threat perceptions during the period (see *FEER*, 23 Apr. [Nakamura Koji, "The Wedge Busters"], 14 May ["Chinese-Soviet Relations: Treading the Siberian Tightrope"]; 28 May ["Chinese Wedge"] 1973; and 18 Oct. 1974 ["Ideological Foes Woo Japan"]). For concurring arguments see Harako, 79–96; and Sato Seizaburo, "Japan-US Relations," 198–99.

29. Hsiao, 173–74; and *FEER*, 19 Mar. 1973 (Nakamura Koji, "The Tanaka Letter"). For other statements by Tanaka to this effect see *Korea Herald*, 6 July 1972; and Ohira, 417.

30. For the summit communiqué see *White Papers of Japan: 1974–75*, 82–84.

31. A number of complications impeded negotiations in the spring of 1974. Generally the Soviets changed the substance of their proposals, and the Japanese became hesitant to make a final commitment without similar participation by the United States (see Curtis, "Tyumen Oil," 147–73).

32. See Harako; Kamiya, "Japanese-US Relations," 721; Kiga; Meyer, 150; and testimony of Robert Scalapino, 4 May 1972 in U.S., Congress, House, Committee on Foreign Affairs, *The New China Policy*, 143.

33. See *White Papers of Japan: 1973–74*, 53–54. These views were echoed in numerous statements during the period by Tanaka and Foreign Minister Ohira. See the September 1972 Nixon-Tanaka summit in *Korea Herald*, 3 Sept. 1972; and *White Papers of Japan: 1972–73*, 69–70; and the August 1973 Nixon-Tanaka summit in *Korea Herald*, 2–3 Aug. 1973. For similar arguments see Kamiya, "Japanese-US Relations," 721; and Sato, "Japan-US Relations," 198–99.

34. The venue for Rogers's statements was the July 1973 United States-Japan Joint Economic Committee meetings (see *Korea Herald*, 17 July 1973). The United States reiterated these assurances at the Tanaka-Nixon summits in September 1972 and August 1973.

35. For the JDA report see *Korea Herald*, 29 Jan. 1974. For the Gaimushō report see *Korea Herald*, 30 June 1974.

36. On these points and Japanese-Vietnamese normalization see Burleson, 12–37; *FEER*, 26 Feb., 11 Mar. 1972; Sato, "Japan-US Relations," 205–6; and *White Papers of Japan: 1974–75*, 72, 74–76. During the period Japan also established diplomatic relations with Mongolia and East Germany and exchanged foreign-ministerial visits with Hungary, Yugoslavia, and Czechoslovakia.

37. Rogers informed Ambassador Ushiba only three hours prior to the airing of Nixon's announcement. Sato, in the midst of a cabinet meeting, received word via Vice-Minister Yasukawa only minutes before the Japanese media carried Nixon's statement (Yasukawa Takeshi, interview by author, 8 July 1972, Tokyo [hereafter Yasukawa interview]; also see U. Alexis Johnson, 553–54; and Meyer, 111–13).

38. This referred to the professed fear of Asakai Koichiro, ambassador to the United States, 1957–63, that Tokyo's allegiance to Taiwan would one day backfire. The ambassador dreamt that he would awake one morning to newspaper headlines announcing U.S. recognition of China (former United States ambassador to Japan, interview by author, 2 Nov. 1994, Stanford, Calif; also see U. Alexis Johnson, 553–54; and Meyer, 113, 134). For government statements see Sato's in *Tokyo Kyodo*, 13 July 1971, in FBIS, 13 July 1971, and *FEER*, 7 Aug. 1971, and Ambassador Ushiba's in *Japan Times*, 13 Aug. 1971.

39. Sunobe interview. For concurring views see Kissinger, 762; Lee and Sato, *U.S. Policy*, 58; and Ambassador Meyer's recalling of events in Meyer, 113, 174.

40. See Ambassador Reischauer's relaying of conversations with Japanese officials in U.S., Congress, House, Committee on Foreign Affairs, *The New China Policy*, 4–10.

41. Testimony of Edwin Reischauer in U.S., Congress, House, Committee on Foreign Affairs, *The New China Policy*, 9, 17. Also see Maruyama, 266–72; and Meyer, 134.

42. Fukuda, "The Future of Japan-US Relations," 242. Prior to the China shock Japan's ties with Taiwan, in deference to U.S. cold-war policies, originated with the December 1951 Yoshida-Dulles letter. Throughout the postwar period LDP conservative elements (e.g., the Kishi, Ishii, and Fukuda factions) and big business supported this position, while liberal LDP elements (e.g., the Miki and Ohira factions) and the *gyōkai* (sectoral associations) favored ties with the PRC. On the Yoshida letter see Acheson, 541, 603–5, 759. On Japanese domestic pressures for relations with China see Baerwald, 195–203; Fukui, "Tanaka Goes to Peking"; Hayashi, 259; Matsumoto, 148–54; and Ogata, 175–203.

43. Nixon, Kissinger, and Rogers personally provided such assurances to Sato, Fukuda, Ushiba, and Emperor Hirohito. A U.S. foreign-policy report issued a week prior to the trip also stated: "Japan is our most important ally in Asia. . . . Our security, our prosperity and our global policies are therefore inextricably interlinked to the US-Japanese relationship" (see Lee and Sato, *U.S. Policy*, 61; and *PPPUS: Nixon*, 72, 232). The Shanghai communiqué's specific reference to the strength of the United States-Japan alliance also squelched any lingering concerns about U.S.-Chinese collusion (for U.S. debriefings see Emmerson, "The United States and Japan," 627; Farnsworth, "Japan 1972," 116; Kamiya, "Japanese-US Relations," 719–20; *Korea Herald*, 1 Mar. 1972; and U.S., Congress, House, Committee on Foreign Affairs, *The New China Policy*, 26–27).

44. Sunobe interview.

45. See Fukuda, "The Future of Japan-US Relations," 238; and Kamiya, "Japanese-US Relations," 719–20.

46. *FEER*, 14 May 1973 (Nakamura Koji, "Interview with Ohira Masayoshi, Japanese Foreign Minister"). For a concurring view see testimony of James W. Morley, 16 May 1972, in U.S., Congress, House, Committee on Foreign Affairs, *The New China Policy*, 156. Nixon's "economic shocks" in August 1971 and Japan's unsuccessful support of Taiwan's UN seat in October 1971 (at the behest of the United States) are two additional events that damaged bilateral relations during the period. However, neither of these raised fears of U.S. abandonment. The economic shocks, while a strain on trade relations, did not undermine confidence in security commitments. Moreover, Japanese officials were not surprised by Nixon's acts, as their lack of cooperation in addressing trade complaints raised anticipation of some form of U.S. retaliation, as related by former Ambassador Reischauer from conversations with Japanese officials (see testimony of Edwin Reischauer in U.S., Congress, House, Committee on Foreign Affairs, *The New China Policy*, 9). Regarding the UN issue, Tokyo did lose political face as a result of the October 1971 defeat of the United States-Japan-sponsored resolution to prevent Taiwan's expulsion; however, this became largely irrelevant after Japan's normalization with China and severing of relations with Taipei. Furthermore, had these events truly constituted U.S. abandonment, popular support for Sato's continued rule would have declined. This was not the case. After these events Sato overwhelmingly defeated a no-confidence vote in the Diet and remained in power for a full year thereafter.

47. Sunobe interview. Sunobe, who was director-general of Asian affairs at the Gaimushō at the time, recalled that on the day of Nixon's China announcement many foreign diplomats asked whether he was upset at the news. Sunobe responded, "I was actually happy because the new U.S. policy had given Japan a free hand to deal with China."

48. Marshall Green, 703–7. A February 1974 Congressional study mission reached similar conclusions (see U.S., Congress, House, Committee on Foreign Affairs, *Report of the Special Study Mission*, 3; also see Overholt, 713; and Whiting, *China Eyes Japan*, 39. For concurring Japanese analyses see Hayashi, 262; Kanazawa, 74; Maruyama, 266–72; and Sato, "Japan-US Relations," 195–206).

49. Lee Tong-won interview, 29 July 1992.

50. See Lee Chong-sik, "The Impact of the Sino-American Detente," 198; and Saito, 25–37.

51. For comments during the Nixon-Zhou summit see *Korea Herald*, 25 Feb. 1972. For additional statements see Park's ROK Military Academy speech (March 1974) in *Korea Herald*, 31 Mar. 1974 (Yun Ik-han, "Park Hits Detente Delusion") and his Armed Forces Day address (October 1974) in *FEER*, 18 Oct. 1974 (Kim Sam-o, "Slapping Down a Political Challenge").

52. The inaugural Red Cross talks went relatively smoothly; however, when negotiations moved to more substantive issues regarding family reunifications,

the delegates could not even agree on an agenda. Regarding the North-South Coordinating Committee, a typical example of this body's ineffectiveness was the March 1973 meetings in which ROK delegation chief Lee Hu-rak and North Korean deputy chief Park Sung-chul became embroiled in heated exchanges over which side was responsible for the Korean war. (For an overview of the talks see *White Paper on South-North Dialogue*; also see *Korea Herald*, 23 Mar. ["2 Sides Swap No Minutes on Confab Results"], 6 Apr. ["South-North Talks Slow to Snail's Pace"] 1973.)

53. North Korean naval activities resulted in armed altercations with ROK coast guard authorities near Cheju Island in February–June 1974. Attacks against ROK fishing vessels occurred off the west coast of the peninsula near the 38th parallel. For these and other North Korean acts see *Korea Herald*, 17 Mar., 27 Dec. 1973 and 12 Feb. 1974; *"Pi'mujang han'guk ŏsŏne taehan pukhanŭi konggyŏk sakŏn"* (North Korea's attack on unarmed ROK fishing boats), 8 Feb. 1974, in ROK-MOFA, *Taehan min'guk woegyo yŏnp'yo: 1974*, 118–26; and U.S., Congress, House, Committee on Foreign Affairs, *Report of the Special Study Mission*, 11.

54. For the assassination attempt see *Korea-Japan Relations and the Attempt on the Life of Korea's President*. For the tunnel discoveries see *FEER*, 29 Nov. 1974; *Korea Herald*, 11 Nov. 1974; and Oberdorfer, *Two Koreas*, 56–59. During the period North Korean defense expenditures increased to 20 percent of GNP, highlighted by a major military modernization program. For additional listings of North Korean actions see "North Korea's Export of Guerrilla Warfare, Seoul, May 24, 1971," in ROK-MOFA, *Taehan min'guk woegyo yŏnp'yo: 1971*, 200–214; "Report of Congressman John M. Murphy, October 23–30, 1975," excerpted in ROK-MOFA, *Woegyo yŏn'guwŏn yŏn'gubu: Pogwanyong* (Archives), 149; and "Addendum to the Memorandum of the ROK on the Question of Korea at the 29th Session of the UNGA, Seoul, November 22, 1974," in ROK-MOFA, *Taehan min'guk woegyo yŏnp'yo: 1974*, 410–15. As Oberdorfer described it, North Korean tunneling practices dated to the Korean war when tunnels were excavated to escape U.S. bombardment. The DMZ tunnels, the first of which was discovered accidentally by routine patrols, were extremely well planned and systematically developed to carry out an underground invasion. The first tunnel, fully equipped with railways, electricity lines, reinforced concrete, and weapons storage areas was estimated to accommodate an invasion flow of five hundred to seven hundred men per hour. A second tunnel, discovered in February 1975, was estimated to ten thousand troops per hour and had already reached three-quarters of a mile into the southern portion of the DMZ. Utilizing high-tech sensors, underground cameras, and seismic listening devices, the U.S. later estimated as many as twenty-two suspected or confirmed tunnel sites (*Two Koreas*, 56–57).

55. See Saito, 29.

56. See *"Che 29 ch'a kukje yŏnhap ch'onghoe che 1 wiwŏnhoe esŏŭi taehan min'guk susŏk taepyo Kim Dongjo woemubu changgwan yŏnsŏlmun, New York, November 29, 1974"* (Statement of Kim Dong-jo, minister of foreign af-

fairs and chair of the ROK delegation at the 1st committee of the 29th session of the UNGA), in ROK-MOFA, *Taehan min'guk woegyo yŏnp'yo: 1974*, 445–71, especially 449–54. For similar statements by Park see *"Pak taet'ongryŏng kakhaŭi nampukhan pulkach'im hyŏpchŏngjeŭi (yŏndu kija hoekyŏn chungesŏ)"* (President Park's Proposal for nonaggression agreement [press conference statements]), Seoul, 18 Jan. 1974; and *"Che 29 ju nyŏn kwangbokchŏl chŭŭmhan Pak taet'ongryŏng kakha kyŏngch'uksa"* (President Park's 29th anniversary National Liberation Day speech), both in ROK-MOFA, *Taehan min'guk woegyo yŏnp'yo: 1974*, 104–13, especially 110, and 265–79, especially 273–74, respectively.

57. U.S., Congress, Senate, Committee on Foreign Relations, *Korea and the Philippines*, 5. For supporting views see testimony of Robert Scalapino, 4 May 1972, in U.S., Congress, House, Committee on Foreign Affairs, *The New China Policy*, 112–31.

58. Nam Joo-hong, 118, 136.

59. See Lee and Sato, *U.S. Policy*, 65; and Nam Joo-hong, 118, 125, 136.

60. These included Chile, Denmark, Indonesia, Iran, Malaysia, and Sweden (see *FEER*, 14 May 1973; and Yung H. Park, 762). On North Korean entry into the IPU and WHO see *FEER*, 14 May 1973; and *Korea Herald*, 18 May 1973 ("WHO Approves N. Korea Entry in 66–41 Vote"). The latter enabled Pyongyang to gain UN permanent-observer status and establish missions in Geneva and New York (South Korea already held permanent-observer status).

61. For example, past proposals submitted by Algeria, Mongolia, and the Soviet Union for withdrawing all foreign troops from Korea were narrowly defeated in 1971 and 1972 (see *Korea Herald*, 25–28 Sept. 1971 and 17–24 Sept. 1972). ROK concerns were justified as the fall of 1973 and 1974 saw the Assembly pass a resolution dissolving the UN political presence in Korea (the Commission for Unification and Rehabilitation, or UNCURK) and eventually pass another resolution in November 1975 for dissolution of the UN Security Command (the latter, however, was not acted upon) (see U.S., Congress, House, Committee on International Relations, *Investigation of Korean-American Relations*, 1977, 43–44). For ROK opposition to these resolutions see *"Che 29 ch'a kukje yŏnhap ch'onghoe han'guk munje egwanhan taehan min'guk kaksŏ"* (Memorandum of the ROK on the question of Korea at the 29th session of the UNGA), 1 Nov. 1974, Seoul, in ROK-MOFA, *Taehan min'guk woegyo yŏnp'yo: 1974*, 360–84.

62. For reactions to Laird's testimony see Chang Doo-song, "Under Four Flags," *FEER*, 10 Sept. 1971. For the Pentagon report see *Korea Herald*, 10 Nov. 1971.

63. In 1971, the first year of the program, U.S. military assistance grants exceeded by $1 million the ROK's $290 million request. However, appropriations for 1972 amounted to only $155 million of $239 million requested; 1973, $149 million of $215 million; and 1974, $94 million of $264 million. Moreover, beginning in 1974, reluctance to appropriate funds grew stronger, as Congress linked cuts in ROK military aid to the Park regime's human rights

violations (e.g., 1975 funds equaled $82 million of $161 million requested). See U.S., Congress, House, Committee on International Relations, *Investigation of Korean-American Relations*, 1977, 45–46, 70–71.

64. *FEER*, 1 July 1974 ("America in Asia 1974" [special supplement], Kim Sam-o, "Credibility Gap"). In line with its abandonment fears the ROK also vehemently opposed any signals of American warming toward the North. In March 1972 Seoul immediately contested U.S. intimations it might lift travel restrictions on North Korea (see *Korea Herald*, 12 Mar. 1972 ["Travel Ban Easing on North Korea Favored"]). In July 1972 Foreign Minister Kim Yong-sik filed strong protests over Secretary Rogers's use of the formal designation DPRK when referring to the North. Both acts by the United States were seen as departures from past practice and were harshly criticized as the first steps toward U.S. recognition of the regime (see *Korea Herald*, 2 July 1972 ["Government Files Protest on N. Korea Name"]; and Saito, 29).

65. On these points see Oberdorfer, *Two Koreas*, 13–15.

66. ROK withdrawals from Vietnam began in 1971 and were completed over a fifteen-month span (see *FEER*, 1 July 1972 ["America in Asia"]; and *Korea Herald*, 4 Sept. 1971). For the Ford-Park proceedings, communiqué, and press statements see *"Ford mitaet'ongryŏngŭl wihan kongsik manch'anhoe esŏŭi Pak Chŏnghŭi taet'ongryŏng kakha yŏnsŏlmun"* (Address by Park Chung Hee, president of the Republic of Korea at the state dinner in honor of Gerald Ford, president of the United States), Seoul, 22 Nov. 1974, and *"Pak Chŏnghŭi taehan min'guk taet'ongryŏng kwa Gerald Ford mihap chungguk taet'ongryŏng kanŭi kongdong sŏngmyŏngsŏ"* (Joint communiqué between Park Chung Hee, president of the Republic of Korea and U.S. president Gerald Ford), Seoul, 23 Nov. 1974, in ROK-MOFA, *Taehan min'guk woegyo yŏnp'yo: 1974*, 430–32 and 438–44, respectively; *FEER*, 6 Dec. 1974 (Roy Whang, "For the President's Ears Only"); and *Korea Herald*, 23 Nov. 1974.

67. For the 1973 SCC communiqué see *"Han-Mi yŏllye anbo hyŏpŭihoe kongdong sŏngmyŏng"* (ROK-US Security Consultative Conference joint statement), in ROK-MOFA, *Taehan min'guk woegyo yŏnp'yo: 1973*, 218–21. For proceedings and press statements see *Korea Herald*, 13–14 Sept. 1973. For the 1974 SCC see *Korea Herald*, 26 Sept. 1974; and *"1974 nyŏn Han-Mi anbo hyŏpŭihoe kongdong sŏngmyŏngsŏ"* (Joint statement of the 1974 annual US-ROK Security Consultative Conference), in ROK-MOFA, *Taehan min'guk woegyo yŏnp'yo: 1974*, 304–9, especially clause 2.

68. Those interviewed included Park, Foreign Minister Kim Dong-jo, Vice-Minister of Defense Choi Kwang-soo, and National Assembly Speaker Chung Il-kwon (U.S., Congress, House, Committee on Foreign Affairs, *Report of the Special Study Mission*, 9).

69. Park Kun interview. Park characterized South Korean attitudes at this time as similar to that of a nervous partner, in constant need of being reassured of the fidelity of a loved one, yet still beset by insecurities. Also see testimony of Marshall Green in U.S., Congress, House, Committee on Foreign Affairs, *The New China Policy*, 36.

70. Interview with Kim Seong Jin in Oberdorfer, *Two Koreas*, 13.

71. This section is based on the following sources: *New York Times*, 29 Jan. 1977, 1 (David Burnham, "South Korea Drops Plan to Buy a Nuclear Plant from France"); 1 Feb., 11 ("Seoul Officials Say Strong U.S. Pressure Forced Cancellation of Plans to Purchase a French Nuclear Plant"); 11 Aug., 3 (Leslie Gelb, "Nuclear Proliferation and the Sale of Arms"); 24 Aug., 9 (Drew Middleton, "U.S. Confident Armies in Korea Are Prepared to Handle Any Attack"); 31 Aug. (David Binder, "U.S. Fears Spread of Atomic Arms in Asia"); Drezner, ch. 8; Sigal, 20; and Spector and Smith, 121–23. For an excellent review of these documents see Oberdorfer, *Two Koreas*, 68–74.

72. On the concept of "recessed deterrence" see Buzan, 36.

73. At that time South Korea relied on the U.S. for its civilian nuclear program but sought non-U.S. help for the more controversial reprocessing technology. Tracking potential proliferation activities by other states had not been a U.S. priority; however, after India's 1974 nuclear test intelligence gathering on such issues increased, and the revelations about South Korea followed shortly thereafter. The U.S. never directly confronted the Koreans on the weapons issue, instead discouraging Seoul's efforts at acquiring the reprocessing technology from a third party. In the end a concerted high-level push was made on Seoul by such American officials as Ambassador Richard Sneider, Defense Secretaries James Schlesinger and later Donald Rumsfeld, and Assistant Secretary of State Philip Habib. A combination of inducements (e.g., guaranteed access to U.S. reprocessing technology when needed by the ROK) and veiled threats (e.g., reconsideration of the alliance and suspension of loans related to the civilian nuclear program) led Park reluctantly to cancel the French reprocessing contract in 1976.

74. Oberdorfer, *Two Koreas*, 71.

75. Richard Sneider, quoted ibid., 73.

76. For the text of the Yusin declaration see "*10/17 taet'ongryŏng ttŭkbyŏl sŏnŏn*" (Special presidential declaration), in ROK-MOFA, *Taehan min'guk woegyo yŏnp'yo: 1972*, 287–98.

77. For fuller discussions of the Yusin system see Clifford, ch. 6; Han Sung-joo, "South Korea in 1974"; Han Sung-joo and Park Yung-chul, "Democratization at Last," especially 165–73; Kim Se-jin; and Sohn, introduction and chs. 2–4, 7–8. Yusin began in December 1971, when Park declared a state of national emergency and railroaded legislation through the Assembly granting him virtual dictatorial powers. Park subsequently declared martial law on October 17, 1972, and installed the Yusin constitution on November 21. The repressive regime ended in 1979 with Park's assassination.

78. See *FEER*, 15 Jan. 1972; U.S., Congress, House, Committee on International Relations, *Investigation of Korean-American Relations*, 1977, 37–38.

79. Lee Tong-won interview, 17 May 1992; Okonogi interview; Park Sang-yong interview, 7 Feb. 1992; and anonymous United States embassy official, interview by author, 12 May 1992, Seoul.

80. For example see Park's December 6, 1971, national emergency speech in *FEER*, 18 Dec. 1971; and *Korea Herald*, 7 Dec. 1971.

81. Ironically Nixon officials, Rogers and Habib, spent more time protesting the explicit link between détente and Yusin in the ROK's planned public statement than they did actually opposing Yusin's imposition. U.S. inaction on Yusin was in part a function of domestic politics. Park, as well as Ferdinand Marcos three weeks earlier in the Philippines, timed their political crackdowns to coincide with the U.S. presidential election campaign, when controversial policy positions against allies were least likely to occur (Oberdorfer, *Two Koreas*, 37–41, especially Kim Jong-pil quotation; also anonymous U.S. embassy official, interview by author, 12 May 1992, Seoul).

82. See testimony of Robert Scalapino, 4 May 1972, in U.S., Congress, House, Committee on Foreign Affairs, *The New China Policy*, 108; idem., *Report of the Special Study Mission*, 12; and U.S., Congress, Senate, Committee on Foreign Relations, *Korea and the Philippines*, 4–10.

83. Sato made the latter point by omitting the phrase "positively and promptly" when asked in Diet sessions to explicate the extent of Japanese base obligations in a second Korean war. Sato's omission was significant as the phrase had been used since his November 1969 National Press Club speech to communicate Japan's immediate and unconditional support for U.S. use of the Okinawan bases for ROK defense (see Emmerson, "The United States and Japan" 631; *Japan Times*, Dec. 9, 1971).

84. See *White Papers of Japan: 1972–73*, 68–69. South Korean and American media recognized this omission as the major news story of the summit (for example, see *Korea Herald*, 11 Jan. 1972).

85. See *Korea Herald*, 12 Jan. 1972 ("Sato Weakened Defense for Taiwan, Korea: Asahi"); and Sato's interview in the *New York Times*, 10 Mar. 1972. Also see *FEER*, 4 Mar. 1972; and *Korea Herald*, 7 Jan. 1972 ("Security in the Far East").

86. See *Japan Times*, 12 Aug. 1971 ("Japan-ROK Communique Highlights"); and ROK-MOFA, *Taehan min'guk woegyo yŏnp'yo: 1971*, 331–37. In place of this clause the communiqué contained a nebulous statement on Japanese acknowledgment of ROK defense efforts.

87. For Kimura's statements see *Japan Times*, 12–13 Aug. 1971.

88. For the Nixon-Tanaka summit see *Korea Herald*, 3 Aug. 1973; and *White Papers of Japan: 1972–73*, 69–71. For the Ford-Tanaka summit see *FEER*, 29 Nov. 1974 (Nakamura Koji, "Ford's 1st Away Game"); and *Korea Herald*, 21 Nov. 1974. During the Nixon-Tanaka summit, press reports indicated the United States intended to ask Japan to provide funds to the ROK for purchase of transport, communications, and noncombat equipment. Whether Japan agreed to this was seen as a vital indicator of Tanaka's support of the Japan-ROK defense link. Secretary Rogers apparently raised the issue with Ohira, but no agreement was reached. Interviews by the author could not confirm the content of these discussions (see *FEER*, 13 Aug. 1973 [Nakamura Koji, "Into

the Breach"]; and *Korea Herald*, 1 Aug. ["US to Request Japanese Aid in Modernizing ROK Army"], 4 Aug. ["US Didn't Ask Japan to Aid Korean Army"] 1973).

89. Kimura, 114.

90. On the link between interpretations of the Korea clause and the Okinawan base agreement see Blaker, 54–55; Lee, *Japan and Korea*, 80; and Yung H. Park, 761–84, especially 767.

91. For the fifth annual joint ministerial conference see *Japan Times*, 11 Aug. 1971; and *Korea Herald*, 10 Aug. 1971 ("Cooperation Subject of ROK-Japan Meet"). For the sixth conference see *Japan Times*, 5 Sept. 1972; and *Korea Herald*, 6, 10 Sept. 1972.

92. *Korea Herald*, 5 Jan. 1972 ("Chung Tells Sato Peking, N. Korea Far East Threats").

93. *Korea Herald*, 7 Jan. 1972 ("Security in the Far East"). For additional South Korean statements see the January 1973 meetings of Foreign Minister Kim Yong-sik with Tanaka and Ohira in *Korea Herald*, 9–12 Jan. 1973.

94. See interview of Kim Jong-pil in *New York Times*, 11 Aug. 1972 (Richard Halloran, "Tokyo's China Bid Unsettles Seoul"); also see *FEER*, 23 Sept. 1972.

95. Illustrating the depth of ROK concerns, Park held emergency cabinet meetings after the Tanaka-Zhou summit to discuss the implications of the normalization agreement on ROK security. A government report stated that the summit made the Korea clause and Okinawan base agreement obsolete and would lead Japan to implement an "equidistance" policy toward Korea (on these points see *Korea Herald*, 5 Oct. 1972). In meetings with Premier Kim Jong-pil, Foreign Minister Kim Yong-sik, and Park, Kimura also presented a letter from Tanaka assuring them that Sino-Japanese normalization would not detract from Japan-ROK relations, but this failed to mollify South Korean anxieties (for Kimura's debriefing see *Korea Herald*, 11–13 Oct. 1972).

96. Methodologically I look here for the absence of cooperation rather than the existence of friction in support of the argument.

97. The state visit was scheduled for November 13–18, 1972, only a couple of weeks after Tanaka's Beijing trip (see statements by senior press secretary Kim Song-jin in *Korea Herald*, 7 Oct. ["Cooperation Hike Seen Major Topic"], 8 Oct. ["Park's November Visit Viewed as Significant"], 1972).

98. Lee Tong-won interview, 29 July 1992.

99. Interviews were conducted by a Senate fact-finding mission with ROK foreign and defense ministers as well as *ch'ŏngwadae* (Blue House) and KCIA officials (see U.S., Congress, Senate, Committee on Foreign Relations, *Korea and the Philippines*, 6; and *Korea Herald*, 18 Oct. 1972).

100. Japan succeeded in deleting the clause on the North Korean security threat from the communiqué. For the communiqué text see ROK-MOFA, *Taehan min'guk woegyo yŏnp'yo: 1971*, 331; for conference statements and proceedings see *Japan Times*, 11–12, 18 Aug. 1971; and *Korea Herald*, 10–12 Aug. 1971.

101. *Korea Herald*, 11 Sept. 1971 ("Japan-North Korean Ties Will Be Discouraged").

102. For Fukuda's statements see his interview with Tonghwa News Agency, as reported in *Korea Herald*, 25 Dec. 1971. For Sato's statements see *Japan Times*, 2 Feb. 1972; and *Korea Herald*, 3 Feb. 1972. While Sato ruled out the possibility of formal normalization with North Korea, his statements were clearly intended to leave open the possibility of de facto political relations.

103. *Japan Times*, 2 Nov. 1972.

104. See Lower House budget sessions, as reported in *Japan Times*, 7 Feb. 1973. For additional examples see *FEER*, 23 Sept. 1972; and interview with Foreign Minister Kimura, "New Directions for Japanese Diplomacy," translated in *Japan Echo* 2, no. 2 (1975): 108–17, 113, 115.

105. The justice ministry enforced this policy by generally declining visa applications for such visits.

106. The meetings, October 25–November 4, 1971, were marked by extreme cordiality, and Kim Il-sung welcomed the visit as an important step toward expansion of Tokyo-Pyongyang relations. See *Japan Times*, 26, 30 Oct., 1 Nov. 1971; and *Korea Herald*, 18 Nov. 1971.

107. See *Korea Herald*, 23 Oct. 1971 ("Japan Ponders Admitting VIP's from North Korea"); also see *Japan Times*, 23 Oct. 1971.

108. LDP legislators coordinated the initial consensus building for the group, formed a significant bloc of thirty-one members and held the chairmanship under Dietman Kuno Chuji. For the league's inauguration and declaration of purpose see *Japan Times*, 17 Nov. 1971. The initial membership of the body included LDP (31), Socialist (155), Democratic-Socialist (15), and Communist (24). In addition, in September 1973 another LDP official, Utsunomiya Tokuma, formed the National Council for the Normalization of Japan-North Korean Relations. Individuals like Kuno and Utsunomiya were also involved in the creation of the League for the Study of Afro-Asian Problems in January 1965 (the other major leftist Diet group). Groups like this were supported by the pro-China Kono, Ono, and Matsumura factions and opposed by the anticommunist conservative factions led by Sato, Kishi, and Ishii (see Yung H. Park, 762–63).

109. The league visit to Pyongyang took place January 15–25, 1972 (see *Japan Times*, 18, 21–22, 26 Jan. 1972; and *Korea Herald*, 14–15, 18 Jan. 1972).

110. The Kōmeitō mission took place June 7, 1972 (see *Japan Times*, 8 June 1972). The January 1972 JSP mission was highlighted by a two-hour, private meeting with Kim Il-sung (see *Japan Times*, 16 Jan. 1972); and the July JSP mission focused on Japan-North Korea normalization, Korean reunification, and trade expansion (see *Japan Times*, 14 July 1972; and *Korea Herald*, 14 July 1972).

111. For example, the first prefectural group, a seventy-member body from Kanagawa dedicated to achieving Japan-North Korea normalization, formed in February 1972 (see *Japan Times*, 12 Feb. 1972). Prefectural officials and labor

leaders also formed the Japan-North Korean Cultural Association in September 1972, which subsequently signed a cultural-exchange agreement with Pyongyang (see *Japan Times*, 6, 8 Sept. 1972; and *Korea Herald*, 27 Sept. 1972). The most prominent among the cultural exchanges was a one hundred-member delegation of athletes, dignitaries, and journalists for the Olympic Winter Games in Sapporo; several groups of scientists; and a North Korean delegation to the Interparliamentary Union convention in Tokyo. For the Olympic delegation see *Korea Herald*, 3 Sept., 4 Dec. 1971. For the North Korean science and parliamentary delegations see *Korea Herald*, 5 July 1973 and 20 Feb. 1974. According to a 1980 study, Japanese approval of North Korean requests to visit Japan increased more than tenfold between 1971 and 1973 from 31 to 315 cases (Hahn, "Asian International Politics," 195, n. 6).

112. For example, LDP Dietmen who visited Pyongyang as part of the Dietmen's League used regular citizen's passports rather than official government passports (see *Japan Times*, 19 Jan. 1972; and *Korea Herald*, 17 Oct. 1972 ["LDP Officials Plan Visit in Early 1973"]).

113. For announcements of the final itinerary see *Japan Times*, 21 Mar. 1973. The visit was heralded as an official mission to develop ties between the Korean Workers Party and LDP. Postponement of the plan was the result of pressure from the Sato government, as it had not yet laid out a definitive policy on relations with the North (see Secretary-General Hashimoto Tomisaburo's statement in *Japan Times*, 15 July 1973; *Korea Herald*, 21 July 1973; and Yung H. Park, 765).

114. *Korea Herald*, 24 Oct. 1971 ("ROK Warns Japanese on North Visits").

115. *Japan Times*, 24 Oct. 1971; and *Korea Herald*, 1, 3, 26 Oct. 1971.

116. For embassy press statements see *Japan Times*, 8 Aug. 1974. For Foreign Minister Kim's protest of the Minobe visit see *Korea Herald*, 19 Nov. 1971.

117. See Maeo's press conference statements in *Japan Times*, 25 Aug. 1971; and *Korea Herald*, 17 Aug. 1971.

118. *Japan Times*, 17 Sept. 1971, and *Korea Herald*, 17 Sept. 1971. The ministry granted eighteen visas in 1971 versus a total of six each year in 1969 and 1970.

119. Visa grantees included the vice-chair and deputy chair of the Chosen Soren and the chair of the North Korean Teachers League in Japan. Activities to be undertaken in Pyongyang included participation in Kim Il-sung's birthday celebrations (*Korea Herald*, 19, 22, 28 Mar. 1972; and *Japan Times*, 18 Aug. 1972).

120. See *Korea Herald*, 1 Sept. 1971 ("Kang Protests Japan Moves on NK Visits").

121. *Korea Herald*, 21 Mar. 1972; also see *Korea Herald*, 18 Mar. 1972 ("Japan Intent Toward NK Concerns ROK").

122. *Korea Herald*, 21 Mar. (Kim Ki-sok, "Political Red Trip Serious Problem"), 22 Mar. 1972.

123. The concept of "incrementalism" was propounded by Yung H. Park, 765–66.

124. The most prominent of these exchanges was North Korea's hosting of a seventeen-member delegation of Japanese journalists in April 1972 and Japan's hosting of a tour of North Korean newsmen in May 1973. These visits marked the first time either government had admitted newspaper delegations on such a large scale apart from any newsworthy event. For the 1972 mission see *Korea Herald*, 24 Mar., 6 Apr. 1972. For the 1973 mission see *Korea Herald*, 6 May 1973 ("Pyongyang Scribes to Tour Japan").

125. *Korea Herald*, 25 Mar. 1972 ("Tokyo-Pyongyang Ties").

126. *FEER*, 23 Sept. 1972; and *Korea Herald*, 9 Sept. 1972. The immediate cause for the closing was an article by correspondent Kato Nobuo which criticized Park's Yusin system and praised the North. For expulsion of the *Yomiuri* newsmen see *Korea Herald*, 12 Sept. 1972.

127. *Korea Herald*, 10 Sept. 1972.

128. See Yun's National Assembly testimony, as reported in *Korea Herald*, 12 Sept. 1972. *Yomiuri* offices were eventually reopened in December 1972 after an apology by the bureau chief. Despite this, the *Yomiuri*, and other major dailies such as the *Asahi Shimbun*, continued to denounce the repressive measures of the Yusin regime. As shall be shown below, this resurfaced as a source of friction in 1973 and 1974.

129. Kim Dae-jung had been living abroad since the imposition of martial law in Korea in 1971. While in Japan, Kim was to meet with LDP officials, Utsunomiya and Kimura, and speak at an anti-ROK government rally in Hibiya Park. He was kidnapped by five Korean-speaking men in the hallway of the Grand Palace Hotel while being accompanied by South Korean opposition politicians Yang Il-dong and Kim Kyung-in. Japanese police found a pistol magazine, anesthetic bottle, three backpacks, and North Korean–made cigarettes at the scene. Despite the last piece of evidence, few believed that any group but the KCIA was responsible. ROK embassy officer Lee Sang-ho (alias Yang Doo-won) in Washington was the KCIA station chief responsible for monitoring Kim's activities abroad and had at one time contemplated a contract murder of Kim in the United States; this led State Department officials in August 1973 to request Lee's expulsion from the United States. Lee Sang-ho and two other Washington-based KCIA operatives, Choi Hong-tae and Park Chung-il, were all in Tokyo at the time of Kim's abduction. In June 1977 Kim Hyung-wook, KCIA director from 1963 to 1969, provided testimony to the United States Congress implicating the following additional individuals in the kidnapping: Lee Hu-rak, KCIA director; Kim Chi-yol, KCIA deputy; Lee Chol-hui, KCIA assistant deputy; Kim Ki-wan (alias Kim Jae-kwon), minister, Korean embassy in Tokyo; Colonel Yun Chin-won, ROK Marine Corps and head of the operations team; Yun Yong-ro, embassy counselor; Kim Tong-won, embassy secretary; Yu Yong-bok, ROK consul, Yokohama; Hong Song-tae, counselor; Yun Chung-guk; and Paek Chol-won (see testimony of Kim Hyung-wook, 22 June

1977 in U.S., Congress, House, Committee on International Relations, *Investigation of Korean-American Relations*, 1977, 39–42, 64–67, 71, 74–75). The KCIA had previously conducted similar operations against overseas Koreans, the most infamous of which were the June 1967 abduction of seventeen Koreans from West Germany and the May 1969 kidnapping of a South Korean businessman from Japan. For U.S. concerns about KCIA activities abroad see *FEER*, 10 Sept. 1973; *Japan Times*, 18 Aug. 1973; and U.S., Congress, House, Committee on International Relations, *Investigation of Korean-American Relations*, 1977, 42. For additional reports and analyses of the Kim kidnapping see Paul Chan, 185–94; Clifford, 85–86; *FEER*, 20 Aug. ("The Kidnapping of Kim"), 10 Sept. ("Backlash to a Kidnapping") 1973 and 29 Apr. 1974 ("Protesting Kim"); *Korea Herald*, 10–11 Aug. 1973; and *New York Times*, 10 Aug. 1973 ("Japan Polices Exit Points After Korean Disappears" and Robert Trumbell, "Japan's Premier Pledges to Press Search for Korean").

130. Correspondence from Francis Underhill, deputy chief-of-mission, U.S. embassy, Seoul, 1971–74, 12 Mar. 1998.

131. Anonymous U.S. intelligence officer, interview by author, Sept. 1992, Cambridge, Mass.; and anonymous *Yomiuri Shimbun* journalist, interview by author, 9 July 1992, Tokyo; Cumings, *Korea's Place in the Sun*, 362; and Oberdorfer, *Two Koreas*, 43. South Korean officials knowledgeable about the incident abstained from comment in interviews with the author. For reports of Kim's reappearance and subsequent house arrest see *FEER*, 20 Aug., 10 Sept. 1973; also see *FEER*, 27 Aug. 1973 ("Official Confusion"); *Japan Times*, 1, 18 Aug. 1973; *Korea Herald*, 14 Aug. 1973; and *Time*, 27 Aug. 1973 ("Bizarre Homecoming"). For Kim's October press conference see *Korea Herald*, 27 Oct. 1973.

132. *New York Times*, 11 Aug. 1973 (Trumbell, "Japan's Premier Pledges to Press Search for Korean").

133. Hogen Shinsaku, interview by author, 11 July 1992, Tokyo (hereafter Hogen interview). Hogen was the point man for the Japanese government during the kidnapping affair. For Japanese requests see *FEER*, 20, 27 Aug. 1973; *Japan Times*, 15, 18 Aug. 1973; and *Korea Herald*, 11, 15 Aug. 1973. In denying each request, the ROK said it would conduct its own investigation and keep Japanese authorities informed of the progress. See letter from Premier Kim Jong-pil to Foreign Minister Ohira and Premier Tanaka in *Japan Times*, 21 Aug. 1973; and *Korea Herald*, 21 Aug. 1973.

134. The South Korean report focused only on the logistics of the abduction and steered clear of efforts to identify the conspirators. This contrasted with a concurrent Japanese investigation that found the vehicles used in the kidnapping to have diplomatic license plates and that KCIA agents, operating under embassy cover at the time of the abduction, had all since returned to Seoul. On these points see *Japan Times*, 15, 23 Aug. 1973; *Korea Herald*, 23, 30 Aug. 1973; *New York Times*, 24 Aug. 1973; and testimony of Kim Hyung-wook, U.S., Congress, House, Committee on International Relations, *Investigation of Korean-American Relations*, 1977, 40–42.

135. Ohira's and Tanaka's protests were the first public expressions of dissatisfaction with the handling of the case. This represented a major change in Tokyo's position, as the government had previously avoided accusations against the ROK despite widespread reports by the Japanese and international media of KCIA complicity. See *FEER*, 10 Sept. 1973 (Richard Halloran, "Japan Postpones Korean Aid Talks over Kidnapping"); *Japan Times*, 25, 29 Aug. 1973; and *New York Times*, 24 Aug. 1973.

136. See *FEER*, 20 Aug. 1973; *Japan Times*, 19, 29 Aug. 1973; *Korea Herald*, 10 Aug. 1973; and *New York Times*, 10–11 Aug. 1973.

137. See *New York Times*, 24 Aug. 1973 (Halloran, "Japan Postpones Korean Aid Talk over Kidnapping"); and *Korea Herald*, 25 Aug. 1973 ("Govt Shuts Down Yomiuri in Seoul"). The ROK took similar actions against other Western journalists (see *FEER*, 10 Sept., 6 Oct. 1973).

138. Hogen interview. Japan initially wanted to keep the Kim case separate from other bilateral issues; however, the ROK's lack of cooperation in the investigation and, moreover, its reluctance to accept evidence implicating the KCIA in the abduction forced Tanaka to expand the issue to the entire relationship. For the postponement of the joint ministerial conference, originally scheduled for September 7–8, see *FEER*, 10 Sept. 1973; *Japan Times*, 3 Sept., 27 Nov. 1973; and *New York Times*, 24 Aug. 1973 (Halloran, "Japan Postpones Korean Aid Talks over Kidnapping"). For Ushiroku's return to Tokyo for consultations see *Japan Times*, 1 Sept. 1973 ("Seoul Reported Mollifying Tokyo over Kidnapping"); and *New York Times*, 1 Sept. 1973.

139. See *Japan Times*, 6–7 Sept. 1973; and *New York Times*, 7 Sept. 1973.

140. Kim Tong-won was later exonerated in a second ROK report on the case (see *Japan Times*, 17 Sept. 1973; and *Korea Herald*, 16, 19 Sept. 1973). For Foreign Minister Kim's protests see *Korea Herald*, 8 Sept. 1973; and *New York Times*, 7 Sept. 1973 (Richard Halloran, "Tokyo Ties 2nd Seoul Aide to Abduction"). Of the officials recalled by the ROK, Japanese police sought several for their suspected role in the kidnapping. Aside from Kim Tong-won, police had evidence implicating Hong Sung-tae, Yun Chung-guk, Yu Yong-bok, and Osaka consulate officials Cho Tong-ki and An Rong-tok (see *FEER*, 17 Sept. 1973 ["Dirty Half-Dozen"]; *Japan Times*, 8, 12 Sept. 1973; and U.S., Congress, House, Committee on International Relations, *Investigation of Korean-American Relations*, 1977, 71).

141. *New York Times*, 7 Sept. 1973.

142. A FEER editorial summarized well what was at stake for Japan in this dispute: "The Japanese government cannot afford to take a moderate attitude over Seoul's violation of Japanese national sovereignty. The insult was so flagrant that unless Premier Kakuei Tanaka demonstrates that South Korea either returns Kim unharmed to Tokyo or faces the stiffest sanctions, Park will have no reason to consider Japan as anything more than neighboring soil on which his hatchetmen can operate. . . . Tokyo should immediately sever all aid programmes to South Korea and give Seoul notice that its commercial ties with Tokyo are in peril as long as Kim Dae Jung remains an involuntary resident of

South Korea. . . . The time has come for diplomatic language to be replaced with economic thumbscrews" (*FEER*, 1 Oct. 1973 ["Tanaka: The Reluctant Wrestler"]).

143. *New York Times*, 10 Oct. 1973 (Richard Halloran, "Tokyo and Seoul Harden Positions").

144. The ROK sorely needed the funds that were to have been provided by Japan at the seventh joint ministerial conference. These had been earmarked for expansion of the ROK steel, shipbuilding, and agricultural industries. Another factor lending toward the attainment of a settlement was quiet pressure from the United States (see *Japan Times*, 27 Oct. 1973).

145. For details of the settlement see *FEER*, 5 Nov. 1973 ("Guilt Lingers On"); *Japan Times*, 27 Oct. 2–3 Nov. 1973; *Korea Herald*, 27 Oct., 2–4 Nov. 1973; *New York Times*, 3 Nov. 1973 (Richard Halloran, "Korean Premier Apologizes").

146. For the seventh joint ministerial conference see *FEER*, 17 Dec. 1973 (Nakamura Koji, "In the Shadow of Kim Dae Jung"); *Japan Times*, 23 Dec. 1973; *Korea Herald*, 27 Dec. 1973; Kim Hosup, "The Politics of Japanese Overseas Development Assistance," 25; Nogami, 165; and Tamaki, 355.

147. For Tanaka's statement see ROK-MOFA, *Ilbon kaehwang*, 372; and *Korea Herald*, 29 Jan., 3 Feb. 1974.

148. See *Korea Herald*, 30 Jan.–3 Feb., 7 Feb. 1974.

149. See *Korea Herald*, 11 Jan. 1974 ("Japanese Scribes Warned Not to Bias").

150. These arrests were part of a nationwide KCIA crackdown on 240 radical student leaders. For details of the charges and July 1974 court martial see *Japan Times*, 28 May, 16 July 1974.

151. For Ohira, Ushiroku, and special envoy Takashima Masuo's initial meetings with Foreign Minister Kim Dong-jo over the issue see *Japan Times*, 26 Apr. 1974; and *Korea Herald*, 28 Apr., 10 May 1974. For Japan's contesting of the verdict see *New York Times*, 16 July 1974.

152. For Kim Dae-jung's arrest and trial see *FEER*, 10 June ("Diplomatic Madness"), 1 July ("Trials of Park Chung Hee"), and 22 July (Rodney Tasker, "Park's Sledgehammer Politics") 1974; *Japan Times*, 4 June 1974; *Korea Herald*, 4–6 June 1974.

153. See Kim Dong-jo and Kim Jong-pil's meetings with Ambassador Ushiroku, as reported in *Korea Herald*, 6, 12, 25–26 June, 20 July 1974. Also see *Japan Times*, 8 June 1974; and *Korea Herald*, 14 July 1974.

154. *Japan Times*, 16, 20 July 1974. Riot police were called out because of the scale of the demonstrations.

155. See *Christian Science Monitor*, 9 July 1974; *FEER*, 24 June 1974; *Japan Times*, 16, 20 July 1974; and *Korea Herald*, 2, 13 July 1974; and *New York Times*, 16 July 1974.

156. It should be noted that in both the Kim Dae-jung affair and the case of the two Japanese students, an alternative, and as of yet unsubstantiated view, purports some Japanese complicity in the events. In the latter case some argue

that conservative LDP elements, business leaders, and right-wing underworld heavies had worked out a script with Park for the arrest of the radical Japanese students, after which they would be quietly deported to Japan. In the former case it is argued that ultra-right-wing individuals in Japanese business and political circles, along with South Korean residents in Japan, may have had prior knowledge of plans to kidnap Kim Dae-jung. Many of the nightspots in Kobe and Osaka were run by South Koreans residing in Japan who had ties with conservative LDP elements and ultra-right-wing members of the Japanese underworld. This group had strong economic interests (e.g., the Shimonoseki-Pusan ferry line) in generally amiable Japan-ROK relations. On the Japanese side members of the conservative *Seiran-kai* (Young Storm Association) within the LDP had similar interests in Japan-ROK business ventures and disliked Kim Dae-jung's anti-Park activities. Such individuals included LDP Dietman Tanaka Tatsuo, the son of former premier-general Tanaka Giichi, and entrepreneur Sasakawa Ryoichi, who had ties with both the South Korean business community and the Seiran-kai. These allegations are, at best, highly speculative. However, if they are accurate and both governments engaged in tacit cooperation, this would pose a strong challenge to my argument.

157. For the official South Korean version of these events see *Korea-Japan Relations and the Attempt on the Life of the South Korean President*. Also see Clifford, 97–98. For an eyewitness account see Oberdorfer, *Two Koreas*, 47–48.

158. South Korean authorities maintained that North Korean agents in Japan had been training Mun since 1972 and that Kim Ho-ryong, a prominent leader of the Osaka branch of the Chosen Soren, provided instructions and funds for the assassination attempt during a secret meeting with Mun aboard a North Korean freighter docked in Osaka in May 1974. Mun was tried in August 1974 and executed December 20 (see *Japan Times*, 18 Aug. 1974; and *Korea Herald*, 18 Aug. 1974; also see text of the prosecution's statements in *FEER*, 30 Aug. 1974 [Russell Spurr, "Bracing for Park's Next Move"]; *Korea Herald*, 9 Oct. 1974; and *Korea Times*, 8 Oct. 1974).

159. See *Korea Herald*, 21 Aug. 1974. The premier reiterated these demands in a letter delivered to Tanaka by Ambassador Kim Yong-son four days later (see *Korea Herald*, 24–25 Aug. 1974). For coverage of the demonstrations see *Japan Times*, 22 Aug. 1974; and *Korea Herald*, 23–29 Aug. 1974.

160. In particular the ROK wanted extradition of the suspected conspirators—Kim Ho-ryong, Yoshii Mikiko, and Yoshii Yukio—to stand trial before a South Korean military court. Japan denied these requests on the ground that there was no prior extradition treaty between the two countries and that these individuals would be dealt with according to Japanese domestic law (*Korea Herald*, 4 Sept. 1974).

161. *Korea Herald*, 29 Aug. 1974 ("Panel Urges Stiff Action Against Japan").

162. For Gaimushō statements see *FEER*, 23 Aug. 1974; *Japan Times*, 22 Aug. 1974; and *Korea Times*, 20 Aug., 1 Sept. 1974. Tanaka attended Mrs.

Park's funeral, and his meetings afterward with ROK leaders were punctuated by emotional exchanges between Tanaka and Foreign Minister Kim Dong-jo over responsibility for the incident (see *Christian Science Monitor*, 19 Aug. 1974; *FEER*, 30 Aug., 11 Oct. 1974; *Korea Herald*, 20–21 Aug. 1974; and *Korea Times*, 17, 20 Aug. 1974).

163. See Kimura, 114; also see *FEER*, 13 Sept. 1974 (Nakamura Koji, "Pressing the Japanese"); *Korea Herald*, 30 Aug. ("No NK Armed Threat to ROK Exists"), 7 Sept. ("Kimura Remarks Spur Seoul Protest") 1974; and Yung H. Park, 767.

164. *Christian Science Monitor*, 8 Sept. 1974; and *FEER*, 27 Sept. 1974 (Nakamura Koji, "Seeing Both Sides of the Coin").

165. See Kimura, 112–16.

166. *Korea Herald*, 31 Aug. 1974 ("Government Files Protest for Irresponsibility").

167. This was an unscheduled, forty-minute meeting, which was extraordinary in the sense that the ultimatum came directly from the chief executive rather than through normal diplomatic channels (see *Korea Herald*, 1 Sept. 1974 ["President Gave Solemn Warning"]; also see *FEER*, 13 Sept. 1974 [Nakamura Koji, "Pressuring the Japanese"]; and *Korea Herald*, 31 Aug., 3 Sept. 1974).

168. Yasukawa interview.

169. *FEER*, 20 Sept. 1974 (Kim Sam-o, "Stirring Up Old Resentments"); and *Korea Herald*, 7 Sept. 1974 ("Angry Seoul Demonstrators Break into Japanese Embassy"). Eighty percent of Japanese tour groups to Seoul were canceled during the demonstrations. The South Korean embassy in Japan also received a rash of bomb threats (see *FEER*, 20 Sept. 1974 ["The Price of Protest"]; and *Korea Herald*, 14 Sept. 1974 ["Mobs Vent Anger Against Japanese"]).

170. See *Korea Herald*, 25 Oct., 5, 25 Dec. 1974. For the recalling of Ushiroku see *Korea Herald*, 7–8 Sept. 1974.

171. "Japan to Remove Families," *Korea Herald*, 15 Sept. 1974. In addition, the embassy issued an advisory to Japanese women and children to return to Japan (14 Sept. 1974).

172. Sneider met with deputy foreign minister Togo Fumihiko. On this meeting and Ford's letter to Park see *Korea Herald*, 3, 15 Sept. 1974.

173. Yasukawa interview; Sunobe interview; and former U.S. embassy official, telephone interview by author, 9 Mar. 1998; also see *FEER*, 11 Oct. 1974 ("Washington's Role in a Settlement"); *Korea Herald*, 3, 6, 15, 17 Sept. 1974; and Oberdorfer, *Two Koreas*, 54–55.

174. As a member of the Japanese press corps for the Shiina mission recalled, the Koreans were extremely upset that Shiina's statement did not contain an explicit condemnation of the Chosen Soren (Oikawa interview).

175. Toyota also reneged on a joint venture on engine plants with Shinjin Motors (see *Japan Times*, 20 July, 15 Dec. 1971). C. Itoh was the first major Japanese trading firm to abide by the Zhou principles (see *Japan Times*, 8 July 1971).

176. For example, Nagano Shigeo was chairman of New Japan Steel, chair of the Japanese Chamber of Commerce, vice-president of Keidanren, and a close associate of Premier Sato.

177. For example, a number of small and medium-size Japanese firms in the fertilizer and steel industries made earlier advances into China. Despite this, big-business leaders such as Nagano did not succumb because of their conservative, anticommunist convictions and close relations with the Sato government. On these points see *FEER*, 25 Sept. 1971; and *Korea Herald*, 4 Sept. 1971.

178. See Ogata, 197–99.

179. For the bank decisions see *Korea Herald*, 10 Oct. 1971 and 14 Jan. 1972. For the Mitsubishi announcement see *Korea Herald*, 13 Nov. 1971. Also see "Business Potentials," 382; Farnsworth, "Japan: The Year of the Shock," 49; and *FEER*, 4 Mar. 1972 (Fukushima Toshitaro, "Politics Not in Command").

180. Ogata, 202.

181. For the July 1971 Cooperation Committee meetings see *FEER*, 31 July 1971; *Japan Times*, 1 Aug. 1971; *Seoul Domestic Press Service*, 23 July 1971, in FBIS, 26 July 1971, E2; and *Tong-A Ilbo*, 23 July 1971. For the March 1972 Economic Cooperation Committee see *Japan Times*, 5 Mar. 1972; and *Korea Herald*, 5 Mar. 1972.

182. See *Japan Times*, 12, 31 ("Japanese Aid to the ROK," editorial) Aug. 1971.

183. The Japanese director-general of Asian affairs at that time concurred with this analysis (Sunobe interview).

184. See *Japan Times*, 26 Aug., 2 Sept. 1971; and *Korea Herald*, 2 Sept. 1971. For the Nichiryū Shōji contract see *Korea Herald*, 22 Oct. 1971; and for the air conditioning deal see *Japan Times*, 19 Nov. 1971.

185. Export sectors targeted by the agreement included Japanese car, computer, and oil-refining plants and North Korean pig iron, coal, and marine products (see *Japan Times*, 23–24 Jan. 1972; *Korea Herald*, 25 Jan. 1972; and Langdon, 179–80).

186. The Japan-North Korea Import-Export Company, established by the Chosen Soren, was responsible for arranging trade missions and negotiating contracts (see *Korea Herald*, 15 Feb. 1972). For the regularization of shipping routes see *Korea Herald*, 30 Jan., 1 Feb. 1972.

187. In March 1972 Hiro Motors concluded a $3.2-million contract for the sale to North Korea of 140 multiton capacity trucks, a significant number given the export of only 4 trucks to the North since 1968 (*Japan Times*, 9 Mar. 1972; *Korea Herald*, 2 Feb. 1972). In October 1972 New Japan Steel agreed to develop the North Korean steel industry, and in July 1973 Shinwa Bussan and a consortium of Japanese banks agreed to finance a $56.6-million cement production plant (*Japan Times*, 20 Oct. 1972 and 21 July 1973; *Korea Herald*, 21 July 1973; and Yung H. Park, 763–65).

188. *Japan Times*, 23, 26 Jan. 1972; and *Korea Herald*, 23 Jan. 1972.

189. For the recalling of Ambassador Lee Ho see *Korea Herald*, 27 Jan.

1972. For ministry protests see *Korea Herald*, 26 Jan. 1972 ("Trade Expansion Deal Serious" and "Japan-North Korean Trade"). Also see *FEER*, 12 Feb. 1972; *Japan Times*, 19, 23 Jan. 1972; and *Korea Herald*, 23, 25 Jan. 1972.

190. This was communicated in a special note to Ushiroku after the inauguration of the Tanaka government (see *FEER*, 23 Sept. 1972; and *Korea Herald*, 5 Aug. 1972).

191. As these meetings took place the same month as the Tanaka-Zhou summit, ROK officials were especially worried that Tokyo-Beijing normalization would adversely affect Japanese attitudes on the EIB issue (see *Korea Herald*, 6, 10 Sept. 1972). ROK officials again raised these points with special envoy Kimura in October 1972 after the Tanaka-Zhou summit. Premier Kim Jong-pil also confronted Tanaka on the EIB issue during a stopover in Tokyo en route from Truman's funeral in the United States in January 1973 (see *Korea Herald*, 11 Oct. 1972 and 12 Jan. 1973).

192. For the December 28 announcement see *Japan Times*, 29 Dec. 1973; and *Korea Herald*, 29 Dec. 1973. Also see Kil Soong-hoom, "Japan in Korean-American Relations," 161.

193. ROK Economic Planning Board reports concluded that Japanese investment accounted for 60–70 percent of total foreign investment in the ROK, while that of the United States decreased to approximately 40 percent (see *Japan Times*, 23 July 1971). For the subway loan agreement see *Japan Times*, 31 Dec. 1971; for the oil exploration pact see *Japan Times*, 29 Apr. 1973 and 26 Jan. 1974; and *Korea Herald*, 5 July 1973.

194. Figures compiled from *Japan Times*, 4–5 Sept. 1972 and 9 Mar. 1974; and *Korea Herald*, 14 Aug. 1973.

195. For the fifth annual joint ministerial conference see ROK-MOFA, *Taehan min'guk woegyo yŏnp'yo: 1971*, 331–37. The 1971 conference resulted in $130 million in credits for the ROK subway and shipbuilding sectors and a commitment to consider future loans for agricultural modernization (also see *Japan Times*, 11–12, 31 Aug. 1971). For the sixth conference see ROK-MOFA, *Taehan min'guk woegyo yŏnp'yo: 1972*, 261–66. The agreement was for $170 million in government loans for agricultural modernization and ROK export and communications industries. ROK requests, however, had been for $700 million.

196. Japan provided only $80 million of the $400 million in credits requested by the ROK in 1973 (see *FEER*, 10 Sept. ["Backlash to a Kidnapping"], 17 Dec. ["In the Shadow of Kim Dae Jung"] 1973; *Japan Times*, 3 Sept. 1973; and *New York Times*, 24 Aug. 1973). For the joint communiqué see ROK-MOFA, *Taehan min'guk woegyo yŏnp'yo: 1973*, 293–95. For statements of South Korean dissatisfaction at the dearth of Japanese economic packages at the 1972 and 1973 conferences see premier Kim Jong-pil's address to the National Assembly, as reported in *Japan Times*, 26 Sept. 1973; *Korea Herald*, 8 Sept. 1972 ("Korea-Japan Partnership," editorial); and ROK statements at the October 1973 Cooperation Committee meetings, as reported in *Japan Times*, 8 Oct. 1973.

197. See *Korea Herald*, 26 Oct., 5, 25 Dec. 1974.

198. *Japan Times*, 9 Mar. 1974; and *Korea Herald*, 19 Mar. 1974. The nine nations composing the IECOK were: Australia, Belgium, Canada, France, Great Britain, Italy, Japan, the United States, and West Germany.

199. For example, IECOK's total recommendation for 1974 was $200 million, while ROK requests from Japan alone for the year equaled $300 million.

200. Newspaper coverage during the Kim Dae-jung affair drew numerous parallels to this case. A legitimate explanation for the disparity in behavior in the two cases is that Kim was an individual of greater public stature than Yun and therefore raised the stakes involved for both governments. However, in a hypothetical posed by the author to Japanese scholars, newsmen, and former government officials involved in the Kim case, most admitted that had Japanese external threat perceptions been similar to those in the 1969–71 period and had the ROK fully informed Japan beforehand of the rationale for the abduction, the controversy might not have reached such grand proportions (Hogen interview; and Oikawa interview).

Chapter 5. Vietnam and the Carter Years

1. Moscow continued to engage in superpower confrontation through proxies in the Middle East. This included Soviet support of Egypt and Syria against United States-backed Israel in the Yom Kippur War (October 1973); its urging of Arab states to embargo U.S. oil; and its pressing OPEC nations to quadruple oil prices in the war's aftermath.

2. The Soviets provided equipment and transportation for fifteen thousand Cuban expeditionary forces in Angola and other African states to support local groups opposed to the United States. For U.S. criticism of these actions see testimony of Winston Lord, director, Policy Planning Staff, Department of State, 23 Mar. 1976, in U.S., Congress, House, Committee on International Relations, *United States-Soviet Union-China: The Great Power Triangle: Summary of Hearings*, 168–75; and "Kissinger Address Before the Economic Club of Detroit, Nov. 24, 1975" (excerpt), in ROK-MOFA, *Woegyo yŏn'guwŏn yŏn'gubu: Pogwanyong*, 39–41.

3. The United States also complained of Soviet violations of the ABM treaty and became increasingly concerned about the growing gap in overall defense expenditures during the period. For figures on Soviet arms buildup after SALT I see U.S., Congress, Senate, Committee on Armed Services, *Detente: An Evaluation*, 7–9. As another Congressional report commented: "SALT agreements brought neither stabilization nor parity, nor curtailments of deployments, development, expenditures, and risks. The SALT debate . . . has degenerated into vituperative and technical accusations of cheating and has given renewed emphasis to the Schlesinger doctrine of selective nuclear strikes, limited nuclear war, and counterforce" (U.S., Congress, House, Committee on International Relations, *United States-Soviet Union-China: The Great Power Triangle*, 42).

4. U.S., Congress, House, Committee on International Relations, *United States-Soviet Union-China: The Great Power Triangle*, 44–45. For additional

arguments on the demise of superpower detente see U.S., Congress, Senate, Committee on Armed Services, *Detente: An Evaluation*, 1–26.

5. See U.S., Congress, House, Committee on International Relations, *United States-Soviet Union-China: The Great Power Triangle*, 40, 42; and testimony of Philip Habib, assistant secretary of state for East Asian and Pacific Affairs, 17 Dec. 1975 in U.S., Congress, House, Committee on International Relations, *United States-China Relations: The Process of Normalization*, 124–26. Among the difficulties in economic relations were a dearth of exportable goods from China to the United States, Beijing's reluctance to permit U.S. long-term credits and foreign investment, and Washington's denial of Chinese requests for the transfer of U.S. dual-use technology. The difficulty in sustaining cultural exchanges largely stemmed from Beijing's growing hesitation in expanding the scope of visits facilitated through the Committee on Scholarly Communication with the PRC and the National Committee on United States-China Relations. This resulted, for example, in the cancellation of a number of scheduled exchanges in 1975. For a list of exchanges from 1972–75 see U.S., Congress, House, Committee on International Relations, *United States-China Relations: The Process of Normalization*, 128–30.

6. This was particularly the case during Secretary Cyrus Vance's August 1977 mission. Vance's meetings with Beijing officials did not produce any new agreements, causing Deputy Premier Deng Xiaopeng to call the visit a "setback" to Sino-American relations. For comments on the lack of success of the Ford and Vance visits see testimony of Philip Habib, 17 Dec. 1975, in U.S., Congress, House, Committee on International Relations, *United States-China Relations: The Process of Normalization*, 108–10; and testimony of A. Doak Barnett, 20 Sept. 1977, in U.S., Congress, House, Committee on International Relations, *Normalization of Relations with the PRC*, 7.

7. U.S., Congress, House, Committee on International Relations, *Normalization of Relations with the PRC*, 7. Also see *FEER*, 1 July 1974 (James Laurie, "The Euphoria of Peking Detente Starts to Fade"); and Oxnam, 24–30.

8. See U.S., Congress, House, Committee on International Relations, *United States-Soviet Union-China: The Great Power Triangle, Summary of Hearings*, 4.

9. See *FEER*, 1 July 1974 (Laurie, "The Euphoria of Peking Detente Starts to Fade"); Oxnam, 24–30; and U.S., Congress, House, Committee on International Relations, *Normalization of Relations with the PRC*, xiv.

10. Testimony of A. Doak Barnett, 20 Sept. 1977, in U.S., Congress, House, Committee on International Relations, *United States-China Relations: The Process of Normalization*, 162–64, also see 135, 149; and testimony of Allen Whiting, 2 Feb. 1976, ibid., 143. China's three preconditions for normalization were (1) withdrawal of U.S. forces from Taiwan, (2) termination of diplomatic relations with Taiwan, and (3) abrogation of the 1954 defense treaty. The last of these was the primary impediment for the United States. See U.S., Congress, House, Committee on International Relations, *Normalization of Relations with the PRC*, x–xiv.

11. See U.S., Congress, House, Committee on International Relations,

United States-Soviet Union-China: The Great Power Triangle, Summary of Hearings, 31–38, 41; U.S., Congress, House, Committee on International Relations, *Normalization of Relations with the PRC*, xvii–xxiv; and testimony of A. Doak Barnett, 20 Sept. 1977, in U.S., Congress, House, Committee on International Relations, *United States-China Relations: The Process of Normalization*, 135–36, 149–59.

12. U.S., Congress, House, Committee on International Relations, *Normalization of Relations with the PRC*, xv. For additional comments on Chinese criticism of the U.S. position on Taiwan at Kissinger and Ford's 1975 meetings and Vance's 1977 meetings see U.S., Congress, House, Committee on International Relations, *United States-Soviet Union-China: The Great Power Triangle: Summary of Hearings*, 37; and testimony of Allen Whiting, 2 Feb. 1976, in U.S., Congress, House, Committee on International Relations, *United States-China Relations: The Process of Normalization*, 143.

13. Testimony of Winston Lord, 23 Mar. 1976, in U.S., Congress, House, Committee on International Relations, *United States-Soviet Union-China: The Great Power Triangle*, 168. Lord's ostensible reason for this change in terminology was the confusion with the term *entente*, however, his admitting of the substantial deterioration in relations with Moscow since the 1972–74 period revealed the more profound meaning behind this change.

14. See comments by Congressman Walter Judd in U.S., Congress, House, Committee on International Relations, *United States-Soviet Union-China: The Great Power Triangle: Summary of Hearings*, 33.

15. The origins of the Carter plan still remain vague even to the former president himself when interviewed about it later (see Oberdorfer's recounting of correspondence with Carter in *Two Koreas*, 85). Carter did have a penchant for undercutting traditional wisdoms about U.S. foreign policy, the overzealous presence of U.S. forces overseas being a prime target, yet there was no immediate precedent for action. The preceding Ford administration did conduct a secret review of Korea policy, including the issue of troop presence, but this study was inconclusive. Nevertheless in a 16 Jan. 1975 *Washington Post* interview Carter stated there was no practical reason to keep U.S. forces in the ROK and that he would remove these troops and U.S. nuclear weapons from the peninsula if elected. He reiterated these campaign promises in a May 1976 PBS television interview and a June 1976 Foreign Policy Association speech (see Nam Joo-hong, 148; and *Washington Post*, 12 June 1977).

16. In conjunction with the Carter plan the United States maintained it would (1) keep air and naval deployments in the region, including the augmentation of U.S. airpower by one squadron of 12 F-4 aircraft; (2) retain certain U.S. intelligence, communications, and logistics personnel in Korea; (3) transfer to Korea at no cost approximately $800-million worth of Second Infantry Division military hardware; (4) provide supplementary foreign military sales credits (approximately $1.1 billion) and give Korea priority in arms sales; (5) make special efforts to support ROK self-sufficiency projects in defense industries; (6) continue joint military exercises; and (7) devise a combined United States-ROK

command structure to augment operational efficiency before the first increment of troop withdrawals. See text of the tenth United States-ROK SCC joint communiqué, in ROK-MOFA, *Taehan min'guk woegyo yŏnp'yo: 1977*, 114–18; and U.S., Congress, Senate, Committee on Armed Services, *Korea: The US Troop Withdrawal Program*, 2.

17. For Carter's press statements see *PPPUS: Carter: 1977*, 343 and 1018–19. For chronologies of these events see Lee and Sato, *U.S. Policy*, 104–46; Nam Joo-hong, 139–74; Oberdorfer, *Two Koreas*, 90; and U.S., Congress, Senate, Committee on Armed Services, *Korea: The US Troop Withdrawal Program*, 1–2.

18. Quoted in Gibney, 160; also see Nam Joo-hong, 143–44, 148–50. For general analyses of the Carter's attempts to infuse American foreign policy with a "new moralism" and respect for human rights see Bell; Hoffmann; Hughes; and Quester.

19. On these points see Nam Joo-hong, 149; *PPPUS: Carter: 1977*, 1018–19; U.S., Congress, House, Committee on International Relations, *Investigation of Korean-American Relations*, 1978, 71–73; and *Washington Post*, 9 Sept. 1977, A15 ("PRM-10 and the Korean Pullout").

20. See Louis Harris poll results cited in Oberdorfer, *Two Koreas*, 87.

21. Singlaub saw Carter's decision as motivated by the need to fulfill campaign promises at home rather than by an accurate understanding of the military balance on the peninsula and warned that the troop withdrawal would lead to war. Also see Lee and Sato, *U.S. Policy*, 109–11; and Nam Joo-hong, 150–51.

22. A June 1977 Senate vote also refused to endorse the plan by a 79–15 margin. In addition, congressional studies such as the January 1978 Humphrey-Glenn report and the January 1979 Senate Armed Services Committee report also called for the maintaining of U.S. troops in Korea (see *Washington Post*, 17 June 1977, A1 [Spencer Rich, "Senate Refuses Endorsement of Korea Pullout"]; *Stars and Stripes*, 26 Jan. 1978, 9 ["Panel Wants to Keep Troops in ROK"]; and *Washington Post*, 23 June 1977, A3 [Terence Hunt, "Brown in Korea to Confer About Pullout, Arms Aid"]). Also see *Korea Herald*, 8 June 1978 ("Carter Decision on Pullout Shocked Military Experts"); Nam Joo-hong, 148; *PPPUS: Carter: 1977*, 343; and U.S., Congress, Senate, Committee on Foreign Relations, *US Troop Withdrawal from the Republic of Korea: A Report to the Committee on Foreign Relations, January 9, 1978, by Hubert Humphrey and John Glenn*, 20.

23. Intelligence reassessments put North Korean tank forces at 80 percent larger and ground forces at 40 percent larger than had been previously estimated. This eventually led Carter reluctantly to issue Presidential Review Memorandum/NSC-45 on 22 January 1979, which called for a new review of Korea policy. By February 1979 Carter announced a temporary freeze on the withdrawal of combat elements pending reassessments of North Korean military capabilities. On July 20, 1979, National Security Advisor Zbigniew Brzezinski announced a postponement of the plan until 1981. For the text of

Brzezinski's statement see *Weekly Compilation of Presidential Documents,* 23 July 1979; also see Nam Joo-hong, 159; and *Washington Star,* 21 July 1979, A3 ("Carter Halts Korea Troop Withdrawal"). For additional announcements of the plan's postponement see "*Che 12 ch'a han-mi yŏllye anjŏng hyŏpŭihoeŭi kongdong sŏngmyŏngsŏ*" (Joint communiqué of the twelfth annual US-ROK Security Consultative Conference), Seoul, Oct. 19, 1979," in ROK-MOFA, *Taehan min'guk woegyo yŏnp'yo: 1979,* 327–29. This decision culminated a period of intense national debate over the merits of the Carter plan. For examples see Gibney, 160–74; LeFever, 245–57; and *New York Times Magazine,* 2 Oct. 1977 (Donald Zagoria, "Why We Still Can't Leave Korea").

24. Defense Secretary Harold Brown, although privately opposed to the plan, made such public statements in defense of Carter's plan as late as July 1979 (see *Stars and Stripes,* 5 July 1979, 8 ["Pullout Question Is When, Not If"]).

25. For discussions of the reassessment of North Korean force structures see Gail, 37–42; U.S., Congress, House, Armed Services Committee, *Impact of the Intelligence Reassessment*; U.S., Congress, Senate, Committee on Armed Services, *Korea: The US Troop Withdrawal Program,* 3–5; Oberdorfer, *Two Koreas,* 101–4; and Weinstein and Kamiya, *The Security of Korea,* 24–38.

26. The United States withdrew one combat battalion of 3,436 troops as part of the first stage of the Carter plan in 1978, cut nuclear weapons from around 700 to around 250, and consolidated these weapons at Kunsan air base.

27. In May 1975 the United States forcibly recaptured a merchant ship seized by Cambodian forces (*New York Times,* 18 May 1975). For U.S. statements on the *Mayaguez* retrieval see text of Secretary of Defense James R. Schlesinger's statement on ABC TV, "Issues and Answers," 18 May 1975, in ROK-MOFA, *Woegyo yŏn'guwŏn yŏn'gubu: Pogwanyong,* 7–12.

28. See "Text of President Ford's Speech at the East-West Center, December 7, 1975," in ROK-MOFA, *Woegyo yŏn'guwŏn yŏn'gubu: Pogwanyong,* 60–73; and UPI release (David Gilmore, "Position of Ford Government Tough on North Korea"), reprinted in *Korea Times,* 23 May 1975.

29. Oberdorfer, *Two Koreas,* 64–65.

30. Although Japan severed relations with Taiwan in 1972, China accused Tokyo of maintaining a two-China policy through its informal political and economic ties with Taipei. This impeded the facilitation of agreements over such issues as civil aviation. Considered by both governments as a key service agreement that would set a precedent for others (i.e., in shipping, fisheries, etc.), civil-aviation negotiations bogged down over Chinese demands that Japan abandon air routes to and from Taipei (see Hsiao, 177; and "Second Stage of Sino-Japanese Relations," 7–9). The slowdown in Sino-Japanese relations was also reflected in such issues as the protracted negotiations over a friendship treaty and the resurgence of Chinese historical animosities toward Japan (e.g., the sovereignty dispute over the Senkaku Islands).

31. Curtis, "Tyumen Oil," 166–67.

32. Havens, 244. The 1975–79 period was marked by growing Soviet intransigence on Japanese borders. The Soviet military buildup in Asia included deployment of SS-20 IRBMs, Backfire bombers, and expansion of the Far East fleet. While Soviet incursions into Japanese airspace were almost absent prior to 1976, they numbered sixty in 1976 and ninety-six in 1977. Naval exercises included the April 1975 Okean naval maneuvers. See Carpenter et al., 21; and Osamu, 53–83. For a comprehensive work on this topic see Solomon and Kosaka, especially 40–93.

33. Carpenter et al., 5, 20; and *Defense of Japan: White Paper, 1976 (Summary)*, 2–3.

34. Taken from the title of the author's work *Fire Across the Sea*.

35. On these two points see Yung H. Park, 771.

36. Respectively, the problem was the prospect of a mass influx of Vietnamese refugees, and the incentive was the new investment potential offered by postwar reconstruction. For a discussion of these two points see Havens, 241–58.

37. Havens, 241; and *Korea Times*, 13 May, 30 Aug. 1975.

38. Kamiya, "The US Presence," 94; and Okonogi interview. For concurring arguments see Kase; and Nacht, 152. The former author, known for his hawkish views, summed up Japanese abandonment fears: "An American military defeat would not have bothered us [Japan] so much. . . . What bothers us is that the United States . . . refused to come to the aid of South Vietnam—even when the South Vietnamese continued to fight against overwhelming odds. . . . I can assure you that the reaction of the political leadership of all parties in Japan and of business and academic leaders was one of real shock. The lesson was obvious. If America could abandon South Vietnam, can we really count on its living up to its commitments to us, not only in the short run, but over time? . . . What I am saying is that for us in Asia, the U.S. abandonment of South Vietnam was a rude awakening to the emergence of the era of American retrenchment" (105–6).

39. See Nam Joo-hong, 141. The War Powers Act of November 1973 effectively limited the president's ability to send U.S. troops to war for more than sixty days without the express approval of Congress.

40. Oberdorfer, *Two Koreas*, 64–67, 86.

41. Highlighting these talks was the first meeting between Kim and Mao Zedong in fourteen years (see *Korea Times*, 20, 27 Apr. 1975).

42. See the Suh-Schlesinger joint communiqué of the eighth SCC (27 Aug. 1975) and Suh-Rumsfeld communiqué of the ninth SCC (26 May 1976), in ROK-MOFA, *Taehan min'guk woegyo yŏnp'yo: 1975*, 265–67 and *Taehan min'guk woegyo yŏnp'yo: 1976*, 148–50, respectively; also see *Korea Times*, 28 Aug. 1975. Evidence pointed to as revealing North Korean aggression included the discovery of additional infiltration tunnels in the DMZ and later the unprovoked North Korean attack on U.S. soldiers pruning a poplar tree in Panmunjom in August 1976 (see Lee and Sato, *U.S. Policy*, 104).

43. See Oberdorfer, *Two Koreas*, 257, on both of these points. U.S. nuclear weapons were deployed on the Korean peninsula since the Eisenhower admini-

stration's 1957 decision to authorize nuclear warheads on Honest John missiles and long-range artillery. They were later removed under the Bush administration.

44. See Chapter 4. Ambassador Richard Sneider and Assistant Secretary of State for East Asia Philip Habib offered the ROK access to U.S. reprocessing technology and a formal science and technology agreement for Park's canceling the contract with France. Sneider held out the possibility of blocking further financing of South Korea's civilian nuclear program and a fundamental reevaluation of the alliance from the U.S. side if the ROK did not oblige.

45. "U.S. Defense Treaty," *Korea Times*, 16 May 1975.

46. Excerpt from the resolution of the ninety-second special parliamentary session, reprinted in *Korea Times*, 21 May 1975.

47. Kim Ki-sok interview.

48. Nam Joo-hong, 141–42. For concurring views see testimony of Robert Scalapino in U.S., Congress, House, Committee on International Relations, *Normalization of Relations with the PRC*, 27; and "Report of Congressman John M. Murphy, Oct. 23–30, 1975" (excerpt), in ROK-MOFA, *Woegyo yŏn'guwŏn yŏn'gubu: Pogwanyong*, 150.

49. The United States formally notified Foreign Minister Park Tong-jin of the decision on March 9, 1977 (see Nam Joo-hong, 148–49).

50. See interviews of ROK government officials in January and May 1977 and February 1978 by U.S. fact-finding teams, as reported in Carpenter et al., 31–32; Han Sung-joo, "South Korea: 1977," 46, 48; *Korea Herald*, 26 Sept. 1978; and Nam Joo-hong, 103–5.

51. The May 1977 Habib-Brown mission to Seoul was mainly to advise Park on PD/NSC-12 and provide reassurances of a viable U.S. defense commitment (anonymous Joint U.S. Military Assistance Group Korea policy officer, 1978–79, interview by author, 21 May 1992, Seoul; *Greensboro Daily News*, 26 May 1977, A-1 ["South Koreans Dislike US Plan to Pull Out Ground Forces"]; and Han, "South Korea: 1977," 45–46).

52. "*Carter mihapchungguk taet'ongryŏng kakha naewoe bunŭl wihan Pak Chŏnghŭi taet'ongryong kakhaŭi manch'anhoe yŏnsŏl, June 30, 1979, Seoul*" (Remarks by President Park Chung Hee at the state dinner in honor of President Carter), in ROK-MOFA, *Taehan min'guk woegyo yŏnp'yo: 1979*, 288–90).

53. The plan designed by White House officials was for Carter to use the Group of Seven meeting in Tokyo as an opportunity to visit Seoul, and in view of the new assessments of North Korean strength, return to Congress expressing the need to reconsider the pullout plan. Carter, however, did not want to discuss the issue with Park (see Oberdorfer, *Two Koreas*, 104).

54. Carter's note, quoted ibid., 106. For an excellent account of these events and the internal battles in the Carter White House opposing the pullout plan see generally 101–8.

55. *Washington Post*, 26 July, A1 (John Saar, "Seoul Given Commitment by Carter"); 27 July, A1 ("Infantry Unit to Be Last Out of Korea") 1977. For

additional examples see Park's 1979 New Year's address to the nation and Foreign Minister Park's February 1979 speech before the Far East-America Council, in ROK-MOFA, *Taehan min'guk woegyo yŏnp'yo: 1979*, 78–80 and 278–87, respectively, especially 283; also see *Korea Herald*, 9 Mar. 1977.

56. Han, "South Korea: 1977," 52, n. 17.

57. Nam Joo-hong, 141–42. For examples of U.S. security guarantees see 21 July 1977 letter from Carter to Park, in ROK-MOFA, *Taehan min'guk woegyo yŏnp'yo: 1977*, 271; joint communiqué of the eleventh SCC, July 1978, in ROK-MOFA, *Taehan min'guk woegyo yŏnp'yo: 1978*, 204–11; and Carter-Park joint communiqué, 1 July 1979, in ROK-MOFA, *Taehan min'guk woegyo yŏnp'yo: 1979*, 316–21, especially clauses 7–8.

58. *Korea Herald*, 26 Sept. 1978, 5 (Kim Yong-soo, "GI Pullout Harms US National Interests"). Gleysteen, while supporting the Carter plan in public, had strong reservations about it in private.

59. For a summary of these programs see U.S., Congress, Senate, Committee on Armed Services, *Korea: The US Troop Withdrawal Program*, 2; and joint communiqué of the tenth SCC, July 26, 1977, in ROK-MOFA, *Taehan min'guk woegyo yŏnp'yo: 1977*, 114–18.

60. See Carpenter et al., 31–32; and Gibney, 164–69.

61. The Koreagate investigations centered on illegal influence peddling in the United States Congress by agents of the ROK government. Largely motivated by the Nixon doctrine and the withdrawal of the Seventh Infantry Division, the Park regime from the early 1970s devised elaborate schemes to bribe American congressmen and persecute unfavorable expatriates in the United States. A key figure in the affair was Park Tong-sun, a businessman in Washington. Park used huge commissions from an exclusive license to sell U.S. rice to Korea (on the order of $9 million), as well as KCIA funds, to line the pockets of certain congressmen and to support his own lavish lifestyle, all in the supposed service of ROK interests. In a related operation, called White Snow, the KCIA in 1974 and 1975 also attempted to bribe House Foreign Affairs Committee members with more than $600,000 to tone down human rights criticisms of the Yusin system. During the investigations the South Korean government refused to heed repeated requests by Congress for the testimony of former Foreign Minister Kim Dong-jo and Park Tong-sun for their roles in Koreagate, thus leading to the 1977 resolution denying armaments transfers and further security assistance. Park eventually testified, was indicted, but escaped conviction, and the resolution passed both houses in 1978. As a long-time news correspondent in Korea noted, the scandal reflected the unprecedented lengths to which the ROK government would go to obtain U.S. policies favorable to ROK interests (Shim interview, 29 Feb. 1992). For the link between Kim's and Park's testimonies and the 1977 resolution see Han, "South Korea: 1977," 48–49; "Joint Statement Regarding Cooperation Between the Governments of the Republic of Korea and the United States Concerning the Case of Mr. Tongsun Park, December 31, 1977 (official translation)," in ROK-MOFA, *Taehan min'guk woegyo yŏnp'yo: 1977*, 372–74; and *Washington Post*, 27 July 1977, A-1 ("In-

fantry Unit to Be Last Out of Korea"). For a monograph on the scandal see Boettcher; for overviews see Clifford, 86–90; Lee and Sato, *U.S. Policy*, 73–94; Nam Koon Woo, 105–7; U.S., Congress, House, Committee on International Relations, *Investigation of Korean-American Relations, 1978*, 5–10, 43–48, 89–113; and U.S., Congress, Senate, Committee on Foreign Relations, *US Troop Withdrawal from the Republic of Korea: A Report to the Committee on Foreign Relations, January 9, 1978, by Hubert Humphrey and John Glenn*.

62. See Nam Koon Woo, 104–5.

63. Anecdotal evidence of how severe ROK anxieties were at the time can be seen in an incident involving the inadvertent straying of a Northwest Airlines passenger jetliner over the Blue House in October 1976. Security forces immediately fired on the plane, missing it, but injuring numerous civilians on the ground from spent antiaircraft shells (see Clifford, 79).

64. C. I. Eugene Kim, 375; also Kim Ki-sok interview. As a 1978 Senate report stated, "Everyone in South Korea opposes withdrawal, even the shoeshine boys," U.S., Congress, Senate, Committee on Foreign Relations, *US Troop Withdrawal from the Republic of Korea: A Report to the Committee on Foreign Relations, January 9, 1978, by Hubert Humphrey and John Glenn*, 20.

65. Anonymous former Joint U.S. Military Assistance Group Korea policy officer, interview by author, 21 May 1992, Seoul. For concurring arguments see Cha Young-koo, 133–47; and Gibney, 164–65, 169.

66. Cited in Havens, 238.

67. On these two points see Kamiya, "The US Presence," 94; and Nam Joo-hong, 172; and interviews with Gaimushō officials by Osamu, 68.

68. Oberdorfer, *Two Koreas*, 85.

69. See interviews with Japanese officials in Carpenter et al., 9–12; and Kamiya, "The US Presence," 94–95. In addition, major foreign-policy statements by Anthony Lake, director, policy-planning staff, State Department, in 1977 and Secretary Vance in 1978 made little reference to U.S. defense priorities in Asia.

70. On these points see Gibney, 162–63; Lee, *Japan and Korea*, 92–93; Hanai, 114; and Olsen, "Japan-South Korea Security Ties," 62. For comments on Korean refugees see Lee and Sato, *U.S. Policy*, 106.

71. Oikawa interview; for similar observations see Sugita, 141.

72. See Lee and Sato, *U.S. Policy*, 106.

73. Fukuda first heard about the plan during a reception at the Okura Hotel in Tokyo (anonymous Central Intelligence Agency officer, formerly stationed in Tokyo, interview by author, 15 Sept. 1992, Cambridge, Mass.). Fukuda replaced Miki as premier in December 1976.

74. See Lee and Sato, *U.S. Policy*, 107; and *Newsweek*, 10 Jan. 1977. Additional evidence of Fukuda's opposition to the plan is given in the section on Japan-ROK bilateral relations below.

75. Tsukamoto interview.

76. *Defense of Japan: White Paper, 1976 (Summary)*, 6. This, the first white paper since 1970, revealed the degree to which Japan saw that thinking about

security in practical terms was something it could no longer avoid. In the end the combination of the Carter plan and the war in Vietnam caused Japan to engage in a wholesale review of alliance ties with the United States, eventually leading to the establishment of consultative mechanisms for United States-SDF operational coordination in August 1975, the Guidelines for Defense Cooperation in November 1978, and the first joint command exercises with the United States in 1985. For the 1977 and 1978 JDA white papers see Carpenter et al., 5, 20; and Lee and Sato, *U.S. Policy*, 106, 110, 117.

77. Comments by Maruyama and Kubo were made during interviews with *Asahi Shimbun* in November 1976. For these as well as Sakata's statements and the JDA white papers see Carpenter et al., 5, 20; and Lee and Sato, *U.S. Policy*, 106, 110, 117.

78. *FEER*, 24 June 1977, 38. As a Japanese newspaper correspondent recalled, this type of reaction was evident during Mondale's 1977 Tokyo trip. Referring to previous statements by Carter that concurrent U.S. force reductions in Europe were only "cutting fat," the Japanese press hounded Mondale with questions as to whether the proposed troop cuts in Asia were cutting, not fat, but muscle (Oikawa interview).

79. For the *Yomiuri* poll see Carpenter et al., 5, 20–21. For the *Asahi* poll see Lee and Sato, *U.S. Policy*, 133.

80. On these points see Carpenter et al., 12; and U.S., Congress, Senate, Committee on Armed Services, *Korea: The US Troop Withdrawal Program*, iv, 6.

81. Solarz went on to say that, even if the United States had conducted withdrawals at a slower pace and in full consultation with Japan, he still believed Japan would have opposed the plan (see testimony of Stephen Solarz, 16 Mar. 1982, in U.S., Congress, House, Committee on Foreign Affairs, *United States-Japan Relations*, 361).

82. Kamiya, "The US Presence," 94.

83. Miki made these statements to Ford and repeated them at press conferences upon his return to Tokyo. As stated earlier, former Premier Tanaka's and Foreign Minister Kimura's reinterpretation of the Korea clause stated that the defense of the entire peninsula, not just South Korea, was essential to Japan (see Chapter 4). For Miki's statements see Lee, *Japan and Korea*, 94; and Yung H. Park, 771. The Miki government succeeded Tanaka in December 1974. For the Miki-Kim meetings see *Tong-A Ilbo*, 29 May 1975; also see Lee, *Japan and Korea*, 94.

84. Yung H. Park, 771, n. 37.

85. For the text of the Miki-Ford communiqué see U.S., State, *Department of State Bulletin*, 8 Sept. 1975, 382–84, especially clause 3. For the Kim-Miyazawa meetings see *Korea Times*, 23–25 July, 7–8 Aug. 1975.

86. This stated that "The security of South Korea is essential to Japan" without the participial phrase referring to peace on the Korean peninsula and in East Asia (see Chapter 3).

87. As stated earlier, with the establishment of the Korea clause in 1969 Japan agreed to allow the United States unlimited use of Okinawa for military

operations in the event of renewed hostilities on the peninsula. Tanaka's reinterpretation of the Korea clause amounted to a separation of Japanese and South Korean security and therefore cast doubt on whether Japanese permission would be forthcoming on use of these facilities for South Korean defense. For statements that the new Korea clause was operationally equivalent to the 1969 text see Assistant Secretary of State Philip Habib's meetings with ROK Ambassador Hahm Pyong-choon, as reported in *Korea Times*, 10 Aug. 1975.

88. Miyazawa's statements were made in plenary sessions with the LDP foreign-policy committee (see *Korea Herald*, 30 Aug. 1975; *Korea Times*, 17, 31 Aug. 1975; Lee, *Japan and Korea*, 96; and Yung H. Park, 772, 779). For similar statements by foreign ministry spokesman Kuroda Mizuo in the immediate aftermath of the North Vietnamese victory see *Korea Times*, 18 Apr. 1975.

89. See testimony of Allen Whiting, 2 Feb. 1976, in U.S., Congress, House, Committee on International Relations, *United States-China Relations: The Process of Normalization*, 145; also see *Korea Times*, 31 Aug. 1975; and Lee, *Japan and Korea*, 96.

90. See interviews conducted by the Strategic Studies Center group (Feb. 1977 and Feb. 1978), as reported in Carpenter et al., 33–34; for concurring arguments see Osamu, 68. Specific measures undertaken by the two governments on defense issues are discussed below in the section on the Carter plan.

91. On Miki's past policy positions on Korea and China see Farnsworth, "Japan: The Year of the Shock," 48; Langdon, 128, 188; Ogata, 195; and Welfield, "A New Balance," 67, especially n. 24. The liberal wing of the LDP included such individuals as Ikeda Hayato, Kono, Matsumura, and Fujiyama, while the conservative wing included Sato Eisaku, Kishi Nobusuke, Ishii, Fukuda Takeo, Nakasone Yasuhiro, and Matsuno (the latter two were in Miki's cabinet).

92. *Korea Times*, 31 Aug. 1975 ("Korea-Japan Talks").

93. As quoted in Yung H. Park, 770.

94. Miyazawa, 5–6.

95. *Korea Times*, 24 July 1975.

96. *Korea Times*, 10 May 1975.

97. On these points see *Korea Times*, 30 Aug., 14–17 Sept. 1975; Lee, *Japan and Korea*, 96; and Yung H. Park, 773–74.

98. Texts for these communiqués ("*Han-Il chŏnggi kang'nyo hoeŭi kongdong sŏngmyŏng*") are in ROK-MOFA, *Taehan min'guk woegyo yŏnp'yo: 1977*, 289–91 (see especially sec. 3); and in *Taehan min'guk woegyo yŏnp'yo: 1978*, 254–56, sec. 5.

99. For example see the June 1975 Japanese opposition parliamentary mission to Seoul reported in *Korea Times*, 8 July 1975.

100. The Cooperation Committee met for the first time in two years in January 1975 (see *Korea Times*, 14 Jan., 8, 11 July 1975; Lee and Sato, *U.S. Policy*, 120; Lee, *Japan and Korea*, 94; and Yung H. Park, 768, 772–73). A distinguishing characteristic of the membership of these groups, particularly that of the Federation of Japan-South Korea Diet Members, was the prominence of

both ruling and opposition party legislators, thereby again reflecting suprapartisan support for better relations. Attitudes toward North Korea are discussed in greater detail below.

101. For background on this issue see Cheong, 35–45; and Kim Kwan-bong, 68–69.

102. Concurrent disputes over fishing rights prompted both governments to express intentions to inhabit the island (Han, "South Korea: 1977," 51).

103. See Chapter 1; and Kim Kwan-bong, 58–64.

104. The extent of ROK protests was a three-paragraph statement (see ROK-MOFA, *Taehan min'guk woegyo yŏnp'yo: 1975*, 276).

105. On the above points see *Korea Times*, 13, 16, 18, 20 Feb. 1975.

106. See *Korea Times*, 11, 23–25 July 1975; Lee, *Japan and Korea*, 94–95; and "Thorn in Japan-ROK Ties."

107. Yung H. Park, 773.

108. Japanese police investigations found Kim Tong-won's fingerprints at the scene of the kidnapping. See Chapter 4 for details.

109. Quoted in Yung H. Park, 774; for concurring arguments see Lee, *Japan and Korea*, 95.

110. For the text of this agreement see ROK-MOFA, *Taehan min'guk woegyo yŏnp'yo: 1975*, 437–40.

111. *Korea Times*, 24 Sept. 1975.

112. These government, yen-denominated loans were 14 billion for the Chŏngju dam project, 4 billion for an electrical transmission project, and 12.6 billion for agriculture (see *"Taehan min'guk chŏngbu wa ilbon chŏngbu ganŭi nong'ŏp kaebal saŏpŭl wihan ch'agwan hyŏpchŏng"* [ROK-Japan agriculture development loan agreement], 10 Feb. 1977, in ROK-MOFA, *Taehan min'guk woegyo yŏnp'yo: 1977*, 383–92). Other major agreements included a March 1976 contract for joint construction of technical training institutes in the ROK, specializing in developing skilled South Korean labor in such light and heavy industry as welding, electrical wiring, and metal fitting (see ROK-MOFA, *Taehan min'guk woegyo yŏnp'yo: 1976*, 511–17), and an agreement on joint continental-shelf exploration and development (see Han, "South Korea: 1977," 51).

113. Tokyo wielded substantial influence in both bodies (see Lee and Sato, *U.S. Policy*, 155).

114. See Yung H. Park, 773.

115. By 1976 it became clear that North Korea was not capable of meeting repayment schedules on debts to Japan. In 1979 and 1983 Tokyo and Pyongyang negotiated an extension of repayment schedules. It should be noted that, while the debt issue lingered throughout the 1975–79 period, the actual rescheduling of payments did not occur until 1979. Therefore, it was not the sole cause of the decline in trade and the suspension of plant exports in the earlier years. On these points see Shin, "Japan's Two-Korea Policy," 269–90, especially 286–87; and Yung H. Park, 768–69.

116. In August 1974 Kimura stated that Seoul was not necessarily the only

legal government on the peninsula, thereby implying de facto political recognition of the North (for details see Chapter 4). On the above points see Baldwin, 112–13; Yung H. Park, 770, 773; and Miki's 1975 New Year's policy address, reported in *Korea Times*, 1 Jan. 1975.

117. Hanai, 114.

118. Oikawa interview.

119. See Lee, *Japan and Korea*, 95; also see Yung H. Park, 768–69.

120. *Korea Times*, 25 July 1975.

121. Low-interest, long-term, government-backed EIB loans enabled Japanese companies to increase the volume of business with North Korea, as Pyongyang could only pay on a deferred basis. South Koreans saw this as Japan's unofficial endorsement of trade with the North.

122. Yung H. Park, 773.

123. Sunobe interview. Sunobe recalled Park's expressing "emotional dissatisfaction" at Carter's lack of prior consultation with either Seoul or Tokyo on the pullout decision.

124. Lee and Sato, *U.S. Policy*, 125.

125. For the relevant sections of the communiqués see ROK-MOFA, *Taehan min'guk woegyo yŏnp'yo: 1977*, 289–91, clause 4; and *Taehan min'guk woegyo yŏnp'yo: 1978*, 254–56, clause 4. For concurring arguments see Sugita, 138–41.

126. For examples see Baldwin, 112–13; *Japan Times*, 14 Nov. 1976; and Lee and Sato, *U.S. Policy*, 106.

127. This declaration was made just prior to the Fukuda-Carter March 1977 summit. Former JDA Vice-Minister Kubo Takuya made similar public statements in November 1976 (see Lee and Sato, *U.S. Policy*, 106, 110; and Lee, *Japan and Korea*, 98).

128. See Baldwin, 112–13; also see Lee, *Japan and Korea*, 98.

129. The Parliamentary Federation sent a second message to Washington in January 1978, reiterating opposition to troop withdrawals. On the above points see Lee and Sato, *U.S. Policy*, 107–10, 118, n. 75.

130. Kim made the following statement in U.S. congressional hearings: "Mr. Quillen (Rep. Tennessee): . . . 'Did the government of South Korea, in its dealings with other nations, develop the same attitude, the same policy, trying to buy favoritism from other nations?' Kim Hyung-wook: 'Yes, we do it to Japan.'" As cited in Lee and Sato, *U.S. Policy*, 87–88. For Kim's actual testimony see U.S., Congress, House, Committee on International Relations, *Korean Influence Investigation*, 115–16. Kim's motives for testifying were hardly noble. Many believe he sought to embarrass the Park regime after having been closed out of the inner circles of power by Lee Hu-rak. Although accurate accounts still remain unavailable, it is believed that Kim's testimony eventually led to his unexplained disappearance in Paris in October 1979, presumably murdered by the KCIA.

131. For example, in 1971 the Park government concluded a major agreement with Mitsubishi for construction of the Seoul metropolitan subway sys-

tem. ROK officials accepted the Mitsubishi bid despite a 20–30 percent lower bid by a French company with the Korean and Japanese governments receiving kickbacks from this differential (see "Thorn in Japan-ROK Ties," 141–44). For a more recent criticism of these ties see Park Jung-mun, "*Chŏngsintae wa komunton somun*" (Comfort women and black money rumors), *Han'gyŏre Sinmun*, 17 Jan. 1992.

132. This involved payoffs to Japanese officials for U.S. air industry contracts, which ultimately led to the resignation and arrest of Premier Tanaka.

133. The December 1977 Diet deliberations focused on the flow of funds between Japanese and Korean private-sector businesses and the government. The Diet blocked passage of legislation critical to implementation of the Japan-ROK continental-shelf-exploration agreement the same year (see Han, "South Korea: 1977," 50–51; Kim, "Policy-Making," 106–8; and "Thorn in Japan-ROK Ties," 143).

134. On these points see Kamiya, "The US Presence," 94; Lee and Sato, *U.S. Policy*, 111, 119–20; Lee, *Japan and Korea*, 98; and *Washington Post*, 28 Mar. 1977, C4 ("No Precipitous Korea Pullout, Fukuda Is Told"). Fukuda did at one point initially state that the pullout issue was a U.S.-ROK bilateral concern that did not involve Japan. However, this formal reaction quickly gave way to Fukuda's true position on the issue (Oikawa interview).

135. See interviews with Ambassador Sunobe Ryōzō and David Blakemore (Korea Desk, Defense Department) in Lee and Sato, *U.S. Policy*, 107, n. 28.

136. For example, in welcoming Fukuda's election to the premiership in December 1976, Seoul also expressed the hope that the Japanese premier would act as a proxy for the ROK in opposing the Carter plan (*Korea Herald*, 26 Dec. 1976).

137. Yasukawa interview. Other analysts of this period aptly summed up these points: "Undeniably, Japan's expressed dissatisfaction with Carter's Korean policy contributed to his policy appraisal. However, South Korea's ability to influence Carter was substantially limited by the embarrassing bribery scandals and human rights controversies. In an effort to exert influence in Washington, the South Koreans relied upon the assistance of the pro-Seoul forces in Japan" (Lee and Sato, *U.S. Policy*, 117–18).

138. Okonogi interview; and Shim interview, 19 Mar. 1992.

139. Kil et al., "*Han-Il kwan'gye ŭi chiha sumaek chindan*" 150; for similar observations see Osamu, 68.

140. Park was assassinated in October 1979; for an outline of the events see Clifford, ch. 10; and Weinstein and Kamiya, 13–15.

141. Oh Kongdan, "Japan-Korea Rapprochement," 29.

142. *Korea Herald*, 7 Apr., 1 May 1979. Also see Lee and Sato, *U.S. Policy*, 125–26; Lee, *Japan and Korea*, 100–101; and Olsen, "Japan-South Korea Security Ties," 62.

143. On these points see *Korea Herald*, 24–27 July 1979; Oh Kongdan, "Japan-Korea Rapprochement," 196–98; and Olsen, "Japan-South Korea Security Ties," 62.

144. Fukuyama interview; and Tsukamoto interview. The former explained how these programs have now become formalized at three of five possible levels: personnel, that is, military officer exchanges; information; and operations. The remaining two are technology/logistics and administration.

145. Oh Kongdan, "Japan-Korea Rapprochement," 197–98.

146. Lee, *Japan and Korea*, 101.

Chapter 6. The 1980s: Evolution and Friction

1. This reversal in U.S. policy actually began in the latter years of the Carter presidency, in particular after the overthrow of the Shah in Iran in January 1979 and the Soviet invasion of Afghanistan the following December. However, it was with the Reagan presidency that this new policy thrust was explicitly stated, sustained, and expanded.

2. Passages extracted from "Message to the Congress on Freedom, Regional Security, and Global Peace, Mar. 14, 1986," in *PPPUS: Reagan: 1986* 1: 341–49; also see *New York Times*, 15 Mar. 1986; and Oye, "Constrained Confidence," 4–5.

3. For the speech in which Reagan introduced this often-cited vision of the Soviets see *Weekly Compilation of Presidential Documents*, 14 Mar. 1983; also see Garthoff, 1015.

4. Weinberger, 690, 696; for other general statements of Reagan's foreign-policy ideology see Kirkpatrick.

5. For analysis and critique of this doctrine see Posen and Van Evera, "Reagan Administration Defense Policy," 75–115; and Smith, 259–85.

6. On these points see Garthoff, 1011, 1019–20; Oye, "Constrained Confidence," 4–5, 13, 21–31; and Rosenfeld, 698–714. For a critical treatment of Reagan's policies see Morris Morley.

7. "Inaugural Address, January 20, 1981," in *PPPUS: Reagan: 1981*, 3. For a cogent elucidation of these views see Jeane Kirkpatrick's address to the Council on Foreign Relations, 10 Mar. 1981, reprinted in Kirkpatrick, 39–45.

8. Human rights concerns gained greater prominence in Asia policy during Reagan's second term. The most dramatic example of this was the withdrawal of U.S. support for the faltering Marcos regime in the Philippines in 1986. In Korea the United States also strongly pressed Chun to fulfill his promise to transfer power in free and fair elections in 1988. These policies, however, did not supersede the renewed alliance commitments established during Reagan's first term. For recent studies on this critical period in South Korea's democratization process see Bedeski, especially ch. 3; Cotton; Lee Manwoo, "Double Patronage," 40–44 and *The Odyssey*; Don Oberdorfer, "U.S. Policy"; and Shultz, 975–82. For an analysis of human rights policy in Reagan's second term see Jacoby, 1066–86.

9. *FEER*, 15 May 1981 ("South Korea: 1981" [special supplement]), 44; for texts of toasts and press statements see *PPPUS: Reagan: 1981*, 66–68.

10. Extracted from clauses 3 and 4 of the communiqué. For the full text see ROK-MOFA, *Taehan min'guk woegyo yŏnp'yo: 1981*, 376–78; *PPPUS: Rea-*

gan: 1981, 68–70; also see *FEER*, 6 Feb. 1981; and Lee and Sato, *U.S. Policy*, 127.

11. Joint exercises for 1981 and 1982, for example, were the largest yet conducted, each involving more than one hundred fifty thousand troops and lasting more than two months. To complement lower-level policy-planning talks, also resumed at this time, the two governments also instituted new dialogue channels between the secretary of state and foreign minister.

12. Lee Manwoo, "Double Patronage," 39.

13. *FEER*, 24 Nov. 1983; *PPPUS: Reagan: 1983* 2: 1588 ("Address Before the Korean National Assembly in Seoul, Nov. 12, 1983") and 2: 1594 ("Remarks to American Troops at Camp Liberty Bell, Republic of Korea, November 13, 1983"); and ROK-MOFA, *Taehan min'guk woegyo yŏnp'yo: 1983*, 214–29. For similar statements at the April 1985 Reagan-Chun summit see Cumings, "American Hegemony," 94, 96; *Diplomacy* 11, no. 5 (25 May 1985), 10–17 (G. Cameron Hurst, "Korean-American Ties More Secure After Chun Visit" and Lee Tong-koi, "Chun, Reagan Walk Arm in Arm on White House Lawn"); *FEER*, 16 May 1985; and ROK-MOFA, *Taehan min'guk woegyo yŏnp'yo: 1985*, 98–99.

14. At these meetings Weinberger personally observed Team Spirit exercises, reiterated support of the ROK's Force Improvement Plan, promised improved terms on ROK foreign military sales credits, and transferred an additional one hundred M48 tanks to the ROK military from the UN Command (see *FEER*, 9 Apr., 18 May ["Focus: South Korea 1982" (special supplement)], and 5 Nov. [Patrick Morgan, "Caspar Strokes Again"] 1982).

15. For the text of Shultz's March 1983 speech see "The US and East Asia: A Partnership for the Future," U.S., State, *Department of State Bulletin*, 83.2073 (Apr. 1983), 31–34; for concurring assessments of the speech see *FEER*, 21 Apr. 1983 (Richard Nations, "A Tilt Towards Tokyo"). In February 1983 Shultz also highlighted his first tour of Northeast Asia with assurances that the United States had no plans to reduce ground forces in Korea (see U.S., State, *Department of State Bulletin* 83.2072 [Mar. 1983]; *FEER*, 24 Feb. 1983; and Kil, "South Korean Policy," 43, n. 30).

16. For the SCC communiqué text see ROK-MOFA, *Taehan min'guk woegyo yŏnp'yo: 1988*, 155–58; also see *FEER*, 23 June 1988.

17. *FEER*, 14 Nov. 1980.

18. Jokes circulated in Seoul that Chun was black and blue from pinching himself to determine whether these events were all a dream (Olsen, *U.S. Policy*, 12); also see John Kie-chiang Oh, "Anti-Americanism," 65–82, especially 74. The domestic politics surrounding the February 1981 U.S.-ROK summit were, of course, much more complex. Rather than an explicit and unadulterated sign of support for the Chun regime, the summit was a secret quid pro quo by the incoming Reagan administration for Chun's commuting of a draconian death sentence levied against opposition figure Kim Dae-Jung in 1980. The historical irony was that the 1981 summit was actually a manifestation of American desires to curb Chun's authoritarian ways rather than to support them.

19. *FEER*, 15 May 1981 ("South Korea: 1981" [special supplement]), 44; also see Chun's summit press conference in ROK-MOFA, *Taehan min'guk woegyo yŏnp'yo: 1981*, 319–22.

20. Gleysteen, 2.

21. The Lance missile system represented an upgrade in force levels from the Honest John and Sergeant missile systems. Other measures in support of the ROK's Force Improvement Plan included the deployment of A10 close-support aircraft around Seoul, additional transfers of military weaponry and equipment (e.g., Stinger air defense systems, Redeye missiles, and M55-1 light tanks), and the stationing of an additional sixteen hundred troops in Korea (see Ahn Byung-joon, "The Security Situation," 124; *Diplomacy* 7, no. 2 [10 Feb. 1981], 44–45 ["Chun, Reagan Meet at White House—Korea, US Vow to Cement Ties"]; *FEER*, 6, 20 Feb. 1981; and ROK-MOFA, *Taehan min'guk woegyo yŏnp'yo: 1981*, 398–99). On the Lance deployments see Olsen, *U.S. Policy*, 88; on the F16 sales see *FEER*, 23 Jan., 6 Feb., 26 June 1986.

22. As stated in the last chapter, Carter's postponement of the troop pullout plan did not comfort Koreans because it merely amounted to an affirmation of the status quo. Reagan's proactive measures, by contrast, upgraded the military balance on the peninsula in the ROK's favor, thus boosting Korean confidence in the U.S. alliance.

23. The Rangoon bombing resulted in the death of fifteen top-level officials, including Foreign Minister Lee Bum-suk. The bomb was inadvertently set off prior to Chun's arrival, sparing the president's life. For a description of this event see ROK-MOFA, *Taehan min'guk woegyo yŏnp'yo: 1983*, 185–206.

24. Shultz, 976. For the Reagan-Chun joint statement see *PPPUS: Reagan: 1983* 2: 1596–99.

25. *FEER*, 24 Nov. 1983; also see Lee Manwoo, "Double Patronage," 40.

26. A discussion of the events in Kwangju is beyond the scope of this work. In addition to the numbers killed in this southwestern city by ROK special forces and regular troops in response to protests against the nationwide imposition of martial law, controversy surrounds the extent to which the United States knew in advance of Chun's intentions and tacitly supported them. On these events see Clark; Oberdorfer, *Two Koreas*, 124–33; and U.S., United States Information Agency, *United States Government Statement on the Events in Kwangju*.

27. Kim Won-soo, director, treaties division, ROK-MOFA, 1992–94, interview by author, 7 June 1995, Stanford, Calif.

28. Over the same period (1976–86) ground forces increased by ten divisions; airpower underwent significant upgrading in both quantity and quality (including deployments of TU-22M Backfire bombers and MiG 31 fighters); and total naval power increased to 1.85 million tons (see *Defense of Japan*, *1986*, 8–14, 26–35; and Pharr, 248).

29. In late 1978 the Soviets deployed twenty-three hundred ground troops on Kunashiri and Etorofu. It also upgraded airpower on the latter island with the addition of MiG-23 fighters and expanded military facilities on Shikotan.

Frequent sightings of Soviet aircraft over the Sea of Japan, harassment of Japanese fishing vessels in regional waters, and the absence of diplomatic progress on resolution of the northern territories issue caused the JDA to declare Soviet actions a serious threat to Japanese security. On the military buildup on the northern territories see *Mainichi Shimbun*, 15 July 1980, in *Daily Summary of the Japanese Press* (hereafter *DSJP*), 15 July 1980, 8; *FEER*, 15 Dec. 1983; and *Nihon Keizai*, 31 Aug. 1983, in *DSJP*, 3–6 Sept. 1983, 15. For JDA statements see *Defense of Japan, 1986*, 171–72; and *FEER*, 23 Jan. 1981.

30. See *PPPUS: Reagan: 1981*, 411 ("Toasts of the President and Prime Minister Suzuki Zenko of Japan at the State Dinner, May 7, 1981"); *FEER*, 15 May 1981; *Mainichi Shimbun*, 24 Mar. 1981, and *Nihon Keizai*, 24 Mar. 1981, both in *DSJP*, 27 Mar. 1981, 9–10, 13–14; *Mainichi Shimbun*, 25 Mar. 1981, in *DSJP*, 31 Mar. 1981, 12.

31. *FEER*, 2 Apr. 1982.

32. *Mainichi Shimbun*, 25 Mar. 1981, in *DSJP*, 31 Mar. 1981, 12. Also see Ito's statements in Diet Upper House Foreign Affairs Committee deliberations in *Asahi Shimbun*, 7 Nov. 1980, in *DSJP*, 15–17 Nov. 1980, 4.

33. The communiqué stirred controversy because of Japan's past hesitance to align itself with the United States fully on such issues, ultimately resulting in Foreign Minister Ito's resignation. For the text of the communiqué see *PPPUS: Reagan: 1981*, 414–16; also see *FEER*, 22 May 1981; and *Yomiuri Shimbun*, 17 May 1981, in *DSJP*, 30 May–1 June 1981, 5–6.

34. *Asahi Shimbun*, 5 May 1981, in *DSJP*, 18 May 1981, 13.

35. *Asahi Shimbun*, 9 May 1981, in *DSJP*, May 18, 1981, 12; and *PPPUS: Reagan: 1981*, 413 ("Remarks of the President and Prime Minister Zenko Suzuki of Japan Following Their Meetings, May 8, 1981").

36. Japanese weapons procurement under the five-year plan included F-15 fighters, P3C antisubmarine aircraft, and T74 tanks. In 1980 the MSDF began participation in RIMPAC (rim of the Pacific) exercises, and in 1986 Keen Edge 87-1 exercises involved all three branches. For the specifics of these policies see *Defense of Japan, 1986*, 175–78; and *FEER*, 15 Oct. 1982, 3 Feb. 1983, 20 Dec. 1984, and 13 November 1986. For more general discussions see Armacost, 82, 88; Mochizuki, "The United States and Japan," 348–57; and Welfield, *An Empire in Eclipse*, 445–46. For the argument that these policies in actuality did not reflect major changes in Japanese defense policy see Pharr.

37. These statements also drew fire from critics in Japan. See *FEER*, 3 Feb. 1983; Pharr, 249; and Thayer, 101–2. For proceedings and statements in the two summits see *FEER*, 3 Feb., 10 Nov. 1983; *PPPUS: Reagan: 1983* 1: 64–65; *PPPUS: Reagan: 1983* 2: 1565–70, 1573–79; and U.S., State, *Department of State Bulletin* 84.2082 (Jan. 1984), 1–11.

38. This was particularly true of Japanese participation at the OECD summits in Williamsburg in May 1983 and Reagan's meetings with Western allies in Los Angeles in January 1985 (see *FEER*, 17 Jan. 1985; Pharr, 249; and Thayer, 102–4).

39. Shultz, 179–82.

40. As stated in Chapter 2, the boosting of internal capabilities can often reflect a state's fear of abandonment with regard to an ally's commitments against an adversarial threat.

41. Reagan's policies drew their inspiration from the 1978 Guidelines for U.S.-Japan Defense Cooperation, however, they went further in both scope and depth in promoting joint planning.

42. Events in Iran and Afghanistan at the end of the 1970s made clear the strategic difficulties of an American response to contingencies in both the Gulf/Indian Ocean region and Asia. In such a scenario Japan was expected to secure air and sea superiority in Northeast Asia while the Seventh Fleet was detained in the Middle East. Operationally this meant holding control of the straits around Japan (e.g., Soya, Tsugaru, and Tsushima) to deny the Soviet ballistic missile submarine fleet access to the Pacific and maintaining air superiority against Soviet Backfire bomber overflights.

43. *Nihon Keizai*, 29 Nov. 1980, in *DSJP*, 6–8 Dec. 1980, 14–16.

44. Mochizuki, "The United States and Japan," 341–48; and Shultz, 189–92.

45. *FEER*, 24 Nov. 1983.

46. *FEER*, 10 Sept. 1987.

47. Mochizuki, "The United States and Japan," 356.

48. Shultz, 189.

49. Quotes are from the text of the September 1984 Nakasone-Chun joint communiqué (Tokyo) and statements by Chun during the 1983 summit (see ROK, Ministry of Information, *Opening A New Era*, 66–68 [esp. clause 3]; and *FEER*, 2 June 1983). For the text of January 1983 Chun-Nakasone joint communiqué (Seoul) see "Source Materials," 718–20.

50. For an excellent analysis of the loan negotiations see Kim, "Policy-Making," 152–93; and Lee, *Japan and Korea*, ch. 5.

51. Emperor Hirohito's "colonial apology" came at a state dinner during the Nakasone-Chun September 1984 summit in Tokyo. For the relevant sections of the text see ROK-MOFA, *Ilbon kaehwang*, 363. Each of the above events is discussed in greater detail below.

52. Japanese sanctions in the aftermath of the October 1983 Rangoon bombing included prohibiting visits by public servants to North Korea, disallowing diplomatic contacts in third countries, and closer scrutiny of visa applications for entry into Japan. Sanctions as a result of the November 1987 KAL 858 bombing included banning of commercial air flights to and from North Korea, restrictions on shore leave for crewmen of visiting North Korean vessels, and additional restrictions on diplomatic contacts and bilateral exchanges. Both sets of sanctions were lifted approximately a year after their imposition (discussed below). In addition to condemning the Soviet 1983 shootdown of KAL 007, the JDA provided critical data that helped U.S. and Korean authorities reconstruct the events that led to the downing of the plane over Sakhalin Island (see *FEER*, 17 Nov. 1983 and 28 Jan. 1988; and Sato Katsumi, 137).

53. A representative sample of authors who make this argument include Bridges; Paul Chan; Colbert; Kim, "Japanese-Korean Relations in the 1980s"; Lee, *Japan and Korea*; and Oh Kongdan, "Japan-Korea Rapprochement."

54. The following exposition of events was compiled from Paul Chan, 262–68; Han, "Convergent and Divergent Interests," 155–59; Lee and Sato, *U.S. Policy*, 158; and Lee, *Japan and Korea*, 110–13. Newspaper accounts of events are individually cited below.

55. For example, more than ten thousand people staged a protest in Hibiya Park the evening after the sentencing (September 17, 1980). In November 1980 Sohyō (Japanese General Council of Trade Unions) initiated a "Save Kim" petition of 1.5 million signatures and announced a boycott of all cargo transports bound for the ROK. More than fifty local city, town, and ward assemblies also adopted resolutions protesting the verdict. See Kim Hong-nak, "After the Park Assassination," 74–75; Lee Chong-sik, "South Korea in 1980," 142; and *Asahi Shimbun*, 5 Oct. 1980, in *DSJP*, 10–14 Oct. 1980, 9–10.

56. The evicted news organizations were *Asahi*, *Jiji*, and *Kyodo* (see *FEER*, 1 Aug. 1980; and *Nihon Keizai*, 18 July 1980, in *DSJP*, 19–21 July 1980, 9–10).

57. Kim was formally arrested on May 18 on the fabricated charge of planning the Kwangju uprising, which, contrary to these charges, was sparked by his arrest (see Oberdorfer, *Two Koreas*, 133).

58. In the 1973 settlement the ROK agreed to excuse Kim from responsibility for political activities in Japan. For coverage of the trial see *FEER*, 29 Aug., 19 Sept. 1980.

59. *Nihon Keizai*, 22 Sept. 1980, in *DSJP*, 27–29 Sept. 1980 (parenthetical insertions in the original); also see *Asahi Shimbun*, 27 Sept. 1980, in *DSJP*, 4–6 Oct. 1980, 2.

60. *FEER*, 26 Sept. 1980. Japanese officials also made numerous inquiries into the nature of the charges against Kim at the time of his arrest in July 1980 (see *FEER*, 11 July 1980 [Ron Richardson, "Seoul Set Out to Topple a Man and a Myth"]; and *Mainichi Shimbun*, 12 July 1980, in *DSJP*, 15 July 1980). In October 1980 press statements Chief Cabinet Secretary Miyazawa described Seoul's response to these inquiries as "unsatisfactory" (see *Tokyo Shimbun*, 9 Oct. 1980, in *DSJP*, 16 Oct. 1980, 6). Technically the ROK was not in violation of the original 1973 settlement, as this included a clause allowing Seoul to detain Kim if he engaged in future antigovernment activities. However, Chun's actions did constitute a breach of trust, as the unwritten understanding at the time of the agreement was that Seoul would never invoke this proviso and would not hold him legally liable for antigovernment acts conducted in Japan (see statements by Asia Bureau Director-General Kiuchi at the October 1980 Upper House Foreign Affairs committee hearings, as reported in *Asahi Shimbun*, 17 Oct. 1980, in *DSJP*, 22 Oct. 1980, 3–4).

61. *Yomiuri Shimbun*, 24 Nov. 1980, in *DSJP*, 26 Nov. 1980, 11–12; also see meetings between Vice-Minister Takashima and ROK embassy officials, as reported in *Asahi Shimbun*, 4 Nov. 1980, in *DSJP*, 11–12 Nov. 1980, 11.

62. Sunobe interview. For the Suzuki-Choi meeting see *Nihon Keizai*, 22 Nov. 1980, in *DSJP*, 26 Nov. 1980, 8; also see *Yomiuri Shimbun*, 5 Dec. 1980, in *DSJP*, 19 Dec. 1980, 5–6. Suzuki also expressed these views to U.S. officials in December 1980 (see *Sankei Shimbun*, 14 Dec. 1980, in *DSJP*, 17 Dec. 1980, 14).

63. Several South Korean groups, including the prominent Federation of Korean Trade Unions, moved to boycott all Japanese products, and rock-throwing demonstrations at the Japanese embassy in Seoul took place. On ROK protests see interview with Ambassador Sunobe in *Mainichi Shimbun*, 30 Nov. 1980, in *DSJP*, 2 Dec. 1980, 12–14; *FEER*, 5 Dec. (Ron Richardson, "Backlash to a Call for Clemency"), 12 Dec. 1980; Kim, "After the Park Assassination," 74; and Lee, "South Korea in 1980," 142.

64. The first target of these sanctions would have been $94 million in Japanese credits negotiated in August 1980 for education and medical facilities (see *FEER*, 19 Dec. 1980; and *Nihon Nogyo Shimbun*, 9 Mar. 1981, in *DSJP*, 14–16 Mar. 1981, 11).

65. After the September 1980 sentencing Carter administration officials made clear to Chun's inner circle of military generals that the United States opposed the execution order against Kim; however, these arguments fell on deaf Korean ears after the November election of Ronald Reagan. In November and December 1980 outgoing Secretary of State Edmund Muskie, Assistant Secretary of State Richard Holbrooke, and senior Deputy Assistant Secretary of State for East Asian Affairs Michael Armacost held a series of discussions with Reagan's incoming national security advisor Richard Allen on the importance of saving Kim's life. With Reagan's authorization Allen held secret meetings in December 1980 with Major General Chung Ho-yong, a special envoy sent by Chun to discuss the Kim case. Despite the Chun regime's initial determination to carry out the sentence, Allen made clear that the Reagan administration could not countenance such an act and warned in very blunt terms that this could undermine any South Korean aspirations for an improvement of U.S.-ROK relations from the Carter period. After three acrimonious meetings on December 9, 18, and January 2 the South Koreans broached the idea of a Reagan-Chun summit in exchange for leniency on Kim's death sentence. The U.S. agreed to this (although the White House later modified Chun's itinerary in such a way that it did not follow the protocol of an official state visit), announcing the February visit on January 21, three days after which Chun commuted the death sentence against Kim. The irony of the situation was that the February 1981 summit was criticized by many as the conservative Reagan administration's stamp of approval on Chun's authoritarian regime and brutal actions in Kwangju at the expense of democracy in Korea. In fact, though, the secret agreement negotiated by Allen that gave rise to the summit preserved Kim as a force for democracy in the country. This account is based on details in *New York Times*, 24 Dec. 1997 (Richard Holbrooke and Michael Armacost, "A Future Leader's Moment of Truth") and 21 Jan. 1998 (Richard V. Allen, "On the Korea Tightrope, 1980"); Oberdorfer, *Two Koreas*, 133–38; and author's phone conversation with M. Armacost, 10 Mar. 1998.

66. Sunobe interview. It should be noted that this dispute arose during the final year of the Carter administration. One might therefore cite this as an instance of *friction* that took place during a period I have described as driven by Japanese-Korean fears of U.S. disengagement and bilateral *cooperation*. However, the Kim affair took place in the autumn of 1980. This was *after* Carter suspended the Korean troop pullout plan (July 1979). Therefore, Japan-ROK fears of U.S. abandonment were no longer salient, and as a result, the likelihood of friction arising was great.

67. The ROK's initial request came at an August 1981 meeting of foreign ministers in Tokyo. This called for $6 billion in government and private loans and was accompanied by a list of nine large-scale projects for which these funds were required.

68. On these points see Bridges, 14; *FEER*, 21, 28 Aug. 1981; Kim, "Policy-Making," 153, 158; Lee, *Japan and Korea*, 116–17; Oh Kongdan, "Japan-Korea Rapprochement," 79–80; and Woo, 186–87.

69. Kim, "After the Park Assassination," 77; and Lee, *Japan and Korea*, 114–15.

70. As noted earlier, the "alliance" terminology that emerged from the Reagan-Suzuki summit drew strong criticism in Japan. The term was later changed under Nakasone to "defense partnership." The comprehensive security strategy essentially argued that Japanese security could be enhanced by nonmilitary (i.e., economic) means.

71. *FEER*, 28 Aug. 1981.

72. *FEER*, 28 Aug. 1981; and *Sankei Shimbun*, 3 Sept. 1981, in *DSJP*, 5–8 Sept. 1981, 16.

73. *FEER*, 28 Aug. 1981 (Shim Jae-hoon, "How to Pin Tokyo Down").

74. *FEER*, 28 Aug. 1981; Kim, "After the Park Assassination," 77–78; and Lee, *Japan and Korea*, 118.

75. *FEER*, 21, 28 Aug. 1981.

76. For ROK arguments see *Nihon Keizai*, 13 Sept. 1981, in *DSJP*, 18 Sept. 1981, 1–2; for Sonoda statements see *FEER*, 18 Sept. 1981; and *Yomiuri Shimbun*, 11 Sept. 1981, in *DSJP*, 19–21 Sept. 1981, 10–13.

77. *Tokyo Shimbun*, 12 Sept. 1981, in *DSJP*, 17 Sept. 1981, 2–3.

78. For joint press statements see *Yomiuri Shimbun*, 11 Sept. 1981, in *DSJP*, 19–21 Sept. 1981, 10–13 and *Yomiuri Shimbun*, 12 Sept. 1981, in *DSJP*, 22 Sept. 1981, 11–12. For additional evaluations of the conference see *FEER*, 18 Sept., 27 Nov. 1981; and *Mainichi Shimbun*, 12 Sept. 1981, in *DSJP*, 22 Sept. 1981, 14.

79. For a study that focuses on this factor as the primary cause of friction during the early 1980s see Kim, "After the Park Assassination."

80. See Kim, "Policy-Making," 187–89; and Lee, *Japan and Korea*, 115–35. The latter also provides an excellent overview of the debates on Japan-Korea historiography (141–64).

81. Protests were delivered to the Japanese ambassador August 3 and 12. See Emmerson and Holland, *The Eagle*, 158–59; *Mainichi Shimbun*, 6 Aug.

1982, in *DSJP*, 13 Aug. 1982, 13–14; and *Sankei Shimbun*, 6 Aug. 1982, in *DSJP*, 13 Aug. 1982, 15–16.

82. Following the breakup of the September 1981 ministerial conference, Seoul and Tokyo both eased their negotiating positions. The former dropped the security-rent argument, and the latter acknowledged that the loan project could fall within the purview of Japan's "comprehensive security" vision. Talks resumed in December 1981, and the Japanese presented a $4-billion-loan package ($1.5 billion in ODA and $2.5 billion in EIB and private loans) in April 1982. Seoul rejected the offer as below its initial request of $6 billion, but in June 1982 agreed to the $4-billion total and proposed a different formula of funds weighted more toward long-term, low-interest commodity loans ($2.3 billion in ODA and $1.7 billion in commodity/bank loans). For a synopsis of the proposals see Kim, "After the Park Assassination," 78–82; and Lee, *Japan and Korea*, 133.

83. In particular National Land Agency Director-General Matsuno Yukiyasu and Education Vice-Minister Misumi Tetsuo pointed to Korean textbook depictions of Japanese colonial administrators as "atrocious colonists" and of the 1909 assassination of Ito Hirobumi by a Korean youth as "heroic" (see *FEER*, 20 Aug. 1982 [Murray Sayle, "A Textbook Case of Aggression"]; and *Nihon Keizai*, 6 Aug. 1982, in *DSJP*, 13 Aug. 1982, 11).

84. See Lee, *Japan and Korea*, 148.

85. Lee, *Japan and Korea*, 146; also see *FEER*, 20 Aug. 1982.

86. On the above points see Paul Chan, 295–98; Kim, "Policy-Making," 187–89; and Lee, *Japan and Korea*, 145–47.

87. *FEER*, 20 Aug. 1982 ("Another Chapter in a History of Mistrust"). Chun's speech recalled such practices as the banning of Korean names and labor conscription. It also explicitly held Japan responsible for the country's division and the Korean war (see Paul Chan, 298–300).

88. See Lee, *Japan and Korea*, 148–49; and October 1982 meetings between Foreign Ministers Lee Bum-suk and Sakurauchi Yoshio in New York in *Yomiuri Shimbun*, 3 Oct. 1982, in *DSJP*, 6 Oct. 1982, 15–16.

89. *FEER*, 30 Jan. 1981.

90. For Suzuki's press club statement see *Asahi Shimbun*, 9 May 1981, in *DSJP*, 18 May 1981, 12; and *Nihon Keizai*, 3 May 1981, in *DSJP*, 14 May 1981, 16. For Chun's invitation see Lee, *Japan and Korea*, 115.

91. *Yomiuri Shimbun*, 15 Sept. 1981, in *DSJP*, 13–14 Sept. 1981, 4.

92. Quotations are from Chun's September 8, 1984, departure statement, in ROK-MOFA, *Taehan min'guk woegyo yŏnp'yo: 1984*, 128. For joint communiqués of the two summits see ROK-MOFA, *Taehan min'guk woegyo yŏnp'yo: 1983*, 59–61 and ROK-MOFA, *Taehan min'guk woegyo yŏnp'yo: 1984*, 117–20; also see ROK, Ministry of Information, *Opening a New Era*, 66–68.

93. See clause 7 of the 1983 communiqué ("Source Materials," 719); *FEER*, 27 Jan. 1983; *Han'guk Ilbo*, 9 Sept. 1984; Kil Soong-hoom, "Two Aspects," 509; and Kim, "Japanese-Korean Relations in the 1980s," 507. The ROK also

unsuccessfully pressed the issue at the foreign ministers' meetings in Seoul in July 1984 (see *Nihon Keizai*, 7 July 1984, in *DSJP*, 12 July 1984, 11–12). The two governments clashed over this issue in 1985 and 1986 after *kyop'o* boycotts of the fingerprint requirement resulted in their arrest and detainment by Japanese immigration authorities. The ROK demanded that Japan not deport these individuals, while Japan accused Seoul of encouraging these groups to violate Japanese domestic law. For examples see *FEER*, 30 May 1985 and 24 July 1986; and *Tokyo Shimbun*, 25 May 1985, in *DSJP*, 4 June 1985, 8.

94. *FEER*, 13 Sept. 1984.

95. Instead it intoned MITI's conventional arguments that the trade deficit was symptomatic of a larger structural problem in which overall growth of the ROK economy was linked with imports of Japanese goods (e.g., intermediate industrial products and capital goods) and that tariff reductions alone could not remedy this problem. In addition, Japan noted that one-third of ROK exports already received preferential treatment under Japan's tariff system, representing a disproportionate 25 percent of Japan's entire GSP list (*Mainichi Shimbun*, 8 July 1984, in *DSJP*, 12 July 1984, 13–14; *Nihon Keizai*, 7 July 1984, in *DSJP*, 2 July 1984, 11–12; and *Yomiuri Shimbun*, 9 Sept. 1984, in *DSJP*, 20 Sept. 1984, 3–4).

96. *FEER*, 13 Sept. 1984; *Mainichi Shimbun*, 31 Aug. 1983, in *DSJP*, 2 Sept. 1983, 15. For a well-balanced synopsis of economic issues salient during the Nakasone-Chun summits see Colbert, 286–89.

97. See Izumi, 192–95; and Ko, 174.

98. For example, during the period the justice ministry approved entry visas for various North Korean delegations to visit Japan. The most notable among these were visits by a trade delegation in 1981 (the first since 1972), a legal delegation to attend an international law conference in 1983, and sports delegations to participate in the Universiad games in Kobe in 1985 and the Niigata table tennis championships in 1988. On these events see *Asahi Shimbun*, 20 May 1983, in *DSJP*, 25 May 1983, 12–13; *FEER*, 19 May 1988; *Nihon Keizai*, 8 May 1981, in *DSJP*, 16–18 May 1981, 7; and *Yomiuri Shimbun*, Aug. 1, 1985, in *DSJP*, 10–12 Aug. 1985, 14.

99. For a description of the Kuno visit see *Tokyo Shimbun*, 1 July 1984, in *DSJP*, 4–5 July 1984, 15. For the Ishibashi visit see ROK-MOFA, *Ilbon kaehwang*, 291; *FEER*, 4 Oct. 1984; and *Nihon Keizai*, 20 Sept. 1984, in *DSJP*, 29 Sept.–1 Oct. 1984, 16.

100. This was announced October 23, 1984, to take effect January 1985 (see *FEER*, 1 Nov. 1984; ROK-MOFA, *Ilbon kaehwang*, 291; *Mainichi Shimbun*, 10 Oct. 1984, in *DSJP*, 20–22 Oct. 1984, 11; and *Nihon Keizai*, 10 Oct. 1984, in *DSJP*, 19 Oct. 1984, 16). For a list of the sanctions see Sato Katsumi, 137.

101. Kim, "Japanese-Korean Relations in the 1980s," 510; and *Nihon Keizai*, 13 June 1985, in *DSJP*, 19 June 1985, 14.

102. On these events see Victor Cha, "National Unification," 92–93.

103. The terrorist bombing of KAL 858 by two North Korean agents took place over the Thailand-Burma border in November 1987.

104. This move was directed particularly at the Iino shipping company, which was a primary carrier of goods to North Korea (see Colbert, 285). For ROK protests at the Chun-Nakasone and annual joint ministerial meetings see Kil, "South Korean Policy," 40–41; and *Nihon Keizai,* 29 Aug. 1983, in *DSJP,* 1 Sept. 1983, 14.

105. See *FEER,* 27 Sept. 1984; Kim, "Japanese-Korean Relations in the 1980s," 507–8; and *Sankei Shimbun,* 9 Sept. 1984, in *DSJP,* 21 Sept. 1984, 4–5.

106. ROK Foreign Minister Lee expressed these views in meetings with Abe at United Nations General Assembly sessions (see *FEER,* 4 Oct. 1984; and *Tokyo Shimbun,* 29 Sept. 1984, in *DSJP,* 10–11 Oct. 1984, 10).

107. Tani also reportedly delivered a letter from Nakasone to Kim Il-sung.

108. *FEER,* 13 Feb. 1986; Kim, "Japanese-Korean Relations in the 1980s," 511–12; *Nihon Keizai,* 19 Jan. 19866, in *DSJP,* 30 Jan. 1986, 13–14; and *Yomiuri Shimbun,* 29 Jan. 1986, in *DSJP,* 8–10 Feb. 1986, 10.

109. Lee, *Japan and Korea,* 120. Protests were raised at the March 1981 and August 1983 foreign ministers meetings and September 1981 joint ministerial conference.

110. The 1979 commitments included participation in United States-led military exercises, joint hardware production, and joint early warning systems (Oh Kongdan, "Japan-Korea Rapprochement," 196–98).

111. *FEER,* 22 Oct. 1982; also see Bridges, 56.

112. For representative examples of ROK protests see Defense Minister Yoon Sung-min's October 1982 National Assembly statements in *FEER,* 22 Oct. 1982, and Foreign Minister Lee Bum-suk's February 1983 meetings with Shultz in Kil, "South Korean Policy," 43.

113. ROK-MOFA, *Ilbon kaehwang,* 363.

114. For Shiina's 1965 apology see Yi, *Taet'ongryŏngŭl kŭrimyŏ,* 207.

115. *Nihon Keizai,* 9 Sept. 1984, in *DSJP,* 21 Sept. 1984, 3–4; and *Tokyo Shimbun,* 8 Sept. 1984, in *DSJP,* 20 Sept. 1984, 2–3.

116. Cited in Kim, "Japanese-Korean Relations in the 1980s," 507.

117. For a discussion of this issue see Kil, "*Han-Il kwan'gye ŭi chiha sumaek chindan*" 146–47; also see Ahn Byung-joon, "Japanese Policy," 265–66; and Bridges, 63. The 1990 Akihito apology is discussed in the Conclusion.

118. Premier Miki visited Yasukuni privately in 1975.

119. *FEER,* 15 Aug. 1985 and 21 Aug. 1986; *Tokyo Shimbun,* 14, 16 Aug. 1985, in *DSJP,* 24–26 Aug. 1985, 3, and 27 Aug. 1985, 13–14, respectively.

120. See *FEER,* 28 Aug. 1986; and *Nihon Keizai,* 10 Jan. 1986, in *DSJP,* 22 Jan. 1986, 14.

121. These criticisms were expressed both in a *Bungei Shunjū* interview (discussed below) and in July 25, 1986, press statements (see *Asahi Shimbun,* 6, 7 Sept. 1988, in *DSJP,* 11 Sept. 1986, 4–7; *FEER,* 14 Aug., 18 Sept. 1986; ROK-MOFA, *Ilbon kaehwang,* 374; and Kim, "Japanese-Korean Relations in the 1980s," 512).

122. *Nihon Keizai*, 2 Aug. 1986, in *DSJP*, 14 Aug. 1986, 13–14.

123. *FEER*, 2 Oct. 1986. Fujio's remarks were historically inaccurate. By 1910 Ito had been assassinated (in 1909 by An Chang-gun), and Kojong no longer held the throne, which he had abdicated in 1907. Fujio was most likely referring to the 1905 protectorate treaty; nevertheless, the basic thrust of his remarks remains the same. On these historical events see Lee Ki-baik, 309–13.

124. Korean newspapers all carried front-page stories rebuking Fujio's arguments as "preposterous."

125. *FEER*, 18 Sept. 1986; Kim, "Japanese-Korean Relations in the 1980s," 512–13; *Korea Herald*, 10 Sept. 1986; and *Tokyo Shimbun*, 27 July 1986, in *DSJP*, 8 Aug. 1986, 6. The foreign ministers' meeting and Naksone's attendance at the Asian Games eventually did happen after Nakasone sacked Fujio on September 8 and apologized for the entire affair; however, residual bitterness was evident in the lack of any substantive accomplishments at these meetings. Chun and Foreign Minister Choi explicitly told their Japanese counterparts that negative feelings and distrust as a result of Fujio's remarks could not be easily erased by settlements at the political level. A major incentive for Japan's swift firing of Fujio was Nakasone's desire to resolve the issue before a November 1986 summit in Beijing. For Chinese criticisms of Fujio's remarks and Nakasone's apologies see *FEER*, 20 Nov. 1986. This issue resurfaced in 1988 when a Japanese cabinet official, Okuno Seisuke, made similar comments evoking further protests from Seoul and Beijing (see *FEER*, 26 May 1988; and ROK-MOFA, *Ilbon kaehwang*, 375).

126. These referred to the March 1 independence movement as an isolated riot and did not note the coercive nature of occupation-period labor conscription programs.

127. The context of this decision was a twenty-year legal battle over the education ministry's rejection of textbooks by the leftist historian Ienaga Saburo in 1962–63. For both events see *FEER*, 10 Apr. 1986.

128. The NCPJ advocated such right-wing policies as autonomous Japanese defense, education based on traditional Japanese foundations, and bold reexamination of the 1946 constitution. The 1982 textbook controversy motivated this group to develop a historical text that defied the dominant leftist theme and instead emphasized veneration and respect for Japan and the emperor (*FEER*, 19 Feb. 1987).

129. Emmerson and Holland, *The Eagle*, 158–59; and *FEER*, 26 June (Bruce Roscoe, "Grappling with History"), 21 Aug. 1986, and 8 Oct. 1987. The NCPJ eventually agreed to make additional revisions of the book before it was fully certified.

130. This was, in fact, what Akihito later did as emperor in 1990 at the Roh-Kaifu summit (see Conclusion).

131. Chun also saw the visit as a high-profile event that could benefit the ruling party in the run-up to the December 1987 presidential elections. At the time the government became increasingly unpopular as it resisted demands for democratic reforms and direct presidential elections. The Japanese government's

conviction to follow through with the visit would have served implicitly as a vote of confidence for the Chun regime.

132. For Sunobe-Chun meetings see *Yomiuri Shimbun*, 21 Aug. 1986, in *DSJP*, 28 Aug. 1986, 9–10. For cancellation of the visit see Bridges, 64; *FEER*, 18 Sept. 1986; and *Tokyo Shimbun*, 21 Aug. 1986, in *DSJP*, 29 Aug. 1986, 13–14.

133. See *FEER*, 23 Feb. (Ian Buruma, "Seoul and Tokyo Scowl Across a Sea of Uncomfortable Similarities"), 29 Nov. (idem., "A Love-Hate Fuse Smolders Beneath Japan's Korea Boom") 1984. The cultural import ban is also discussed in the Conclusion.

Conclusion: Quasi Allies or Adversaries?

1. See Chapter 2 for the assumptions underlying these hypotheses as well as the operationalization of abandonment and entrapment for Japan and Korea.

2. A 1964 memo from R. W. Komer to Johnson conveying instructions for Winthrop Brown, the new ambassador to Korea, is representative: "You give top priority to the long-delayed Korea-Japan settlement. Let's get Japan to start sharing the burden. Aside from $600 million in Jap aid which a settlement would bring, we want to redevelop the natural economic ties between Korea and Japan. . . . [Tell Brown] [y]ou are personally inclined to cut our 50,000 U.S. troops in Korea; our needs are more in Southeast Asia. Defense of Korea is vital; but can't we do it with fewer men? . . . You've held off on these cuts because they might give the wrong signal to the Chicoms just now, but Brown should keep a close eye on when it might be feasible" (memo, Komer-the President, 31 July 1964 [secret, declassified 23 June 1993], "Korea, Vol. II," KCF, NSF, Box 254, LBJ Library).

3. As a memo from George Ball to Johnson stated, the funds were "no more than we plan to provide in any event over the next three fiscal years, but its announcement at this time may be crucial to the Korea-Japan settlement" (memo, Ball-the President, 13 May 1965 [secret, declassified 7 Aug. 1992], "Park Visit Briefing Book," KCF, NSF, Box 256, LBJ library, 2).

4. It is important to note that this argument does not apply to private-sector activities, where governments are relatively less capable of pushing their policy priorities on profit-oriented businesses.

5. Post–cold war issues are discussed later in this chapter.

6. I thank Jon Mercer for insights on these points.

7. As Snyder states, lesser powers that are assured of a security commitment from the superpower enjoy a "freedom of irresponsibility" to indulge their preferences in a manner that would not be otherwise available to them (Snyder, "Alliance Theory, 121).

8. With regard to the Korean case it should be remembered that on the two occasions that the United States removed or contemplated removing ground forces from the Korean peninsula (i.e., Nixon's pullout of one division in 1970–71 and Carter's plan for a total troop withdrawal in 1977) the South Koreans seriously pursued nuclear weaponization.

9. In line with the dictates of the Nunn-Warner bill, EASI called for a three-phased reduction of U.S. troops in Korea, beginning with seven thousand ground and air personnel in 1990–92, six thousand to seven thousand additional troops in 1993–95, and further reductions to be determined from 1995 (see Grinter; and *Stars and Stripes*, 6 Apr. 1990 and 23 Oct. 1991).

10. EASI was postponed in September 1992 over the North Korean nuclear issue (see *Chosŏn Ilbo*, 17 Dec. 1994, 1, in FBIS, 94-243, 19 Dec. 1994, 55–56; and *New York Times*, 9 Nov. 1992). For U.S. statements see Nye; and U.S., Department of Defense, *A Strategic Framework*. Also see the November 1993 Clinton-Kim press conference in ROK-MOFA, *Taehan min'guk woegyo yŏnp'yo: 1993*, 548–56, and the joint communiqué of the twenty-sixth United States-ROK SCC, in ROK-MOFA, *Taehan min'guk woegyo yŏnp'yo: 1994*, 259–62.

11. Armacost, 247.

12. For a concise overview of the North's missile program see Wiencik.

13. For representative examples of this argument see Betts; Huntington, "America's Changing Strategic Interests"; McNaugher; and Roy.

14. For the Yamashita visit see Chapter 5. In November 1990 JDA Director-General Ishikawa Yozo visited Panmunjom and toured North Korean-dug infiltration tunnels in a gesture of support for South Korean defense. This visit was reciprocated the following month by ROK Defense Minister Lee Jong-koo with inspections of SDF forces (see *Korea Herald*, 11 Nov., 8 Dec. 1990).

15. Bridges, 56; *Korea Herald*, 12 Oct. 1991; *Korea Times*, 3 Nov. 1991; and Mochizuki, "Japan as an Asia-Pacific Power," 144. The policy-planning talks take place at the assistant foreign minister level.

16. James Sterngold, "Japan and Korea Fear a Vacuum if Clinton Turns the US Inward," *New York Times*, 9 Nov. 1992. Also see Kang Sung-chul, "US Presence Still Important for Asia: Roh, Miyazawa Hold Informal Talks," *Korea Herald*, 10 Nov. 1992.

17. Republic of Korea, Ministry of National Defense, *Defense White Paper: 1992–93*, 30; and *The Modality of the Security and Defense Capability of Japan*, 9. Also see Bridges, 56; and Takesada, 189. For reports on the 1995 JDA white paper see *Korea Herald*, 23 June 1996. These views were also reiterated in the Review of U.S.-Japan Defense Guidelines in 1997 (see statements by JDA Director Kyuma Fumio, reported in *Yomiuri Shimbun*, 29 Apr. 1997, 5).

18. On these points see *Korea Herald*, 27 Sept. ("SK, Japan Held Secret Military Talks in July: Official"), 10 Oct. ("So. Korea-Japan Defense Policy Talks to Open in Tokyo"), 13 Oct. ("Seoul, Tokyo Plan Regular Meeting on Military Info") 1995; *Korea Update*, 6, no. 1 (9 Jan. 1995), 3; and Yonhap (newswire), 20 Dec. 1994, in FBIS, 20 Dec. 1994, 54–55.

19. This dialogue was intended to complement the existing summit and foreign-ministerial meetings (see *Chosŏn Ilbo*, 15 Apr. 1997; *Korea Herald*, 15 Apr. 1997; and *Korea Press Service*, 15 Apr. 1997).

20. For example, see Otsuka Umio, "Prospects of Japan-Korea Defense Cooperation: Partners or Rivals," paper presented at the Conference on Japan-Korea-U.S. Trilateral Dialogue, Tokyo, 5–6 Dec. 1997.

21. LDP leader Kanemaru Shin's meetings with Kim Il-sung in 1990, followed by the start of normalization talks, raised complaints in Seoul about how Japan's "rushing" to engage Pyongyang undermined North-South dialogue. See Armacost, 145–49; *Japan Times* (International Weekly edition), 8–14 Oct. 1990 (Henry Cutter, "North Korea Warms to Japan"); Kim, "Japanese-North Korean Relations"; *Korea Update* 1, no. 5 (15 Oct. 1990; "Japan Visit to North Korea Creates ROK Furor"); and Yi Pyŏngsun, 60–63.

22. See *Japan Times* (International Weekly edition), 3–9 Dec. 1990 ("Nations Inch Toward Better Relations"); *New York Times*, 26 Nov. 1990, A5 (Steven Weisman, "Japan Weighs Aid to North Koreans"); and Okonogi, "Japan-North Korean Negotiations," 204–5.

23. A full exposition of this dispute is beyond the scope of this work. I provide a very basic chronology of events and discussion of Seoul-Tokyo interaction over the issue. For background see Bermudez; Victor Cha, "Geneva"; Cheng; Harrison; Koh, "Trends"; Mack; Mazarr, "Going Just a Little Nuclear"; Oberdorfer, "North Korea"; and Oh Kong-dan, "Background and Options." For more technical discussions see Albright and Hibbs, "North Korea's Plutonium Puzzle," 37–40; idem., "What's North Korea Up To," 10–11. For an authoritative new account see Sigal.

24. See *New York Times*, 30 Mar. (David Sanger, "Seoul Eases Stand on Nuclear Inspections of North"), 31 Mar. (idem., "Neighbors Differ on How to Chasten North Korea"), 1993.

25. On the concept of "recessed deterrence" see Buzan, 35–36. Also see Ball; and Manning and Stern.

26. For examples see *Korea Times*, 12 Nov. 1995 ("ROK Navy Pursues Blue Water Ambition"); Lee, "Naval Power"; and *Wall Street Journal*, 17 Jan. 1995.

27. See *Korea Herald*, 15 Nov. 1995 and 14 Mar. 1996; and *Washington Post*, 14 Nov. 1995.

28. Regarding the latter point, a important indicator of Japanese cooperation in the event of sanctions will be the extent to which it restricts the remittances of hard currency to Pyongyang from the Chosen Soren. While exact figures are not known, this transfer of funds, passed through dummy corporations and third-country accounts, ranges in the hundreds of millions of dollars per year and constitutes a substantial source of North Korea's foreign capital. This may be the West's only lever in using sanctions, especially if Chinese participation is absent. On the former point conditions on the disbursement of monies resulting from Tokyo-Pyongyang normalization would be a key topic of debate between Japan and the ROK. Seoul would demand that such funds not be used to enhance the North's war potential. Tokyo would desire the same restrictions, but the two may disagree on the stringency of these conditions.

29. As discussed below, this includes mutual compromise and conciliation on such delicate historical issues as *chŏngsintae* (comfort women).

30. Similarly, some argue that the ROK's opposition to a larger Japanese role in the Gulf War and UN peacekeeping operations stemmed as much from

the resulting pressures this would put on the ROK to increase its burden in such operations as from any fears of uncorking Japanese militarism (Bridges, 57).

31. This section benefited from discussions with Michael Green.

32. These include trilateral cooperation projects by the Okazaki Institute (Japan), the Pacific Forum (U.S.), and the Yoido Society (ROK); the Korea Institute of Defense Analysis (ROK), the National Institute of Defense Studies (Japan), and RAND (United States); and the Center for Strategic Studies (United States), the Korean Institute for National Unification (ROK), and the Research Institute for Peace and Security (Japan). On an elaboration of these points see Michael Green, 12–14.

33. Otsuka, 18–21; and Michael Green, 21–22.

34. The minister's statements were in direct response to a *Wall Street Journal* article (17 Jan. 1995) which cited the ROK defense buildup as directed against Japan (see *Joongang Ilbo*, 23 Jan. 1995, 4, in FBIS, 23 Jan. 1995, 47–48).

35. Cited in "Revitalizing the US-Japan Alliance," 7.

36. *Yomiuri Shimbun*, 6 Nov. 1996 (Takahama Tatou, "Time to Consider the Unimaginable").

37. A expansive discussion of the problems and prospects of Korean unification is beyond the scope of this book. I focus on certain aspects of unification as they affect Korean foreign policy and security alignments in the region. For background see Cha, "National Unification," Foster-Carter; Henriksen and Lho; and Kihl.

38. These arguments either explicitly or implicitly inform much of the discussion on post–cold war East Asian security. For representative examples see Betts; Friedberg; Olsen, "Korea's Reunification," and Roy. The ensuing discussion excludes Russia. This is not because Russia is unimportant to future security equations in East Asia, but because much of its current energies are focused inward. Barring major territorial disputes on the Sino-Soviet border or with Japan over the northern territories, Russia's interest lies in maintaining as benign a security environment as possible while cultivating economic interests in the region.

39. On the ROK's zero-sum mentality and classically Realist conceptions of security see Victor Cha, "Realism."

40. Fitzpatrick, 430.

41. Kim Won-soo interview by author, 26 Oct. 1994, Stanford, Calif. The only reference agreeable to China was to the "abnormal" state of past relations (*bijŏngsang kwan'gye*) (see the Roh-Yang Shangkun communiqué in ROK-MOFA, *Taehan min'guk woegyo yŏnp'yo: 1992*, 560–61).

42. Hao and Qubing, 1137.

43. *Korea Herald*, 10 Nov. 1992 ("Chinese Military Wary of Naval Buildup of Japan, Korea").

44. See Korean coverage of the CPC report in *Mal* ([Free] Speech), Oct. 1994, in FBIS-EAS 94-245, 21 Dec. 1994, 38–46.

45. See *Korea Herald*, 11 Oct. 1995 ("Beijing Asks Seoul to Curb Activities

of Korean Civilian Body in Manchuria"); and *Wall Street Journal,* 9 Oct. 1995 ("After 1300 Years, White Collar Armies Target Manchuria"). On Roh's Korean community concept see Cha, "National Unification," 99.

46. By contrast, meetings with expatriate communities are a standard itinerary item in ROK summit visits to Japan, the United States, South America, and Europe (Kim Won-soo, interview by author, 26 Oct. 1994, Stanford, Calif.).

47. Glaser, 261–62. China-ROK economic issues are elaborated below.

48. Mearsheimer, "The Case for a Ukrainian Nuclear Deterrent," 54.

49. It is interesting to note that in a 1993 trip to Beijing ROK Foreign Minister Han Sung-joo explicitly stated that, while Japan once administered Korea as a colony, it was no longer seen as threatening (see *FEER,* 11 Nov. 1993 [Frank Ching, "Securing Northeast Asia"]).

50. While these relations do not constitute "institutions" in the formal sense of a European NATO or EC, they do breed a familiarity between Japanese and Korean leaders. For a related point on how such institutions engendered a familiarity among European leaders that mollified anxieties about German reunification see Friedberg, 13.

51. Steve Chan, 79.

52. Dollar, 1168–69; and Qin, 156–59.

53. This view was also confirmed in the author's discussions with chairmen of several Korean conglomerates in April and August 1993 and June 1996, Seoul. For a concurring argument see McNaugher, 12–17.

54. See *Korea Times,* 3 Mar. 1993. Another report by the government-backed Korea Development Institute in 1991 estimated the investment burden to bring North Korean production levels to 60 percent of the ROK over ten years to be $816.7 billion. For more recent independent estimates that put the cost even higher (in the range of $1 to $2 trillion) see Hwang; Noland; and Rhee, especially 372–73.

55. While Germany's unification cost (estimated around $1 trillion) occupied only 10 percent of the national budget, a low-end figure of $500 billion for Korea's unification is over ten times Seoul's national budget. In addition, while West Germany was geographically larger and four times more populous than its counterpart, the ROK is 25 percent smaller in area and only twice as populous as the North. This presages a relatively heavier burden in terms of infrastructure and social welfare costs. For other comparative indicators see Fitzpatrick, 416–18; and Foster-Carter, 103–4.

56. Domestic financing would be in the form of a "unification tax" and private capital; however, a substantial portion of the funds would have to come through government bond sales, international borrowing, and foreign aid and investment.

57. For estimates that put total U.S. and international organization contributions at a paltry $20 billion see Hufbauer.

58. The latter is largely through trading companies set up by the Chosen Soren and memo arrangements dating back to the 1970s.

59. One of the main reasons Japanese aid and investment shifted from the

ROK to Southeast Asia in the 1980s was that labor costs in South Korea had grown too high (see Kim Hosup, "The End of the Cold War," 225–26). Japan would be eager to take part in infrastructural projects such as expansion of the $8-billion Seoul-Pusan high-speed railway. Another major area of investment will be tourism (e.g., the development of Kumgang-san and Paekdu-san as resorts). A third area will be development of the eastern coast of the peninsula stretching from Wonsan to Najin for trade and manufacturing. As one knowledgeable observer found in interviews with business and government elites in the region, the Japanese banking sector has been the most active in drawing up plans of action for Korean unification (Paal, 6).

60. This argument derives from the "boomerang" effect, in which certain South Korean industries have become so successful as a result of Japanese aid and technology that they now challenge Japan for market share.

61. James Morley, "Dynamics," 8.

62. This figure is based on the traditional benchmark of military forces as approximately 1 percent of total population.

63. One could argue that the United States "shocked" the region during the 1975–79 period with its abandonment of South Vietnam and with the Carter plan. However, these policies led to Japan-Korea cooperation because the cold-war structures of the time left the two states without alternative partners to deal with their security scarcity. In the post–cold war era similar constraints do not exist and therefore may not result in consolidation of the Japan-Korea axis.

64. In addition, reforms have been instituted to expunge corruption, root out the military's influence in politics, and enhance civil liberties (see Victor Cha, "Politics and Democracy"; and Han Sung-joo, "Korea's Democratic Experiment," 63–78).

65. As Huntington states, the "critical point" in the democratization process of a political system is the accession to power of a government chosen in a "free, open, and fair election" (see Huntington, The Third Wave, 9). Democracy is defined below.

66. This assessment is in accordance with the generally accepted definition of a democratic system as one in which (1) leaders are chosen through fair, honest, and periodic elections; (2) candidates freely compete for votes; (3) the right to vote is accorded to the majority of citizens; and (4) basic civil liberties of free speech and the right to assemble are preserved (see Huntington, The Third Wave, 7; also see Dahl).

67. As Russett states, "The norms of regulated political competition, compromise solutions to political conflicts, and peaceful transfer of power are externalized by democracies in their dealing with other national actors in world politics." See Russett, 33; also see Brown; Dixon; and Doyle. I am indebted to Bob Jervis for suggesting the application of this literature to Japan and Korea.

68. Although a discussion of domestic political factors falls outside this book's largely structural treatment of Japan-Korea relations, it is not necessarily inconsistent with it. In both structural and domestic arguments for Japan-Korea interaction, the focus is on *perceptions* as a key causal variable. In the former

case perceptions of U.S. abandonment are important; and in the latter, perceptions of one another as liberal democracies. On the causal significance of perceptions in explaining democratic peace see Owen, "Liberalism." For Owen's assessment of the Japan-ROK case, which differs from this book's, see Owen, *Liberal Peace*, 217–21.

69. For agreements relating to the Kobe earthquake, civilian nuclear energy, and sea-related search-and-rescue operations see ROK-MOFA, *Taehan min'guk choyakjip: yangja choyak: 1990*, 13: 361–76; and ROK-MOFA, *Taehan min'guk woegyo yŏnp'yo: 1993*, 205–9.

70. Interviews by author with *Yomiuri Shimbun* journalists who covered the South Korean and Japanese foreign ministries during the 1970s, 31 Jan., 9 July 1992, Tokyo; and Shim interview, 19 Mar. 1992.

71. See Kil et al., "*Han-Il kwan'gye ŭi chiha sumaek chindan*," 149–50; and "Japan's Korea Boom," *Korea Herald*, 8 Sept. 1988.

72. Lee Jong-suk, 92.

73. Hoffman, 489.

74. For example, the language used at bilateral meetings in the 1950s–70s was often Japanese, as the older generation of South Korean leaders had attained fluency during the occupation. This tainted every conversation with the colonial legacy. However, with the new generation of leaders either an interpreter is present at meetings or English is used (Cho interview; also see Tamaki, 354; Oh Kongdan, "Japan-Korea Rapprochement," 82–83; and Kil et al., "*Han-Il kwan'gye ŭi chiha sumaek chindan*," 145).

75. Russett, 30.

76. For a study of this during the Rhee years see Cheong. A contemporary example is the multimillion dollar project to raze the National Museum in central Seoul, formerly the structure that housed Japanese occupation headquarters. In addition, in the spring 1992 legislative elections a handful of candidates ran on anti-Japan platforms (albeit with limited success).

77. See Kim Sŏnyŏp.

78. Lee Jong-suk, 89.

79. *FEER*, 12 June 1997 (Allan Song, "Diplomacy and Yakuza Films").

80. In particular Akihito stated: "I think of the suffering your people underwent during the unfortunate period, which was brought about by my country, and cannot help but feel the deepest regret" (for this text and the apologies by the former premiers see ROK-MOFA, *Ilbon kaehwang*, 365). ROK officials admitted that this was a more direct statement of contrition than the 1984 Shōwa apology (see statements by presidential advisor Kim Chong-whi in *Korea Newsreview*, 26 May 1990). For very positive ROK reactions to Hashimoto's 1996 apology see *Korea Herald*, 25 June 1996 ("Looking Ahead").

81. See ROK-MOFA, *Ilbon kaehwang*, 353–55. The former example refers to 1991 agreements that exempted third-generation Korean residents from the much-despised fingerprinting registration required of previous generations. South Koreans perceived this as an important first step toward more democratic and equitable treatment of the ethnic Korean minority in Japan (also see Lee

Jung-hoon, 175–76; *New York Times*, 11 Jan. 1991 ["Japan Eases Rule on Korean Aliens"]). Regarding the latter example, in January 1992 historical records were found implicating the Japanese Imperial Army in conscripting Korean women to serve in "comfort stations" during the Second World War. Tokyo had previously denied any responsibility, asserting that private companies were involved in these practices (*Han'gyŏre Sinmun*, 17 Jan. 1992; and *Korea Herald*, 15, 17–18 Jan. 1992). Although this issue represented an emotional powderkeg for relations, the two governments conducted dialogue in a businesslike fashion. There was no emotional invective from Seoul, and immediately after the revelations Japanese Premier Miyazawa offered an uncharacteristically prompt apology. Tokyo also committed to revising history textbooks to include explicit recognition of Japanese wartime aggression and supported compensation of *chŏngsintae* victims through private organizations (Cho interview; and Shim interview, 19 Mar. 1992). See *Han'gyŏre Sinmun*, 17 Jan. 1992, for criticism by women's and human rights groups of Seoul's atypically subdued attitude during this dispute.

82. Bridges, 63; *Chosŏn Ilbo*, 15 Apr. 1997; *Korea Herald*, 25 June 1996 ("Japan Offers Joint History Study with Korea") and 15 July 1997 ("Korea, Japan to Hold Research Talks").

83. Cho interview; and anonymous official of the Japanese embassy in Seoul, political section, interview by author, 15 Mar. 1992, Seoul.

84. *Korea Herald*, 25 June 1996 ("Looking Ahead").

85. See *FEER*, 11 Nov. 1993 (Charles Smith, "New Men, Old Ghosts").

86. This included a major policy initiative in March 1991 to invest $2.13 billion in development of targeted technological fields through 1995 and an earlier initiative requiring Korean conglomerates to establish technology research centers, now numbering in the range of 150. See *Korea Newsreview*, 23 Mar. 1991; also see *FEER*, 14 Feb. 1991, 62 (Mark Clifford, "Samsung's Springboard"); and Kim Dong-hyun, 20–27.

87. See *Korea Newsreview*, 25 Jan. 1992; and *Korea Times*, 15 Oct. 1991, 8 ("ROK, Japan Businessmen to Expand Technological Cooperation"); and *Korea Update* 3, no. 2 (27 Jan. 1992).

88. Lee, *Japan Faces China*; and Morley, *Japan and Korea*.

89. Lee, *Japan and Korea*; and Whiting, *China Eyes Japan*.

Works Cited

Acheson, Dean. *Present at Creation: My Years in the State Department.* New York: Norton, 1969.

Advisory Group on Defense Issues. *The Modality of the Security and Defense Capability of Japan: Outlook for the 21st Century,* 12 Aug. 1994.

Ahn, Byong-man. "The Internal Political Change in Japan and Its Foreign Policy Toward Korea." *Korea and World Affairs* 2, no. 2 (summer 1978): 179–97.

Ahn, Byung-joon. "Japanese Policy Toward Korea." In Gerald L. Curtis, ed., *Japan's Foreign Policy After the Cold War,* 263–73. Armonk, N.Y.: Sharpe, 1993.

———. "Political and Economic Development in Korea and Korea-Japan Relations." In Chin-wee Chung, Ky-moon Ohm, Suk-ryul Yu, and Dal-joong Chang, eds., *Korea and Japan in World Politics.* Seoul: Korean Association of International Relations, 1985.

———. "The Security Situation on the Korean Peninsula in Global Perspective." In Bae-ho Hahn, ed., *Korea-Japan Relations in Transition.* Seoul: Asiatic Research Center, Korea University, 1982.

———. "The United States and Korean-Japanese Relations." In Gerald Curtis and Sung-joo Han, eds., *The U.S.-South Korean Alliance: Evolving Patterns in Security Relations.* Lexington, Mass.: Heath, 1983.

Aichi, Kiichi. "Japan's Destiny of Change." *Foreign Affairs* 48, no. 1 (Oct. 1969): 21–38.

Albright, David, and Mark Hibbs. "North Korea's Plutonium Puzzle." *The Bulletin of the Atomic Scientists* 48, no. 6 (Nov. 1992): 37–40.

———. "What's North Korea Up To, Anyway?" *The Bulletin of the Atomic Scientists* 47, no. 6 (Dec. 1991): 10–11.

Armacost, Michael H. *Friends or Rivals? The Insider's Account of U.S.-Japan Relations.* New York: Columbia University Press, 1996.

Baerwald, Hans. "Aspects of Sino-Japanese Normalization." *Pacific Community* 4, no. 2 (Jan. 1973): 195–203.

Baldwin, Frank. "US-Japan-South Korea Relations—Japan: Roadblock on the Way out of Korea." *Korean Review* 2, nos. 4–5 (July–Oct. 1978): 111–19.

Ball, Desmond. "Arms and Affluence: Military Acquisitions in the Asia-Pacific Region." *International Security* 18, no. 3 (winter 1993–94): 78–112.

Barnett, A. Doak. "The Changing Strategic Balance in Asia." In Gene T. Hsiao, ed., *Sino-American Detente and Its Policy Implications*. New York: Praeger, 1974.

Barnett, Michael, and Jack Levy. "Domestic Sources of Alliances and Alignments: The Case of Egypt, 1962–1973." *International Organization* 45, no. 3 (summer 1991): 369–95.

Bedeski, Robert. *The Transformation of South Korea: Reform and Reconstruction in the Sixth Republic Under Roh Tae Woo 1987–1992*. London: Routledge, 1994.

Bell, Coral. *President Carter and Foreign Policy: The Cost of Virtue*. Canberra: Australian National University Press, 1980.

Bennett, Andrew, Joseph Lepgold, and Daniel Unger. "Burden-sharing in the Persian Gulf War." *International Organization* 48, no. 1 (winter 1994): 39–75.

Berger, Thomas U. "From Sword to Chrysanthemum: Japan's Culture of Anti-Militarism." *International Security* 17, no. 4 (spring 1993): 119–50.

Bermudez, Joseph. "N. Korea: Set to Join the Nuclear Club?" *Jane's Defence Weekly* (23 Sept. 1989).

Bernstein, Thomas, and Andrew Nathan. "The Soviet Union, China, and Korea." In Gerald Curtis and Han Sung-joo, eds., *The U.S.-South Korean Alliance*, 89–128. Lexington, Mass.: Heath, 1983.

Betts, Richard. "Wealth, Power, and Instability: East Asia and the United States After the Cold War." *International Security* 18, no. 3 (winter 1993–94): 34–77.

Bix, Herbert. "Regional Integration: Japan and South Korea in America's Asian Policy." In Frank Baldwin, ed., *Without Parallel: The American-Korean Relationship Since 1945*. New York: Pantheon, 1974.

Blaker, Michael K. "US-Japanese Security Relations." In *Framework for an Alliance: Options for US-Japanese Security Relations, Report of the Task Forces of the United Nations Association of the USA and the Asia-Pacific Association of Japan, UNA-USA Policy Panel Report*. New York: United Nations Association of the USA and the Asia-Pacific Association of Japan, Aug. 1975.

Boettcher, Robert. *Gifts of Deceit: Sun Myung Moon, Tongsun Park, and the Korean Scandal*. New York: Holt, Rinehart and Winston, 1980.

Bridges, Brian. *Japan and Korea in the 1990s: From Antagonism to Adjustment*. Cambridge: Cambridge University Press, 1993.

Brown, Michael, ed. *Debating the Democratic Peace*. Cambridge, Mass.: MIT Press, 1996.

Bueno de Mesquita, Bruce, and J. David Singer. "Alliances, Capabilities, and War." In *Political Science Annual*. Vol. 4. New York: Bobbs-Merrill, 1973.

Burleson, Hugh. "The Nixon Doctrine in Northeast Asia: Strategic Implications of Japanese Reactions." Monograph of the United States Army War College, Carlisle Barracks, Pa., 18 Apr. 1973.

"Business Potentials in China," *Japan Quarterly* 18, no. 4 (Oct.–Dec. 1971): 380–83.

Buzan, Barry. "Japan's Defence Problematique." *Pacific Review* 8, no. 1 (1995): 25–43.

Carpenter, William M., James E. Dornan, Jr., Garrett N. Scalera, and Richard G. Stillwell. *US Strategy in Northeast Asia*. Report of the Strategic Studies Center, SRI International. Arlington, Va.: SRI International, 1978.

Cha, Victor D. "Bridging the Gap: The Strategic Context of Korea-Japan Normalization." *Korean Studies* 20 (1996): 123–60.

———. "Forgotten by History: The Plight of the *P'ip'okja*." *Fulbright Korea* 1, no. 7 (May 1992): 3.

———. "The Geneva Framework Agreement and Korea's Future." EAI Reports. New York: East Asian Institute, Columbia University, June 1995.

———. "National Unification: The Long and Winding Road." *In Depth* 4, no. 2 (spring 1994): 89–123.

———. "1965 nyŏn Hanil sugyo hyŏpchŏng ch'egyŏle taehan hyŏnsil juuijŏk koch'al" (A Realist analysis of the conclusion to the 1965 Korea-Japan normalization negotiation). *Han'guk kwa kukje chŏngch'i* 13, no. 1 (spring/summer 1997): 263–97.

———. "Politics and Democracy Under the Kim Young Sam Government: Something Old, Something New." *Asian Survey* 33, no. 9 (Sept. 1993): 849–63.

———. "Realism, Liberalism, and the Durability of the U.S.-South Korean Alliance." *Asian Survey* 37, no. 7 (July 1997): 609–22.

Cha, Young-koo. "U.S.-ROK Security Relations: A Korean Perspective." In Robert Scalapino and Sung-joo Han, eds., *United States–Korean Relations*. Berkeley: University of California Press, 1986.

Chan, Paul Huen. "From Colony to Neighbor: Relations Between Japan and South Korea, 1945–1985." Ph.D. diss., Johns Hopkins University, 1988.

Chan, Steve. *East Asian Dynamism: Growth, Order, and Security in the Pacific Region*. 2nd ed. Boulder, Colo.: Westview, 1993.

Chang, Dal-joong. "Integration and Conflict in Japan's Corporate Expansion into South Korea." *Korea and World Affairs* 7, no. 1 (spring 1983): 114–36.

Cheng, Dean. "The North Korean Nuclear Program and Japan." Working Paper of the MIT Japan Program (MITJP 92-08). Aug. 1992.

Cheong, Sung-hwa. *The Politics of Anti-Japanese Sentiment in Korea: Japanese-South Korean Relations Under the American Occupation, 1949–1952*. New York: Greenwood Press, 1991.

Cho, Soon. "A Korean View of Korean-Japan Economic Relations." In Chinwee Chung, Ky-moon Ohm, Suk-ryul Yu, and Dal-joong Chang, eds., *Korea and Japan in World Politics*. Seoul: Korean Association of International Relations, 1985.

Christensen, Thomas J. "Perceptions and Alliances in Europe, 1865–1940." *International Organization* 51, no. 1 (winter 1997): 65–97.

Christensen, Thomas J., and Jack Snyder. "Chain Gangs and Passed Bucks: Predicting Alliance Patterns in Multipolarity." *International Organization* 44, no. 2 (spring 1990): 137–68.

"Chronology of Relations Between Korea and Japan: 1965–1984." *Korea and World Affairs* 8, no. 3 (fall 1984): 685–715.

Clark, Donald, ed. *The Kwangju Uprising.* Boulder, Colo.: Westview, 1988.

Claude, Inis L., Jr. *Power and International Relations.* New York: Random House, 1962.

Clifford, Mark L. *Troubled Tiger: Businessmen, Bureaucrats, and Generals in South Korea.* Armonk, N.Y.: Sharpe, 1994.

Clough, Ralph N. *East Asia and U.S. Security.* Washington, D.C.: Brookings Institution, 1975.

Colbert, Evelyn. "Japan and the Republic of Korea: Yesterday, Today, and Tomorrow." *Asian Survey* 26, no. 3 (Mar. 1986): 273–91.

Conroy, Hilary. *The Japanese Seizure of Korea 1868–1910.* Philadelphia: University of Pennsylvania Press, 1960.

Cotton, James, ed. *Politics and Policy in the New Korean State.* New York: St. Martin's, 1995.

Cross, John G. "Some Theoretical Characteristics of Economic and Political Coalitions." *Journal of Conflict Resolution* 11, no. 2 (June 1967): 184–95.

Cumings, Bruce. "American Hegemony in Northeast Asia." In Morris H. Morley, ed., *Crisis and Confrontation: Ronald Reagan's Foreign Policy.* Totowa, N.J.: Rowman and Littlefield, 1988.

———. *Korea's Place in the Sun: A Modern History.* New York: Norton, 1997.

Curtis, Gerald. "The Tyumen Oil Development Project and Japanese Foreign Policy Decision-Making." In Robert A. Scalapino, ed., *The Foreign Policy of Modern Japan.* Berkeley: University of California Press, 1977.

Dahl, Robert A. *Polyarchy: Participation and Opposition.* New Haven: Yale University Press, 1971.

David, Stephen. "Explaining Third World Alignment." *World Politics* 43, no. 2 (Jan. 1991): 233–56.

Davies, Derek. "Will Japan's Accommodation with China Work?" *Pacific Community* 4, no. 3 (Apr. 1973): 340–55.

Dawson, Raymond, and Richard Rosecrance. "Theory and Reality in the Anglo-American Alliance." *World Politics* 19, no. 1 (Oct. 1966): 21–51.

DeConde, Alexander. *A History of American Foreign Policy.* Vol. 1. New York: Charles Scribner's Sons, 1978.

Direction of Trade. Vols. for 1967, 1975. Washington, D.C.: International Monetary Fund.

Direction of Trade Statistics. Vols. for 1981, 1988, 1995. Washington, D.C.: International Monetary Fund.

Dixon, William. "Democracy and the Peaceful Settlement of International Conflict." *American Political Science Review* 88, no. 1 (Mar. 1994): 14–32.

Dollar, David. "South Korea-China Trade Relations: Problems and Prospects." *Asian Survey* 29, no. 12 (Dec. 1989): 1167–76.

Doyle, Michael. "Liberalism and World Politics." *American Political Science Review* 80 (Dec. 1986): 1151–69.

Drezner, Dan. *Economic Statecraft and International Relations.* Cambridge: Cambridge University Press, forthcoming.

Duffield, John. "International Regimes and Alliance Behavior: Explaining NATO Conventional Force Levels." *International Organization* 46, no. 4 (autumn 1992): 819–55.

Duncan, George, and Randolph M. Siverson. "Flexibility of Alliance Partner Choice in a Multipolar System." *International Studies Quarterly* 26, no. 4 (Dec. 1982): 511–38.

Eckert, Carter J., Ki-baik Lee, Young Ick Lew, Michael Robinson, and Edward W. Wagner. *Korea Old and New: A History.* Seoul: Ilchokak and Harvard University, 1990.

Eckstein, Harry. "Case Studies and Theory in Political Science." In Fred I. Greenstein and Nelson W. Polsby, eds., *Handbook of Political Science.* Vol. 7. Reading, Mass.: Addison-Wesley, 1975.

Emmerson, John K. *Arms, Yen and Power: The Japanese Dilemma.* New York: Dunellen, 1971.

———. *The Japanese Thread: A Life in the U.S. Foreign Service.* New York: Holt, Rinehart and Winston, 1978.

———. "The United States and Japan: Uneasy Partnership?" *Pacific Community* 3, no. 4 (July 1972): 625–35.

Emmerson, John K., and Harrison M. Holland. *The Eagle and the Rising Sun: America and Japan in the Twentieth Century.* Stanford, Calif.: Stanford Alumni Association, 1987.

Farnham, Barbara. "Single Case Studies and Theory Building: The Historical Case Study as a Plausibility Probe." Paper presented at Hunter College, 8 Mar. 1990.

Farnsworth, Lee. "Japan: The Year of the Shock." *Asian Survey* 12, no. 1 (Jan. 1972): 46–55.

———. "Japan 1972: New Faces and New Friends." *Asian Survey* 13, no. 1 (Jan. 1973): 113–25.

Fitzpatrick, Mark. "Why Japan and the United States Will Welcome Korean Unification." *Korea and World Affairs* 15, no. 3 (fall 1991): 415–41.

Foster-Carter, Aidan. *Korea's Coming Reunification: Another East Asian Superpower?* Economist Intelligence Unit, Special Report no. M212. London: Economist Intelligence Unit, Apr. 1992.

Fox, William T. R., and Annette Baker Fox. *NATO and the Range of American Choice.* New York: Columbia University Press, 1962.

Freeman, Charles, Jr. "The Process of Rapprochement: Achievements and Problems." In Gene T. Hsiao and Michael Witunski, eds., *Sino-American Normalization and Its Policy Implications.* New York: Praeger, 1983.

Friedberg, Aaron. "Ripe for Rivalry: Prospects for Peace in a Multipolar Asia." *International Security* 18, no. 3 (winter 1993–94): 5–33.

Fuccello, Charles. "South Korean-Japanese Relations in the Cold War: A Journey to Normalization." Ph.D. diss., New School for Social Research, 1977.

Fukuda, Takeo. "The Future of Japan-US Relations." *Pacific Community* 3, no. 2 (Jan. 1972): 237–46.

———. "Japan in the 1970's." *Pacific Community* 1, no. 2 (Jan. 1970): 137–48.

Fukui, Haruhiro. *Party in Power: The Japanese Liberal Democrats and Policy Making.* Berkeley: University of California Press, 1970.

———. "Tanaka Goes to Peking." In T. J. Pempel, ed., *Policymaking in Contemporary Japan.* Ithaca: Cornell University Press, 1977.

Gail, Bridget. "The Korean Balance and the U.S. Withdrawal." *Armed Forces Journal International* (Apr. 1978).

Garthoff, Raymond L. *Detente and Confrontation: American-Soviet Relations from Nixon to Reagan.* Washington, D.C.: Brookings Institution, 1985.

George, Alexander. "Case Studies and Theory Development: The Method of Structured Focused Comparison." In Paul Gordon Lauren, ed., *Diplomacy: New Approaches.* New York: Free Press, 1979.

Gibney, Frank. "The Ripple Effect in Korea." *Foreign Affairs* 56, no. 1 (Oct. 1977): 160–74.

Glaser, Bonnie. "China's Security Perceptions: Interests and Ambitions." *Asian Survey* 33, no. 3 (Mar. 1993): 252–71.

Gleysteen, William. "The United States and South Korea." In *Asia Society Media Briefings.* New York: Asia Society, 1983.

Goldstein, Avery. "Discounting the Free Ride: Alliances and Security in the Postwar World." *International Organization* 49, no. 1 (winter 1995): 39–71.

Gonzalez, Edward. "Castro's Revolution, Cuban Communist Appeals, and the Soviet Response." *World Politics* 21, no. 1 (Oct. 1968): 39–68.

Grajdanzev, Andrew. *Modern Korea.* New York: Day, 1944.

Graves, James E. "If South Korea Falls, Will Japan Be Next?" U.S. Army War College, Carlisle Barracks, Pa., Oct. 17, 1975. Photocopy.

Green, Marshall. "Mutual Trust and Security in US-Japan Relations." *Department of State Bulletin* (18 Dec. 1972): 703–7.

Green, Michael. "U.S.-Japan-ROK Trilateral Security Cooperation: Prospects and Pitfalls." Paper presented at the annual meeting of the American Political Science Association, Washington, D.C., 28–31 Aug. 1997.

Gregor, A. James. *Land of the Morning Calm: Korean and American Security.* Boston: University Press of America, 1990.

Grinter, Lawrence. "East Asia and the United States into the 21st Century." *CADRE Report.* Maxwell Air Force Base, Ala., Nov. 1991.

Gulick, Edward. *Europe's Classical Balance of Power.* New York: Norton, 1967.

Hahn, Bae-ho. "Asian International Politics and the Future of Korea-Japan Relations." In Bae-ho Hahn, ed., *Korea-Japan Relations: Issues and Future Prospects.* Seoul: Asiatic Research Center, Korea University, 1980.

———. "Japan's International Role: Asian and Non-Asian Views." In Bae-ho

Hahn, ed., *Korea-Japan Relations in Transition: Challenges and Opportunities*. Seoul: Asiatic Research Center, Korea University, 1982.

———. "Policy Toward Japan." In Youngnok Koo and Sung-joo Han, eds., *The Foreign Policy of the Republic of Korea*. New York: Columbia University Press, 1985.

———, ed. *Korea-Japan Relations in Transition: Challenges and Opportunities*. Seoul: Asiatic Research Center, Korea University, 1982.

———, ed. *Korea-Japan Relations: Issues and Future Prospects*. Seoul: Asiatic Research Center, Korea University, 1980.

Hahn, Bae-ho, and Tadashi Yamamoto, eds. *Korea-Japan Relations: A New Dialogue Across the Channel*. Seoul: Asiatic Research Center, Korea University, 1978.

Han, Luke. "Han: Unquenched Woes of the Oppressed." *Korea Times*, 5 Dec. 1990.

Han, Sung-joo. "Convergent and Divergent Interests in Korean-Japanese Relations." In Bae-ho Hahn, ed., *Korea-Japan Relations in Transition: Challenges and Opportunities*. Seoul: Asiatic Research Center, Korea University, 1982.

———. "Korea's Democratic Experiment, 1987–1991." In *Democratic Institutions: 1992*. Vol. 1. New York: Carnegie Council on Ethics and International Affairs, 1991.

———. "South Korea in 1974: The Korean 'Democracy' on Trial." *Asian Survey* 15, no. 1 (Jan. 1975): 35–42.

———. "South Korea: 1977, Preparing for Self-Reliance." *Asian Survey* 18, no. 1 (Jan. 1978): 45–57.

———. "South Korea and the United States: Past, Present, and Future." In Gerald Curtis and Sung-joo Han, eds., *The U.S.-South Korean Alliance*. Lexington, Mass.: Heath, 1983.

———. "South Korea's Participation in the Vietnam Conflict: An Analysis of the US-Korean Alliance." *Orbis* 21, no. 4 (winter 1978): 893–912.

Han, Sung-joo, and Yung-chul Park. "South Korea: Democratization at Last." In James W. Morley, ed., *Driven By Growth: Political Change in the Asia-Pacific Region*. Armonk, N.Y.: Sharpe, 1993.

Han, Y. C. "The 1969 Constitutional Revision and Party Politics in South Korea." *Pacific Affairs* 44, no. 2 (summer 1971): 242–58.

Hanai, Hitoshi. "An Open Korean Peninsula." Translated in *Japan Echo* 2, no. 4 (1975): 111–20.

Han-Il kwan'gye charyojip (Collected materials on Korea-Japan relations). Vols. 1 and 2. Seoul: Asiatic Research Center, Korea University, 1977.

Hao, Jia, and Shuang Qubing. "China's Policy Toward the Korean Peninsula." *Asian Survey* 32, no. 12 (Dec. 1992): 1137–56.

Harako, Rinjaro. "Japan-Soviet Relations and Japan's Choice." *Pacific Community* 4, no. 1 (Oct. 1972): 79–96.

Harrison, Selig. "The North Korean Nuclear Crisis: From Stalemate to Breakthrough." *Arms Control Today* (Nov. 1994): 18–20.

Havens, Thomas R. H. *Fire Across the Sea: The Vietnam War and Japan 1965–1975*. Princeton: Princeton University Press, 1987.

Hayashi, Risuke. "Where Do We Go From Here?" *Japan Quarterly* 21, no. 3 (July–Sept. 1974): 258–64.

Hellmann, Donald C. *Japan and East Asia: The New International Order*. New York: Praeger, 1972.

————. "Japanese Security and Postwar Japanese Foreign Policy." In Robert A. Scalapino, ed., *The Foreign Policy of Modern Japan*. Berkeley: University of California Press, 1977.

————. "US-Korean Relations: The Japan Factor." In Robert A. Scalapino and Sung-joo Han, eds., *United States-Korea Relations*. Berkeley: University of California Press, 1986.

Henriksen, Thomas, and Kyongsoo Lho, eds. *One Korea?* Stanford, Calif.: Hoover Institution Press, 1994.

Herz, John. *Political Realism and Political Idealism*. Chicago: University of Chicago Press, 1951.

Hirasawa, Kazushige. "Japan's Future World Role and Japanese-American Relations." *Orbis* 15, no. 1 (spring 1971): 338–50.

Hirono, Ryokichi. "A Japanese View on Korea-Japan Economic Relations." In Chin-wee Chung, Ky-moon Ohm, Suk-ryul Yu, and Dal-joong Chang, eds., *Korea and Japan in World Politics*. Seoul: Korean Association of International Relations, 1985.

Hoffman, Diane. "Changing Faces, Changing Places: The New Koreans in Japan." *Japan Quarterly* 39, no. 4 (Oct.–Dec. 1992): 472–89.

Hoffmann, Stanley. "The Hell of Good Intentions." *Foreign Policy* 29 (winter 1977–78): 3–26.

Holsti, Ole R., P. Terrence Hopmann, and John D. Sullivan. *Unity and Disintegration in International Alliances: Comparative Studies*. New York: Wiley, 1973.

Hong, Sung-chick. "Japanese in the Minds of Korean People." In Bae-ho Hahn and Tadashi Yamamoto, eds., *Korea and Japan: A New Dialogue Across the Channel*. Seoul: Asiatic Research Center, Korea University, 1978.

Hsiao, Gene T. "The Sino-Japanese Rapprochement: A Relationship of Ambivalence." In Gene T. Hsiao, ed., *Sino-American Detente and Its Policy Implications*. New York: Praeger, 1974.

Hufbauer, Gary. "What Role Might the International Community Play in the Process of Korean Unification?" Paper presented at the KIEP-*Korea Herald* Conference on International Economic Implications of Korean Unification, Seoul, 28–29 June 1996.

Hughes, Thomas L. "Carter and the Management of Contradictions." *Foreign Policy* 31 (summer 1978): 34–55.

Huntington, Samuel P. "America's Changing Strategic Interests." *Survival* 33, no. 1 (Jan.–Feb. 1991): 3–17.

————. *The Third Wave: Democratization in the Late Twentieth Century*. Norman: University of Oklahoma Press, 1991.

Hurst, Cameron. "The United States and Korea-Japan Relations." In Chin-wee Chung, Ky-moon Ohm, Suk-ryul Yu, and Dal-joong Chang, eds., *Korea and Japan in World Politics*. Seoul: Korean Association of International Relations, 1985.

Huth, Paul, and Bruce Russett. "What Makes Deterrence Work? Cases from 1900 to 1980." *World Politics* 36 (Dec. 1984): 496–526.

Hwang, Eui-guk. "How Will Unification Affect Korea's Participation in the World Economy?" Paper presented at the KIEP-*Korea Herald* Conference on the International Economic Implications of Korean Unification, Seoul, 28–29 June 1996.

Imazu, Hiroshi. "A New Era in Japanese-South Korean Relations." *Japan Quarterly* 31, no. 4 (Oct.–Dec. 1984): 355–63.

———. "Uniting a Divided Korea: Will Japan Help?" *Japan Quarterly* 37, no. 2 (Apr.–June 1990): 136–44.

Itō, Kobun. "Japan's Security in the 1970's." *Asian Survey* 10, no. 12 (Dec. 1970): 1031–36.

Izumi, Hajime. "American Policy Toward North Korea and Japan's Role." In Masao Okonogi, ed., *North Korea at the Crossroads*. Tokyo: Japan Institute of International Affairs, 1988.

Jacoby, Tamar. "The Reagan Turnaround on Human Rights." *Foreign Affairs* 64, no. 5 (summer 1986): 1066–86.

Japan. Defense Agency. *Defense of Japan: White Paper, 1976 (Summary)*. Tokyo, June 1976.

———. *Defense of Japan, 1986*. Tokyo, n.d.

Japan. Ministry of Finance. *The Budget in Brief, 1970*. Tokyo, 1970.

———. *The Budget in Brief, 1971*. Tokyo, 1971.

Japan. Ministry of Foreign Affairs. Economic Affairs Bureau. *Statistical Survey of Japan's Economy*. Vols. for 1972–82. Tokyo.

Japan. Ministry of International Trade and Industry. *Statistics on Japanese Industries*. Vols. for 1967, 1972, 1975, 1978, 1982, 1989, 1991. Tokyo.

Jervis, Robert. "Cooperation Under the Security Dilemma." *World Politics* 30, no. 2 (Jan. 1978): 167–214.

———. *Perception and Misperception in International Politics*. Princeton: Princeton University Press, 1976.

Johnson, Lyndon Baines. *The Vantage Point: Perspectives of the Presidency 1963–1969*. New York: Holt, Rinehart and Winston, 1971.

Johnson, U. Alexis. *The Right Hand of Power*. Englewood Cliffs, N.J.: Prentice-Hall, 1984.

"Joint Communique Between President Richard Nixon and Prime Minister Eisaku Sato." United States Embassy transcript, Washington, D.C., 21 Nov. 1969.

Kahn, Robert A. "Alliances Versus Ententes." *World Politics* 28, no. 4 (July 1976): 611–21.

Kamiya, Fuji. "Japanese-US Relations and the Security Treaty: A Japanese Perspective." *Asian Survey* 12, no. 9 (Sept. 1972): 717–25.

———. "The US Presence in the Republic of Korea as Foreign Policy: The

Withdrawal Decision and Its Repercussions." Translated in *Japan Echo* 4, no. 3 (autumn 1977): 92–105.

Kanazawa, Masao. "Japan and the Balance of Power in Asia." *Pacific Community* 4, no. 1 (Oct. 1972): 71–78.

Kase, Hideaki. "Northeast Asian Security: A View from Japan." In Richard Foster, ed., *Security and Strategy in Northeast Asia*. New York: Crane, Russack, 1979.

Kegley, Charles, and Gregory Raymond. "Alliance Norms and War: A New Piece in an Old Puzzle." *International Studies Quarterly* 26, no. 4 (Dec. 1982): 572–95.

———. "Alliances and the Preservation of Peace: Weighing the Contribution." In Charles Kegley, ed., *The Long Postwar Peace: Contending Explanations and Projections*. New York: HarperCollins, 1991.

Keohane, Robert O. "The Big Influence of Small Allies." *Foreign Policy*, no. 2 (spring 1971): 161–82.

———. *International Institutions and State Power*. Boulder, Colo.: Westview, 1989.

Kiga, Kenzo. "Russo-Japanese Economic Cooperation and Its International Environment." *Pacific Community* 4, no. 3 (Apr. 1973): 452–70.

Kihl, Young-whan, ed. *Korea and the World: Beyond the Cold War*. Boulder, Colo.: Westview, 1994.

Kil, Soong-hoom. "Japan in American-Korean Relations." In Koo Youngnok and Suh Dae-sook, eds., *Korea and the U.S.: A Century of Cooperation*. Honolulu: University of Hawaii Press, 1984.

———. "South Korean Policy Toward Japan." *Journal of Northeast Asian Studies* 2, no. 3 (Sept. 1983): 35–51.

———. "Two Aspects of Korea-Japan Relations." *Korea and World Affairs* 8, no. 3 (fall 1984): 505–13.

Kil Sŭnghŭm (Kil Soong-hoom). "Han-Il kukkyo chŏngsanghwa 20-nyŏn ŭi pansŏng" (Reflections on 20 years of normalization between Korea and Japan). *Sin Tong-A* (June 1985): 146–53.

Kil Sŭnghŭm, Yun Chŏngsŏk, and Hwang Pyŏngnyŏl. "Han-Il kwan'gye ŭi chiha sumaek chindan" (Examining the hidden pulse of Korea-Japan relations). *Chŏnggyŏng Munhwa* (Sept. 1984): 144–55.

Kim, C. I. Eugene. "Emergency, Development, and Human Rights: South Korea." *Asian Survey* 28, no. 4 (Apr. 1978): 363–78.

Kim, Dong-hyun. "The Development of Indigenous Science and Technology Capabilities in Korea." *Korea Journal* 30, no. 2 (Feb. 1990): 20–27.

Kim, Hong-nak. "Japanese-Korean Relations in the 1980s." *Asian Survey* 27, no. 2 (May 1987): 497–514.

———. "Japanese-North Korean Relations: Problems and Prospects." *Korea Observer* 22, no. 2 (summer 1991): 189–205.

———. "Japanese-South Korean Relations After the Park Assassination." *Journal of Northeast Asian Studies* 1, no. 4 (Dec. 1982): 71–90.

———. "Japanese-South Korean Relations in the 1980s." *Korea Observer* 16, no. 2 (summer 1985): 117–33.

———. "Japan's Policy Toward the Korean Peninsula Since 1965." In Tae-hwan Kwak and Wayne Patterson, eds., *The Two Koreas in World Politics*. Seoul: Kyungnam University Press, 1983.

Kim, Hosup. "The End of the Cold War and Korea-Japan Relations: Old Perceptions, New Issues." In Manwoo Lee and Richard Mansbach, eds., *The Changing Order in Northeast Asia and the Korean Peninsula*. Seoul: Institute for Far Eastern Studies, Kyungnam University, 1993.

———. "Policy-Making of Japanese Official Development Assistance to the Republic of Korea, 1965–1983." Ph.D. diss., University of Michigan, 1987.

Kim, Jiyul. "U.S. and Korea in Vietnam and the Japan-Korea Treaty: Search for Security, Prosperity, and Influence." M.A. thesis, Harvard University, 1991.

Kim, Kwan-bong. *The Korea-Japan Treaty Crisis and the Instability of the Korean Political System*. New York: Praeger, 1971.

Kim, Se-jin. *The Politics of Military Revolution in Korea*. Chapel Hill: University of North Carolina Press, 1971.

Kim Sŏnyŏp. "Waesaek munhwa, Han'guksŏ hwalkaetchit" (Japanese culture swaggers in Korea). *Sisa Chŏnŏl* (23 Aug. 1990).

Kim Tongjo (Kim Dong-jo). *Hoesang Samsimnyŏn, Han-Il Hoedam* (Recollections of thirty years of Korea-Japan talks). Seoul: Chungang Ilbosa, 1986.

Kim Tongsŏn. "Ilbon ŭn uri ege muŏsinga" (What Japan means to us). *Sisa Chŏnŏl* (23 Aug. 1990).

Kim, Young C., ed. *Major Powers in Korea*. Silver Springs, Md.: Research Institute on Korean Affairs, 1973.

Kimura, Toshio. "New Directions for Japanese Diplomacy." Translated in *Japan Echo* 2, no. 2 (1975): 108–17.

Kirkpatrick, Jeane J. *The Reagan Phenomenon*. Washington, D.C.: American Enterprise Institute, 1983.

Kissinger, Henry. *White House Years*. New York: Little, Brown, 1979.

Ko, Seung-kyun. "Japan and Two Koreas: Japanese Policy Toward South Korea's New Nordpolitik." *Korea Observer* 22, no. 2 (summer 1991): 173–88.

Kobayashi, Katsumi. "The Nixon Doctrine and US-Japanese Relations." Paper presented at the Conference on the Future of U.S.-Japanese Relations, Palm Springs, California, Arms Control and Foreign Policy Seminar, 5–8 Jan. 1975.

Kobayashi, Keiji, Yamaoka Kunihiro, Yasuo Yoshiteru, and Hong In'gun. "Han-Il ŭng'ŏri nŭn min'gan kyoryuro p'urŏya" (The Korea-Japan tangle must be untied by people-to-people exchange). *Sin Tong-A* (June 1985): 260–75.

Koh, Byung-chul. *The Foreign Policy Systems of North and South Korea*. Berkeley: University of California Press, 1984.

———. "The *Pueblo* Incident in Perspective." *Asian Survey* 9, no. 4 (Apr. 1969): 264–80.

———. "Trends in North Korean Foreign Policy." *Journal of Northeast Asian Studies* 13, no. 2 (summer 1994): 61–74.

Korea-Japan Relations and the Attempt on the Life of Korea's President. Seoul: Pan-National Council for the Probe into the August 15 [1974] Incident, n.d.

Kubota, Akira. "Transferring Technology to Asia." *Japan Quarterly* 33, no. 1 (Jan. 1986): 37–44.

Langdon, Frank C. *Japan's Foreign Policy*. Vancouver: University of British Columbia Press, 1973.

Lee, Chae-jin. *Japan Faces China: Political and Economic Relations in the Postwar Era*. Baltimore: Johns Hopkins University Press, 1976.

Lee, Chae-jin, and Hideo Sato. *US Policy Toward Japan and Korea: A Changing Influence Partnership*. New York: Praeger, 1982.

Lee, Changsoo, and George de Vos. *Koreans in Japan: Ethnic Conflict and Accommodation*. Berkeley: University of California Press, 1981.

Lee, Chong-sik. "The Impact of the Sino-American Detente on Korea." In Gene T. Hsiao, ed., *Sino-American Detente and Its Policy Implications*. New York: Praeger, 1974.

———. *Japan and Korea: The Political Dimension*. Stanford, Calif.: Hoover Institution Press, 1985.

———. "South Korea in 1980: The Emergence of a New Authoritarian Order." *Asian Survey* 21, no. 1 (Jan. 1981): 125–43.

Lee, Hy-sang. "Japanese-South Korean Economic Relations on Troubled Economic Waters." *Korea Observer* 16, no. 2 (summer 1985): 166–88.

Lee, Jong-suk. "Measures on the Import of Japanese Pop Culture." *Korea Focus* 5, no. 1 (Jan.–Feb. 1997): 83–96.

Lee, Jung-hoon. "Korean-Japanese Relations: The Past, Present, and Future." *Korea Observer* 21, no. 2 (summer 1990): 159–78.

Lee, Ki-baik. *A New History of Korea*. Cambridge, Mass.: Harvard University Press, 1984.

Lee, Manwoo. "Double Patronage Toward South Korea: Security Vs. Democracy and Human Rights." In Manwoo Lee, Ronald McLaurin, and Chung-in Moon, *Alliance Under Tension: The Evolution of South-Korean-U.S. Relations*. Boulder, Colo.: Westview and Kyungnam University, 1988.

———. *The Odyssey of Korean Democracy*. New York: Praeger, 1990.

Lee, Seo-hang. "Naval Power as an Instrument of Foreign Policy: The Case of Korea." *Korea Focus* 5, no. 2 (March–April 1997): 26–36.

LeFever, Ernest. "Carter, Korea, and the Decline of the West." *Korea and World Affairs* 1, no. 3 (fall 1977): 245–57.

Levin, Norman D., and Richard L. Sneider. "Korea in Postwar U.S. Security Policy." In Gerald Curtis and Sung-joo Han, eds., *The U.S.-South Korean Alliance*. Lexington, Mass.: Heath, 1983.

Levy, Jack. "Alliance Formation and War Behavior: An Analysis of the Great Powers, 1495–1975." *Journal of Conflict Resolution* 25 (Dec. 1981): 581–613.

Lijphart, Arend. "Comparative Politics and the Comparative Method." *American Political Science Review* 65, no. 3 (Sept. 1971): 682–93.

Liska, George. *Nations in Alliance: The Limits of Interdependence*. Baltimore: Johns Hopkins University Press, 1962.

Mack, Andrew. "North Korea and the Bomb." *Foreign Policy* 83 (summer 1991): 87–104.

Makato, Momoi. "Basic Trends in Japanese Security Policies." In Robert A. Scalapino, ed., *The Foreign Policy of Modern Japan*. Berkeley: University of California Press, 1977.

Mandelbaum, Michael. *The Nuclear Revolution: International Politics Before and After Hiroshima*. New York: Cambridge University Press, 1981.

Manning, Robert, and Paula Stern. "The Myth of the Pacific Community." *Foreign Affairs* 73, no. 6 (Nov.–Dec. 1994): 79–93.

Maruyama, Shizuo. "The Nixon Doctrine and Ping-Pong Diplomacy." *Japan Quarterly* 18, no. 3 (July–Sept. 1971): 266–72.

Matsumoto, Shunichi. "Our Neighbor China." *Japan Quarterly* 18, no. 2 (Apr.–June 1971): 148–54.

Mazarr, Michael. "Going Just a Little Nuclear: Nonproliferation Lessons from North Korea." *International Security* 20, no. 2 (fall 1995): 92–122.

McCalla, Robert. "NATO's Persistence After the Cold War." *International Organization* 50, no. 3 (summer 1996): 445–76.

McKinney, William Robert. "Japan-South Korean Relations Under the Nixon Doctrine." M.A. thesis, University of Colorado, 1972.

McNaugher, Thomas. "Reforging Northeast Asia's Dagger?" *The Brookings Review* 2, no. 3 (summer 1993): 12–17.

Mearsheimer, John. "The Case for a Ukrainian Nuclear Deterrent." *Foreign Affairs* 72, no. 3 (summer 1993): 50–66.

———. "The False Promise of International Institutions." *International Security* 19, no. 3 (winter 1994–95): 5–49.

Mercer, Jonathan. *Reputation and International Politics*. Ithaca: Cornell University Press, 1996.

Meyer, Armin. *Assignment Tokyo: An Ambassador's Journal*. New York: Bobbs-Merrill, 1974.

The Military Balance 1996–97. London: International Institute for Strategic Studies, Oct. 1996.

Miyazawa, Kiichi. "Japan's Diplomacy in Today's World." Speech presented by Foreign Minister Miyazawa Kiichi at the Foreign Correspondents' Club of Japan, Tokyo, 10 July 1975.

Mochizuki, Mike M. "Japan as an Asia-Pacific Power." In Robert Ross, ed., *East Asia in Transition*. Armonk, N.Y.: Sharpe, 1995.

———. "The United States and Japan: Conflict and Cooperation Under Mr. Reagan." In Kenneth A. Oye, Robert J. Lieber, and Donald Rothchild, eds., *Eagle Resurgent? The Reagan Era in American Foreign Policy*. Boston: Little, Brown, 1987.

Modelski, George. "The Study of Alliances: A Review." *Journal of Conflict Resolution* 7, no. 4 (Dec. 1963): 769–76.

Moon, Chung-in. "International Quasi-Crisis: Theory and a Case of Japan-South Korean Bilateral Friction." *Asian Perspective* 15, no. 2 (fall–winter 1992): 99–123.

Morgenthau, Hans. "Alliances in Theory and Practice." In Arnold Wolfers, ed., *Alliance Policy in the Cold War*. Baltimore: Johns Hopkins University Press, 1959.

————. *Politics Among Nations*. New York: Knopf, 1973.

Morley, James W., ed. *Driven by Growth: Political Change in the Asia-Pacific Region*. Armonk, N.Y.: Sharpe, 1993.

————. "The Dynamics of the Korean Connection." In Gerald Curtis and Sung-joo Han, eds., *The U.S.-South Korean Alliance*. Lexington, Mass.: Heath, 1983.

————. *Japan and Korea: America's Allies in the Pacific*. New York: Walker, 1965.

Morley, Morris H., ed. *Crisis and Confrontation: Ronald Reagan's Foreign Policy*. Totowa, N.J.: Rowman and Littlefield, 1988.

Morrow, James. "Arms Versus Allies: Trade-offs in the Search for Security." *International Organization* 47, no. 2 (spring 1993): 207–33.

Nacht, Michael. "United States-Japanese Relations," *Current History* 87, no. 501 (Apr. 1988): 149–54.

Nakasone Yasuhiro. "Defense of Japan." Speech presented at the Foreign Correspondents' Club of Japan, Tokyo, 1 Dec. 1970.

Nam, Joo-hong. *America's Commitment to South Korea: The First Decade of the Nixon Doctrine*. Cambridge: Cambridge University Press, 1986.

Nam, Koon Woo. *South Korean Politics: The Search for Political Consensus and Stability*. Lanham, Md.: University Press of America, 1989.

Niou, Emerson M. S., Peter C. Ordeshook, and Gregory F. Rose. *The Balance of Power: Stability in International Systems*. New York: Cambridge University Press, 1989.

Nixon, Richard. "Asia After Viet Nam." *Foreign Affairs* 46, no. 1 (Oct. 1967): 111–25.

————. *RN: Memoirs of Richard Nixon*. New York: Grosset and Dunlap, 1978.

————. *Setting the Course: The First Year, Major Policy Statements by President Richard Nixon*. Commentary by Richard Wilson. New York: Frank and Wagnalis, 1970.

————. *United States Foreign Policy for the 1970's: A New Strategy for Peace, A Report to Congress by the President of the United States*. Washington D.C.: GPO, 18 Feb. 1970.

Nogami, Tadashi. "The Korean Caper." *Japan Quarterly* 21, no. 2 (Apr.–June 1974): 160–67.

Noland, Marcus. "Modeling Economic Reform in North Korea." Paper presented at the KIEP-*Korea Herald* Conference on the International Economic Implications of Korean Unification, Seoul, 28–29 June 1996.

Nye, Joseph. "The Case for Deep Engagement." *Foreign Affairs* 74, no. 4 (July–Aug. 1995): 90–102.

Oberdorfer, Don. "North Korea and Its Not-So-Secret Weapon." *Washington Post National Weekly Edition* (2–8 Mar. 1992).

————. *The Two Koreas: A Contemporary History* (Reading, Mass.: Addison-Wesley, 1997).

————. "U.S. Policy Toward Korea in the 1987 Crisis Compared with Other Allies." In Robert A. Scalapino and Hongkoo Lee, eds., *Korea-U.S. Relations: The Politics of Trade and Security*. Berkeley: University of California Press, 1988.

Ogata, Sadako. "The Business Community and Japanese Foreign Policy: Normalization of Relations with the Peoples' Republic of China." In Robert A. Scalapino, ed., *Foreign Policy of Modern Japan*. Berkeley: University of California Press, 1977.

Oh, John Kie-chiang. "Anti-Americanism and Anti-Authoritarian Politics in Korea." *In Depth* 4, no. 2 (spring 1994), 65–82.

————. *Korea: Democracy on Trial*. Ithaca: Cornell University Press, 1968.

Oh, Kongdan. "Background and Options for Nuclear Arms Control on the Korean Peninsula." RAND Note N-3475-USDP. Prepared for the Assistant Secretary of Defense, Office of the Under Secretary of Defense for Policy. Santa Monica: RAND, 1992.

————. "Japan-Korea Rapprochement: A Study in Political, Cultural, and Economic Cooperation in the 1980's." Ph.D. diss., University of California, Berkeley, 1986.

Ohira, Masayoshi. "A New Foreign Policy for Japan." *Pacific Community* 3, no. 3 (Apr. 1972): 405–18.

Okonogi, Masao. "A Japanese Perspective on Korea-Japan Relations." In Chinwee Chung, Ky-moon Ohm, Suk-ryul Yu, and Dal-joong Chang, eds., *Korea and Japan in World Politics*. Seoul: Korean Association of International Relations, 1985.

————. "Japan-North Korean Negotiations for Normalization: An Overview." In Manwoo Lee and Richard Mansbach, eds., *The Changing Order in Northeast Asia and the Korean Peninsula*. Seoul: Institute for Far Eastern Studies, Kyungnam University, 1993.

————, ed. *North Korea at the Crossroads*. Tokyo: Japan Institute of International Affairs, 1988.

Oliver, Robert T. *Syngman Rhee: The Man Behind the Myth*. New York: Dodd Mead, 1954.

Olsen, Edward A. "Japan and Korea." In W. Arnold and R. Ozaki, eds., *Japan's Foreign Economic Relations in the 1980s*. Lexington, Mass.: Lexington Books, 1984.

————. "Japan-South Korea Security Ties," *Air University Review* 32, no. 4 (May–June 1981): 60–66.

————. "Korea's Reunification: Implications for the U.S.-ROK Alliance." In Thomas Henriksen and Kyongsoo Lho, eds., *One Korea?* Stanford, Calif.: Hoover Institution Press, 1994.

————. *U.S. Policy and the Two Koreas*. Boulder, Colo.: Westview, 1988.

Olson, Mancur, and Richard Zeckhauser. "An Economic Theory of Alliances." *Review of Economics and Statistics* 48, no. 3 (Aug. 1966): 266–79.

Oral Histories of the Johnson Administration, 1963–1969 Part I: The White

House and Executive Departments. Microfiche from the Holdings of the Lyndon Baines Johnson Library, Austin, Tex. Frederick, Md.: University Publications of America, 1986.

Osamu, Miyoshi. "Growth of Soviet Power and the Security of Japan." In Richard Foster, ed., *Strategy and Security in Northeast Asia.* New York: Crane, Russack, 1979.

Osgood, Robert E. *Alliances and American Foreign Policy.* Baltimore: Johns Hopkins University Press, 1968.

———. *The Weary and the Wary.* SAIS Studies in International Affairs, no. 10. Baltimore: Johns Hopkins University Press, 1972.

Otsuka, Umio. "Prospects of Japan-Korea Defense Cooperation: Partners or Rivals." Paper presented at the Conference on Japan-Korea-U.S. Trilateral Dialogue, Tokyo, 5–6 Dec. 1997.

Overholt, William. "President Nixon's Trip to China and Its Consequences." *Asian Survey* 13, no. 7 (July 1973): 707–21.

Owen, John M. "How Liberalism Produces Democratic Peace." *International Security* 19, no. 2 (fall 1994): 87–125.

———. *Liberal Peace, Liberal War: American Politics and International Security.* Ithaca: Cornell University Press, 1997.

Oxnam, Robert. "Sino-American Relations in Historical Perspective." In Michel Oksenberg and Robert Oxnam, eds., *Dragon and Eagle, US-China Relations: Past and Future.* New York: Basic Books, 1978.

Oye, Kenneth. "Constrained Confidence and the Evolution of Reagan Foreign Policy." In Kenneth Oye, Robert Lieber, and Donald Rothchild, eds., *Eagle Resurgent? The Reagan Era in American Foreign Policy.* Boston: Little, Brown, 1987.

Paal, Douglas. "The Regional Political Context of Korean Unification." Paper presented at the KIEP-*Korea Herald* Conference on International Economic Implications of Korean Unification, Seoul, 28–29 June 1996.

Packard, George. *Protest in Tokyo: The Security Treaty Crisis of 1960.* Princeton: Princeton University Press, 1966.

Park, Chang-jin. "The Influence of Small States on the Superpowers." *World Politics* 28, no. 1 (Oct. 1975): 97–117.

Park, Yung H. "Japan's Perspectives and Expectations Regarding America's Role in Korea." *Orbis* 20, no. 3 (fall 1976): 761–84.

Pharr, Susan J. "Japan's Defensive Foreign Policy and the Politics of Burden-Sharing." In Gerald Curtis, ed., *Japan's Foreign Policy After the Cold War.* Armonk, N.Y.: Sharpe, 1993.

P'ohang Chech'ŏl Simnyŏnsa (A ten-year history of the POSCO Project). P'ohang: P'ohang Chonghap Chech'ŏl Chusik hoesa, 1979.

Posen, Barry R. *Sources of Military Doctrine.* Ithaca: Cornell University Press, 1984.

Posen, Barry R., and Stephen Van Evera. "Reagan Administration Defense Policy: Departure from Containment." In Kenneth Oye, Robert Lieber, and

Donald Rothchild, eds., *Eagle Resurgent? The Reagan Era in American Foreign Policy*. Boston: Little, Brown, 1987.

Public Papers of the Presidents of the United States, Jimmy Carter, 1977. Book I. Washington, D.C.: GPO, 1977.

Public Papers of the Presidents of the United States, Richard Nixon: 1969. Washington, D.C.: GPO, 1971

Public Papers of the Presidents of the United States, Ronald Reagan: 1981. Washington, D.C.: GPO, 1982.

Public Papers of the Presidents of the United States, Ronald Reagan: 1983. Books I and II. Washington, D.C.: GPO, 1984.

Public Papers of the Presidents of the United States, Ronald Reagan: 1986. Book 1. Washington, D.C.: GPO, 1987.

Qin, Yongchun. "China-ROK Relations in a New Period." *Korean Journal of International Studies* 25, no. 2 (1994): 147–59.

Quester, George. "The Malaise of American Foreign Policy: Relating the Past to Future." *World Politics* 33, no. 1 (Oct. 1980): 82–95.

Reischauer, Edwin O. *My Life Between Japan and America*. New York: Harper and Row, 1986.

Reiter, Dan. "Learning, Realism, and Alliances: The Weight of the Shadow of the Past." *World Politics* 46, no. 4 (July 1994): 490–526.

Republic of Korea. Economic Planning Board. *Major Statistics of the Korean Economy*. Seoul, 1982.

Republic of Korea. National Statistical Office. *Major Statistics of the Korean Economy*, Sept. 1996.

Republic of Korea. Ministry of Foreign Affairs. *Ilbon kaehwang* (Summary status: Japan). Government Publication no. 17000-20030-67-9607. Seoul, Feb. 1996.

———. *Korea-Japan Relations: Korean Views, Related Documents, Proposed Agreements and Statements*. Confidential reference material FPA no. 15. Declassified, n.d. Seoul, 1957.

———. *Korea-US Relations: Defense Commitments and Other Related Matters: July 1970–June 1975*. Seoul, n.d.

———. *Status of Overseas Koreans*. Seoul, 1995.

———. *Taehan min'guk woegyo yŏnp'yo: 1965–1993 bu juyo munhŏn*. (Major and minor diplomatic documents annual of the Republic of Korea). Vols. for 1965–93. Seoul.

———. *Woegyo yŏn'guwŏn yŏn'gubu: Pogwanyong* (Archives of the Foreign Ministry Research Institute, Research Department), *Statements Concerning the Defense of the Republic of Korea by Leaders of the United States Government, May 1975–January 1976*. Seoul, n.d.

Republic of Korea. Ministry of Foreign Affairs. International Treaties Division. *Taehan min'guk choyakjip: yangja choyak* (Bilateral treaties and agreements of the Republic of Korea). Government publication no. 17000-25100-17-9459. Vols. 2–14 (1962–91). Seoul.

Republic of Korea. Ministry of Information. *Opening A New Era in Korea-Japan Relations*. Seoul: Korean Overseas Information Service, Dec. 1984.

Republic of Korea. Ministry of National Defense. *Defense White Paper: 1992–1993*. Seoul, 1993.

"Revitalizing the US-Japan Alliance: Workshop III Report." Ralph Bunche Institute, CUNY, and Himeji Dokkyo University, n.d.

Rhee, Kang-suk. "Korea's Unification: The Applicability of the German Experience." *Asian Survey* 33, no. 4 (Apr. 1993): 360–75.

Riker, William H. *The Theory of Political Coalitions*. New Haven: Yale University Press, 1962.

Rosenfeld, Stephen S. "The Guns of July." *Foreign Affairs* 64, no. 4 (spring 1986): 698–714.

Rothstein, Robert L. *Alliances and Small Powers*. New York: Columbia University Press, 1968.

Roy, Denny. "Hegemon on the Horizon: China's Threat to East Asian Security." *International Security* 19, no. 1 (summer 1994): 149–68.

Rusk, Dean. *As I Saw It*. New York: Norton, 1990.

Russett, Bruce. *Grasping the Democratic Peace: Principles for a Post–Cold War World*. Princeton: Princeton University Press, 1993.

Ryang, Sonia. *North Koreans in Japan: Language, Ideology, and Identity*. Boulder, Colo.: Westview, 1997.

Sabrosky, Alan Ned, ed. *Alliances in US Foreign Policy: Issues in the Quest for Collective Defense*. Boulder, Colo.: Westview, 1988.

Saiki, Toshio. "Detente in Asia—Some Thoughts on the Asian Situation." *Pacific Community* 4, no. 4 (July 1973): 602–24.

Saito, Takashi. "Japan and Korean Unification." *Japan Interpreter* 8, no. 1 (winter 1973): 25–37.

Sato, Eisaku. "New Pacific Age." *Pacific Quarterly* 1, no. 2 (Jan. 1970): 333–40.

Sato, Katsumi. "Current Status and Problems of Japan-North Korea Relations." In Masao Okonogi, ed., *North Korea at the Crossroads*. Tokyo: Japan Institute of International Affairs, 1988.

Sato, Seizaburo. "Indispensable but Uneasy Partnership." In Chin-wee Chung, Ky-moon Ohm, Suk-ryul Yu, and Dal-joong Chang, eds., *Korea and Japan in World Politics*. Seoul: Korean Association of International Relations, 1985.

———. "Japan-US Relations—Yesterday and Tomorrow." Translated in *The Silent Power: Japan's Identity and World Role*, by the Japan Center for International Exchange. Tokyo: Simul Press, 1976.

Schweller, Randall. "Bandwagoning for Profit: Bringing the Revisionist State Back In." *International Security* 19, no. 1 (summer 1994): 72–107.

———. "Tripolarity and the Second World War." *International Studies Quarterly* 37, no. 1 (Mar. 1993): 73–103.

"Second Stage of Sino-Japanese Relations," *Japan Quarterly* 11, no. 1 (Jan.–Mar. 1974): 7–9.

Shin, Jung-hyun. *Japanese-North Korean Relations: Linkage Politics in the Regional System of East Asia*. Seoul: Kyunghee University Press, 1981.

———. "Japan's Two-Korea Policy and Korea-Japan Relations." In Chin-wee Chung, Ky-moon Ohm, Suk-ryul Yu, and Dal-joong Chang, eds., *Korea and Japan in World Politics*. Seoul: Korean Association of International Relations, 1985.

Shultz, George P. *Turmoil and Triumph: My Years as Secretary of State*. New York: Scribners, 1993.

Sigal, Leon V. *Disarming Strangers: Nuclear Diplomacy with North Korea*. Princeton: Princeton University Press, 1998.

Sigur, Gaston, and Young C. Kim, eds. *Japanese and US Policy in Asia*. New York: Praeger, 1982.

Singer, J. David, and Melvin Small. "Alliance Aggregation and the Onset of War: 1815–1945." In J. David Singer, ed., *Quantitative International Politics: Insights and Evidence*. New York: Free Press, 1968.

Smith, Michael. "The Reagan Presidency and Foreign Policy," In Joseph Hogan, ed., *The Reagan Years: The Record in Presidential Leadership*. Manchester: Manchester University Press, 1990.

Sneider, Richard. *US-Japanese Security Relations: A Historical Perspective*. Occasional Papers of the East Asian Institute, Columbia University. New York: East Asian Institute, Columbia University, 1982.

Snyder, Glenn. "Alliances, Balance, and Stability." *International Organization* 45, no. 1 (winter 1991): 121–42.

———. *Alliance Politics*. Ithaca: Cornell University Press, 1997.

———. "Alliance Theory: A Neorealist First Cut." *International Organization* 45, no. 1 (winter 1991): 121–42.

———. "Alliances, Balance, and Stability." *Journal of International Affairs* 44, no. 1 (spring 1990): 103–24.

———. "The Security Dilemma in Alliance Politics." *World Politics* 36, no. 4 (July 1984): 461–96.

Sohn, Hak-kyu. *Authoritarianism and Opposition in South Korea*. London: Routledge, 1989.

Solomon, Richard H., and Masataka Kosaka, eds. *The Soviet Far East Military Buildup: Nuclear Dilemmas and Asian Security*. Dover, Mass.: Auburn House, 1986.

"Source Materials on Korea-Japan Relations: 1965–1984." *Korea and World Affairs* 8, no. 3 (fall 1984): 716–42.

Spector, Leonard S., and Jacqueline R. Smith. *Nuclear Ambitions: The Spread of Nuclear Weapons 1989–1990*. Boulder, Colo.: Westview, 1990.

Stockwin, J. A. A. *The Japanese Socialist Party and Neutralism*. London: Cambridge University Press, 1968.

Sugita, I. "Japanese Perspectives on Security." In Richard Foster, ed., *Strategy and Security in Northeast Asia*. New York: Crane, Russack, 1979.

Summary Report of the Conference on US-Japanese Political and Security Rela-

tions: Implications for the 1970's, February 4–5, 1975. New York: Foreign Policy Research Institute and the Japan Society, n.d.

Takesada, Hideshi. "Japan's Defense Role: A Change in Defense Policy?" In Manwoo Lee and Richard Mansbach, eds., The Changing Order in Northeast Asia and the Korean Peninsula. Seoul: Institute for Far Eastern Studies, Kyungnam University, 1993.

Tamaki, Motoi. "Close but Distant Neighbors," Japan Quarterly 21, no. 4 (Oct.–Dec. 1974): 349–55.

Tanaka, Akira. "Japan and Korea—Relations Between Two Peripheral Cultures." Japan Quarterly 28, no. 1 (Mar. 1981): 30–38.

Tanaka, Yasumasa. "Japanese Perceptions of the World of Politics: An Analysis of Subjective Political Culture." In Bae-ho Hahn and Tadashi Yamamoto, eds., Korea and Japan: A New Dialogue Across the Channel. Seoul: Asiatic Research Center, Korea University, 1978.

Thayer, Nathaniel B. "Japanese Foreign Policy in the Nakasone Years." In Gerald Curtis, ed., Japan's Foreign Policy After the Cold War. Armonk, N.Y.: Sharpe, 1993.

"Thorn in Japan-ROK Ties." Japan Quarterly 25, no. 2 (Apr.–June 1978): 141–44.

Totten, George O. "Japan's Reaction to China's Bomb." The Correspondent, no. 33 (winter 1965): 13–15.

Tsujimara, Akira. "Japanese Perceptions of South Korea." Translated in Japan Echo 8, special issue (1981): 75–78.

United States. Central Intelligence Agency. "Special Report: The Future of Korean-Japanese Relations." 18 Mar. 1966. Declassified, 18 Sept. 1979. Washington, D.C.: Office of Current Intelligence, SC no. 00761 66A.

United States. Congress. House. Armed Services Committee. Impact of the Intelligence Reassessment on the Withdrawal of US Troops from Korea. 96th Cong., 1st sess., 1979.

United States Congress. House. Committee on Foreign Affairs. American-Korean Relations. 92nd Cong., 1st sess., 1971.

———. National Security Policy and the Changing Power Alignment. 92nd Cong., 2nd sess., 1972.

———. The New China Policy: Its Impact on the United States and Asia: Hearings Before the Subcommittee on Asian and Pacific Affairs. 92nd Cong., 2nd sess., 1972.

———. Detente: Hearings Before the Subcommittee on Europe. 93rd Cong., 2nd sess., 1974.

———. Report of the Special Study Mission to Japan, Taiwan and Korea, April 10, 1974. 93rd Cong., 2nd sess., 1974.

———. United States-Japan Relations, Hearings Before the Committee on Foreign Affairs. 97th Cong., 2nd sess., 1982.

United States. Congress. House. Committee on International Relations. *United States-China Relations: The Process of Normalization of Relations, Hearings Before the Special Subcommittee on Investigation.* 94th Cong., 1st and 2nd sess., 1976.

———. *United States-Soviet Union-China: The Great Power Triangle, Hearings Before the Subcommittee on Future Foreign Policy Research and Development, Part I.* 94th Cong., 1st sess., 1976.

———. *United States-Soviet Union-China: The Great Power Triangle, Hearings Before the Subcommittee on Future Foreign Policy Research and Development, Part II.* 94th Cong., 2nd sess., 1976.

———. *Investigation of Korean-American Relations, Hearings Before the Subcommittee on International Organizations.* 95th Cong., 1st sess., 1977.

———. *Normalization of Relations with the PRC: Practical Implications, Hearings Before the Subcommittee on Asia and Pacific Affairs.* 95th Cong., 1st sess., 1977.

———. *United States-Soviet Union-China: The Great Power Triangle, Summary of Hearings, Subcommittee on Future Foreign Policy Research and Development, October–December 1975, March–June 1976.* 95th Cong., 1st sess., 1977.

———. *Investigation of Korean-American Relations, Appendices to the Report of the Subcommittee on International Organizations.* 95th Cong., 2nd sess., 1978.

———. *Investigation of Korean-American Relations, Hearings Before the Subcommittee on International Organizations.* 95th Cong., 2nd sess., 1978.

United States. Congress. House. Committee on Standards of Official Conduct. *Korean Influence Investigation: Report.* 95th Cong., 2nd sess., 1978.

United States. Congress. Senate. Committee on Armed Services. *Detente: An Evaluation, Subcommittee on Arms Control.* 93rd Cong., 2nd sess., 1974.

———. *Korea: The US Troop Withdrawal Program, Report of the Pacific Study Group, January 23, 1979.* 96th Cong., 1st sess., 1979.

United States. Congress. Senate. Committee on Foreign Relations. *United States Security Agreements and Commitments Abroad, Vol. II, Part 5, Japan and Okinawa.* 91st Cong., 2nd sess., 1971.

———. *United States Security Agreements and Commitments Abroad, Vol. II, Part 6, Republic of Korea.* 91st Cong., 2nd sess., 1971.

———. *Korea and the Philippines, November 1972: A Staff Report, February 18, 1973.* 93rd Cong., 1st sess., 1973.

———. *Detente.* 93rd Cong., 2nd sess., 1975.

———. *US Troop Withdrawal from the Republic of Korea: A Report to the Committee on Foreign Relations, January 9, 1978, by Hubert Humphrey and John Glenn.* 95th Cong., 1st sess., 1978.

United States. Department of Defense. *A Strategic Framework for the Asian Pacific Rim: Report to Congress.* Washington, D.C.: Department of Defense, 1992.

United States. Department of State. *American Foreign Policy: Current Documents, 1964.* Washington, D.C.: GPO, 1967.

————. *American Foreign Policy: Current Documents, 1965*. Washington, D.C.: GPO, 1968.

————. *United States Foreign Policy, 1969–1970: A Report of the Secretary of State*. Washington, D.C.: GPO, 1971.

————. *United States Foreign Policy, 1971: A Report of the Secretary of State*. Washington, D.C.: GPO, 1972.

United States. United States Information Agency. *United States Government Statement on the Events in Kwangju, Republic of Korea, May 1980*. Seoul, United States Embassy, 19 June 1989.

United States Treaties and Other International Agreements, 1972. Vol. 23. Washington, D.C.: GPO, 1973.

Vasquez, John. "The Steps to War: Toward a Scientific Explanation of Correlates of War Findings." *World Politics* 40 (Oct. 1987): 108–45.

Wagner, Harrison. "The Theory of Games and the Problem of International Cooperation." *American Political Science Review* 77 (June 1983): 330–46.

Wakasuki, Yasuo. "Sasil kwa hŏgu waŭi ch'airŭl ara" (Knowing the difference between fact and fiction). *Han'guk Nondan* (Mar. 1992): 45–51.

Walt, Stephen M. *The Origins of Alliances*. Ithaca: Cornell University Press, 1987.

Waltz, Kenneth. *Man, the State and War: A Theoretical Analysis*. New York: Columbia University Press, 1954.

————. *Theory of International Politics*. New York: Random House, 1979.

Warr, Peter G. "Korea's Masan Free Export Zone: Benefits and Costs." Occasional paper no. 36. Australian National University, 1983.

Watanabe, Akio. "Political Change in Japan and Korea-Japan Relations." In Chin-wee Chung, Ky-moon Ohm, Suk-ryul Yu, and Dal-joong Chang, eds., *Korea and Japan in World Politics*. Seoul: Korean Association of International Relations, 1985.

Weinberger, Caspar W. "U.S. Defense Strategy." *Foreign Affairs* 64, no. 4 (spring 1986): 675–97.

Weinstein, Franklin B. "The Concept of Commitment in International Relations." *Journal of Conflict Resolution* 13, no. 1 (Mar. 1969): 39–56.

Weinstein, Franklin B., and Fuji Kamiya, eds., *The Security of Korea: US and Japanese Perspectives on the 1980's*. Boulder, Colo.: Westview, 1980.

Welfield, John. *An Empire in Eclipse: Japan in the Postwar American Alliance System*. London: Athlone, 1988.

————. "A New Balance: Japan Versus China?" *Pacific Community* 4, no. 1 (Oct. 1972): 54–70.

White Paper on South-North Dialogue. Seoul: South-North Coordinating Committee, 31 Dec. 1979.

White Papers of Japan. Tokyo: Japan Institute of International Affairs. Vols. for 1968–78.

Whiting, Allen. *China Eyes Japan*. Berkeley: University of California Press, 1989.

————. "Japan and Sino-American Relations." In Michel Oksenberg and Robert Oxnam, eds., *Dragon and Eagle, US-China Relations: Past and Future.* New York: Basic Books, 1978.

——. "New Perspectives on Asia." *Pacific Community* 3, no. 2 (Jan. 1972): 261–76.

Wiencik, David G. "Missile Proliferation in Asia." In William Carpenter and David Wiencik, eds., *Asian Security Handbook.* Armonk, N.Y.: Sharpe, 1996.

Wolfers, Arnold. "Alliances." In David L. Sills, ed., *International Encyclopedia of the Social Sciences.* New York: Macmillan, 1968.

——. *Discord and Collaboration: Essays on International Politics.* Baltimore: Johns Hopkins University Press, 1962.

Woo, Jung-en. *Race to the Swift: State and Finance in Korean Industrialization.* New York: Columbia University Press, 1991.

Yi Chŏngsik (Lee Chong-sik). *Han'guk kwa Ilbon: chŏngch'ijŏk kwan'gye ŭi chŏm'yŏng* (Korea and Japan: The political dimension). Seoul: Kyobo Mun'go, 1986.

Yi Pyŏngsun. "Pukhan-Ilbon sugyo hoedam ŭi chŏnmang" (Outlook on Japan–North Korean friendship conferences). *Mal* (Apr. 1991): 60–63.

Yi Tongwŏn (Lee Tong-won). *Taet'ongryŏngŭl kŭrimyŏ* (Yearning for the president). Seoul: Koryŏwŏn, 1992.

Yi Tongwŏn and Fukuda Takeo. "Han-Il kukkyo chŏngsanghwa: kŭnal kwa ŏnŭl" (The Korea-Japan normalization: Yesterday and today). *Sin Tong-A* (June 1985): 244–58.

Yoshitsu, Michael. *Japan and the San Francisco Peace Settlement.* New York: Columbia University Press, 1983.

Youn, Jung-sik. "Korea-Japan Relations—20 Years of Normalization." *Korea and World Affairs* 9, no. 3 (fall 1985): 421–44.

Zagoria, Donald. "Why We Still Can't Leave Korea." *New York Times Magazine,* 2 Oct. 1977.

Zinnes, Dina. "Coalition Theories and the Balance of Power." In S. Groennings, E. W. Kelley, and M. Leiserson, eds., *The Study of Coalition Behavior.* New York: Holt, Rinehart and Winston, 1970.

Index

In this index an "f" after a number indicates a separate reference on the next page, and an "ff" indicates separate references on the next two pages. A continuous discussion over two or more pages is indicated by a span of page numbers, e.g., "57–59." *Passim* is used for a cluster of references in close but not consecutive sequence.

Abandonment, 37, 199, 255n12; asymmetrical structure of, 46, 48, 54, 101, 133, 135, 139, 200, 206; behavior and, 43, 260n78; bluffing, 44, 265n41; concerns about, 38, 48, 255n21, 256n30; cooperation and, 79, 200, 206; entrapment and, 47–48; fear of, 2, 4, 38–60 *passim*, 85, 89, 115, 133, 135, 162, 178, 200f, 209, 231; friction and, 207, 213; impact of, 50, 58; influences on, 40, 43; Japan and, 50–54, 58, 68–73, 107–8, 109, 116, 146f, 152, 154, 166, 192, 229; Japan-ROK relations and, 98–99, 202, 205; mutual, 44, 258nn48, 49; quasi-alliance model and, 203; ROK and, 50–58 *passim*, 64–67, 73, 100–101, 110–14, 117, 142, 146–54 *passim*, 166, 173, 192, 229; symmetrical structure of, 46–47, 200, 206; by U.S., 57, 60, 64–67, 72, 73, 79, 85, 89, 93, 100–101, 107–13, 115, 133, 135, 142, 146, 153, 166, 180, 190, 192, 197, 200, 214, 230

Abe Shintaro, 191, 196
Abe Sukuya, 274n149, 325n106
ABM, *see* Anti–Ballistic Missile treaty
Adachi Tadashi, 250n56
"Admiration-enmity" complex, 20
Adversary game, 39
Advisory Defense Council Report for Japan, 209–10

Agency for Defense Development, 83, 113
Agnew, Spiro, 66, 69, 265–66n45
Agreed Framework, 211f
Aichi Kiichi, 267n62, 270n92, 272n123; EC-121 incident and, 68; economic cooperation and, 96; Korea clause and, 78; North Korea and, 84; Okinawa and, 75; on peacekeeping responsibilities, 70; troop reductions and, 71, 79
Akihito, Prince/Emperor, 16, 196, 198, 326n130; apology by, 227, 245n21, 333n80
Alignment, 4, 255n21, 258n52; abandonment/entrapment and, 40; gradations of, 37
Allen, Richard: Kim Dae-jung and, 321n65
Alliance game: abandonment/entrapment fear in, 54, 260n78; dynamics of, 45–48; strategies in, 43–45; threats/promises and, 202
Alliances, 45; commitment to, 38, 42–43; international relations and, 37; obligations and, 40; security and, 40f; structure and, 204; tightness/looseness of, 37
Alliance theory, 2–3, 5; foreign-policy behavior and, 38; Japan-ROK and, 57; quasi-alliance model and, 4
An Chang-gun, 326n123
Ando Toyoroku, 250n56
Angolan Resolution (1975), 148

An Rong-tok, 295n140
Anti–Ballistic Missile (ABM) treaty, 102, 301n3
Anti-Japanism, 179, 185–86, 187, 226, 227; Korean nationalism and, 26, 231; public support/political capital and, 19
Anxieties: balance of, 40–43; intra-/extra-alliance, 45
Anzai Masao, 250n56
Appeasement, 43; internal balancing and, 258n49
Arita Kiichi, security issues and, 81
Armacost, Michael: Kim Dae-jung and, 321n65
Asahi Shimbun: banning of, 128; on U.S. commitment, 154; Yusin regime and, 293n128
Asakai Koichiro, 283n38
Asian Development Bank, 160
Asian Games, 195
Association for the Protection of Human Rights of Korean Residents in Japan, 276n171
Association of International Lawyers, 276n172
Atsugi naval base, 71, 269n87

Baker, James, 209
Balance-of-power theories, 4, 37, 54, 102
Balance-of-threat theory, 9, 202, 204, 243n2, 244n4, 258n52; abandonment and, 49; commitment and, 49; quasi alliances and, 48–50, 49 (fig.)
Balance-of-trade deficit, Japan-ROK, 11–12, 16
Balancing, 255n9; bandwagoning and, 258n52; internal, 43, 47, 256n32, 258n49
Basic Agreement on Reconciliation (1991), 207
Behavior, *see* Foreign-policy behavior
Berger, Samuel, 30–31
Bilateral agreements/meetings, language issue and, 243n2, 333n74
Bilateral issues, 2, 21–22, 254n86, 259n65; private channels and, 244n3
Bilateral relations, 23, 163, 279n1; abandonment and, 47; cooperation in, 3, 169; pragmatism in, 102; stability and, 3
Blue House, 110, 112, 290n99; Northwest Airlines flight over, 309n63; raid at, 63, 65, 113f, 151, 262n17, 264n32

Boomerang effect, 96, 97, 260n68, 332n60
Brezhnev, Leonid, 105, 280n10; fishing rights issue and, 147
Brown, George: Carter plan and, 150
Brown, Harold, 145, 150–51, 305n24
Brown, Winthrop, 31f, 252n72, 262n13, 327n2
Brzezinski, Zbigniew, 145, 152, 304–5n23
Bulwark-of-defense argument, 52f, 185, 259n62
Bundy, McGeorge, 252n72, 253n75
Bundy, William, 32f
Bungei Shunjū, on Japan-Korea unification, 195
Burden sharing, 55, 70, 184, 281n18
Bush, George, 208f

Calcutta agreement, 90, 276n178
Carter, Jimmy, 169, 211; disengagement and, 141; human rights and, 172, 304n18; Kim Il-sung and, 151; Park and, 150, 172, 307n53, 313n123; ROK and, 149–54, 174, 303n15; Shanghai communiqué and, 143f
Carter-Fukuda summit, 165, 313n27
Carter plan, 161f, 174, 202f; disengagement and, 144–46; Japan and, 152–53, 154, 176; Japan-ROK relations and, 163–68, 332n63; origins of, 303n15; points of, 145, 303–4n16; rejection of, 165, 172f, 177, 192, 314n137, 317n22; ROK and, 149–54; security issues and, 166
Center for Strategic Studies, projects by, 330n32
Chang Key-young, 85, 243n3
Chang Myon, 28
Cheju Island, 82, 248nn34, 37, 285n52
China: long-term concerns about, 208–9; nuclear capability for, 29, 266n54; relationship with, 9, 281n20; trade principles of, 97
China-Japan-ROK triangle, 216, 222–23; security and, 221
China-ROK relations, 216–19 *passim*; Japan and, 220–21
China shock, 115; Japan and, 107–8, 280n15
Ch'in han p'a (friends of Korea), 250nn54, 56
Choi Hong-tae, 293n129
Choi Kwang-soo, 195, 287n68

Choi Kyu-hah, 77, 264n34, 326n125; reversion and, 74–75; Yanagida and, 92
Choi Kyung-nok, Kim Dae-jung affair and, 183
Cholera epidemic, 92
Chong Chae-ho, 249n49
Chŏ ngju dam project, loans for, 312n112
Chongsintae (comfort women), 22, 227, 329n29, 334n81
Chosen Soren, 53, 91, 133, 259n66, 277n179; cultural delegation of, 90; Japanese and, 59, 132; pro–North Korean activities of, 182; reentry visas and, 122; restrictions on, 140, 162; trading companies by, 331n58
Chosŏn Ilbo, analysis by, 91
Cho Tong-ki, 295n140
Cho Yong-su, 276n171
Chu'munjin, commando infiltration at, 82
Chun Doo-hwan: Akihito visit and, 196; assassination attempt on, 175; authoritarianism of, 316n18; Hirohito apology and, 180, 194; historical animosity and, 186, 193; human rights and, 172; Japan-ROK relations and, 15–16, 181, 187, 188–90, 197; Kim Dae-jung and, 320n60, 321n65; Nakasone and, 180; Rangoon bombing and, 181, 317n23; Reagan and, 169–74 passim; security rent and, 184
Chung Ho-yong, Kim Dae-jung and, 321n65
Chung Il-kwon, 26f, 264n34, 270nn89, 92; Sato and, 117–18; threat by, 66; Yodo incident and, 83f
Chun-Nakasone summits, 191, 196f, 319nn49, 51; Japan-ROK relations and, 188–89, 192, 198; North Korea and, 190; protesting, 325n104
Chun-Suzuki summit, 187, 198
CIA, Carter plan and, 146
C. Itoh, 134f; Zhou principles and, 298n175
Clark, Mark, 249n42
Clinton, Bill: North Korea/reactors and, 211; ROK and, 208
COCOM, see Coordinating Committee for Export to Communist Countries
Colonial legacy, 20, 22, 245n10; apologizing for, 32, 227
Comfort women, see Chongsintae
Commitment: abandonment and, 44–45, 48; balance-of-threat theory and, 49;

downgrading, 42–43; entrapment and, 45; strong/weak, 38, 46, 256n29; U.S., 55–56, 57, 96, 99, 154, 214
Committee on Scholarly Communication, 302n5
Committees: formation of, 59; Japan-ROK, 86 (table)
Communication, growth in, 225 (table)
Communist Party Central Committee, China-ROK relations and, 217
Conciliation, risks of, 44f
Congruence method, 58
Consultations: defense, 265n30; emphasis on, 224–25; growth in, 225 (table)
Cooperation, 60, 75, 272n125, 322n66; abandonment and, 79, 91, 98–99, 200, 206; counterpressures against, 96–97; disengagement and, 200, 213; engagement and, 200–201; explaining, 38, 199–200; friction and, 17, 23, 58; gradual finality and, 213; Japan-ROK, 73–87 passim, 97, 98–99, 100, 154–55, 158, 198, 200–205 passim; political, 85, 87; quasi-alliance model and, 203–4
Coordinating Committee for Export to Communist Countries (COCOM), 179; North Korea and, 92f; Yanagida and, 93
Cultural issues, 87, 196, 327n133; Japan-ROK, 9, 191, 225, 226–27
Cultural Revolution, 68; China–North Korea relations and, 266n56

Daiichi-Kangyō Bank, Taiwan and, 134
Daikin Kōgyō Company, 136
Damansky (Zhenbao) Island, clash at, 102
Dawson, Raymond, on U.S.-British relations, 42
Defense issues, 41, 178, 322n70; Japan-ROK, 52–53, 100, 116, 193, 209
Defense White Paper (JDA), 71
DeGaulle, Charles, abandonment fear and, 43
Demilitarized Zone (DMZ), 175, 262n16; incidents at, 64 (table), 151; pullback from, 62, 66; tunnels under, 110, 167, 285n54, 306n42, 328n14
Democratic Lawyers Association, 276n172
Democratic maturation, East Asian, 223–29
Democratic Republican Party (DRP), 30, 277n190; Japanese funds for, 251n68
Deng Xiaoping, 143, 302n6
Detente, 170, 197, 202, 247n33; abandon-

ment and, 133; demise of, 141, 142–46, 162; dynamic/strategic imperatives and, 103; Japan and, 103–6, 108–9, 140; Japan-ROK relations and, 6; proliferation of, 101–4; ROK and, 100, 106, 109–15

Dietmen's League for Japan–North Korean Friendship, 120–22, 190f; trade agreement by, 136

Diplomatic ties, 158–59; establishment of, 59; future-oriented, 227

Disengagement: concerns about, 56, 207, 322n66; cooperation and, 200, 213; Japan and, 178; Japan-ROK relations and, 168, 205; quasi-alliance model and, 209; ROK and, 149–54; by U.S., 61–63, 69f, 103, 111, 117, 123, 141, 144–46, 166, 171, 200–213 passim, 222–23, 230

DMZ, see Demilitarized Zone

Doi Masaharu, 278n211

Doko Toshio, 250n56

Domestic politics: Japan-ROK relations and, 87–89, 181–83, 187; liberalization of, 224

DRP, see Democratic Republican Party

Dulles, John Foster, 25, 29

East Asian Strategic Initiative (EASI), 208, 328n9

EC-121 incident, 64, 75, 81, 151, 263nn22, 29, 264n32, 269n88; criticism of, 68; Japan and, 80

Economic aid, 61; colonial restitutions and, 247n31; Japan and, 59, 79, 332n60; for ROK, 59, 250n62; security and, 156

"Economic animal" mentality, 12, 135

Economic growth, ROK, 55–56, 88, 96, 186

Economic Planning Board, 300n193; Masan and, 94; P'ohang and, 278n198

Economic relations: China-ROK, 219–20; Japan–North Korea, 222 (table); Japan-ROK, 11, 12–13, 53, 85, 93–99, 133–40, 160, 184–85, 198, 201, 222 (table), 228, 237–38 (table); perceptual gaps and, 17; policy initiatives on, 93–94; positive, 13, 16, 95f

Education Ministry, 259n63; revision by, 22; textbook issue and, 186, 187

EIB, see Export-Import Bank

Entrapment, 37, 38–43, 199, 255n12, 257n39; abandonment and, 47–48; asymmetrical structure of, 46, 48, 54,

101, 133, 135, 139, 200, 206; avoiding, 44–45, 101, 135; behavior and, 43, 260n78; fear of, 2, 4, 38–46 passim, 50, 54, 255n21; foreign-policy outcomes and, 58; friction and, 207; immunity from, 41; Japan and, 50–54, 58, 119, 135–40 passim, 202, 229; likelihood of, 40, 256n30; multipolarity and, 42; quasi-alliance model and, 203; ROK and, 50–54, 58, 123, 202, 229

Entry, determinants of, 41–42

Equidistance policy, 16, 19, 123, 140, 158, 290n95

Ericson, Richard, Japan-ROK relations and, 132

Esaki Masumi, burden sharing and, 281n18

Eto Seishiro, 210

Exit, determinants of, 41–42

Expectations: abandonment/entrapment and, 40; mutual, 39–40

Export-Import Bank (EIB), 163, 323n82; Japan and, 300n191; loans from, 160, 180, 278n198, 281n20, 313n121; North Korea and, 137–38, 162, 202

External-threat perceptions, 133, 135; internal balancing and, 256n32

Far East clause, 70

Federation of Economic Organizations, 250n56

Federation of Japan-South Korea Diet Members, 157, 311–12n100

Federation of Korean Trade Unions, boycott by, 321n63

Fisheries issue, 32, 110, 192, 246n28, 248nn34, 35, 37, 253n78; friction over, 158; ROK and, 59; Soviet-Japanese, 147

Five-year development plans, 79, 87f, 157, 160

Force Improvement Plan (ROK), 174, 316n14, 317n21

Ford, Gerald, 112, 310n81; abandonment and, 148; Japan-ROK relations and, 132; Korea policy of, 303n15; Shanghai communiqué and, 144; Sino-American relations and, 143, 302n6; Team Spirit exercises and, 149; Vietnam withdrawal and, 146f

Ford-Miki summit, 155

Ford-Tanaka communiqué, 116

Foreign Affairs, Aichi in, 70

Foreign Assistance Act (1961), 249n48

Foreign ministry-defense agency meetings, 180, 267n62
Foreign Policy Association, Carter at, 145
Foreign-policy behavior: abandonment/ entrapment and, 43, 58; alliance theory and, 38; contentious/cooperative, 5; psycho-historical explanation for, 23
Four Party Talks, 207
Free Bar Association, 276n172
Friction, 22, 206, 229, 322n66; abandonment/entrapment and, 207, 213; circumventing, 58, 82–85, 91, 93; cooperation and, 17, 23, 58; disagreements and, 274n143; intensification of, 128–29; psycho-historical explanation for, 23; quasi-alliance model and, 197, 203–4
Friendship Society of Japan-ROK Legislators, 157
Fuji Bank, Taiwan and, 134
Fujio Masayuki, 196, 326nn123, 125; controversy over, 194–95; on education reform, 195
Fujiyama Aiichiro, 311n91
Fukuda Takeo, 15, 28, 104, 165, 181, 281n19, 283nn42, 43; Carter plan and, 153, 314n136; on China isolation, 107–8; Japan–North Korea relations and, 120, 161; Japan-ROK relations and, 120, 159, 165; political reconciliation and, 157
Funada Naka, 244n3, 249n54, 250n56, 275nn158, 162

G-7, 178, 307n53
Gallucci, Robert, 211
Gang of Four, 143
Generalized System of Preferences, Korean goods and, 189
Germ controversy, 91–92, 93
Gleysteen, William: Carter plan and, 308n58; on U.S. commitment/ROK, 151
Gorbachev, Mikhail, 207
Gradual finality, 204–15; cooperation and, 213; U.S.-Japan-ROK triangle and, 214
Grants, 248n34, 249n48
Green, Marshall, 66, 69, 261n5, 270n89
Gregg, Donald, 132
Gromyko, Andrei, 105, 282n28
Guideline for Defense Cooperation, 310n76, 319n41
Gulf of Tonkin resolution, 29

Habib, Philip, 288n73, 307n44, 311n87; Carter plan and, 150; Japan-ROK relations and, 132; Kim kidnapping and, 125; Yusin and, 114, 289n81
Hahm Pyong-choon, 311n87
Haig, Alexander, 171–76 passim
Han (unredeemed resentment), 20, 126, 128
Han'guk Ilbo, 90, 276n177; on Hirohito apology, 194
Han'gŭl generation, 185–86
Han-Il ŭng'ŏri (Korea-Japan tangle), 21
Hanmintong, 182
Han Sung-joo, 65, 331n49
Hasegawa Jin, 244n3
Hasegawa Norishige, 134, 275n158
Hashimoto Ryutaro, apology by, 227
Havens, Thomas, on Vietnam withdrawal/Japan, 147
Hayakawa Yoshiharu, 129, 159
Herter, Christian, 269n85
Hideyoshi Toyotomi, 19
Hirobumi Ito, 195
Hirohito, Emperor, 283n43; apology by, 16, 169, 180, 188, 194, 196, 319n51; historical animosity, 193; Japan-ROK relations and, 194, 198
Historical animosities, 19–23, 27, 60, 128, 167; friction from, 180, 206f; Japan-ROK relations and, 34ff; normalization and, 25–26; persistence of, 193–98 passim; realpolitik and, 231; state behavior and, 232; textbook dispute and, 185–88
Historical emotionalism, 188, 195–96, 228–32 passim
History committees, 227
Hitachi, 135, 250n57
Ho Dam, 191f, 259n58
Hogen Shinsaku, 125, 128, 275n166
Holbrooke, Richard, 146, 321n65
Hondonami formula, 75, 268–69n81
Hong Song-ha, 275n158
Hong Sung-tae, 293n129, 295n140
Hori Shigeru, 87, 267n62
Hosokawa Morihiro, 223, 227f
Hua Kuofeng, 143
Human rights, 171f, 304n18; concerns about, 308n61, 314n137, 315n8; military assistance and, 286–87n63; violation of, 131, 160, 165f, 266n45

IAEA, see International Atomic Energy Agency

IECOK, *see* International Economic Consultation Group on Korea

Ienaga Saburo, 326n127

IFANS, *see* Institute of Foreign Affairs and National Security

Iguchi Sadao, Japan-ROK relations and, 245n20

Ikeda Hayato, 251n66, 311n91

Industrial development, Japanese aid for, 79, 94, 116, 138, 160

Institute of Foreign Affairs and National Security (IFANS), 215

Internal balancing, 43, 47, 256n32, 258n49

International Atomic Energy Agency (IAEA), North Korea and, 211

International Bank for Reconstruction and Development, 95, 160

International Economic Consultation Group on Korea (IECOK), 139

International relations, 2–3; alliances and, 36–37; Realist school of, 199; theoretical models of, 229–30

Interparliamentary Union, 111, 292n111

Intervention, automatic, 67, 149

Investment: interdependence and, 9; Japan-ROK, 93, 138–40

Iseki Yujiro, 244n3, 249n54

Ishibashi Masashi, 190f

Ishii Mitsujiro, 244n3, 249n54, 250n56, 275nn158, 162, 281n19, 283n42, 291n108

Ishikawa Yozo, 328n14

Itazuke air base, 71, 269n87

Ito Hirobumi, 323n83

Ito Masayoshi, 318n33; Kim Dae-jung affair and, 182; U.S.-Japan alliance and, 176

Iwasa Yoshizane, 134

Japan Chamber of Commerce, 134, 250n56

Japanese Communist party, 90, 273n128

Japanese Defense Agency (JDA), 210, 273n139; budget cuts for, 82; Carter plan and, 106, 153; defense plan by, 71, 82, 177, 214, 281n18; Korea attaches and, 274n141; Soviets and, 147, 318n29

Japanese Maritime Safety Agency, Yanagida and, 91

Japan Federation of Employer Associations, 250n56

Japan–North Korea Import-Export Company, 299n186

Japan–North Korean Cultural Association, 292n111

Japan–North Korea relations, 59, 115, 128, 212, 291n110; improvement in, 293n124; ROK and, 89–93, 118, 119–22, 191; trade and, 136–38, 160–63 *passim*

Japan–North Korea Trade Association, 90

Japan-ROK Cooperation Committee, 74, 85, 87, 118; cholera epidemic and, 92; Zhou principles and, 97f, 135

Japan-ROK Economic Cooperation Committee, 97, 134f, 158, 160; Masan and, 94

Japan-ROK Parliamentarians Conference, 74

Japan-ROK Parliamentary Federation, 164, 313n129

Japan-ROK relations: abandonment/entrapment and, 133, 154, 180, 200, 205; analysis of, 1–5, 7, 36, 54f, 229, 244n6; cooperation and, 169–70, 201–2; democratization and, 225–26; disengagement and, 168, 205; domestic politics and, 17, 19, 332–33n68; future of, 207, 212–13, 215, 223–29, 230; improvements in, 142, 156–59, 180–96, 197; peace through strength and, 170–71; policy fora for, 224 (table); private channels of, 243–44n3; problems in, 3–16 *passim*, 115–33, 138, 139–40, 180–96, 199; quasi-alliance model and, 5f, 54–58, 201 (table), 229; realism/reality of, 17, 18 (fig.), 19; strategies for, 54; terrorist attacks and, 181, 193; theoretical model for, 199, 206 (fig.); U.S. and, 28–34, 180, 204–13

Japan Socialist Party (JSP): no-confidence motion by, 253n75, 291n110; North Korea and, 121, 191

Japan-Taiwan Cooperation Committee, 98

Japan-Unified Korea relations, 207, 215–23

JDA, *see* Japanese Defense Agency

Jilin province, Koreans in, 218

Johnson, Lyndon B., 31, 263n19; Gulf of Tonkin resolution and, 29; Japan-ROK treaty and, 252n72; normalization and, 29–30, 33; ROK aid and, 201

Johnson, U. Alexis, 76

Joint Chiefs of Staff, Carter plan and, 146, 150

Joint Parliamentary Security Consultative Council, 166

Joint U.S. Military Assistance Group-Korea, 152

Joongang Ilbo, on troop withdrawal, 152

JSP, *see* Japan Socialist Party

Jung Nae-hyuk, SCC and, 66

KAL 007 downing, 175, 319n52

KAL 858 bombing, 191, 325n103; impact of, 181, 190, 319n52

Kanayama Augustin, P'ohang and, 95

Kanemaru Shin, 329n21; fishing rights issue and, 147

Kanghwa Treaty (1876), 10

Kang Ryang-wook, 121

Kang Sok-ju, 211

Kankoku būmu (Korea boom), 196, 225

Kato Nobuo, on Yusin system, 293n126

Kawashima Shojiro, 87

Kaya Okinori, 244n3, 275n158

KCIA, *see* Korean Central Intelligence Agency

KEDO, *see* Korean Energy Development Organization

Keen Edge 87-1 exercises, 318n36

Keidanren, 134, 243–44n3

Kim Chi-yol, 293n129

Kim Chong Pil, 252n70; opposition and, 31; riots against, 251n68

Kim Chong-tae, Zhou principles and, 98

Kim Chong-whi, 333n80

Kim Chu-in, 275n158

Kim Dae-jung, 88, 137, 139, 157; arrest of, 129, 133, 182, 320nn57, 58, 60, 321n65; controversy over, 138, 160, 181–83, 188, 198, 203; election of, 223; Japan-ROK relations and, 181–83; kidnapping of, 15, 89, 124–27, 128, 140, 159, 166, 182, 225; *Seiran-kai* and, 297n156

Kim Dong-jo, 128, 287n68, 296n151, 298n162; Japan–North Korea relations and, 162; Japan-ROK relations and, 132; Kim kidnapping and, 127; Korea clause and, 155; Koreagate and, 308n61; Mun affair and, 130; on North-South communiqué, 110; political reconciliation and, 157

Kim Hak-ryul, 95, 272n123

Kim-Hashimoto summit, 227

Kim Ho-ryong, 297nn158, 160

Kim Hyung-wook, 164, 293n129, 313n130

Kim Il-sung, 91, 191, 211, 217, 292n119, 325n107; Blue House raid and, 262n17;

Carter and, 151; Japan and, 68, 120f, 291n106; Kanemaru and, 329n21; Mao and, 306n41; meetings with, 190, 291n110; Sino–North Korean relations and, 148

Kim Jong-pil, 25, 27, 120, 290n95; on Japanese China policy, 118; Kim kidnapping and, 127; Korea clause and, 154; Mun affair and, 130, 132; normalization and, 30–31; on North-South communiqué, 110; political reconciliation and, 157; Tanaka/EIB and, 300n191; Yusin and, 114

Kim Jong-whan, 166

Kim Kwan-bong, 250n59

Kim Kye-won, 81

Kim Kyong-in, 125, 293n129

Kimpo airport, hijacking at, 83–84

Kim Sang-yong, 275n158

Kim Song-kun, 244n3, 275n158

Kim Sung-eun, 65

Kim Tong-won: exoneration of, 159, 295n140; kidnapping and, 126, 295n140, 312n108

Kim U-jong, 190

Kimura Toshio, 13, 104, 135, 275n166, 290n95; Japan–North Korea relations and, 161; on Japanese investment, 116; Mun affair and, 130f; on security, 116–17; Sino-Japanese relations and, 118

Kim Yong-sik, 287n64, 290n95; Japan–North Korea relations and, 119–20, 137; Kim kidnapping and, 126; Sino-Japanese relations and, 122

Kim Yong-son, 130f, 297n159

Kim Young-sam, 223, 228

Kim-Zhou summit, 111

Kinugasa Hayao, 273n139

Kirkpatrick, Jeane, 171

Kisaeng houses, informal diplomacy at, 181

Kishi Nobusuke, 69, 243n3, 249n54, 250n56; award for, 275n162; Japan-ROK Cooperation Committee and, 85; on Park, 250n55; repatriation agreement and, 24–25, 91; reversion and, 74

Kissinger, Henry, 173, 252n70, 283n43; abandonment and, 101; China and, 101–7 *passim*, 112, 141, 143, 279n3; EC-121 incident and, 64

Kiuchi Aritane, 185, 320n60

Kojong, 195, 326n123

Kokumin Kaigi, 195

Kōmeitō party, 121, 273n128, 291n110
Komer, Robert, 252n72, 327n2
Kono Ichiro, 244n3, 291n108, 311n91
Korea clause, 13, 73–80 passim, 271nn105, 109; acknowledgment of, 271n104; Japan and, 51–52, 77ff, 117, 123, 140, 311n87; new, 154–56; revisiting, 115–19; ROK and, 52, 79, 311n87
Korea Development Institute, report by, 331n54
Koreagate, 151, 165f, 308n61
Korea Institute of Defense Analysis, 330n32
Korea-Japan Basic Relations Treaty, 33ff; opposition to, 59; signing of, 24, 59
Korean Businessmen's Association, 249n49
Korean Central Intelligence Agency (KCIA), 165, 280n12, 290n99; crackdown by, 296n150; kidnapping by, 276n171, 293–94n129, 294n134, 295nn135, 138; Kim kidnapping and, 15, 89, 124–27 passim; Koreagate and, 164, 308n61; overseas operations by, 293–94n129; Yun kidnapping and, 88–89, 140
Korean Energy Development Organization (KEDO), 211–12
Korean Institute for National Unification, projects by, 330n32
Koreans, overseas, 21f, 189, 218, 218 (table), 225, 260n66
Korean War: economic aid during, 249n49; Japan-ROK relations during, 10; Okinawa and, 270n88
Korean Workers Party, LDP and, 121, 292n113
Kosaka Zentaro, Carter plan and, 153, 163
Kubota Kanichiro, 24
Kubo Takuya, 313n127; Carter plan and, 153; Japan–North Korea relations and, 161
Kuno Chuji, 190, 291n108
Kuraray Company, North Korea trade and, 136
Kwangju air base, 80, 268n74
Kwangju uprisings, 174f, 320nn57, 58, 321n65
Kwangyang Steel complex, 260n68

Laird, Melvin, 111, 263n23, 264n36
Lake, Anthony, 309n69
LDP, see Liberal Democratic Party
League for the Study of Afro-Asian Problems, 291n108

League of Nations, United States and, 257n39
Lee Bum-suk, 317n23, 325nn106, 112
Lee Byong-chol, 249n49
Lee Byong-tae, 210
Lee Chae-jin, 229
Lee Chol-hui, 293n129
Lee Chong-rim, 249n49
Lee Chong-sik, 187, 229
Lee Han-ung, 249n49
Lee Ho, 122
Lee Hu-rak, 78, 285n52, 293n129
Lee Jae-hyon, 164
Lee Jong-koo, 328n14
Lee Sang-ho (Yang Doo-won), 293n129
Lee-Shiina joint communiqué, 247n33, 248n37
Lee Tong-won, 25, 31, 244n3, 247n35, 275nn158, 162; on antitreaty sentiment, 254n87; Japan-ROK relations and, 119; Japan visit of, 32–33; Kim kidnapping and, 125; Nixon-Sato communiqué and, 272n120; normalization and, 27; U.S. visit of, 33
Lee Yang-ho, 210
Lho Shin-yong, on security rent, 184
Liberal Democratic Party (LDP), 281n19, 283n42; bribery and, 164; China policy and, 98; economic/security interest and, 19; former colonial officials in, 249n54; Japan–North Korea relations and, 13, 121; Korean Worker's Party and, 121, 292n113; Okinawa reversion and, 272n116; ROK and, 14, 162, 244n9; security issues and, 147–48
Liska, George: on alliances, 36–37; on ambivalence, 255n16
Lord, Winston, detente and, 144, 303n13

MacArthur line, 246n28
Maeda Toshikazu, Carter plan and, 177
Maeo Shigesaburo, 120, 122
Mainichi Shimbun, Park in, 155
Makita Yoichiro, 278n211
Mao Zedong, 143; Kim and, 306n41; Nixon/China and, 101; Sino-Japanese relations and, 105
Marcos, Ferdinand, 289n81, 315n8
Market-oriented, sector-specific (MOSS) talks, 179
Marubeni Trading, 250n57
Maruyama Takashi, Carter plan and, 153

Masan Free Export Zone, 94
Matsumoto Shun'ichi, 266n55
Matsumura, 291n108, 311n91
Matsuno Yukiyasu, 311n91, 323n83
Meyer, Armin, 71, 268n71; on Japan-ROK security link, 272n111; security issues and, 77
Miki Takeo, 159, 190, 203, 281n19, 283n42; Carter plan and, 153; China relations and, 156; fishing rights issue and, 147; Japan–North Korea relations and, 162; Korea clause and, 154f; North Korea trade and, 161; political reconciliation and, 157; Vietnam withdrawal and, 148; Yasukuni and, 325n118
Militarism, Japanese, 68, 212f, 330n30
Military Armistice Commission, 111
Military assistance: human rights and, 286–87n63; for ROK, 50, 67, 250n62; U.S., 55, 67
Military Information Consultative System, 210
Ministerial conferences, 16, 296n144; postponement/suspension of, 2
Ministry of International Trade and Industry (MITI), 279n198, 281n20, 324n95; North Korea and, 90, 137–38; P'ohang and, 95
Minobe Ryokichi, visit by, 120–22
Misawa air base, 71, 269n87
Misumi Tetsuo, 323n83
MITI, see Ministry of International Trade and Industry
Mitsubishi, 135, 250n57, 313–14n131
Mitsui, 135
Miyazawa Kiichi, 311n88, 334n81; Japan–North Korea relations and, 162; Kim and, 320n60; Korea clause and, 155; political reconciliation and, 156–57, 159; Roh and, 209; security issues and, 147–48, 185
Monbushō (Education Ministry), 259n63; revision by, 22; textbook issue and, 186f
Mondale, Walter: Japan trip of, 150, 164, 165, 310n78; troop withdrawals and, 153
Morley, James, 229
MOSS, see Market-oriented, sector-specific talks
MSDF, RIMPAC and, 318n36
Multilateral, defined, 279n1
Mun Hyong-tae, 81, 273n136

Mun Se-kwang, 139, 157, 203, 297n158; assassination attempt by, 129–33, 182
Murayama Tatsuo, apology by, 227
Murphy, Robert, Rhee and, 26
Muskie, Edmund, 321n65
Mutual distrust, 60, 188, 231f

Nagano Shigeo, 167, 244n3, 275n158; influence of, 134; Sato and, 299nn176, 177; Zhou principles and, 98
Nakagawa Ichiro, 244n3
Nakahira Noburo, 275n166
Nakamura Kikuo, 244n3, 275n158
Nakasone Yasuhiro, 71, 81, 259n58, 267n62, 268n76; at Asian Games, 326n125; Chun and, 180; defense partnership and, 322n70; Japan-ROK relations and, 15–16, 181, 188–90, 193, 197; North Korea relations and, 120; North-South dialogue and, 191; Reagan and, 169, 177–78; trade issues and, 179, 189–90
National Assembly: Tanaka and, 126; Yusin and, 114
National Assembly Defense Committee, security issues and, 81
National Committee on United States-China Relations, 302n5
National Council for the Normalization of Japan–North Korean Relations, 291n108
National Institute of Defense Studies, projects by, 330n32
National Security Council (NSC), 144; Carter plan and, 62, 146
National Security Decision Memorandum 48, 62
NDP, boycotting by, 277n190
New Japan Steel, 299n187
Newsweek: on Carter plan, 163; Fukuda in, 153
New York Times: Brzezinski in, 152; on Kim kidnapping, 127; Park in, 155
Nikkan Mondai Kondankai (Roundtable on the South Korean problem), 250n54
Nikkan yuchaku controversy, 164–65, 166, 184
Nippon Electric, 135
Nippon Kōei, 250n57
Nippon Steel, 135
Nishiyama Akira, Japan–North Korea relations and, 161
Nisshō Trading, 250n57

Nixon, Richard, 173, 283n43; alliances and, 69–70; Asian tour by, 60; China and, 101–12 passim, 116, 119, 135f, 141, 143, 279n5, 280n16; EC-121 incident and, 64; economic shocks by, 284n46; Japan and, 108; Moscow visit of, 102; one-China principle and, 102; retrenchment and, 74, 93; reversion and, 74, 76
Nixon-Brezhnev summit, 102
Nixon doctrine, 66, 75, 78, 96, 117, 202, 230, 308n61; impact of, 60–64, 69–70, 87; Japan and, 68–72 passim, 77, 81–82; Japan-ROK relations and, 6; ROK and, 67, 77, 81–82, 110f; U.S. alliances and, 61
Nixon-Park communiqué, 66
Nixon-Sato communiqué, 70, 258n56, 272nn116, 120; Korea clause of, 75, 79
Nixon-Sato summit, 77, 115–16, 270n99, 271nn104, 108, 109; Korea clause and, 51, 117; Taiwan clause and, 68
Nixon-Tanaka summit, 116, 282n34, 289n88
Nixon-Zhou meetings, 109, 142, 144
Noda Uichi, 275n158
Noguchi Uichi, 249n54
Nonaggression, 102, 246n27
Non-Proliferation Treaty, 211
Nordpolitik, 207
Normalization, 22, 158, 201, 217, 250n57, 254n86, 261n3, 329n21; China's preconditions for, 302n10; importance of, 30, 254n88; Japan–North Korea, 329n28; Japan-ROK, 31–32, 35; occupation and, 22; problems with, 1–2, 25–28 passim; realpolitik and, 24–28; U.S. role in, 28–34
Northern Territories, dispute over, 105
North Korea: defense spending by, 285n54; encirclement fear of, 52–53; Japan-ROK relations and, 190–93, 210–13; normalization talks with, 207, 291n110; nuclear weapons for, 208–11 passim; provocations by, 12, 53, 63–64, 208; relationship with, 9, 56, 119–20, 161
North Korea-Japan Friendship Association, 190
North-South communiqué, 109f, 115
North-South Coordinating Committee, 103, 110, 285n52
North-South dialogue, 191; Japan-ROK relations and, 210; problems with, 109–10

North Vietnam, Japan and, 106–7, 163
NSC, see National Security Council
Nuclear program, civilian, 288n73, 307n44
Nuclear weapons, 55f, 72f, 208f, 327n8; Japan-ROK relations and, 210–13; on Korean peninsula, 306–7n43; reintroduction of, 269n86; ROK and, 113–15, 145
Nunn, Sam, Carter plan and, 154
Nunn-Warner bill, 328n9

Oberdorfer, Don, 280n12; on North Korean tunneling, 285n54
Obligations, 40, 42; minimizing, 46. See also Entrapment
Occupation, 2, 333n74; han of, 20, 126; Japanese language and, 243n2; normalization treaty and, 22; polls on, 21
OECD, see Organization for Economic Cooperation and Development
Ohira Masayoshi, 25, 30, 129, 259n65; Carter plan and, 154; Japan–North Korea trade and, 137; on Japanese foreign policy, 108; Kim kidnapping and, 125, 126; protest by, 295n135; on quintipolar world, 267n65
Okazaki Institute, projects by, 330n32
Okinawa, 70, 72, 259n61, 269n87; abandonment fears and, 270n89; Korean War and, 270n88; reversion of, 73–75, 87, 269n83, 269n84, 269n86; ROK and, 13, 15, 51, 55, 75; security and, 75
Okinawan bases; agreement on, 51, 77–80 passim, 115, 117, 140, 271nn105, 109; Korea clause and, 76; restrictions on, 73f; ROK and, 117
Okonogi Masao, 76, 243n3
Okuno Seisuke, 326n125
Olympic Games, 1, 21, 191, 225f, 292n111
One-China principle, 102
One-Korea policy, 13, 19
Ono Banboku, 244n3, 249n54, 250n56
Operation Focus Retina, 67, 80, 265n43
Operation Freedom Vault, 67, 80, 265n43
Operation White Snow, 308n61
Organization for Economic Cooperation and Development (OECD), 178; China and, 220; ROK and, 226

Pacific Doctrine, 146
Packard, David, 270n89
Paek Chol-won, 293n129
Paek Nam-ok, 244n3, 275n158

Paik Tu-jin, 244n3, 275n158
Pak Hung-shik, 249n49, 252n72
Park, Yung H., incrementalism and, 293n123
Park Chung-hee, 12, 25, 30, 33, 181; abandonment and, 110, 113, 119; antitreaty attacks and, 33; assassination attempt on, 15, 63, 110, 129–33, 182; assassination of, 15, 174, 314n140; Carter and, 150f, 172, 307n53, 313n123; constitutional limits and, 87; criticism of, 159, 166; defense issues and, 83; on detente, 111; development plans of, 11, 27f, 34; election of, 87–88, 275–76n167; human rights and, 150, 165f, 266n45, 286–87n63; Japan–North Korea relations and, 123; Japan-ROK Cooperation Committee and, 85; Japan-ROK relations and, 26, 119, 132; Kim and, 125, 139, 295n142; Korea clause and, 117–18, 140; normalization and, 26f, 34; nuclear weapons and, 113, 266n48; political opposition and, 14–15, 159; retaliation and, 65; security and, 80–81, 82, 155; Sino-U.S. rapprochement and, 112–13; Vietnam withdrawal and, 147; Yanagida and, 92; *Yodo* incident and, 83–84; Yusin and, 114, 128, 139
Park Chung-il, 293n129
Park Kun, 125, 263–64n30, 287n69
Park Sung-chul, 285n52
Park Tae-joon, 26, 278n198
Park Tong-jin, 307n49
Park Tong-sun, 308n61
Patriotism, Korean, 20, 231
Payne, R. Douglas, 252n70
Peace dividends, 209
Peaceful coexistence, 101f, 142, 197; ROK and, 111; Sino-Japanese, 105
Peace line, violation of, 24
Peace through strength, 170–71, 176
Peoples' diplomacy, 121
P'ohang Iron and Steel Complex, 134, 202, 260n68, 272n126; EIB money for, 160; Japan and, 94–97; loan suspension for, 139
Policy coordination, importance of, 69
Policy fora: Japan-ROK, 224 (table); proliferation of, 224–25
Political issues, Japan-ROK, 13–15, 158
Porter, William, 62, 262n18; assassination attempt against, 63; troop withdrawals and, 261n10

Predictions, reality of, 18 (fig.)
Presidential Directive/NSC-12 (PD/NSC-12), 145
Presidential Review Memorandum/NSC 13 (PRM-13), 144
Prior-consultation issue, 76, 269n85
Process tracing, historical data for, 58
Pukch'in t'ongil (march north) strategy, 27

Quasi-alliance model, 36, 47, 100, 169f, 206, 216, 231; abandonment and, 49; alliances and, 4, 204; balance-of-threat theory and, 48–50, 49 (fig.); cooperation/friction and, 197, 203–4; development of, 2–3, 50, 197–98, 230; disengagement and, 209; future of, 207–8; Japan-ROK relations and, 55, 57, 197, 199, 201 (table), 223, 228–29; Japan-ROK-U.S. relations and, 167–68; policy behavior and, 58; post–Cold War era and, 207–10; as theory-building exercise, 4

RAND, projects by, 330n32
Rangoon bombing, 175, 181, 190f, 317n23, 319n52
Reagan, Ronald, 143, 174, 321n65; Carter plan and, 177, 192; defense spending by, 171; human rights and, 171; Japan-ROK relations and, 188, 198; Kim Dae-jung affair and, 183; peace through strength and, 169, 176; ROK and, 172–75 *passim*; U.S.-Japan alliance and, 176; vision of, 168, 169–71, 205
Reagan-Chun summit, 174, 184, 187, 321n65
Reagan-Suzuki communiqué, 176
Reagan-Suzuki summit, 184, 322n70
Realism, 199, 229; anomalous behavior and, 5; Japan-ROK relations and, 2, 9; predictions of, 18 (fig.); reality and, 17, 19
Realpolitik: historical animosity and, 231; normalization and, 24–28
Recessed deterrence, 212, 288n72, 329n25
Red Cross, 110, 284–85n52; family unification/visitation programs and, 103; Japan–North Korea agreement by, 90–91
Reentry visas, 122–23
Reischauer, Edwin O., 250n60, 252n72, 253n78; on China policy/Japan, 107; normalization and, 30, 32

Reparations; negotiations over, 247n29; normalization and, 28

Repatriation, 246n27, 247n30

Research Institute for Peace and Security, projects by, 330n32

Resolution 195 (III) (United Nations), 247n33

Retrenchment, 43, 208; ROK, 152–54; U.S., 60–64, 70, 72–74, 93, 149, 152, 197, 215

Rhee line, 24, 248nn34, 37

Rhee Syngman, 10, 34, 167, 257n43; anti-Japan sentiment of, 25, 244n8; antipathy for, 26; Japan-ROK relations and, 245n20; normalization and, 26; sovereign waters and, 24

RIMPAC exercises, MSDF and, 318n36

Rogers, William P., 263n23, 264n34, 283nn37, 43, 289n88; detente/Yusin and, 289n81; Nixon doctrine and, 95; North Korea and, 287n64; policy statement by, 106; reversion and, 74; troop reductions and, 71; Vietnam War Allies Conference and, 268n77

Roh Tae-woo, 209, 218

ROK-Japan relations, see Japan-ROK relations

ROK military: Japan and, 222; modernization of, 112, 148, 151; self-sufficiency for, 231

ROK Ministry of Defense, defense dialogue and, 214

Rosecrance, Richard, on U.S.-British relations, 42

Rumsfeld, Donald, 288n73

Rusk, Dean; Asia visit by, 251n66; normalization and, 30–34 passim

Ryūkyū Islands, reversion of, 72–75 passim

Sakata Michita, 152; Carter plan and, 153, 163; Korea clause and, 155

SALT, see Strategic Arms Limitation accords

Samch'ŏk, commando infiltration at, 82

Sano Hirohiro, 277n186

Sasakawa Ryoichi, 297n156

Sasebo naval base, 68, 80, 269n87

Sato Eisaku, 181, 243n3, 253n75, 258n56, 259n65; bilateral trade and, 15; concerns of, 72–73; criticism of, 77–78; EC-121 incident and, 68; Japan–North Korea relations and, 89; Japan-ROK Cooperation Committee and, 85; Japan-ROK relations

and, 78, 120; Korea clause and, 77f, 271n109; National Press Club speech by, 76f; Nixon and, 72, 108, 270n99, 280n16; North Korea and, 84; Okinawa reversion and, 74, 77, 269n83, 272n116, 274n155; one-Korea policy and, 13; Park and, 87f, 203; prior-consultation issue and, 76; security issues and, 81f, 115–16; Sino-American rapprochement and, 104; Sino-Japanese relations and, 104, 122; troop reductions and, 71; Yodo incident and, 84; Yun abduction and, 88; Zhou principles and, 98

SCAP, 246n28, 247n29

SCC, see U.S.-ROK Security Consultative Conference

Schlesinger, James, 147, 288n73, 301n3; Korea clause and, 155; nuclear weapons and, 148–49; Vietnam withdrawal and, 148

SDF, see Self-Defense Forces

SDI, see Strategic Defense Initiative

Second Infantry Division, pullback of, 62, 66, 145, 261n12

Second Track Security Dialogue (Track II), 214

Security, 3, 13, 43f, 140, 221; abandonment/entrapment and, 39; alliances and, 40f; alternative arrangements for, 47f; Carter plan and, 166; competition and, 219; comprehensive strategy for, 260n69, 322n70; economic aid and, 156; Japan and, 68, 108, 116–17, 138, 192, 197, 222; Japan-ROK, 1–2, 9, 11–14, 52–53, 59, 73–85, 87, 97, 106–7, 116f, 139, 142, 155–58 passim, 163, 192–93, 201f, 208–16 passim, 223; mutual, 230, 272n125; needs for, 42, 53–54; ROK and, 65, 67, 83, 175; U.S. and, 55–56, 57, 61, 65, 108, 214–19 passim, 230; U.S.-Japan, 179, 268n72; U.S.-Japan-ROK, 199, 230–31; U.S.-ROK, 74

Security rent, 53, 184, 186, 197, 259n62

Seikei bunri, 54, 90

Seiran-kai (Young Storm Association), 297n156

Self-Defense Forces (SDF), 80f, 177, 212

Senkaku (Diaoyutai) Islands, dispute over, 105, 305n30

Seoul-Pusan high-speed railway, 332n59

Seoul-Pusan highway, 96

Seoul subway system, 96, 138

Seventh Fleet, 50, 56, 178, 269n87
Seventh Infantry Division, 82, 261n12, 308n61; withdrawal of, 62, 71, 79, 81, 113f, 163
Shanghai communiqué, 101, 141, 144, 283n43; antihegemony clause of, 280n10; reneging on, 143
Shibusawa Keizo, 250n56
Shiina Etsusaburo, 25, 31, 33, 244n3, 247n32, 248n35; antitreaty sentiment and, 254n87; apology by, 193; Korea clause and, 155; Korea visit by, 32; Mun affair and, 131–32
Shim Jae-hoon, 93
Shimonoseki-Pusan ferry line, 275n162, 297n156
Shinin Kinai, 275n158
Shinjin Motors, Toyota and, 298n175
Shintō worship, 19, 186
Shinwa Bussan, 299n187
Shultz, George, 173, 316n15; on Rangoon bombing/Reagan visit, 175; on U.S.-Japan relations, 179
Singlaub, John, Carter plan and, 146, 304n21
Sino-American relations, 101–3, 110, 112–13; decline of, 141, 142–44; Japan and, 104; North Korea and, 138; ROK and, 111–12; Taiwan and, 144
Sino-Japanese relations, 10, 93, 104–9 passim, 115, 135; normalization of, 230, 250n61, 282n28, 290n95, 300n191; ROK and, 118–19, 122; stagnation of, 147; trade and, 137
Sino-Soviet conflict, 60, 102
Sneider, Richard, 148, 288n73, 298n172, 307n44; Japan-ROK relations and, 132
Snyder, Glenn, 327n7; on abandonment/entrapment, 37; on alignment gradations, 37; on balance-of-power theories, 37; quasi-alliance model and, 38
Sogang River dam project, 96
Sohyō (Japanese General Council of Trade Unions), 276n172; "Save Kim" petition of, 320n55
Solarz, Stephen, Carter plan and, 154, 310n81
Sonoda Sunao, 166; Carter plan and, 154; security issues and, 185
Southern Kurile Islands, dispute over, 105
South Vietnamese military, modernization of, 62

Soviet-Japanese relations, 105–9 passim, 147
Soviet Union: Asian military buildup by, 306n32; deterring, 170; relationship with, 9, 101
Straddle strategy, 45
Strategic Arms Limitation accords (SALT), 102, 142, 301n3
Strategic Arms Reduction Talks, 171
Strategic Defense Initiative (SDI), 171
Structural differences: alliances and, 204; perceptual gaps and, 17
Suh Chong-chol, 148, 273n139
Sukimiji Cho, 244n3
Sunobe Ryozo, 243n3, 270n92, 274n151, 275n156; Akihito visit and, 196; Kim Dae-jung affair and, 182–83; on Park/Carter, 313n123
Support, defining, 58
Suzuki-Choi meeting, 183
Suzuki Zenko, 16; Japan-ROK relations and, 187f; Kim Dae-jung affair and, 182; security issues and, 185; U.S.-Japan alliance and, 176, 177

Tachikawa Masaki, 129, 159
Taejon World Expo, 225, 277n179
Taft-Katsura agreement (1904), 10
Taiwan: Japan and, 230, 305n30; rhetoric on, 29; security/political commitments to, 143–44; Sino-Japanese relations and, 147; Sino-U.S. relations and, 144
Taiwan clause, 68f, 104
Takagi Masao, 26
Takashima Masuo, 296n151; Kim Dae-jung affair and, 182
Tanaka Giichi, 297n156
Tanaka Isaji, 125
Tanaka Kakuei: China and, 104, 118; EIB and, 300n191; entrapment and, 123, 138; equidistance policy of, 16, 158; Japan-ROK relations and, 120, 126; joint ministerial conference and, 138–39; Kim kidnapping and, 125f, 138, 295nn135, 138, 142; Korea clause and, 13, 155, 311n87; Mun affair and, 130; normalization and, 259n58; North Korea trade and, 137
Tanaka Tatsuo, 275n158
Tanaka-Zhou summit, 105, 118, 290n95, 300n191
Tani Yoichi, 191–92, 259n58, 325n107

Task Force 71, 80; EC-121 incident and, 64, 68
Team Spirit exercises, 149, 316n14
Technological training centers, plans for, 12
Territorial waters, demarcation of, 246nn27, 28
Textbook dispute, 185–88, 195f
"Time to Consider the Unimaginable" (IFANS), 215
Togo Fumihiko, 298n172; Carter plan and, 163; North Korea trade and, 163
Tokto/Takeshima Island, claims to, 158, 192, 212
Tokuyasu Chijucho, 244n3
Tong-a/Asahi newspaper, polls by, 21
Tong-A Ilbo, on national security, 78
Toshiba affair, 179
Toyota, 135; Japan-ROK Economic Cooperation Committee and, 134; Shinjin Motors and, 298n175
Track II, see Second Track Security Dialogue
Trade/trade issues, 9, 13, 15; China-ROK, 219–20; Japan–North Korea, 136, 236–37 (table); Japan-ROK, 13, 94, 161, 189, 228, 235–36 (table); U.S.-Japan, 178–80
Triangular alliance dynamic, 279n1; Japan-ROK and, 50, 54–58; U.S. and, 3
Troop reductions, 153, 163, 174, 201; Asian theater, 61–63, 61 (table); concerns about, 67; Japan and, 68, 70–73; ROK and, 65–67, 71, 78–79
Tsuchiya Yoshihiko, 78, 81
Tsukamoto Katsuichi, 243n3, 273nn136, 137, 139; on JDA/ROK, 274n142
Two-China policy, 305n30
Tyumen petroleum project, Japan and, 105f

Uemura Kentaro, 275n158
Uemura Kogoro, 134, 243n3, 250n56, 275n158; zaikai mission of, 160; Zhou principles and, 98
Ulchin, commando infiltration at, 82
Ulsan shipyard, construction of, 96
Unification, 4, 332n59; China and, 218–19; economics of, 219–21, 331nn55, 56; Japan and, 221; myths of, 221–23; overseas Koreans and, 218
United Nations, ROK and, 226
U.S.-China–Soviet Union strategic triangle, 103

U.S. Department of Defense: Carter plan and, 146; defense dialogue and, 214
U.S.-Japan relations, 107–8; consolidation/expansion of, 176–77; Japan-ROK relations and, 180; problems in, 178–80
U.S.-Japan-ROK relations, 54–58, 68, 184, 198, 213–15; analyzing, 229; gradual finality and, 214; quasi-alliance model and, 167–68, 205; two-tiered model of, 206–7
U.S.-Japan security treaty, 68, 77, 105, 116
U.S.-ROK relations, 164; abandonment and, 112–14; reaffirmation of, 172–75; tests for, 64–67, 175
U.S.-ROK Security Consultative Conference (SCC), 66, 112, 172, 174; communiqué by, 173; U.S.-ROK security issues and, 265n39
U.S. State Department: Carter plan and, 146; policy planning by, 214
Ushiba Nobuhiko, 267n62, 283nn37, 43
Ushiroku Torao, 128f, 247n33, 296n151, 300n190; Japan–North Korea relations and, 123; Japan-ROK relations and, 132; Kim kidnapping and, 125; Mun affair and, 131; Yomiuri incident and, 124, 126
USS Mayaguez incident, 146, 148
USS Pueblo seizure, 63, 80, 114, 151, 264n32, 269n88; retaliation for, 65; ROK and, 264n32
Utsunomiya Tokuma, 291n108, 293n29

Vance, Cyrus, 145, 309n69; Pueblo seizure and, 63; retaliation and, 65; Sino-American relations and, 302n6
Vietnamization, 62f, 70
Vietnam War Allies Conference, 268n77
Vietnam withdrawal, 141, 143; allied reaction to, 146–49; Japan and, 106, 148, 176; ROK and, 148, 201
Visits, official/unofficial, 238–40 (table)

Wajima Ejii, on Koreans in Japan, 21
Walt, Stephen: balance-of-threat logic and, 243n2; on balancing/bandwagoning, 258n52
War Powers Act (1973), 148, 306n39
Weapons Exploitation Committee, 113
Weinberger, Caspar, 173, 316n14; U.S.-Japan alliance and, 176
Whiting, Allen, 229
World Bank, 96, 139

World Cup, ROK and, 226
World Health Organization (WHO), 111;
Yanagida and, 92–93

Xinjiang/Kazakhstan border, clash at, 102

Yagi Nobuo, 249n54
Yamada Masao, visit by, 81, 273n136
Yamamura Shinjiro, 274n149; *Yodo* inci-
dent and, 83f
Yamanaka Sadanori, 161
Yamashita Ganri: Carter plan and, 154; Ja-
pan-ROK relations and, 193; visit by,
167, 209
Yanagida Trading Company, 277n186;
COCOM and, 93; investigations of, 91–
92; WHO and, 92–93
Yang Doo-won, *see* Lee Sang-ho
Yang Il-dong, 125, 293n129
Yasukawa Takeshi, 132, 243n3, 283n37;
Carter plan and, 166
Yasukuni shrine, 195f; Miki and, 325n118;
Nakasone at, 194
Yatsugi Kazuo, 94, 244n3, 275n158
Yi Son-kun, 275n158
Yodo incident, 83–85
Yoido Society, cooperation projects by,
330n32
Yokota air base, 71, 269n87
Yomiuri Shimbun, 153, 162, 294n131;
ROK closing of, 123–24, 126, 133; on
U.S. commitment, 154; Yusin regime and,
293n128

Yon Ha-gu, 247n33
Yoon Sung-min, 325n112
Yoshida Shigeru, 34, 249n54; anti-Korean
sentiment of, 25–26; Korea clause and,
271n104; ROK relations and, 11
Yoshii Mikiko, 297n160
Yoshii Yukio, 297n160
Young Lawyers Association, 276n172
Young Storm Association (*Seiran-kai*),
297n156
Yu Kun-chang, visit by, 81
Yun Chin-won, 293n129, 301n199
Yun Chung-guk, 293n129, 295n140,
301n199
Yun Duk Min, on security issues, 215
Yun Ju-young, *Yomiuri* incident and, 126
Yun Suk-huen, 122, 125; Japan–North Ko-
rea relations and, 123; *Yomiuri* incident
and, 124
Yun Yu-gil, abduction of, 88–89, 140
Yusin system, 113–15, 128, 182, 308n61;
criticism of, 124, 293n126; imposition of,
119
Yu Yong-bok, 293n129, 295n140

Zhou Enlai, 143; Japanese militarism and,
68; Nixon/China and, 101, 109; one-
China principle and, 102; Sino-Japanese
relations and, 105; U.S.-Japan security
treaty and, 105
Zhou principles, 133–36, 160, 298n175;
friction over, 135–36; Japan-ROK economic relations and, 97–98

Library of Congress Cataloging-in-Publication Data

Cha, Victor D.
    Alignment despite antagonism : the United States–Korea–Japan
security triangle / Victor D. Cha.
      p.   cm. — (Studies of the East Asian Institute, Columbia
University)
    Includes bibliographical references and index.
      ISBN 0-8047-3191-8 (cl. : alk. paper) : ISBN 0-8047-3192-6 (pbk. : alk. paper)
      1. United States—Relations—Korea (South).   2. Korea (South)—
Relations—United States.   3. United States—Relations—Japan.
4. Japan—Relations—United States.   5. Korea (South)—Relations—
Japan.   6. Japan—Relations—Korea (South).   7. United States—
Foreign relations—1945–1989.   8. United States—Foreign relations—
1989– .   I. Title.   II. Series: Studies of the East Asian Institute.

E183.8.K7C395   1999
327.7305'09'045—dc21   98-35015
                                                                CIP

This book is printed on acid-free, recycled paper.

Original printing 1999
Last figure below indicates year of this printing:
08   07   06   05   04   03   02   01   00